Structure and Interpretation of Computer Programs

Structure and Interpretation of Computer Programs

second edition

Harold Abelson and Gerald Jay Sussman
with Julie Sussman

foreword by Alan J. Perlis

The MIT Press
Cambridge, Massachusetts   London, England

The McGraw-Hill Companies, Inc.
New York   St. Louis   San Francisco   Montreal   Toronto

McGraw-Hill

A Division of The McGraw·Hill Companies

This book is one of a series of texts written by faculty of the Electrical Engineering and Computer Science Department at the Massachusetts Institute of Technology. It was edited and produced by The MIT Press under a joint production-distribution arrangement with The McGraw-Hill Companies, Inc.

Ordering Information:

North America
Text orders should be addressed to:
The McGraw-Hill Companies
Order Services
P.O. Box 545
Blacklick, OH 43004-0545
For toll-free customer service, call 1-800-338-3987

All other orders should be addressed to:
The MIT Press
55 Hayward Street
Cambridge, MA 02142
or at the toll-free number 1-800-356-0343

Outside North America
All orders should be addressed to The MIT Press or its local distributor.

This book was set by the authors using the LATEX typesetting system and was printed and bound in the United States of America.

This book is printed on acid-free paper.

8 9 10 DOC/DOC 0 9 8 7

ISBN: 978-0-07-000484-9
MHID: 0-07-000484-6

Library of Congress Cataloging-in-Publication Data
Abelson, Harold
    Structure and interpretation of computer programs / Harold Abelson
and Gerald Jay Sussman, with Julie Sussman.—2nd ed.
    p. cm.—(Electrical engineering and computer science series)
    Includes bibliographical references and index.
    ISBN 0-262-01153-0 (MIT Press hardcover)
    ISBN 0-07-000484-6 (McGraw-Hill hardcover)
    1. Electronic digital computers—Programming. 2. LISP (Computer
program language) I. Sussman, Gerald Jay. II. Sussman, Julie.
III. Title. IV. Series: MIT electrical engineering and computer
science series.
QA76.6.A255   1996
005.13'3—dc20   96-17756

This book is dedicated, in respect and admiration, to the spirit that lives in the computer.

"I think that it's extraordinarily important that we in computer science keep fun in computing. When it started out, it was an awful lot of fun. Of course, the paying customers got shafted every now and then, and after a while we began to take their complaints seriously. We began to feel as if we really were responsible for the successful, error-free perfect use of these machines. I don't think we are. I think we're responsible for stretching them, setting them off in new directions, and keeping fun in the house. I hope the field of computer science never loses its sense of fun. Above all, I hope we don't become missionaries. Don't feel as if you're Bible salesmen. The world has too many of those already. What you know about computing other people will learn. Don't feel as if the key to successful computing is only in your hands. What's in your hands, I think and hope, is intelligence: the ability to see the machine as more than when you were first led up to it, that you can make it more."

Alan J. Perlis (April 1, 1922–February 7, 1990)

Contents

Foreword

Educators, generals, dieticians, psychologists, and parents program. Armies, students, and some societies are programmed. An assault on large problems employs a succession of programs, most of which spring into existence en route. These programs are rife with issues that appear to be particular to the problem at hand. To appreciate programming as an intellectual activity in its own right you must turn to computer programming; you must read and write computer programs—many of them. It doesn't matter much what the programs are about or what applications they serve. What does matter is how well they perform and how smoothly they fit with other programs in the creation of still greater programs. The programmer must seek both perfection of part and adequacy of collection. In this book the use of "program" is focused on the creation, execution, and study of programs written in a dialect of Lisp for execution on a digital computer. Using Lisp we restrict or limit not what we may program, but only the notation for our program descriptions.

Our traffic with the subject matter of this book involves us with three foci of phenomena: the human mind, collections of computer programs, and the computer. Every computer program is a model, hatched in the mind, of a real or mental process. These processes, arising from human experience and thought, are huge in number, intricate in detail, and at any time only partially understood. They are modeled to our permanent satisfaction rarely by our computer programs. Thus even though our programs are carefully handcrafted discrete collections of symbols, mosaics of interlocking functions, they continually evolve: we change them as our perception of the model deepens, enlarges, generalizes until the model ultimately attains a metastable place within still another model with which we struggle. The source of the exhilaration associated with computer programming is the continual unfolding within the mind and on the computer of mechanisms expressed as programs and the explosion of perception they generate. If art interprets our dreams, the computer executes them in the guise of programs!

For all its power, the computer is a harsh taskmaster. Its programs must be correct, and what we wish to say must be said accurately in every detail. As in every other symbolic activity, we become convinced of program truth through argument. Lisp itself can be assigned a semantics (another model, by the way), and if a program's function can be specified, say, in the predicate calculus, the proof methods of logic can be used to make an acceptable correctness argument. Unfortunately, as programs get large and complicated, as they almost always do, the adequacy, consistency, and correctness of the specifications themselves become open to doubt, so that complete formal arguments of correctness seldom accompany large programs. Since large programs grow from small ones, it is crucial that we develop an arsenal of standard program structures of whose correctness we have become sure—we call them idioms—and learn to combine them into larger structures using organizational techniques of proven value. These techniques are treated at length in this book, and understanding them is essential to participation in the Promethean enterprise called programming. More than anything else, the uncovering and mastery of powerful organizational techniques accelerates our ability to create large, significant programs. Conversely, since writing large programs is very taxing, we are stimulated to invent new methods of reducing the mass of function and detail to be fitted into large programs.

Unlike programs, computers must obey the laws of physics. If they wish to perform rapidly—a few nanoseconds per state change—they must transmit electrons only small distances (at most $1\frac{1}{2}$ feet). The heat generated by the huge number of devices so concentrated in space has to be removed. An exquisite engineering art has been developed balancing between multiplicity of function and density of devices. In any event, hardware always operates at a level more primitive than that at which we care to program. The processes that transform our Lisp programs to "machine" programs are themselves abstract models which we program. Their study and creation give a great deal of insight into the organizational programs associated with programming arbitrary models. Of course the computer itself can be so modeled. Think of it: the behavior of the smallest physical switching element is modeled by quantum mechanics described by differential equations whose detailed behavior is captured by numerical approximations represented in computer programs executing on computers composed of ... !

It is not merely a matter of tactical convenience to separately identify the three foci. Even though, as they say, it's all in the head, this logical separation induces an acceleration of symbolic traffic between these foci whose richness, vitality, and potential is exceeded in human experience only by the evolution of life itself. At best, relationships between the foci are metastable. The computers are never large enough or fast enough. Each breakthrough in hardware technology leads to more massive programming enterprises, new organizational principles, and an enrichment of abstract models. Every reader should ask himself periodically "Toward what end, toward what end?"—but do not ask it too often lest you pass up the fun of programming for the constipation of bittersweet philosophy.

Among the programs we write, some (but never enough) perform a precise mathematical function such as sorting or finding the maximum of a sequence of numbers, determining primality, or finding the square root. We call such programs algorithms, and a great deal is known of their optimal behavior, particularly with respect to the two important parameters of execution time and data storage requirements. A programmer should acquire good algorithms and idioms. Even though some programs resist precise specifications, it is the responsibility of the programmer to estimate, and always to attempt to improve, their performance.

Lisp is a survivor, having been in use for about a quarter of a century. Among the active programming languages only Fortran has had a longer life. Both languages have supported the programming needs of important areas of application, Fortran for scientific and engineering computation and Lisp for artificial intelligence. These two areas continue to be important, and their programmers are so devoted to these two languages that Lisp and Fortran may well continue in active use for at least another quarter-century.

Lisp changes. The Scheme dialect used in this text has evolved from the original Lisp and differs from the latter in several important ways, including static scoping for variable binding and permitting functions to yield functions as values. In its semantic structure Scheme is as closely akin to Algol 60 as to early Lisps. Algol 60, never to be an active language again, lives on in the genes of Scheme and Pascal. It would be difficult to find two languages that are the communicating coin of two more different cultures than those gathered around these two languages. Pascal is for building pyramids—imposing, breathtaking, static structures built by armies pushing heavy blocks into place. Lisp is for building organisms—imposing, breathtaking, dynamic structures built by squads fitting fluctuating myriads of simpler organisms into place. The organizing principles used are the same in both cases, except for one extraordinarily important difference: The discretionary exportable functionality entrusted to the individual Lisp programmer is more than an order of magnitude greater than that to be found within Pascal enterprises. Lisp programs inflate libraries with functions whose utility transcends the application that produced them. The list, Lisp's native data structure, is largely responsible for such growth of utility. The simple structure and natural applicability of lists are reflected in functions that are amazingly nonidiosyncratic. In Pascal the plethora of declarable data structures induces a specialization within functions that inhibits and penalizes casual cooperation. It is better to have 100 functions operate on one data structure than to have 10 functions operate on 10 data structures. As a result the pyramid must stand unchanged for a millennium; the organism must evolve or perish.

To illustrate this difference, compare the treatment of material and exercises within this book with that in any first-course text using Pascal. Do not labor under the illusion that this is a text digestible at MIT only, peculiar to the breed found there. It is precisely what a serious book on programming Lisp must be, no matter who the student is or where it is used.

Note that this is a text about programming, unlike most Lisp books, which are used as a preparation for work in artificial intelligence. After all, the critical programming concerns of software engineering and artificial intelligence tend to coalesce as the systems under investigation become larger. This explains why there is such growing interest in Lisp outside of artificial intelligence.

As one would expect from its goals, artificial intelligence research generates many significant programming problems. In other programming cultures this spate of problems spawns new languages. Indeed, in any very large programming task a useful organizing principle is to control and isolate traffic within the task modules via the invention of language. These languages tend to become less primitive as one approaches the boundaries of the system where we humans interact most often. As a result, such systems contain complex language-processing functions replicated many times. Lisp has such a simple syntax and semantics that parsing can be treated as an elementary task. Thus parsing technology plays almost no role in Lisp programs, and the construction of language processors is rarely an impediment to the rate of growth and change of large Lisp systems. Finally, it is this very simplicity of syntax and semantics that is responsible for the burden and freedom borne by all Lisp programmers. No Lisp program of any size beyond a few lines can be written without being saturated with discretionary functions. Invent and fit; have fits and reinvent! We toast the Lisp programmer who pens his thoughts within nests of parentheses.

Alan J. Perlis
New Haven, Connecticut

Preface to the Second Edition

> Is it possible that software is not like anything else, that
> it is meant to be discarded: that the whole point is to
> always see it as a soap bubble?

Alan J. Perlis

The material in this book has been the basis of MIT's entry-level computer science subject since 1980. We had been teaching this material for four years when the first edition was published, and twelve more years have elapsed until the appearance of this second edition. We are pleased that our work has been widely adopted and incorporated into other texts. We have seen our students take the ideas and programs in this book and build them in as the core of new computer systems and languages. In literal realization of an ancient Talmudic pun, our students have become our builders. We are lucky to have such capable students and such accomplished builders.

In preparing this edition, we have incorporated hundreds of clarifications suggested by our own teaching experience and the comments of colleagues at MIT and elsewhere. We have redesigned most of the major programming systems in the book, including the generic-arithmetic system, the interpreters, the register-machine simulator, and the compiler; and we have rewritten all the program examples to ensure that any Scheme implementation conforming to the IEEE Scheme standard (IEEE 1990) will be able to run the code.

This edition emphasizes several new themes. The most important of these is the central role played by different approaches to dealing with time in computational models: objects with state, concurrent programming, functional programming, lazy evaluation, and nondeterministic programming. We have included new sections on concurrency and nondeterminism, and we have tried to integrate this theme throughout the book.

The first edition of the book closely followed the syllabus of our MIT one-semester subject. With all the new material in the second edition, it will not be possible to cover everything in a single semester, so the instructor will have to pick and choose. In our own teaching, we sometimes skip the section on logic programming (section 4.4), we have students use the register-machine simulator but we do not cover its implementation (section 5.2), and we give only a cursory overview of the compiler (section 5.5). Even so, this is still an intense course. Some instructors may wish to cover only the first three or four chapters, leaving the other material for subsequent courses.

The World-Wide-Web site `www-mitpress.mit.edu/sicp` provides support for users of this book. This includes programs from the book, sample programming assignments, supplementary materials, and downloadable implementations of the Scheme dialect of Lisp.

Preface to the First Edition

> A computer is like a violin. You can imagine a novice
> trying first a phonograph and then a violin. The latter, he
> says, sounds terrible. That is the argument we have heard
> from our humanists and most of our computer scientists.
> Computer programs are good, they say, for particular
> purposes, but they aren't flexible. Neither is a violin, or a
> typewriter, until you learn how to use it.
>
> Marvin Minsky, "Why Programming Is a Good
> Medium for Expressing Poorly-Understood and
> Sloppily-Formulated Ideas"

"The Structure and Interpretation of Computer Programs" is the entry-level subject in computer science at the Massachusetts Institute of Technology. It is required of all students at MIT who major in electrical engineering or in computer science, as one-fourth of the "common core curriculum," which also includes two subjects on circuits and linear systems and a subject on the design of digital systems. We have been involved in the development of this subject since 1978, and we have taught this material in its present form since the fall of 1980 to between 600 and 700 students each year. Most of these students have had little or no prior formal training in computation, although many have played with computers a bit and a few have had extensive programming or hardware-design experience.

Our design of this introductory computer-science subject reflects two major concerns. First, we want to establish the idea that a computer language is not just a way of getting a computer to perform operations but rather that it is a novel formal medium for expressing ideas about methodology. Thus, programs must be written for people to read, and only incidentally for machines to execute. Second, we believe that the essential material to be addressed by a subject at this level is not the syntax of particular programming-language constructs, nor clever algorithms for computing particular functions efficiently, nor even the mathematical analysis of algorithms and the foundations of computing, but rather the techniques used to control the intellectual complexity of large software systems.

Our goal is that students who complete this subject should have a good feel for the elements of style and the aesthetics of programming. They should have command of the major techniques for controlling complexity in a large system. They should be capable of reading a 50-page-long program, if it is written in an exemplary style. They should know what not to read, and what they need not understand at any moment. They should feel secure about modifying a program, retaining the spirit and style of the original author.

These skills are by no means unique to computer programming. The techniques we teach and draw upon are common to all of engineering design. We control complexity by building abstractions that hide details when appropriate. We control complexity by establishing conventional interfaces that enable us to construct systems by combining standard, well-understood pieces in a "mix and match" way. We control complexity by establishing new languages for describing a design, each of which emphasizes particular aspects of the design and deemphasizes others.

Underlying our approach to this subject is our conviction that "computer science" is not a science and that its significance has little to do with computers. The computer revolution is a revolution in the way we think and in the way we express what we think. The essence of this change is the emergence of what might best be called *procedural epistemology*—the study of the structure of knowledge from an imperative point of view, as opposed to the more declarative point of view taken by classical mathematical subjects. Mathematics provides a framework for dealing precisely with notions of "what is." Computation provides a framework for dealing precisely with notions of "how to."

In teaching our material we use a dialect of the programming language Lisp. We never formally teach the language, because we don't have to. We just use it, and students pick it up in a few days. This is one great advantage of Lisp-like languages: They have very few ways of forming compound expressions, and almost no syntactic structure. All of the formal properties can be covered in an hour, like the rules of chess. After a short time we forget about syntactic details of the language (because there are none) and get on with the real issues—figuring out what we want to compute, how we will decompose problems into manageable parts, and how we will work on the parts. Another advantage of Lisp is that it supports (but does not enforce) more of the large-scale strategies for modular decomposition of programs than any other language we know. We can make procedural and data abstractions, we can use higher-order functions to capture common patterns of usage, we can model local state using assignment and data mutation, we can link parts of a program with streams and delayed evaluation, and we can easily implement embedded languages. All of this is embedded in an interactive environment with excellent support for incremental program design, construction, testing, and debugging. We thank all the generations of Lisp wizards, starting with John McCarthy, who have fashioned a fine tool of unprecedented power and elegance.

Scheme, the dialect of Lisp that we use, is an attempt to bring together the power and elegance of Lisp and Algol. From Lisp we take the metalinguistic power that derives from the simple syntax, the uniform representation of programs as data objects, and the garbage-collected heap-allocated data. From Algol we take lexical scoping and block structure, which are gifts from the pioneers of programming-language design who were on the Algol committee. We wish to cite John Reynolds and Peter Landin for their insights into the relationship of Church's lambda calculus to the structure of programming languages. We also recognize our debt to the mathematicians who scouted out this territory decades before computers appeared on the scene. These pioneers include Alonzo Church, Barkley Rosser, Stephen Kleene, and Haskell Curry.

Acknowledgments

We would like to thank the many people who have helped us develop this book and this curriculum.

Our subject is a clear intellectual descendant of "6.231," a wonderful subject on programming linguistics and the lambda calculus taught at MIT in the late 1960s by Jack Wozencraft and Arthur Evans, Jr.

We owe a great debt to Robert Fano, who reorganized MIT's introductory curriculum in electrical engineering and computer science to emphasize the principles of engineering design. He led us in starting out on this enterprise and wrote the first set of subject notes from which this book evolved.

Much of the style and aesthetics of programming that we try to teach were developed in conjunction with Guy Lewis Steele Jr., who collaborated with Gerald Jay Sussman in the initial development of the Scheme language. In addition, David Turner, Peter Henderson, Dan Friedman, David Wise, and Will Clinger have taught us many of the techniques of the functional programming community that appear in this book.

Joel Moses taught us about structuring large systems. His experience with the Macsyma system for symbolic computation provided the insight that one should avoid complexities of control and concentrate on organizing the data to reflect the real structure of the world being modeled.

Marvin Minsky and Seymour Papert formed many of our attitudes about programming and its place in our intellectual lives. To them we owe the understanding that computation provides a means of expression for exploring ideas that would otherwise be too complex to deal with precisely. They emphasize that a student's ability to write and modify programs provides a powerful medium in which exploring becomes a natural activity.

We also strongly agree with Alan Perlis that programming is lots of fun and we had better be careful to support the joy of programming. Part of this joy derives from observing great masters at work. We are fortunate to have been apprentice programmers at the feet of Bill Gosper and Richard Greenblatt.

It is difficult to identify all the people who have contributed to the development of our curriculum. We thank all the lecturers, recitation instructors, and tutors who have worked with us over the past fifteen years and put in many extra hours on our subject, especially Bill Siebert, Albert Meyer, Joe Stoy, Randy Davis, Louis Braida, Eric Grimson, Rod Brooks, Lynn Stein, and Peter Szolovits. We would like to specially acknowledge the outstanding teaching contributions of Franklyn Turbak, now at Wellesley; his work in undergraduate instruction set a standard that we can all aspire to. We are grateful to Jerry Saltzer and Jim Miller for helping us grapple with the mysteries of concurrency, and to Peter Szolovits and David McAllester for their contributions to the exposition of nondeterministic evaluation in chapter 4.

Many people have put in significant effort presenting this material at other universities. Some of the people we have worked closely with are Jacob Katzenelson at the Technion, Hardy Mayer at the University of California at Irvine, Joe Stoy at Oxford, Elisha Sacks at Purdue, and Jan Komorowski at the Norwegian University of Science and Technology. We are exceptionally proud of our colleagues who have received major teaching awards for their adaptations of this subject at other universities, including Kenneth Yip at Yale, Brian Harvey at the University of California at Berkeley, and Dan Huttenlocher at Cornell.

Al Moyé arranged for us to teach this material to engineers at Hewlett-Packard, and for the production of videotapes of these lectures. We would like to thank the talented instructors—in particular Jim Miller, Bill Siebert, and Mike Eisenberg—who have designed continuing education courses incorporating these tapes and taught them at universities and industry all over the world.

Many educators in other countries have put in significant work translating the first edition. Michel Briand, Pierre Chamard, and André Pic produced a French edition; Susanne Daniels-Herold produced a German edition; and Fumio Motoyoshi produced a Japanese edition. We do not know who produced the Chinese edition, but we consider it an honor to have been selected as the subject of an "unauthorized" translation.

It is hard to enumerate all the people who have made technical contributions to the development of the Scheme systems we use for instructional purposes. In addition to Guy Steele, principal wizards have included Chris Hanson, Joe Bowbeer, Jim Miller, Guillermo Rozas, and Stephen Adams. Others who have put in significant time are Richard Stallman, Alan Bawden, Kent Pitman, Jon Taft, Neil Mayle, John Lamping, Gwyn Osnos, Tracy Larrabee, George Carrette, Soma Chaudhuri, Bill Chiarchiaro, Steven Kirsch, Leigh Klotz, Wayne Noss, Todd Cass, Patrick O'Donnell, Kevin Theobald, Daniel Weise, Kenneth Sinclair, Anthony Courtemanche, Henry M. Wu, Andrew Berlin, and Ruth Shyu.

Beyond the MIT implementation, we would like to thank the many people who worked on the IEEE Scheme standard, including William Clinger and Jonathan Rees, who edited the R^4RS, and Chris Haynes, David Bartley, Chris Hanson, and Jim Miller, who prepared the IEEE standard.

Dan Friedman has been a long-time leader of the Scheme community. The community's broader work goes beyond issues of language design to encompass significant educational innovations, such as the high-school curriculum based on EdScheme by Schemer's Inc., and the wonderful books by Mike Eisenberg and by Brian Harvey and Matthew Wright.

We appreciate the work of those who contributed to making this a real book, especially Terry Ehling, Larry Cohen, and Paul Bethge at the MIT Press. Ella Mazel found the wonderful cover image. For the second edition we are particularly grateful to Bernard and Ella Mazel for help with the book design, and to David Jones, TEX wizard extraordinaire. We also are indebted to those readers who made penetrating comments on the new draft: Jacob Katzenelson, Hardy Mayer, Jim Miller, and especially Brian Harvey, who did unto this book as Julie did unto his book *Simply Scheme*.

Finally, we would like to acknowledge the support of the organizations that have encouraged this work over the years, including suppport from Hewlett-Packard, made possible by Ira Goldstein and Joel Birnbaum, and support from DARPA, made possible by Bob Kahn.

Structure and Interpretation
of Computer Programs

1

Building Abstractions with Procedures

> The acts of the mind, wherein it exerts its power over simple ideas, are chiefly these three: 1. Combining several simple ideas into one compound one, and thus all complex ideas are made. 2. The second is bringing two ideas, whether simple or complex, together, and setting them by one another so as to take a view of them at once, without uniting them into one, by which it gets all its ideas of relations. 3. The third is separating them from all other ideas that accompany them in their real existence: this is called abstraction, and thus all its general ideas are made.
>
> John Locke, *An Essay Concerning Human Understanding* (1690)

We are about to study the idea of a *computational process*. Computational processes are abstract beings that inhabit computers. As they evolve, processes manipulate other abstract things called *data*. The evolution of a process is directed by a pattern of rules called a *program*. People create programs to direct processes. In effect, we conjure the spirits of the computer with our spells.

A computational process is indeed much like a sorcerer's idea of a spirit. It cannot be seen or touched. It is not composed of matter at all. However, it is very real. It can perform intellectual work. It can answer questions. It can affect the world by disbursing money at a bank or by controlling a robot arm in a factory. The programs we use to conjure processes are like a sorcerer's spells. They are carefully composed from symbolic expressions in arcane and esoteric *programming languages* that prescribe the tasks we want our processes to perform.

A computational process, in a correctly working computer, executes programs precisely and accurately. Thus, like the sorcerer's apprentice, novice programmers must learn to understand and to anticipate the consequences of their conjuring. Even small errors (usually called *bugs* or *glitches*) in programs can have complex and unanticipated consequences.

Fortunately, learning to program is considerably less dangerous than learning sorcery, because the spirits we deal with are conveniently contained in a secure way. Real-world programming, however, requires care, expertise, and wisdom. A small bug in a computer-aided design program, for example, can lead to the catastrophic collapse of an airplane or a dam or the self-destruction of an industrial robot.

Master software engineers have the ability to organize programs so that they can be reasonably sure that the resulting processes will perform the tasks intended. They can visualize the behavior of their systems in advance. They know how to structure programs so that unanticipated problems do not lead to catastrophic consequences, and when problems do arise, they can *debug* their programs. Well-designed computational systems, like well-designed automobiles or nuclear reactors, are designed in a modular manner, so that the parts can be constructed, replaced, and debugged separately.

Programming in Lisp

We need an appropriate language for describing processes, and we will use for this purpose the programming language Lisp. Just as our everyday thoughts are usually expressed in our natural language (such as English, French, or Japanese), and descriptions of quantitative phenomena are expressed with mathematical notations, our procedural thoughts will be expressed in Lisp. Lisp was invented in the late 1950s as a formalism for reasoning about the use of certain kinds of logical expressions, called *recursion equations*, as a model for computation. The language was conceived by John McCarthy and is based on his paper "Recursive Functions of Symbolic Expressions and Their Computation by Machine" (McCarthy 1960).

Despite its inception as a mathematical formalism, Lisp is a practical programming language. A Lisp *interpreter* is a machine that carries out processes described in the Lisp language. The first Lisp interpreter was implemented by McCarthy with the help of colleagues and students in the Artificial Intelligence Group of the MIT Research Laboratory of Electronics and in the MIT Computation Center.[1] Lisp, whose name is an acronym for LISt Processing, was designed to provide symbol-manipulating capabilities for attacking programming problems such as the symbolic differentiation and integration of algebraic expressions. It

---

[1] The *Lisp 1 Programmer's Manual* appeared in 1960, and the *Lisp 1.5 Programmer's Manual* (McCarthy 1965) was published in 1962. The early history of Lisp is described in McCarthy 1978.

included for this purpose new data objects known as atoms and lists, which most strikingly set it apart from all other languages of the period.

Lisp was not the product of a concerted design effort. Instead, it evolved informally in an experimental manner in response to users' needs and to pragmatic implementation considerations. Lisp's informal evolution has continued through the years, and the community of Lisp users has traditionally resisted attempts to promulgate any "official" definition of the language. This evolution, together with the flexibility and elegance of the initial conception, has enabled Lisp, which is the second oldest language in widespread use today (only Fortran is older), to continually adapt to encompass the most modern ideas about program design. Thus, Lisp is by now a family of dialects, which, while sharing most of the original features, may differ from one another in significant ways. The dialect of Lisp used in this book is called Scheme.[2]

Because of its experimental character and its emphasis on symbol manipulation, Lisp was at first very inefficient for numerical computations, at least in comparison with Fortran. Over the years, however, Lisp compilers have been developed that translate programs into machine code that can perform numerical computations reasonably efficiently. And for special applications, Lisp has been used with great effectiveness.[3] Although Lisp has not yet overcome its old reputation as hopelessly inefficient, Lisp is now used in many applications where efficiency is not the central concern. For example, Lisp has become a language of choice for

---

[2]The two dialects in which most major Lisp programs of the 1970s were written are MacLisp (Moon 1978; Pitman 1983), developed at the MIT Project MAC, and Interlisp (Teitelman 1974), developed at Bolt Beranek and Newman Inc. and the Xerox Palo Alto Research Center. Portable Standard Lisp (Hearn 1969; Griss 1981) was a Lisp dialect designed to be easily portable between different machines. MacLisp spawned a number of subdialects, such as Franz Lisp, which was developed at the University of California at Berkeley, and Zetalisp (Moon 1981), which was based on a special-purpose processor designed at the MIT Artificial Intelligence Laboratory to run Lisp very efficiently. The Lisp dialect used in this book, called Scheme (Steele 1975), was invented in 1975 by Guy Lewis Steele Jr. and Gerald Jay Sussman of the MIT Artificial Intelligence Laboratory and later reimplemented for instructional use at MIT. Scheme became an IEEE standard in 1990 (IEEE 1990). The Common Lisp dialect (Steele 1982, Steele 1990) was developed by the Lisp community to combine features from the earlier Lisp dialects to make an industrial standard for Lisp. Common Lisp became an ANSI standard in 1994 (ANSI 1994).

[3]One such special application was a breakthrough computation of scientific importance— an integration of the motion of the Solar System that extended previous results by nearly two orders of magnitude, and demonstrated that the dynamics of the Solar System is chaotic. This computation was made possible by new integration algorithms, a special-purpose compiler, and a special-purpose computer all implemented with the aid of software tools written in Lisp (Abelson et al. 1992; Sussman and Wisdom 1992).

operating-system shell languages and for extension languages for editors and computer-aided design systems.

If Lisp is not a mainstream language, why are we using it as the framework for our discussion of programming? Because the language possesses unique features that make it an excellent medium for studying important programming constructs and data structures and for relating them to the linguistic features that support them. The most significant of these features is the fact that Lisp descriptions of processes, called *procedures*, can themselves be represented and manipulated as Lisp data. The importance of this is that there are powerful program-design techniques that rely on the ability to blur the traditional distinction between "passive" data and "active" processes. As we shall discover, Lisp's flexibility in handling procedures as data makes it one of the most convenient languages in existence for exploring these techniques. The ability to represent procedures as data also makes Lisp an excellent language for writing programs that must manipulate other programs as data, such as the interpreters and compilers that support computer languages. Above and beyond these considerations, programming in Lisp is great fun.

1.1   The Elements of Programming

A powerful programming language is more than just a means for instructing a computer to perform tasks. The language also serves as a framework within which we organize our ideas about processes. Thus, when we describe a language, we should pay particular attention to the means that the language provides for combining simple ideas to form more complex ideas. Every powerful language has three mechanisms for accomplishing this:

- **primitive expressions**, which represent the simplest entities the language is concerned with,

- **means of combination**, by which compound elements are built from simpler ones, and

- **means of abstraction**, by which compound elements can be named and manipulated as units.

In programming, we deal with two kinds of elements: procedures and data. (Later we will discover that they are really not so distinct.) Informally, data is "stuff" that we want to manipulate, and procedures are descriptions of the rules for manipulating the data. Thus, any powerful programming language should be able to describe primitive data and primitive procedures and should have methods for combining and abstracting procedures and data.

In this chapter we will deal only with simple numerical data so that we can focus on the rules for building procedures.[4] In later chapters we will see that these same rules allow us to build procedures to manipulate compound data as well.

1.1.1   Expressions

One easy way to get started at programming is to examine some typical interactions with an interpreter for the Scheme dialect of Lisp. Imagine that you are sitting at a computer terminal. You type an *expression*, and the interpreter responds by displaying the result of its *evaluating* that expression.

One kind of primitive expression you might type is a number. (More precisely, the expression that you type consists of the numerals that represent the number in base 10.) If you present Lisp with a number

486

the interpreter will respond by printing[5]

486

Expressions representing numbers may be combined with an expression representing a primitive procedure (such as + or *) to form a com-

---

[4]The characterization of numbers as "simple data" is a barefaced bluff. In fact, the treatment of numbers is one of the trickiest and most confusing aspects of any programming language. Some typical issues involved are these: Some computer systems distinguish *integers*, such as 2, from *real numbers*, such as 2.71. Is the real number 2.00 different from the integer 2? Are the arithmetic operations used for integers the same as the operations used for real numbers? Does 6 divided by 2 produce 3, or 3.0? How large a number can we represent? How many decimal places of accuracy can we represent? Is the range of integers the same as the range of real numbers? Above and beyond these questions, of course, lies a collection of issues concerning roundoff and truncation errors—the entire science of numerical analysis. Since our focus in this book is on large-scale program design rather than on numerical techniques, we are going to ignore these problems. The numerical examples in this chapter will exhibit the usual roundoff behavior that one observes when using arithmetic operations that preserve a limited number of decimal places of accuracy in noninteger operations.

[5]Throughout this book, when we wish to emphasize the distinction between the input typed by the user and the response printed by the interpreter, we will show the latter in slanted characters.

pound expression that represents the application of the procedure to those numbers. For example:

```
(+ 137 349)
486

(- 1000 334)
666

(* 5 99)
495

(/ 10 5)
2

(+ 2.7 10)
12.7
```

Expressions such as these, formed by delimiting a list of expressions within parentheses in order to denote procedure application, are called *combinations*. The leftmost element in the list is called the *operator*, and the other elements are called *operands*. The value of a combination is obtained by applying the procedure specified by the operator to the *arguments* that are the values of the operands.

The convention of placing the operator to the left of the operands is known as *prefix notation*, and it may be somewhat confusing at first because it departs significantly from the customary mathematical convention. Prefix notation has several advantages, however. One of them is that it can accommodate procedures that may take an arbitrary number of arguments, as in the following examples:

```
(+ 21 35 12 7)
75

(* 25 4 12)
1200
```

No ambiguity can arise, because the operator is always the leftmost element and the entire combination is delimited by the parentheses.

A second advantage of prefix notation is that it extends in a straightforward way to allow combinations to be *nested*, that is, to have combinations whose elements are themselves combinations:

```
(+ (* 3 5) (- 10 6))
19
```

There is no limit (in principle) to the depth of such nesting and to the overall complexity of the expressions that the Lisp interpreter can evaluate. It is we humans who get confused by still relatively simple expressions such as

```
(+ (* 3 (+ (* 2 4) (+ 3 5))) (+ (- 10 7) 6))
```

which the interpreter would readily evaluate to be 57. We can help ourselves by writing such an expression in the form

```
(+ (* 3
      (+ (* 2 4)
         (+ 3 5)))
   (+ (- 10 7)
      6))
```

following a formatting convention known as *pretty-printing*, in which each long combination is written so that the operands are aligned vertically. The resulting indentations display clearly the structure of the expression.[6]

Even with complex expressions, the interpreter always operates in the same basic cycle: It reads an expression from the terminal, evaluates the expression, and prints the result. This mode of operation is often expressed by saying that the interpreter runs in a *read-eval-print loop*. Observe in particular that it is not necessary to explicitly instruct the interpreter to print the value of the expression.[7]

1.1.2   Naming and the Environment

A critical aspect of a programming language is the means it provides for using names to refer to computational objects. We say that the name identifies a *variable* whose *value* is the object.

In the Scheme dialect of Lisp, we name things with `define`. Typing

```
(define size 2)
```

---

[6]Lisp systems typically provide features to aid the user in formatting expressions. Two especially useful features are one that automatically indents to the proper pretty-print position whenever a new line is started and one that highlights the matching left parenthesis whenever a right parenthesis is typed.

[7]Lisp obeys the convention that every expression has a value. This convention, together with the old reputation of Lisp as an inefficient language, is the source of the quip by Alan Perlis (paraphrasing Oscar Wilde) that "Lisp programmers know the value of everything but the cost of nothing."

causes the interpreter to associate the value 2 with the name size.[8] Once
the name size has been associated with the number 2, we can refer to
the value 2 by name:

```
size
2

(* 5 size)
10
```

Here are further examples of the use of define:

```
(define pi 3.14159)

(define radius 10)

(* pi (* radius radius))
314.159

(define circumference (* 2 pi radius))

circumference
62.8318
```

Define is our language's simplest means of abstraction, for it allows
us to use simple names to refer to the results of compound operations,
such as the circumference computed above. In general, computational
objects may have very complex structures, and it would be extremely
inconvenient to have to remember and repeat their details each time we
want to use them. Indeed, complex programs are constructed by building,
step by step, computational objects of increasing complexity. The interpreter makes this step-by-step program construction particularly convenient because name-object associations can be created incrementally in
successive interactions. This feature encourages the incremental development and testing of programs and is largely responsible for the fact
that a Lisp program usually consists of a large number of relatively simple procedures.

It should be clear that the possibility of associating values with symbols and later retrieving them means that the interpreter must maintain
some sort of memory that keeps track of the name-object pairs. This
memory is called the *environment* (more precisely the *global environ-*

---

[8]In this book, we do not show the interpreter's response to evaluating definitions, since
this is highly implementation-dependent.

ment, since we will see later that a computation may involve a number of different environments).[9]

1.1.3   Evaluating Combinations

One of our goals in this chapter is to isolate issues about thinking procedurally. As a case in point, let us consider that, in evaluating combinations, the interpreter is itself following a procedure.

- To evaluate a combination, do the following:

1. Evaluate the subexpressions of the combination.

2. Apply the procedure that is the value of the leftmost subexpression (the operator) to the arguments that are the values of the other subexpressions (the operands).

Even this simple rule illustrates some important points about processes in general. First, observe that the first step dictates that in order to accomplish the evaluation process for a combination we must first perform the evaluation process on each element of the combination. Thus, the evaluation rule is *recursive* in nature; that is, it includes, as one of its steps, the need to invoke the rule itself.[10]

Notice how succinctly the idea of recursion can be used to express what, in the case of a deeply nested combination, would otherwise be viewed as a rather complicated process. For example, evaluating

```
(* (+ 2 (* 4 6))
   (+ 3 5 7))
```

requires that the evaluation rule be applied to four different combinations. We can obtain a picture of this process by representing the combination in the form of a tree, as shown in figure 1.1. Each combination is represented by a node with branches corresponding to the operator and the operands of the combination stemming from it. The terminal nodes (that is, nodes with no branches stemming from them) represent

---

[9]Chapter 3 will show that this notion of environment is crucial, both for understanding how the interpreter works and for implementing interpreters.

[10]It may seem strange that the evaluation rule says, as part of the first step, that we should evaluate the leftmost element of a combination, since at this point that can only be an operator such as + or * representing a built-in primitive procedure such as addition or multiplication. We will see later that it is useful to be able to work with combinations whose operators are themselves compound expressions.

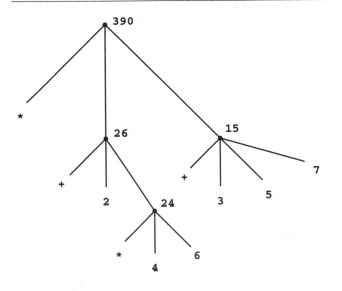

Figure 1.1   Tree representation, showing the value of each subcombination.

either operators or numbers. Viewing evaluation in terms of the tree, we can imagine that the values of the operands percolate upward, starting from the terminal nodes and then combining at higher and higher levels. In general, we shall see that recursion is a very powerful technique for dealing with hierarchical, treelike objects. In fact, the "percolate values upward" form of the evaluation rule is an example of a general kind of process known as *tree accumulation*.

Next, observe that the repeated application of the first step brings us to the point where we need to evaluate, not combinations, but primitive expressions such as numerals, built-in operators, or other names. We take care of the primitive cases by stipulating that

• the values of numerals are the numbers that they name,

• the values of built-in operators are the machine instruction sequences that carry out the corresponding operations, and

• the values of other names are the objects associated with those names in the environment.

We may regard the second rule as a special case of the third one by stipulating that symbols such as + and * are also included in the global environment, and are associated with the sequences of machine instructions that are their "values." The key point to notice is the role of the environment in determining the meaning of the symbols in expressions. In an interactive language such as Lisp, it is meaningless to speak of the value of an expression such as (+ x 1) without specifying any information about the environment that would provide a meaning for the symbol x (or even for the symbol +). As we shall see in chapter 3, the general notion of the environment as providing a context in which evaluation takes place will play an important role in our understanding of program execution.

Notice that the evaluation rule given above does not handle definitions. For instance, evaluating (define x 3) does not apply define to two arguments, one of which is the value of the symbol x and the other of which is 3, since the purpose of the define is precisely to associate x with a value. (That is, (define x 3) is not a combination.)

Such exceptions to the general evaluation rule are called *special forms*. Define is the only example of a special form that we have seen so far, but we will meet others shortly. Each special form has its own evaluation rule. The various kinds of expressions (each with its associated evaluation rule) constitute the syntax of the programming language. In comparison with most other programming languages, Lisp has a very simple syntax; that is, the evaluation rule for expressions can be described by a simple general rule together with specialized rules for a small number of special forms.[11]

1.1.4   Compound Procedures

We have identified in Lisp some of the elements that must appear in any powerful programming language:

- Numbers and arithmetic operations are primitive data and procedures.

- Nesting of combinations provides a means of combining operations.

- Definitions that associate names with values provide a limited means of abstraction.

---

[11]Special syntactic forms that are simply convenient alternative surface structures for things that can be written in more uniform ways are sometimes called *syntactic sugar*, to use a phrase coined by Peter Landin. In comparison with users of other languages, Lisp programmers, as a rule, are less concerned with matters of syntax. (By contrast, examine any Pascal manual and notice how much of it is devoted to descriptions of syntax.) This disdain for syntax is due partly to the flexibility of Lisp, which makes it easy to change surface syntax, and partly to the observation that many "convenient" syntactic constructs, which make the language less uniform, end up causing more trouble than they are worth when programs become large and complex. In the words of Alan Perlis, "Syntactic sugar causes cancer of the semicolon."

Now we will learn about *procedure definitions*, a much more powerful abstraction technique by which a compound operation can be given a name and then referred to as a unit.

We begin by examining how to express the idea of "squaring." We might say, "To square something, multiply it by itself." This is expressed in our language as

```
(define (square x) (* x x))
```

We can understand this in the following way:

```
(define (square  x)        (*       x     x))
   ↑         ↑     ↑         ↑        ↑     ↑
   To     square something, multiply it by itself.
```

We have here a *compound procedure*, which has been given the name square. The procedure represents the operation of multiplying something by itself. The thing to be multiplied is given a local name, x, which plays the same role that a pronoun plays in natural language. Evaluating the definition creates this compound procedure and associates it with the name square.[12]

The general form of a procedure definition is

```
(define (⟨name⟩ ⟨formal parameters⟩) ⟨body⟩)
```

The ⟨*name*⟩ is a symbol to be associated with the procedure definition in the environment.[13] The ⟨*formal parameters*⟩ are the names used within the body of the procedure to refer to the corresponding arguments of the procedure. The ⟨*body*⟩ is an expression that will yield the value of the procedure application when the formal parameters are replaced by the actual arguments to which the procedure is applied.[14] The ⟨*name*⟩ and

---

[12]Observe that there are two different operations being combined here: we are creating the procedure, and we are giving it the name square. It is possible, indeed important, to be able to separate these two notions—to create procedures without naming them, and to give names to procedures that have already been created. We will see how to do this in section 1.3.2.

[13]Throughout this book, we will describe the general syntax of expressions by using italic symbols delimited by angle brackets—e.g., ⟨*name*⟩—to denote the "slots" in the expression to be filled in when such an expression is actually used.

[14]More generally, the body of the procedure can be a sequence of expressions. In this case, the interpreter evaluates each expression in the sequence in turn and returns the value of the final expression as the value of the procedure application.

the ⟨*formal parameters*⟩ are grouped within parentheses, just as they would be in an actual call to the procedure being defined.

Having defined `square`, we can now use it:

```
(square 21)
441

(square (+ 2 5))
49

(square (square 3))
81
```

We can also use `square` as a building block in defining other procedures. For example, $x^2 + y^2$ can be expressed as

```
(+ (square x) (square y))
```

We can easily define a procedure `sum-of-squares` that, given any two numbers as arguments, produces the sum of their squares:

```
(define (sum-of-squares x y)
  (+ (square x) (square y)))

(sum-of-squares 3 4)
25
```

Now we can use `sum-of-squares` as a building block in constructing further procedures:

```
(define (f a)
  (sum-of-squares (+ a 1) (* a 2)))

(f 5)
136
```

Compound procedures are used in exactly the same way as primitive procedures. Indeed, one could not tell by looking at the definition of `sum-of-squares` given above whether `square` was built into the interpreter, like + and *, or defined as a compound procedure.

1.1.5   The Substitution Model for Procedure Application

To evaluate a combination whose operator names a compound procedure, the interpreter follows much the same process as for combinations whose operators name primitive procedures, which we described in sec-

tion 1.1.3. That is, the interpreter evaluates the elements of the combination and applies the procedure (which is the value of the operator of the
combination) to the arguments (which are the values of the operands of
the combination).

We can assume that the mechanism for applying primitive procedures
to arguments is built into the interpreter. For compound procedures, the
application process is as follows:

• To apply a compound procedure to arguments, evaluate the body of
the procedure with each formal parameter replaced by the corresponding
argument.

To illustrate this process, let's evaluate the combination

```
(f 5)
```

where f is the procedure defined in section 1.1.4. We begin by retrieving
the body of f:

```
(sum-of-squares (+ a 1) (* a 2))
```

Then we replace the formal parameter a by the argument 5:

```
(sum-of-squares (+ 5 1) (* 5 2))
```

Thus the problem reduces to the evaluation of a combination with two
operands and an operator sum-of-squares. Evaluating this combination involves three subproblems. We must evaluate the operator to get
the procedure to be applied, and we must evaluate the operands to get
the arguments. Now (+ 5 1) produces 6 and (* 5 2) produces 10,
so we must apply the sum-of-squares procedure to 6 and 10. These
values are substituted for the formal parameters x and y in the body of
sum-of-squares, reducing the expression to

```
(+ (square 6) (square 10))
```

If we use the definition of square, this reduces to

```
(+ (* 6 6) (* 10 10))
```

which reduces by multiplication to

```
(+ 36 100)
```

and finally to

136

The process we have just described is called the *substitution model* for procedure application. It can be taken as a model that determines the "meaning" of procedure application, insofar as the procedures in this chapter are concerned. However, there are two points that should be stressed:

• The purpose of the substitution is to help us think about procedure application, not to provide a description of how the interpreter really works. Typical interpreters do not evaluate procedure applications by manipulating the text of a procedure to substitute values for the formal parameters. In practice, the "substitution" is accomplished by using a local environment for the formal parameters. We will discuss this more fully in chapters 3 and 4 when we examine the implementation of an interpreter in detail.

• Over the course of this book, we will present a sequence of increasingly elaborate models of how interpreters work, culminating with a complete implementation of an interpreter and compiler in chapter 5. The substitution model is only the first of these models—a way to get started thinking formally about the evaluation process. In general, when modeling phenomena in science and engineering, we begin with simplified, incomplete models. As we examine things in greater detail, these simple models become inadequate and must be replaced by more refined models. The substitution model is no exception. In particular, when we address in chapter 3 the use of procedures with "mutable data," we will see that the substitution model breaks down and must be replaced by a more complicated model of procedure application.[15]

Applicative order versus normal order

According to the description of evaluation given in section 1.1.3, the interpreter first evaluates the operator and operands and then applies the

---

[15]Despite the simplicity of the substitution idea, it turns out to be surprisingly complicated to give a rigorous mathematical definition of the substitution process. The problem arises from the possibility of confusion between the names used for the formal parameters of a procedure and the (possibly identical) names used in the expressions to which the procedure may be applied. Indeed, there is a long history of erroneous definitions of *substitution* in the literature of logic and programming semantics. See Stoy 1977 for a careful discussion of substitution.

resulting procedure to the resulting arguments. This is not the only way
to perform evaluation. An alternative evaluation model would not evaluate the operands until their values were needed. Instead it would first
substitute operand expressions for parameters until it obtained an expression involving only primitive operators, and would then perform the
evaluation. If we used this method, the evaluation of

```
(f 5)
```

would proceed according to the sequence of expansions

```
(sum-of-squares (+ 5 1) (* 5 2))

(+      (square (+ 5 1))        (square (* 5 2))   )

(+      (* (+ 5 1) (+ 5 1))     (* (* 5 2) (* 5 2)))
```

followed by the reductions

```
(+           (* 6 6)              (* 10 10))

(+             36                   100)
```

$$136$$

This gives the same answer as our previous evaluation model, but the process is different. In particular, the evaluations of (+ 5 1) and (* 5 2)
are each performed twice here, corresponding to the reduction of the expression

```
(* x x)
```

with x replaced respectively by (+ 5 1) and (* 5 2).

   This alternative "fully expand and then reduce" evaluation method is
known as *normal-order evaluation*, in contrast to the "evaluate the arguments and then apply" method that the interpreter actually uses, which
is called *applicative-order evaluation*. It can be shown that, for procedure applications that can be modeled using substitution (including all
the procedures in the first two chapters of this book) and that yield legitimate values, normal-order and applicative-order evaluation produce
the same value. (See exercise 1.5 for an instance of an "illegitimate"
value where normal-order and applicative-order evaluation do not give
the same result.)

Lisp uses applicative-order evaluation, partly because of the additional efficiency obtained from avoiding multiple evaluations of expressions such as those illustrated with (+ 5 1) and (* 5 2) above and, more significantly, because normal-order evaluation becomes much more complicated to deal with when we leave the realm of procedures that can be modeled by substitution. On the other hand, normal-order evaluation can be an extremely valuable tool, and we will investigate some of its implications in chapters 3 and 4.[16]

1.1.6   Conditional Expressions and Predicates

The expressive power of the class of procedures that we can define at this point is very limited, because we have no way to make tests and to perform different operations depending on the result of a test. For instance, we cannot define a procedure that computes the absolute value of a number by testing whether the number is positive, negative, or zero and taking different actions in the different cases according to the rule

$$|x| = \begin{cases} x & \text{if } x > 0 \\ 0 & \text{if } x = 0 \\ -x & \text{if } x < 0 \end{cases}$$

This construct is called a *case analysis,* and there is a special form in Lisp for notating such a case analysis. It is called cond (which stands for "conditional"), and it is used as follows:

```
(define (abs x)
  (cond ((> x 0) x)
        ((= x 0) 0)
        ((< x 0) (- x)))))
```

The general form of a conditional expression is

```
(cond (⟨p₁⟩ ⟨e₁⟩)
      (⟨p₂⟩ ⟨e₂⟩)
        ⋮
      (⟨pₙ⟩ ⟨eₙ⟩)))
```

---

[16]In chapter 3 we will introduce *stream processing*, which is a way of handling apparently "infinite" data structures by incorporating a limited form of normal-order evaluation. In section 4.2 we will modify the Scheme interpreter to produce a normal-order variant of Scheme.

consisting of the symbol cond followed by parenthesized pairs of ex-
pressions ($\langle p \rangle$ $\langle e \rangle$) called *clauses*. The first expression in each pair is
a *predicate*—that is, an expression whose value is interpreted as either
true or false.[17]

Conditional expressions are evaluated as follows. The predicate $\langle p_1 \rangle$
is evaluated first. If its value is false, then $\langle p_2 \rangle$ is evaluated. If $\langle p_2 \rangle$'s
value is also false, then $\langle p_3 \rangle$ is evaluated. This process continues until
a predicate is found whose value is true, in which case the interpreter
returns the value of the corresponding *consequent expression* $\langle e \rangle$ of the
clause as the value of the conditional expression. If none of the $\langle p \rangle$'s is
found to be true, the value of the cond is undefined.

The word *predicate* is used for procedures that return true or false,
as well as for expressions that evaluate to true or false. The absolute-
value procedure abs makes use of the primitive predicates >, <, and =.[18]
These take two numbers as arguments and test whether the first number
is, respectively, greater than, less than, or equal to the second number,
returning true or false accordingly.

Another way to write the absolute-value procedure is

```
(define (abs x)
  (cond ((< x 0) (- x))
        (else x)))
```

which could be expressed in English as "If x is less than zero return $-x$;
otherwise return x." Else is a special symbol that can be used in place of
the $\langle p \rangle$ in the final clause of a cond. This causes the cond to return as its
value the value of the corresponding $\langle e \rangle$ whenever all previous clauses
have been bypassed. In fact, any expression that always evaluates to a
true value could be used as the $\langle p \rangle$ here.

Here is yet another way to write the absolute-value procedure:

```
(define (abs x)
  (if (< x 0)
      (- x)
      x))
```

---

[17]"Interpreted as either true or false" means this: In Scheme, there are two distinguished
values that are denoted by the constants #t and #f. When the interpreter checks a predicate's value, it interprets #f as false. Any other value is treated as true. (Thus, providing
#t is logically unnecessary, but it is convenient.) In this book we will use names true and
false, which are associated with the values #t and #f respectively.

[18]Abs also uses the "minus" operator -, which, when used with a single operand, as in
(- x), indicates negation.

This uses the special form `if`, a restricted type of conditional that can be used when there are precisely two cases in the case analysis. The general form of an `if` expression is

(if ⟨*predicate*⟩ ⟨*consequent*⟩ ⟨*alternative*⟩)

To evaluate an `if` expression, the interpreter starts by evaluating the ⟨*predicate*⟩ part of the expression. If the ⟨*predicate*⟩ evaluates to a true value, the interpreter then evaluates the ⟨*consequent*⟩ and returns its value. Otherwise it evaluates the ⟨*alternative*⟩ and returns its value.[19]

In addition to primitive predicates such as <, =, and >, there are logical composition operations, which enable us to construct compound predicates. The three most frequently used are these:

- (and ⟨e_1⟩ ... ⟨e_n⟩)

The interpreter evaluates the expressions ⟨*e*⟩ one at a time, in left-to-right order. If any ⟨*e*⟩ evaluates to false, the value of the and expression is false, and the rest of the ⟨*e*⟩'s are not evaluated. If all ⟨*e*⟩'s evaluate to true values, the value of the and expression is the value of the last one.

- (or ⟨e_1⟩ ... ⟨e_n⟩)

The interpreter evaluates the expressions ⟨*e*⟩ one at a time, in left-to-right order. If any ⟨*e*⟩ evaluates to a true value, that value is returned as the value of the or expression, and the rest of the ⟨*e*⟩'s are not evaluated. If all ⟨*e*⟩'s evaluate to false, the value of the or expression is false.

- (not ⟨*e*⟩)

The value of a not expression is true when the expression ⟨*e*⟩ evaluates to false, and false otherwise.

Notice that and and or are special forms, not procedures, because the subexpressions are not necessarily all evaluated. Not is an ordinary procedure.

As an example of how these are used, the condition that a number x be in the range $5 < x < 10$ may be expressed as

(and (> x 5) (< x 10))

---

[19]A minor difference between `if` and `cond` is that the ⟨*e*⟩ part of each cond clause may be a sequence of expressions. If the corresponding ⟨*p*⟩ is found to be true, the expressions ⟨*e*⟩ are evaluated in sequence and the value of the final expression in the sequence is returned as the value of the cond. In an `if` expression, however, the ⟨*consequent*⟩ and ⟨*alternative*⟩ must be single expressions.

As another example, we can define a predicate to test whether one number is greater than or equal to another as

```
(define (>= x y)
  (or (> x y) (= x y)))
```

or alternatively as

```
(define (>= x y)
  (not (< x y)))
```

Exercise 1.1

Below is a sequence of expressions. What is the result printed by the interpreter in response to each expression? Assume that the sequence is to be evaluated in the order in which it is presented.

```
10

(+ 5 3 4)

(- 9 1)

(/ 6 2)

(+ (* 2 4) (- 4 6))

(define a 3)

(define b (+ a 1))

(+ a b (* a b))

(= a b)

(if (and (> b a) (< b (* a b)))
    b
    a)

(cond ((= a 4) 6)
      ((= b 4) (+ 6 7 a))
      (else 25))

(+ 2 (if (> b a) b a))

(* (cond ((> a b) a)
         ((< a b) b)
         (else -1))
   (+ a 1))
```

Exercise 1.2

Translate the following expression into prefix form

$$\frac{5 + 4 + \left(2 - \left(3 - \left(6 + \frac{4}{5}\right)\right)\right)}{3(6 - 2)(2 - 7)}$$

Exercise 1.3

Define a procedure that takes three numbers as arguments and returns the sum of the squares of the two larger numbers.

Exercise 1.4

Observe that our model of evaluation allows for combinations whose operators are compound expressions. Use this observation to describe the behavior of the following procedure:

```
(define (a-plus-abs-b a b)
  ((if (> b 0) + -) a b))
```

Exercise 1.5

Ben Bitdiddle has invented a test to determine whether the interpreter he is faced with is using applicative-order evaluation or normal-order evaluation. He defines the following two procedures:

```
(define (p) (p))

(define (test x y)
  (if (= x 0)
      0
      y))
```

Then he evaluates the expression

```
(test 0 (p))
```

What behavior will Ben observe with an interpreter that uses applicative-order evaluation? What behavior will he observe with an interpreter that uses normal-order evaluation? Explain your answer. (Assume that the evaluation rule for the special form `if` is the same whether the interpreter is using normal or applicative order: The predicate expression is evaluated first, and the result determines whether to evaluate the consequent or the alternative expression.)

1.1.7   Example: Square Roots by Newton's Method

Procedures, as introduced above, are much like ordinary mathematical functions. They specify a value that is determined by one or more parameters. But there is an important difference between mathematical functions and computer procedures. Procedures must be effective.

As a case in point, consider the problem of computing square roots. We can define the square-root function as

$$\sqrt{x} = \text{the } y \text{ such that } y \geq 0 \text{ and } y^2 = x$$

This describes a perfectly legitimate mathematical function. We could use it to recognize whether one number is the square root of another, or to derive facts about square roots in general. On the other hand, the definition does not describe a procedure. Indeed, it tells us almost nothing about how to actually find the square root of a given number. It will not help matters to rephrase this definition in pseudo-Lisp:

```
(define (sqrt x)
  (the y (and (>= y 0)
              (= (square y) x))))
```

This only begs the question.

The contrast between function and procedure is a reflection of the general distinction between describing properties of things and describing how to do things, or, as it is sometimes referred to, the distinction between declarative knowledge and imperative knowledge. In mathematics we are usually concerned with declarative (what is) descriptions, whereas in computer science we are usually concerned with imperative (how to) descriptions.[20]

How does one compute square roots? The most common way is to use Newton's method of successive approximations, which says that whenever we have a guess y for the value of the square root of a number x, we can perform a simple manipulation to get a better guess (one closer to

---

[20]Declarative and imperative descriptions are intimately related, as indeed are mathematics and computer science. For instance, to say that the answer produced by a program is "correct" is to make a declarative statement about the program. There is a large amount of research aimed at establishing techniques for proving that programs are correct, and much of the technical difficulty of this subject has to do with negotiating the transition between imperative statements (from which programs are constructed) and declarative statements (which can be used to deduce things). In a related vein, an important current area in programming-language design is the exploration of so-called very high-level languages, in which one actually programs in terms of declarative statements. The idea is to make interpreters sophisticated enough so that, given "what is" knowledge specified by the programmer, they can generate "how to" knowledge automatically. This cannot be done in general, but there are important areas where progress has been made. We shall revisit this idea in chapter 4.

the actual square root) by averaging y with x/y.[21] For example, we can compute the square root of 2 as follows. Suppose our initial guess is 1:

Guess	Quotient	Average
1	$\dfrac{2}{1} = 2$	$\dfrac{(2+1)}{2} = 1.5$
1.5	$\dfrac{2}{1.5} = 1.3333$	$\dfrac{(1.3333 + 1.5)}{2} = 1.4167$
1.4167	$\dfrac{2}{1.4167} = 1.4118$	$\dfrac{(1.4167 + 1.4118)}{2} = 1.4142$
1.4142 ...		...

Continuing this process, we obtain better and better approximations to the square root.

Now let's formalize the process in terms of procedures. We start with a value for the radicand (the number whose square root we are trying to compute) and a value for the guess. If the guess is good enough for our purposes, we are done; if not, we must repeat the process with an improved guess. We write this basic strategy as a procedure:

```
(define (sqrt-iter guess x)
  (if (good-enough? guess x)
      guess
      (sqrt-iter (improve guess x)
                 x)))
```

A guess is improved by averaging it with the quotient of the radicand and the old guess:

```
(define (improve guess x)
  (average guess (/ x guess)))
```

where

```
(define (average x y)
  (/ (+ x y) 2))
```

---

[21]This square-root algorithm is actually a special case of Newton's method, which is a general technique for finding roots of equations. The square-root algorithm itself was developed by Heron of Alexandria in the first century A.D. We will see how to express the general Newton's method as a Lisp procedure in section 1.3.4.

We also have to say what we mean by "good enough." The following will
do for illustration, but it is not really a very good test. (See exercise 1.7.)
The idea is to improve the answer until it is close enough so that its
square differs from the radicand by less than a predetermined tolerance
(here 0.001):[22]

```
(define (good-enough? guess x)
  (< (abs (- (square guess) x)) 0.001))
```

Finally, we need a way to get started. For instance, we can always guess
that the square root of any number is 1:[23]

```
(define (sqrt x)
  (sqrt-iter 1.0 x))
```

If we type these definitions to the interpreter, we can use sqrt just as we
can use any procedure:

```
(sqrt 9)
3.00009155413138

(sqrt (+ 100 37))
11.704699917758145

(sqrt (+ (sqrt 2) (sqrt 3)))
1.7739279023207892

(square (sqrt 1000))
1000.000369924366
```

The sqrt program also illustrates that the simple procedural language
we have introduced so far is sufficient for writing any purely numerical
program that one could write in, say, C or Pascal. This might seem sur-

---

[22]We will usually give predicates names ending with question marks, to help us remember
that they are predicates. This is just a stylistic convention. As far as the interpreter is
concerned, the question mark is just an ordinary character.

[23]Observe that we express our initial guess as 1.0 rather than 1. This would not make any
difference in many Lisp implementations. MIT Scheme, however, distinguishes between
exact integers and decimal values, and dividing two integers produces a rational number
rather than a decimal. For example, dividing 10 by 6 yields 5/3, while dividing 10.0 by
6.0 yields 1.6666666666666667. (We will learn how to implement arithmetic on rational
numbers in section 2.1.1.) If we start with an initial guess of 1 in our square-root program,
and x is an exact integer, all subsequent values produced in the square-root computation
will be rational numbers rather than decimals. Mixed operations on rational numbers
and decimals always yield decimals, so starting with an initial guess of 1.0 forces all
subsequent values to be decimals.

prising, since we have not included in our language any iterative (looping) constructs that direct the computer to do something over and over again. Sqrt-iter, on the other hand, demonstrates how iteration can be accomplished using no special construct other than the ordinary ability to call a procedure.[24]

Exercise 1.6

Alyssa P. Hacker doesn't see why if needs to be provided as a special form. "Why can't I just define it as an ordinary procedure in terms of cond?" she asks. Alyssa's friend Eva Lu Ator claims this can indeed be done, and she defines a new version of if:

```
(define (new-if predicate then-clause else-clause)
  (cond (predicate then-clause)
        (else else-clause)))
```

Eva demonstrates the program for Alyssa:

```
(new-if (= 2 3) 0 5)
5

(new-if (= 1 1) 0 5)
0
```

Delighted, Alyssa uses new-if to rewrite the square-root program:

```
(define (sqrt-iter guess x)
  (new-if (good-enough? guess x)
          guess
          (sqrt-iter (improve guess x)
                     x)))
```

What happens when Alyssa attempts to use this to compute square roots? Explain.

Exercise 1.7

The good-enough? test used in computing square roots will not be very effective for finding the square roots of very small numbers. Also, in real computers, arithmetic operations are almost always performed with limited precision. This makes our test inadequate for very large numbers. Explain these statements, with examples showing how the test fails for small and large numbers. An alternative strategy for implementing good-enough? is to watch how guess changes from one iteration to the next and to stop when the change is a very small fraction of the guess. Design a square-root procedure that uses this kind of end test. Does this work better for small and large numbers?

---

[24]Readers who are worried about the efficiency issues involved in using procedure calls to implement iteration should note the remarks on "tail recursion" in section 1.2.1.

Exercise 1.8

Newton's method for cube roots is based on the fact that if y is an approximation to the cube root of x, then a better approximation is given by the value

$$\frac{x/y^2 + 2y}{3}$$

Use this formula to implement a cube-root procedure analogous to the square-root procedure. (In section 1.3.4 we will see how to implement Newton's method in general as an abstraction of these square-root and cube-root procedures.)

1.1.8   Procedures as Black-Box Abstractions

Sqrt is our first example of a process defined by a set of mutually defined procedures. Notice that the definition of sqrt-iter is *recursive*; that is, the procedure is defined in terms of itself. The idea of being able to define a procedure in terms of itself may be disturbing; it may seem unclear how such a "circular" definition could make sense at all, much less specify a well-defined process to be carried out by a computer. This will be addressed more carefully in section 1.2. But first let's consider some other important points illustrated by the sqrt example.

Observe that the problem of computing square roots breaks up naturally into a number of subproblems: how to tell whether a guess is good enough, how to improve a guess, and so on. Each of these tasks is accomplished by a separate procedure. The entire sqrt program can be viewed as a cluster of procedures (shown in figure 1.2) that mirrors the decomposition of the problem into subproblems.

The importance of this decomposition strategy is not simply that one is dividing the program into parts. After all, we could take any large program and divide it into parts—the first ten lines, the next ten lines, the next ten lines, and so on. Rather, it is crucial that each procedure accomplishes an identifiable task that can be used as a module in defining other procedures. For example, when we define the good-enough? procedure in terms of square, we are able to regard the square procedure as a "black box." We are not at that moment concerned with *how* the procedure computes its result, only with the fact that it computes the square. The details of how the square is computed can be suppressed, to be considered at a later time. Indeed, as far as the good-enough? procedure is concerned, square is not quite a procedure but rather an abstraction of a procedure, a so-called *procedural abstraction*. At this level of abstraction, any procedure that computes the square is equally good.

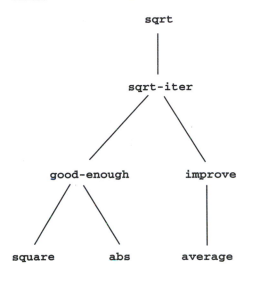

Figure 1.2   Procedural decomposition of the `sqrt` program.

Thus, considering only the values they return, the following two procedures for squaring a number should be indistinguishable. Each takes a numerical argument and produces the square of that number as the value.[25]

```
(define (square x) (* x x))
```

```
(define (square x)
  (exp (double (log x)))))
```

```
(define (double x) (+ x x))
```

So a procedure definition should be able to suppress detail. The users of the procedure may not have written the procedure themselves, but may have obtained it from another programmer as a black box. A user should not need to know how the procedure is implemented in order to use it.

Local names

One detail of a procedure's implementation that should not matter to the user of the procedure is the implementer's choice of names for the

---

[25] It is not even clear which of these procedures is a more efficient implementation. This depends upon the hardware available. There are machines for which the "obvious" implementation is the less efficient one. Consider a machine that has extensive tables of logarithms and antilogarithms stored in a very efficient manner.

procedure's formal parameters. Thus, the following procedures should not be distinguishable:

```
(define (square x) (* x x))

(define (square y) (* y y))
```

This principle—that the meaning of a procedure should be independent of the parameter names used by its author—seems on the surface to be self-evident, but its consequences are profound. The simplest consequence is that the parameter names of a procedure must be local to the body of the procedure. For example, we used square in the definition of good-enough? in our square-root procedure:

```
(define (good-enough? guess x)
  (< (abs (- (square guess) x)) 0.001))
```

The intention of the author of good-enough? is to determine if the square of the first argument is within a given tolerance of the second argument. We see that the author of good-enough? used the name guess to refer to the first argument and x to refer to the second argument. The argument of square is guess. If the author of square used x (as above) to refer to that argument, we see that the x in good-enough? must be a different x than the one in square. Running the procedure square must not affect the value of x that is used by good-enough?, because that value of x may be needed by good-enough? after square is done computing.

If the parameters were not local to the bodies of their respective procedures, then the parameter x in square could be confused with the parameter x in good-enough?, and the behavior of good-enough? would depend upon which version of square we used. Thus, square would not be the black box we desired.

A formal parameter of a procedure has a very special role in the procedure definition, in that it doesn't matter what name the formal parameter has. Such a name is called a *bound variable*, and we say that the procedure definition *binds* its formal parameters. The meaning of a procedure definition is unchanged if a bound variable is consistently renamed throughout the definition.[26] If a variable is not bound, we say that it is *free*. The set of expressions for which a binding defines a name is called the *scope* of that name. In a procedure definition, the bound variables

---

[26]The concept of consistent renaming is actually subtle and difficult to define formally. Famous logicians have made embarrassing errors here.

declared as the formal parameters of the procedure have the body of the procedure as their scope.

In the definition of good-enough? above, guess and x are bound variables but <, -, abs, and square are free. The meaning of good-enough? should be independent of the names we choose for guess and x so long as they are distinct and different from <, -, abs, and square. (If we renamed guess to abs we would have introduced a bug by *capturing* the variable abs. It would have changed from free to bound.) The meaning of good-enough? is not independent of the names of its free variables, however. It surely depends upon the fact (external to this definition) that the symbol abs names a procedure for computing the absolute value of a number. Good-enough? will compute a different function if we substitute cos for abs in its definition.

Internal definitions and block structure

We have one kind of name isolation available to us so far: The formal parameters of a procedure are local to the body of the procedure. The square-root program illustrates another way in which we would like to control the use of names. The existing program consists of separate procedures:

```
(define (sqrt x)
  (sqrt-iter 1.0 x))

(define (sqrt-iter guess x)
  (if (good-enough? guess x)
      guess
      (sqrt-iter (improve guess x) x)))

(define (good-enough? guess x)
  (< (abs (- (square guess) x)) 0.001))

(define (improve guess x)
  (average guess (/ x guess)))
```

The problem with this program is that the only procedure that is important to users of sqrt is sqrt. The other procedures (sqrt-iter, good-enough?, and improve) only clutter up their minds. They may not define any other procedure called good-enough? as part of another program to work together with the square-root program, because sqrt needs it. The problem is especially severe in the construction of large systems by many separate programmers. For example, in the construction of a large library of numerical procedures, many numerical functions are computed as successive approximations and thus might have procedures named good-enough? and improve as auxiliary procedures. We would like to localize the subprocedures, hiding them inside sqrt so that sqrt could coexist with other successive approximations, each having its own private good-enough? procedure. To make this possible, we allow a procedure to have internal definitions that are local to that procedure. For example, in the square-root problem we can write

```
(define (sqrt x)
  (define (good-enough? guess x)
    (< (abs (- (square guess) x)) 0.001))
  (define (improve guess x)
    (average guess (/ x guess)))
  (define (sqrt-iter guess x)
    (if (good-enough? guess x)
        guess
        (sqrt-iter (improve guess x) x)))
  (sqrt-iter 1.0 x))
```

Such nesting of definitions, called *block structure*, is basically the right solution to the simplest name-packaging problem. But there is a better idea lurking here. In addition to internalizing the definitions of the auxiliary procedures, we can simplify them. Since x is bound in the definition of sqrt, the procedures good-enough?, improve, and sqrt-iter, which are defined internally to sqrt, are in the scope of x. Thus, it is not necessary to pass x explicitly to each of these procedures. Instead, we allow x to be a free variable in the internal definitions, as shown below. Then x gets its value from the argument with which the enclosing procedure sqrt is called. This discipline is called *lexical scoping.*[27]

```
(define (sqrt x)
  (define (good-enough? guess)
    (< (abs (- (square guess) x)) 0.001))
  (define (improve guess)
    (average guess (/ x guess)))
  (define (sqrt-iter guess)
    (if (good-enough? guess)
        guess
        (sqrt-iter (improve guess))))
  (sqrt-iter 1.0))
```

---

[27]Lexical scoping dictates that free variables in a procedure are taken to refer to bindings made by enclosing procedure definitions; that is, they are looked up in the environment in which the procedure was defined. We will see how this works in detail in chapter 3 when we study environments and the detailed behavior of the interpreter.

We will use block structure extensively to help us break up large programs into tractable pieces.[28] The idea of block structure originated with the programming language Algol 60. It appears in most advanced programming languages and is an important tool for helping to organize the construction of large programs.

1.2   Procedures and the Processes They Generate

We have now considered the elements of programming: We have used primitive arithmetic operations, we have combined these operations, and we have abstracted these composite operations by defining them as compound procedures. But that is not enough to enable us to say that we know how to program. Our situation is analogous to that of someone who has learned the rules for how the pieces move in chess but knows nothing of typical openings, tactics, or strategy. Like the novice chess player, we don't yet know the common patterns of usage in the domain. We lack the knowledge of which moves are worth making (which procedures are worth defining). We lack the experience to predict the consequences of making a move (executing a procedure).

The ability to visualize the consequences of the actions under consideration is crucial to becoming an expert programmer, just as it is in any synthetic, creative activity. In becoming an expert photographer, for example, one must learn how to look at a scene and know how dark each region will appear on a print for each possible choice of exposure and development conditions. Only then can one reason backward, planning framing, lighting, exposure, and development to obtain the desired effects. So it is with programming, where we are planning the course of action to be taken by a process and where we control the process by means of a program. To become experts, we must learn to visualize the processes generated by various types of procedures. Only after we have developed such a skill can we learn to reliably construct programs that exhibit the desired behavior.

A procedure is a pattern for the *local evolution* of a computational process. It specifies how each stage of the process is built upon the previous stage. We would like to be able to make statements about the overall, or *global*, behavior of a process whose local evolution has been specified by a procedure. This is very difficult to do in general, but we can at least try to describe some typical patterns of process evolution.

---

[28]Embedded definitions must come first in a procedure body. The management is not responsible for the consequences of running programs that intertwine definition and use.

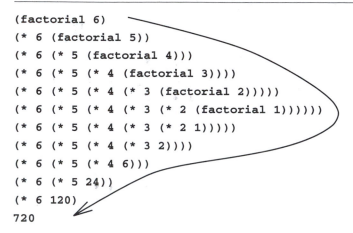

```
(factorial 6)
(* 6 (factorial 5))
(* 6 (* 5 (factorial 4)))
(* 6 (* 5 (* 4 (factorial 3))))
(* 6 (* 5 (* 4 (* 3 (factorial 2)))))
(* 6 (* 5 (* 4 (* 3 (* 2 (factorial 1))))))
(* 6 (* 5 (* 4 (* 3 (* 2 1)))))
(* 6 (* 5 (* 4 (* 3 2))))
(* 6 (* 5 (* 4 6)))
(* 6 (* 5 24))
(* 6 120)
720
```

Figure 1.3   A linear recursive process for computing 6!.

In this section we will examine some common "shapes" for processes generated by simple procedures. We will also investigate the rates at which these processes consume the important computational resources of time and space. The procedures we will consider are very simple. Their role is like that played by test patterns in photography: as oversimplified prototypical patterns, rather than practical examples in their own right.

1.2.1   Linear Recursion and Iteration

We begin by considering the factorial function, defined by

$$n! = n \cdot (n - 1) \cdot (n - 2) \cdots 3 \cdot 2 \cdot 1$$

There are many ways to compute factorials. One way is to make use of the observation that $n!$ is equal to n times $(n - 1)!$ for any positive integer n:

$$n! = n \cdot [(n - 1) \cdot (n - 2) \cdots 3 \cdot 2 \cdot 1] = n \cdot (n - 1)!$$

Thus, we can compute $n!$ by computing $(n - 1)!$ and multiplying the result by n. If we add the stipulation that 1! is equal to 1, this observation translates directly into a procedure:

```
(define (factorial n)
  (if (= n 1)
      1
      (* n (factorial (- n 1)))))
```

```
(factorial 6)
(fact-iter    1 1 6)
(fact-iter    1 2 6)
(fact-iter    2 3 6)
(fact-iter    6 4 6)
(fact-iter   24 5 6)
(fact-iter  120 6 6)
(fact-iter  720 7 6)
720
```

Figure 1.4   A linear iterative process for computing 6!.

We can use the substitution model of section 1.1.5 to watch this procedure in action computing 6!, as shown in figure 1.3.

Now let's take a different perspective on computing factorials. We
could describe a rule for computing $n!$ by specifying that we first multiply 1 by 2, then multiply the result by 3, then by 4, and so on until we
reach n. More formally, we maintain a running product, together with a
counter that counts from 1 up to n. We can describe the computation by
saying that the counter and the product simultaneously change from one
step to the next according to the rule

product $\leftarrow$ counter $\cdot$ product

counter $\leftarrow$ counter $+$ 1

and stipulating that $n!$ is the value of the product when the counter exceeds n.

Once again, we can recast our description as a procedure for computing factorials:[29]

---

[29]In a real program we would probably use the block structure introduced in the last section
to hide the definition of `fact-iter`:

```
(define (factorial n)
  (define (iter product counter)
    (if (> counter n)
        product
        (iter (* counter product)
              (+ counter 1))))
  (iter 1 1))
```

We avoided doing this here so as to minimize the number of things to think about at once.

```
(define (factorial n)
  (fact-iter 1 1 n))

(define (fact-iter product counter max-count)
  (if (> counter max-count)
      product
      (fact-iter (* counter product)
                 (+ counter 1)
                 max-count)))
```

As before, we can use the substitution model to visualize the process of computing 6!, as shown in figure 1.4.

Compare the two processes. From one point of view, they seem hardly different at all. Both compute the same mathematical function on the same domain, and each requires a number of steps proportional to *n* to compute *n*!. Indeed, both processes even carry out the same sequence of multiplications, obtaining the same sequence of partial products. On the other hand, when we consider the "shapes" of the two processes, we find that they evolve quite differently.

Consider the first process. The substitution model reveals a shape of expansion followed by contraction, indicated by the arrow in figure 1.3. The expansion occurs as the process builds up a chain of *deferred operations* (in this case, a chain of multiplications). The contraction occurs as the operations are actually performed. This type of process, characterized by a chain of deferred operations, is called a *recursive process*. Carrying out this process requires that the interpreter keep track of the operations to be performed later on. In the computation of *n*!, the length of the chain of deferred multiplications, and hence the amount of information needed to keep track of it, grows linearly with *n* (is proportional to *n*), just like the number of steps. Such a process is called a *linear recursive process*.

By contrast, the second process does not grow and shrink. At each step, all we need to keep track of, for any *n*, are the current values of the variables product, counter, and max-count. We call this an *iterative process*. In general, an iterative process is one whose state can be summarized by a fixed number of *state variables*, together with a fixed rule that describes how the state variables should be updated as the process moves from state to state and an (optional) end test that specifies conditions under which the process should terminate. In computing *n*!, the number of steps required grows linearly with *n*. Such a process is called a *linear iterative process*.

The contrast between the two processes can be seen in another way. In the iterative case, the program variables provide a complete description of the state of the process at any point. If we stopped the computation between steps, all we would need to do to resume the computation is to supply the interpreter with the values of the three program variables. Not so with the recursive process. In this case there is some additional "hidden" information, maintained by the interpreter and not contained in the program variables, which indicates "where the process is" in negotiating the chain of deferred operations. The longer the chain, the more information must be maintained.[30]

In contrasting iteration and recursion, we must be careful not to confuse the notion of a recursive *process* with the notion of a recursive *procedure*. When we describe a procedure as recursive, we are referring to the syntactic fact that the procedure definition refers (either directly or indirectly) to the procedure itself. But when we describe a process as following a pattern that is, say, linearly recursive, we are speaking about how the process evolves, not about the syntax of how a procedure is written. It may seem disturbing that we refer to a recursive procedure such as `fact-iter` as generating an iterative process. However, the process really is iterative: Its state is captured completely by its three state variables, and an interpreter need keep track of only three variables in order to execute the process.

One reason that the distinction between process and procedure may be confusing is that most implementations of common languages (including Ada, Pascal, and C) are designed in such a way that the interpretation of any recursive procedure consumes an amount of memory that grows with the number of procedure calls, even when the process described is, in principle, iterative. As a consequence, these languages can describe iterative processes only by resorting to special-purpose "looping constructs" such as `do`, `repeat`, `until`, `for`, and `while`. The implementation of Scheme we shall consider in chapter 5 does not share this defect. It will execute an iterative process in constant space, even if the iterative process is described by a recursive procedure. An implementation with this property is called *tail-recursive*. With a tail-recursive implementation,

---

[30]When we discuss the implementation of procedures on register machines in chapter 5, we will see that any iterative process can be realized "in hardware" as a machine that has a fixed set of registers and no auxiliary memory. In contrast, realizing a recursive process requires a machine that uses an auxiliary data structure known as a *stack*.

iteration can be expressed using the ordinary procedure call mechanism, so that special iteration constructs are useful only as syntactic sugar.[31]

Exercise 1.9

Each of the following two procedures defines a method for adding two positive integers in terms of the procedures inc, which increments its argument by 1, and dec, which decrements its argument by 1.

```
(define (+ a b)
  (if (= a 0)
      b
      (inc (+ (dec a) b))))
(define (+ a b)
  (if (= a 0)
      b
      (+ (dec a) (inc b))))
```

Using the substitution model, illustrate the process generated by each procedure in evaluating (+ 4 5). Are these processes iterative or recursive?

Exercise 1.10

The following procedure computes a mathematical function called Ackermann's function.

```
(define (A x y)
  (cond ((= y 0) 0)
        ((= x 0) (* 2 y))
        ((= y 1) 2)
        (else (A (- x 1)
                 (A x (- y 1))))))
```

What are the values of the following expressions?

(A 1 10)

(A 2 4)

(A 3 3)

---

[31] Tail recursion has long been known as a compiler optimization trick. A coherent semantic basis for tail recursion was provided by Carl Hewitt (1977), who explained it in terms of the "message-passing" model of computation that we shall discuss in chapter 3. Inspired by this, Gerald Jay Sussman and Guy Lewis Steele Jr. (see Steele 1975) constructed a tail-recursive interpreter for Scheme. Steele later showed how tail recursion is a consequence of the natural way to compile procedure calls (Steele 1977). The IEEE standard for Scheme requires that Scheme implementations be tail-recursive.

Consider the following procedures, where A is the procedure defined above:

```
(define (f n) (A 0 n))
```

```
(define (g n) (A 1 n))
```

```
(define (h n) (A 2 n))
```

```
(define (k n) (* 5 n n))
```

Give concise mathematical definitions for the functions computed by the procedures f, g, and h for positive integer values of *n*. For example, (k n) computes $5n^2$.

1.2.2 Tree Recursion

Another common pattern of computation is called *tree recursion*. As an example, consider computing the sequence of Fibonacci numbers, in which each number is the sum of the preceding two:

$0, 1, 1, 2, 3, 5, 8, 13, 21, \ldots$

In general, the Fibonacci numbers can be defined by the rule

$$\text{Fib}(n) = \begin{cases} 0 & \text{if } n = 0 \\ 1 & \text{if } n = 1 \\ \text{Fib}(n-1) + \text{Fib}(n-2) & \text{otherwise} \end{cases}$$

We can immediately translate this definition into a recursive procedure for computing Fibonacci numbers:

```
(define (fib n)
  (cond ((= n 0) 0)
        ((= n 1) 1)
        (else (+ (fib (- n 1))
                 (fib (- n 2))))))
```

Consider the pattern of this computation. To compute (fib 5), we compute (fib 4) and (fib 3). To compute (fib 4), we compute (fib 3) and (fib 2). In general, the evolved process looks like a tree, as shown in figure 1.5. Notice that the branches split into two at each level (except at the bottom); this reflects the fact that the fib procedure calls itself twice each time it is invoked.

This procedure is instructive as a prototypical tree recursion, but it is a terrible way to compute Fibonacci numbers because it does so much

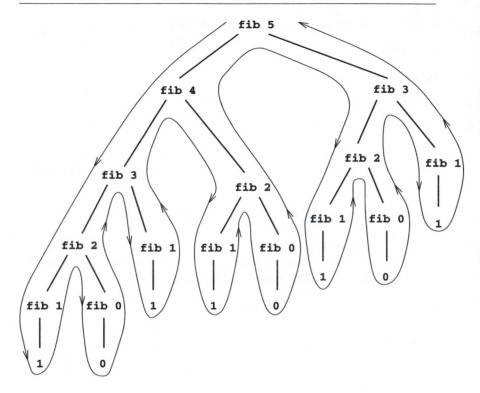

Figure 1.5   The tree-recursive process generated in computing (`fib 5`).

redundant computation. Notice in figure 1.5 that the entire computation of (`fib 3`)—almost half the work—is duplicated. In fact, it is not hard to show that the number of times the procedure will compute (`fib 1`) or (`fib 0`) (the number of leaves in the above tree, in general) is precisely Fib($n+1$). To get an idea of how bad this is, one can show that the value of Fib(n) grows exponentially with n. More precisely (see exercise 1.13), Fib(n) is the closest integer to $\phi^n/\sqrt{5}$, where

$$\phi = (1 + \sqrt{5})/2 \approx 1.6180$$

is the *golden ratio*, which satisfies the equation

$$\phi^2 = \phi + 1$$

Thus, the process uses a number of steps that grows exponentially with the input. On the other hand, the space required grows only linearly with the input, because we need keep track only of which nodes are above us in the tree at any point in the computation. In general, the number of steps required by a tree-recursive process will be proportional to the number of nodes in the tree, while the space required will be proportional to the maximum depth of the tree.

We can also formulate an iterative process for computing the Fibonacci numbers. The idea is to use a pair of integers a and b, initialized to Fib(1) = 1 and Fib(0) = 0, and to repeatedly apply the simultaneous transformations

$$a \leftarrow a + b$$
$$b \leftarrow a$$

It is not hard to show that, after applying this transformation n times, a and b will be equal, respectively, to Fib($n + 1$) and Fib(n). Thus, we can compute Fibonacci numbers iteratively using the procedure

```
(define (fib n)
  (fib-iter 1 0 n))

(define (fib-iter a b count)
  (if (= count 0)
      b
      (fib-iter (+ a b) a (- count 1))))
```

This second method for computing Fib(n) is a linear iteration. The difference in number of steps required by the two methods—one linear in n, one growing as fast as Fib(n) itself—is enormous, even for small inputs.

One should not conclude from this that tree-recursive processes are useless. When we consider processes that operate on hierarchically structured data rather than numbers, we will find that tree recursion is a natural and powerful tool.[32] But even in numerical operations, tree-recursive processes can be useful in helping us to understand and design programs. For instance, although the first `fib` procedure is much less efficient than the second one, it is more straightforward, being little more than a translation into Lisp of the definition of the Fibonacci sequence. To formulate the iterative algorithm required noticing that the computation could be recast as an iteration with three state variables.

---

[32] An example of this was hinted at in section 1.1.3: The interpreter itself evaluates expressions using a tree-recursive process.

Example: Counting change

It takes only a bit of cleverness to come up with the iterative Fibonacci algorithm. In contrast, consider the following problem: How many different ways can we make change of $1.00, given half-dollars, quarters, dimes, nickels, and pennies? More generally, can we write a procedure to compute the number of ways to change any given amount of money?

This problem has a simple solution as a recursive procedure. Suppose we think of the types of coins available as arranged in some order. Then the following relation holds:

The number of ways to change amount a using n kinds of coins equals

• the number of ways to change amount a using all but the first kind of coin, plus

• the number of ways to change amount $a - d$ using all n kinds of coins, where d is the denomination of the first kind of coin.

To see why this is true, observe that the ways to make change can be divided into two groups: those that do not use any of the first kind of coin, and those that do. Therefore, the total number of ways to make change for some amount is equal to the number of ways to make change for the amount without using any of the first kind of coin, plus the number of ways to make change assuming that we do use the first kind of coin. But the latter number is equal to the number of ways to make change for the amount that remains after using a coin of the first kind.

Thus, we can recursively reduce the problem of changing a given amount to the problem of changing smaller amounts using fewer kinds of coins. Consider this reduction rule carefully, and convince yourself that we can use it to describe an algorithm if we specify the following degenerate cases:[33]

• If a is exactly 0, we should count that as 1 way to make change.

• If a is less than 0, we should count that as 0 ways to make change.

• If n is 0, we should count that as 0 ways to make change.

We can easily translate this description into a recursive procedure:

```
(define (count-change amount)
  (cc amount 5))
```

---

[33] For example, work through in detail how the reduction rule applies to the problem of making change for 10 cents using pennies and nickels.

```
(define (cc amount kinds-of-coins)
  (cond ((= amount 0) 1)
        ((or (< amount 0) (= kinds-of-coins 0)) 0)
        (else (+ (cc amount
                     (- kinds-of-coins 1))
                 (cc (- amount
                        (first-denomination kinds-of-coins))
                     kinds-of-coins)))))

(define (first-denomination kinds-of-coins)
  (cond ((= kinds-of-coins 1) 1)
        ((= kinds-of-coins 2) 5)
        ((= kinds-of-coins 3) 10)
        ((= kinds-of-coins 4) 25)
        ((= kinds-of-coins 5) 50)))
```

(The `first-denomination` procedure takes as input the number of kinds of coins available and returns the denomination of the first kind. Here we are thinking of the coins as arranged in order from largest to smallest, but any order would do as well.) We can now answer our original question about changing a dollar:

```
(count-change 100)
292
```

Count-change generates a tree-recursive process with redundancies similar to those in our first implementation of `fib`. (It will take quite a while for that 292 to be computed.) On the other hand, it is not obvious how to design a better algorithm for computing the result, and we leave this problem as a challenge. The observation that a tree-recursive process may be highly inefficient but often easy to specify and understand has led people to propose that one could get the best of both worlds by designing a "smart compiler" that could transform tree-recursive procedures into more efficient procedures that compute the same result.[34]

---

[34]One approach to coping with redundant computations is to arrange matters so that we automatically construct a table of values as they are computed. Each time we are asked to apply the procedure to some argument, we first look to see if the value is already stored in the table, in which case we avoid performing the redundant computation. This strategy, known as *tabulation* or *memoization*, can be implemented in a straightforward way. Tabulation can sometimes be used to transform processes that require an exponential number of steps (such as `count-change`) into processes whose space and time requirements grow linearly with the input. See exercise 3.27.

Exercise 1.11

A function f is defined by the rule that $f(n) = n$ if $n < 3$ and $f(n) = f(n-1) + 2f(n-2) + 3f(n-3)$ if $n \geq 3$. Write a procedure that computes f by means of a recursive process. Write a procedure that computes f by means of an iterative process.

Exercise 1.12

The following pattern of numbers is called *Pascal's triangle*.

```
        1
      1   1
    1   2   1
  1   3   3   1
1   4   6   4   1
      . . .
```

The numbers at the edge of the triangle are all 1, and each number inside the triangle is the sum of the two numbers above it.[35] Write a procedure that computes elements of Pascal's triangle by means of a recursive process.

Exercise 1.13

Prove that Fib(n) is the closest integer to $\phi^n/\sqrt{5}$, where $\phi = (1 + \sqrt{5})/2$. Hint: Let $\psi = (1 - \sqrt{5})/2$. Use induction and the definition of the Fibonacci numbers (see section 1.2.2) to prove that Fib(n) = $(\phi^n - \psi^n)/\sqrt{5}$.

1.2.3   Orders of Growth

The previous examples illustrate that processes can differ considerably in the rates at which they consume computational resources. One convenient way to describe this difference is to use the notion of *order of growth* to obtain a gross measure of the resources required by a process as the inputs become larger.

Let n be a parameter that measures the size of the problem, and let $R(n)$ be the amount of resources the process requires for a problem of size n. In our previous examples we took n to be the number for which a given function is to be computed, but there are other possibilities. For instance, if our goal is to compute an approximation to the square root of

---

[35]The elements of Pascal's triangle are called the *binomial coefficients*, because the nth row consists of the coefficients of the terms in the expansion of $(x + y)^n$. This pattern for computing the coefficients appeared in Blaise Pascal's 1653 seminal work on probability theory, *Traité du triangle arithmétique*. According to Knuth (1973), the same pattern appears in the *Szu-yuen Yü-chien* ("The Precious Mirror of the Four Elements"), published by the Chinese mathematician Chu Shih-chieh in 1303, in the works of the twelfth-century Persian poet and mathematician Omar Khayyam, and in the works of the twelfth-century Hindu mathematician Bháscara Áchárya.

a number, we might take n to be the number of digits accuracy required. For matrix multiplication we might take n to be the number of rows in the matrices. In general there are a number of properties of the problem with respect to which it will be desirable to analyze a given process. Similarly, $R(n)$ might measure the number of internal storage registers used, the number of elementary machine operations performed, and so on. In computers that do only a fixed number of operations at a time, the time required will be proportional to the number of elementary machine operations performed.

We say that $R(n)$ has order of growth $\Theta(f(n))$, written $R(n) = \Theta(f(n))$ (pronounced "theta of $f(n)$"), if there are positive constants k_1 and k_2 independent of n such that

$$k_1 f(n) \leq R(n) \leq k_2 f(n)$$

for any sufficiently large value of n. (In other words, for large n, the value $R(n)$ is sandwiched between $k_1 f(n)$ and $k_2 f(n)$.)

For instance, with the linear recursive process for computing factorial described in section 1.2.1 the number of steps grows proportionally to the input n. Thus, the steps required for this process grows as $\Theta(n)$. We also saw that the space required grows as $\Theta(n)$. For the iterative factorial, the number of steps is still $\Theta(n)$ but the space is $\Theta(1)$—that is, constant.[36] The tree-recursive Fibonacci computation requires $\Theta(\phi^n)$ steps and space $\Theta(n)$, where ϕ is the golden ratio described in section 1.2.2.

Orders of growth provide only a crude description of the behavior of a process. For example, a process requiring n^2 steps and a process requiring $1000n^2$ steps and a process requiring $3n^2 + 10n + 17$ steps all have $\Theta(n^2)$ order of growth. On the other hand, order of growth provides a useful indication of how we may expect the behavior of the process to change as we change the size of the problem. For a $\Theta(n)$ (linear) process, doubling the size will roughly double the amount of resources used. For an exponential process, each increment in problem size will multiply the resource utilization by a constant factor. In the remainder of section 1.2 we will examine two algorithms whose order of growth is logarithmic, so that doubling the problem size increases the resource requirement by a constant amount.

---

[36]These statements mask a great deal of oversimplification. For instance, if we count process steps as "machine operations" we are making the assumption that the number of machine operations needed to perform, say, a multiplication is independent of the size of the numbers to be multiplied, which is false if the numbers are sufficiently large. Similar remarks hold for the estimates of space. Like the design and description of a process, the analysis of a process can be carried out at various levels of abstraction.

Exercise 1.14

Draw the tree illustrating the process generated by the count-change procedure of section 1.2.2 in making change for 11 cents. What are the orders of growth of the space and number of steps used by this process as the amount to be changed increases?

Exercise 1.15

The sine of an angle (specified in radians) can be computed by making use of the approximation $\sin x \approx x$ if x is sufficiently small, and the trigonometric identity

$$\sin x = 3\sin\frac{x}{3} - 4\sin^3\frac{x}{3}$$

to reduce the size of the argument of sin. (For purposes of this exercise an angle is considered "sufficiently small" if its magnitude is not greater than 0.1 radians.) These ideas are incorporated in the following procedures:

```
(define (cube x) (* x x x))

(define (p x) (- (* 3 x) (* 4 (cube x))))

(define (sine angle)
   (if (not (> (abs angle) 0.1))
       angle
       (p (sine (/ angle 3.0))))))
```

a. How many times is the procedure p applied when (sine 12.15) is evaluated?

b. What is the order of growth in space and number of steps (as a function of a) used by the process generated by the sine procedure when (sine a) is evaluated?

1.2.4   Exponentiation

Consider the problem of computing the exponential of a given number. We would like a procedure that takes as arguments a base b and a positive integer exponent n and computes b^n. One way to do this is via the recursive definition

$$b^n = b \cdot b^{n-1}$$
$$b^0 = 1$$

which translates readily into the procedure

```
(define (expt b n)
   (if (= n 0)
       1
       (* b (expt b (- n 1)))))
```

This is a linear recursive process, which requires $\Theta(n)$ steps and $\Theta(n)$ space. Just as with factorial, we can readily formulate an equivalent linear iteration:

```
(define (expt b n)
  (expt-iter b n 1))

(define (expt-iter b counter product)
  (if (= counter 0)
      product
      (expt-iter b
                 (- counter 1)
                 (* b product))))
```

This version requires $\Theta(n)$ steps and $\Theta(1)$ space.

We can compute exponentials in fewer steps by using successive squaring. For instance, rather than computing b^8 as

$$b \cdot (b \cdot (b \cdot (b \cdot (b \cdot (b \cdot (b \cdot b))))))$$

we can compute it using three multiplications:

$$b^2 = b \cdot b$$
$$b^4 = b^2 \cdot b^2$$
$$b^8 = b^4 \cdot b^4$$

This method works fine for exponents that are powers of 2. We can also take advantage of successive squaring in computing exponentials in general if we use the rule

$$b^n = (b^{b/2})^2 \qquad \text{if } n \text{ is even}$$
$$b^n = b \cdot b^{n-1} \qquad \text{if } n \text{ is odd}$$

We can express this method as a procedure:

```
(define (fast-expt b n)
  (cond ((= n 0) 1)
        ((even? n) (square (fast-expt b (/ n 2))))
        (else (* b (fast-expt b (- n 1))))))
```

where the predicate to test whether an integer is even is defined in terms of the primitive procedure `remainder` by

```
(define (even? n)
  (= (remainder n 2) 0))
```

The process evolved by `fast-expt` grows logarithmically with n in both space and number of steps. To see this, observe that computing b^{2n} using `fast-expt` requires only one more multiplication than computing b^n. The size of the exponent we can compute therefore doubles (approximately) with every new multiplication we are allowed. Thus, the number of multiplications required for an exponent of n grows about as fast as the logarithm of n to the base 2. The process has $\Theta(\log n)$ growth.[37]

The difference between $\Theta(\log n)$ growth and $\Theta(n)$ growth becomes striking as n becomes large. For example, `fast-expt` for $n = 1000$ requires only 14 multiplications.[38] It is also possible to use the idea of successive squaring to devise an iterative algorithm that computes exponentials with a logarithmic number of steps (see exercise 1.16), although, as is often the case with iterative algorithms, this is not written down so straightforwardly as the recursive algorithm.[39]

Exercise 1.16

Design a procedure that evolves an iterative exponentiation process that uses successive squaring and uses a logarithmic number of steps, as does `fast-expt`. (Hint: Using the observation that $(b^{n/2})^2 = (b^2)^{n/2}$, keep, along with the exponent n and the base b, an additional state variable a, and define the state transformation in such a way that the product ab^n is unchanged from state to state. At the beginning of the process a is taken to be 1, and the answer is given by the value of a at the end of the process. In general, the technique of defining an *invariant quantity* that remains unchanged from state to state is a powerful way to think about the design of iterative algorithms.)

Exercise 1.17

The exponentiation algorithms in this section are based on performing exponentiation by means of repeated multiplication. In a similar way, one can perform integer multiplication by means of repeated addition. The following multiplication procedure (in which it is assumed that our language can only add, not multiply) is analogous to the `expt` procedure:

```
(define (* a b)
  (if (= b 0)
      0
      (+ a (* a (- b 1)))))
```

---

[37]More precisely, the number of multiplications required is equal to 1 less than the log base 2 of n plus the number of ones in the binary representation of n. This total is always less than twice the log base 2 of n. The arbitrary constants k_1 and k_2 in the definition of order notation imply that, for a logarithmic process, the base to which logarithms are taken does not matter, so all such processes are described as $\Theta(\log n)$.

[38]You may wonder why anyone would care about raising numbers to the 1000th power. See section 1.2.6.

[39]This iterative algorithm is ancient. It appears in the *Chandah-sutra* by Áchárya Pingala, written before 200 B.C. See Knuth 1981, section 4.6.3, for a full discussion and analysis of this and other methods of exponentiation.

This algorithm takes a number of steps that is linear in b. Now suppose we include, together with addition, operations double, which doubles an integer, and halve, which divides an (even) integer by 2. Using these, design a multiplication procedure analogous to fast-expt that uses a logarithmic number of steps.

Exercise 1.18

Using the results of exercises 1.16 and 1.17, devise a procedure that generates an iterative process for multiplying two integers in terms of adding, doubling, and halving and uses a logarithmic number of steps.[40]

Exercise 1.19

There is a clever algorithm for computing the Fibonacci numbers in a logarithmic number of steps. Recall the transformation of the state variables a and b in the fib-iter process of section 1.2.2: $a \leftarrow a+b$ and $b \leftarrow a$. Call this transformation T, and observe that applying T over and over again n times, starting with 1 and 0, produces the pair $Fib(n + 1)$ and $Fib(n)$. In other words, the Fibonacci numbers are produced by applying T^n, the nth power of the transformation T, starting with the pair $(1, 0)$. Now consider T to be the special case of $p = 0$ and $q = 1$ in a family of transformations T_{pq}, where T_{pq} transforms the pair (a, b) according to $a \leftarrow bq + aq + ap$ and $b \leftarrow bp + aq$. Show that if we apply such a transformation T_{pq} twice, the effect is the same as using a single transformation $T_{p'q'}$ of the same form, and compute p' and q' in terms of p and q. This gives us an explicit way to square these transformations, and thus we can compute T^n using successive squaring, as in the fast-expt procedure. Put this all together to complete the following procedure, which runs in a logarithmic number of steps:[41]

```
(define (fib n)
  (fib-iter 1 0 0 1 n))

(define (fib-iter a b p q count)
  (cond ((= count 0) b)
        ((even? count)
         (fib-iter a
                   b
                   ⟨??⟩          ; compute p'
                   ⟨??⟩          ; compute q'
                   (/ count 2)))
        (else (fib-iter (+ (* b q) (* a q) (* a p))
                        (+ (* b p) (* a q))
                        p
                        q
                        (- count 1)))))
```

---

[40]This algorithm, which is sometimes known as the "Russian peasant method" of multiplication, is ancient. Examples of its use are found in the Rhind Papyrus, one of the two oldest mathematical documents in existence, written about 1700 B.C. (and copied from an even older document) by an Egyptian scribe named A'h-mose.

[41]This exercise was suggested to us by Joe Stoy, based on an example in Kaldewaij 1990.

1.2.5   Greatest Common Divisors

The greatest common divisor (GCD) of two integers a and b is defined to be the largest integer that divides both a and b with no remainder. For example, the GCD of 16 and 28 is 4. In chapter 2, when we investigate how to implement rational-number arithmetic, we will need to be able to compute GCDs in order to reduce rational numbers to lowest terms. (To reduce a rational number to lowest terms, we must divide both the numerator and the denominator by their GCD. For example, 16/28 reduces to 4/7.) One way to find the GCD of two integers is to factor them and search for common factors, but there is a famous algorithm that is much more efficient.

The idea of the algorithm is based on the observation that, if r is the remainder when a is divided by b, then the common divisors of a and b are precisely the same as the common divisors of b and r. Thus, we can use the equation

$$\text{GCD}(a, b) = \text{GCD}(b, r)$$

to successively reduce the problem of computing a GCD to the problem of computing the GCD of smaller and smaller pairs of integers. For example,

$$
\begin{aligned}
\text{GCD}(206, 40) &= \text{GCD}(40, 6) \\
&= \text{GCD}(6, 4) \\
&= \text{GCD}(4, 2) \\
&= \text{GCD}(2, 0) \\
&= 2
\end{aligned}
$$

reduces GCD(206,40) to GCD(2,0), which is 2. It is possible to show that starting with any two positive integers and performing repeated reductions will always eventually produce a pair where the second number is 0. Then the GCD is the other number in the pair. This method for computing the GCD is known as *Euclid's Algorithm*.[42]

---

[42]Euclid's Algorithm is so called because it appears in Euclid's *Elements* (Book 7, ca. 300 B.C.). According to Knuth (1973), it can be considered the oldest known nontrivial algorithm. The ancient Egyptian method of multiplication (exercise 1.18) is surely older, but, as Knuth explains, Euclid's algorithm is the oldest known to have been presented as a general algorithm, rather than as a set of illustrative examples.

It is easy to express Euclid's Algorithm as a procedure:

```
(define (gcd a b)
  (if (= b 0)
      a
      (gcd b (remainder a b)))))
```

This generates an iterative process, whose number of steps grows as the logarithm of the numbers involved.

The fact that the number of steps required by Euclid's Algorithm has logarithmic growth bears an interesting relation to the Fibonacci numbers:

Lamé's Theorem: If Euclid's Algorithm requires k steps to compute the GCD of some pair, then the smaller number in the pair must be greater than or equal to the kth Fibonacci number.[43]

We can use this theorem to get an order-of-growth estimate for Euclid's Algorithm. Let n be the smaller of the two inputs to the procedure. If the process takes k steps, then we must have $n \geq \text{Fib}(k) \approx \phi^k / \sqrt{5}$. Therefore the number of steps k grows as the logarithm (to the base ϕ) of n. Hence, the order of growth is $\Theta(\log n)$.

Exercise 1.20

The process that a procedure generates is of course dependent on the rules used by the interpreter. As an example, consider the iterative gcd procedure given above. Suppose we were to interpret this procedure using normal-order evaluation, as discussed in section 1.1.5. (The normal-order-evaluation rule for if is described in exercise 1.5.) Using the substitution method (for nor-

---

[43]This theorem was proved in 1845 by Gabriel Lamé, a French mathematician and engineer known chiefly for his contributions to mathematical physics. To prove the theorem, we consider pairs (a_k, b_k), where $a_k \geq b_k$, for which Euclid's Algorithm terminates in k steps. The proof is based on the claim that, if $(a_{k+1}, b_{k+1}) \rightarrow (a_k, b_k) \rightarrow (a_{k-1}, b_{k-1})$ are three successive pairs in the reduction process, then we must have $b_{k+1} \geq b_k + b_{k-1}$. To verify the claim, consider that a reduction step is defined by applying the transformation $a_{k-1} = b_k$, $b_{k-1} = $ remainder of a_k divided by b_k. The second equation means that $a_k = qb_k + b_{k-1}$ for some positive integer q. And since q must be at least 1 we have $a_k = qb_k + b_{k-1} \geq b_k + b_{k-1}$. But in the previous reduction step we have $b_{k+1} = a_k$. Therefore, $b_{k+1} = a_k \geq b_k + b_{k-1}$. This verifies the claim. Now we can prove the theorem by induction on k, the number of steps that the algorithm requires to terminate. The result is true for $k = 1$, since this merely requires that b be at least as large as $\text{Fib}(1) = 1$. Now, assume that the result is true for all integers less than or equal to k and establish the result for $k + 1$. Let $(a_{k+1}, b_{k+1}) \rightarrow (a_k, b_k) \rightarrow (a_{k-1}, b_{k-1})$ be successive pairs in the reduction process. By our induction hypotheses, we have $b_{k-1} \geq \text{Fib}(k - 1)$ and $b_k \geq \text{Fib}(k)$. Thus, applying the claim we just proved together with the definition of the Fibonacci numbers gives $b_{k+1} \geq b_k + b_{k-1} \geq \text{Fib}(k) + \text{Fib}(k - 1) = \text{Fib}(k + 1)$, which completes the proof of Lamé's Theorem.

mal order), illustrate the process generated in evaluating (gcd 206 40) and
indicate the `remainder` operations that are actually performed. How many
`remainder` operations are actually performed in the normal-order evaluation
of (gcd 206 40)? In the applicative-order evaluation?

1.2.6   Example: Testing for Primality

This section describes two methods for checking the primality of an integer n, one with order of growth $\Theta(\sqrt{n})$, and a "probabilistic" algorithm
with order of growth $\Theta(\log n)$. The exercises at the end of this section
suggest programming projects based on these algorithms.

Searching for divisors

Since ancient times, mathematicians have been fascinated by problems
concerning prime numbers, and many people have worked on the problem of determining ways to test if numbers are prime. One way to test if a
number is prime is to find the number's divisors. The following program
finds the smallest integral divisor (greater than 1) of a given number n.
It does this in a straightforward way, by testing n for divisibility by successive integers starting with 2.

```
(define (smallest-divisor n)
  (find-divisor n 2))

(define (find-divisor n test-divisor)
  (cond ((> (square test-divisor) n) n)
        ((divides? test-divisor n) test-divisor)
        (else (find-divisor n (+ test-divisor 1)))))

(define (divides? a b)
  (= (remainder b a) 0))
```

We can test whether a number is prime as follows: n is prime if and
only if n is its own smallest divisor.

```
(define (prime? n)
  (= n (smallest-divisor n)))
```

The end test for `find-divisor` is based on the fact that if n is not
prime it must have a divisor less than or equal to $\sqrt{n}$.[44] This means that
the algorithm need only test divisors between 1 and $\sqrt{n}$. Consequently,
the number of steps required to identify n as prime will have order of
growth $\Theta(\sqrt{n})$.

---

[44] If d is a divisor of n, then so is n/d. But d and n/d cannot both be greater than $\sqrt{n}$.

The Fermat test

The $\Theta(\log n)$ primality test is based on a result from number theory known as Fermat's Little Theorem.[45]

Fermat's Little Theorem: If n is a prime number and a is any positive integer less than n, then a raised to the nth power is congruent to a modulo n.

(Two numbers are said to be *congruent modulo n* if they both have the same remainder when divided by n. The remainder of a number a when divided by n is also referred to as the *remainder of a modulo n*, or simply as *a modulo n*.)

If n is not prime, then, in general, most of the numbers $a < n$ will not satisfy the above relation. This leads to the following algorithm for testing primality: Given a number n, pick a random number $a < n$ and compute the remainder of a^n modulo n. If the result is not equal to a, then n is certainly not prime. If it is a, then chances are good that n is prime. Now pick another random number a and test it with the same method. If it also satisfies the equation, then we can be even more confident that n is prime. By trying more and more values of a, we can increase our confidence in the result. This algorithm is known as the Fermat test.

To implement the Fermat test, we need a procedure that computes the exponential of a number modulo another number:

```
(define (expmod base exp m)
  (cond ((= exp 0) 1)
        ((even? exp)
         (remainder (square (expmod base (/ exp 2) m))
                    m))
        (else
         (remainder (* base (expmod base (- exp 1) m))
                    m))))
```

---

[45]Pierre de Fermat (1601–1665) is considered to be the founder of modern number theory. He obtained many important number-theoretic results, but he usually announced just the results, without providing his proofs. Fermat's Little Theorem was stated in a letter he wrote in 1640. The first published proof was given by Euler in 1736 (and an earlier, identical proof was discovered in the unpublished manuscripts of Leibniz). The most famous of Fermat's results—known as Fermat's Last Theorem—was jotted down in 1637 in his copy of the book *Arithmetic* (by the third-century Greek mathematician Diophantus) with the remark "I have discovered a truly remarkable proof, but this margin is too small to contain it." Finding a proof of Fermat's Last Theorem became one of the most famous challenges in number theory. A complete solution was finally given in 1995 by Andrew Wiles of Princeton University.

This is very similar to the `fast-expt` procedure of section 1.2.4. It uses successive squaring, so that the number of steps grows logarithmically with the exponent.[46]

The Fermat test is performed by choosing at random a number a between 1 and $n - 1$ inclusive and checking whether the remainder modulo n of the nth power of a is equal to a. The random number a is chosen using the procedure `random`, which we assume is included as a primitive in Scheme. Random returns a nonnegative integer less than its integer input. Hence, to obtain a random number between 1 and $n - 1$, we call random with an input of $n - 1$ and add 1 to the result:

```
(define (fermat-test n)
  (define (try-it a)
    (= (expmod a n n) a))
  (try-it (+ 1 (random (- n 1)))))
```

The following procedure runs the test a given number of times, as specified by a parameter. Its value is true if the test succeeds every time, and false otherwise.

```
(define (fast-prime? n times)
  (cond ((= times 0) true)
        ((fermat-test n) (fast-prime? n (- times 1)))
        (else false)))
```

Probabilistic methods

The Fermat test differs in character from most familiar algorithms, in which one computes an answer that is guaranteed to be correct. Here, the answer obtained is only probably correct. More precisely, if n ever fails the Fermat test, we can be certain that n is not prime. But the fact that n passes the test, while an extremely strong indication, is still not a guarantee that n is prime. What we would like to say is that for any number n, if we perform the test enough times and find that n always passes the test, then the probability of error in our primality test can be made as small as we like.

---

[46]The reduction steps in the cases where the exponent e is greater than 1 are based on the fact that, for any integers x, y, and m, we can find the remainder of x times y modulo m by computing separately the remainders of x modulo m and y modulo m, multiplying these, and then taking the remainder of the result modulo m. For instance, in the case where e is even, we compute the remainder of $b^{e/2}$ modulo m, square this, and take the remainder modulo m. This technique is useful because it means we can perform our computation without ever having to deal with numbers much larger than m. (Compare exercise 1.25.)

Unfortunately, this assertion is not quite correct. There do exist numbers that fool the Fermat test: numbers n that are not prime and yet have the property that a^n is congruent to a modulo n for all integers $a < n$. Such numbers are extremely rare, so the Fermat test is quite reliable in practice.[47] There are variations of the Fermat test that cannot be fooled. In these tests, as with the Fermat method, one tests the primality of an integer n by choosing a random integer $a < n$ and checking some condition that depends upon n and a. (See exercise 1.28 for an example of such a test.) On the other hand, in contrast to the Fermat test, one can prove that, for any n, the condition does not hold for most of the integers $a < n$ unless n is prime. Thus, if n passes the test for some random choice of a, the chances are better than even that n is prime. If n passes the test for two random choices of a, the chances are better than 3 out of 4 that n is prime. By running the test with more and more randomly chosen values of a we can make the probability of error as small as we like.

The existence of tests for which one can prove that the chance of error becomes arbitrarily small has sparked interest in algorithms of this type, which have come to be known as *probabilistic algorithms*. There is a great deal of research activity in this area, and probabilistic algorithms have been fruitfully applied to many fields.[48]

Exercise 1.21

Use the `smallest-divisor` procedure to find the smallest divisor of each of the following numbers: 199, 1999, 19999.

---

[47]Numbers that fool the Fermat test are called *Carmichael numbers*, and little is known about them other than that they are extremely rare. There are 255 Carmichael numbers below 100,000,000. The smallest few are 561, 1105, 1729, 2465, 2821, and 6601. In testing primality of very large numbers chosen at random, the chance of stumbling upon a value that fools the Fermat test is less than the chance that cosmic radiation will cause the computer to make an error in carrying out a "correct" algorithm. Considering an algorithm to be inadequate for the first reason but not for the second illustrates the difference between mathematics and engineering.

[48]One of the most striking applications of probabilistic prime testing has been to the field of cryptography. Although it is now computationally infeasible to factor an arbitrary 200-digit number, the primality of such a number can be checked in a few seconds with the Fermat test. This fact forms the basis of a technique for constructing "unbreakable codes" suggested by Rivest, Shamir, and Adleman (1977). The resulting *RSA algorithm* has become a widely used technique for enhancing the security of electronic communications. Because of this and related developments, the study of prime numbers, once considered the epitome of a topic in "pure" mathematics to be studied only for its own sake, now turns out to have important practical applications to cryptography, electronic funds transfer, and information retrieval.

Exercise 1.22

Most Lisp implementations include a primitive called `runtime` that returns an integer that specifies the amount of time the system has been running (measured, for example, in microseconds). The following `timed-prime-test` procedure, when called with an integer n, prints n and checks to see if n is prime. If n is prime, the procedure prints three asterisks followed by the amount of time used in performing the test.

```
(define (timed-prime-test n)
  (newline)
  (display n)
  (start-prime-test n (runtime)))

(define (start-prime-test n start-time)
  (if (prime? n)
      (report-prime (- (runtime) start-time))))

(define (report-prime elapsed-time)
  (display " *** ")
  (display elapsed-time))
```

Using this procedure, write a procedure `search-for-primes` that checks the primality of consecutive odd integers in a specified range. Use your procedure to find the three smallest primes larger than 1000; larger than 10,000; larger than 100,000; larger than 1,000,000. Note the time needed to test each prime. Since the testing algorithm has order of growth of $\Theta(\sqrt{n})$, you should expect that testing for primes around 10,000 should take about $\sqrt{10}$ times as long as testing for primes around 1000. Do your timing data bear this out? How well do the data for 100,000 and 1,000,000 support the $\sqrt{n}$ prediction? Is your result compatible with the notion that programs on your machine run in time proportional to the number of steps required for the computation?

Exercise 1.23

The `smallest-divisor` procedure shown at the start of this section does lots of needless testing: After it checks to see if the number is divisible by 2 there is no point in checking to see if it is divisible by any larger even numbers. This suggests that the values used for `test-divisor` should not be 2, 3, 4, 5, 6, ..., but rather 2, 3, 5, 7, 9, ... To implement this change, define a procedure `next` that returns 3 if its input is equal to 2 and otherwise returns its input plus 2. Modify the `smallest-divisor` procedure to use `(next test-divisor)` instead of `(+ test-divisor 1)`. With `timed-prime-test` incorporating this modified version of `smallest-divisor`, run the test for each of the 12 primes found in exercise 1.22. Since this modification halves the number of test steps, you should expect it to run about twice as fast. Is this expectation confirmed? If not, what is the observed ratio of the speeds of the two algorithms, and how do you explain the fact that it is different from 2?

Exercise 1.24

Modify the `timed-prime-test` procedure of exercise 1.22 to use `fast-prime?` (the Fermat method), and test each of the 12 primes you found in that exercise. Since the Fermat test has $\Theta(\log n)$ growth, how would you expect the time to test primes near 1,000,000 to compare with the time needed to test primes near 1000? Do your data bear this out? Can you explain any discrepancy you find?

Exercise 1.25

Alyssa P. Hacker complains that we went to a lot of extra work in writing `expmod`. After all, she says, since we already know how to compute exponentials, we could have simply written

```
(define (expmod base exp m)
  (remainder (fast-expt base exp) m))
```

Is she correct? Would this procedure serve as well for our fast prime tester? Explain.

Exercise 1.26

Louis Reasoner is having great difficulty doing exercise 1.24. His `fast-prime?` test seems to run more slowly than his `prime?` test. Louis calls his friend Eva Lu Ator over to help. When they examine Louis's code, they find that he has rewritten the `expmod` procedure to use an explicit multiplication, rather than calling `square`:

```
(define (expmod base exp m)
  (cond ((= exp 0) 1)
        ((even? exp)
         (remainder (* (expmod base (/ exp 2) m)
                       (expmod base (/ exp 2) m))
                    m))
        (else
         (remainder (* base (expmod base (- exp 1) m))
                    m))))
```

"I don't see what difference that could make," says Louis. "I do." says Eva. "By writing the procedure like that, you have transformed the $\Theta(\log n)$ process into a $\Theta(n)$ process." Explain.

Exercise 1.27

Demonstrate that the Carmichael numbers listed in footnote 47 really do fool the Fermat test. That is, write a procedure that takes an integer n and tests whether a^n is congruent to a modulo n for every $a < n$, and try your procedure on the given Carmichael numbers.

Exercise 1.28

One variant of the Fermat test that cannot be fooled is called the *Miller-Rabin test* (Miller 1976; Rabin 1980). This starts from an alternate form of Fermat's Little Theorem, which states that if n is a prime number and a is any positive integer less than n, then a raised to the $(n-1)$st power is congruent to 1 modulo n. To test the primality of a number n by the Miller-Rabin test, we pick a random number $a < n$ and raise a to the $(n-1)$st power modulo n using the expmod procedure. However, whenever we perform the squaring step in expmod, we check to see if we have discovered a "nontrivial square root of 1 modulo n," that is, a number not equal to 1 or $n-1$ whose square is equal to 1 modulo n. It is possible to prove that if such a nontrivial square root of 1 exists, then n is not prime. It is also possible to prove that if n is an odd number that is not prime, then, for at least half the numbers $a < n$, computing a^{n-1} in this way will reveal a nontrivial square root of 1 modulo n. (This is why the Miller-Rabin test cannot be fooled.) Modify the expmod procedure to signal if it discovers a nontrivial square root of 1, and use this to implement the Miller-Rabin test with a procedure analogous to fermat-test. Check your procedure by testing various known primes and non-primes. Hint: One convenient way to make expmod signal is to have it return 0.

1.3   Formulating Abstractions with Higher-Order Procedures

We have seen that procedures are, in effect, abstractions that describe compound operations on numbers independent of the particular numbers. For example, when we

```
(define (cube x) (* x x x))
```

we are not talking about the cube of a particular number, but rather about a method for obtaining the cube of any number. Of course we could get along without ever defining this procedure, by always writing expressions such as

```
(* 3 3 3)
(* x x x)
(* y y y)
```

and never mentioning cube explicitly. This would place us at a serious disadvantage, forcing us to work always at the level of the particular operations that happen to be primitives in the language (multiplication, in this case) rather than in terms of higher-level operations. Our programs would be able to compute cubes, but our language would lack the ability to express the concept of cubing. One of the things we should demand from a powerful programming language is the ability to build abstractions by assigning names to common patterns and then to work in terms of the abstractions directly. Procedures provide this ability. This is why all but the most primitive programming languages include mechanisms for defining procedures.

Yet even in numerical processing we will be severely limited in our ability to create abstractions if we are restricted to procedures whose parameters must be numbers. Often the same programming pattern will be used with a number of different procedures. To express such patterns as concepts, we will need to construct procedures that can accept procedures as arguments or return procedures as values. Procedures that manipulate procedures are called *higher-order procedures*. This section shows how higher-order procedures can serve as powerful abstraction mechanisms, vastly increasing the expressive power of our language.

1.3.1 Procedures as Arguments

Consider the following three procedures. The first computes the sum of the integers from a through b:

```
(define (sum-integers a b)
  (if (> a b)
      0
      (+ a (sum-integers (+ a 1) b))))
```

The second computes the sum of the cubes of the integers in the given range:

```
(define (sum-cubes a b)
  (if (> a b)
      0
      (+ (cube a) (sum-cubes (+ a 1) b))))
```

The third computes the sum of a sequence of terms in the series

$$\frac{1}{1\cdot 3} + \frac{1}{5\cdot 7} + \frac{1}{9\cdot 11} + \cdots$$

which converges to $\pi/8$ (very slowly):[49]

```
(define (pi-sum a b)
  (if (> a b)
      0
      (+ (/ 1.0 (* a (+ a 2))) (pi-sum (+ a 4) b))))
```

---

[49]This series, usually written in the equivalent form $\frac{\pi}{4} = 1 - \frac{1}{3} + \frac{1}{5} - \frac{1}{7} + \cdots$, is due to Leibniz. We'll see how to use this as the basis for some fancy numerical tricks in section 3.5.3.

These three procedures clearly share a common underlying pattern. They are for the most part identical, differing only in the name of the procedure, the function of a used to compute the term to be added, and the function that provides the next value of a. We could generate each of the procedures by filling in slots in the same template:

```
(define (⟨name⟩ a b)
  (if (> a b)
      0
      (+ (⟨term⟩ a)
         (⟨name⟩ (⟨next⟩ a) b))))
```

The presence of such a common pattern is strong evidence that there is a useful abstraction waiting to be brought to the surface. Indeed, mathematicians long ago identified the abstraction of *summation of a series* and invented "sigma notation," for example

$$\sum_{n=a}^{b} f(n) = f(a) + \cdots + f(b)$$

to express this concept. The power of sigma notation is that it allows mathematicians to deal with the concept of summation itself rather than only with particular sums—for example, to formulate general results about sums that are independent of the particular series being summed.

Similarly, as program designers, we would like our language to be powerful enough so that we can write a procedure that expresses the concept of summation itself rather than only procedures that compute particular sums. We can do so readily in our procedural language by taking the common template shown above and transforming the "slots" into formal parameters:

```
(define (sum term a next b)
  (if (> a b)
      0
      (+ (term a)
         (sum term (next a) next b))))
```

Notice that sum takes as its arguments the lower and upper bounds a and b together with the procedures term and next. We can use sum just as we would any procedure. For example, we can use it (along with a procedure inc that increments its argument by 1) to define sum-cubes:

```
(define (inc n) (+ n 1))
```

```
(define (sum-cubes a b)
  (sum cube a inc b))
```

Using this, we can compute the sum of the cubes of the integers from 1 to 10:

```
(sum-cubes 1 10)
3025
```

With the aid of an identity procedure to compute the term, we can define sum-integers in terms of sum:

```
(define (identity x) x)
```

```
(define (sum-integers a b)
  (sum identity a inc b))
```

Then we can add up the integers from 1 to 10:

```
(sum-integers 1 10)
55
```

We can also define pi-sum in the same way:[50]

```
(define (pi-sum a b)
  (define (pi-term x)
    (/ 1.0 (* x (+ x 2))))
  (define (pi-next x)
    (+ x 4))
  (sum pi-term a pi-next b))
```

Using these procedures, we can compute an approximation to π:

```
(* 8 (pi-sum 1 1000))
3.139592655589783
```

Once we have sum, we can use it as a building block in formulating further concepts. For instance, the definite integral of a function f between the limits a and b can be approximated numerically using the formula

$$\int_a^b f = \left[f\left(a + \frac{dx}{2}\right) + f\left(a + dx + \frac{dx}{2}\right) + f\left(a + 2dx + \frac{dx}{2}\right) + \cdots \right] dx$$

for small values of dx. We can express this directly as a procedure:

---

[50]Notice that we have used block structure (section 1.1.8) to embed the definitions of pi-next and pi-term within pi-sum, since these procedures are unlikely to be useful for any other purpose. We will see how to get rid of them altogether in section 1.3.2.

```
(define (integral f a b dx)
  (define (add-dx x) (+ x dx))
  (* (sum f (+ a (/ dx 2.0)) add-dx b)
     dx))

(integral cube 0 1 0.01)
.24998750000000042

(integral cube 0 1 0.001)
.249999875000001
```

(The exact value of the integral of cube between 0 and 1 is 1/4.)

Exercise 1.29

Simpson's Rule is a more accurate method of numerical integration than the method illustrated above. Using Simpson's Rule, the integral of a function f between a and b is approximated as

$$\frac{h}{3}[y_0 + 4y_1 + 2y_2 + 4y_3 + 2y_4 + \cdots + 2y_{n-2} + 4y_{n-1} + y_n]$$

where $h = (b - a)/n$, for some even integer n, and $y_k = f(a + kh)$. (Increasing n increases the accuracy of the approximation.) Define a procedure that takes as arguments f, a, b, and n and returns the value of the integral, computed using Simpson's Rule. Use your procedure to integrate cube between 0 and 1 (with $n = 100$ and $n = 1000$), and compare the results to those of the integral procedure shown above.

Exercise 1.30

The sum procedure above generates a linear recursion. The procedure can be rewritten so that the sum is performed iteratively. Show how to do this by filling in the missing expressions in the following definition:

```
(define (sum term a next b)
  (define (iter a result)
    (if ⟨??⟩
        ⟨??⟩
        (iter ⟨??⟩ ⟨??⟩)))
  (iter ⟨??⟩ ⟨??⟩))
```

Exercise 1.31

a. The sum procedure is only the simplest of a vast number of similar abstractions that can be captured as higher-order procedures.[51] Write an analogous

---

[51] The intent of exercises 1.31–1.33 is to demonstrate the expressive power that is attained by using an appropriate abstraction to consolidate many seemingly disparate operations. However, though accumulation and filtering are elegant ideas, our hands are somewhat tied in using them at this point since we do not yet have data structures to provide suitable means of combination for these abstractions. We will return to these ideas in section 2.2.3

procedure called `product` that returns the product of the values of a function at points over a given range. Show how to define `factorial` in terms of `product`. Also use `product` to compute approximations to π using the formula[52]

$$\frac{\pi}{4} = \frac{2 \cdot 4 \cdot 4 \cdot 6 \cdot 6 \cdot 8 \cdots}{3 \cdot 3 \cdot 5 \cdot 5 \cdot 7 \cdot 7 \cdots}$$

b. If your `product` procedure generates a recursive process, write one that generates an iterative process. If it generates an iterative process, write one that generates a recursive process.

Exercise 1.32

a. Show that `sum` and `product` (exercise 1.31) are both special cases of a still more general notion called `accumulate` that combines a collection of terms, using some general accumulation function:

```
(accumulate combiner null-value term a next b)
```

`Accumulate` takes as arguments the same term and range specifications as `sum` and `product`, together with a `combiner` procedure (of two arguments) that specifies how the current term is to be combined with the accumulation of the preceding terms and a `null-value` that specifies what base value to use when the terms run out. Write `accumulate` and show how `sum` and `product` can both be defined as simple calls to `accumulate`.

b. If your `accumulate` procedure generates a recursive process, write one that generates an iterative process. If it generates an iterative process, write one that generates a recursive process.

Exercise 1.33

You can obtain an even more general version of `accumulate` (exercise 1.32) by introducing the notion of a *filter* on the terms to be combined. That is, combine only those terms derived from values in the range that satisfy a specified condition. The resulting `filtered-accumulate` abstraction takes the same arguments as `accumulate`, together with an additional predicate of one argument that specifies the filter. Write `filtered-accumulate` as a procedure. Show how to express the following using `filtered-accumulate`:

a. the sum of the squares of the prime numbers in the interval *a* to *b* (assuming that you have a `prime?` predicate already written)

b. the product of all the positive integers less than *n* that are relatively prime to *n* (i.e., all positive integers $i < n$ such that $GCD(i, n) = 1$).

---

when we show how to use *sequences* as interfaces for combining filters and accumulators to build even more powerful abstractions. We will see there how these methods really come into their own as a powerful and elegant approach to designing programs.

[52]This formula was discovered by the seventeenth-century English mathematician John Wallis.

1.3.2   Constructing Procedures Using Lambda

In using sum as in section 1.3.1, it seems terribly awkward to have to define trivial procedures such as pi-term and pi-next just so we can use them as arguments to our higher-order procedure. Rather than define pi-next and pi-term, it would be more convenient to have a way to directly specify "the procedure that returns its input incremented by 4" and "the procedure that returns the reciprocal of its input times its input plus 2." We can do this by introducing the special form lambda, which creates procedures. Using lambda we can describe what we want as

```
(lambda (x) (+ x 4))
```

and

```
(lambda (x) (/ 1.0 (* x (+ x 2))))
```

Then our pi-sum procedure can be expressed without defining any auxiliary procedures as

```
(define (pi-sum a b)
  (sum (lambda (x) (/ 1.0 (* x (+ x 2))))
       a
       (lambda (x) (+ x 4))
       b))
```

Again using lambda, we can write the integral procedure without having to define the auxiliary procedure add-dx:

```
(define (integral f a b dx)
  (* (sum f
          (+ a (/ dx 2.0))
          (lambda (x) (+ x dx))
          b)
     dx))
```

In general, lambda is used to create procedures in the same way as define, except that no name is specified for the procedure:

```
(lambda (⟨formal-parameters⟩) ⟨body⟩)
```

The resulting procedure is just as much a procedure as one that is created using define. The only difference is that it has not been associated with any name in the environment. In fact,

```
(define (plus4 x) (+ x 4))
```

is equivalent to

```
(define plus4 (lambda (x) (+ x 4)))
```

We can read a lambda expression as follows:

```
(lambda                    (x)                    (+    x    4))
   ↑                        ↑                      ↑    ↑    ↑
the procedure       of an argument x      that adds   x and 4
```

Like any expression that has a procedure as its value, a lambda expression can be used as the operator in a combination such as

```
((lambda (x y z) (+ x y (square z))) 1 2 3)
12
```

or, more generally, in any context where we would normally use a procedure name.[53]

Using let to create local variables

Another use of lambda is in creating local variables. We often need local variables in our procedures other than those that have been bound as formal parameters. For example, suppose we wish to compute the function

$$f(x, y) = x(1 + xy)^2 + y(1 - y) + (1 + xy)(1 - y)$$

which we could also express as

$$a = 1 + xy$$
$$b = 1 - y$$
$$f(x, y) = xa^2 + yb + ab$$

In writing a procedure to compute f, we would like to include as local variables not only x and y but also the names of intermediate quantities like a and b. One way to accomplish this is to use an auxiliary procedure to bind the local variables:

---

[53] It would be clearer and less intimidating to people learning Lisp if a name more obvious than lambda, such as make-procedure, were used. But the convention is firmly entrenched. The notation is adopted from the λ calculus, a mathematical formalism introduced by the mathematical logician Alonzo Church (1941). Church developed the λ calculus to provide a rigorous foundation for studying the notions of function and function application. The λ calculus has become a basic tool for mathematical investigations of the semantics of programming languages.

```
(define (f x y)
  (define (f-helper a b)
    (+ (* x (square a))
       (* y b)
       (* a b)))
  (f-helper (+ 1 (* x y))
            (- 1 y)))
```

Of course, we could use a lambda expression to specify an anonymous procedure for binding our local variables. The body of f then becomes a single call to that procedure:

```
(define (f x y)
  ((lambda (a b)
     (+ (* x (square a))
        (* y b)
        (* a b)))
   (+ 1 (* x y))
   (- 1 y)))
```

This construct is so useful that there is a special form called let to make its use more convenient. Using let, the f procedure could be written as

```
(define (f x y)
  (let ((a (+ 1 (* x y)))
        (b (- 1 y)))
    (+ (* x (square a))
       (* y b)
       (* a b))))
```

The general form of a let expression is

$$
\begin{aligned}
&\texttt{(let } ((\langle var_1 \rangle \ \langle exp_1 \rangle) \\
&\qquad\quad (\langle var_2 \rangle \ \langle exp_2 \rangle) \\
&\qquad\qquad \vdots \\
&\qquad\quad (\langle var_n \rangle \ \langle exp_n \rangle)) \\
&\quad\ \langle body \rangle)
\end{aligned}
$$

which can be thought of as saying

let $\langle var_1 \rangle$ have the value $\langle exp_1 \rangle$ and

         $\langle var_2 \rangle$ have the value $\langle exp_2 \rangle$ and

         $\vdots$

         $\langle var_n \rangle$ have the value $\langle exp_n \rangle$

in $\langle body \rangle$

The first part of the let expression is a list of name-expression pairs. When the let is evaluated, each name is associated with the value of the corresponding expression. The body of the let is evaluated with these names bound as local variables. The way this happens is that the let expression is interpreted as an alternate syntax for

```
((lambda (⟨var₁⟩ ... ⟨varₙ⟩)
    ⟨body⟩)
 ⟨exp₁⟩
    ⋮
 ⟨expₙ⟩))
```

No new mechanism is required in the interpreter in order to provide local variables. A let expression is simply syntactic sugar for the underlying lambda application.

We can see from this equivalence that the scope of a variable specified by a let expression is the body of the let. This implies that:

• Let allows one to bind variables as locally as possible to where they are to be used. For example, if the value of x is 5, the value of the expression

```
(+ (let ((x 3))
     (+ x (* x 10)))
   x)
```

is 38. Here, the x in the body of the let is 3, so the value of the let expression is 33. On the other hand, the x that is the second argument to the outermost + is still 5.

• The variables' values are computed outside the let. This matters when the expressions that provide the values for the local variables depend upon variables having the same names as the local variables themselves. For example, if the value of x is 2, the expression

```
(let ((x 3)
      (y (+ x 2)))
  (* x y))
```

will have the value 12 because, inside the body of the let, x will be 3 and y will be 4 (which is the outer x plus 2).

Sometimes we can use internal definitions to get the same effect as with let. For example, we could have defined the procedure f above as

```
(define (f x y)
  (define a (+ 1 (* x y)))
  (define b (- 1 y))
  (+ (* x (square a))
     (* y b)
     (* a b)))
```

We prefer, however, to use let in situations like this and to use internal define only for internal procedures.[54]

Exercise 1.34

Suppose we define the procedure

```
(define (f g)
  (g 2))
```

Then we have

```
(f square)
```
4

```
(f (lambda (z) (* z (+ z 1))))
```
6

What happens if we (perversely) ask the interpreter to evaluate the combination (f f)? Explain.

1.3.3   Procedures as General Methods

We introduced compound procedures in section 1.1.4 as a mechanism for abstracting patterns of numerical operations so as to make them independent of the particular numbers involved. With higher-order procedures, such as the integral procedure of section 1.3.1, we began to see a more powerful kind of abstraction: procedures used to express general methods of computation, independent of the particular functions involved. In this section we discuss two more elaborate examples—general methods for finding zeros and fixed points of functions—and show how these methods can be expressed directly as procedures.

---

[54]Understanding internal definitions well enough to be sure a program means what we intend it to mean requires a more elaborate model of the evaluation process than we have presented in this chapter. The subtleties do not arise with internal definitions of procedures, however. We will return to this issue in section 4.1.6, after we learn more about evaluation.

Finding roots of equations by the half-interval method

The *half-interval method* is a simple but powerful technique for finding roots of an equation $f(x) = 0$, where f is a continuous function. The idea is that, if we are given points a and b such that $f(a) < 0 < f(b)$, then f must have at least one zero between a and b. To locate a zero, let x be the average of a and b and compute $f(x)$. If $f(x) > 0$, then f must have a zero between a and x. If $f(x) < 0$, then f must have a zero between x and b. Continuing in this way, we can identify smaller and smaller intervals on which f must have a zero. When we reach a point where the interval is small enough, the process stops. Since the interval of uncertainty is reduced by half at each step of the process, the number of steps required grows as $\Theta(\log(L/T))$, where L is the length of the original interval and T is the error tolerance (that is, the size of the interval we will consider "small enough"). Here is a procedure that implements this strategy:

```
(define (search f neg-point pos-point)
  (let ((midpoint (average neg-point pos-point)))
    (if (close-enough? neg-point pos-point)
        midpoint
        (let ((test-value (f midpoint)))
          (cond ((positive? test-value)
                 (search f neg-point midpoint))
                ((negative? test-value)
                 (search f midpoint pos-point))
                (else midpoint))))))
```

We assume that we are initially given the function f together with points at which its values are negative and positive. We first compute the midpoint of the two given points. Next we check to see if the given interval is small enough, and if so we simply return the midpoint as our answer. Otherwise, we compute as a test value the value of f at the midpoint. If the test value is positive, then we continue the process with a new interval running from the original negative point to the midpoint. If the test value is negative, we continue with the interval from the midpoint to the positive point. Finally, there is the possibility that the test value is 0, in which case the midpoint is itself the root we are searching for.

To test whether the endpoints are "close enough" we can use a procedure similar to the one used in section 1.1.7 for computing square roots:[55]

---

[55]We have used 0.001 as a representative "small" number to indicate a tolerance for the acceptable error in a calculation. The appropriate tolerance for a real calculation depends upon the problem to be solved and the limitations of the computer and the algorithm. This is often a very subtle consideration, requiring help from a numerical analyst or some other kind of magician.

```
(define (close-enough? x y)
  (< (abs (- x y)) 0.001))
```

Search is awkward to use directly, because we can accidentally give it points at which f's values do not have the required sign, in which case we get a wrong answer. Instead we will use search via the following procedure, which checks to see which of the endpoints has a negative function value and which has a positive value, and calls the search procedure accordingly. If the function has the same sign on the two given points, the half-interval method cannot be used, in which case the procedure signals an error.[56]

```
(define (half-interval-method f a b)
  (let ((a-value (f a))
        (b-value (f b)))
    (cond ((and (negative? a-value) (positive? b-value))
           (search f a b))
          ((and (negative? b-value) (positive? a-value))
           (search f b a))
          (else
           (error "Values are not of opposite sign" a b)))))
```

The following example uses the half-interval method to approximate π as the root between 2 and 4 of $\sin x = 0$:

```
(half-interval-method sin 2.0 4.0)
3.14111328125
```

Here is another example, using the half-interval method to search for a root of the equation $x^3 - 2x - 3 = 0$ between 1 and 2:

```
(half-interval-method (lambda (x) (- (* x x x) (* 2 x) 3))
                      1.0
                      2.0)
1.89306640625
```

Finding fixed points of functions

A number x is called a *fixed point* of a function f if x satisfies the equation $f(x) = x$. For some functions f we can locate a fixed point by beginning with an initial guess and applying f repeatedly,

$$f(x), f(f(x)), f(f(f(x))), \ldots$$

---

[56]This can be accomplished using error, which takes as arguments a number of items that are printed as error messages.

until the value does not change very much. Using this idea, we can devise a procedure `fixed-point` that takes as inputs a function and an initial guess and produces an approximation to a fixed point of the function. We apply the function repeatedly until we find two successive values whose difference is less than some prescribed tolerance:

```
(define tolerance 0.00001)
```

```
(define (fixed-point f first-guess)
  (define (close-enough? v1 v2)
    (< (abs (- v1 v2)) tolerance))
  (define (try guess)
    (let ((next (f guess)))
      (if (close-enough? guess next)
          next
          (try next))))
  (try first-guess))
```

For example, we can use this method to approximate the fixed point of the cosine function, starting with 1 as an initial approximation:[57]

```
(fixed-point cos 1.0)
.7390822985224023
```

Similarly, we can find a solution to the equation $y = \sin y + \cos y$:

```
(fixed-point (lambda (y) (+ (sin y) (cos y)))
             1.0)
1.2587315962971173
```

The fixed-point process is reminiscent of the process we used for finding square roots in section 1.1.7. Both are based on the idea of repeatedly improving a guess until the result satisfies some criterion. In fact, we can readily formulate the square-root computation as a fixed-point search. Computing the square root of some number x requires finding a y such that $y^2 = x$. Putting this equation into the equivalent form $y = x/y$, we recognize that we are looking for a fixed point of the function[58] $y \mapsto x/y$, and we can therefore try to compute square roots as

```
(define (sqrt x)
  (fixed-point (lambda (y) (/ x y))
               1.0))
```

---

[57] Try this during a boring lecture: Set your calculator to radians mode and then repeatedly press the cos button until you obtain the fixed point.

[58] $\mapsto$ (pronounced "maps to") is the mathematician's way of writing `lambda`. $y \mapsto x/y$ means `(lambda(y) (/ x y))`, that is, the function whose value at y is x/y.

Unfortunately, this fixed-point search does not converge. Consider an initial guess y_1. The next guess is $y_2 = x/y_1$ and the next guess is $y_3 = x/y_2 = x/(x/y_1) = y_1$. This results in an infinite loop in which the two guesses y_1 and y_2 repeat over and over, oscillating about the answer.

One way to control such oscillations is to prevent the guesses from changing so much. Since the answer is always between our guess y and x/y, we can make a new guess that is not as far from y as x/y by averaging y with x/y, so that the next guess after y is $\frac{1}{2}(y+x/y)$ instead of x/y. The process of making such a sequence of guesses is simply the process of looking for a fixed point of $y \mapsto \frac{1}{2}(y + x/y)$:

```
(define (sqrt x)
  (fixed-point (lambda (y) (average y (/ x y)))
               1.0))
```

(Note that $y = \frac{1}{2}(y + x/y)$ is a simple transformation of the equation $y = x/y$; to derive it, add y to both sides of the equation and divide by 2.)

With this modification, the square-root procedure works. In fact, if we unravel the definitions, we can see that the sequence of approximations to the square root generated here is precisely the same as the one generated by our original square-root procedure of section 1.1.7. This approach of averaging successive approximations to a solution, a technique we that we call *average damping*, often aids the convergence of fixed-point searches.

Exercise 1.35

Show that the golden ratio ϕ (section 1.2.2) is a fixed point of the transformation $x \mapsto 1 + 1/x$, and use this fact to compute ϕ by means of the `fixed-point` procedure.

Exercise 1.36

Modify `fixed-point` so that it prints the sequence of approximations it generates, using the `newline` and `display` primitives shown in exercise 1.22. Then find a solution to $x^x = 1000$ by finding a fixed point of $x \mapsto \log(1000)/\log(x)$. (Use Scheme's primitive `log` procedure, which computes natural logarithms.) Compare the number of steps this takes with and without average damping. (Note that you cannot start `fixed-point` with a guess of 1, as this would cause division by $\log(1) = 0$.)

Exercise 1.37

a. An infinite *continued fraction* is an expression of the form

$$
f = \cfrac{N_1}{D_1 + \cfrac{N_2}{D_2 + \cfrac{N_3}{D_3 + \cdots}}}
$$

As an example, one can show that the infinite continued fraction expansion with the N_i and the D_i all equal to 1 produces $1/\phi$, where ϕ is the golden ratio (described in section 1.2.2). One way to approximate an infinite continued fraction is to truncate the expansion after a given number of terms. Such a truncation—a so-called *k-term finite continued fraction*—has the form

$$
\cfrac{N_1}{D_1 + \cfrac{N_2}{\cfrac{\ddots}{ + \cfrac{N_K}{D_K}}}}
$$

Suppose that n and d are procedures of one argument (the term index i) that return the N_i and D_i of the terms of the continued fraction. Define a procedure cont-frac such that evaluating (cont-frac n d k) computes the value of the k-term finite continued fraction. Check your procedure by approximating $1/\phi$ using

```
(cont-frac (lambda (i) 1.0)
           (lambda (i) 1.0)
           k)
```

for successive values of k. How large must you make k in order to get an approximation that is accurate to 4 decimal places?

b. If your cont-frac procedure generates a recursive process, write one that generates an iterative process. If it generates an iterative process, write one that generates a recursive process.

Exercise 1.38

In 1737, the Swiss mathematician Leonhard Euler published a memoir *De Fractionibus Continuis*, which included a continued fraction expansion for $e - 2$, where e is the base of the natural logarithms. In this fraction, the N_i are all 1, and the D_i are successively 1, 2, 1, 1, 4, 1, 1, 6, 1, 1, 8, ... Write a program that uses your cont-frac procedure from exercise 1.37 to approximate e, based on Euler's expansion.

Exercise 1.39

A continued fraction representation of the tangent function was published in 1770 by the German mathematician J.H. Lambert:

$$\tan x = \cfrac{x}{1 - \cfrac{x^2}{3 - \cfrac{x^2}{5 - \ddots}}}$$

where x is in radians. Define a procedure (tan-cf x k) that computes an approximation to the tangent function based on Lambert's formula. K specifies the number of terms to compute, as in exercise 1.37.

1.3.4   Procedures as Returned Values

The above examples demonstrate how the ability to pass procedures as arguments significantly enhances the expressive power of our programming language. We can achieve even more expressive power by creating procedures whose returned values are themselves procedures.

We can illustrate this idea by looking again at the fixed-point example described at the end of section 1.3.3. We formulated a new version of the square-root procedure as a fixed-point search, starting with the observation that $\sqrt{x}$ is a fixed-point of the function $y \mapsto x/y$. Then we used average damping to make the approximations converge. Average damping is a useful general technique in itself. Namely, given a function f, we consider the function whose value at x is equal to the average of x and $f(x)$.

We can express the idea of average damping by means of the following procedure:

```
(define (average-damp f)
  (lambda (x) (average x (f x))))
```

Average-damp is a procedure that takes as its argument a procedure f and returns as its value a procedure (produced by the lambda) that, when applied to a number x, produces the average of x and (f x). For example, applying average-damp to the square procedure produces a procedure whose value at some number x is the average of x and x^2. Applying this resulting procedure to 10 returns the average of 10 and 100, or 55:[59]

---

[59]Observe that this is a combination whose operator is itself a combination. Exercise 1.4 already demonstrated the ability to form such combinations, but that was only a toy example. Here we begin to see the real need for such combinations—when applying a procedure that is obtained as the value returned by a higher-order procedure.

```
((average-damp square) 10)
55
```

Using `average-damp`, we can reformulate the square-root procedure as follows:

```
(define (sqrt x)
  (fixed-point (average-damp (lambda (y) (/ x y)))
               1.0))
```

Notice how this formulation makes explicit the three ideas in the method: fixed-point search, average damping, and the function $y \mapsto x/y$. It is instructive to compare this formulation of the square-root method with the original version given in section 1.1.7. Bear in mind that these procedures express the same process, and notice how much clearer the idea becomes when we express the process in terms of these abstractions. In general, there are many ways to formulate a process as a procedure. Experienced programmers know how to choose procedural formulations that are particularly perspicuous, and where useful elements of the process are exposed as separate entities that can be reused in other applications. As a simple example of reuse, notice that the cube root of x is a fixed point of the function $y \mapsto x/y^2$, so we can immediately generalize our square-root procedure to one that extracts cube roots:[60]

```
(define (cube-root x)
  (fixed-point (average-damp (lambda (y) (/ x (square y))))
               1.0))
```

Newton's method

When we first introduced the square-root procedure, in section 1.1.7, we mentioned that this was a special case of *Newton's method*. If $x \mapsto g(x)$ is a differentiable function, then a solution of the equation $g(x) = 0$ is a fixed point of the function $x \mapsto f(x)$ where

$$f(x) = x - \frac{g(x)}{Dg(x)}$$

and $Dg(x)$ is the derivative of g evaluated at x. Newton's method is the use of the fixed-point method we saw above to approximate a solution of the equation by finding a fixed point of the function f.[61] For many func-

---

[60] See exercise 1.45 for a further generalization.

[61] Elementary calculus books usually describe Newton's method in terms of the sequence of approximations $x_{n+1} = x_n - g(x_n)/Dg(x_n)$. Having language for talking about processes and using the idea of fixed points simplifies the description of the method.

tions g and for sufficiently good initial guesses for x, Newton's method converges very rapidly to a solution of $g(x) = 0$.[62]

In order to implement Newton's method as a procedure, we must first express the idea of derivative. Note that "derivative," like average damping, is something that transforms a function into another function. For instance, the derivative of the function $x \mapsto x^3$ is the function $x \mapsto 3x^2$. In general, if g is a function and dx is a small number, then the derivative Dg of g is the function whose value at any number x is given (in the limit of small dx) by

$$Dg(x) = \frac{g(x + dx) - g(x)}{dx}$$

Thus, we can express the idea of derivative (taking dx to be, say, 0.00001) as the procedure

```
(define (deriv g)
  (lambda (x)
    (/ (- (g (+ x dx)) (g x))
       dx)))
```

along with the definition

```
(define dx 0.00001)
```

Like `average-damp`, `deriv` is a procedure that takes a procedure as argument and returns a procedure as value. For example, to approximate the derivative of $x \mapsto x^3$ at 5 (whose exact value is 75) we can evaluate

```
(define (cube x) (* x x x))
```

```
((deriv cube) 5)
75.00014999664018
```

With the aid of `deriv`, we can express Newton's method as a fixed-point process:

```
(define (newton-transform g)
  (lambda (x)
    (- x (/ (g x) ((deriv g) x)))))
```

---

[62]Newton's method does not always converge to an answer, but it can be shown that in favorable cases each iteration doubles the number-of-digits accuracy of the approximation to the solution. In such cases, Newton's method will converge much more rapidly than the half-interval method.

```
(define (newtons-method g guess)
  (fixed-point (newton-transform g) guess))
```

The newton-transform procedure expresses the formula at the beginning of this section, and newtons-method is readily defined in terms
of this. It takes as arguments a procedure that computes the function for
which we want to find a zero, together with an initial guess. For instance,
to find the square root of x, we can use Newton's method to find a zero
of the function $y \mapsto y^2 - x$ starting with an initial guess of 1.[63] This
provides yet another form of the square-root procedure:

```
(define (sqrt x)
  (newtons-method (lambda (y) (- (square y) x))
                  1.0))
```

Abstractions and first-class procedures

We've seen two ways to express the square-root computation as an instance of a more general method, once as a fixed-point search and once
using Newton's method. Since Newton's method was itself expressed
as a fixed-point process, we actually saw two ways to compute square
roots as fixed points. Each method begins with a function and finds a
fixed point of some transformation of the function. We can express this
general idea itself as a procedure:

```
(define (fixed-point-of-transform g transform guess)
  (fixed-point (transform g) guess))
```

This very general procedure takes as its arguments a procedure g that
computes some function, a procedure that transforms g, and an initial
guess. The returned result is a fixed point of the transformed function.
   Using this abstraction, we can recast the first square-root computation
from this section (where we look for a fixed point of the average-damped
version of $y \mapsto x/y$) as an instance of this general method:

```
(define (sqrt x)
  (fixed-point-of-transform (lambda (y) (/ x y))
                            average-damp
                            1.0))
```

---

[63] For finding square roots, Newton's method converges rapidly to the correct solution from
any starting point.

Similarly, we can express the second square-root computation from this section (an instance of Newton's method that finds a fixed point of the Newton transform of $y \mapsto y^2 - x$) as

```
(define (sqrt x)
  (fixed-point-of-transform (lambda (y) (- (square y) x))
                            newton-transform
                            1.0))
```

We began section 1.3 with the observation that compound procedures are a crucial abstraction mechanism, because they permit us to express general methods of computing as explicit elements in our programming language. Now we've seen how higher-order procedures permit us to manipulate these general methods to create further abstractions.

As programmers, we should be alert to opportunities to identify the underlying abstractions in our programs and to build upon them and generalize them to create more powerful abstractions. This is not to say that one should always write programs in the most abstract way possible; expert programmers know how to choose the level of abstraction appropriate to their task. But it is important to be able to think in terms of these abstractions, so that we can be ready to apply them in new contexts. The significance of higher-order procedures is that they enable us to represent these abstractions explicitly as elements in our programming language, so that they can be handled just like other computational elements.

In general, programming languages impose restrictions on the ways in which computational elements can be manipulated. Elements with the fewest restrictions are said to have *first-class* status. Some of the "rights and privileges" of first-class elements are:[64]

- They may be named by variables.

- They may be passed as arguments to procedures.

- They may be returned as the results of procedures.

- They may be included in data structures.[65]

---

[64]The notion of first-class status of programming-language elements is due to the British computer scientist Christopher Strachey (1916–1975).

[65]We'll see examples of this after we introduce data structures in chapter 2.

Lisp, unlike other common programming languages, awards procedures full first-class status. This poses challenges for efficient implementation, but the resulting gain in expressive power is enormous.[66]

Exercise 1.40

Define a procedure `cubic` that can be used together with the `newtons-method` procedure in expressions of the form

```
(newtons-method (cubic a b c) 1)
```

to approximate zeros of the cubic $x^3 + ax^2 + bx + c$.

Exercise 1.41

Define a procedure `double` that takes a procedure of one argument as argument and returns a procedure that applies the original procedure twice. For example, if `inc` is a procedure that adds 1 to its argument, then (`double inc`) should be a procedure that adds 2. What value is returned by

```
(((double (double double)) inc) 5)
```

Exercise 1.42

Let f and g be two one-argument functions. The *composition* f after g is defined to be the function $x \mapsto f(g(x))$. Define a procedure `compose` that implements composition. For example, if `inc` is a procedure that adds 1 to its argument,

```
((compose square inc) 6)
```
49

Exercise 1.43

If f is a numerical function and n is a positive integer, then we can form the nth repeated application of f, which is defined to be the function whose value at x is $f(f(\ldots(f(x))\ldots))$. For example, if f is the function $x \mapsto x + 1$, then the nth repeated application of f is the function $x \mapsto x + n$. If f is the operation of squaring a number, then the nth repeated application of f is the function that raises its argument to the 2^nth power. Write a procedure that takes as inputs a procedure that computes f and a positive integer n and returns the procedure that computes the nth repeated application of f. Your procedure should be able to be used as follows:

```
((repeated square 2) 5)
```
625

Hint: You may find it convenient to use `compose` from exercise 1.42.

---

[66]The major implementation cost of first-class procedures is that allowing procedures to be returned as values requires reserving storage for a procedure's free variables even while the procedure is not executing. In the Scheme implementation we will study in section 4.1, these variables are stored in the procedure's environment.

Exercise 1.44

The idea of *smoothing* a function is an important concept in signal processing. If f is a function and dx is some small number, then the smoothed version of f is the function whose value at a point x is the average of $f(x - dx)$, $f(x)$, and $f(x + dx)$. Write a procedure smooth that takes as input a procedure that computes f and returns a procedure that computes the smoothed f. It is sometimes valuable to repeatedly smooth a function (that is, smooth the smoothed function, and so on) to obtained the *n-fold smoothed function*. Show how to generate the n-fold smoothed function of any given function using smooth and repeated from exercise 1.43.

Exercise 1.45

We saw in section 1.3.3 that attempting to compute square roots by naively finding a fixed point of $y \mapsto x/y$ does not converge, and that this can be fixed by average damping. The same method works for finding cube roots as fixed points of the average-damped $y \mapsto x/y^2$. Unfortunately, the process does not work for fourth roots—a single average damp is not enough to make a fixed-point search for $y \mapsto x/y^3$ converge. On the other hand, if we average damp twice (i.e., use the average damp of the average damp of $y \mapsto x/y^3$) the fixed-point search does converge. Do some experiments to determine how many average damps are required to compute nth roots as a fixed-point search based upon repeated average damping of $y \mapsto x/y^{n-1}$. Use this to implement a simple procedure for computing nth roots using fixed-point, average-damp, and the repeated procedure of exercise 1.43. Assume that any arithmetic operations you need are available as primitives.

Exercise 1.46

Several of the numerical methods described in this chapter are instances of an extremely general computational strategy known as *iterative improvement*. Iterative improvement says that, to compute something, we start with an initial guess for the answer, test if the guess is good enough, and otherwise improve the guess and continue the process using the improved guess as the new guess. Write a procedure iterative-improve that takes two procedures as arguments: a method for telling whether a guess is good enough and a method for improving a guess. Iterative-improve should return as its value a procedure that takes a guess as argument and keeps improving the guess until it is good enough. Rewrite the sqrt procedure of section 1.1.7 and the fixed-point procedure of section 1.3.3 in terms of iterative-improve.

2

Building Abstractions with Data

> We now come to the decisive step of mathematical
> abstraction: we forget about what the symbols stand for.
> ...[The mathematician] need not be idle; there are many
> operations which he may carry out with these symbols,
> without ever having to look at the things they stand for.
>
> Hermann Weyl, *The Mathematical Way of Thinking*

We concentrated in chapter 1 on computational processes and on the
role of procedures in program design. We saw how to use primitive
data (numbers) and primitive operations (arithmetic operations), how to
combine procedures to form compound procedures through composition,
conditionals, and the use of parameters, and how to abstract procedures
by using define. We saw that a procedure can be regarded as a pattern
for the local evolution of a process, and we classified, reasoned about,
and performed simple algorithmic analyses of some common patterns
for processes as embodied in procedures. We also saw that higher-order
procedures enhance the power of our language by enabling us to manipulate, and thereby to reason in terms of, general methods of computation.
This is much of the essence of programming.

In this chapter we are going to look at more complex data. All the
procedures in chapter 1 operate on simple numerical data, and simple
data are not sufficient for many of the problems we wish to address using computation. Programs are typically designed to model complex
phenomena, and more often than not one must construct computational
objects that have several parts in order to model real-world phenomena
that have several aspects. Thus, whereas our focus in chapter 1 was on
building abstractions by combining procedures to form compound procedures, we turn in this chapter to another key aspect of any programming
language: the means it provides for building abstractions by combining
data objects to form *compound data*.

Why do we want compound data in a programming language? For the
same reasons that we want compound procedures: to elevate the conceptual level at which we can design our programs, to increase the modular-

ity of our designs, and to enhance the expressive power of our language. Just as the ability to define procedures enables us to deal with processes at a higher conceptual level than that of the primitive operations of the language, the ability to construct compound data objects enables us to deal with data at a higher conceptual level than that of the primitive data objects of the language.

Consider the task of designing a system to perform arithmetic with rational numbers. We could imagine an operation add-rat that takes two rational numbers and produces their sum. In terms of simple data, a rational number can be thought of as two integers: a numerator and a denominator. Thus, we could design a program in which each rational number would be represented by two integers (a numerator and a denominator) and where add-rat would be implemented by two procedures (one producing the numerator of the sum and one producing the denominator). But this would be awkward, because we would then need to explicitly keep track of which numerators corresponded to which denominators. In a system intended to perform many operations on many rational numbers, such bookkeeping details would clutter the programs substantially, to say nothing of what they would do to our minds. It would be much better if we could "glue together" a numerator and denominator to form a pair—a *compound data object*—that our programs could manipulate in a way that would be consistent with regarding a rational number as a single conceptual unit.

The use of compound data also enables us to increase the modularity of our programs. If we can manipulate rational numbers directly as objects in their own right, then we can separate the part of our program that deals with rational numbers per se from the details of how rational numbers may be represented as pairs of integers. The general technique of isolating the parts of a program that deal with how data objects are represented from the parts of a program that deal with how data objects are used is a powerful design methodology called *data abstraction*. We will see how data abstraction makes programs much easier to design, maintain, and modify.

The use of compound data leads to a real increase in the expressive power of our programming language. Consider the idea of forming a "linear combination" $ax + by$. We might like to write a procedure that would accept a, b, x, and y as arguments and return the value of $ax + by$. This presents no difficulty if the arguments are to be numbers, because we can readily define the procedure

```
(define (linear-combination a b x y)
  (+ (* a x) (* b y)))
```

But suppose we are not concerned only with numbers. Suppose we would like to express, in procedural terms, the idea that one can form linear combinations whenever addition and multiplication are defined—for rational numbers, complex numbers, polynomials, or whatever. We could express this as a procedure of the form

```
(define (linear-combination a b x y)
  (add (mul a x) (mul b y)))
```

where add and mul are not the primitive procedures + and * but rather more complex things that will perform the appropriate operations for whatever kinds of data we pass in as the arguments a, b, x, and y. The key point is that the only thing linear-combination should need to know about a, b, x, and y is that the procedures add and mul will perform the appropriate manipulations. From the perspective of the procedure linear-combination, it is irrelevant what a, b, x, and y are and even more irrelevant how they might happen to be represented in terms of more primitive data. This same example shows why it is important that our programming language provide the ability to manipulate compound objects directly: Without this, there is no way for a procedure such as linear-combination to pass its arguments along to add and mul without having to know their detailed structure.[1]

We begin this chapter by implementing the rational-number arithmetic system mentioned above. This will form the background for our discussion of compound data and data abstraction. As with compound procedures, the main issue to be addressed is that of abstraction as a technique for coping with complexity, and we will see how data abstraction enables us to erect suitable *abstraction barriers* between different parts of a program.

---

[1]The ability to directly manipulate procedures provides an analogous increase in the expressive power of a programming language. For example, in section 1.3.1 we introduced the sum procedure, which takes a procedure term as an argument and computes the sum of the values of term over some specified interval. In order to define sum, it is crucial that we be able to speak of a procedure such as term as an entity in its own right, without regard for how term might be expressed with more primitive operations. Indeed, if we did not have the notion of "a procedure," it is doubtful that we would ever even think of the possibility of defining an operation such as sum. Moreover, insofar as performing the summation is concerned, the details of how term may be constructed from more primitive operations are irrelevant.

We will see that the key to forming compound data is that a programming language should provide some kind of "glue" so that data objects can be combined to form more complex data objects. There are many possible kinds of glue. Indeed, we will discover how to form compound data using no special "data" operations at all, only procedures. This will further blur the distinction between "procedure" and "data," which was already becoming tenuous toward the end of chapter 1. We will also explore some conventional techniques for representing sequences and trees. One key idea in dealing with compound data is the notion of *closure*—that the glue we use for combining data objects should allow us to combine not only primitive data objects, but compound data objects as well. Another key idea is that compound data objects can serve as *conventional interfaces* for combining program modules in mix-and-match ways. We illustrate some of these ideas by presenting a simple graphics language that exploits closure.

We will then augment the representational power of our language by introducing *symbolic expressions*—data whose elementary parts can be arbitrary symbols rather than only numbers. We explore various alternatives for representing sets of objects. We will find that, just as a given numerical function can be computed by many different computational processes, there are many ways in which a given data structure can be represented in terms of simpler objects, and the choice of representation can have significant impact on the time and space requirements of processes that manipulate the data. We will investigate these ideas in the context of symbolic differentiation, the representation of sets, and the encoding of information.

Next we will take up the problem of working with data that may be represented differently by different parts of a program. This leads to the need to implement *generic operations*, which must handle many different types of data. Maintaining modularity in the presence of generic operations requires more powerful abstraction barriers than can be erected with simple data abstraction alone. In particular, we introduce *data-directed programming* as a technique that allows individual data representations to be designed in isolation and then combined *additively* (i.e., without modification). To illustrate the power of this approach to system design, we close the chapter by applying what we have learned to the implementation of a package for performing symbolic arithmetic on polynomials, in which the coefficients of the polynomials can be integers, rational numbers, complex numbers, and even other polynomials.

2.1   Introduction to Data Abstraction

In section 1.1.8, we noted that a procedure used as an element in creating a more complex procedure could be regarded not only as a collection of particular operations but also as a procedural abstraction. That is, the details of how the procedure was implemented could be suppressed, and the particular procedure itself could be replaced by any other procedure with the same overall behavior. In other words, we could make an abstraction that would separate the way the procedure would be used from the details of how the procedure would be implemented in terms of more primitive procedures. The analogous notion for compound data is called *data abstraction*. Data abstraction is a methodology that enables us to isolate how a compound data object is used from the details of how it is constructed from more primitive data objects.

The basic idea of data abstraction is to structure the programs that are to use compound data objects so that they operate on "abstract data." That is, our programs should use data in such a way as to make no assumptions about the data that are not strictly necessary for performing the task at hand. At the same time, a "concrete" data representation is defined independent of the programs that use the data. The interface between these two parts of our system will be a set of procedures, called *selectors* and *constructors*, that implement the abstract data in terms of the concrete representation. To illustrate this technique, we will consider how to design a set of procedures for manipulating rational numbers.

2.1.1   Example: Arithmetic Operations for Rational Numbers

Suppose we want to do arithmetic with rational numbers. We want to be able to add, subtract, multiply, and divide them and to test whether two rational numbers are equal.

Let us begin by assuming that we already have a way of constructing a rational number from a numerator and a denominator. We also assume that, given a rational number, we have a way of extracting (or selecting) its numerator and its denominator. Let us further assume that the constructor and selectors are available as procedures:

- (make-rat $\langle n \rangle$ $\langle d \rangle$) returns the rational number whose numerator is the integer $\langle n \rangle$ and whose denominator is the integer $\langle d \rangle$.

- (numer $\langle x \rangle$) returns the numerator of the rational number $\langle x \rangle$.

- (denom $\langle x \rangle$) returns the denominator of the rational number $\langle x \rangle$.

We are using here a powerful strategy of synthesis: *wishful thinking*. We haven't yet said how a rational number is represented, or how the procedures numer, denom, and make-rat should be implemented. Even so, if we did have these three procedures, we could then add, subtract, multiply, divide, and test equality by using the following relations:

$$\frac{n_1}{d_1} + \frac{n_2}{d_2} = \frac{n_1 d_2 + n_2 d_1}{d_1 d_2}$$

$$\frac{n_1}{d_1} - \frac{n_2}{d_2} = \frac{n_1 d_2 - n_2 d_1}{d_1 d_2}$$

$$\frac{n_1}{d_1} \cdot \frac{n_2}{d_2} = \frac{n_1 n_2}{d_1 d_2}$$

$$\frac{n_1/d_1}{n_2/d_2} = \frac{n_1 d_2}{d_1 n_2}$$

$$\frac{n_1}{d_1} = \frac{n_2}{d_2} \text{ if and only if } n_1 d_2 = n_2 d_1$$

We can express these rules as procedures:

```
(define (add-rat x y)
  (make-rat (+ (* (numer x) (denom y))
               (* (numer y) (denom x)))
            (* (denom x) (denom y))))

(define (sub-rat x y)
  (make-rat (- (* (numer x) (denom y))
               (* (numer y) (denom x)))
            (* (denom x) (denom y))))

(define (mul-rat x y)
  (make-rat (* (numer x) (numer y))
            (* (denom x) (denom y))))

(define (div-rat x y)
  (make-rat (* (numer x) (denom y))
            (* (denom x) (numer y))))

(define (equal-rat? x y)
  (= (* (numer x) (denom y))
     (* (numer y) (denom x))))
```

Now we have the operations on rational numbers defined in terms of the selector and constructor procedures numer, denom, and make-rat.

But we haven't yet defined these. What we need is some way to glue together a numerator and a denominator to form a rational number.

Pairs

To enable us to implement the concrete level of our data abstraction, our language provides a compound structure called a *pair*, which can be constructed with the primitive procedure cons. This procedure takes two arguments and returns a compound data object that contains the two arguments as parts. Given a pair, we can extract the parts using the primitive procedures car and cdr.[2] Thus, we can use cons, car, and cdr as follows:

```
(define x (cons 1 2))

(car x)
1

(cdr x)
2
```

Notice that a pair is a data object that can be given a name and manipulated, just like a primitive data object. Moreover, cons can be used to form pairs whose elements are pairs, and so on:

```
(define x (cons 1 2))

(define y (cons 3 4))

(define z (cons x y))

(car (car z))
1

(car (cdr z))
3
```

In section 2.2 we will see how this ability to combine pairs means that pairs can be used as general-purpose building blocks to create all sorts of complex data structures. The single compound-data primitive *pair*, implemented by the procedures cons, car, and cdr, is the only glue we need. Data objects constructed from pairs are called *list-structured* data.

---

[2]The name cons stands for "construct." The names car and cdr derive from the original implementation of Lisp on the IBM 704. That machine had an addressing scheme that allowed one to reference the "address" and "decrement" parts of a memory location. Car stands for "Contents of Address part of Register" and cdr (pronounced "could-er") stands for "Contents of Decrement part of Register."

Representing rational numbers

Pairs offer a natural way to complete the rational-number system. Simply represent a rational number as a pair of two integers: a numerator and a denominator. Then make-rat, numer, and denom are readily implemented as follows:[3]

```
(define (make-rat n d) (cons n d))

(define (numer x) (car x))

(define (denom x) (cdr x))
```

Also, in order to display the results of our computations, we can print rational numbers by printing the numerator, a slash, and the denominator:[4]

```
(define (print-rat x)
  (newline)
  (display (numer x))
  (display "/")
  (display (denom x)))
```

Now we can try our rational-number procedures:

```
(define one-half (make-rat 1 2))

(print-rat one-half)
1/2

(define one-third (make-rat 1 3))
```

---

[3] Another way to define the selectors and constructor is

```
(define make-rat cons)
(define numer car)
(define denom cdr)
```

The first definition associates the name make-rat with the value of the expression cons, which is the primitive procedure that constructs pairs. Thus make-rat and cons are names for the same primitive constructor.

Defining selectors and constructors in this way is efficient: Instead of make-rat *calling* cons, make-rat *is* cons, so there is only one procedure called, not two, when make-rat is called. On the other hand, doing this defeats debugging aids that trace procedure calls or put breakpoints on procedure calls: You may want to watch make-rat being called, but you certainly don't want to watch every call to cons.

We have chosen not to use this style of definition in this book.

[4] Display is the Scheme primitive for printing data. The Scheme primitive newline starts a new line for printing. Neither of these procedures returns a useful value, so in the uses of print-rat below, we show only what print-rat prints, not what the interpreter prints as the value returned by print-rat.

```
(print-rat (add-rat one-half one-third))
5/6
```

```
(print-rat (mul-rat one-half one-third))
1/6
```

```
(print-rat (add-rat one-third one-third))
6/9
```

As the final example shows, our rational-number implementation does not reduce rational numbers to lowest terms. We can remedy this by changing make-rat. If we have a gcd procedure like the one in section 1.2.5 that produces the greatest common divisor of two integers, we can use gcd to reduce the numerator and the denominator to lowest terms before constructing the pair:

```
(define (make-rat n d)
  (let ((g (gcd n d)))
    (cons (/ n g) (/ d g))))
```

Now we have

```
(print-rat (add-rat one-third one-third))
2/3
```

as desired. This modification was accomplished by changing the constructor make-rat without changing any of the procedures (such as add-rat and mul-rat) that implement the actual operations.

Exercise 2.1

Define a better version of make-rat that handles both positive and negative arguments. Make-rat should normalize the sign so that if the rational number is positive, both the numerator and denominator are positive, and if the rational number is negative, only the numerator is negative.

2.1.2 Abstraction Barriers

Before continuing with more examples of compound data and data abstraction, let us consider some of the issues raised by the rational-number example. We defined the rational-number operations in terms of a constructor make-rat and selectors numer and denom. In general, the underlying idea of data abstraction is to identify for each type of data object a basic set of operations in terms of which all manipulations of data objects of that type will be expressed, and then to use only those operations in manipulating the data.

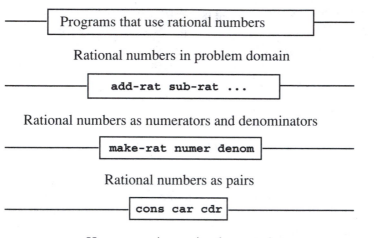

Figure 2.1   Data-abstraction barriers in the rational-number package.

We can envision the structure of the rational-number system as shown in figure 2.1. The horizontal lines represent *abstraction barriers* that isolate different "levels" of the system. At each level, the barrier separates the programs (above) that use the data abstraction from the programs (below) that implement the data abstraction. Programs that use rational numbers manipulate them solely in terms of the procedures supplied "for public use" by the rational-number package: add-rat, sub-rat, mul-rat, div-rat, and equal-rat?. These, in turn, are implemented solely in terms of the constructor and selectors make-rat, numer, and denom, which themselves are implemented in terms of pairs. The details of how pairs are implemented are irrelevant to the rest of the rational-number package so long as pairs can be manipulated by the use of cons, car, and cdr. In effect, procedures at each level are the interfaces that define the abstraction barriers and connect the different levels.

This simple idea has many advantages. One advantage is that it makes programs much easier to maintain and to modify. Any complex data structure can be represented in a variety of ways with the primitive data structures provided by a programming language. Of course, the choice of representation influences the programs that operate on it; thus, if the representation were to be changed at some later time, all such programs might have to be modified accordingly. This task could be time-consuming and expensive in the case of large programs unless the dependence on the representation were to be confined by design to a very few program modules.

For example, an alternate way to address the problem of reducing rational numbers to lowest terms is to perform the reduction whenever we access the parts of a rational number, rather than when we construct it. This leads to different constructor and selector procedures:

```
(define (make-rat n d)
  (cons n d))

(define (numer x)
  (let ((g (gcd (car x) (cdr x))))
    (/ (car x) g)))

(define (denom x)
  (let ((g (gcd (car x) (cdr x))))
    (/ (cdr x) g)))
```

The difference between this implementation and the previous one lies in when we compute the gcd. If in our typical use of rational numbers we access the numerators and denominators of the same rational numbers many times, it would be preferable to compute the gcd when the rational numbers are constructed. If not, we may be better off waiting until access time to compute the gcd. In any case, when we change from one representation to the other, the procedures add-rat, sub-rat, and so on do not have to be modified at all.

Constraining the dependence on the representation to a few interface procedures helps us design programs as well as modify them, because it allows us to maintain the flexibility to consider alternate implementations. To continue with our simple example, suppose we are designing a rational-number package and we can't decide initially whether to perform the gcd at construction time or at selection time. The data-abstraction methodology gives us a way to defer that decision without losing the ability to make progress on the rest of the system.

Exercise 2.2

Consider the problem of representing line segments in a plane. Each segment is represented as a pair of points: a starting point and an ending point. Define a constructor make-segment and selectors start-segment and end-segment that define the representation of segments in terms of points. Furthermore, a point can be represented as a pair of numbers: the x coordinate and the y coordinate. Accordingly, specify a constructor make-point and selectors x-point and y-point that define this representation. Finally, using your selectors and constructors, define a procedure `midpoint-segment` that takes a line segment as argument and returns its midpoint (the point whose coordinates are the average of the coordinates of the endpoints). To try your procedures, you'll need a way to print points:

```
(define (print-point p)
  (newline)
  (display "(")
  (display (x-point p))
  (display ",")
  (display (y-point p))
  (display ")"))
```

Exercise 2.3

Implement a representation for rectangles in a plane. (Hint: You may want to make use of exercise 2.2.) In terms of your constructors and selectors, create procedures that compute the perimeter and the area of a given rectangle. Now implement a different representation for rectangles. Can you design your system with suitable abstraction barriers, so that the same perimeter and area procedures will work using either representation?

2.1.3   What Is Meant by Data?

We began the rational-number implementation in section 2.1.1 by implementing the rational-number operations `add-rat`, `sub-rat`, and so on in terms of three unspecified procedures: `make-rat`, `numer`, and `denom`. At that point, we could think of the operations as being defined in terms of data objects—numerators, denominators, and rational numbers—whose behavior was specified by the latter three procedures.

But exactly what is meant by *data*? It is not enough to say "whatever is implemented by the given selectors and constructors." Clearly, not every arbitrary set of three procedures can serve as an appropriate basis for the rational-number implementation. We need to guarantee that, if we construct a rational number x from a pair of integers n and d, then extracting the `numer` and the `denom` of x and dividing them should yield the same result as dividing n by d. In other words, `make-rat`, `numer`, and `denom` must satisfy the condition that, for any integer n and any non-zero integer d, if x is (`make-rat` n d), then

$$\frac{(\text{numer } x)}{(\text{denom } x)} = \frac{n}{d}$$

In fact, this is the only condition `make-rat`, `numer`, and `denom` must fulfill in order to form a suitable basis for a rational-number representation. In general, we can think of data as defined by some collection of selectors and constructors, together with specified conditions that these procedures must fulfill in order to be a valid representation.[5]

This point of view can serve to define not only "high-level" data objects, such as rational numbers, but lower-level objects as well. Consider the notion of a pair, which we used in order to define our rational numbers. We never actually said what a pair was, only that the language supplied procedures cons, car, and cdr for operating on pairs. But the only thing we need to know about these three operations is that if we glue two objects together using cons we can retrieve the objects using car and cdr. That is, the operations satisfy the condition that, for any objects x and y, if z is (cons x y) then (car z) is x and (cdr z) is y. Indeed, we mentioned that these three procedures are included as primitives in our language. However, any triple of procedures that satisfies the above condition can be used as the basis for implementing pairs. This point is illustrated strikingly by the fact that we could implement cons, car, and cdr without using any data structures at all but only using procedures. Here are the definitions:

```
(define (cons x y)
  (define (dispatch m)
    (cond ((= m 0) x)
          ((= m 1) y)
          (else (error "Argument not 0 or 1 -- CONS" m))))
  dispatch)

(define (car z) (z 0))

(define (cdr z) (z 1))
```

This use of procedures corresponds to nothing like our intuitive notion of what data should be. Nevertheless, all we need to do to show that this

---

[5]Surprisingly, this idea is very difficult to formulate rigorously. There are two approaches to giving such a formulation. One, pioneered by C. A. R. Hoare (1972), is known as the method of *abstract models*. It formalizes the "procedures plus conditions" specification as outlined in the rational-number example above. Note that the condition on the rational-number representation was stated in terms of facts about integers (equality and division). In general, abstract models define new kinds of data objects in terms of previously defined types of data objects. Assertions about data objects can therefore be checked by reducing them to assertions about previously defined data objects. Another approach, introduced by Zilles at MIT, by Goguen, Thatcher, Wagner, and Wright at IBM (see Thatcher, Wagner, and Wright 1978), and by Guttag at Toronto (see Guttag 1977), is called *algebraic specification*. It regards the "procedures" as elements of an abstract algebraic system whose behavior is specified by axioms that correspond to our "conditions," and uses the techniques of abstract algebra to check assertions about data objects. Both methods are surveyed in the paper by Liskov and Zilles (1975).

is a valid way to represent pairs is to verify that these procedures satisfy the condition given above.

The subtle point to notice is that the value returned by (cons x y) is a procedure—namely the internally defined procedure dispatch, which takes one argument and returns either x or y depending on whether the argument is 0 or 1. Correspondingly, (car z) is defined to apply z to 0. Hence, if z is the procedure formed by (cons x y), then z applied to 0 will yield x. Thus, we have shown that (car (cons x y)) yields x, as desired. Similarly, (cdr (cons x y)) applies the procedure returned by (cons x y) to 1, which returns y. Therefore, this procedural implementation of pairs is a valid implementation, and if we access pairs using only cons, car, and cdr we cannot distinguish this implementation from one that uses "real" data structures.

The point of exhibiting the procedural representation of pairs is not that our language works this way (Scheme, and Lisp systems in general, implement pairs directly, for efficiency reasons) but that it could work this way. The procedural representation, although obscure, is a perfectly adequate way to represent pairs, since it fulfills the only conditions that pairs need to fulfill. This example also demonstrates that the ability to manipulate procedures as objects automatically provides the ability to represent compound data. This may seem a curiosity now, but procedural representations of data will play a central role in our programming repertoire. This style of programming is often called *message passing*, and we will be using it as a basic tool in chapter 3 when we address the issues of modeling and simulation.

Exercise 2.4

Here is an alternative procedural representation of pairs. For this representation, verify that (car (cons x y)) yields x for any objects x and y.

```
(define (cons x y)
  (lambda (m) (m x y)))

(define (car z)
  (z (lambda (p q) p)))
```

What is the corresponding definition of cdr? (Hint: To verify that this works, make use of the substitution model of section 1.1.5.)

Exercise 2.5

Show that we can represent pairs of nonnegative integers using only numbers and arithmetic operations if we represent the pair a and b as the integer that is the product $2^a 3^b$. Give the corresponding definitions of the procedures cons, car, and cdr.

Exercise 2.6

In case representing pairs as procedures wasn't mind-boggling enough, consider that, in a language that can manipulate procedures, we can get by without numbers (at least insofar as nonnegative integers are concerned) by implementing 0 and the operation of adding 1 as

```
(define zero (lambda (f) (lambda (x) x)))
```

```
(define (add-1 n)
  (lambda (f) (lambda (x) (f ((n f) x)))))
```

This representation is known as *Church numerals*, after its inventor, Alonzo Church, the logician who invented the λ calculus.

Define one and two directly (not in terms of zero and add-1). (Hint: Use substitution to evaluate (add-1 zero)). Give a direct definition of the addition procedure + (not in terms of repeated application of add-1).

2.1.4   Extended Exercise: Interval Arithmetic

Alyssa P. Hacker is designing a system to help people solve engineering problems. One feature she wants to provide in her system is the ability to manipulate inexact quantities (such as measured parameters of physical devices) with known precision, so that when computations are done with such approximate quantities the results will be numbers of known precision.

Electrical engineers will be using Alyssa's system to compute electrical quantities. It is sometimes necessary for them to compute the value of a parallel equivalent resistance R_p of two resistors R_1 and R_2 using the formula

$$R_p = \frac{1}{1/R_1 + 1/R_2}$$

Resistance values are usually known only up to some tolerance guaranteed by the manufacturer of the resistor. For example, if you buy a resistor labeled "6.8 ohms with 10% tolerance" you can only be sure that the resistor has a resistance between $6.8 - 0.68 = 6.12$ and $6.8 + 0.68 = 7.48$ ohms. Thus, if you have a 6.8-ohm 10% resistor in parallel with a 4.7-ohm 5% resistor, the resistance of the combination can range from about 2.58 ohms (if the two resistors are at the lower bounds) to about 2.97 ohms (if the two resistors are at the upper bounds).

Alyssa's idea is to implement "interval arithmetic" as a set of arithmetic operations for combining "intervals" (objects that represent the range of possible values of an inexact quantity). The result of adding, subtracting, multiplying, or dividing two intervals is itself an interval, representing the range of the result.

Alyssa postulates the existence of an abstract object called an "interval" that has two endpoints: a lower bound and an upper bound. She also presumes that, given the endpoints of an interval, she can construct the interval using the data constructor make-interval. Alyssa first writes a procedure for adding two intervals. She reasons that the minimum value the sum could be is the sum of the two lower bounds and the maximum value it could be is the sum of the two upper bounds:

```
(define (add-interval x y)
  (make-interval (+ (lower-bound x) (lower-bound y))
                 (+ (upper-bound x) (upper-bound y))))
```

Alyssa also works out the product of two intervals by finding the minimum and the maximum of the products of the bounds and using them as the bounds of the resulting interval. (Min and max are primitives that find the minimum or maximum of any number of arguments.)

```
(define (mul-interval x y)
  (let ((p1 (* (lower-bound x) (lower-bound y)))
        (p2 (* (lower-bound x) (upper-bound y)))
        (p3 (* (upper-bound x) (lower-bound y)))
        (p4 (* (upper-bound x) (upper-bound y))))
    (make-interval (min p1 p2 p3 p4)
                   (max p1 p2 p3 p4))))
```

To divide two intervals, Alyssa multiplies the first by the reciprocal of the second. Note that the bounds of the reciprocal interval are the reciprocal of the upper bound and the reciprocal of the lower bound, in that order.

```
(define (div-interval x y)
  (mul-interval x
                (make-interval (/ 1.0 (upper-bound y))
                               (/ 1.0 (lower-bound y)))))
```

Exercise 2.7

Alyssa's program is incomplete because she has not specified the implementation of the interval abstraction. Here is a definition of the interval constructor:

```
(define (make-interval a b) (cons a b))
```

Define selectors upper-bound and lower-bound to complete the implementation.

Exercise 2.8

Using reasoning analogous to Alyssa's, describe how the difference of two intervals may be computed. Define a corresponding subtraction procedure, called `sub-interval`.

Exercise 2.9

The *width* of an interval is half of the difference between its upper and lower bounds. The width is a measure of the uncertainty of the number specified by the interval. For some arithmetic operations the width of the result of combining two intervals is a function only of the widths of the argument intervals, whereas for others the width of the combination is not a function of the widths of the argument intervals. Show that the width of the sum (or difference) of two intervals is a function only of the widths of the intervals being added (or subtracted). Give examples to show that this is not true for multiplication or division.

Exercise 2.10

Ben Bitdiddle, an expert systems programmer, looks over Alyssa's shoulder and comments that it is not clear what it means to divide by an interval that spans zero. Modify Alyssa's code to check for this condition and to signal an error if it occurs.

Exercise 2.11

In passing, Ben also cryptically comments: "By testing the signs of the endpoints of the intervals, it is possible to break `mul-interval` into nine cases, only one of which requires more than two multiplications." Rewrite this procedure using Ben's suggestion.

After debugging her program, Alyssa shows it to a potential user, who complains that her program solves the wrong problem. He wants a program that can deal with numbers represented as a center value and an additive tolerance; for example, he wants to work with intervals such as 3.5 ± 0.15 rather than $[3.35, 3.65]$. Alyssa returns to her desk and fixes this problem by supplying an alternate constructor and alternate selectors:

```
(define (make-center-width c w)
  (make-interval (- c w) (+ c w)))

(define (center i)
  (/ (+ (lower-bound i) (upper-bound i)) 2))

(define (width i)
  (/ (- (upper-bound i) (lower-bound i)) 2))
```

Unfortunately, most of Alyssa's users are engineers. Real engineering situations usually involve measurements with only a small uncertainty, measured as the ratio of the width of the interval to the midpoint of the interval. Engineers usually specify percentage tolerances on the parameters of devices, as in the resistor specifications given earlier.

Exercise 2.12

Define a constructor `make-center-percent` that takes a center and a percentage tolerance and produces the desired interval. You must also define a selector `percent` that produces the percentage tolerance for a given interval. The `center` selector is the same as the one shown above.

Exercise 2.13

Show that under the assumption of small percentage tolerances there is a simple formula for the approximate percentage tolerance of the product of two intervals in terms of the tolerances of the factors. You may simplify the problem by assuming that all numbers are positive.

After considerable work, Alyssa P. Hacker delivers her finished system. Several years later, after she has forgotten all about it, she gets a frenzied call from an irate user, Lem E. Tweakit. It seems that Lem has noticed that the formula for parallel resistors can be written in two algebraically equivalent ways:

$$\frac{R_1 R_2}{R_1 + R_2}$$

and

$$\frac{1}{1/R_1 + 1/R_2}$$

He has written the following two programs, each of which computes the parallel-resistors formula differently:

```
(define (par1 r1 r2)
  (div-interval (mul-interval r1 r2)
                (add-interval r1 r2)))

(define (par2 r1 r2)
  (let ((one (make-interval 1 1)))
    (div-interval one
                  (add-interval (div-interval one r1)
                                (div-interval one r2)))))
```

Lem complains that Alyssa's program gives different answers for the two ways of computing. This is a serious complaint.

Exercise 2.14

Demonstrate that Lem is right. Investigate the behavior of the system on a variety of arithmetic expressions. Make some intervals A and B, and use them in computing the expressions A/A and A/B. You will get the most insight by using intervals whose width is a small percentage of the center value. Examine the results of the computation in center-percent form (see exercise 2.12).

Exercise 2.15

Eva Lu Ator, another user, has also noticed the different intervals computed by different but algebraically equivalent expressions. She says that a formula to compute with intervals using Alyssa's system will produce tighter error bounds if it can be written in such a form that no variable that represents an uncertain number is repeated. Thus, she says, par2 is a "better" program for parallel resistances than par1. Is she right? Why?

Exercise 2.16

Explain, in general, why equivalent algebraic expressions may lead to different answers. Can you devise an interval-arithmetic package that does not have this shortcoming, or is this task impossible? (Warning: This problem is very difficult.)

2.2 Hierarchical Data and the Closure Property

As we have seen, pairs provide a primitive "glue" that we can use to construct compound data objects. Figure 2.2 shows a standard way to visualize a pair—in this case, the pair formed by (cons 1 2). In this representation, which is called *box-and-pointer notation*, each object is shown as a *pointer* to a box. The box for a primitive object contains a representation of the object. For example, the box for a number contains a numeral. The box for a pair is actually a double box, the left part containing (a pointer to) the car of the pair and the right part containing the cdr.

We have already seen that cons can be used to combine not only numbers but pairs as well. (You made use of this fact, or should have, in doing exercises 2.2 and 2.3.) As a consequence, pairs provide a universal building block from which we can construct all sorts of data structures. Figure 2.3 shows two ways to use pairs to combine the numbers 1, 2, 3, and 4.

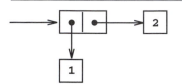

Figure 2.2   Box-and-pointer representation of (cons 1 2).

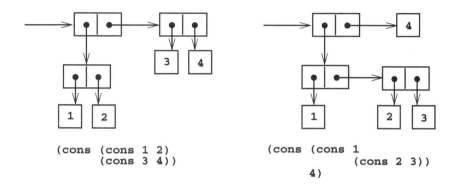

Figure 2.3   Two ways to combine 1, 2, 3, and 4 using pairs.

The ability to create pairs whose elements are pairs is the essence of list structure's importance as a representational tool. We refer to this ability as the *closure property* of cons. In general, an operation for combining data objects satisfies the closure property if the results of combining things with that operation can themselves be combined using the same operation.[6] Closure is the key to power in any means of combination because it permits us to create *hierarchical* structures—structures made up of parts, which themselves are made up of parts, and so on.

From the outset of chapter 1, we've made essential use of closure in dealing with procedures, because all but the very simplest programs rely on the fact that the elements of a combination can themselves be combinations. In this section, we take up the consequences of closure for com-

---

[6]The use of the word "closure" here comes from abstract algebra, where a set of elements is said to be closed under an operation if applying the operation to elements in the set produces an element that is again an element of the set. The Lisp community also (unfortunately) uses the word "closure" to describe a totally unrelated concept: A closure is an implementation technique for representing procedures with free variables. We do not use the word "closure" in this second sense in this book.

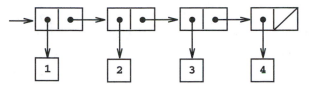

Figure 2.4   The sequence 1, 2, 3, 4 represented as a chain of pairs.

pound data. We describe some conventional techniques for using pairs
to represent sequences and trees, and we exhibit a graphics language that
illustrates closure in a vivid way.[7]

2.2.1   Representing Sequences

One of the useful structures we can build with pairs is a *sequence*—an
ordered collection of data objects. There are, of course, many ways to
represent sequences in terms of pairs. One particularly straightforward
representation is illustrated in figure 2.4, where the sequence 1, 2, 3, 4 is
represented as a chain of pairs. The car of each pair is the corresponding
item in the chain, and the cdr of the pair is the next pair in the chain.
The cdr of the final pair signals the end of the sequence by pointing to
a distinguished value that is not a pair, represented in box-and-pointer
diagrams as a diagonal line and in programs as the value of the variable
nil. The entire sequence is constructed by nested cons operations:

```
(cons 1
      (cons 2
            (cons 3
                  (cons 4 nil))))
```

---

[7]The notion that a means of combination should satisfy closure is a straightforward idea.
Unfortunately, the data combiners provided in many popular programming languages do
not satisfy closure, or make closure cumbersome to exploit. In Fortran or Basic, one typically combines data elements by assembling them into arrays—but one cannot form arrays
whose elements are themselves arrays. Pascal and C admit structures whose elements are
structures. However, this requires that the programmer manipulate pointers explicitly, and
adhere to the restriction that each field of a structure can contain only elements of a prespecified form. Unlike Lisp with its pairs, these languages have no built-in general-purpose
glue that makes it easy to manipulate compound data in a uniform way. This limitation
lies behind Alan Perlis's comment in his foreword to this book: "In Pascal the plethora
of declarable data structures induces a specialization within functions that inhibits and penalizes casual cooperation. It is better to have 100 functions operate on one data structure
than to have 10 functions operate on 10 data structures."

Such a sequence of pairs, formed by nested conses, is called a *list*, and Scheme provides a primitive called `list` to help in constructing lists.[8] The above sequence could be produced by (`list 1 2 3 4`). In general,

(`list` $\langle a_1 \rangle$ $\langle a_2 \rangle$ ... $\langle a_n \rangle$)

is equivalent to

(`cons` $\langle a_1 \rangle$ (`cons` $\langle a_2 \rangle$ (`cons` ... (`cons` $\langle a_n \rangle$ `nil`) ...)))

Lisp systems conventionally print lists by printing the sequence of elements, enclosed in parentheses. Thus, the data object in figure 2.4 is printed as (1 2 3 4):

```
(define one-through-four (list 1 2 3 4))
```

```
one-through-four
(1 2 3 4)
```

Be careful not to confuse the expression (`list 1 2 3 4`) with the list (1 2 3 4), which is the result obtained when the expression is evaluated. Attempting to evaluate the expression (1 2 3 4) will signal an error when the interpreter tries to apply the procedure 1 to arguments 2, 3, and 4.

We can think of `car` as selecting the first item in the list, and of `cdr` as selecting the sublist consisting of all but the first item. Nested applications of `car` and `cdr` can be used to extract the second, third, and subsequent items in the list.[9] The constructor `cons` makes a list like the original one, but with an additional item at the beginning.

```
(car one-through-four)
1
```

```
(cdr one-through-four)
(2 3 4)
```

---

[8]In this book, we use *list* to mean a chain of pairs terminated by the end-of-list marker. In contrast, the term *list structure* refers to any data structure made out of pairs, not just to lists.

[9]Since nested applications of `car` and `cdr` are cumbersome to write, Lisp dialects provide abbreviations for them—for instance,

(`cadr` $\langle arg \rangle$) = (`car` (`cdr` $\langle arg \rangle$))

The names of all such procedures start with c and end with r. Each a between them stands for a `car` operation and each d for a `cdr` operation, to be applied in the same order in which they appear in the name. The names `car` and `cdr` persist because simple combinations like `cadr` are pronounceable.

```
(car (cdr one-through-four))
2
```

```
(cons 10 one-through-four)
(10 1 2 3 4)
```

```
(cons 5 one-through-four)
(5 1 2 3 4)
```

The value of `nil`, used to terminate the chain of pairs, can be thought of as a sequence of no elements, the *empty list*. The word *nil* is a contraction of the Latin word *nihil*, which means "nothing."[10]

List operations

The use of pairs to represent sequences of elements as lists is accompanied by conventional programming techniques for manipulating lists by successively "cdring down" the lists. For example, the procedure `list-ref` takes as arguments a list and a number n and returns the nth item of the list. It is customary to number the elements of the list beginning with 0. The method for computing `list-ref` is the following:

- For $n = 0$, `list-ref` should return the `car` of the list.

- Otherwise, `list-ref` should return the $(n-1)$st item of the `cdr` of the list.

```
(define (list-ref items n)
  (if (= n 0)
      (car items)
      (list-ref (cdr items) (- n 1))))
```

```
(define squares (list 1 4 9 16 25))
```

```
(list-ref squares 3)
16
```

---

[10]It's remarkable how much energy in the standardization of Lisp dialects has been dissipated in arguments that are literally over nothing: Should `nil` be an ordinary name? Should the value of `nil` be a symbol? Should it be a list? Should it be a pair? In Scheme, `nil` is an ordinary name, which we use in this section as a variable whose value is the end-of-list marker (just as `true` is an ordinary variable that has a true value). Other dialects of Lisp, including Common Lisp, treat `nil` as a special symbol. The authors of this book, who have endured too many language standardization brawls, would like to avoid the entire issue. Once we have introduced quotation in section 2.3, we will denote the empty list as '() and dispense with the variable `nil` entirely.

Often we `cdr` down the whole list. To aid in this, Scheme includes a primitive predicate `null?`, which tests whether its argument is the empty list. The procedure `length`, which returns the number of items in a list, illustrates this typical pattern of use:

```
(define (length items)
  (if (null? items)
      0
      (+ 1 (length (cdr items)))))

(define odds (list 1 3 5 7))

(length odds)
4
```

The `length` procedure implements a simple recursive plan. The reduction step is:

• The `length` of any list is 1 plus the `length` of the `cdr` of the list.

This is applied successively until we reach the base case:

• The `length` of the empty list is 0.

We could also compute `length` in an iterative style:

```
(define (length items)
  (define (length-iter a count)
    (if (null? a)
        count
        (length-iter (cdr a) (+ 1 count))))
  (length-iter items 0))
```

Another conventional programming technique is to "cons up" an answer list while `cdr`ing down a list, as in the procedure `append`, which takes two lists as arguments and combines their elements to make a new list:

```
(append squares odds)
(1 4 9 16 25 1 3 5 7)

(append odds squares)
(1 3 5 7 1 4 9 16 25)
```

Append is also implemented using a recursive plan. To append lists `list1` and `list2`, do the following:

• If list1 is the empty list, then the result is just list2.

• Otherwise, append the cdr of list1 and list2, and cons the car of list1 onto the result:

```
(define (append list1 list2)
  (if (null? list1)
      list2
      (cons (car list1) (append (cdr list1) list2))))
```

Exercise 2.17

Define a procedure last-pair that returns the list that contains only the last element of a given (nonempty) list:

```
(last-pair (list 23 72 149 34))
(34)
```

Exercise 2.18

Define a procedure reverse that takes a list as argument and returns a list of the same elements in reverse order:

```
(reverse (list 1 4 9 16 25))
(25 16 9 4 1)
```

Exercise 2.19

Consider the change-counting program of section 1.2.2. It would be nice to be able to easily change the currency used by the program, so that we could compute the number of ways to change a British pound, for example. As the program is written, the knowledge of the currency is distributed partly into the procedure first-denomination and partly into the procedure count-change (which knows that there are five kinds of U.S. coins). It would be nicer to be able to supply a list of coins to be used for making change.

We want to rewrite the procedure cc so that its second argument is a list of the values of the coins to use rather than an integer specifying which coins to use. We could then have lists that defined each kind of currency:

```
(define us-coins (list 50 25 10 5 1))
```

```
(define uk-coins (list 100 50 20 10 5 2 1 0.5))
```

We could then call cc as follows:

```
(cc 100 us-coins)
292
```

To do this will require changing the program cc somewhat. It will still have the same form, but it will access its second argument differently, as follows:

```
(define (cc amount coin-values)
  (cond ((= amount 0) 1)
        ((or (< amount 0) (no-more? coin-values)) 0)
        (else
          (+ (cc amount
                 (except-first-denomination coin-values))
             (cc (- amount
                    (first-denomination coin-values))
                 coin-values)))))
```

Define the procedures first-denomination, except-first-denomination, and no-more? in terms of primitive operations on list structures. Does the order of the list coin-values affect the answer produced by cc? Why or why not?

Exercise 2.20

The procedures +, *, and list take arbitrary numbers of arguments. One way to define such procedures is to use define with *dotted-tail notation*. In a procedure definition, a parameter list that has a dot before the last parameter name indicates that, when the procedure is called, the initial parameters (if any) will have as values the initial arguments, as usual, but the final parameter's value will be a *list* of any remaining arguments. For instance, given the definition

```
(define (f x y . z) ⟨body⟩)
```

the procedure f can be called with two or more arguments. If we evaluate

```
(f 1 2 3 4 5 6)
```

then in the body of f, x will be 1, y will be 2, and z will be the list (3 4 5 6). Given the definition

```
(define (g . w) ⟨body⟩)
```

the procedure g can be called with zero or more arguments. If we evaluate

```
(g 1 2 3 4 5 6)
```

then in the body of g, w will be the list (1 2 3 4 5 6).[11]

Use this notation to write a procedure same-parity that takes one or more integers and returns a list of all the arguments that have the same even-odd parity as the first argument. For example,

```
(same-parity 1 2 3 4 5 6 7)
(1 3 5 7)

(same-parity 2 3 4 5 6 7)
(2 4 6)
```

---

[11]To define f and g using lambda we would write

```
(define f (lambda (x y . z) ⟨body⟩))
(define g (lambda w ⟨body⟩))
```

Mapping over lists

One extremely useful operation is to apply some transformation to each
element in a list and generate the list of results. For instance, the following procedure scales each number in a list by a given factor:

```
(define (scale-list items factor)
  (if (null? items)
      nil
      (cons (* (car items) factor)
            (scale-list (cdr items) factor))))

(scale-list (list 1 2 3 4 5) 10)
(10 20 30 40 50)
```

We can abstract this general idea and capture it as a common pattern
expressed as a higher-order procedure, just as in section 1.3. The higher-
order procedure here is called map. Map takes as arguments a procedure
of one argument and a list, and returns a list of the results produced by
applying the procedure to each element in the list:[12]

```
(define (map proc items)
  (if (null? items)
      nil
      (cons (proc (car items))
            (map proc (cdr items)))))

(map abs (list -10 2.5 -11.6 17))
(10 2.5 11.6 17)

(map (lambda (x) (* x x))
     (list 1 2 3 4))
(1 4 9 16)
```

---

[12]Scheme standardly provides a map procedure that is more general than the one described
here. This more general map takes a procedure of *n* arguments, together with *n* lists, and
applies the procedure to all the first elements of the lists, all the second elements of the
lists, and so on, returning a list of the results. For example:

```
(map + (list 1 2 3) (list 40 50 60) (list 700 800 900))
(741 852 963)

(map (lambda (x y) (+ x (* 2 y)))
     (list 1 2 3)
     (list 4 5 6))
(9 12 15)
```

Now we can give a new definition of `scale-list` in terms of map:

```
(define (scale-list items factor)
  (map (lambda (x) (* x factor))
       items))
```

Map is an important construct, not only because it captures a common pattern, but because it establishes a higher level of abstraction in dealing with lists. In the original definition of `scale-list`, the recursive structure of the program draws attention to the element-by-element processing of the list. Defining `scale-list` in terms of map suppresses that level of detail and emphasizes that scaling transforms a list of elements to a list of results. The difference between the two definitions is not that the computer is performing a different process (it isn't) but that we think about the process differently. In effect, map helps establish an abstraction barrier that isolates the implementation of procedures that transform lists from the details of how the elements of the list are extracted and combined. Like the barriers shown in figure 2.1, this abstraction gives us the flexibility to change the low-level details of how sequences are implemented, while preserving the conceptual framework of operations that transform sequences to sequences. Section 2.2.3 expands on this use of sequences as a framework for organizing programs.

Exercise 2.21

The procedure `square-list` takes a list of numbers as argument and returns a list of the squares of those numbers.

```
(square-list (list 1 2 3 4))
(1 4 9 16)
```

Here are two different definitions of `square-list`. Complete both of them by filling in the missing expressions:

```
(define (square-list items)
  (if (null? items)
      nil
      (cons ⟨??⟩ ⟨??⟩)))

(define (square-list items)
  (map ⟨??⟩ ⟨??⟩))
```

Exercise 2.22

Louis Reasoner tries to rewrite the first `square-list` procedure of exercise 2.21 so that it evolves an iterative process:

```
(define (square-list items)
  (define (iter things answer)
    (if (null? things)
        answer
        (iter (cdr things)
              (cons (square (car things))
                    answer)))))
  (iter items nil))
```

Unfortunately, defining `square-list` this way produces the answer list in the reverse order of the one desired. Why?

Louis then tries to fix his bug by interchanging the arguments to `cons`:

```
(define (square-list items)
  (define (iter things answer)
    (if (null? things)
        answer
        (iter (cdr things)
              (cons answer
                    (square (car things)))))))
  (iter items nil))
```

This doesn't work either. Explain.

Exercise 2.23

The procedure `for-each` is similar to `map`. It takes as arguments a procedure and a list of elements. However, rather than forming a list of the results, `for-each` just applies the procedure to each of the elements in turn, from left to right. The values returned by applying the procedure to the elements are not used at all—`for-each` is used with procedures that perform an action, such as printing. For example,

```
(for-each (lambda (x) (newline) (display x))
          (list 57 321 88))
57
321
88
```

The value returned by the call to `for-each` (not illustrated above) can be something arbitrary, such as true. Give an implementation of `for-each`.

2.2.2   Hierarchical Structures

The representation of sequences in terms of lists generalizes naturally to represent sequences whose elements may themselves be sequences. For example, we can regard the object `((1 2) 3 4)` constructed by

```
(cons (list 1 2) (list 3 4))
```

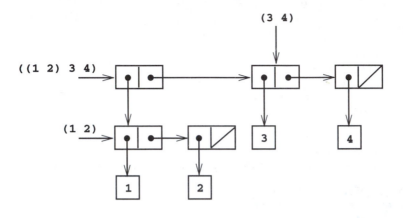

Figure 2.5 Structure formed by `(cons (list 1 2) (list 3 4))`.

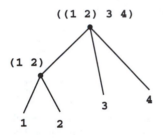

Figure 2.6 The list structure in figure 2.5 viewed as a tree.

as a list of three items, the first of which is itself a list, (1 2). Indeed, this is suggested by the form in which the result is printed by the interpreter. Figure 2.5 shows the representation of this structure in terms of pairs.

Another way to think of sequences whose elements are sequences is as *trees*. The elements of the sequence are the branches of the tree, and elements that are themselves sequences are subtrees. Figure 2.6 shows the structure in figure 2.5 viewed as a tree.

Recursion is a natural tool for dealing with tree structures, since we can often reduce operations on trees to operations on their branches, which reduce in turn to operations on the branches of the branches, and so on, until we reach the leaves of the tree. As an example, compare the `length` procedure of section 2.2.1 with the `count-leaves` procedure, which returns the total number of leaves of a tree:

```
(define x (cons (list 1 2) (list 3 4)))

(length x)
3
```

```
(count-leaves x)
4

(list x x)
(((1 2) 3 4) ((1 2) 3 4))

(length (list x x))
2

(count-leaves (list x x))
8
```

To implement count-leaves, recall the recursive plan for computing length:

- Length of a list x is 1 plus length of the cdr of x.

- Length of the empty list is 0.

Count-leaves is similar. The value for the empty list is the same:

- Count-leaves of the empty list is 0.

But in the reduction step, where we strip off the car of the list, we must take into account that the car may itself be a tree whose leaves we need to count. Thus, the appropriate reduction step is

- Count-leaves of a tree x is count-leaves of the car of x plus count-leaves of the cdr of x.

Finally, by taking cars we reach actual leaves, so we need another base case:

- Count-leaves of a leaf is 1.

To aid in writing recursive procedures on trees, Scheme provides the primitive predicate pair?, which tests whether its argument is a pair. Here is the complete procedure:[13]

```
(define (count-leaves x)
  (cond ((null? x) 0)
        ((not (pair? x)) 1)
        (else (+ (count-leaves (car x))
                 (count-leaves (cdr x))))))
```

---

[13]The order of the first two clauses in the cond matters, since the empty list satisfies null? and also is not a pair.

Exercise 2.24

Suppose we evaluate the expression (list 1 (list 2 (list 3 4))). Give the result printed by the interpreter, the corresponding box-and-pointer structure, and the interpretation of this as a tree (as in figure 2.6).

Exercise 2.25

Give combinations of cars and cdrs that will pick 7 from each of the following lists:

(1 3 (5 7) 9)

((7))

(1 (2 (3 (4 (5 (6 7))))))

Exercise 2.26

Suppose we define x and y to be two lists:

(define x (list 1 2 3))

(define y (list 4 5 6))

What result is printed by the interpreter in response to evaluating each of the following expressions:

(append x y)

(cons x y)

(list x y)

Exercise 2.27

Modify your reverse procedure of exercise 2.18 to produce a deep-reverse procedure that takes a list as argument and returns as its value the list with its elements reversed and with all sublists deep-reversed as well. For example,

(define x (list (list 1 2) (list 3 4)))

x
((1 2) (3 4))

(reverse x)
((3 4) (1 2))

(deep-reverse x)
((4 3) (2 1))

Exercise 2.28

Write a procedure `fringe` that takes as argument a tree (represented as a list) and returns a list whose elements are all the leaves of the tree arranged in left-to-right order. For example,

```
(define x (list (list 1 2) (list 3 4)))

(fringe x)
(1 2 3 4)

(fringe (list x x))
(1 2 3 4 1 2 3 4)
```

Exercise 2.29

A binary mobile consists of two branches, a left branch and a right branch. Each branch is a rod of a certain length, from which hangs either a weight or another binary mobile. We can represent a binary mobile using compound data by constructing it from two branches (for example, using `list`):

```
(define (make-mobile left right)
  (list left right))
```

A branch is constructed from a `length` (which must be a number) together with a `structure`, which may be either a number (representing a simple weight) or another mobile:

```
(define (make-branch length structure)
  (list length structure))
```

a. Write the corresponding selectors `left-branch` and `right-branch`, which return the branches of a mobile, and `branch-length` and `branch-structure`, which return the components of a branch.

b. Using your selectors, define a procedure `total-weight` that returns the total weight of a mobile.

c. A mobile is said to be *balanced* if the torque applied by its top-left branch is equal to that applied by its top-right branch (that is, if the length of the left rod multiplied by the weight hanging from that rod is equal to the corresponding product for the right side) and if each of the submobiles hanging off its branches is balanced. Design a predicate that tests whether a binary mobile is balanced.

d. Suppose we change the representation of mobiles so that the constructors are

```
(define (make-mobile left right)
  (cons left right))

(define (make-branch length structure)
  (cons length structure))
```

How much do you need to change your programs to convert to the new representation?

Mapping over trees

Just as map is a powerful abstraction for dealing with sequences, map together with recursion is a powerful abstraction for dealing with trees. For instance, the scale-tree procedure, analogous to scale-list of section 2.2.1, takes as arguments a numeric factor and a tree whose leaves are numbers. It returns a tree of the same shape, where each number is multiplied by the factor. The recursive plan for scale-tree is similar to the one for count-leaves:

```
(define (scale-tree tree factor)
  (cond ((null? tree) nil)
        ((not (pair? tree)) (* tree factor))
        (else (cons (scale-tree (car tree) factor)
                    (scale-tree (cdr tree) factor)))))

(scale-tree (list 1 (list 2 (list 3 4) 5) (list 6 7))
            10)
(10 (20 (30 40) 50) (60 70))
```

Another way to implement scale-tree is to regard the tree as a sequence of sub-trees and use map. We map over the sequence, scaling each sub-tree in turn, and return the list of results. In the base case, where the tree is a leaf, we simply multiply by the factor:

```
(define (scale-tree tree factor)
  (map (lambda (sub-tree)
         (if (pair? sub-tree)
             (scale-tree sub-tree factor)
             (* sub-tree factor)))
       tree))
```

Many tree operations can be implemented by similar combinations of sequence operations and recursion.

Exercise 2.30

Define a procedure square-tree analogous to the square-list procedure of exercise 2.21. That is, square-list should behave as follows:

```
(square-tree
 (list 1
       (list 2 (list 3 4) 5)
       (list 6 7)))
(1 (4 (9 16) 25) (36 49))
```

Define square-tree both directly (i.e., without using any higher-order procedures) and also by using map and recursion.

Exercise 2.31

Abstract your answer to exercise 2.30 to produce a procedure `tree-map` with the property that `square-tree` could be defined as

```
(define (square-tree tree) (tree-map square tree))
```

Exercise 2.32

We can represent a set as a list of distinct elements, and we can represent the set of all subsets of the set as a list of lists. For example, if the set is (1 2 3), then the set of all subsets is (() (3) (2) (2 3) (1) (1 3) (1 2) (1 2 3)). Complete the following definition of a procedure that generates the set of subsets of a set and give a clear explanation of why it works:

```
(define (subsets s)
  (if (null? s)
      (list nil)
      (let ((rest (subsets (cdr s))))
        (append rest (map ⟨??⟩ rest)))))
```

2.2.3 Sequences as Conventional Interfaces

In working with compound data, we've stressed how data abstraction permits us to design programs without becoming enmeshed in the details of data representations, and how abstraction preserves for us the flexibility to experiment with alternative representations. In this section, we introduce another powerful design principle for working with data structures—the use of *conventional interfaces*.

In section 1.3 we saw how program abstractions, implemented as higher-order procedures, can capture common patterns in programs that deal with numerical data. Our ability to formulate analogous operations for working with compound data depends crucially on the style in which we manipulate our data structures. Consider, for example, the following procedure, analogous to the `count-leaves` procedure of section 2.2.2, which takes a tree as argument and computes the sum of the squares of the leaves that are odd:

```
(define (sum-odd-squares tree)
  (cond ((null? tree) 0)
        ((not (pair? tree))
         (if (odd? tree) (square tree) 0))
        (else (+ (sum-odd-squares (car tree))
                 (sum-odd-squares (cdr tree))))))
```

On the surface, this procedure is very different from the following one, which constructs a list of all the even Fibonacci numbers Fib(k), where k is less than or equal to a given integer n:

```
(define (even-fibs n)
  (define (next k)
    (if (> k n)
        nil
        (let ((f (fib k)))
          (if (even? f)
              (cons f (next (+ k 1)))
              (next (+ k 1))))))
  (next 0))
```

Despite the fact that these two procedures are structurally very different, a more abstract description of the two computations reveals a great deal of similarity. The first program

- enumerates the leaves of a tree;
- filters them, selecting the odd ones;
- squares each of the selected ones; and
- accumulates the results using +, starting with 0.

The second program

- enumerates the integers from 0 to n;
- computes the Fibonacci number for each integer;
- filters them, selecting the even ones; and
- accumulates the results using cons, starting with the empty list.

A signal-processing engineer would find it natural to conceptualize these processes in terms of signals flowing through a cascade of stages, each of which implements part of the program plan, as shown in figure 2.7. In sum-odd-squares, we begin with an *enumerator*, which generates a "signal" consisting of the leaves of a given tree. This signal is passed through a *filter*, which eliminates all but the odd elements. The resulting signal is in turn passed through a *map*, which is a "transducer" that applies the square procedure to each element. The output of the map is then fed to an *accumulator*, which combines the elements using +, starting from an initial 0. The plan for even-fibs is analogous.

Unfortunately, the two procedure definitions above fail to exhibit this signal-flow structure. For instance, if we examine the sum-odd-squares

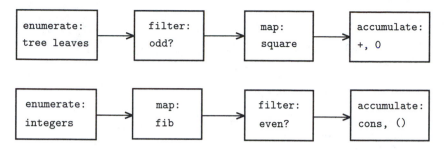

Figure 2.7   The signal-flow plans for the procedures `sum-odd-squares` (top) and `even-fibs` (bottom) reveal the commonality between the two programs.

procedure, we find that the enumeration is implemented partly by the `null?` and `pair?` tests and partly by the tree-recursive structure of the procedure. Similarly, the accumulation is found partly in the tests and partly in the addition used in the recursion. In general, there are no distinct parts of either procedure that correspond to the elements in the signal-flow description. Our two procedures decompose the computations in a different way, spreading the enumeration over the program and mingling it with the map, the filter, and the accumulation. If we could organize our programs to make the signal-flow structure manifest in the procedures we write, this would increase the conceptual clarity of the resulting code.

Sequence Operations

The key to organizing programs so as to more clearly reflect the signal-flow structure is to concentrate on the "signals" that flow from one stage in the process to the next. If we represent these signals as lists, then we can use list operations to implement the processing at each of the stages. For instance, we can implement the mapping stages of the signal-flow diagrams using the `map` procedure from section 2.2.1:

```
(map square (list 1 2 3 4 5))
(1 4 9 16 25)
```

Filtering a sequence to select only those elements that satisfy a given predicate is accomplished by

```
(define (filter predicate sequence)
  (cond ((null? sequence) nil)
        ((predicate (car sequence))
         (cons (car sequence)
               (filter predicate (cdr sequence))))
        (else (filter predicate (cdr sequence)))))
```

For example,

```
(filter odd? (list 1 2 3 4 5))
(1 3 5)
```

Accumulations can be implemented by

```
(define (accumulate op initial sequence)
  (if (null? sequence)
      initial
      (op (car sequence)
          (accumulate op initial (cdr sequence)))))

(accumulate + 0 (list 1 2 3 4 5))
15

(accumulate * 1 (list 1 2 3 4 5))
120

(accumulate cons nil (list 1 2 3 4 5))
(1 2 3 4 5)
```

All that remains to implement signal-flow diagrams is to enumerate the sequence of elements to be processed. For even-fibs, we need to generate the sequence of integers in a given range, which we can do as follows:

```
(define (enumerate-interval low high)
  (if (> low high)
      nil
      (cons low (enumerate-interval (+ low 1) high))))

(enumerate-interval 2 7)
(2 3 4 5 6 7)
```

To enumerate the leaves of a tree, we can use[14]

```
(define (enumerate-tree tree)
  (cond ((null? tree) nil)
        ((not (pair? tree)) (list tree))
        (else (append (enumerate-tree (car tree))
                      (enumerate-tree (cdr tree))))))

(enumerate-tree (list 1 (list 2 (list 3 4)) 5))
(1 2 3 4 5)
```

---

[14]This is, in fact, precisely the fringe procedure from exercise 2.28. Here we've renamed it to emphasize that it is part of a family of general sequence-manipulation procedures.

Now we can reformulate `sum-odd-squares` and `even-fibs` as in the signal-flow diagrams. For `sum-odd-squares`, we enumerate the sequence of leaves of the tree, filter this to keep only the odd numbers in the sequence, square each element, and sum the results:

```
(define (sum-odd-squares tree)
  (accumulate +
              0
              (map square
                   (filter odd?
                           (enumerate-tree tree)))))
```

For `even-fibs`, we enumerate the integers from 0 to *n*, generate the Fibonacci number for each of these integers, filter the resulting sequence to keep only the even elements, and accumulate the results into a list:

```
(define (even-fibs n)
  (accumulate cons
              nil
              (filter even?
                      (map fib
                           (enumerate-interval 0 n)))))
```

The value of expressing programs as sequence operations is that this helps us make program designs that are modular, that is, designs that are constructed by combining relatively independent pieces. We can encourage modular design by providing a library of standard components together with a conventional interface for connecting the components in flexible ways.

Modular construction is a powerful strategy for controlling complexity in engineering design. In real signal-processing applications, for example, designers regularly build systems by cascading elements selected from standardized families of filters and transducers. Similarly, sequence operations provide a library of standard program elements that we can mix and match. For instance, we can reuse pieces from the `sum-odd-squares` and `even-fibs` procedures in a program that constructs a list of the squares of the first *n* + 1 Fibonacci numbers:

```
(define (list-fib-squares n)
  (accumulate cons
              nil
              (map square
                   (map fib
                        (enumerate-interval 0 n)))))
```

```
(list-fib-squares 10)
(0 1 1 4 9 25 64 169 441 1156 3025)
```

We can rearrange the pieces and use them in computing the product of the odd integers in a sequence:

```
(define (product-of-squares-of-odd-elements sequence)
  (accumulate *
              1
              (map square
                   (filter odd? sequence))))
```

```
(product-of-squares-of-odd-elements (list 1 2 3 4 5))
225
```

We can also formulate conventional data-processing applications in terms of sequence operations. Suppose we have a sequence of personnel records and we want to find the salary of the highest-paid programmer. Assume that we have a selector salary that returns the salary of a record, and a predicate programmer? that tests if a record is for a programmer. Then we can write

```
(define (salary-of-highest-paid-programmer records)
  (accumulate max
              0
              (map salary
                   (filter programmer? records))))
```

These examples give just a hint of the vast range of operations that can be expressed as sequence operations.[15]

Sequences, implemented here as lists, serve as a conventional interface that permits us to combine processing modules. Additionally, when we uniformly represent structures as sequences, we have localized the data-structure dependencies in our programs to a small number of sequence operations. By changing these, we can experiment with alternative representations of sequences, while leaving the overall design of our programs intact. We will exploit this capability in section 3.5, when we generalize the sequence-processing paradigm to admit infinite sequences.

---

[15]Richard Waters (1979) developed a program that automatically analyzes traditional Fortran programs, viewing them in terms of maps, filters, and accumulations. He found that fully 90 percent of the code in the Fortran Scientific Subroutine Package fits neatly into this paradigm. One of the reasons for the success of Lisp as a programming language is that lists provide a standard medium for expressing ordered collections so that they can be manipulated using higher-order operations. The programming language APL owes much of its power and appeal to a similar choice. In APL all data are represented as arrays, and there is a universal and convenient set of generic operators for all sorts of array operations.

Exercise 2.33

Fill in the missing expressions to complete the following definitions of some basic list-manipulation operations as accumulations:

```
(define (map p sequence)
  (accumulate (lambda (x y) ⟨??⟩) nil sequence))

(define (append seq1 seq2)
  (accumulate cons ⟨??⟩ ⟨??⟩))

(define (length sequence)
  (accumulate ⟨??⟩ 0 sequence))
```

Exercise 2.34

Evaluating a polynomial in x at a given value of x can be formulated as an accumulation. We evaluate the polynomial

$$a_n x^n + a_{n-1} x^{n-1} + \cdots + a_1 x + a_0$$

using a well-known algorithm called *Horner's rule*, which structures the computation as

$$(\cdots (a_n x + a_{n-1}) x + \cdots + a_1) x + a_0$$

In other words, we start with a_n, multiply by x, add a_{n-1}, multiply by x, and so on, until we reach a_0.[16] Fill in the following template to produce a procedure that evaluates a polynomial using Horner's rule. Assume that the coefficients of the polynomial are arranged in a sequence, from a_0 through a_n.

```
(define (horner-eval x coefficient-sequence)
  (accumulate (lambda (this-coeff higher-terms) ⟨??⟩)
              0
              coefficient-sequence))
```

For example, to compute $1 + 3x + 5x^3 + x^5$ at $x = 2$ you would evaluate

```
(horner-eval 2 (list 1 3 0 5 0 1))
```

---

[16] According to Knuth (1981), this rule was formulated by W. G. Horner early in the nineteenth century, but the method was actually used by Newton over a hundred years earlier. Horner's rule evaluates the polynomial using fewer additions and multiplications than does the straightforward method of first computing $a_n x^n$, then adding $a_{n-1} x^{n-1}$, and so on. In fact, it is possible to prove that any algorithm for evaluating arbitrary polynomials must use at least as many additions and multiplications as does Horner's rule, and thus Horner's rule is an optimal algorithm for polynomial evaluation. This was proved (for the number of additions) by A. M. Ostrowski in a 1954 paper that essentially founded the modern study of optimal algorithms. The analogous statement for multiplications was proved by V. Y. Pan in 1966. The book by Borodin and Munro (1975) provides an overview of these and other results about optimal algorithms.

Exercise 2.35

Redefine `count-leaves` from section 2.2.2 as an accumulation:

```
(define (count-leaves t)
  (accumulate ⟨??⟩ ⟨??⟩ (map ⟨??⟩ ⟨??⟩)))
```

Exercise 2.36

The procedure `accumulate-n` is similar to `accumulate` except that it takes as its third argument a sequence of sequences, which are all assumed to have the same number of elements. It applies the designated accumulation procedure to combine all the first elements of the sequences, all the second elements of the sequences, and so on, and returns a sequence of the results. For instance, if s is a sequence containing four sequences, `((1 2 3) (4 5 6) (7 8 9) (10 11 12))`, then the value of `(accumulate-n + 0 s)` should be the sequence `(22 26 30)`. Fill in the missing expressions in the following definition of `accumulate-n`:

```
(define (accumulate-n op init seqs)
  (if (null? (car seqs))
      nil
      (cons (accumulate op init ⟨??⟩)
            (accumulate-n op init ⟨??⟩))))
```

Exercise 2.37

Suppose we represent vectors $v = (v_i)$ as sequences of numbers, and matrices $m = (m_{ij})$ as sequences of vectors (the rows of the matrix). For example, the matrix

$$\begin{bmatrix} 1 & 2 & 3 & 4 \\ 4 & 5 & 6 & 6 \\ 6 & 7 & 8 & 9 \end{bmatrix}$$

is represented as the sequence `((1 2 3 4) (4 5 6 6) (6 7 8 9))`. With this representation, we can use sequence operations to concisely express the basic matrix and vector operations. These operations (which are described in any book on matrix algebra) are the following:

`(dot-product v w)`	returns the sum $\sum_i v_i w_i$;
`(matrix-*-vector m v)`	returns the vector t, where $t_i = \sum_j m_{ij} v_j$;
`(matrix-*-matrix m n)`	returns the matrix p, where $p_{ij} = \sum_k m_{ik} n_{kj}$;
`(transpose m)`	returns the matrix n, where $n_{ij} = m_{ji}$.

We can define the dot product as[17]

```
(define (dot-product v w)
  (accumulate + 0 (map * v w)))
```

Fill in the missing expressions in the following procedures for computing the other matrix operations. (The procedure `accumulate-n` is defined in exercise 2.36.)

```
(define (matrix-*-vector m v)
  (map ⟨??⟩ m))

(define (transpose mat)
  (accumulate-n ⟨??⟩ ⟨??⟩ mat))

(define (matrix-*-matrix m n)
  (let ((cols (transpose n)))
    (map ⟨??⟩ m)))
```

Exercise 2.38

The `accumulate` procedure is also known as `fold-right`, because it combines the first element of the sequence with the result of combining all the elements to the right. There is also a `fold-left`, which is similar to `fold-right`, except that it combines elements working in the opposite direction:

```
(define (fold-left op initial sequence)
  (define (iter result rest)
    (if (null? rest)
        result
        (iter (op result (car rest))
              (cdr rest))))
  (iter initial sequence))
```

What are the values of

```
(fold-right / 1 (list 1 2 3))

(fold-left / 1 (list 1 2 3))

(fold-right list nil (list 1 2 3))

(fold-left list nil (list 1 2 3))
```

Give a property that op should satisfy to guarantee that `fold-right` and `fold-left` will produce the same values for any sequence.

---

[17]This definition uses the extended version of map described in footnote 12.

Exercise 2.39

Complete the following definitions of reverse (exercise 2.18) in terms of fold-right and fold-left from exercise 2.38:

```
(define (reverse sequence)
  (fold-right (lambda (x y) ⟨??⟩) nil sequence))

(define (reverse sequence)
  (fold-left (lambda (x y) ⟨??⟩) nil sequence))
```

Nested Mappings

We can extend the sequence paradigm to include many computations that are commonly expressed using nested loops.[18] Consider this problem: Given a positive integer n, find all ordered pairs of distinct positive integers i and j, where $1 \le j < i \le n$, such that $i + j$ is prime. For example, if n is 6, then the pairs are the following:

i	2	3	4	4	5	6	6
j	1	2	1	3	2	1	5
$i + j$	3	5	5	7	7	7	11

A natural way to organize this computation is to generate the sequence of all ordered pairs of positive integers less than or equal to n, filter to select those pairs whose sum is prime, and then, for each pair (i, j) that passes through the filter, produce the triple $(i, j, i + j)$.

Here is a way to generate the sequence of pairs: For each integer $i \le n$, enumerate the integers $j < i$, and for each such i and j generate the pair (i, j). In terms of sequence operations, we map along the sequence (enumerate-interval 1 n). For each i in this sequence, we map along the sequence (enumerate-interval 1 (- i 1)). For each j in this latter sequence, we generate the pair (list i j). This gives us a sequence of pairs for each i. Combining all the sequences for all the i (by accumulating with append) produces the required sequence of pairs:[19]

---

[18]This approach to nested mappings was shown to us by David Turner, whose languages KRC and Miranda provide elegant formalisms for dealing with these constructs. The examples in this section (see also exercise 2.42) are adapted from Turner 1981. In section 3.5.3, we'll see how this approach generalizes to infinite sequences.

[19]We're representing a pair here as a list of two elements rather than as a Lisp pair. Thus, the "pair" (i, j) is represented as (list i j), not (cons i j).

```
(accumulate append
            nil
            (map (lambda (i)
                   (map (lambda (j) (list i j))
                        (enumerate-interval 1 (- i 1))))
                 (enumerate-interval 1 n)))
```

The combination of mapping and accumulating with append is so common in this sort of program that we will isolate it as a separate procedure:

```
(define (flatmap proc seq)
  (accumulate append nil (map proc seq)))
```

Now filter this sequence of pairs to find those whose sum is prime. The filter predicate is called for each element of the sequence; its argument is a pair and it must extract the integers from the pair. Thus, the predicate to apply to each element in the sequence is

```
(define (prime-sum? pair)
  (prime? (+ (car pair) (cadr pair))))
```

Finally, generate the sequence of results by mapping over the filtered pairs using the following procedure, which constructs a triple consisting of the two elements of the pair along with their sum:

```
(define (make-pair-sum pair)
  (list (car pair) (cadr pair) (+ (car pair) (cadr pair))))
```

Combining all these steps yields the complete procedure:

```
(define (prime-sum-pairs n)
  (map make-pair-sum
       (filter prime-sum?
               (flatmap
                (lambda (i)
                  (map (lambda (j) (list i j))
                       (enumerate-interval 1 (- i 1))))
                (enumerate-interval 1 n)))))
```

Nested mappings are also useful for sequences other than those that enumerate intervals. Suppose we wish to generate all the permutations of a set S; that is, all the ways of ordering the items in the set. For instance, the permutations of $\{1, 2, 3\}$ are $\{1, 2, 3\}$, $\{1, 3, 2\}$, $\{2, 1, 3\}$, $\{2, 3, 1\}$, $\{3, 1, 2\}$, and $\{3, 2, 1\}$. Here is a plan for generating the permutations of S: For each item x in S, recursively generate the sequence of permutations of $S - x$,[20] and adjoin x to the front of each one. This yields, for each x in S, the sequence of permutations of S that begin with x. Combining these sequences for all x gives all the permutations of S:[21]

```
(define (permutations s)
  (if (null? s)                          ; empty set?
      (list nil)                         ; sequence containing empty set
      (flatmap (lambda (x)
                 (map (lambda (p) (cons x p))
                      (permutations (remove x s))))
               s)))
```

Notice how this strategy reduces the problem of generating permutations of S to the problem of generating the permutations of sets with fewer elements than S. In the terminal case, we work our way down to the empty list, which represents a set of no elements. For this, we generate (list nil), which is a sequence with one item, namely the set with no elements. The remove procedure used in permutations returns all the items in a given sequence except for a given item. This can be expressed as a simple filter:

```
(define (remove item sequence)
  (filter (lambda (x) (not (= x item)))
          sequence))
```

Exercise 2.40

Define a procedure unique-pairs that, given an integer n, generates the sequence of pairs (i, j) with $1 \le j < i \le n$. Use unique-pairs to simplify the definition of prime-sum-pairs given above.

Exercise 2.41

Write a procedure to find all ordered triples of distinct positive integers i, j, and k less than or equal to a given integer n that sum to a given integer s.

Exercise 2.42

The "eight-queens puzzle" asks how to place eight queens on a chessboard so that no queen is in check from any other (i.e., no two queens are in the same row, column, or diagonal). One possible solution is shown in figure 2.8. One way to solve the puzzle is to work across the board, placing a queen in each column. Once we have placed $k - 1$ queens, we must place the kth queen in a position where it does not check any of the queens already on the board. We can

---

[20]The set $S - x$ is the set of all elements of S, excluding x.

[21]Semicolons in Scheme code are used to introduce *comments*. Everything from the semicolon to the end of the line is ignored by the interpreter. In this book we don't use many comments; we try to make our programs self-documenting by using descriptive names.

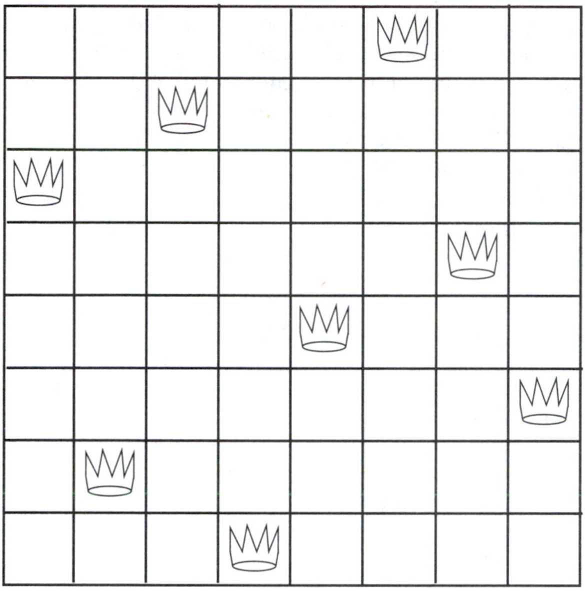

Figure 2.8   A solution to the eight-queens puzzle.

formulate this approach recursively: Assume that we have already generated the sequence of all possible ways to place $k - 1$ queens in the first $k - 1$ columns of the board. For each of these ways, generate an extended set of positions by placing a queen in each row of the kth column. Now filter these, keeping only the positions for which the queen in the kth column is safe with respect to the other queens. This produces the sequence of all ways to place k queens in the first k columns. By continuing this process, we will produce not only one solution, but all solutions to the puzzle.

We implement this solution as a procedure queens, which returns a sequence of all solutions to the problem of placing n queens on an $n \times n$ chessboard. Queens has an internal procedure queen-cols that returns the sequence of all ways to place queens in the first k columns of the board.

```
(define (queens board-size)
  (define (queen-cols k)
    (if (= k 0)
        (list empty-board)
        (filter
         (lambda (positions) (safe? k positions))
         (flatmap
          (lambda (rest-of-queens)
            (map (lambda (new-row)
                   (adjoin-position new-row k rest-of-queens))
                 (enumerate-interval 1 board-size)))
          (queen-cols (- k 1))))))
  (queen-cols board-size))
```

In this procedure `rest-of-queens` is a way to place $k - 1$ queens in the first $k - 1$ columns, and `new-row` is a proposed row in which to place the queen for the kth column. Complete the program by implementing the representation for sets of board positions, including the procedure `adjoin-position`, which adjoins a new row-column position to a set of positions, and `empty-board`, which represents an empty set of positions. You must also write the procedure `safe?`, which determines for a set of positions, whether the queen in the kth column is safe with respect to the others. (Note that we need only check whether the new queen is safe—the other queens are already guaranteed safe with respect to each other.)

Exercise 2.43

Louis Reasoner is having a terrible time doing exercise 2.42. His `queens` procedure seems to work, but it runs extremely slowly. (Louis never does manage to wait long enough for it to solve even the 6×6 case.) When Louis asks Eva Lu Ator for help, she points out that he has interchanged the order of the nested mappings in the `flatmap`, writing it as

```
(flatmap
 (lambda (new-row)
   (map (lambda (rest-of-queens)
          (adjoin-position new-row k rest-of-queens))
        (queen-cols (- k 1))))
 (enumerate-interval 1 board-size))
```

Explain why this interchange makes the program run slowly. Estimate how long it will take Louis's program to solve the eight-queens puzzle, assuming that the program in exercise 2.42 solves the puzzle in time T.

2.2.4 Example: A Picture Language

This section presents a simple language for drawing pictures that illustrates the power of data abstraction and closure, and also exploits higher-order procedures in an essential way. The language is designed to make it easy to experiment with patterns such as the ones in figure 2.9, which are composed of repeated elements that are shifted and scaled.[22] In this language, the data objects being combined are represented as procedures rather than as list structure. Just as `cons`, which satisfies the closure property, allowed us to easily build arbitrarily complicated list structure, the operations in this language, which also satisfy the closure property, allow us to easily build arbitrarily complicated patterns.

---

[22]The picture language is based on the language Peter Henderson created to construct images like M.C. Escher's "Square Limit" woodcut (see Henderson 1982). The woodcut incorporates a repeated scaled pattern, similar to the arrangements drawn using the `square-limit` procedure in this section.

Figure 2.9   Designs generated with the picture language.

The picture language

When we began our study of programming in section 1.1, we emphasized the importance of describing a language by focusing on the language's primitives, its means of combination, and its means of abstraction. We'll follow that framework here.

Part of the elegance of this picture language is that there is only one kind of element, called a *painter*. A painter draws an image that is shifted and scaled to fit within a designated parallelogram-shaped frame. For example, there's a primitive painter we'll call wave that makes a crude line drawing, as shown in figure 2.10. The actual shape of the drawing depends on the frame—all four images in figure 2.10 are produced by the same wave painter, but with respect to four different frames. Painters can be more elaborate than this: The primitive painter called rogers paints a picture of MIT's founder, William Barton Rogers, as shown in figure 2.11.[23] The four images in figure 2.11 are drawn with respect to the same four frames as the wave images in figure 2.10.

---

[23] William Barton Rogers (1804–1882) was the founder and first president of MIT. A geologist and talented teacher, he taught at William and Mary College and at the University of Virginia. In 1859 he moved to Boston, where he had more time for research, worked on a plan for establishing a "polytechnic institute," and served as Massachusetts's first State Inspector of Gas Meters.

When MIT was established in 1861, Rogers was elected its first president. Rogers espoused an ideal of "useful learning" that was different from the university education of the time, with its overemphasis on the classics, which, as he wrote, "stand in the way of the broader, higher and more practical instruction and discipline of the natural and social sciences." This education was likewise to be different from narrow trade-school education. In Rogers's words:

To combine images, we use various operations that construct new painters from given painters. For example, the `beside` operation takes two painters and produces a new, compound painter that draws the first painter's image in the left half of the frame and the second painter's image in the right half of the frame. Similarly, `below` takes two painters and produces a compound painter that draws the first painter's image below the second painter's image. Some operations transform a single painter to produce a new painter. For example, `flip-vert` takes a painter and produces a painter that draws its image upside-down, and `flip-horiz` produces a painter that draws the original painter's image left-to-right reversed.

Figure 2.12 shows the drawing of a painter called `wave4` that is built up in two stages starting from `wave`:

```
(define wave2 (beside wave (flip-vert wave)))
(define wave4 (below wave2 wave2))
```

The world-enforced distinction between the practical and the scientific worker is utterly futile, and the whole experience of modern times has demonstrated its utter worthlessness.

Rogers served as president of MIT until 1870, when he resigned due to ill health. In 1878 the second president of MIT, John Runkle, resigned under the pressure of a financial crisis brought on by the Panic of 1873 and strain of fighting off attempts by Harvard to take over MIT. Rogers returned to hold the office of president until 1881.

Rogers collapsed and died while addressing MIT's graduating class at the commencement exercises of 1882. Runkle quoted Rogers's last words in a memorial address delivered that same year:

"As I stand here today and see what the Institute is, . . . I call to mind the beginnings of science. I remember one hundred and fifty years ago Stephen Hales published a pamphlet on the subject of illuminating gas, in which he stated that his researches had demonstrated that 128 grains of bituminous coal—"

"Bituminous coal," these were his last words on earth. Here he bent forward, as if consulting some notes on the table before him, then slowly regaining an erect position, threw up his hands, and was translated from the scene of his earthly labors and triumphs to "the tomorrow of death," where the mysteries of life are solved, and the disembodied spirit finds unending satisfaction in contemplating the new and still unfathomable mysteries of the infinite future.

In the words of Francis A. Walker (MIT's third president):

All his life he had borne himself most faithfully and heroically, and he died as so good a knight would surely have wished, in harness, at his post, and in the very part and act of public duty.

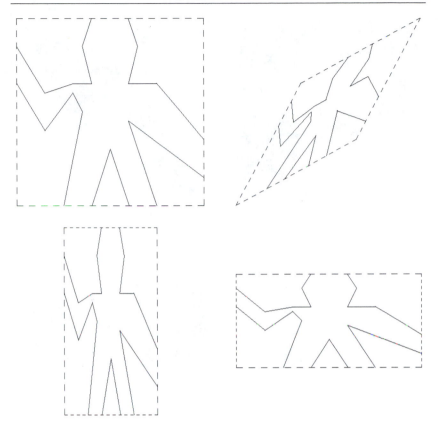

Figure 2.10   Images produced by the wave painter, with respect to four different frames. The frames, shown with dotted lines, are not part of the images.

In building up a complex image in this manner we are exploiting the fact that painters are closed under the language's means of combination. The beside or below of two painters is itself a painter; therefore, we can use it as an element in making more complex painters. As with building up list structure using cons, the closure of our data under the means of combination is crucial to the ability to create complex structures while using only a few operations.

Once we can combine painters, we would like to be able to abstract typical patterns of combining painters. We will implement the painter operations as Scheme procedures. This means that we don't need a spe-

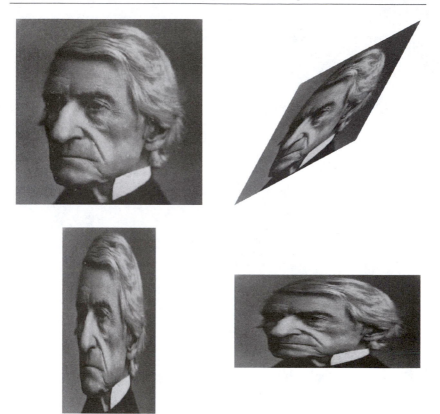

Figure 2.11   Images of William Barton Rogers, founder and first president of MIT, painted with respect to the same four frames as in figure 2.10 (original image reprinted with the permission of the MIT Museum).

cial abstraction mechanism in the picture language: Since the means of combination are ordinary Scheme procedures, we automatically have the capability to do anything with painter operations that we can do with procedures. For example, we can abstract the pattern in wave4 as

```
(define (flipped-pairs painter)
  (let ((painter2 (beside painter (flip-vert painter))))
    (below painter2 painter2)))
```

and define wave4 as an instance of this pattern:

```
(define wave4 (flipped-pairs wave))
```

We can also define recursive operations. Here's one that makes painters split and branch towards the right as shown in figures 2.13 and 2.14:

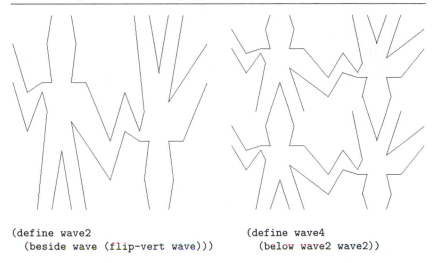

```
(define wave2                    (define wave4
  (beside wave (flip-vert wave)))   (below wave2 wave2))
```

Figure 2.12   Creating a complex figure, starting from the wave painter of figure 2.10.

identity	right-split $n-1$
	right-split $n-1$

right-split n

up-split $n-1$	up-split $n-1$	corner-split $n-1$
identity		right-split $n-1$
		right-split $n-1$

corner-split n

Figure 2.13   Recursive plans for `right-split` and `corner-split`.

```
(define (right-split painter n)
  (if (= n 0)
      painter
      (let ((smaller (right-split painter (- n 1))))
        (beside painter (below smaller smaller)))))
```

We can produce balanced patterns by branching upwards as well as towards the right (see exercise 2.44 and figures 2.13 and 2.14):

```
(define (corner-split painter n)
  (if (= n 0)
      painter
      (let ((up (up-split painter (- n 1)))
            (right (right-split painter (- n 1))))
        (let ((top-left (beside up up))
              (bottom-right (below right right))
              (corner (corner-split painter (- n 1))))
          (beside (below painter top-left)
                  (below bottom-right corner)))))))
```

By placing four copies of a corner-split appropriately, we obtain a pattern called square-limit, whose application to wave and rogers is shown in figure 2.9:

```
(define (square-limit painter n)
  (let ((quarter (corner-split painter n)))
    (let ((half (beside (flip-horiz quarter) quarter)))
      (below (flip-vert half) half))))
```

Exercise 2.44
Define the procedure up-split used by corner-split. It is similar to right-split, except that it switches the roles of below and beside.

Higher-order operations
In addition to abstracting patterns of combining painters, we can work at a higher level, abstracting patterns of combining painter operations. That is, we can view the painter operations as elements to manipulate and can write means of combination for these elements—procedures that take painter operations as arguments and create new painter operations.

For example, flipped-pairs and square-limit each arrange four copies of a painter's image in a square pattern; they differ only in how they orient the copies. One way to abstract this pattern of painter combination is with the following procedure, which takes four one-argument painter operations and produces a painter operation that transforms a given painter with those four operations and arranges the results in a square. Tl, tr, bl, and br are the transformations to apply to the top left copy, the top right copy, the bottom left copy, and the bottom right copy, respectively.

```
(define (square-of-four tl tr bl br)
  (lambda (painter)
    (let ((top (beside (tl painter) (tr painter)))
          (bottom (beside (bl painter) (br painter))))
      (below bottom top))))
```

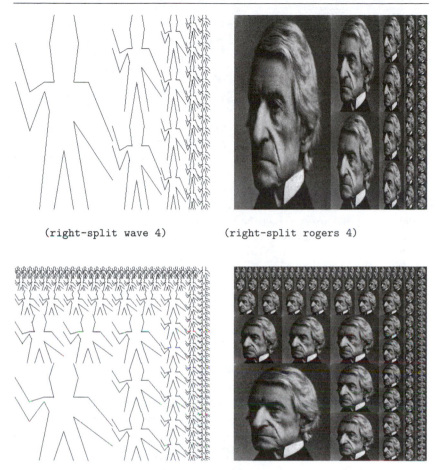

(right-split wave 4)   (right-split rogers 4)

(corner-split wave 4)   (corner-split rogers 4)

Figure 2.14 The recursive operations `right-split` and `corner-split` applied to the painters `wave` and `rogers`. Combining four `corner-split` figures produces symmetric `square-limit` designs as shown in figure 2.9.

Then `flipped-pairs` can be defined in terms of `square-of-four` as follows:[24]

---

[24]Equivalently, we could write

```
(define flipped-pairs
  (square-of-four identity flip-vert identity flip-vert))
```

```
(define (flipped-pairs painter)
  (let ((combine4 (square-of-four identity flip-vert
                                  identity flip-vert)))
    (combine4 painter)))
```

and square-limit can be expressed as[25]

```
(define (square-limit painter n)
  (let ((combine4 (square-of-four flip-horiz identity
                                  rotate180 flip-vert)))
    (combine4 (corner-split painter n))))
```

Exercise 2.45

Right-split and up-split can be expressed as instances of a general splitting operation. Define a procedure split with the property that evaluating

```
(define right-split (split beside below))
(define up-split (split below beside))
```

produces procedures right-split and up-split with the same behaviors as the ones already defined.

Frames

Before we can show how to implement painters and their means of combination, we must first consider frames. A frame can be described by three vectors—an origin vector and two edge vectors. The origin vector specifies the offset of the frame's origin from some absolute origin in the plane, and the edge vectors specify the offsets of the frame's corners from its origin. If the edges are perpendicular, the frame will be rectangular. Otherwise the frame will be a more general parallelogram.

Figure 2.15 shows a frame and its associated vectors. In accordance with data abstraction, we need not be specific yet about how frames are represented, other than to say that there is a constructor make-frame, which takes three vectors and produces a frame, and three corresponding selectors origin-frame, edge1-frame, and edge2-frame (see exercise 2.47).

We will use coordinates in the unit square ($0 \leq x, y \leq 1$) to specify images. With each frame, we associate a *frame coordinate map*, which will be used to shift and scale images to fit the frame. The map trans-

---

[25]Rotate180 rotates a painter by 180 degrees (see exercise 2.50). Instead of rotate180 we could say (compose flip-vert flip-horiz), using the compose procedure from exercise 1.42.

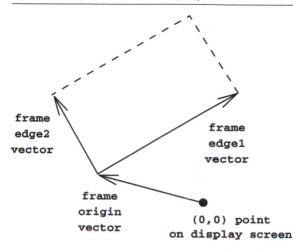

Figure 2.15   A frame is described by three vectors—an origin and two edges.

forms the unit square into the frame by mapping the vector $\mathbf{v} = (x, y)$ to the vector sum

$$\text{Origin(Frame)} + x \cdot \text{Edge}_1\text{(Frame)} + y \cdot \text{Edge}_2\text{(Frame)}$$

For example, $(0, 0)$ is mapped to the origin of the frame, $(1, 1)$ to the vertex diagonally opposite the origin, and $(0.5, 0.5)$ to the center of the frame. We can create a frame's coordinate map with the following procedure:[26]

```
(define (frame-coord-map frame)
  (lambda (v)
    (add-vect
     (origin-frame frame)
     (add-vect (scale-vect (xcor-vect v)
                           (edge1-frame frame))
              (scale-vect (ycor-vect v)
                          (edge2-frame frame))))))
```

Observe that applying `frame-coord-map` to a frame returns a procedure that, given a vector, returns a vector. If the argument vector is in the unit square, the result vector will be in the frame. For example,

---

[26]`Frame-coord-map` uses the vector operations described in exercise 2.46 below, which we assume have been implemented using some representation for vectors. Because of data abstraction, it doesn't matter what this vector representation is, so long as the vector operations behave correctly.

```
((frame-coord-map a-frame) (make-vect 0 0))
```

returns the same vector as

```
(origin-frame a-frame)
```

Exercise 2.46

A two-dimensional vector **v** running from the origin to a point can be represented as a pair consisting of an x-coordinate and a y-coordinate. Implement a data abstraction for vectors by giving a constructor make-vect and corresponding selectors xcor-vect and ycor-vect. In terms of your selectors and constructor, implement procedures add-vect, sub-vect, and scale-vect that perform the operations vector addition, vector subtraction, and multiplying a vector by a scalar:

$$(x_1, y_1) + (x_2, y_2) = (x_1 + x_2, y_1 + y_2)$$
$$(x_1, y_1) - (x_2, y_2) = (x_1 - x_2, y_1 - y_2)$$
$$s \cdot (x, y) = (sx, sy)$$

Exercise 2.47

Here are two possible constructors for frames:

```
(define (make-frame origin edge1 edge2)
  (list origin edge1 edge2))

(define (make-frame origin edge1 edge2)
  (cons origin (cons edge1 edge2)))
```

For each constructor supply the appropriate selectors to produce an implementation for frames.

Painters

A painter is represented as a procedure that, given a frame as argument, draws a particular image shifted and scaled to fit the frame. That is to say, if p is a painter and f is a frame, then we produce p's image in f by calling p with f as argument.

The details of how primitive painters are implemented depend on the particular characteristics of the graphics system and the type of image to be drawn. For instance, suppose we have a procedure draw-line that draws a line on the screen between two specified points. Then we can create painters for line drawings, such as the wave painter in figure 2.10, from lists of line segments as follows:[27]

---

[27]Segments->painter uses the representation for line segments described in exercise 2.48 below. It also uses the for-each procedure described in exercise 2.23.

```
(define (segments->painter segment-list)
  (lambda (frame)
    (for-each
     (lambda (segment)
       (draw-line
         ((frame-coord-map frame) (start-segment segment))
         ((frame-coord-map frame) (end-segment segment))))
     segment-list)))
```

The segments are given using coordinates with respect to the unit square. For each segment in the list, the painter transforms the segment endpoints with the frame coordinate map and draws a line between the transformed points.

Representing painters as procedures erects a powerful abstraction barrier in the picture language. We can create and intermix all sorts of primitive painters, based on a variety of graphics capabilities. The details of their implementation do not matter. Any procedure can serve as a painter, provided that it takes a frame as argument and draws something scaled to fit the frame.[28]

Exercise 2.48

A directed line segment in the plane can be represented as a pair of vectors—the vector running from the origin to the start-point of the segment, and the vector running from the origin to the end-point of the segment. Use your vector representation from exercise 2.46 to define a representation for segments with a constructor make-segment and selectors start-segment and end-segment.

Exercise 2.49

Use segments->painter to define the following primitive painters:

a. The painter that draws the outline of the designated frame.

b. The painter that draws an "X" by connecting opposite corners of the frame.

c. The painter that draws a diamond shape by connecting the midpoints of the sides of the frame.

d. The wave painter.

---

[28] For example, the rogers painter of figure 2.11 was constructed from a gray-level image. For each point in a given frame, the rogers painter determines the point in the image that is mapped to it under the frame coordinate map, and shades it accordingly. By allowing different types of painters, we are capitalizing on the abstract data idea discussed in section 2.1.3, where we argued that a rational-number representation could be anything at all that satisfies an appropriate condition. Here we're using the fact that a painter can be implemented in any way at all, so long as it draws something in the designated frame. Section 2.1.3 also showed how pairs could be implemented as procedures. Painters are our second example of a procedural representation for data.

Transforming and combining painters

An operation on painters (such as `flip-vert` or `beside`) works by creating a painter that invokes the original painters with respect to frames derived from the argument frame. Thus, for example, `flip-vert` doesn't have to know how a painter works in order to flip it—it just has to know how to turn a frame upside down: The flipped painter just uses the original painter, but in the inverted frame.

Painter operations are based on the procedure `transform-painter`, which takes as arguments a painter and information on how to transform a frame and produces a new painter. The transformed painter, when called on a frame, transforms the frame and calls the original painter on the transformed frame. The arguments to `transform-painter` are points (represented as vectors) that specify the corners of the new frame: When mapped into the frame, the first point specifies the new frame's origin and the other two specify the ends of its edge vectors. Thus, arguments within the unit square specify a frame contained within the original frame.

```
(define (transform-painter painter origin corner1 corner2)
  (lambda (frame)
    (let ((m (frame-coord-map frame)))
      (let ((new-origin (m origin)))
        (painter
          (make-frame new-origin
                      (sub-vect (m corner1) new-origin)
                      (sub-vect (m corner2) new-origin)))))))
```

Here's how to flip painter images vertically:

```
(define (flip-vert painter)
  (transform-painter painter
                     (make-vect 0.0 1.0)    ; new origin
                     (make-vect 1.0 1.0)    ; new end of edge1
                     (make-vect 0.0 0.0)))  ; new end of edge2
```

Using `transform-painter`, we can easily define new transformations. For example, we can define a painter that shrinks its image to the upper-right quarter of the frame it is given:

```
(define (shrink-to-upper-right painter)
  (transform-painter painter
                     (make-vect 0.5 0.5)
                     (make-vect 1.0 0.5)
                     (make-vect 0.5 1.0)))
```

Other transformations rotate images counterclockwise by 90 degrees[29]

```
(define (rotate90 painter)
  (transform-painter painter
                     (make-vect 1.0 0.0)
                     (make-vect 1.0 1.0)
                     (make-vect 0.0 0.0)))
```

or squash images towards the center of the frame:[30]

```
(define (squash-inwards painter)
  (transform-painter painter
                     (make-vect 0.0 0.0)
                     (make-vect 0.65 0.35)
                     (make-vect 0.35 0.65)))
```

Frame transformation is also the key to defining means of combining two or more painters. The beside procedure, for example, takes
two painters, transforms them to paint in the left and right halves of
an argument frame respectively, and produces a new, compound painter.
When the compound painter is given a frame, it calls the first transformed
painter to paint in the left half of the frame and calls the second transformed painter to paint in the right half of the frame:

```
(define (beside painter1 painter2)
  (let ((split-point (make-vect 0.5 0.0)))
    (let ((paint-left
           (transform-painter painter1
                              (make-vect 0.0 0.0)
                              split-point
                              (make-vect 0.0 1.0)))
          (paint-right
           (transform-painter painter2
                              split-point
                              (make-vect 1.0 0.0)
                              (make-vect 0.5 1.0))))
      (lambda (frame)
        (paint-left frame)
        (paint-right frame)))))
```

---

[29]Rotate90 is a pure rotation only for square frames, because it also stretches and shrinks
the image to fit into the rotated frame.

[30]The diamond-shaped images in figures 2.10 and 2.11 were created with squash-
inwards applied to wave and rogers.

Observe how the painter data abstraction, and in particular the representation of painters as procedures, makes `beside` easy to implement. The `beside` procedure need not know anything about the details of the component painters other than that each painter will draw something in its designated frame.

Exercise 2.50

Define the transformation `flip-horiz`, which flips painters horizontally, and transformations that rotate painters counterclockwise by 180 degrees and 270 degrees.

Exercise 2.51

Define the `below` operation for painters. `Below` takes two painters as arguments. The resulting painter, given a frame, draws with the first painter in the bottom of the frame and with the second painter in the top. Define `below` in two different ways—first by writing a procedure that is analogous to the `beside` procedure given above, and again in terms of `beside` and suitable rotation operations (from exercise 2.50).

Levels of language for robust design

The picture language exercises some of the critical ideas we've introduced about abstraction with procedures and data. The fundamental data abstractions, painters, are implemented using procedural representations, which enables the language to handle different basic drawing capabilities in a uniform way. The means of combination satisfy the closure property, which permits us to easily build up complex designs. Finally, all the tools for abstracting procedures are available to us for abstracting means of combination for painters.

We have also obtained a glimpse of another crucial idea about languages and program design. This is the approach of *stratified design*, the notion that a complex system should be structured as a sequence of levels that are described using a sequence of languages. Each level is constructed by combining parts that are regarded as primitive at that level, and the parts constructed at each level are used as primitives at the next level. The language used at each level of a stratified design has primitives, means of combination, and means of abstraction appropriate to that level of detail.

Stratified design pervades the engineering of complex systems. For example, in computer engineering, resistors and transistors are combined (and described using a language of analog circuits) to produce parts such as and-gates and or-gates, which form the primitives of a language for digital-circuit design.[31] These parts are combined to build processors, bus structures, and memory systems, which are in turn combined to form computers, using languages appropriate to computer architecture. Computers are combined to form distributed systems, using languages appropriate for describing network interconnections, and so on.

As a tiny example of stratification, our picture language uses primitive elements (primitive painters) that are created using a language that specifies points and lines to provide the lists of line segments for `segments->painter`, or the shading details for a painter like `rogers`. The bulk of our description of the picture language focused on combining these primitives, using geometric combiners such as `beside` and `below`. We also worked at a higher level, regarding `beside` and `below` as primitives to be manipulated in a language whose operations, such as `square-of-four`, capture common patterns of combining geometric combiners.

Stratified design helps make programs *robust*, that is, it makes it likely that small changes in a specification will require correspondingly small changes in the program. For instance, suppose we wanted to change the image based on `wave` shown in figure 2.9. We could work at the lowest level to change the detailed appearance of the `wave` element; we could work at the middle level to change the way `corner-split` replicates the wave; we could work at the highest level to change how `square-limit` arranges the four copies of the corner. In general, each level of a stratified design provides a different vocabulary for expressing the characteristics of the system, and a different kind of ability to change it.

Exercise 2.52

Make changes to the square limit of `wave` shown in figure 2.9 by working at each of the levels described above. In particular:

a. Add some segments to the primitive `wave` painter of exercise 2.49 (to add a smile, for example).

b. Change the pattern constructed by `corner-split` (for example, by using only one copy of the `up-split` and `right-split` images instead of two).

c. Modify the version of `square-limit` that uses `square-of-four` so as to assemble the corners in a different pattern. (For example, you might make the big Mr. Rogers look outward from each corner of the square.)

---

[31] Section 3.3.4 describes one such language.

2.3   Symbolic Data

All the compound data objects we have used so far were constructed ultimately from numbers. In this section we extend the representational capability of our language by introducing the ability to work with arbitrary symbols as data.

2.3.1   Quotation

If we can form compound data using symbols, we can have lists such as

```
(a b c d)
(23 45 17)
((Norah 12) (Molly 9) (Anna 7) (Lauren 6) (Charlotte 4))
```

Lists containing symbols can look just like the expressions of our language:

```
(* (+ 23 45) (+ x 9))

(define (fact n) (if (= n 1) 1 (* n (fact (- n 1)))))
```

In order to manipulate symbols we need a new element in our language: the ability to *quote* a data object. Suppose we want to construct the list (a b). We can't accomplish this with (list a b), because this expression constructs a list of the *values* of a and b rather than the symbols themselves. This issue is well known in the context of natural languages, where words and sentences may be regarded either as semantic entities or as character strings (syntactic entities). The common practice in natural languages is to use quotation marks to indicate that a word or a sentence is to be treated literally as a string of characters. For instance, the first letter of "John" is clearly "J." If we tell somebody "say your name aloud," we expect to hear that person's name. However, if we tell somebody "say 'your name' aloud," we expect to hear the words "your name." Note that we are forced to nest quotation marks to describe what somebody else might say.[32]

---

[32] Allowing quotation in a language wreaks havoc with the ability to reason about the language in simple terms, because it destroys the notion that equals can be substituted for equals. For example, three is one plus two, but the word "three" is not the phrase "one plus two." Quotation is powerful because it gives us a way to build expressions that manipulate other expressions (as we will see when we write an interpreter in chapter 4). But allowing statements in a language that talk about other statements in that language makes it very difficult to maintain any coherent principle of what "equals can be substituted for equals" should mean. For example, if we know that the evening star is the morning star, then

We can follow this same practice to identify lists and symbols that are to be treated as data objects rather than as expressions to be evaluated. However, our format for quoting differs from that of natural languages in that we place a quotation mark (traditionally, the single quote symbol ') only at the beginning of the object to be quoted. We can get away with this in Scheme syntax because we rely on blanks and parentheses to delimit objects. Thus, the meaning of the single quote character is to quote the next object.[33]

Now we can distinguish between symbols and their values:

```
(define a 1)

(define b 2)

(list a b)
(1 2)

(list 'a 'b)
(a b)

(list 'a b)
(a 2)
```

Quotation also allows us to type in compound objects, using the conventional printed representation for lists:[34]

from the statement "the evening star is Venus" we can deduce "the morning star is Venus." However, given that "John knows that the evening star is Venus" we cannot infer that "John knows that the morning star is Venus."

[33] The single quote is different from the double quote we have been using to enclose character strings to be printed. Whereas the single quote can be used to denote lists or symbols, the double quote is used only with character strings. In this book, the only use for character strings is as items to be printed.

[34] Strictly, our use of the quotation mark violates the general rule that all compound expressions in our language should be delimited by parentheses and look like lists. We can recover this consistency by introducing a special form quote, which serves the same purpose as the quotation mark. Thus, we would type (quote a) instead of 'a, and we would type (quote (a b c)) instead of '(a b c). This is precisely how the interpreter works. The quotation mark is just a single-character abbreviation for wrapping the next complete expression with quote to form (quote ⟨*expression*⟩). This is important because it maintains the principle that any expression seen by the interpreter can be manipulated as a data object. For instance, we could construct the expression (car '(a b c)), which is the same as (car (quote (a b c))), by evaluating (list 'car (list 'quote '(a b c))).

```
(car '(a b c))
```
a

```
(cdr '(a b c))
```
(b c)

In keeping with this, we can obtain the empty list by evaluating ' (), and thus dispense with the variable `nil`.

One additional primitive used in manipulating symbols is eq?, which takes two symbols as arguments and tests whether they are the same.[35] Using eq?, we can implement a useful procedure called memq. This takes two arguments, a symbol and a list. If the symbol is not contained in the list (i.e., is not eq? to any item in the list), then memq returns false. Otherwise, it returns the sublist of the list beginning with the first occurrence of the symbol:

```
(define (memq item x)
  (cond ((null? x) false)
        ((eq? item (car x)) x)
        (else (memq item (cdr x)))))
```

For example, the value of

```
(memq 'apple '(pear banana prune))
```

is false, whereas the value of

```
(memq 'apple '(x (apple sauce) y apple pear))
```

is (apple pear).

Exercise 2.53

What would the interpreter print in response to evaluating each of the following expressions?

```
(list 'a 'b 'c)
```

```
(list (list 'george))
```

```
(cdr '((x1 x2) (y1 y2)))
```

```
(cadr '((x1 x2) (y1 y2)))
```

---

[35]We can consider two symbols to be "the same" if they consist of the same characters in the same order. Such a definition skirts a deep issue that we are not yet ready to address: the meaning of "sameness" in a programming language. We will return to this in chapter 3 (section 3.1.3).

```
(pair? (car '(a short list)))

(memq 'red '((red shoes) (blue socks)))

(memq 'red '(red shoes blue socks))
```

Exercise 2.54

Two lists are said to be equal? if they contain equal elements arranged in the same order. For example,

```
(equal? '(this is a list) '(this is a list))
```

is true, but

```
(equal? '(this is a list) '(this (is a) list))
```

is false. To be more precise, we can define equal? recursively in terms of the basic eq? equality of symbols by saying that a and b are equal? if they are both symbols and the symbols are eq?, or if they are both lists such that (car a) is equal? to (car b) and (cdr a) is equal? to (cdr b). Using this idea, implement equal? as a procedure.[36]

Exercise 2.55

Eva Lu Ator types to the interpreter the expression

```
(car ''abracadabra)
```

To her surprise, the interpreter prints back quote. Explain.

2.3.2 Example: Symbolic Differentiation

As an illustration of symbol manipulation and a further illustration of data abstraction, consider the design of a procedure that performs symbolic differentiation of algebraic expressions. We would like the procedure to take as arguments an algebraic expression and a variable and to return the derivative of the expression with respect to the variable. For example, if the arguments to the procedure are $ax^2 + bx + c$ and x, the procedure should return $2ax + b$. Symbolic differentiation is of special historical significance in Lisp. It was one of the motivating examples behind the development of a computer language for symbol manipula-

---

[36] In practice, programmers use equal? to compare lists that contain numbers as well as symbols. Numbers are not considered to be symbols. The question of whether two numerically equal numbers (as tested by =) are also eq? is highly implementation-dependent. A better definition of equal? (such as the one that comes as a primitive in Scheme) would also stipulate that if a and b are both numbers, then a and b are equal? if they are numerically equal.

tion. Furthermore, it marked the beginning of the line of research that led to the development of powerful systems for symbolic mathematical work, which are currently being used by a growing number of applied mathematicians and physicists.

In developing the symbolic-differentiation program, we will follow the same strategy of data abstraction that we followed in developing the rational-number system of section 2.1.1. That is, we will first define a differentiation algorithm that operates on abstract objects such as "sums," "products," and "variables" without worrying about how these are to be represented. Only afterward will we address the representation problem.

The differentiation program with abstract data

In order to keep things simple, we will consider a very simple symbolic-differentiation program that handles expressions that are built up using only the operations of addition and multiplication with two arguments. Differentiation of any such expression can be carried out by applying the following reduction rules:

$$\frac{dc}{dx} = 0 \text{ for } c \text{ a constant or a variable different from } x$$

$$\frac{dx}{dx} = 1$$

$$\frac{d(u + v)}{dx} = \frac{du}{dx} + \frac{dv}{dx}$$

$$\frac{d(uv)}{dx} = u \left(\frac{dv}{dx}\right) + v \left(\frac{du}{dx}\right)$$

Observe that the latter two rules are recursive in nature. That is, to obtain the derivative of a sum we first find the derivatives of the terms and add them. Each of the terms may in turn be an expression that needs to be decomposed. Decomposing into smaller and smaller pieces will eventually produce pieces that are either constants or variables, whose derivatives will be either 0 or 1.

To embody these rules in a procedure we indulge in a little wishful thinking, as we did in designing the rational-number implementation. If we had a means for representing algebraic expressions, we should be able to tell whether an expression is a sum, a product, a constant, or a variable. We should be able to extract the parts of an expression. For a sum, for example we want to be able to extract the addend (first term) and the augend (second term). We should also be able to construct expressions from parts. Let us assume that we already have procedures to implement the following selectors, constructors, and predicates:

`(variable? e)`	Is e a variable?
`(same-variable? v1 v2)`	Are v1 and v2 the same variable?
`(sum? e)`	Is e a sum?
`(addend e)`	Addend of the sum e.
`(augend e)`	Augend of the sum e.
`(make-sum a1 a2)`	Construct the sum of a1 and a2.
`(product? e)`	Is e a product?
`(multiplier e)`	Multiplier of the product e.
`(multiplicand e)`	Multiplicand of the product e.
`(make-product m1 m2)`	Construct the product of m1 and m2.

Using these, and the primitive predicate number?, which identifies numbers, we can express the differentiation rules as the following procedure:

```
(define (deriv exp var)
  (cond ((number? exp) 0)
        ((variable? exp)
         (if (same-variable? exp var) 1 0))
        ((sum? exp)
         (make-sum (deriv (addend exp) var)
                   (deriv (augend exp) var)))
        ((product? exp)
         (make-sum
           (make-product (multiplier exp)
                         (deriv (multiplicand exp) var))
           (make-product (deriv (multiplier exp) var)
                         (multiplicand exp))))
        (else
         (error "unknown expression type -- DERIV" exp))))
```

This `deriv` procedure incorporates the complete differentiation algorithm. Since it is expressed in terms of abstract data, it will work no matter how we choose to represent algebraic expressions, as long as we design a proper set of selectors and constructors. This is the issue we must address next.

Representing algebraic expressions

We can imagine many ways to use list structure to represent algebraic expressions. For example, we could use lists of symbols that mirror the usual algebraic notation, representing $ax + b$ as the list (a * x + b). However, one especially straightforward choice is to use the same parenthesized prefix notation that Lisp uses for combinations; that is, to represent $ax + b$ as (+ (* a x) b). Then our data representation for the differentiation problem is as follows:

- The variables are symbols. They are identified by the primitive predicate symbol?:

```
(define (variable? x) (symbol? x))
```

- Two variables are the same if the symbols representing them are eq?:

```
(define (same-variable? v1 v2)
  (and (variable? v1) (variable? v2) (eq? v1 v2)))
```

- Sums and products are constructed as lists:

```
(define (make-sum a1 a2) (list '+ a1 a2))

(define (make-product m1 m2) (list '* m1 m2))
```

- A sum is a list whose first element is the symbol +:

```
(define (sum? x)
  (and (pair? x) (eq? (car x) '+)))
```

- The addend is the second item of the sum list:

```
(define (addend s) (cadr s))
```

- The augend is the third item of the sum list:

```
(define (augend s) (caddr s))
```

- A product is a list whose first element is the symbol *:

```
(define (product? x)
  (and (pair? x) (eq? (car x) '*)))
```

- The multiplier is the second item of the product list:

```
(define (multiplier p) (cadr p))
```

- The multiplicand is the third item of the product list:

```
(define (multiplicand p) (caddr p))
```

Thus, we need only combine these with the algorithm as embodied by deriv in order to have a working symbolic-differentiation program. Let us look at some examples of its behavior:

```
(deriv '(+ x 3) 'x)
(+ 1 0)

(deriv '(* x y) 'x)
(+ (* x 0) (* 1 y))

(deriv '(* (* x y) (+ x 3)) 'x)
(+ (* (* x y) (+ 1 0))
   (* (+ (* x 0) (* 1 y))
      (+ x 3)))
```

The program produces answers that are correct; however, they are un-simplified. It is true that

$$\frac{d(xy)}{dx} = x \cdot 0 + 1 \cdot y$$

but we would like the program to know that $x \cdot 0 = 0$, $1 \cdot y = y$, and $0 + y = y$. The answer for the second example should have been simply y. As the third example shows, this becomes a serious issue when the expressions are complex.

Our difficulty is much like the one we encountered with the rational-number implementation: we haven't reduced answers to simplest form. To accomplish the rational-number reduction, we needed to change only the constructors and the selectors of the implementation. We can adopt a similar strategy here. We won't change deriv at all. Instead, we will change make-sum so that if both summands are numbers, make-sum will add them and return their sum. Also, if one of the summands is 0, then make-sum will return the other summand.

```
(define (make-sum a1 a2)
  (cond ((=number? a1 0) a2)
        ((=number? a2 0) a1)
        ((and (number? a1) (number? a2)) (+ a1 a2))
        (else (list '+ a1 a2))))
```

This uses the procedure =number?, which checks whether an expression is equal to a given number:

```
(define (=number? exp num)
  (and (number? exp) (= exp num)))
```

Similarly, we will change make-product to build in the rules that 0 times anything is 0 and 1 times anything is the thing itself:

```
(define (make-product m1 m2)
  (cond ((or (=number? m1 0) (=number? m2 0)) 0)
        ((=number? m1 1) m2)
        ((=number? m2 1) m1)
        ((and (number? m1) (number? m2)) (* m1 m2))
        (else (list '* m1 m2))))
```

Here is how this version works on our three examples:

```
(deriv '(+ x 3) 'x)
1

(deriv '(* x y) 'x)
y

(deriv '(* (* x y) (+ x 3)) 'x)
(+ (* x y) (* y (+ x 3)))
```

Although this is quite an improvement, the third example shows that there is still a long way to go before we get a program that puts expressions into a form that we might agree is "simplest." The problem of algebraic simplification is complex because, among other reasons, a form that may be simplest for one purpose may not be for another.

Exercise 2.56

Show how to extend the basic differentiator to handle more kinds of expressions. For instance, implement the differentiation rule

$$\frac{d(u^n)}{dx} = nu^{n-1}\left(\frac{du}{dx}\right)$$

by adding a new clause to the deriv program and defining appropriate procedures exponentiation?, base, exponent, and make-exponentiation. (You may use the symbol ** to denote exponentiation.) Build in the rules that anything raised to the power 0 is 1 and anything raised to the power 1 is the thing itself.

Exercise 2.57

Extend the differentiation program to handle sums and products of arbitrary numbers of (two or more) terms. Then the last example above could be expressed as

```
(deriv '(* x y (+ x 3)) 'x)
```

Try to do this by changing only the representation for sums and products, without changing the deriv procedure at all. For example, the addend of a sum would be the first term, and the augend would be the sum of the rest of the terms.

Exercise 2.58

Suppose we want to modify the differentiation program so that it works with ordinary mathematical notation, in which + and * are infix rather than prefix operators. Since the differentiation program is defined in terms of abstract data, we can modify it to work with different representations of expressions solely by changing the predicates, selectors, and constructors that define the representation of the algebraic expressions on which the differentiator is to operate.

a. Show how to do this in order to differentiate algebraic expressions presented in infix form, such as (x + (3 * (x + (y + 2)))). To simplify the task, assume that + and * always take two arguments and that expressions are fully parenthesized.

b. The problem becomes substantially harder if we allow standard algebraic notation, such as (x + 3 * (x + y + 2)), which drops unnecessary parentheses and assumes that multiplication is done before addition. Can you design appropriate predicates, selectors, and constructors for this notation such that our derivative program still works?

2.3.3   Example: Representing Sets

In the previous examples we built representations for two kinds of compound data objects: rational numbers and algebraic expressions. In one of these examples we had the choice of simplifying (reducing) the expressions at either construction time or selection time, but other than that the choice of a representation for these structures in terms of lists was straightforward. When we turn to the representation of sets, the choice of a representation is not so obvious. Indeed, there are a number of possible representations, and they differ significantly from one another in several ways.

Informally, a set is simply a collection of distinct objects. To give a more precise definition we can employ the method of data abstraction. That is, we define "set" by specifying the operations that are to be used on sets. These are union-set, intersection-set, element-of-set?, and adjoin-set. Element-of-set? is a predicate that determines whether a given element is a member of a set. Adjoin-set takes an object and a set as arguments and returns a set that contains the elements of the original set and also the adjoined element. Union-set computes the union of two sets, which is the set containing each element that appears in either argument. Intersection-set computes the intersection of two sets, which is the set containing only elements that appear in both arguments. From the viewpoint of data abstraction, we are free to design any representation that implements these operations in a way consistent with the interpretations given above.[37]

Sets as unordered lists

One way to represent a set is as a list of its elements in which no element appears more than once. The empty set is represented by the empty list. In this representation, element-of-set? is similar to the procedure memq of section 2.3.1. It uses equal? instead of eq? so that the set elements need not be symbols:

```
(define (element-of-set? x set)
  (cond ((null? set) false)
        ((equal? x (car set)) true)
        (else (element-of-set? x (cdr set)))))
```

Using this, we can write adjoin-set. If the object to be adjoined is already in the set, we just return the set. Otherwise, we use cons to add the object to the list that represents the set:

```
(define (adjoin-set x set)
  (if (element-of-set? x set)
      set
      (cons x set)))
```

For intersection-set we can use a recursive strategy. If we know how to form the intersection of set2 and the cdr of set1, we only need to

---

[37]If we want to be more formal, we can specify "consistent with the interpretations given above" to mean that the operations satisfy a collection of rules such as these:

• For any set S and any object x, (element-of-set? x (adjoin-set x S)) is true (informally: "Adjoining an object to a set produces a set that contains the object").

• For any sets S and T and any object x, (element-of-set? x (union-set S T)) is equal to (or (element-of-set? x S) (element-of-set? x T)) (informally: "The elements of (union S T) are the elements that are in S or in T").

• For any object x, (element-of-set? x '()) is false (informally: "No object is an element of the empty set").

decide whether to include the `car` of `set1` in this. But this depends on whether `(car set1)` is also in `set2`. Here is the resulting procedure:

```
(define (intersection-set set1 set2)
  (cond ((or (null? set1) (null? set2)) '())
        ((element-of-set? (car set1) set2)
         (cons (car set1)
               (intersection-set (cdr set1) set2)))
        (else (intersection-set (cdr set1) set2))))
```

In designing a representation, one of the issues we should be concerned with is efficiency. Consider the number of steps required by our set operations. Since they all use `element-of-set?`, the speed of this operation has a major impact on the efficiency of the set implementation as a whole. Now, in order to check whether an object is a member of a set, `element-of-set?` may have to scan the entire set. (In the worst case, the object turns out not to be in the set.) Hence, if the set has n elements, `element-of-set?` might take up to n steps. Thus, the number of steps required grows as $\Theta(n)$. The number of steps required by `adjoin-set`, which uses this operation, also grows as $\Theta(n)$. For `intersection-set`, which does an `element-of-set?` check for each element of `set1`, the number of steps required grows as the product of the sizes of the sets involved, or $\Theta(n^2)$ for two sets of size n. The same will be true of `union-set`.

Exercise 2.59

Implement the `union-set` operation for the unordered-list representation of sets.

Exercise 2.60

We specified that a set would be represented as a list with no duplicates. Now suppose we allow duplicates. For instance, the set {1, 2, 3} could be represented as the list (2 3 2 1 3 2 2). Design procedures `element-of-set?`, `adjoin-set`, `union-set`, and `intersection-set` that operate on this representation. How does the efficiency of each compare with the corresponding procedure for the non-duplicate representation? Are there applications for which you would use this representation in preference to the non-duplicate one?

Sets as ordered lists

One way to speed up our set operations is to change the representation so that the set elements are listed in increasing order. To do this, we need some way to compare two objects so that we can say which is bigger. For example, we could compare symbols lexicographically, or we could

agree on some method for assigning a unique number to an object and
then compare the elements by comparing the corresponding numbers.
To keep our discussion simple, we will consider only the case where
the set elements are numbers, so that we can compare elements using
> and <. We will represent a set of numbers by listing its elements in
increasing order. Whereas our first representation above allowed us to
represent the set {1, 3, 6, 10} by listing the elements in any order, our
new representation allows only the list (1 3 6 10).

One advantage of ordering shows up in `element-of-set?`: In checking for the presence of an item, we no longer have to scan the entire set.
If we reach a set element that is larger than the item we are looking for,
then we know that the item is not in the set:

```
(define (element-of-set? x set)
  (cond ((null? set) false)
        ((= x (car set)) true)
        ((< x (car set)) false)
        (else (element-of-set? x (cdr set)))))
```

How many steps does this save? In the worst case, the item we are looking for may be the largest one in the set, so the number of steps is the
same as for the unordered representation. On the other hand, if we search
for items of many different sizes we can expect that sometimes we will
be able to stop searching at a point near the beginning of the list and that
other times we will still need to examine most of the list. On the average
we should expect to have to examine about half of the items in the set.
Thus, the average number of steps required will be about $n/2$. This is
still $\Theta(n)$ growth, but it does save us, on the average, a factor of 2 in
number of steps over the previous implementation.

We obtain a more impressive speedup with `intersection-set`. In
the unordered representation this operation required $\Theta(n^2)$ steps, because we performed a complete scan of `set2` for each element of `set1`.
But with the ordered representation, we can use a more clever method.
Begin by comparing the initial elements, `x1` and `x2`, of the two sets. If
`x1` equals `x2`, then that gives an element of the intersection, and the rest
of the intersection is the intersection of the `cdr`s of the two sets. Suppose, however, that `x1` is less than `x2`. Since `x2` is the smallest element
in `set2`, we can immediately conclude that `x1` cannot appear anywhere
in `set2` and hence is not in the intersection. Hence, the intersection is
equal to the intersection of `set2` with the `cdr` of `set1`. Similarly, if `x2`
is less than `x1`, then the intersection is given by the intersection of `set1`
with the `cdr` of `set2`. Here is the procedure:

```
(define (intersection-set set1 set2)
  (if (or (null? set1) (null? set2))
      '()
      (let ((x1 (car set1)) (x2 (car set2)))
        (cond ((= x1 x2)
               (cons x1
                     (intersection-set (cdr set1)
                                       (cdr set2))))
              ((< x1 x2)
               (intersection-set (cdr set1) set2))
              ((< x2 x1)
               (intersection-set set1 (cdr set2)))))))
```

To estimate the number of steps required by this process, observe that at each step we reduce the intersection problem to computing intersections of smaller sets—removing the first element from set1 or set2 or both. Thus, the number of steps required is at most the sum of the sizes of set1 and set2, rather than the product of the sizes as with the unordered representation. This is $\Theta(n)$ growth rather than $\Theta(n^2)$—a considerable speedup, even for sets of moderate size.

Exercise 2.61

Give an implementation of adjoin-set using the ordered representation. By analogy with element-of-set? show how to take advantage of the ordering to produce a procedure that requires on the average about half as many steps as with the unordered representation.

Exercise 2.62

Give a $\Theta(n)$ implementation of union-set for sets represented as ordered lists.

Sets as binary trees

We can do better than the ordered-list representation by arranging the set elements in the form of a tree. Each node of the tree holds one element of the set, called the "entry" at that node, and a link to each of two other (possibly empty) nodes. The "left" link points to elements smaller than the one at the node, and the "right" link to elements greater than the one at the node. Figure 2.16 shows some trees that represent the set $\{1, 3, 5, 7, 9, 11\}$. The same set may be represented by a tree in a number of different ways. The only thing we require for a valid representation is that all elements in the left subtree be smaller than the node entry and that all elements in the right subtree be larger.

The advantage of the tree representation is this: Suppose we want to check whether a number x is contained in a set. We begin by comparing

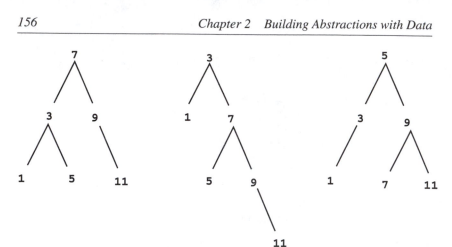

Figure 2.16   Various binary trees that represent the set $\{1, 3, 5, 7, 9, 11\}$.

x with the entry in the top node. If x is less than this, we know that we need only search the left subtree; if x is greater, we need only search the right subtree. Now, if the tree is "balanced," each of these subtrees will be about half the size of the original. Thus, in one step we have reduced the problem of searching a tree of size n to searching a tree of size $n/2$. Since the size of the tree is halved at each step, we should expect that the number of steps needed to search a tree of size n grows as $\Theta(\log n)$.[38] For large sets, this will be a significant speedup over the previous representations.

We can represent trees by using lists. Each node will be a list of three items: the entry at the node, the left subtree, and the right subtree. A left or a right subtree of the empty list will indicate that there is no subtree connected there. We can describe this representation by the following procedures:[39]

```
(define (entry tree) (car tree))
```

```
(define (left-branch tree) (cadr tree))
```

---

[38] Halving the size of the problem at each step is the distinguishing characteristic of logarithmic growth, as we saw with the fast-exponentiation algorithm of section 1.2.4 and the half-interval search method of section 1.3.3.

[39] We are representing sets in terms of trees, and trees in terms of lists—in effect, a data abstraction built upon a data abstraction. We can regard the procedures `entry`, `left-branch`, `right-branch`, and `make-tree` as a way of isolating the abstraction of a "binary tree" from the particular way we might wish to represent such a tree in terms of list structure.

```
(define (right-branch tree) (caddr tree))

(define (make-tree entry left right)
  (list entry left right))
```

Now we can write the `element-of-set?` procedure using the strategy described above:

```
(define (element-of-set? x set)
  (cond ((null? set) false)
        ((= x (entry set)) true)
        ((< x (entry set))
         (element-of-set? x (left-branch set)))
        ((> x (entry set))
         (element-of-set? x (right-branch set)))))
```

Adjoining an item to a set is implemented similarly and also requires $\Theta(\log n)$ steps. To adjoin an item x, we compare x with the node entry to determine whether x should be added to the right or to the left branch, and having adjoined x to the appropriate branch we piece this newly constructed branch together with the original entry and the other branch. If x is equal to the entry, we just return the node. If we are asked to adjoin x to an empty tree, we generate a tree that has x as the entry and empty right and left branches. Here is the procedure:

```
(define (adjoin-set x set)
  (cond ((null? set) (make-tree x '() '()))
        ((= x (entry set)) set)
        ((< x (entry set))
         (make-tree (entry set)
                    (adjoin-set x (left-branch set))
                    (right-branch set)))
        ((> x (entry set))
         (make-tree (entry set)
                    (left-branch set)
                    (adjoin-set x (right-branch set))))))
```

The above claim that searching the tree can be performed in a logarithmic number of steps rests on the assumption that the tree is "balanced," i.e., that the left and the right subtree of every tree have approximately the same number of elements, so that each subtree contains about half the elements of its parent. But how can we be certain that the trees we construct will be balanced? Even if we start with a balanced tree, adding elements with `adjoin-set` may produce an unbalanced result. Since the position of a newly adjoined element depends on how the element com-

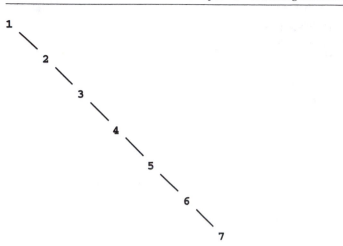

Figure 2.17   Unbalanced tree produced by adjoining 1 through 7 in sequence.

pares with the items already in the set, we can expect that if we add elements "randomly" the tree will tend to be balanced on the average. But
this is not a guarantee. For example, if we start with an empty set and
adjoin the numbers 1 through 7 in sequence we end up with the highly
unbalanced tree shown in figure 2.17. In this tree all the left subtrees
are empty, so it has no advantage over a simple ordered list. One way to
solve this problem is to define an operation that transforms an arbitrary
tree into a balanced tree with the same elements. Then we can perform
this transformation after every few `adjoin-set` operations to keep our
set in balance. There are also other ways to solve this problem, most
of which involve designing new data structures for which searching and
insertion both can be done in $\Theta(\log n)$ steps.[40]

Exercise 2.63

Each of the following two procedures converts a binary tree to a list.

```
(define (tree->list-1 tree)
  (if (null? tree)
      '()
      (append (tree->list-1 (left-branch tree))
              (cons (entry tree)
                    (tree->list-1 (right-branch tree))))))
```

[40]Examples of such structures include *B-trees* and *red-black trees*. There is a large literature on data structures devoted to this problem. See Cormen, Leiserson, and Rivest
1990.

```
(define (tree->list-2 tree)
  (define (copy-to-list tree result-list)
    (if (null? tree)
        result-list
        (copy-to-list (left-branch tree)
                      (cons (entry tree)
                            (copy-to-list (right-branch tree)
                                          result-list)))))
  (copy-to-list tree '()))
```

a. Do the two procedures produce the same result for every tree? If not, how
do the results differ? What lists do the two procedures produce for the trees in
figure 2.16?

b. Do the two procedures have the same order of growth in the number of steps
required to convert a balanced tree with n elements to a list? If not, which one
grows more slowly?

Exercise 2.64

The following procedure list->tree converts an ordered list to a balanced binary tree. The helper procedure partial-tree takes as arguments an integer n
and list of at least n elements and constructs a balanced tree containing the first n
elements of the list. The result returned by partial-tree is a pair (formed with
cons) whose car is the constructed tree and whose cdr is the list of elements
not included in the tree.

```
(define (list->tree elements)
  (car (partial-tree elements (length elements))))

(define (partial-tree elts n)
  (if (= n 0)
      (cons '() elts)
      (let ((left-size (quotient (- n 1) 2)))
        (let ((left-result (partial-tree elts left-size)))
          (let ((left-tree (car left-result))
                (non-left-elts (cdr left-result))
                (right-size (- n (+ left-size 1))))
            (let ((this-entry (car non-left-elts))
                  (right-result (partial-tree (cdr non-left-elts)
                                              right-size)))
              (let ((right-tree (car right-result))
                    (remaining-elts (cdr right-result)))
                (cons (make-tree this-entry left-tree right-tree)
                      remaining-elts)))))))))
```

a. Write a short paragraph explaining as clearly as you can how partial-tree
works. Draw the tree produced by list->tree for the list (1 3 5 7 9 11).

b. What is the order of growth in the number of steps required by list->tree
to convert a list of n elements?

Exercise 2.65

Use the results of exercises 2.63 and 2.64 to give $\Theta(n)$ implementations of `union-set` and `intersection-set` for sets implemented as (balanced) binary trees.[41]

Sets and information retrieval

We have examined options for using lists to represent sets and have seen how the choice of representation for a data object can have a large impact on the performance of the programs that use the data. Another reason for concentrating on sets is that the techniques discussed here appear again and again in applications involving information retrieval.

Consider a data base containing a large number of individual records, such as the personnel files for a company or the transactions in an accounting system. A typical data-management system spends a large amount of time accessing or modifying the data in the records and therefore requires an efficient method for accessing records. This is done by identifying a part of each record to serve as an identifying *key*. A key can be anything that uniquely identifies the record. For a personnel file, it might be an employee's ID number. For an accounting system, it might be a transaction number. Whatever the key is, when we define the record as a data structure we should include a `key` selector procedure that retrieves the key associated with a given record.

Now we represent the data base as a set of records. To locate the record with a given key we use a procedure `lookup`, which takes as arguments a key and a data base and which returns the record that has that key, or false if there is no such record. Lookup is implemented in almost the same way as `element-of-set?`. For example, if the set of records is implemented as an unordered list, we could use

```
(define (lookup given-key set-of-records)
  (cond ((null? set-of-records) false)
        ((equal? given-key (key (car set-of-records)))
         (car set-of-records))
        (else (lookup given-key (cdr set-of-records)))))
```

Of course, there are better ways to represent large sets than as unordered lists. Information-retrieval systems in which records have to be "randomly accessed" are typically implemented by a tree-based method, such as the binary-tree representation discussed previously. In designing such a system the methodology of data abstraction can be a great

---

[41] Exercises 2.63–2.65 are due to Paul Hilfinger.

help. The designer can create an initial implementation using a simple, straightforward representation such as unordered lists. This will be unsuitable for the eventual system, but it can be useful in providing a "quick and dirty" data base with which to test the rest of the system. Later on, the data representation can be modified to be more sophisticated. If the data base is accessed in terms of abstract selectors and constructors, this change in representation will not require any changes to the rest of the system.

Exercise 2.66

Implement the `lookup` procedure for the case where the set of records is structured as a binary tree, ordered by the numerical values of the keys.

2.3.4   Example: Huffman Encoding Trees

This section provides practice in the use of list structure and data abstraction to manipulate sets and trees. The application is to methods for representing data as sequences of ones and zeros (bits). For example, the ASCII standard code used to represent text in computers encodes each character as a sequence of seven bits. Using seven bits allows us to distinguish 2^7, or 128, possible different characters. In general, if we want to distinguish n different symbols, we will need to use $\log_2 n$ bits per symbol. If all our messages are made up of the eight symbols A, B, C, D, E, F, G, and H, we can choose a code with three bits per character, for example

A 000	C 010	E 100	G 110
B 001	D 011	F 101	H 111

With this code, the message

BACADAEAFABBAAAGAH

is encoded as the string of 54 bits

001000010000011000100000101000001001000000000110000111

Codes such as ASCII and the A-through-H code above are known as *fixed-length* codes, because they represent each symbol in the message with the same number of bits. It is sometimes advantageous to use *variable-length* codes, in which different symbols may be represented by different numbers of bits. For example, Morse code does not use the same number of dots and dashes for each letter of the alphabet. In particular, E, the most frequent letter, is represented by a single dot. In general, if our messages are such that some symbols appear very frequently and some very rarely, we can encode data more efficiently (i.e., using fewer bits per message) if we assign shorter codes to the frequent symbols. Consider the following alternative code for the letters A through H:

A 0   C 1010   E 1100   G 1110
B 100   D 1011   F 1101   H 1111

With this code, the same message as above is encoded as the string

100010100101101100011010100100000111001111

This string contains 42 bits, so it saves more than 20% in space in comparison with the fixed-length code shown above.

One of the difficulties of using a variable-length code is knowing when you have reached the end of a symbol in reading a sequence of zeros and ones. Morse code solves this problem by using a special *separator code* (in this case, a pause) after the sequence of dots and dashes for each letter. Another solution is to design the code in such a way that no complete code for any symbol is the beginning (or *prefix*) of the code for another symbol. Such a code is called a *prefix code*. In the example above, A is encoded by 0 and B is encoded by 100, so no other symbol can have a code that begins with 0 or with 100.

In general, we can attain significant savings if we use variable-length prefix codes that take advantage of the relative frequencies of the symbols in the messages to be encoded. One particular scheme for doing this is called the Huffman encoding method, after its discoverer, David Huffman. A Huffman code can be represented as a binary tree whose leaves are the symbols that are encoded. At each non-leaf node of the tree there is a set containing all the symbols in the leaves that lie below the node. In addition, each symbol at a leaf is assigned a weight (which is its relative frequency), and each non-leaf node contains a weight that is the sum of all the weights of the leaves lying below it. The weights are not used in the encoding or the decoding process. We will see below how they are used to help construct the tree.

Figure 2.18 shows the Huffman tree for the A-through-H code given above. The weights at the leaves indicate that the tree was designed for messages in which A appears with relative frequency 8, B with relative frequency 3, and the other letters each with relative frequency 1.

Given a Huffman tree, we can find the encoding of any symbol by starting at the root and moving down until we reach the leaf that holds the symbol. Each time we move down a left branch we add a 0 to the code, and each time we move down a right branch we add a 1. (We decide which branch to follow by testing to see which branch either is the leaf node for the symbol or contains the symbol in its set.) For example, starting from the root of the tree in figure 2.18, we arrive at the leaf for D

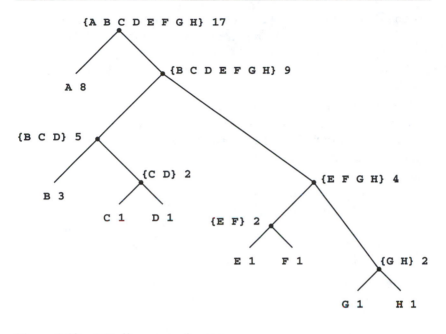

Figure 2.18 A Huffman encoding tree.

by following a right branch, then a left branch, then a right branch, then a right branch; hence, the code for D is 1011.

To decode a bit sequence using a Huffman tree, we begin at the root and use the successive zeros and ones of the bit sequence to determine whether to move down the left or the right branch. Each time we come to a leaf, we have generated a new symbol in the message, at which point we start over from the root of the tree to find the next symbol. For example, suppose we are given the tree above and the sequence 10001010. Starting at the root, we move down the right branch, (since the first bit of the string is 1), then down the left branch (since the second bit is 0), then down the left branch (since the third bit is also 0). This brings us to the leaf for B, so the first symbol of the decoded message is B. Now we start again at the root, and we make a left move because the next bit in the string is 0. This brings us to the leaf for A. Then we start again at the root with the rest of the string 1010, so we move right, left, right, left and reach C. Thus, the entire message is BAC.

Generating Huffman trees

Given an "alphabet" of symbols and their relative frequencies, how do we construct the "best" code? (In other words, which tree will encode messages with the fewest bits?) Huffman gave an algorithm for doing this and showed that the resulting code is indeed the best variable-length code for messages where the relative frequency of the symbols matches the frequencies with which the code was constructed. We will not prove this optimality of Huffman codes here, but we will show how Huffman trees are constructed.[42]

The algorithm for generating a Huffman tree is very simple. The idea is to arrange the tree so that the symbols with the lowest frequency appear farthest away from the root. Begin with the set of leaf nodes, containing symbols and their frequencies, as determined by the initial data from which the code is to be constructed. Now find two leaves with the lowest weights and merge them to produce a node that has these two nodes as its left and right branches. The weight of the new node is the sum of the two weights. Remove the two leaves from the original set and replace them by this new node. Now continue this process. At each step, merge two nodes with the smallest weights, removing them from the set and replacing them with a node that has these two as its left and right branches. The process stops when there is only one node left, which is the root of the entire tree. Here is how the Huffman tree of figure 2.18 was generated:

Initial leaves	{(A 8) (B 3) (C 1) (D 1) (E 1) (F 1) (G 1) (H 1)}
Merge	{(A 8) (B 3) ({C D} 2) (E 1) (F 1) (G 1) (H 1)}
Merge	{(A 8) (B 3) ({C D} 2) ({E F} 2) (G 1) (H 1)}
Merge	{(A 8) (B 3) ({C D} 2) ({E F} 2) ({G H} 2)}
Merge	{(A 8) (B 3) ({C D} 2) ({E F G H} 4)}
Merge	{(A 8) ({B C D} 5) ({E F G H} 4)}
Merge	{(A 8) ({B C D E F G H} 9)}
Final merge	{(({A B C D E F G H} 17)}

The algorithm does not always specify a unique tree, because there may not be unique smallest-weight nodes at each step. Also, the choice of the order in which the two nodes are merged (i.e., which will be the right branch and which will be the left branch) is arbitrary.

Representing Huffman trees

In the exercises below we will work with a system that uses Huffman trees to encode and decode messages and generates Huffman trees according to the algorithm outlined above. We will begin by discussing how trees are represented.

---

[42] See Hamming 1980 for a discussion of the mathematical properties of Huffman codes.

Leaves of the tree are represented by a list consisting of the symbol leaf, the symbol at the leaf, and the weight:

```
(define (make-leaf symbol weight)
  (list 'leaf symbol weight))

(define (leaf? object)
  (eq? (car object) 'leaf))

(define (symbol-leaf x) (cadr x))

(define (weight-leaf x) (caddr x))
```

A general tree will be a list of a left branch, a right branch, a set of symbols, and a weight. The set of symbols will be simply a list of the symbols, rather than some more sophisticated set representation. When we make a tree by merging two nodes, we obtain the weight of the tree as the sum of the weights of the nodes, and the set of symbols as the union of the sets of symbols for the nodes. Since our symbol sets are represented as lists, we can form the union by using the append procedure we defined in section 2.2.1:

```
(define (make-code-tree left right)
  (list left
        right
        (append (symbols left) (symbols right))
        (+ (weight left) (weight right))))
```

If we make a tree in this way, we have the following selectors:

```
(define (left-branch tree) (car tree))

(define (right-branch tree) (cadr tree))

(define (symbols tree)
  (if (leaf? tree)
      (list (symbol-leaf tree))
      (caddr tree)))

(define (weight tree)
  (if (leaf? tree)
      (weight-leaf tree)
      (cadddr tree)))
```

The procedures symbols and weight must do something slightly different depending on whether they are called with a leaf or a general tree.

These are simple examples of *generic procedures* (procedures that can handle more than one kind of data), which we will have much more to say about in sections 2.4 and 2.5.

The decoding procedure

The following procedure implements the decoding algorithm. It takes as arguments a list of zeros and ones, together with a Huffman tree.

```
(define (decode bits tree)
  (define (decode-1 bits current-branch)
    (if (null? bits)
        '()
        (let ((next-branch
                (choose-branch (car bits) current-branch)))
          (if (leaf? next-branch)
              (cons (symbol-leaf next-branch)
                    (decode-1 (cdr bits) tree))
              (decode-1 (cdr bits) next-branch)))))
  (decode-1 bits tree))

(define (choose-branch bit branch)
  (cond ((= bit 0) (left-branch branch))
        ((= bit 1) (right-branch branch))
        (else (error "bad bit -- CHOOSE-BRANCH" bit))))
```

The procedure decode-1 takes two arguments: the list of remaining bits and the current position in the tree. It keeps moving "down" the tree, choosing a left or a right branch according to whether the next bit in the list is a zero or a one. (This is done with the procedure choose-branch.) When it reaches a leaf, it returns the symbol at that leaf as the next symbol in the message by consing it onto the result of decoding the rest of the message, starting at the root of the tree. Note the error check in the final clause of choose-branch, which complains if the procedure finds something other than a zero or a one in the input data.

Sets of weighted elements

In our representation of trees, each non-leaf node contains a set of symbols, which we have represented as a simple list. However, the tree-generating algorithm discussed above requires that we also work with sets of leaves and trees, successively merging the two smallest items. Since we will be required to repeatedly find the smallest item in a set, it is convenient to use an ordered representation for this kind of set.

We will represent a set of leaves and trees as a list of elements, arranged in increasing order of weight. The following adjoin-set procedure for constructing sets is similar to the one described in exercise 2.61;

however, items are compared by their weights, and the element being added to the set is never already in it.

```
(define (adjoin-set x set)
  (cond ((null? set) (list x))
        ((< (weight x) (weight (car set))) (cons x set))
        (else (cons (car set)
                    (adjoin-set x (cdr set))))))
```

The following procedure takes a list of symbol-frequency pairs such as ((A 4) (B 2) (C 1) (D 1)) and constructs an initial ordered set of leaves, ready to be merged according to the Huffman algorithm:

```
(define (make-leaf-set pairs)
  (if (null? pairs)
      '()
      (let ((pair (car pairs)))
        (adjoin-set (make-leaf (car pair)      ; symbol
                               (cadr pair))    ; frequency
                    (make-leaf-set (cdr pairs))))))
```

Exercise 2.67

Define an encoding tree and a sample message:

```
(define sample-tree
  (make-code-tree (make-leaf 'A 4)
                  (make-code-tree
                   (make-leaf 'B 2)
                   (make-code-tree (make-leaf 'D 1)
                                   (make-leaf 'C 1)))))

(define sample-message '(0 1 1 0 0 1 0 1 0 1 1 1 0))
```

Use the decode procedure to decode the message, and give the result.

Exercise 2.68

The encode procedure takes as arguments a message and a tree and produces the list of bits that gives the encoded message.

```
(define (encode message tree)
  (if (null? message)
      '()
      (append (encode-symbol (car message) tree)
              (encode (cdr message) tree))))
```

Encode-symbol is a procedure, which you must write, that returns the list of bits that encodes a given symbol according to a given tree. You should design encode-symbol so that it signals an error if the symbol is not in the tree at all. Test your procedure by encoding the result you obtained in exercise 2.67 with the sample tree and seeing whether it is the same as the original sample message.

Exercise 2.69

The following procedure takes as its argument a list of symbol-frequency pairs (where no symbol appears in more than one pair) and generates a Huffman encoding tree according to the Huffman algorithm.

```
(define (generate-huffman-tree pairs)
  (successive-merge (make-leaf-set pairs)))
```

Make-leaf-set is the procedure given above that transforms the list of pairs into an ordered set of leaves. Successive-merge is the procedure you must write, using make-code-tree to successively merge the smallest-weight elements of the set until there is only one element left, which is the desired Huffman tree. (This procedure is slightly tricky, but not really complicated. If you find yourself designing a complex procedure, then you are almost certainly doing something wrong. You can take significant advantage of the fact that we are using an ordered set representation.)

Exercise 2.70

The following eight-symbol alphabet with associated relative frequencies was designed to efficiently encode the lyrics of 1950s rock songs. (Note that the "symbols" of an "alphabet" need not be individual letters.)

A	2	NA	16
BOOM	1	SHA	3
GET	2	YIP	9
JOB	2	WAH	1

Use generate-huffman-tree (exercise 2.69) to generate a corresponding Huffman tree, and use encode (exercise 2.68) to encode the following message:

Get a job
Sha na na na na na na na na
Get a job
Sha na na na na na na na na
Wah yip yip yip yip yip yip yip yip yip
Sha boom

How many bits are required for the encoding? What is the smallest number of bits that would be needed to encode this song if we used a fixed-length code for the eight-symbol alphabet?

Exercise 2.71

Suppose we have a Huffman tree for an alphabet of n symbols, and that the relative frequencies of the symbols are $1, 2, 4, \ldots, 2^{n-1}$. Sketch the tree for $n=5$; for $n=10$. In such a tree (for general n) how may bits are required to encode the most frequent symbol? the least frequent symbol?

Exercise 2.72

Consider the encoding procedure that you designed in exercise 2.68. What is
the order of growth in the number of steps needed to encode a symbol? Be
sure to include the number of steps needed to search the symbol list at each
node encountered. To answer this question in general is difficult. Consider the
special case where the relative frequencies of the n symbols are as described in
exercise 2.71, and give the order of growth (as a function of n) of the number
of steps needed to encode the most frequent and least frequent symbols in the
alphabet.

2.4   Multiple Representations for Abstract Data

We have introduced data abstraction, a methodology for structuring systems in such a way that much of a program can be specified independent
of the choices involved in implementing the data objects that the program manipulates. For example, we saw in section 2.1.1 how to separate
the task of designing a program that uses rational numbers from the task
of implementing rational numbers in terms of the computer language's
primitive mechanisms for constructing compound data. The key idea was
to erect an abstraction barrier—in this case, the selectors and constructors for rational numbers (`make-rat`, `numer`, `denom`)—that isolates the
way rational numbers are used from their underlying representation in
terms of list structure. A similar abstraction barrier isolates the details
of the procedures that perform rational arithmetic (`add-rat`, `sub-rat`,
`mul-rat`, and `div-rat`) from the "higher-level" procedures that use rational numbers. The resulting program has the structure shown in figure 2.1.

These data-abstraction barriers are powerful tools for controlling complexity. By isolating the underlying representations of data objects, we
can divide the task of designing a large program into smaller tasks that
can be performed separately. But this kind of data abstraction is not yet
powerful enough, because it may not always make sense to speak of "the
underlying representation" for a data object.

For one thing, there might be more than one useful representation for
a data object, and we might like to design systems that can deal with multiple representations. To take a simple example, complex numbers may
be represented in two almost equivalent ways: in rectangular form (real
and imaginary parts) and in polar form (magnitude and angle). Some-

times rectangular form is more appropriate and sometimes polar form is more appropriate. Indeed, it is perfectly plausible to imagine a system in which complex numbers are represented in both ways, and in which the procedures for manipulating complex numbers work with either representation.

More importantly, programming systems are often designed by many people working over extended periods of time, subject to requirements that change over time. In such an environment, it is simply not possible for everyone to agree in advance on choices of data representation. So in addition to the data-abstraction barriers that isolate representation from use, we need abstraction barriers that isolate different design choices from each other and permit different choices to coexist in a single program. Furthermore, since large programs are often created by combining pre-existing modules that were designed in isolation, we need conventions that permit programmers to incorporate modules into larger systems *additively*, that is, without having to redesign or reimplement these modules.

In this section, we will learn how to cope with data that may be represented in different ways by different parts of a program. This requires constructing *generic procedures*—procedures that can operate on data that may be represented in more than one way. Our main technique for building generic procedures will be to work in terms of data objects that have *type tags*, that is, data objects that include explicit information about how they are to be processed. We will also discuss *data-directed* programming, a powerful and convenient implementation strategy for additively assembling systems with generic operations.

We begin with the simple complex-number example. We will see how type tags and data-directed style enable us to design separate rectangular and polar representations for complex numbers while maintaining the notion of an abstract "complex-number" data object. We will accomplish this by defining arithmetic procedures for complex numbers (`add-complex`, `sub-complex`, `mul-complex`, and `div-complex`) in terms of generic selectors that access parts of a complex number independent of how the number is represented. The resulting complex-number system, as shown in figure 2.19, contains two different kinds of abstraction barriers. The "horizontal" abstraction barriers play the same role as the ones in figure 2.1. They isolate "higher-level" operations from "lower-level" representations. In addition, there is a "vertical" barrier that gives us the ability to separately design and install alternative representations.

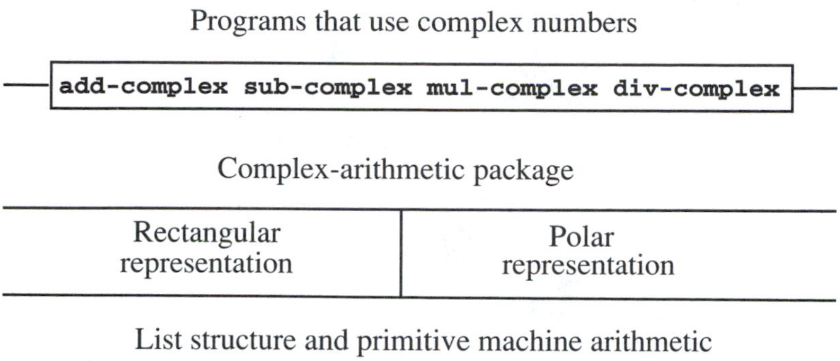

Programs that use complex numbers

```
add-complex sub-complex mul-complex div-complex
```

Complex-arithmetic package

Rectangular representation	Polar representation

List structure and primitive machine arithmetic

Figure 2.19   Data-abstraction barriers in the complex-number system.

In section 2.5 we will show how to use type tags and data-directed style to develop a generic arithmetic package. This provides procedures (add, mul, and so on) that can be used to manipulate all sorts of "numbers" and can be easily extended when a new kind of number is needed. In section 2.5.3, we'll show how to use generic arithmetic in a system that performs symbolic algebra.

2.4.1   Representations for Complex Numbers

We will develop a system that performs arithmetic operations on complex numbers as a simple but unrealistic example of a program that uses generic operations. We begin by discussing two plausible representations for complex numbers as ordered pairs: rectangular form (real part and imaginary part) and polar form (magnitude and angle).[43] Section 2.4.2 will show how both representations can be made to coexist in a single system through the use of type tags and generic operations.

Like rational numbers, complex numbers are naturally represented as ordered pairs. The set of complex numbers can be thought of as a two-dimensional space with two orthogonal axes, the "real" axis and the "imaginary" axis. (See figure 2.20.) From this point of view, the complex number $z = x + iy$ (where $i^2 = -1$) can be thought of as the point in the plane whose real coordinate is x and whose imaginary coordinate is y.

---

[43]In actual computational systems, rectangular form is preferable to polar form most of the time because of roundoff errors in conversion between rectangular and polar form. This is why the complex-number example is unrealistic. Nevertheless, it provides a clear illustration of the design of a system using generic operations and a good introduction to the more substantial systems to be developed later in this chapter.

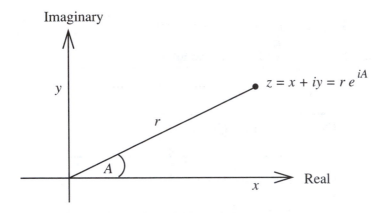

Figure 2.20   Complex numbers as points in the plane.

Addition of complex numbers reduces in this representation to addition of coordinates:

Real-part$(z_1 + z_2)$ = Real-part(z_1) + Real-part(z_2)

Imaginary-part$(z_1 + z_2)$ = Imaginary-part(z_1) + Imaginary-part(z_2)

When multiplying complex numbers, it is more natural to think in terms of representing a complex number in polar form, as a magnitude and an angle (r and A in figure 2.20). The product of two complex numbers is the vector obtained by stretching one complex number by the length of the other and then rotating it through the angle of the other:

Magnitude$(z_1 \cdot z_2)$ = Magnitude(z_1) · Magnitude(z_2)

Angle$(z_1 \cdot z_2)$ = Angle(z_1) + Angle(z_2)

Thus, there are two different representations for complex numbers, which are appropriate for different operations. Yet, from the viewpoint of someone writing a program that uses complex numbers, the principle of data abstraction suggests that all the operations for manipulating complex numbers should be available regardless of which representation is used by the computer. For example, it is often useful to be able to find the magnitude of a complex number that is specified by rectangular coordinates. Similarly, it is often useful to be able to determine the real part of a complex number that is specified by polar coordinates.

To design such a system, we can follow the same data-abstraction strategy we followed in designing the rational-number package in section 2.1.1. Assume that the operations on complex numbers are implemented in terms of four selectors: `real-part`, `imag-part`, `magnitude`, and `angle`. Also assume that we have two procedures for constructing complex numbers: `make-from-real-imag` returns a complex number with specified real and imaginary parts, and `make-from-mag-ang` returns a complex number with specified magnitude and angle. These procedures have the property that, for any complex number z, both

```
(make-from-real-imag (real-part z) (imag-part z))
```

and

```
(make-from-mag-ang (magnitude z) (angle z))
```

produce complex numbers that are equal to z.

Using these constructors and selectors, we can implement arithmetic on complex numbers using the "abstract data" specified by the constructors and selectors, just as we did for rational numbers in section 2.1.1. As shown in the formulas above, we can add and subtract complex numbers in terms of real and imaginary parts while multiplying and dividing complex numbers in terms of magnitudes and angles:

```
(define (add-complex z1 z2)
  (make-from-real-imag (+ (real-part z1) (real-part z2))
                       (+ (imag-part z1) (imag-part z2))))

(define (sub-complex z1 z2)
  (make-from-real-imag (- (real-part z1) (real-part z2))
                       (- (imag-part z1) (imag-part z2))))

(define (mul-complex z1 z2)
  (make-from-mag-ang (* (magnitude z1) (magnitude z2))
                     (+ (angle z1) (angle z2))))

(define (div-complex z1 z2)
  (make-from-mag-ang (/ (magnitude z1) (magnitude z2))
                     (- (angle z1) (angle z2))))
```

To complete the complex-number package, we must choose a representation and we must implement the constructors and selectors in terms of primitive numbers and primitive list structure. There are two obvious ways to do this: We can represent a complex number in "rectangular form" as a pair (real part, imaginary part) or in "polar form" as a pair (magnitude, angle). Which shall we choose?

In order to make the different choices concrete, imagine that there are two programmers, Ben Bitdiddle and Alyssa P. Hacker, who are independently designing representations for the complex-number system. Ben chooses to represent complex numbers in rectangular form. With this choice, selecting the real and imaginary parts of a complex number is straightforward, as is constructing a complex number with given real and imaginary parts. To find the magnitude and the angle, or to construct a complex number with a given magnitude and angle, he uses the trigonometric relations

$$x = r \, \cos A \qquad\qquad r = \sqrt{x^2 + y^2}$$

$$y = r \, \sin A \qquad\qquad A = \arctan(y, x)$$

which relate the real and imaginary parts (x, y) to the magnitude and the angle (r, A).[44] Ben's representation is therefore given by the following selectors and constructors:

```
(define (real-part z) (car z))

(define (imag-part z) (cdr z))

(define (magnitude z)
  (sqrt (+ (square (real-part z)) (square (imag-part z)))))

(define (angle z)
  (atan (imag-part z) (real-part z)))

(define (make-from-real-imag x y) (cons x y))

(define (make-from-mag-ang r a)
  (cons (* r (cos a)) (* r (sin a))))
```

Alyssa, in contrast, chooses to represent complex numbers in polar form. For her, selecting the magnitude and angle is straightforward, but she has to use the trigonometric relations to obtain the real and imaginary parts. Alyssa's representation is:

```
(define (real-part z)
  (* (magnitude z) (cos (angle z))))
```

---

[44]The arctangent function referred to here, computed by Scheme's `atan` procedure, is defined so as to take two arguments y and x and to return the angle whose tangent is y/x. The signs of the arguments determine the quadrant of the angle.

```
(define (imag-part z)
  (* (magnitude z) (sin (angle z))))

(define (magnitude z) (car z))

(define (angle z) (cdr z))

(define (make-from-real-imag x y)
  (cons (sqrt (+ (square x) (square y)))
        (atan y x)))

(define (make-from-mag-ang r a) (cons r a))
```

The discipline of data abstraction ensures that the same implementation of `add-complex`, `sub-complex`, `mul-complex`, and `div-complex` will work with either Ben's representation or Alyssa's representation.

2.4.2   Tagged data

One way to view data abstraction is as an application of the "principle of least commitment." In implementing the complex-number system in section 2.4.1, we can use either Ben's rectangular representation or Alyssa's polar representation. The abstraction barrier formed by the selectors and constructors permits us to defer to the last possible moment the choice of a concrete representation for our data objects and thus retain maximum flexibility in our system design.

The principle of least commitment can be carried to even further extremes. If we desire, we can maintain the ambiguity of representation even *after* we have designed the selectors and constructors, and elect to use both Ben's representation *and* Alyssa's representation. If both representations are included in a single system, however, we will need some way to distinguish data in polar form from data in rectangular form. Otherwise, if we were asked, for instance, to find the `magnitude` of the pair (3, 4), we wouldn't know whether to answer 5 (interpreting the number in rectangular form) or 3 (interpreting the number in polar form). A straightforward way to accomplish this distinction is to include a *type tag*—the symbol `rectangular` or `polar`—as part of each complex number. Then when we need to manipulate a complex number we can use the tag to decide which selector to apply.

In order to manipulate tagged data, we will assume that we have procedures `type-tag` and `contents` that extract from a data object the tag and the actual contents (the polar or rectangular coordinates, in the case of a complex number). We will also postulate a procedure `attach-tag` that takes a tag and contents and produces a tagged data object. A straight-forward way to implement this is to use ordinary list structure:

```
(define (attach-tag type-tag contents)
  (cons type-tag contents))

(define (type-tag datum)
  (if (pair? datum)
      (car datum)
      (error "Bad tagged datum -- TYPE-TAG" datum)))

(define (contents datum)
  (if (pair? datum)
      (cdr datum)
      (error "Bad tagged datum -- CONTENTS" datum)))
```

Using these procedures, we can define predicates `rectangular?` and `polar?`, which recognize polar and rectangular numbers, respectively:

```
(define (rectangular? z)
  (eq? (type-tag z) 'rectangular))

(define (polar? z)
  (eq? (type-tag z) 'polar))
```

With type tags, Ben and Alyssa can now modify their code so that their two different representations can coexist in the same system. Whenever Ben constructs a complex number, he tags it as rectangular. Whenever Alyssa constructs a complex number, she tags it as polar. In addition, Ben and Alyssa must make sure that the names of their procedures do not conflict. One way to do this is for Ben to append the suffix `rectangular` to the name of each of his representation procedures and for Alyssa to append `polar` to the names of hers. Here is Ben's revised rectangular representation from section 2.4.1:

```
(define (real-part-rectangular z) (car z))

(define (imag-part-rectangular z) (cdr z))

(define (magnitude-rectangular z)
  (sqrt (+ (square (real-part-rectangular z))
           (square (imag-part-rectangular z)))))

(define (angle-rectangular z)
  (atan (imag-part-rectangular z)
        (real-part-rectangular z)))
```

```
(define (make-from-real-imag-rectangular x y)
  (attach-tag 'rectangular (cons x y)))

(define (make-from-mag-ang-rectangular r a)
  (attach-tag 'rectangular
                (cons (* r (cos a)) (* r (sin a)))))
```

and here is Alyssa's revised polar representation:

```
(define (real-part-polar z)
  (* (magnitude-polar z) (cos (angle-polar z))))

(define (imag-part-polar z)
  (* (magnitude-polar z) (sin (angle-polar z))))

(define (magnitude-polar z) (car z))

(define (angle-polar z) (cdr z))

(define (make-from-real-imag-polar x y)
  (attach-tag 'polar
                (cons (sqrt (+ (square x) (square y)))
                      (atan y x))))

(define (make-from-mag-ang-polar r a)
  (attach-tag 'polar (cons r a)))
```

Each generic selector is implemented as a procedure that checks the tag of its argument and calls the appropriate procedure for handling data of that type. For example, to obtain the real part of a complex number, `real-part` examines the tag to determine whether to use Ben's `real-part-rectangular` or Alyssa's `real-part-polar`. In either case, we use `contents` to extract the bare, untagged datum and send this to the rectangular or polar procedure as required:

```
(define (real-part z)
  (cond ((rectangular? z)
         (real-part-rectangular (contents z)))
        ((polar? z)
         (real-part-polar (contents z)))
        (else (error "Unknown type -- REAL-PART" z))))

(define (imag-part z)
  (cond ((rectangular? z)
         (imag-part-rectangular (contents z)))
        ((polar? z)
         (imag-part-polar (contents z)))
        (else (error "Unknown type -- IMAG-PART" z))))
```

```
(define (magnitude z)
  (cond ((rectangular? z)
         (magnitude-rectangular (contents z)))
        ((polar? z)
         (magnitude-polar (contents z)))
        (else (error "Unknown type -- MAGNITUDE" z))))

(define (angle z)
  (cond ((rectangular? z)
         (angle-rectangular (contents z)))
        ((polar? z)
         (angle-polar (contents z)))
        (else (error "Unknown type -- ANGLE" z))))
```

To implement the complex-number arithmetic operations, we can use the same procedures `add-complex`, `sub-complex`, `mul-complex`, and `div-complex` from section 2.4.1, because the selectors they call are generic, and so will work with either representation. For example, the procedure `add-complex` is still

```
(define (add-complex z1 z2)
  (make-from-real-imag (+ (real-part z1) (real-part z2))
                       (+ (imag-part z1) (imag-part z2))))
```

Finally, we must choose whether to construct complex numbers using Ben's representation or Alyssa's representation. One reasonable choice is to construct rectangular numbers whenever we have real and imaginary parts and to construct polar numbers whenever we have magnitudes and angles:

```
(define (make-from-real-imag x y)
  (make-from-real-imag-rectangular x y))

(define (make-from-mag-ang r a)
  (make-from-mag-ang-polar r a))
```

The resulting complex-number system has the structure shown in figure 2.21. The system has been decomposed into three relatively independent parts: the complex-number-arithmetic operations, Alyssa's polar implementation, and Ben's rectangular implementation. The polar and rectangular implementations could have been written by Ben and Alyssa working separately, and both of these can be used as underlying representations by a third programmer implementing the complex-arithmetic procedures in terms of the abstract constructor/selector interface.

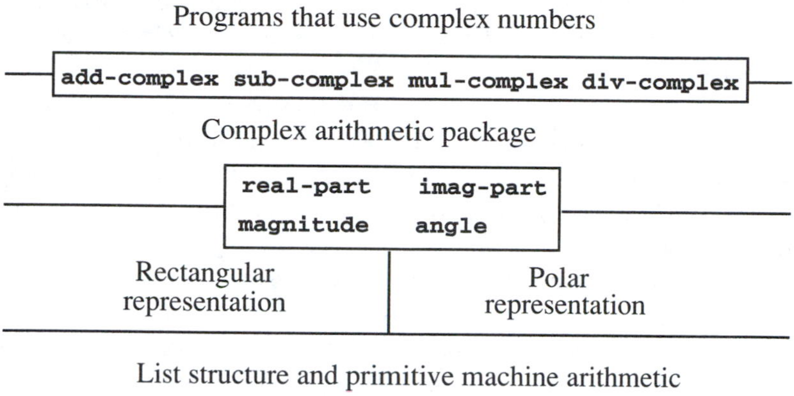

Programs that use complex numbers

```
┌─────────────────────────────────────────────────┐
│ add-complex sub-complex mul-complex div-complex  │
└─────────────────────────────────────────────────┘
```

Complex arithmetic package

```
       ┌──────────────────────────────┐
       │ real-part     imag-part      │
       │ magnitude     angle          │
       └──────────────────────────────┘
```

| Rectangular representation | Polar representation |

List structure and primitive machine arithmetic

Figure 2.21   Structure of the generic complex-arithmetic system.

Since each data object is tagged with its type, the selectors operate on the data in a generic manner. That is, each selector is defined to have a behavior that depends upon the particular type of data it is applied to. Notice the general mechanism for interfacing the separate representations: Within a given representation implementation (say, Alyssa's polar package) a complex number is an untyped pair (magnitude, angle). When a generic selector operates on a number of polar type, it strips off the tag and passes the contents on to Alyssa's code. Conversely, when Alyssa constructs a number for general use, she tags it with a type so that it can be appropriately recognized by the higher-level procedures. This discipline of stripping off and attaching tags as data objects are passed from level to level can be an important organizational strategy, as we shall see in section 2.5.

2.4.3   Data-Directed Programming and Additivity

The general strategy of checking the type of a datum and calling an appropriate procedure is called *dispatching on type*. This is a powerful strategy for obtaining modularity in system design. On the other hand, implementing the dispatch as in section 2.4.2 has two significant weaknesses. One weakness is that the generic interface procedures (real-part, imag-part, magnitude, and angle) must know about all the different representations. For instance, suppose we wanted to incorporate a new representation for complex numbers into our complex-number system. We would need to identify this new representation with a type, and then add a clause to each of the generic interface procedures to check for the new type and apply the appropriate selector for that representation.

Another weakness of the technique is that even though the individual representations can be designed separately, we must guarantee that no two procedures in the entire system have the same name. This is why Ben and Alyssa had to change the names of their original procedures from section 2.4.1.

The issue underlying both of these weaknesses is that the technique for implementing generic interfaces is not *additive*. The person implementing the generic selector procedures must modify those procedures each time a new representation is installed, and the people interfacing the individual representations must modify their code to avoid name conflicts. In each of these cases, the changes that must be made to the code are straightforward, but they must be made nonetheless, and this is a source of inconvenience and error. This is not much of a problem for the complex-number system as it stands, but suppose there were not two but hundreds of different representations for complex numbers. And suppose that there were many generic selectors to be maintained in the abstract-data interface. Suppose, in fact, that no one programmer knew all the interface procedures or all the representations. The problem is real and must be addressed in such programs as large-scale data-base-management systems.

What we need is a means for modularizing the system design even further. This is provided by the programming technique known as *data-directed programming*. To understand how data-directed programming works, begin with the observation that whenever we deal with a set of generic operations that are common to a set of different types we are, in effect, dealing with a two-dimensional table that contains the possible operations on one axis and the possible types on the other axis. The entries in the table are the procedures that implement each operation for each type of argument presented. In the complex-number system developed in the previous section, the correspondence between operation name, data type, and actual procedure was spread out among the various conditional clauses in the generic interface procedures. But the same information could have been organized in a table, as shown in figure 2.22.

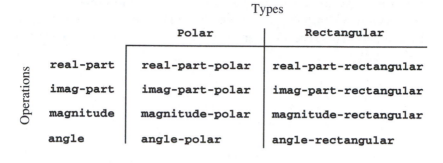

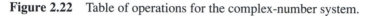

Figure 2.22   Table of operations for the complex-number system.

Data-directed programming is the technique of designing programs to work with such a table directly. Previously, we implemented the mechanism that interfaces the complex-arithmetic code with the two representation packages as a set of procedures that each perform an explicit dispatch on type. Here we will implement the interface as a single procedure that looks up the combination of the operation name and argument type in the table to find the correct procedure to apply, and then applies it to the contents of the argument. If we do this, then to add a new representation package to the system we need not change any existing procedures; we need only add new entries to the table.

To implement this plan, assume that we have two procedures, put and get, for manipulating the operation-and-type table:

- (put ⟨*op*⟩ ⟨*type*⟩ ⟨*item*⟩)

installs the ⟨*item*⟩ in the table, indexed by the ⟨*op*⟩ and the ⟨*type*⟩.

- (get ⟨*op*⟩ ⟨*type*⟩)

looks up the ⟨*op*⟩, ⟨*type*⟩ entry in the table and returns the item found there. If no item is found, get returns false.

For now, we can assume that put and get are included in our language. In chapter 3 (section 3.3.3, exercise 3.24) we will see how to implement these and other operations for manipulating tables.

Here is how data-directed programming can be used in the complex-number system. Ben, who developed the rectangular representation, implements his code just as he did originally. He defines a collection of procedures, or a *package*, and interfaces these to the rest of the system by adding entries to the table that tell the system how to operate on rectangular numbers. This is accomplished by calling the following procedure:

```
(define (install-rectangular-package)
  ;; internal procedures
  (define (real-part z) (car z))
  (define (imag-part z) (cdr z))
  (define (make-from-real-imag x y) (cons x y))
  (define (magnitude z)
    (sqrt (+ (square (real-part z))
             (square (imag-part z)))))
  (define (angle z)
    (atan (imag-part z) (real-part z)))
  (define (make-from-mag-ang r a)
    (cons (* r (cos a)) (* r (sin a))))

  ;; interface to the rest of the system
  (define (tag x) (attach-tag 'rectangular x))
  (put 'real-part '(rectangular) real-part)
  (put 'imag-part '(rectangular) imag-part)
  (put 'magnitude '(rectangular) magnitude)
  (put 'angle '(rectangular) angle)
  (put 'make-from-real-imag 'rectangular
       (lambda (x y) (tag (make-from-real-imag x y))))
  (put 'make-from-mag-ang 'rectangular
       (lambda (r a) (tag (make-from-mag-ang r a))))
  'done)
```

Notice that the internal procedures here are the same procedures from section 2.4.1 that Ben wrote when he was working in isolation. No changes are necessary in order to interface them to the rest of the system. Moreover, since these procedure definitions are internal to the installation procedure, Ben needn't worry about name conflicts with other procedures outside the rectangular package. To interface these to the rest of the system, Ben installs his `real-part` procedure under the operation name `real-part` and the type `(rectangular)`, and similarly for the other selectors.[45] The interface also defines the constructors to be used by the external system.[46] These are identical to Ben's internally defined constructors, except that they attach the tag.

---

[45] We use the list `(rectangular)` rather than the symbol `rectangular` to allow for the possibility of operations with multiple arguments, not all of the same type.

[46] The type the constructors are installed under needn't be a list because a constructor is always used to make an object of one particular type.

Alyssa's polar package is analogous:

```
(define (install-polar-package)
  ;; internal procedures
  (define (magnitude z) (car z))
  (define (angle z) (cdr z))
  (define (make-from-mag-ang r a) (cons r a))
  (define (real-part z)
    (* (magnitude z) (cos (angle z))))
  (define (imag-part z)
    (* (magnitude z) (sin (angle z))))
  (define (make-from-real-imag x y)
    (cons (sqrt (+ (square x) (square y)))
          (atan y x)))

  ;; interface to the rest of the system
  (define (tag x) (attach-tag 'polar x))
  (put 'real-part '(polar) real-part)
  (put 'imag-part '(polar) imag-part)
  (put 'magnitude '(polar) magnitude)
  (put 'angle '(polar) angle)
  (put 'make-from-real-imag 'polar
       (lambda (x y) (tag (make-from-real-imag x y))))
  (put 'make-from-mag-ang 'polar
       (lambda (r a) (tag (make-from-mag-ang r a))))
  'done)
```

Even though Ben and Alyssa both still use their original procedures defined with the same names as each other's (e.g., real-part), these definitions are now internal to different procedures (see section 1.1.8), so there is no name conflict.

The complex-arithmetic selectors access the table by means of a general "operation" procedure called apply-generic, which applies a generic operation to some arguments. Apply-generic looks in the table under the name of the operation and the types of the arguments and applies the resulting procedure if one is present:[47]

---

[47] Apply-generic uses the dotted-tail notation described in exercise 2.20, because different generic operations may take different numbers of arguments. In apply-generic, op has as its value the first argument to apply-generic and args has as its value a list of the remaining arguments.

Apply-generic also uses the primitive procedure apply, which takes two arguments, a procedure and a list. Apply applies the procedure, using the elements in the list as arguments. For example,

```
(apply + (list 1 2 3 4))
```

returns 10.

```
(define (apply-generic op . args)
  (let ((type-tags (map type-tag args)))
    (let ((proc (get op type-tags)))
      (if proc
          (apply proc (map contents args))
          (error
            "No method for these types -- APPLY-GENERIC"
            (list op type-tags))))))
```

Using `apply-generic`, we can define our generic selectors as follows:

```
(define (real-part z) (apply-generic 'real-part z))
(define (imag-part z) (apply-generic 'imag-part z))
(define (magnitude z) (apply-generic 'magnitude z))
(define (angle z) (apply-generic 'angle z))
```

Observe that these do not change at all if a new representation is added to the system.

We can also extract from the table the constructors to be used by the programs external to the packages in making complex numbers from real and imaginary parts and from magnitudes and angles. As in section 2.4.2, we construct rectangular numbers whenever we have real and imaginary parts, and polar numbers whenever we have magnitudes and angles:

```
(define (make-from-real-imag x y)
  ((get 'make-from-real-imag 'rectangular) x y))

(define (make-from-mag-ang r a)
  ((get 'make-from-mag-ang 'polar) r a))
```

Exercise 2.73

Section 2.3.2 described a program that performs symbolic differentiation:

```
(define (deriv exp var)
  (cond ((number? exp) 0)
        ((variable? exp) (if (same-variable? exp var) 1 0))
        ((sum? exp)
         (make-sum (deriv (addend exp) var)
                   (deriv (augend exp) var)))
        ((product? exp)
         (make-sum
           (make-product (multiplier exp)
                         (deriv (multiplicand exp) var))
           (make-product (deriv (multiplier exp) var)
                         (multiplicand exp)))))
        ⟨ more rules can be added here ⟩
        (else (error "unknown expression type -- DERIV" exp))))
```

We can regard this program as performing a dispatch on the type of the expression to be differentiated. In this situation the "type tag" of the datum is the algebraic operator symbol (such as +) and the operation being performed is `deriv`. We can transform this program into data-directed style by rewriting the basic derivative procedure as

```
(define (deriv exp var)
   (cond ((number? exp) 0)
         ((variable? exp) (if (same-variable? exp var) 1 0))
         (else ((get 'deriv (operator exp)) (operands exp)
                                            var))))

(define (operator exp) (car exp))

(define (operands exp) (cdr exp))
```

a. Explain what was done above. Why can't we assimilate the predicates `number?` and `same-variable?` into the data-directed dispatch?

b. Write the procedures for derivatives of sums and products, and the auxiliary code required to install them in the table used by the program above.

c. Choose any additional differentiation rule that you like, such as the one for exponents (exercise 2.56), and install it in this data-directed system.

d. In this simple algebraic manipulator the type of an expression is the algebraic operator that binds it together. Suppose, however, we indexed the procedures in the opposite way, so that the dispatch line in `deriv` looked like

```
((get (operator exp) 'deriv) (operands exp) var)
```

What corresponding changes to the derivative system are required?

Exercise 2.74

Insatiable Enterprises, Inc., is a highly decentralized conglomerate company consisting of a large number of independent divisions located all over the world. The company's computer facilities have just been interconnected by means of a clever network-interfacing scheme that makes the entire network appear to any user to be a single computer. Insatiable's president, in her first attempt to exploit the ability of the network to extract administrative information from division files, is dismayed to discover that, although all the division files have been implemented as data structures in Scheme, the particular data structure used varies from division to division. A meeting of division managers is hastily called to search for a strategy to integrate the files that will satisfy headquarters' needs while preserving the existing autonomy of the divisions.

Show how such a strategy can be implemented with data-directed programming. As an example, suppose that each division's personnel records consist of a single file, which contains a set of records keyed on employees' names.

The structure of the set varies from division to division. Furthermore, each employee's record is itself a set (structured differently from division to division) that contains information keyed under identifiers such as `address` and `salary`. In particular:

a. Implement for headquarters a `get-record` procedure that retrieves a specified employee's record from a specified personnel file. The procedure should be applicable to any division's file. Explain how the individual divisions' files should be structured. In particular, what type information must be supplied?

b. Implement for headquarters a `get-salary` procedure that returns the salary information from a given employee's record from any division's personnel file. How should the record be structured in order to make this operation work?

c. Implement for headquarters a `find-employee-record` procedure. This should search all the divisions' files for the record of a given employee and return the record. Assume that this procedure takes as arguments an employee's name and a list of all the divisions' files.

d. When Insatiable takes over a new company, what changes must be made in order to incorporate the new personnel information into the central system?

Message passing

The key idea of data-directed programming is to handle generic operations in programs by dealing explicitly with operation-and-type tables, such as the table in figure 2.22. The style of programming we used in section 2.4.2 organized the required dispatching on type by having each operation take care of its own dispatching. In effect, this decomposes the operation-and-type table into rows, with each generic operation procedure representing a row of the table.

An alternative implementation strategy is to decompose the table into columns and, instead of using "intelligent operations" that dispatch on data types, to work with "intelligent data objects" that dispatch on operation names. We can do this by arranging things so that a data object, such as a rectangular number, is represented as a procedure that takes as input the required operation name and performs the operation indicated. In such a discipline, `make-from-real-imag` could be written as

```
(define (make-from-real-imag x y)
  (define (dispatch op)
    (cond ((eq? op 'real-part) x)
          ((eq? op 'imag-part) y)
          ((eq? op 'magnitude)
           (sqrt (+ (square x) (square y))))
          ((eq? op 'angle) (atan y x))
          (else
           (error "Unknown op -- MAKE-FROM-REAL-IMAG" op))))
  dispatch)
```

The corresponding `apply-generic` procedure, which applies a generic operation to an argument, now simply feeds the operation's name to the data object and lets the object do the work:[48]

```
(define (apply-generic op arg) (arg op))
```

Note that the value returned by `make-from-real-imag` is a procedure— the internal `dispatch` procedure. This is the procedure that is invoked when `apply-generic` requests an operation to be performed.

   This style of programming is called *message passing*. The name comes from the image that a data object is an entity that receives the requested operation name as a "message." We have already seen an example of message passing in section 2.1.3, where we saw how `cons`, `car`, and `cdr` could be defined with no data objects but only procedures. Here we see that message passing is not a mathematical trick but a useful technique for organizing systems with generic operations. In the remainder of this chapter we will continue to use data-directed programming, rather than message passing, to discuss generic arithmetic operations. In chapter 3 we will return to message passing, and we will see that it can be a powerful tool for structuring simulation programs.

Exercise 2.75

Implement the constructor `make-from-mag-ang` in message-passing style. This procedure should be analogous to the `make-from-real-imag` procedure given above.

Exercise 2.76

As a large system with generic operations evolves, new types of data objects or new operations may be needed. For each of the three strategies—generic operations with explicit dispatch, data-directed style, and message-passing-style— describe the changes that must be made to a system in order to add new types or new operations. Which organization would be most appropriate for a system in which new types must often be added? Which would be most appropriate for a system in which new operations must often be added?

2.5   Systems with Generic Operations

In the previous section, we saw how to design systems in which data objects can be represented in more than one way. The key idea is to link the code that specifies the data operations to the several representations by

---

[48]One limitation of this organization is it permits only generic procedures of one argument.

Programs that use numbers

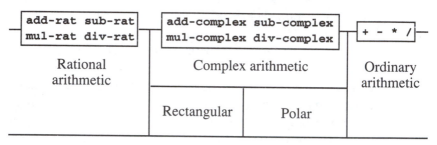

Generic arithmetic package

List structure and primitive machine arithmetic

Figure 2.23   Generic arithmetic system.

means of generic interface procedures. Now we will see how to use this same idea not only to define operations that are generic over different representations but also to define operations that are generic over different kinds of arguments. We have already seen several different packages of arithmetic operations: the primitive arithmetic (+, -, *, /) built into our language, the rational-number arithmetic (add-rat, sub-rat, mul-rat, div-rat) of section 2.1.1, and the complex-number arithmetic that we implemented in section 2.4.3. We will now use data-directed techniques to construct a package of arithmetic operations that incorporates all the arithmetic packages we have already constructed.

Figure 2.23 shows the structure of the system we shall build. Notice the abstraction barriers. From the perspective of someone using "numbers," there is a single procedure add that operates on whatever numbers are supplied. Add is part of a generic interface that allows the separate ordinary-arithmetic, rational-arithmetic, and complex-arithmetic packages to be accessed uniformly by programs that use numbers. Any individual arithmetic package (such as the complex package) may itself be accessed through generic procedures (such as add-complex) that combine packages designed for different representations (such as rectangular and polar). Moreover, the structure of the system is additive, so that one can design the individual arithmetic packages separately and combine them to produce a generic arithmetic system.

2.5.1   Generic Arithmetic Operations

The task of designing generic arithmetic operations is analogous to that of designing the generic complex-number operations. We would like, for instance, to have a generic addition procedure add that acts like ordinary primitive addition + on ordinary numbers, like add-rat on rational numbers, and like add-complex on complex numbers. We can implement add, and the other generic arithmetic operations, by following the same strategy we used in section 2.4.3 to implement the generic selectors for complex numbers. We will attach a type tag to each kind of number and cause the generic procedure to dispatch to an appropriate package according to the data type of its arguments.

The generic arithmetic procedures are defined as follows:

```
(define (add x y) (apply-generic 'add x y))
(define (sub x y) (apply-generic 'sub x y))
(define (mul x y) (apply-generic 'mul x y))
(define (div x y) (apply-generic 'div x y))
```

We begin by installing a package for handling *ordinary* numbers, that is, the primitive numbers of our language. We will tag these with the symbol scheme-number. The arithmetic operations in this package are the primitive arithmetic procedures (so there is no need to define extra procedures to handle the untagged numbers). Since these operations each take two arguments, they are installed in the table keyed by the list (scheme-number scheme-number):

```
(define (install-scheme-number-package)
  (define (tag x)
    (attach-tag 'scheme-number x))
  (put 'add '(scheme-number scheme-number)
       (lambda (x y) (tag (+ x y))))
  (put 'sub '(scheme-number scheme-number)
       (lambda (x y) (tag (- x y))))
  (put 'mul '(scheme-number scheme-number)
       (lambda (x y) (tag (* x y))))
  (put 'div '(scheme-number scheme-number)
       (lambda (x y) (tag (/ x y))))
  (put 'make 'scheme-number
       (lambda (x) (tag x)))
  'done)
```

Users of the Scheme-number package will create (tagged) ordinary numbers by means of the procedure:

```
(define (make-scheme-number n)
  ((get 'make 'scheme-number) n))
```

Now that the framework of the generic arithmetic system is in place, we can readily include new kinds of numbers. Here is a package that performs rational arithmetic. Notice that, as a benefit of additivity, we can use without modification the rational-number code from section 2.1.1 as the internal procedures in the package:

```
(define (install-rational-package)
  ;; internal procedures
  (define (numer x) (car x))
  (define (denom x) (cdr x))
  (define (make-rat n d)
    (let ((g (gcd n d)))
      (cons (/ n g) (/ d g))))
  (define (add-rat x y)
    (make-rat (+ (* (numer x) (denom y))
                 (* (numer y) (denom x)))
              (* (denom x) (denom y))))
  (define (sub-rat x y)
    (make-rat (- (* (numer x) (denom y))
                 (* (numer y) (denom x)))
              (* (denom x) (denom y))))
  (define (mul-rat x y)
    (make-rat (* (numer x) (numer y))
              (* (denom x) (denom y))))
  (define (div-rat x y)
    (make-rat (* (numer x) (denom y))
              (* (denom x) (numer y))))

  ;; interface to rest of the system
  (define (tag x) (attach-tag 'rational x))
  (put 'add '(rational rational)
       (lambda (x y) (tag (add-rat x y))))
  (put 'sub '(rational rational)
       (lambda (x y) (tag (sub-rat x y))))
  (put 'mul '(rational rational)
       (lambda (x y) (tag (mul-rat x y))))
  (put 'div '(rational rational)
       (lambda (x y) (tag (div-rat x y))))

  (put 'make 'rational
       (lambda (n d) (tag (make-rat n d))))
  'done)

(define (make-rational n d)
  ((get 'make 'rational) n d))
```

We can install a similar package to handle complex numbers, using the tag `complex`. In creating the package, we extract from the table the operations `make-from-real-imag` and `make-from-mag-ang` that were defined by the rectangular and polar packages. Additivity permits us to use, as the internal operations, the same `add-complex`, `sub-complex`, `mul-complex`, and `div-complex` procedures from section 2.4.1.

```
(define (install-complex-package)
  ;; imported procedures from rectangular and polar packages
  (define (make-from-real-imag x y)
    ((get 'make-from-real-imag 'rectangular) x y))
  (define (make-from-mag-ang r a)
    ((get 'make-from-mag-ang 'polar) r a))

  ;; internal procedures
  (define (add-complex z1 z2)
    (make-from-real-imag (+ (real-part z1) (real-part z2))
                         (+ (imag-part z1) (imag-part z2))))
  (define (sub-complex z1 z2)
    (make-from-real-imag (- (real-part z1) (real-part z2))
                         (- (imag-part z1) (imag-part z2))))
  (define (mul-complex z1 z2)
    (make-from-mag-ang (* (magnitude z1) (magnitude z2))
                       (+ (angle z1) (angle z2))))
  (define (div-complex z1 z2)
    (make-from-mag-ang (/ (magnitude z1) (magnitude z2))
                       (- (angle z1) (angle z2))))

  ;; interface to rest of the system
  (define (tag z) (attach-tag 'complex z))
  (put 'add '(complex complex)
       (lambda (z1 z2) (tag (add-complex z1 z2))))
  (put 'sub '(complex complex)
       (lambda (z1 z2) (tag (sub-complex z1 z2))))
  (put 'mul '(complex complex)
       (lambda (z1 z2) (tag (mul-complex z1 z2))))
  (put 'div '(complex complex)
       (lambda (z1 z2) (tag (div-complex z1 z2))))
  (put 'make-from-real-imag 'complex
       (lambda (x y) (tag (make-from-real-imag x y))))
  (put 'make-from-mag-ang 'complex
       (lambda (r a) (tag (make-from-mag-ang r a))))
  'done)
```

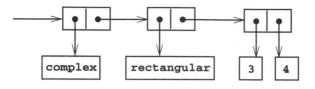

Figure 2.24   Representation of $3 + 4i$ in rectangular form.

Programs outside the complex-number package can construct complex numbers either from real and imaginary parts or from magnitudes and angles. Notice how the underlying procedures, originally defined in the rectangular and polar packages, are exported to the complex package, and exported from there to the outside world.

```
(define (make-complex-from-real-imag x y)
  ((get 'make-from-real-imag 'complex) x y))

(define (make-complex-from-mag-ang r a)
  ((get 'make-from-mag-ang 'complex) r a))
```

What we have here is a two-level tag system. A typical complex number, such as $3 + 4i$ in rectangular form, would be represented as shown in figure 2.24. The outer tag (`complex`) is used to direct the number to the complex package. Once within the complex package, the next tag (`rectangular`) is used to direct the number to the rectangular package. In a large and complicated system there might be many levels, each interfaced with the next by means of generic operations. As a data object is passed "downward," the outer tag that is used to direct it to the appropriate package is stripped off (by applying `contents`) and the next level of tag (if any) becomes visible to be used for further dispatching.

In the above packages, we used `add-rat`, `add-complex`, and the other arithmetic procedures exactly as originally written. Once these definitions are internal to different installation procedures, however, they no longer need names that are distinct from each other: we could simply name them `add`, `sub`, `mul`, and `div` in both packages.

Exercise 2.77

Louis Reasoner tries to evaluate the expression (`magnitude z`) where z is the object shown in figure 2.24. To his surprise, instead of the answer 5 he gets an error message from `apply-generic`, saying there is no method for the operation `magnitude` on the types (`complex`). He shows this interaction to Alyssa P. Hacker, who says "The problem is that the complex-number selectors were never

defined for `complex` numbers, just for `polar` and `rectangular` numbers. All
you have to do to make this work is add the following to the `complex` package:"

```
(put 'real-part '(complex) real-part)
(put 'imag-part '(complex) imag-part)
(put 'magnitude '(complex) magnitude)
(put 'angle '(complex) angle)
```

Describe in detail why this works. As an example, trace through all the procedures called in evaluating the expression (`magnitude z`) where z is the object
shown in figure 2.24. In particular, how many times is `apply-generic` invoked? What procedure is dispatched to in each case?

Exercise 2.78

The internal procedures in the `scheme-number` package are essentially nothing
more than calls to the primitive procedures +, -, etc. It was not possible to use
the primitives of the language directly because our type-tag system requires that
each data object have a type attached to it. In fact, however, all Lisp implementations do have a type system, which they use internally. Primitive predicates
such as `symbol?` and `number?` determine whether data objects have particular
types. Modify the definitions of `type-tag`, `contents`, and `attach-tag` from
section 2.4.2 so that our generic system takes advantage of Scheme's internal
type system. That is to say, the system should work as before except that ordinary numbers should be represented simply as Scheme numbers rather than as
pairs whose `car` is the symbol `scheme-number`.

Exercise 2.79

Define a generic equality predicate `equ?` that tests the equality of two numbers,
and install it in the generic arithmetic package. This operation should work for
ordinary numbers, rational numbers, and complex numbers.

Exercise 2.80

Define a generic predicate `=zero?` that tests if its argument is zero, and install
it in the generic arithmetic package. This operation should work for ordinary
numbers, rational numbers, and complex numbers.

2.5.2   Combining Data of Different Types

We have seen how to define a unified arithmetic system that encompasses
ordinary numbers, complex numbers, rational numbers, and any other
type of number we might decide to invent, but we have ignored an important issue. The operations we have defined so far treat the different
data types as being completely independent. Thus, there are separate
packages for adding, say, two ordinary numbers, or two complex numbers. What we have not yet considered is the fact that it is meaningful to
define operations that cross the type boundaries, such as the addition of

a complex number to an ordinary number. We have gone to great pains to introduce barriers between parts of our programs so that they can be developed and understood separately. We would like to introduce the cross-type operations in some carefully controlled way, so that we can support them without seriously violating our module boundaries.

One way to handle cross-type operations is to design a different procedure for each possible combination of types for which the operation is valid. For example, we could extend the complex-number package so that it provides a procedure for adding complex numbers to ordinary numbers and installs this in the table using the tag (complex scheme-number):[49]

```
;; to be included in the complex package
(define (add-complex-to-schemenum z x)
  (make-from-real-imag (+ (real-part z) x)
                       (imag-part z)))

(put 'add '(complex scheme-number)
     (lambda (z x) (tag (add-complex-to-schemenum z x))))
```

This technique works, but it is cumbersome. With such a system, the cost of introducing a new type is not just the construction of the package of procedures for that type but also the construction and installation of the procedures that implement the cross-type operations. This can easily be much more code than is needed to define the operations on the type itself. The method also undermines our ability to combine separate packages additively, or least to limit the extent to which the implementors of the individual packages need to take account of other packages. For instance, in the example above, it seems reasonable that handling mixed operations on complex numbers and ordinary numbers should be the responsibility of the complex-number package. Combining rational numbers and complex numbers, however, might be done by the complex package, by the rational package, or by some third package that uses operations extracted from these two packages. Formulating coherent policies on the division of responsibility among packages can be an overwhelming task in designing systems with many packages and many cross-type operations.

---

[49]We also have to supply an almost identical procedure to handle the types (scheme-number complex).

Coercion

In the general situation of completely unrelated operations acting on completely unrelated types, implementing explicit cross-type operations, cumbersome though it may be, is the best that one can hope for. Fortunately, we can usually do better by taking advantage of additional structure that may be latent in our type system. Often the different data types are not completely independent, and there may be ways by which objects of one type may be viewed as being of another type. This process is called *coercion*. For example, if we are asked to arithmetically combine an ordinary number with a complex number, we can view the ordinary number as a complex number whose imaginary part is zero. This transforms the problem to that of combining two complex numbers, which can be handled in the ordinary way by the complex-arithmetic package.

In general, we can implement this idea by designing coercion procedures that transform an object of one type into an equivalent object of another type. Here is a typical coercion procedure, which transforms a given ordinary number to a complex number with that real part and zero imaginary part:

```
(define (scheme-number->complex n)
  (make-complex-from-real-imag (contents n) 0))
```

We install these coercion procedures in a special coercion table, indexed under the names of the two types:

```
(put-coercion 'scheme-number 'complex scheme-number->complex)
```

(We assume that there are `put-coercion` and `get-coercion` procedures available for manipulating this table.) Generally some of the slots in the table will be empty, because it is not generally possible to coerce an arbitrary data object of each type into all other types. For example, there is no way to coerce an arbitrary complex number to an ordinary number, so there will be no general `complex->scheme-number` procedure included in the table.

Once the coercion table has been set up, we can handle coercion in a uniform manner by modifying the `apply-generic` procedure of section 2.4.3. When asked to apply an operation, we first check whether the operation is defined for the arguments' types, just as before. If so, we dispatch to the procedure found in the operation-and-type table. Otherwise, we try coercion. For simplicity, we consider only the case where

there are two arguments.[50] We check the coercion table to see if objects
of the first type can be coerced to the second type. If so, we coerce the
first argument and try the operation again. If objects of the first type
cannot in general be coerced to the second type, we try the coercion the
other way around to see if there is a way to coerce the second argument
to the type of the first argument. Finally, if there is no known way to
coerce either type to the other type, we give up. Here is the procedure:

```
(define (apply-generic op . args)
  (let ((type-tags (map type-tag args)))
    (let ((proc (get op type-tags)))
      (if proc
          (apply proc (map contents args))
          (if (= (length args) 2)
              (let ((type1 (car type-tags))
                    (type2 (cadr type-tags))
                    (a1 (car args))
                    (a2 (cadr args)))
                (let ((t1->t2 (get-coercion type1 type2))
                      (t2->t1 (get-coercion type2 type1)))
                  (cond (t1->t2
                         (apply-generic op (t1->t2 a1) a2))
                        (t2->t1
                         (apply-generic op a1 (t2->t1 a2)))
                        (else
                         (error "No method for these types"
                                (list op type-tags))))))
              (error "No method for these types"
                     (list op type-tags)))))))
```

    This coercion scheme has many advantages over the method of defin-
ing explicit cross-type operations, as outlined above. Although we still
need to write coercion procedures to relate the types (possibly n^2 procedures for a system with n types), we need to write only one procedure for
each pair of types rather than a different procedure for each collection of
types and each generic operation.[51] What we are counting on here is the

---

[50] See exercise 2.82 for generalizations.

[51] If we are clever, we can usually get by with fewer than n^2 coercion procedures. For
instance, if we know how to convert from type 1 to type 2 and from type 2 to type 3, then
we can use this knowledge to convert from type 1 to type 3. This can greatly decrease the
number of coercion procedures we need to supply explicitly when we add a new type to the
system. If we are willing to build the required amount of sophistication into our system,
we can have it search the "graph" of relations among types and automatically generate
those coercion procedures that can be inferred from the ones that are supplied explicitly.

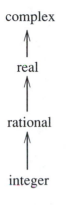

Figure 2.25   A tower of types.

fact that the appropriate transformation between types depends only on the types themselves, not on the operation to be applied.

On the other hand, there may be applications for which our coercion scheme is not general enough. Even when neither of the objects to be combined can be converted to the type of the other it may still be possible to perform the operation by converting both objects to a third type. In order to deal with such complexity and still preserve modularity in our programs, it is usually necessary to build systems that take advantage of still further structure in the relations among types, as we discuss next.

Hierarchies of types

The coercion scheme presented above relied on the existence of natural relations between pairs of types. Often there is more "global" structure in how the different types relate to each other. For instance, suppose we are building a generic arithmetic system to handle integers, rational numbers, real numbers, and complex numbers. In such a system, it is quite natural to regard an integer as a special kind of rational number, which is in turn a special kind of real number, which is in turn a special kind of complex number. What we actually have is a so-called *hierarchy of types*, in which, for example, integers are a *subtype* of rational numbers (i.e., any operation that can be applied to a rational number can automatically be applied to an integer). Conversely, we say that rational numbers form a *supertype* of integers. The particular hierarchy we have here is of a very simple kind, in which each type has at most one supertype and at most one subtype. Such a structure, called a *tower*, is illustrated in figure 2.25.

If we have a tower structure, then we can greatly simplify the problem of adding a new type to the hierarchy, for we need only specify how the new type is embedded in the next supertype above it and how it is the supertype of the type below it. For example, if we want to add an integer to a complex number, we need not explicitly define a special coercion procedure `integer->complex`. Instead, we define how an integer can be transformed into a rational number, how a rational number is transformed into a real number, and how a real number is transformed into a complex number. We then allow the system to transform the integer into a complex number through these steps and then add the two complex numbers.

We can redesign our `apply-generic` procedure in the following way: For each type, we need to supply a `raise` procedure, which "raises" objects of that type one level in the tower. Then when the system is required to operate on objects of different types it can successively raise the lower types until all the objects are at the same level in the tower. (Exercises 2.83 and 2.84 concern the details of implementing such a strategy.)

Another advantage of a tower is that we can easily implement the notion that every type "inherits" all operations defined on a supertype. For instance, if we do not supply a special procedure for finding the real part of an integer, we should nevertheless expect that `real-part` will be defined for integers by virtue of the fact that integers are a subtype of complex numbers. In a tower, we can arrange for this to happen in a uniform way by modifying `apply-generic`. If the required operation is not directly defined for the type of the object given, we raise the object to its supertype and try again. We thus crawl up the tower, transforming our argument as we go, until we either find a level at which the desired operation can be performed or hit the top (in which case we give up).

Yet another advantage of a tower over a more general hierarchy is that it gives us a simple way to "lower" a data object to the simplest representation. For example, if we add $2 + 3i$ to $4 - 3i$, it would be nice to obtain the answer as the integer 6 rather than as the complex number $6 + 0i$. Exercise 2.85 discusses a way to implement such a lowering operation. (The trick is that we need a general way to distinguish those objects that can be lowered, such as $6 + 0i$, from those that cannot, such as $6 + 2i$.)

Inadequacies of hierarchies

If the data types in our system can be naturally arranged in a tower, this greatly simplifies the problems of dealing with generic operations on different types, as we have seen. Unfortunately, this is usually not the case.

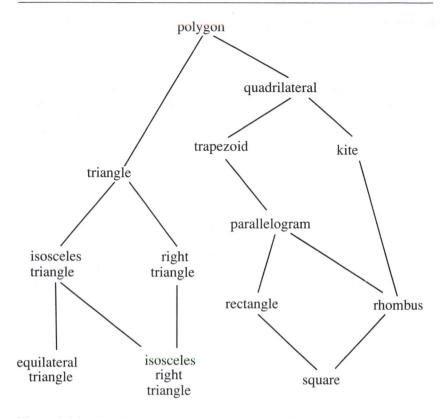

Figure 2.26   Relations among types of geometric figures.

Figure 2.26 illustrates a more complex arrangement of mixed types, this one showing relations among different types of geometric figures. We see that, in general, a type may have more than one subtype. Triangles and quadrilaterals, for instance, are both subtypes of polygons. In addition, a type may have more than one supertype. For example, an isosceles right triangle may be regarded either as an isosceles triangle or as a right triangle. This multiple-supertypes issue is particularly thorny, since it means that there is no unique way to "raise" a type in the hierarchy. Finding the "correct" supertype in which to apply an operation to an object may involve considerable searching through the entire type network on the part of a procedure such as `apply-generic`. Since there generally are multiple subtypes for a type, there is a similar problem in coercing a value "down" the type hierarchy. Dealing with large numbers of interrelated types while still preserving modularity in the design of large systems is very difficult, and is an area of much current research.[52]

Exercise 2.81

Louis Reasoner has noticed that `apply-generic` may try to coerce the arguments to each other's type even if they already have the same type. Therefore, he reasons, we need to put procedures in the coercion table to "coerce" arguments of each type to their own type. For example, in addition to the `scheme-number->complex` coercion shown above, he would do:

```
(define (scheme-number->scheme-number n) n)
(define (complex->complex z) z)
(put-coercion 'scheme-number 'scheme-number
              scheme-number->scheme-number)
(put-coercion 'complex 'complex complex->complex)
```

a. With Louis's coercion procedures installed, what happens if `apply-generic` is called with two arguments of type `scheme-number` or two arguments of type `complex` for an operation that is not found in the table for those types? For example, assume that we've defined a generic exponentiation operation:

```
(define (exp x y) (apply-generic 'exp x y))
```

and have put a procedure for exponentiation in the Scheme-number package but not in any other package:

```
;; following added to Scheme-number package
(put 'exp '(scheme-number scheme-number)
     (lambda (x y) (tag (expt x y))))  ; using primitive expt
```

What happens if we call `exp` with two complex numbers as arguments?

b. Is Louis correct that something had to be done about coercion with arguments of the same type, or does `apply-generic` work correctly as is?

c. Modify `apply-generic` so that it doesn't try coercion if the two arguments have the same type.

---

[52]This statement, which also appears in the first edition of this book, is just as true now as it was when we wrote it twelve years ago. Developing a useful, general framework for expressing the relations among different types of entities (what philosophers call "ontology") seems intractably difficult. The main difference between the confusion that existed ten years ago and the confusion that exists now is that now a variety of inadequate ontological theories have been embodied in a plethora of correspondingly inadequate programming languages. For example, much of the complexity of object-oriented programming languages—and the subtle and confusing differences among contemporary object-oriented languages—centers on the treatment of generic operations on interrelated types. Our own discussion of computational objects in chapter 3 avoids these issues entirely. Readers familiar with object-oriented programming will notice that we have much to say in chapter 3 about local state, but we do not even mention "classes" or "inheritance." In fact, we suspect that these problems cannot be adequately addressed in terms of computer-language design alone, without also drawing on work in knowledge representation and automated reasoning.

Exercise 2.82

Show how to generalize `apply-generic` to handle coercion in the general case of multiple arguments. One strategy is to attempt to coerce all the arguments to the type of the first argument, then to the type of the second argument, and so on. Give an example of a situation where this strategy (and likewise the two-argument version given above) is not sufficiently general. (Hint: Consider the case where there are some suitable mixed-type operations present in the table that will not be tried.)

Exercise 2.83

Suppose you are designing a generic arithmetic system for dealing with the tower of types shown in figure 2.25: integer, rational, real, complex. For each type (except complex), design a procedure that raises objects of that type one level in the tower. Show how to install a generic `raise` operation that will work for each type (except complex).

Exercise 2.84

Using the `raise` operation of exercise 2.83, modify the `apply-generic` procedure so that it coerces its arguments to have the same type by the method of successive raising, as discussed in this section. You will need to devise a way to test which of two types is higher in the tower. Do this in a manner that is "compatible" with the rest of the system and will not lead to problems in adding new levels to the tower.

Exercise 2.85

This section mentioned a method for "simplifying" a data object by lowering it in the tower of types as far as possible. Design a procedure `drop` that accomplishes this for the tower described in exercise 2.83. The key is to decide, in some general way, whether an object can be lowered. For example, the complex number $1.5 + 0i$ can be lowered as far as `real`, the complex number $1 + 0i$ can be lowered as far as `integer`, and the complex number $2 + 3i$ cannot be lowered at all. Here is a plan for determining whether an object can be lowered: Begin by defining a generic operation `project` that "pushes" an object down in the tower. For example, projecting a complex number would involve throwing away the imaginary part. Then a number can be dropped if, when we `project` it and `raise` the result back to the type we started with, we end up with something equal to what we started with. Show how to implement this idea in detail, by writing a `drop` procedure that drops an object as far as possible. You will need to design the various projection operations[53] and install `project` as a generic operation in the system. You will also need to make use of a generic equality predicate, such as described in exercise 2.79. Finally, use `drop` to rewrite `apply-generic` from exercise 2.84 so that it "simplifies" its answers.

---

[53] A real number can be projected to an integer using the `round` primitive, which returns the closest integer to its argument.

Exercise 2.86

Suppose we want to handle complex numbers whose real parts, imaginary parts, magnitudes, and angles can be either ordinary numbers, rational numbers, or other numbers we might wish to add to the system. Describe and implement the changes to the system needed to accommodate this. You will have to define operations such as `sine` and `cosine` that are generic over ordinary numbers and rational numbers.

2.5.3   Example: Symbolic Algebra

The manipulation of symbolic algebraic expressions is a complex process that illustrates many of the hardest problems that occur in the design of large-scale systems. An algebraic expression, in general, can be viewed as a hierarchical structure, a tree of operators applied to operands. We can construct algebraic expressions by starting with a set of primitive objects, such as constants and variables, and combining these by means of algebraic operators, such as addition and multiplication. As in other languages, we form abstractions that enable us to refer to compound objects in simple terms. Typical abstractions in symbolic algebra are ideas such as linear combination, polynomial, rational function, or trigonometric function. We can regard these as compound "types," which are often useful for directing the processing of expressions. For example, we could describe the expression

$$x^2 \sin(y^2 + 1) + x \, \cos 2y + \cos(y^3 - 2y^2)$$

as a polynomial in x with coefficients that are trigonometric functions of polynomials in y whose coefficients are integers.

We will not attempt to develop a complete algebraic-manipulation system here. Such systems are exceedingly complex programs, embodying deep algebraic knowledge and elegant algorithms. What we will do is look at a simple but important part of algebraic manipulation: the arithmetic of polynomials. We will illustrate the kinds of decisions the designer of such a system faces, and how to apply the ideas of abstract data and generic operations to help organize this effort.

Arithmetic on polynomials

Our first task in designing a system for performing arithmetic on polynomials is to decide just what a polynomial is. Polynomials are normally defined relative to certain variables (the *indeterminates* of the polynomial). For simplicity, we will restrict ourselves to polynomials having just one indeterminate (*univariate polynomials*).[54] We will define a polynomial to be a sum of terms, each of which is either a coefficient, a power of the indeterminate, or a product of a coefficient and a power of the indeterminate. A coefficient is defined as an algebraic expression that is not dependent upon the indeterminate of the polynomial. For example,

$$5x^2 + 3x + 7$$

is a simple polynomial in x, and

$$(y^2 + 1)x^3 + (2y)x + 1$$

is a polynomial in x whose coefficients are polynomials in y.

Already we are skirting some thorny issues. Is the first of these polynomials the same as the polynomial $5y^2 + 3y + 7$, or not? A reasonable answer might be "yes, if we are considering a polynomial purely as a mathematical function, but no, if we are considering a polynomial to be a syntactic form." The second polynomial is algebraically equivalent to a polynomial in y whose coefficients are polynomials in x. Should our system recognize this, or not? Furthermore, there are other ways to represent a polynomial—for example, as a product of factors, or (for a univariate polynomial) as the set of roots, or as a listing of the values of the polynomial at a specified set of points.[55] We can finesse these questions by deciding that in our algebraic-manipulation system a "polynomial" will be a particular syntactic form, not its underlying mathematical meaning.

Now we must consider how to go about doing arithmetic on polynomials. In this simple system, we will consider only addition and multiplication. Moreover, we will insist that two polynomials to be combined must have the same indeterminate.

We will approach the design of our system by following the familiar discipline of data abstraction. We will represent polynomials using a data

---

[54]On the other hand, we will allow polynomials whose coefficients are themselves polynomials in other variables. This will give us essentially the same representational power as a full multivariate system, although it does lead to coercion problems, as discussed below.

[55]For univariate polynomials, giving the value of a polynomial at a given set of points can be a particularly good representation. This makes polynomial arithmetic extremely simple. To obtain, for example, the sum of two polynomials represented in this way, we need only add the values of the polynomials at corresponding points. To transform back to a more familiar representation, we can use the Lagrange interpolation formula, which shows how to recover the coefficients of a polynomial of degree n given the values of the polynomial at $n + 1$ points.

structure called a *poly*, which consists of a variable and a collection of terms. We assume that we have selectors variable and term-list that extract those parts from a poly and a constructor make-poly that assembles a poly from a given variable and a term list. A variable will be just a symbol, so we can use the same-variable? procedure of section 2.3.2 to compare variables. The following procedures define addition and multiplication of polys:

```
(define (add-poly p1 p2)
  (if (same-variable? (variable p1) (variable p2))
      (make-poly (variable p1)
                 (add-terms (term-list p1)
                            (term-list p2)))
      (error "Polys not in same var -- ADD-POLY"
             (list p1 p2))))

(define (mul-poly p1 p2)
  (if (same-variable? (variable p1) (variable p2))
      (make-poly (variable p1)
                 (mul-terms (term-list p1)
                            (term-list p2)))
      (error "Polys not in same var -- MUL-POLY"
             (list p1 p2))))
```

To incorporate polynomials into our generic arithmetic system, we need to supply them with type tags. We'll use the tag polynomial, and install appropriate operations on tagged polynomials in the operation table. We'll embed all our code in an installation procedure for the polynomial package, similar to the ones in section 2.5.1:

```
(define (install-polynomial-package)
  ;; internal procedures
  ;; representation of poly
  (define (make-poly variable term-list)
    (cons variable term-list))
  (define (variable p) (car p))
  (define (term-list p) (cdr p))
  ⟨procedures same-variable? and variable? from section 2.3.2⟩

  ;; representation of terms and term lists
  ⟨procedures adjoin-term ... coeff from text below⟩

  ;; continued on next page
```

```
(define (add-poly p1 p2) ...)
⟨procedures used by add-poly⟩
(define (mul-poly p1 p2) ...)
⟨procedures used by mul-poly⟩

;; interface to rest of the system
(define (tag p) (attach-tag 'polynomial p))
(put 'add '(polynomial polynomial)
     (lambda (p1 p2) (tag (add-poly p1 p2))))
(put 'mul '(polynomial polynomial)
     (lambda (p1 p2) (tag (mul-poly p1 p2))))
(put 'make 'polynomial
     (lambda (var terms) (tag (make-poly var terms))))
'done)
```

Polynomial addition is performed termwise. Terms of the same order (i.e., with the same power of the indeterminate) must be combined. This is done by forming a new term of the same order whose coefficient is the sum of the coefficients of the addends. Terms in one addend for which there are no terms of the same order in the other addend are simply accumulated into the sum polynomial being constructed.

In order to manipulate term lists, we will assume that we have a constructor `the-empty-termlist` that returns an empty term list and a constructor `adjoin-term` that adjoins a new term to a term list. We will also assume that we have a predicate `empty-termlist?` that tells if a given term list is empty, a selector `first-term` that extracts the highest-order term from a term list, and a selector `rest-terms` that returns all but the highest-order term. To manipulate terms, we will suppose that we have a constructor `make-term` that constructs a term with given order and coefficient, and selectors `order` and `coeff` that return, respectively, the order and the coefficient of the term. These operations allow us to consider both terms and term lists as data abstractions, whose concrete representations we can worry about separately.

Here is the procedure that constructs the term list for the sum of two polynomials:[56]

---

[56]This operation is very much like the ordered `union-set` operation we developed in exercise 2.62. In fact, if we think of the terms of the polynomial as a set ordered according to the power of the indeterminate, then the program that produces the term list for a sum is almost identical to `union-set`.

```
(define (add-terms L1 L2)
  (cond ((empty-termlist? L1) L2)
        ((empty-termlist? L2) L1)
        (else
         (let ((t1 (first-term L1)) (t2 (first-term L2)))
           (cond ((> (order t1) (order t2))
                  (adjoin-term
                   t1 (add-terms (rest-terms L1) L2)))
                 ((< (order t1) (order t2))
                  (adjoin-term
                   t2 (add-terms L1 (rest-terms L2))))
                 (else
                  (adjoin-term
                   (make-term (order t1)
                              (add (coeff t1) (coeff t2)))
                   (add-terms (rest-terms L1)
                              (rest-terms L2)))))))))
```

The most important point to note here is that we used the generic addition procedure add to add together the coefficients of the terms being combined. This has powerful consequences, as we will see below.

In order to multiply two term lists, we multiply each term of the first list by all the terms of the other list, repeatedly using mul-term-by-all-terms, which multiplies a given term by all terms in a given term list. The resulting term lists (one for each term of the first list) are accumulated into a sum. Multiplying two terms forms a term whose order is the sum of the orders of the factors and whose coefficient is the product of the coefficients of the factors:

```
(define (mul-terms L1 L2)
  (if (empty-termlist? L1)
      (the-empty-termlist)
      (add-terms (mul-term-by-all-terms (first-term L1) L2)
                 (mul-terms (rest-terms L1) L2))))

(define (mul-term-by-all-terms t1 L)
  (if (empty-termlist? L)
      (the-empty-termlist)
      (let ((t2 (first-term L)))
        (adjoin-term
         (make-term (+ (order t1) (order t2))
                    (mul (coeff t1) (coeff t2)))
         (mul-term-by-all-terms t1 (rest-terms L))))))
```

This is really all there is to polynomial addition and multiplication. Notice that, since we operate on terms using the generic procedures add and `mul`, our polynomial package is automatically able to handle any type of coefficient that is known about by the generic arithmetic package. If we include a coercion mechanism such as one of those discussed in section 2.5.2, then we also are automatically able to handle operations on polynomials of different coefficient types, such as

$$\left[3x^2 + (2 + 3i)x + 7\right] \cdot \left[x^4 + \frac{2}{3}x^2 + (5 + 3i)\right]$$

Because we installed the polynomial addition and multiplication procedures `add-poly` and `mul-poly` in the generic arithmetic system as the add and mul operations for type `polynomial`, our system is also automatically able to handle polynomial operations such as

$$\left[(y + 1)x^2 + (y^2 + 1)x + (y - 1)\right] \cdot \left[(y - 2)x + (y^3 + 7)\right]$$

The reason is that when the system tries to combine coefficients, it will dispatch through add and mul. Since the coefficients are themselves polynomials (in y), these will be combined using `add-poly` and `mul-poly`. The result is a kind of "data-directed recursion" in which, for example, a call to `mul-poly` will result in recursive calls to `mul-poly` in order to multiply the coefficients. If the coefficients of the coefficients were themselves polynomials (as might be used to represent polynomials in three variables), the data direction would ensure that the system would follow through another level of recursive calls, and so on through as many levels as the structure of the data dictates.[57]

Representing term lists

Finally, we must confront the job of implementing a good representation for term lists. A term list is, in effect, a set of coefficients keyed by the order of the term. Hence, any of the methods for representing sets, as discussed in section 2.3.3, can be applied to this task. On the other hand, our procedures `add-terms` and `mul-terms` always access term lists sequentially from highest to lowest order. Thus, we will use some kind of ordered list representation.

---

[57]To make this work completely smoothly, we should also add to our generic arithmetic system the ability to coerce a "number" to a polynomial by regarding it as a polynomial of degree zero whose coefficient is the number. This is necessary if we are going to perform operations such as

$$\left[x^2 + (y + 1)x + 5\right] + \left[x^2 + 2x + 1\right]$$

which requires adding the coefficient $y + 1$ to the coefficient 2.

How should we structure the list that represents a term list? One consideration is the "density" of the polynomials we intend to manipulate. A polynomial is said to be *dense* if it has nonzero coefficients in terms of most orders. If it has many zero terms it is said to be *sparse*. For example,

$$A : \quad x^5 + 2x^4 + 3x^2 - 2x - 5$$

is a dense polynomial, whereas

$$B : \quad x^{100} + 2x^2 + 1$$

is sparse.

The term lists of dense polynomials are most efficiently represented as lists of the coefficients. For example, A above would be nicely represented as (1 2 0 3 -2 -5). The order of a term in this representation is the length of the sublist beginning with that term's coefficient, decremented by 1.[58] This would be a terrible representation for a sparse polynomial such as B: There would be a giant list of zeros punctuated by a few lonely nonzero terms. A more reasonable representation of the term list of a sparse polynomial is as a list of the nonzero terms, where each term is a list containing the order of the term and the coefficient for that order. In such a scheme, polynomial B is efficiently represented as ((100 1) (2 2) (0 1)). As most polynomial manipulations are performed on sparse polynomials, we will use this method. We will assume that term lists are represented as lists of terms, arranged from highest-order to lowest-order term. Once we have made this decision, implementing the selectors and constructors for terms and term lists is straightforward:[59]

---

[58] In these polynomial examples, we assume that we have implemented the generic arithmetic system using the type mechanism suggested in exercise 2.78. Thus, coefficients that are ordinary numbers will be represented as the numbers themselves rather than as pairs whose car is the symbol scheme-number.

[59] Although we are assuming that term lists are ordered, we have implemented adjoin-term to simply cons the new term onto the existing term list. We can get away with this so long as we guarantee that the procedures (such as add-terms) that use adjoin-term always call it with a higher-order term than appears in the list. If we did not want to make such a guarantee, we could have implemented adjoin-term to be similar to the adjoin-set constructor for the ordered-list representation of sets (exercise 2.61).

```
(define (adjoin-term term term-list)
  (if (=zero? (coeff term))
      term-list
      (cons term term-list)))

(define (the-empty-termlist) '())
(define (first-term term-list) (car term-list))
(define (rest-terms term-list) (cdr term-list))
(define (empty-termlist? term-list) (null? term-list))

(define (make-term order coeff) (list order coeff))
(define (order term) (car term))
(define (coeff term) (cadr term))
```

where =zero? is as defined in exercise 2.80. (See also exercise 2.87 below.)

Users of the polynomial package will create (tagged) polynomials by means of the procedure:

```
(define (make-polynomial var terms)
  ((get 'make 'polynomial) var terms))
```

Exercise 2.87

Install =zero? for polynomials in the generic arithmetic package. This will allow adjoin-term to work for polynomials with coefficients that are themselves polynomials.

Exercise 2.88

Extend the polynomial system to include subtraction of polynomials. (Hint: You may find it helpful to define a generic negation operation.)

Exercise 2.89

Define procedures that implement the term-list representation described above as appropriate for dense polynomials.

Exercise 2.90

Suppose we want to have a polynomial system that is efficient for both sparse and dense polynomials. One way to do this is to allow both kinds of term-list representations in our system. The situation is analogous to the complex-number example of section 2.4, where we allowed both rectangular and polar representations. To do this we must distinguish different types of term lists and make the operations on term lists generic. Redesign the polynomial system to implement this generalization. This is a major effort, not a local change.

Exercise 2.91

A univariate polynomial can be divided by another one to produce a polynomial quotient and a polynomial remainder. For example,

$$\frac{x^5 - 1}{x^2 - 1} = x^3 + x, \text{ remainder } x - 1$$

Division can be performed via long division. That is, divide the highest-order term of the dividend by the highest-order term of the divisor. The result is the first term of the quotient. Next, multiply the result by the divisor, subtract that from the dividend, and produce the rest of the answer by recursively dividing the difference by the divisor. Stop when the order of the divisor exceeds the order of the dividend and declare the dividend to be the remainder. Also, if the dividend ever becomes zero, return zero as both quotient and remainder.

We can design a `div-poly` procedure on the model of `add-poly` and `mul-poly`. The procedure checks to see if the two polys have the same variable. If so, `div-poly` strips off the variable and passes the problem to `div-terms`, which performs the division operation on term lists. Div-poly finally reattaches the variable to the result supplied by `div-terms`. It is convenient to design `div-terms` to compute both the quotient and the remainder of a division. Div-terms can take two term lists as arguments and return a list of the quotient term list and the remainder term list.

Complete the following definition of `div-terms` by filling in the missing expressions. Use this to implement `div-poly`, which takes two polys as arguments and returns a list of the quotient and remainder polys.

```
(define (div-terms L1 L2)
  (if (empty-termlist? L1)
      (list (the-empty-termlist) (the-empty-termlist))
      (let ((t1 (first-term L1))
            (t2 (first-term L2)))
        (if (> (order t2) (order t1))
            (list (the-empty-termlist) L1)
            (let ((new-c (div (coeff t1) (coeff t2)))
                  (new-o (- (order t1) (order t2))))
              (let ((rest-of-result
                     ⟨compute rest of result recursively⟩
                     ))
                ⟨form complete result⟩
                ))))))
```

Hierarchies of types in symbolic algebra

Our polynomial system illustrates how objects of one type (polynomials) may in fact be complex objects that have objects of many different types as parts. This poses no real difficulty in defining generic operations. We need only install appropriate generic operations for performing the necessary manipulations of the parts of the compound types. In fact, we saw that polynomials form a kind of "recursive data abstraction," in that parts of a polynomial may themselves be polynomials. Our generic operations and our data-directed programming style can handle this complication without much trouble.

On the other hand, polynomial algebra is a system for which the data types cannot be naturally arranged in a tower. For instance, it is possible to have polynomials in x whose coefficients are polynomials in y. It is also possible to have polynomials in y whose coefficients are polynomials in x. Neither of these types is "above" the other in any natural way, yet it is often necessary to add together elements from each set. There are several ways to do this. One possibility is to convert one polynomial to the type of the other by expanding and rearranging terms so that both polynomials have the same principal variable. One can impose a tower-like structure on this by ordering the variables and thus always converting any polynomial to a "canonical form" with the highest-priority variable dominant and the lower-priority variables buried in the coefficients. This strategy works fairly well, except that the conversion may expand a polynomial unnecessarily, making it hard to read and perhaps less efficient to work with. The tower strategy is certainly not natural for this domain or for any domain where the user can invent new types dynamically using old types in various combining forms, such as trigonometric functions, power series, and integrals.

It should not be surprising that controlling coercion is a serious problem in the design of large-scale algebraic-manipulation systems. Much of the complexity of such systems is concerned with relationships among diverse types. Indeed, it is fair to say that we do not yet completely understand coercion. In fact, we do not yet completely understand the concept of a data type. Nevertheless, what we know provides us with powerful structuring and modularity principles to support the design of large systems.

Exercise 2.92

By imposing an ordering on variables, extend the polynomial package so that addition and multiplication of polynomials works for polynomials in different variables. (This is not easy!)

Extended exercise: Rational functions

We can extend our generic arithmetic system to include *rational functions*. These are "fractions" whose numerator and denominator are polynomials, such as

$$\frac{x + 1}{x^3 - 1}$$

The system should be able to add, subtract, multiply, and divide rational functions, and to perform such computations as

$$\frac{x+1}{x^3-1} + \frac{x}{x^2-1} = \frac{x^3+2x^2+3x+1}{x^4+x^3-x-1}$$

(Here the sum has been simplified by removing common factors. Ordinary "cross multiplication" would have produced a fourth-degree polynomial over a fifth-degree polynomial.)

If we modify our rational-arithmetic package so that it uses generic operations, then it will do what we want, except for the problem of reducing fractions to lowest terms.

Exercise 2.93

Modify the rational-arithmetic package to use generic operations, but change make-rat so that it does not attempt to reduce fractions to lowest terms. Test your system by calling make-rational on two polynomials to produce a rational function

```
(define p1 (make-polynomial 'x '((2 1)(0 1))))
(define p2 (make-polynomial 'x '((3 1)(0 1))))
(define rf (make-rational p2 p1))
```

Now add rf to itself, using add. You will observe that this addition procedure does not reduce fractions to lowest terms.

We can reduce polynomial fractions to lowest terms using the same idea we used with integers: modifying make-rat to divide both the numerator and the denominator by their greatest common divisor. The notion of "greatest common divisor" makes sense for polynomials. In fact, we can compute the GCD of two polynomials using essentially the same Euclid's Algorithm that works for integers.[60] The integer version is

```
(define (gcd a b)
  (if (= b 0)
      a
      (gcd b (remainder a b)))))
```

---

[60]The fact that Euclid's Algorithm works for polynomials is formalized in algebra by saying that polynomials form a kind of algebraic domain called a *Euclidean ring*. A Euclidean ring is a domain that admits addition, subtraction, and commutative multiplication, together with a way of assigning to each element x of the ring a positive integer "measure" $m(x)$ with the properties that $m(xy) \geq m(x)$ for any nonzero x and y and that, given any x and y, there exists a q such that $y = qx + r$ and either $r = 0$ or $m(r) < m(x)$. From an abstract point of view, this is what is needed to prove that Euclid's Algorithm works. For the domain of integers, the measure m of an integer is the absolute value of the integer itself. For the domain of polynomials, the measure of a polynomial is its degree.

Using this, we could make the obvious modification to define a GCD
operation that works on term lists:

```
(define (gcd-terms a b)
  (if (empty-termlist? b)
      a
      (gcd-terms b (remainder-terms a b))))
```

where `remainder-terms` picks out the remainder component of the list
returned by the term-list division operation `div-terms` that was implemented in exercise 2.91.

Exercise 2.94

Using `div-terms`, implement the procedure `remainder-terms` and use this to
define `gcd-terms` as above. Now write a procedure `gcd-poly` that computes
the polynomial GCD of two polys. (The procedure should signal an error if the
two polys are not in the same variable.) Install in the system a generic operation
`greatest-common-divisor` that reduces to `gcd-poly` for polynomials and to
ordinary gcd for ordinary numbers. As a test, try

```
(define p1 (make-polynomial 'x '((4 1) (3 -1) (2 -2) (1 2))))
(define p2 (make-polynomial 'x '((3 1) (1 -1))))
(greatest-common-divisor p1 p2)
```

and check your result by hand.

Exercise 2.95

Define P_1, P_2, and P_3 to be the polynomials

$P_1:$ $x^2 - 2x + 1$

$P_2:$ $11x^2 + 7$

$P_3:$ $13x + 5$

Now define Q_1 to be the product of P_1 and P_2 and Q_2 to be the product of P_1
and P_3, and use `greatest-common-divisor` (exercise 2.94) to compute the
GCD of Q_1 and Q_2. Note that the answer is not the same as P_1. This example
introduces noninteger operations into the computation, causing difficulties with
the GCD algorithm.[61] To understand what is happening, try tracing `gcd-terms`
while computing the GCD or try performing the division by hand.

---

[61] In an implementation like MIT Scheme, this produces a polynomial that is indeed a
divisor of Q_1 and Q_2, but with rational coefficients. In many other Scheme systems, in
which division of integers can produce limited-precision decimal numbers, we may fail to
get a valid divisor.

We can solve the problem exhibited in exercise 2.95 if we use the following modification of the GCD algorithm (which really works only in the case of polynomials with integer coefficients). Before performing any polynomial division in the GCD computation, we multiply the dividend by an integer constant factor, chosen to guarantee that no fractions will arise during the division process. Our answer will thus differ from the actual GCD by an integer constant factor, but this does not matter in the case of reducing rational functions to lowest terms; the GCD will be used to divide both the numerator and denominator, so the integer constant factor will cancel out.

More precisely, if P and Q are polynomials, let O_1 be the order of P (i.e., the order of the largest term of P) and let O_2 be the order of Q. Let c be the leading coefficient of Q. Then it can be shown that, if we multiply P by the *integerizing factor* $c^{1+O_1-O_2}$, the resulting polynomial can be divided by Q by using the `div-terms` algorithm without introducing any fractions. The operation of multiplying the dividend by this constant and then dividing is sometimes called the *pseudodivision* of P by Q. The remainder of the division is called the *pseudoremainder*.

Exercise 2.96

a.   Implement the procedure `pseudoremainder-terms`, which is just like `remainder-terms` except that it multiplies the dividend by the integerizing factor described above before calling `div-terms`. Modify `gcd-terms` to use `pseudoremainder-terms`, and verify that `greatest-common-divisor` now produces an answer with integer coefficients on the example in exercise 2.95.

b.   The GCD now has integer coefficients, but they are larger than those of P_1. Modify `gcd-terms` so that it removes common factors from the coefficients of the answer by dividing all the coefficients by their (integer) greatest common divisor.

Thus, here is how to reduce a rational function to lowest terms:

• Compute the GCD of the numerator and denominator, using the version of `gcd-terms` from exercise 2.96.

• When you obtain the GCD, multiply both numerator and denominator by the same integerizing factor before dividing through by the GCD, so that division by the GCD will not introduce any noninteger coefficients. As the factor you can use the leading coefficient of the GCD raised to the power $1 + O_1 - O_2$, where O_2 is the order of the GCD and O_1 is the maximum of the orders of the numerator and denominator. This will ensure that dividing the numerator and denominator by the GCD will not introduce any fractions.

• The result of this operation will be a numerator and denominator with integer coefficients. The coefficients will normally be very large because of all of the integerizing factors, so the last step is to remove the redundant factors by computing the (integer) greatest common divisor of all the coefficients of the numerator and the denominator and dividing through by this factor.

Exercise 2.97

a. Implement this algorithm as a procedure `reduce-terms` that takes two term lists n and d as arguments and returns a list nn, dd, which are n and d reduced to lowest terms via the algorithm given above. Also write a procedure `reduce-poly`, analogous to `add-poly`, that checks to see if the two polys have the same variable. If so, `reduce-poly` strips off the variable and passes the problem to `reduce-terms`, then reattaches the variable to the two term lists supplied by `reduce-terms`.

b. Define a procedure analogous to `reduce-terms` that does what the original `make-rat` did for integers:

```
(define (reduce-integers n d)
  (let ((g (gcd n d)))
    (list (/ n g) (/ d g))))
```

and define `reduce` as a generic operation that calls `apply-generic` to dispatch to either `reduce-poly` (for `polynomial` arguments) or `reduce-integers` (for `scheme-number` arguments). You can now easily make the rational-arithmetic package reduce fractions to lowest terms by having `make-rat` call `reduce` before combining the given numerator and denominator to form a rational number. The system now handles rational expressions in either integers or polynomials. To test your program, try the example at the beginning of this extended exercise:

```
(define p1 (make-polynomial 'x '((1 1)(0 1))))
(define p2 (make-polynomial 'x '((3 1)(0 -1))))
(define p3 (make-polynomial 'x '((1 1))))
(define p4 (make-polynomial 'x '((2 1)(0 -1))))

(define rf1 (make-rational p1 p2))
(define rf2 (make-rational p3 p4))

(add rf1 rf2)
```

See if you get the correct answer, correctly reduced to lowest terms.

The GCD computation is at the heart of any system that does operations on rational functions. The algorithm used above, although mathematically straightforward, is extremely slow. The slowness is due partly to the large number of division operations and partly to the enormous size of the intermediate coefficients generated by the pseudodivisions. One of the active areas in the development of algebraic-manipulation systems is the design of better algorithms for computing polynomial GCDs.[62]

---

[62]One extremely efficient and elegant method for computing polynomial GCDs was discovered by Richard Zippel (1979). The method is a probabilistic algorithm, as is the fast test for primality that we discussed in chapter 1. Zippel's book (1993) describes this method, together with other ways to compute polynomial GCDs.

3

Modularity, Objects, and State

Μεταβάλλον ἀναπαύεται
(Even while it changes, it stands still.)

Heraclitus

Plus ça change, plus c'est la même chose.

Alphonse Karr

The preceding chapters introduced the basic elements from which programs are made. We saw how primitive procedures and primitive data are combined to construct compound entities, and we learned that abstraction is vital in helping us to cope with the complexity of large systems. But these tools are not sufficient for designing programs. Effective program synthesis also requires organizational principles that can guide us in formulating the overall design of a program. In particular, we need strategies to help us structure large systems so that they will be *modular*, that is, so that they can be divided "naturally" into coherent parts that can be separately developed and maintained.

One powerful design strategy, which is particularly appropriate to the construction of programs for modeling physical systems, is to base the structure of our programs on the structure of the system being modeled. For each object in the system, we construct a corresponding computational object. For each system action, we define a symbolic operation in our computational model. Our hope in using this strategy is that extending the model to accommodate new objects or new actions will require no strategic changes to the program, only the addition of the new symbolic analogs of those objects or actions. If we have been successful in our system organization, then to add a new feature or debug an old one we will have to work on only a localized part of the system.

To a large extent, then, the way we organize a large program is dictated by our perception of the system to be modeled. In this chapter we will investigate two prominent organizational strategies arising from two rather different "world views" of the structure of systems. The first organizational strategy concentrates on *objects*, viewing a large system as a collection of distinct objects whose behaviors may change over time. An alternative organizational strategy concentrates on the *streams* of information that flow in the system, much as an electrical engineer views a signal-processing system.

Both the object-based approach and the stream-processing approach raise significant linguistic issues in programming. With objects, we must be concerned with how a computational object can change and yet maintain its identity. This will force us to abandon our old substitution model of computation (section 1.1.5) in favor of a more mechanistic but less theoretically tractable *environment model* of computation. The difficulties of dealing with objects, change, and identity are a fundamental consequence of the need to grapple with time in our computational models. These difficulties become even greater when we allow the possibility of concurrent execution of programs. The stream approach can be most fully exploited when we decouple simulated time in our model from the order of the events that take place in the computer during evaluation. We will accomplish this using a technique known as *delayed evaluation*.

3.1   Assignment and Local State

We ordinarily view the world as populated by independent objects, each of which has a state that changes over time. An object is said to "have state" if its behavior is influenced by its history. A bank account, for example, has state in that the answer to the question "Can I withdraw $100?" depends upon the history of deposit and withdrawal transactions. We can characterize an object's state by one or more *state variables*, which among them maintain enough information about history to determine the object's current behavior. In a simple banking system, we could characterize the state of an account by a current balance rather than by remembering the entire history of account transactions.

In a system composed of many objects, the objects are rarely completely independent. Each may influence the states of others through interactions, which serve to couple the state variables of one object to those of other objects. Indeed, the view that a system is composed of separate objects is most useful when the state variables of the system can be grouped into closely coupled subsystems that are only loosely coupled to other subsystems.

This view of a system can be a powerful framework for organizing computational models of the system. For such a model to be modular, it should be decomposed into computational objects that model the actual objects in the system. Each computational object must have its own *local state variables* describing the actual object's state. Since the states of objects in the system being modeled change over time, the state variables of the corresponding computational objects must also change. If we choose to model the flow of time in the system by the elapsed time in the computer, then we must have a way to construct computational objects whose behaviors change as our programs run. In particular, if we wish to model state variables by ordinary symbolic names in the programming language, then the language must provide an *assignment operator* to enable us to change the value associated with a name.

3.1.1   Local State Variables

To illustrate what we mean by having a computational object with time-varying state, let us model the situation of withdrawing money from a bank account. We will do this using a procedure withdraw, which takes as argument an amount to be withdrawn. If there is enough money in the account to accommodate the withdrawal, then withdraw should return the balance remaining after the withdrawal. Otherwise, withdraw should return the message *Insufficient funds*. For example, if we begin with $100 in the account, we should obtain the following sequence of responses using withdraw:

```
(withdraw 25)
75

(withdraw 25)
50

(withdraw 60)
"Insufficient funds"

(withdraw 15)
35
```

Observe that the expression (withdraw 25), evaluated twice, yields different values. This is a new kind of behavior for a procedure. Until now, all our procedures could be viewed as specifications for computing mathematical functions. A call to a procedure computed the value of the function applied to the given arguments, and two calls to the same procedure with the same arguments always produced the same result.[1]

To implement `withdraw`, we can use a variable `balance` to indicate the balance of money in the account and define `withdraw` as a procedure that accesses `balance`. The `withdraw` procedure checks to see if `balance` is at least as large as the requested `amount`. If so, `withdraw` decrements `balance` by `amount` and returns the new value of `balance`. Otherwise, `withdraw` returns the *Insufficient funds* message. Here are the definitions of `balance` and `withdraw`:

```
(define balance 100)

(define (withdraw amount)
  (if (>= balance amount)
      (begin (set! balance (- balance amount))
             balance)
      "Insufficient funds"))
```

Decrementing `balance` is accomplished by the expression

```
(set! balance (- balance amount))
```

This uses the `set!` special form, whose syntax is

```
(set! ⟨name⟩ ⟨new-value⟩)
```

Here ⟨*name*⟩ is a symbol and ⟨*new-value*⟩ is any expression. `Set!` changes ⟨*name*⟩ so that its value is the result obtained by evaluating ⟨*new-value*⟩. In the case at hand, we are changing `balance` so that its new value will be the result of subtracting `amount` from the previous value of `balance`.[2]

`Withdraw` also uses the `begin` special form to cause two expressions to be evaluated in the case where the `if` test is true: first decrementing

---

[1] Actually, this is not quite true. One exception was the random-number generator in section 1.2.6. Another exception involved the operation/type tables we introduced in section 2.4.3, where the values of two calls to `get` with the same arguments depended on intervening calls to `put`. On the other hand, until we introduce assignment, we have no way to create such procedures ourselves.

[2] The value of a `set!` expression is implementation-dependent. `Set!` should be used only for its effect, not for its value.

The name `set!` reflects a naming convention used in Scheme: Operations that change the values of variables (or that change data structures, as we will see in section 3.3) are given names that end with an exclamation point. This is similar to the convention of designating predicates by names that end with a question mark.

balance and then returning the value of balance. In general, evaluating the expression

(begin ⟨*exp₁*⟩ ⟨*exp₂*⟩ ... ⟨*expₖ*⟩)

causes the expressions ⟨*exp₁*⟩ through ⟨*expₖ*⟩ to be evaluated in sequence and the value of the final expression ⟨*expₖ*⟩ to be returned as the value of the entire begin form.[3]

Although withdraw works as desired, the variable balance presents a problem. As specified above, balance is a name defined in the global environment and is freely accessible to be examined or modified by any procedure. It would be much better if we could somehow make balance internal to withdraw, so that withdraw would be the only procedure that could access balance directly and any other procedure could access balance only indirectly (through calls to withdraw). This would more accurately model the notion that balance is a local state variable used by withdraw to keep track of the state of the account.

We can make balance internal to withdraw by rewriting the definition as follows:

```
(define new-withdraw
  (let ((balance 100))
    (lambda (amount)
      (if (>= balance amount)
          (begin (set! balance (- balance amount))
                 balance)
          "Insufficient funds"))))
```

What we have done here is use let to establish an environment with a local variable balance, bound to the initial value 100. Within this local environment, we use lambda to create a procedure that takes amount as an argument and behaves like our previous withdraw procedure. This procedure—returned as the result of evaluating the let expression—is new-withdraw, which behaves in precisely the same way as withdraw but whose variable balance is not accessible by any other procedure.[4]

---

[3]We have already used begin implicitly in our programs, because in Scheme the body of a procedure can be a sequence of expressions. Also, the ⟨*consequent*⟩ part of each clause in a cond expression can be a sequence of expressions rather than a single expression.

[4]In programming-language jargon, the variable balance is said to be *encapsulated* within the new-withdraw procedure. Encapsulation reflects the general system-design principle known as the *hiding principle*: One can make a system more modular and robust by protecting parts of the system from each other; that is, by providing information access only to those parts of the system that have a "need to know."

Combining `set!` with local variables is the general programming
technique we will use for constructing computational objects with local state. Unfortunately, using this technique raises a serious problem:
When we first introduced procedures, we also introduced the substitution model of evaluation (section 1.1.5) to provide an interpretation of
what procedure application means. We said that applying a procedure
should be interpreted as evaluating the body of the procedure with the
formal parameters replaced by their values. The trouble is that, as soon
as we introduce assignment into our language, substitution is no longer
an adequate model of procedure application. (We will see why this is so
in section 3.1.3.) As a consequence, we technically have at this point no
way to understand why the `new-withdraw` procedure behaves as claimed
above. In order to really understand a procedure such as `new-withdraw`,
we will need to develop a new model of procedure application. In section 3.2 we will introduce such a model, together with an explanation of
`set!` and local variables. First, however, we examine some variations on
the theme established by `new-withdraw`.

The following procedure, `make-withdraw`, creates "withdrawal processors." The formal parameter `balance` in `make-withdraw` specifies
the initial amount of money in the account.[5]

```
(define (make-withdraw balance)
  (lambda (amount)
    (if (>= balance amount)
        (begin (set! balance (- balance amount))
               balance)
        "Insufficient funds")))
```

`Make-withdraw` can be used as follows to create two objects W1 and W2:

```
(define W1 (make-withdraw 100))
(define W2 (make-withdraw 100))

(W1 50)
50

(W2 70)
30
```

---

[5]In contrast with `new-withdraw` above, we do not have to use `let` to make `balance` a
local variable, since formal parameters are already local. This will be clearer after the
discussion of the environment model of evaluation in section 3.2. (See also exercise 3.10.)

(W2 40)
"Insufficient funds"

(W1 40)
10

Observe that W1 and W2 are completely independent objects, each with its own local state variable balance. Withdrawals from one do not affect the other.

We can also create objects that handle deposits as well as withdrawals, and thus we can represent simple bank accounts. Here is a procedure that returns a "bank-account object" with a specified initial balance:

```
(define (make-account balance)
  (define (withdraw amount)
    (if (>= balance amount)
        (begin (set! balance (- balance amount))
               balance)
        "Insufficient funds"))
  (define (deposit amount)
    (set! balance (+ balance amount))
    balance)
  (define (dispatch m)
    (cond ((eq? m 'withdraw) withdraw)
          ((eq? m 'deposit) deposit)
          (else (error "Unknown request -- MAKE-ACCOUNT"
                       m))))
  dispatch)
```

Each call to make-account sets up an environment with a local state variable balance. Within this environment, make-account defines procedures deposit and withdraw that access balance and an additional procedure dispatch that takes a "message" as input and returns one of the two local procedures. The dispatch procedure itself is returned as the value that represents the bank-account object. This is precisely the *message-passing* style of programming that we saw in section 2.4.3, although here we are using it in conjunction with the ability to modify local variables.

Make-account can be used as follows:

```
(define acc (make-account 100))
```

```
((acc 'withdraw) 50)
```
50

```
((acc 'withdraw) 60)
"Insufficient funds"

((acc 'deposit) 40)
90

((acc 'withdraw) 60)
30
```

Each call to acc returns the locally defined deposit or withdraw procedure, which is then applied to the specified amount. As was the case with make-withdraw, another call to make-account

```
(define acc2 (make-account 100))
```

will produce a completely separate account object, which maintains its own local balance.

Exercise 3.1

An *accumulator* is a procedure that is called repeatedly with a single numeric argument and accumulates its arguments into a sum. Each time it is called, it returns the currently accumulated sum. Write a procedure make-accumulator that generates accumulators, each maintaining an independent sum. The input to make-accumulator should specify the initial value of the sum; for example

```
(define A (make-accumulator 5))

(A 10)
15

(A 10)
25
```

Exercise 3.2

In software-testing applications, it is useful to be able to count the number of times a given procedure is called during the course of a computation. Write a procedure make-monitored that takes as input a procedure, f, that itself takes one input. The result returned by make-monitored is a third procedure, say mf, that keeps track of the number of times it has been called by maintaining an internal counter. If the input to mf is the special symbol how-many-calls?, then mf returns the value of the counter. If the input is the special symbol reset-count, then mf resets the counter to zero. For any other input, mf returns the result of calling f on that input and increments the counter. For instance, we could make a monitored version of the sqrt procedure:

```
(define s (make-monitored sqrt))

(s 100)
10

(s 'how-many-calls?)
1
```

Exercise 3.3

Modify the make-account procedure so that it creates password-protected accounts. That is, make-account should take a symbol as an additional argument, as in

```
(define acc (make-account 100 'secret-password))
```

The resulting account object should process a request only if it is accompanied by the password with which the account was created, and should otherwise return a complaint:

```
((acc 'secret-password 'withdraw) 40)
60

((acc 'some-other-password 'deposit) 50)
"Incorrect password"
```

Exercise 3.4

Modify the make-account procedure of exercise 3.3 by adding another local state variable so that, if an account is accessed more than seven consecutive times with an incorrect password, it invokes the procedure call-the-cops.

3.1.2   The Benefits of Introducing Assignment

As we shall see, introducing assignment into our programming language leads us into a thicket of difficult conceptual issues. Nevertheless, viewing systems as collections of objects with local state is a powerful technique for maintaining a modular design. As a simple example, consider the design of a procedure rand that, whenever it is called, returns an integer chosen at random.

It is not at all clear what is meant by "chosen at random." What we presumably want is for successive calls to rand to produce a sequence of numbers that has statistical properties of uniform distribution. We will not discuss methods for generating suitable sequences here. Rather, let us assume that we have a procedure rand-update that has the property that if we start with a given number x_1 and form

```
x₂ = (rand-update x₁)
x₃ = (rand-update x₂)
```
$$x_2 = (\text{rand-update } x_1)$$
$$x_3 = (\text{rand-update } x_2)$$

then the sequence of values $x_1, x_2, x_3, \ldots$, will have the desired statistical properties.[6]

We can implement rand as a procedure with a local state variable x that is initialized to some fixed value random-init. Each call to rand computes rand-update of the current value of x, returns this as the random number, and also stores this as the new value of x.

```
(define rand
  (let ((x random-init))
    (lambda ()
      (set! x (rand-update x))
      x)))
```

Of course, we could generate the same sequence of random numbers without using assignment by simply calling rand-update directly. However, this would mean that any part of our program that used random numbers would have to explicitly remember the current value of x to be passed as an argument to rand-update. To realize what an annoyance this would be, consider using random numbers to implement a technique called *Monte Carlo simulation*.

The Monte Carlo method consists of choosing sample experiments at random from a large set and then making deductions on the basis of the probabilities estimated from tabulating the results of those experiments. For example, we can approximate π using the fact that $6/\pi^2$ is the probability that two integers chosen at random will have no factors in common; that is, that their greatest common divisor will be 1.[7] To obtain the approximation to π, we perform a large number of experiments. In each experiment we choose two integers at random and perform a test to see

---

[6]One common way to implement rand-update is to use the rule that x is updated to $ax + b$ modulo m, where a, b, and m are appropriately chosen integers. Chapter 3 of Knuth 1981 includes an extensive discussion of techniques for generating sequences of random numbers and establishing their statistical properties. Notice that the rand-update procedure computes a mathematical function: Given the same input twice, it produces the same output. Therefore, the number sequence produced by rand-update certainly is not "random," if by "random" we insist that each number in the sequence is unrelated to the preceding number. The relation between "real randomness" and so-called *pseudo-random* sequences, which are produced by well-determined computations and yet have suitable statistical properties, is a complex question involving difficult issues in mathematics and philosophy. Kolmogorov, Solomonoff, and Chaitin have made great progress in clarifying these issues; a discussion can be found in Chaitin 1975.

[7]This theorem is due to E. Cesàro. See section 4.5.2 of Knuth 1981 for a discussion and a proof.

if their GCD is 1. The fraction of times that the test is passed gives us our estimate of $6/\pi^2$, and from this we obtain our approximation to π.

The heart of our program is a procedure `monte-carlo`, which takes as arguments the number of times to try an experiment, together with the experiment, represented as a no-argument procedure that will return either true or false each time it is run. `Monte-carlo` runs the experiment for the designated number of trials and returns a number telling the fraction of the trials in which the experiment was found to be true.

```
(define (estimate-pi trials)
  (sqrt (/ 6 (monte-carlo trials cesaro-test))))

(define (cesaro-test)
  (= (gcd (rand) (rand)) 1))

(define (monte-carlo trials experiment)
  (define (iter trials-remaining trials-passed)
    (cond ((= trials-remaining 0)
           (/ trials-passed trials))
          ((experiment)
           (iter (- trials-remaining 1) (+ trials-passed 1)))
          (else
           (iter (- trials-remaining 1) trials-passed))))
  (iter trials 0))
```

Now let us try the same computation using `rand-update` directly rather than `rand`, the way we would be forced to proceed if we did not use assignment to model local state:

```
(define (estimate-pi trials)
  (sqrt (/ 6 (random-gcd-test trials random-init))))

(define (random-gcd-test trials initial-x)
  (define (iter trials-remaining trials-passed x)
    (let ((x1 (rand-update x)))
      (let ((x2 (rand-update x1)))
        (cond ((= trials-remaining 0)
               (/ trials-passed trials))
              ((= (gcd x1 x2) 1)
               (iter (- trials-remaining 1)
                     (+ trials-passed 1)
                     x2))
              (else
               (iter (- trials-remaining 1)
                     trials-passed
                     x2))))))
  (iter trials 0 initial-x))
```

While the program is still simple, it betrays some painful breaches of modularity. In our first version of the program, using rand, we can express the Monte Carlo method directly as a general monte-carlo procedure that takes as an argument an arbitrary experiment procedure. In our second version of the program, with no local state for the random-number generator, random-gcd-test must explicitly manipulate the random numbers x1 and x2 and recycle x2 through the iterative loop as the new input to rand-update. This explicit handling of the random numbers intertwines the structure of accumulating test results with the fact that our particular experiment uses two random numbers, whereas other Monte Carlo experiments might use one random number or three. Even the top-level procedure estimate-pi has to be concerned with supplying an initial random number. The fact that the random-number generator's insides are leaking out into other parts of the program makes it difficult for us to isolate the Monte Carlo idea so that it can be applied to other tasks. In the first version of the program, assignment encapsulates the state of the random-number generator within the rand procedure, so that the details of random-number generation remain independent of the rest of the program.

The general phenomenon illustrated by the Monte Carlo example is this: From the point of view of one part of a complex process, the other parts appear to change with time. They have hidden time-varying local state. If we wish to write computer programs whose structure reflects this decomposition, we make computational objects (such as bank accounts and random-number generators) whose behavior changes with time. We model state with local state variables, and we model the changes of state with assignments to those variables.

It is tempting to conclude this discussion by saying that, by introducing assignment and the technique of hiding state in local variables, we are able to structure systems in a more modular fashion than if all state had to be manipulated explicitly, by passing additional parameters. Unfortunately, as we shall see, the story is not so simple.

Exercise 3.5

Monte Carlo integration is a method of estimating definite integrals by means of Monte Carlo simulation. Consider computing the area of a region of space described by a predicate $P(x, y)$ that is true for points (x, y) in the region and false for points not in the region. For example, the region contained within a circle of radius 3 centered at $(5, 7)$ is described by the predicate that tests whether $(x - 5)^2 + (y - 7)^2 \leq 3^2$. To estimate the area of the region described by such a predicate, begin by choosing a rectangle that contains the region. For example, a rectangle with diagonally opposite corners at $(2, 4)$ and $(8, 10)$ contains the circle above. The desired integral is the area of that portion of the rectangle that lies in the region. We can estimate the integral by picking, at random, points (x, y) that lie in the rectangle, and testing $P(x, y)$ for each point to determine whether the point lies in the region. If we try this with many points, then the fraction of points that fall in the region should give an estimate of the proportion of the rectangle that lies in the region. Hence, multiplying this fraction by the area of the entire rectangle should produce an estimate of the integral.

Implement Monte Carlo integration as a procedure `estimate-integral` that takes as arguments a predicate P, upper and lower bounds x1, x2, y1, and y2 for the rectangle, and the number of trials to perform in order to produce the estimate. Your procedure should use the same `monte-carlo` procedure that was used above to estimate π. Use your `estimate-integral` to produce an estimate of π by measuring the area of a unit circle.

You will find it useful to have a procedure that returns a number chosen at random from a given range. The following `random-in-range` procedure implements this in terms of the `random` procedure used in section 1.2.6, which returns a nonnegative number less than its input.[8]

```
(define (random-in-range low high)
  (let ((range (- high low)))
    (+ low (random range))))
```

Exercise 3.6

It is useful to be able to reset a random-number generator to produce a sequence starting from a given value. Design a new `rand` procedure that is called with an argument that is either the symbol generate or the symbol reset and behaves as follows: (`rand` 'generate) produces a new random number; ((`rand` 'reset) ⟨*new-value*⟩) resets the internal state variable to the designated ⟨*new-value*⟩. Thus, by resetting the state, one can generate repeatable sequences. These are very handy to have when testing and debugging programs that use random numbers.

3.1.3   The Costs of Introducing Assignment

As we have seen, the `set!` operation enables us to model objects that have local state. However, this advantage comes at a price. Our programming language can no longer be interpreted in terms of the substitution model of procedure application that we introduced in section 1.1.5. Moreover, no simple model with "nice" mathematical properties can be an adequate framework for dealing with objects and assignment in programming languages.

---

[8]MIT Scheme provides such a procedure. If `random` is given an exact integer (as in section 1.2.6) it returns an exact integer, but if it is given a decimal value (as in this exercise) it returns a decimal value.

So long as we do not use assignments, two evaluations of the same procedure with the same arguments will produce the same result, so that procedures can be viewed as computing mathematical functions. Programming without any use of assignments, as we did throughout the first two chapters of this book, is accordingly known as *functional programming*.

To understand how assignment complicates matters, consider a simplified version of the make-withdraw procedure of section 3.1.1 that does not bother to check for an insufficient amount:

```
(define (make-simplified-withdraw balance)
  (lambda (amount)
    (set! balance (- balance amount))
    balance))

(define W (make-simplified-withdraw 25))

(W 20)
5

(W 10)
-5
```

Compare this procedure with the following make-decrementer procedure, which does not use set!:

```
(define (make-decrementer balance)
  (lambda (amount)
    (- balance amount)))
```

Make-decrementer returns a procedure that subtracts its input from a designated amount balance, but there is no accumulated effect over successive calls, as with make-simplified-withdraw:

```
(define D (make-decrementer 25))

(D 20)
5

(D 10)
15
```

We can use the substitution model to explain how make-decrementer works. For instance, let us analyze the evaluation of the expression

```
((make-decrementer 25) 20)
```

We first simplify the operator of the combination by substituting 25 for `balance` in the body of `make-decrementer`. This reduces the expression to

```
((lambda (amount) (- 25 amount)) 20)
```

Now we apply the operator by substituting 20 for `amount` in the body of the `lambda` expression:

```
(- 25 20)
```

The final answer is 5.

Observe, however, what happens if we attempt a similar substitution analysis with `make-simplified-withdraw`:

```
((make-simplified-withdraw 25) 20)
```

We first simplify the operator by substituting 25 for `balance` in the body of `make-simplified-withdraw`. This reduces the expression to[9]

```
((lambda (amount) (set! balance (- 25 amount))) 25) 20)
```

Now we apply the operator by substituting 20 for `amount` in the body of the `lambda` expression:

```
(set! balance (- 25 20)) 25
```

If we adhered to the substitution model, we would have to say that the meaning of the procedure application is to first set `balance` to 5 and then return 25 as the value of the expression. This gets the wrong answer. In order to get the correct answer, we would have to somehow distinguish the first occurrence of `balance` (before the effect of the `set!`) from the second occurrence of `balance` (after the effect of the `set!`), and the substitution model cannot do this.

The trouble here is that substitution is based ultimately on the notion that the symbols in our language are essentially names for values. But as soon as we introduce `set!` and the idea that the value of a variable can change, a variable can no longer be simply a name. Now a variable somehow refers to a place where a value can be stored, and the value stored at this place can change. In section 3.2 we will see how environments play this role of "place" in our computational model.

---

[9]We don't substitute for the occurrence of `balance` in the `set!` expression because the ⟨*name*⟩ in a `set!` is not evaluated. If we did substitute for it, we would get `(set! 25 (- 25 amount))`, which makes no sense.

Sameness and change

The issue surfacing here is more profound than the mere breakdown of a particular model of computation. As soon as we introduce change into our computational models, many notions that were previously straight-forward become problematical. Consider the concept of two things being "the same."

Suppose we call make-decrementer twice with the same argument to create two procedures:

```
(define D1 (make-decrementer 25))

(define D2 (make-decrementer 25))
```

Are D1 and D2 the same? An acceptable answer is yes, because D1 and D2 have the same computational behavior—each is a procedure that sub-tracts its input from 25. In fact, D1 could be substituted for D2 in any computation without changing the result.

Contrast this with making two calls to make-simplified-withdraw:

```
(define W1 (make-simplified-withdraw 25))

(define W2 (make-simplified-withdraw 25))
```

Are W1 and W2 the same? Surely not, because calls to W1 and W2 have distinct effects, as shown by the following sequence of interactions:

```
(W1 20)
5

(W1 20)
−15

(W2 20)
5
```

Even though W1 and W2 are "equal" in the sense that they are both created by evaluating the same expression, (make-simplified-withdraw 25), it is not true that W1 could be substituted for W2 in any expression without changing the result of evaluating the expression.

A language that supports the concept that "equals can be substituted for equals" in an expresssion without changing the value of the expression is said to be *referentially transparent*. Referential transparency is violated when we include `set!` in our computer language. This makes it tricky to determine when we can simplify expressions by substituting equivalent expressions. Consequently, reasoning about programs that use assignment becomes drastically more difficult.

Once we forgo referential transparency, the notion of what it means for computational objects to be "the same" becomes difficult to capture in a formal way. Indeed, the meaning of "same" in the real world that our programs model is hardly clear in itself. In general, we can determine that two apparently identical objects are indeed "the same one" only by modifying one object and then observing whether the other object has changed in the same way. But how can we tell if an object has "changed" other than by observing the "same" object twice and seeing whether some property of the object differs from one observation to the next? Thus, we cannot determine "change" without some *a priori* notion of "sameness," and we cannot determine sameness without observing the effects of change.

As an example of how this issue arises in programming, consider the situation where Peter and Paul have a bank account with $100 in it. There is a substantial difference between modeling this as

```
(define peter-acc (make-account 100))
(define paul-acc (make-account 100))
```

and modeling it as

```
(define peter-acc (make-account 100))
(define paul-acc peter-acc)
```

In the first situation, the two bank accounts are distinct. Transactions made by Peter will not affect Paul's account, and vice versa. In the second situation, however, we have defined `paul-acc` to be *the same thing* as `peter-acc`. In effect, Peter and Paul now have a joint bank account, and if Peter makes a withdrawal from `peter-acc` Paul will observe less money in `paul-acc`. These two similar but distinct situations can cause confusion in building computational models. With the shared account, in particular, it can be especially confusing that there is one object (the bank account) that has two different names (`peter-acc` and `paul-acc`); if we are searching for all the places in our program where `paul-acc` can be changed, we must remember to look also at things that change peter-acc.[10]

With reference to the above remarks on "sameness" and "change," observe that if Peter and Paul could only examine their bank balances, and could not perform operations that changed the balance, then the issue of whether the two accounts are distinct would be moot. In general, so long as we never modify data objects, we can regard a compound data object to be precisely the totality of its pieces. For example, a rational number is determined by giving its numerator and its denominator. But this view is no longer valid in the presence of change, where a compound data object has an "identity" that is something different from the pieces of which it is composed. A bank account is still "the same" bank account even if we change the balance by making a withdrawal; conversely, we could have two different bank accounts with the same state information. This complication is a consequence, not of our programming language, but of our perception of a bank account as an object. We do not, for example, ordinarily regard a rational number as a changeable object with identity, such that we could change the numerator and still have "the same" rational number.

Pitfalls of imperative programming

In contrast to functional programming, programming that makes extensive use of assignment is known as *imperative programming*. In addition to raising complications about computational models, programs written in imperative style are susceptible to bugs that cannot occur in functional programs. For example, recall the iterative factorial program from section 1.2.1:

```
(define (factorial n)
  (define (iter product counter)
    (if (> counter n)
        product
        (iter (* counter product)
              (+ counter 1))))
  (iter 1 1))
```

---

[10]The phenomenon of a single computational object being accessed by more than one name is known as *aliasing*. The joint bank account situation illustrates a very simple example of an alias. In section 3.3 we will see much more complex examples, such as "distinct" compound data structures that share parts. Bugs can occur in our programs if we forget that a change to an object may also, as a "side effect," change a "different" object because the two "different" objects are actually a single object appearing under different aliases. These so-called *side-effect bugs* are so difficult to locate and to analyze that some people have proposed that programming languages be designed in such a way as to not allow side effects or aliasing (Lampson et al. 1981; Morris, Schmidt, and Wadler 1980).

Instead of passing arguments in the internal iterative loop, we could adopt a more imperative style by using explicit assignment to update the values of the variables product and counter:

```
(define (factorial n)
  (let ((product 1)
        (counter 1))
    (define (iter)
      (if (> counter n)
          product
          (begin (set! product (* counter product))
                 (set! counter (+ counter 1))
                 (iter))))
    (iter)))
```

This does not change the results produced by the program, but it does introduce a subtle trap. How do we decide the order of the assignments? As it happens, the program is correct as written. But writing the assignments in the opposite order

```
(set! counter (+ counter 1))
(set! product (* counter product))
```

would have produced a different, incorrect result. In general, programming with assignment forces us to carefully consider the relative orders of the assignments to make sure that each statement is using the correct version of the variables that have been changed. This issue simply does not arise in functional programs.[11]

The complexity of imperative programs becomes even worse if we consider applications in which several processes execute concurrently. We will return to this in section 3.4. First, however, we will address the issue of providing a computational model for expressions that involve assignment, and explore the uses of objects with local state in designing simulations.

---

[11] In view of this, it is ironic that introductory programming is most often taught in a highly imperative style. This may be a vestige of a belief, common throughout the 1960s and 1970s, that programs that call procedures must inherently be less efficient than programs that perform assignments. (Steele (1977) debunks this argument.) Alternatively it may reflect a view that step-by-step assignment is easier for beginners to visualize than procedure call. Whatever the reason, it often saddles beginning programmers with "should I set this variable before or after that one" concerns that can complicate programming and obscure the important ideas.

Exercise 3.7

Consider the bank account objects created by make-account, with the password modification described in exercise 3.3. Suppose that our banking system requires the ability to make joint accounts. Define a procedure make-joint that accomplishes this. Make-joint should take three arguments. The first is a password-protected account. The second argument must match the password with which the account was defined in order for the make-joint operation to proceed. The third argument is a new password. Make-joint is to create an additional access to the original account using the new password. For example, if peter-acc is a bank account with password open-sesame, then

```
(define paul-acc
  (make-joint peter-acc 'open-sesame 'rosebud))
```

will allow one to make transactions on peter-acc using the name paul-acc and the password rosebud. You may wish to modify your solution to exercise 3.3 to accommodate this new feature.

Exercise 3.8

When we defined the evaluation model in section 1.1.3, we said that the first step in evaluating an expression is to evaluate its subexpressions. But we never specified the order in which the subexpressions should be evaluated (e.g., left to right or right to left). When we introduce assignment, the order in which the arguments to a procedure are evaluated can make a difference to the result. Define a simple procedure f such that evaluating (+ (f 0) (f 1)) will return 0 if the arguments to + are evaluated from left to right but will return 1 if the arguments are evaluated from right to left.

3.2   The Environment Model of Evaluation

When we introduced compound procedures in chapter 1, we used the substitution model of evaluation (section 1.1.5) to define what is meant by applying a procedure to arguments:

• To apply a compound procedure to arguments, evaluate the body of the procedure with each formal parameter replaced by the corresponding argument.

Once we admit assignment into our programming language, such a definition is no longer adequate. In particular, section 3.1.3 argued that, in the presence of assignment, a variable can no longer be considered to be merely a name for a value. Rather, a variable must somehow designate a "place" in which values can be stored. In our new model of evaluation, these places will be maintained in structures called *environments*.

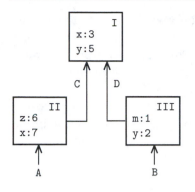

Figure 3.1   A simple environment structure.

An environment is a sequence of *frames*. Each frame is a table (possibly empty) of *bindings*, which associate variable names with their corresponding values. (A single frame may contain at most one binding for any variable.) Each frame also has a pointer to its *enclosing environment*, unless, for the purposes of discussion, the frame is considered to be *global*. The *value of a variable* with respect to an environment is the value given by the binding of the variable in the first frame in the environment that contains a binding for that variable. If no frame in the sequence specifies a binding for the variable, then the variable is said to be *unbound* in the environment.

Figure 3.1 shows a simple environment structure consisting of three frames, labeled I, II, and III. In the diagram, A, B, C, and D are pointers to environments. C and D point to the same environment. The variables z and x are bound in frame II, while y and x are bound in frame I. The value of x in environment D is 3. The value of x with respect to environment B is also 3. This is determined as follows: We examine the first frame in the sequence (frame III) and do not find a binding for x, so we proceed to the enclosing environment D and find the binding in frame I. On the other hand, the value of x in environment A is 7, because the first frame in the sequence (frame II) contains a binding of x to 7. With respect to environment A, the binding of x to 7 in frame II is said to *shadow* the binding of x to 3 in frame I.

The environment is crucial to the evaluation process, because it determines the context in which an expression should be evaluated. Indeed, one could say that expressions in a programming language do not, in themselves, have any meaning. Rather, an expression acquires a meaning only with respect to some environment in which it is evaluated. Even the interpretation of an expression as straightforward as (+ 1 1) depends on an understanding that one is operating in a context in which + is the symbol for addition. Thus, in our model of evaluation we will always speak of evaluating an expression with respect to some environment. To describe interactions with the interpreter, we will suppose that there is a global environment, consisting of a single frame (with no enclosing environment) that includes values for the symbols associated with the primitive procedures. For example, the idea that + is the symbol for addition is captured by saying that the symbol + is bound in the global environment to the primitive addition procedure.

3.2.1   The Rules for Evaluation

The overall specification of how the interpreter evaluates a combination remains the same as when we first introduced it in section 1.1.3:

• To evaluate a combination:

1. Evaluate the subexpressions of the combination.[12]

2. Apply the value of the operator subexpression to the values of the operand subexpressions.

The environment model of evaluation replaces the substitution model in specifying what it means to apply a compound procedure to arguments.

In the environment model of evaluation, a procedure is always a pair consisting of some code and a pointer to an environment. Procedures are created in one way only: by evaluating a lambda expression. This produces a procedure whose code is obtained from the text of the lambda expression and whose environment is the environment in which the lambda expression was evaluated to produce the procedure. For example, consider the procedure definition

```
(define (square x)
  (* x x))
```

---

[12]Assignment introduces a subtlety into step 1 of the evaluation rule. As shown in exercise 3.8, the presence of assignment allows us to write expressions that will produce different values depending on the order in which the subexpressions in a combination are evaluated. Thus, to be precise, we should specify an evaluation order in step 1 (e.g., left to right or right to left). However, this order should always be considered to be an implementation detail, and one should never write programs that depend on some particular order. For instance, a sophisticated compiler might optimize a program by varying the order in which subexpressions are evaluated.

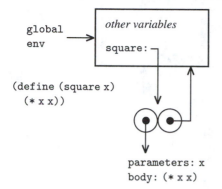

(define (square x)
    (* x x))

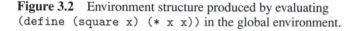

parameters: x
body: (* x x)

Figure 3.2   Environment structure produced by evaluating
(define (square x) (* x x)) in the global environment.

evaluated in the global environment. The procedure definition syntax
is just syntactic sugar for an underlying implicit lambda expression. It
would have been equivalent to have used

(define square
    (lambda (x) (* x x)))

which evaluates (lambda (x) (* x x)) and binds square to the resulting value, all in the global environment.

Figure 3.2 shows the result of evaluating this define expression. The
procedure object is a pair whose code specifies that the procedure has
one formal parameter, namely x, and a procedure body (* x x). The
environment part of the procedure is a pointer to the global environment, since that is the environment in which the lambda expression was
evaluated to produce the procedure. A new binding, which associates
the procedure object with the symbol square, has been added to the
global frame. In general, define creates definitions by adding bindings
to frames.

Now that we have seen how procedures are created, we can describe
how procedures are applied. The environment model specifies: To apply
a procedure to arguments, create a new environment containing a frame
that binds the parameters to the values of the arguments. The enclosing
environment of this frame is the environment specified by the procedure.
Now, within this new environment, evaluate the procedure body.

To show how this rule is followed, figure 3.3 illustrates the environment structure created by evaluating the expression (square 5) in the

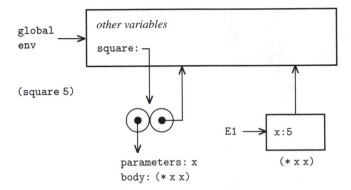

(square 5)

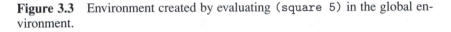

Figure 3.3   Environment created by evaluating (square 5) in the global environment.

global environment, where square is the procedure generated in figure 3.2. Applying the procedure results in the creation of a new environment, labeled E1 in the figure, that begins with a frame in which x, the formal parameter for the procedure, is bound to the argument 5. The pointer leading upward from this frame shows that the frame's enclosing environment is the global environment. The global environment is chosen here, because this is the environment that is indicated as part of the square procedure object. Within E1, we evaluate the body of the procedure, (* x x). Since the value of x in E1 is 5, the result is (* 5 5), or 25.

The environment model of procedure application can be summarized by two rules:

• A procedure object is applied to a set of arguments by constructing a frame, binding the formal parameters of the procedure to the arguments of the call, and then evaluating the body of the procedure in the context of the new environment constructed. The new frame has as its enclosing environment the environment part of the procedure object being applied.

• A procedure is created by evaluating a lambda expression relative to a given environment. The resulting procedure object is a pair consisting of the text of the lambda expression and a pointer to the environment in which the procedure was created.

We also specify that defining a symbol using define creates a binding in the current environment frame and assigns to the symbol the indicated value.[13] Finally, we specify the behavior of set!, the operation that forced us to introduce the environment model in the first place. Evaluating the expression (set! ⟨*variable*⟩ ⟨*value*⟩) in some environment locates the binding of the variable in the environment and changes that binding to indicate the new value. That is, one finds the first frame in the environment that contains a binding for the variable and modifies that frame. If the variable is unbound in the environment, then set! signals an error.

These evaluation rules, though considerably more complex than the substitution model, are still reasonably straightforward. Moreover, the evaluation model, though abstract, provides a correct description of how the interpreter evaluates expressions. In chapter 4 we shall see how this model can serve as a blueprint for implementing a working interpreter. The following sections elaborate the details of the model by analyzing some illustrative programs.

3.2.2 Applying Simple Procedures

When we introduced the substitution model in section 1.1.5 we showed how the combination (f 5) evaluates to 136, given the following procedure definitions:

```
(define (square x)
  (* x x))

(define (sum-of-squares x y)
  (+ (square x) (square y)))

(define (f a)
  (sum-of-squares (+ a 1) (* a 2)))
```

We can analyze the same example using the environment model. Figure 3.4 shows the three procedure objects created by evaluating the definitions of f, square, and sum-of-squares in the global environment. Each procedure object consists of some code, together with a pointer to the global environment.

---

[13]If there is already a binding for the variable in the current frame, then the binding is changed. This is convenient because it allows redefinition of symbols; however, it also means that define can be used to change values, and this brings up the issues of assignment without explicitly using set!. Because of this, some people prefer redefinitions of existing symbols to signal errors or warnings.

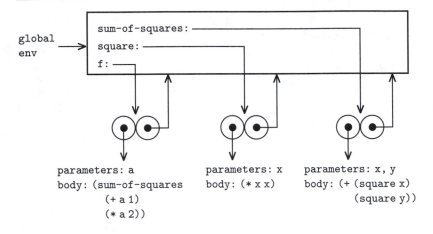

Figure 3.4   Procedure objects in the global frame.

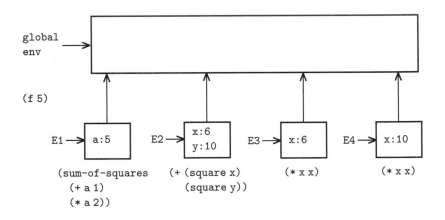

Figure 3.5   Environments created by evaluating (f 5) using the procedures in figure 3.4.

In figure 3.5 we see the environment structure created by evaluating the expression (f 5). The call to f creates a new environment E1 beginning with a frame in which a, the formal parameter of f, is bound to the argument 5. In E1, we evaluate the body of f:

```
(sum-of-squares (+ a 1) (* a 2))
```

To evaluate this combination, we first evaluate the subexpressions. The first subexpression, sum-of-squares, has a value that is a procedure object. (Notice how this value is found: We first look in the first frame of

E1, which contains no binding for sum-of-squares. Then we proceed to the enclosing environment, i.e. the global environment, and find the binding shown in figure 3.4.) The other two subexpressions are evaluated by applying the primitive operations + and * to evaluate the two combinations (+ a 1) and (* a 2) to obtain 6 and 10, respectively.

Now we apply the procedure object sum-of-squares to the arguments 6 and 10. This results in a new environment E2 in which the formal parameters x and y are bound to the arguments. Within E2 we evaluate the combination (+ (square x) (square y)). This leads us to evaluate (square x), where square is found in the global frame and x is 6. Once again, we set up a new environment, E3, in which x is bound to 6, and within this we evaluate the body of square, which is (* x x). Also as part of applying sum-of-squares, we must evaluate the subexpression (square y), where y is 10. This second call to square creates another environment, E4, in which x, the formal parameter of square, is bound to 10. And within E4 we must evaluate (* x x).

The important point to observe is that each call to square creates a new environment containing a binding for x. We can see here how the different frames serve to keep separate the different local variables all named x. Notice that each frame created by square points to the global environment, since this is the environment indicated by the square procedure object.

After the subexpressions are evaluated, the results are returned. The values generated by the two calls to square are added by sum-of-squares, and this result is returned by f. Since our focus here is on the environment structures, we will not dwell on how these returned values are passed from call to call; however, this is also an important aspect of the evaluation process, and we will return to it in detail in chapter 5.

Exercise 3.9

In section 1.2.1 we used the substitution model to analyze two procedures for computing factorials, a recursive version

```
(define (factorial n)
  (if (= n 1)
      1
      (* n (factorial (- n 1)))))
```

and an iterative version

```
(define (factorial n)
  (fact-iter 1 1 n))
```

```
(define (fact-iter product counter max-count)
  (if (> counter max-count)
      product
      (fact-iter (* counter product)
                 (+ counter 1)
                 max-count)))
```

Show the environment structures created by evaluating (factorial 6) using each version of the factorial procedure.[14]

3.2.3   Frames as the Repository of Local State

We can turn to the environment model to see how procedures and assignment can be used to represent objects with local state. As an example, consider the "withdrawal processor" from section 3.1.1 created by calling the procedure

```
(define (make-withdraw balance)
  (lambda (amount)
    (if (>= balance amount)
        (begin (set! balance (- balance amount))
               balance)
        "Insufficient funds")))
```

Let us describe the evaluation of

```
(define W1 (make-withdraw 100))
```

followed by

```
(W1 50)
50
```

Figure 3.6 shows the result of defining the make-withdraw procedure in the global environment. This produces a procedure object that contains a pointer to the global environment. So far, this is no different from the examples we have already seen, except that the body of the procedure is itself a lambda expression.

The interesting part of the computation happens when we apply the procedure make-withdraw to an argument:

```
(define W1 (make-withdraw 100))
```

---

[14]The environment model will not clarify our claim in section 1.2.1 that the interpreter can execute a procedure such as fact-iter in a constant amount of space using tail recursion. We will discuss tail recursion when we deal with the control structure of the interpreter in section 5.4.

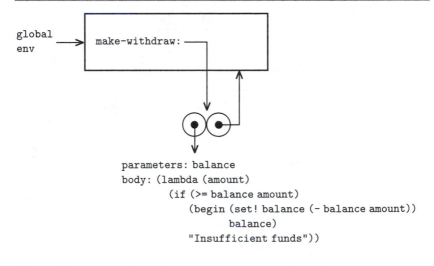

Figure 3.6   Result of defining `make-withdraw` in the global environment.

We begin, as usual, by setting up an environment E1 in which the formal parameter `balance` is bound to the argument 100. Within this environment, we evaluate the body of `make-withdraw`, namely the `lambda` expression. This constructs a new procedure object, whose code is as specified by the `lambda` and whose environment is E1, the environment in which the `lambda` was evaluated to produce the procedure. The resulting procedure object is the value returned by the call to `make-withdraw`. This is bound to W1 in the global environment, since the `define` itself is being evaluated in the global environment. Figure 3.7 shows the resulting environment structure.

Now we can analyze what happens when W1 is applied to an argument:

```
(W1 50)
50
```

We begin by constructing a frame in which `amount`, the formal parameter of W1, is bound to the argument 50. The crucial point to observe is that this frame has as its enclosing environment not the global environment, but rather the environment E1, because this is the environment that is specified by the W1 procedure object. Within this new environment, we evaluate the body of the procedure:

```
(if (>= balance amount)
    (begin (set! balance (- balance amount))
           balance)
    "Insufficient funds")
```

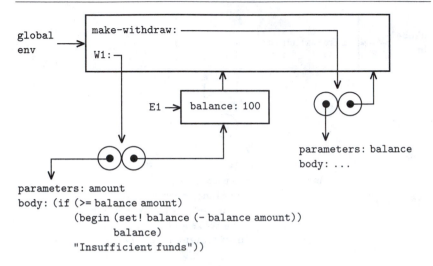

parameters: amount
body: (if (>= balance amount)
            (begin (set! balance (- balance amount))
                    balance)
            "Insufficient funds"))

Figure 3.7   Result of evaluating (define W1 (make-withdraw 100)).

The resulting environment structure is shown in figure 3.8. The expression being evaluated references both amount and balance. Amount will be found in the first frame in the environment, while balance will be found by following the enclosing-environment pointer to E1.

When the set! is executed, the binding of balance in E1 is changed. At the completion of the call to W1, balance is 50, and the frame that contains balance is still pointed to by the procedure object W1. The frame that binds amount (in which we executed the code that changed balance) is no longer relevant, since the procedure call that constructed it has terminated, and there are no pointers to that frame from other parts of the environment. The next time W1 is called, this will build a new frame that binds amount and whose enclosing environment is E1. We see that E1 serves as the "place" that holds the local state variable for the procedure object W1. Figure 3.9 shows the situation after the call to W1.

Observe what happens when we create a second "withdraw" object by making another call to make-withdraw:

(define W2 (make-withdraw 100))

This produces the environment structure of figure 3.10, which shows that W2 is a procedure object, that is, a pair with some code and an environment. The environment E2 for W2 was created by the call to make-withdraw. It contains a frame with its own local binding for balance. On the other hand, W1 and W2 have the same code: the code

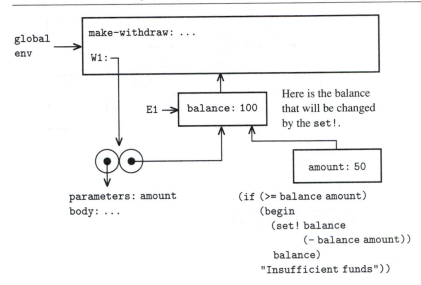

Here is the balance
that will be changed
by the set!.

parameters: amount
body: ...

```
(if (>= balance amount)
    (begin
      (set! balance
            (- balance amount))
      balance)
    "Insufficient funds"))
```

Figure 3.8   Environments created by applying the procedure object W1.

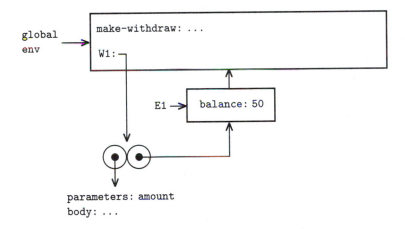

parameters: amount
body: ...

Figure 3.9   Environments after the call to W1.

specified by the lambda expression in the body of make-withdraw.[15]
We see here why W1 and W2 behave as independent objects. Calls to W1
reference the state variable balance stored in E1, whereas calls to W2
reference the balance stored in E2. Thus, changes to the local state of
one object do not affect the other object.

---

[15]Whether W1 and W2 share the same physical code stored in the computer, or whether
they each keep a copy of the code, is a detail of the implementation. For the interpreter we
implement in chapter 4, the code is in fact shared.

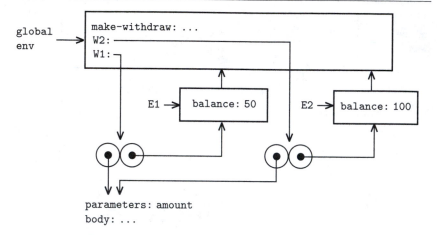

Figure 3.10 Using (define W2 (make-withdraw 100)) to create a second object.

Exercise 3.10

In the make-withdraw procedure, the local variable balance is created as a parameter of make-withdraw. We could also create the local state variable explicitly, using let, as follows:

```
(define (make-withdraw initial-amount)
  (let ((balance initial-amount))
    (lambda (amount)
      (if (>= balance amount)
          (begin (set! balance (- balance amount))
                 balance)
          "Insufficient funds"))))
```

Recall from section 1.3.2 that let is simply syntactic sugar for a procedure call:

(let (((*var*) (*exp*))) (*body*))

is interpreted as an alternate syntax for

((lambda ((*var*)) (*body*)) (*exp*))

Use the environment model to analyze this alternate version of make-withdraw, drawing figures like the ones above to illustrate the interactions

(define W1 (make-withdraw 100))

(W1 50)

(define W2 (make-withdraw 100))

Show that the two versions of make-withdraw create objects with the same behavior. How do the environment structures differ for the two versions?

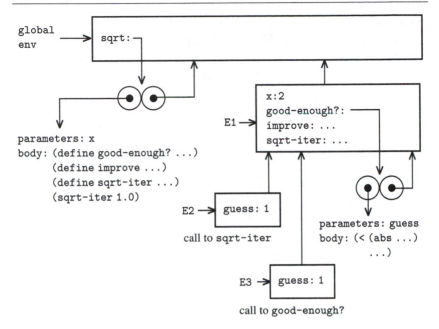

Figure 3.11   Sqrt procedure with internal definitions.

3.2.4   **Internal Definitions**

Section 1.1.8 introduced the idea that procedures can have internal definitions, thus leading to a block structure as in the following procedure to compute square roots:

```
(define (sqrt x)
  (define (good-enough? guess)
    (< (abs (- (square guess) x)) 0.001))
  (define (improve guess)
    (average guess (/ x guess)))
  (define (sqrt-iter guess)
    (if (good-enough? guess)
        guess
        (sqrt-iter (improve guess))))
  (sqrt-iter 1.0))
```

Now we can use the environment model to see why these internal definitions behave as desired. Figure 3.11 shows the point in the evaluation of the expression (sqrt 2) where the internal procedure good-enough? has been called for the first time with guess equal to 1.

Observe the structure of the environment. Sqrt is a symbol in the global environment that is bound to a procedure object whose associated environment is the global environment. When sqrt was called, a new environment E1 was formed, subordinate to the global environment, in which the parameter x is bound to 2. The body of sqrt was then evaluated in E1. Since the first expression in the body of sqrt is

```
(define (good-enough? guess)
  (< (abs (- (square guess) x)) 0.001))
```

evaluating this expression defined the procedure good-enough? in the environment E1. To be more precise, the symbol good-enough? was added to the first frame of E1, bound to a procedure object whose associated environment is E1. Similarly, improve and sqrt-iter were defined as procedures in E1. For conciseness, figure 3.11 shows only the procedure object for good-enough?.

After the local procedures were defined, the expression (sqrt-iter 1.0) was evaluated, still in environment E1. So the procedure object bound to sqrt-iter in E1 was called with 1 as an argument. This created an environment E2 in which guess, the parameter of sqrt-iter, is bound to 1. Sqrt-iter in turn called good-enough? with the value of guess (from E2) as the argument for good-enough?. This set up another environment, E3, in which guess (the parameter of good-enough?) is bound to 1. Although sqrt-iter and good-enough? both have a parameter named guess, these are two distinct local variables located in different frames. Also, E2 and E3 both have E1 as their enclosing environment, because the sqrt-iter and good-enough? procedures both have E1 as their environment part. One consequence of this is that the symbol x that appears in the body of good-enough? will reference the binding of x that appears in E1, namely the value of x with which the original sqrt procedure was called.

The environment model thus explains the two key properties that make local procedure definitions a useful technique for modularizing programs:

• The names of the local procedures do not interfere with names external to the enclosing procedure, because the local procedure names will be bound in the frame that the procedure creates when it is run, rather than being bound in the global environment.

• The local procedures can access the arguments of the enclosing procedure, simply by using parameter names as free variables. This is because the body of the local procedure is evaluated in an environment that is subordinate to the evaluation environment for the enclosing procedure.

Exercise 3.11

In section 3.2.3 we saw how the environment model described the behavior of procedures with local state. Now we have seen how internal definitions work. A typical message-passing procedure contains both of these aspects. Consider the bank account procedure of section 3.1.1:

```
(define (make-account balance)
  (define (withdraw amount)
    (if (>= balance amount)
        (begin (set! balance (- balance amount))
               balance)
        "Insufficient funds"))
  (define (deposit amount)
    (set! balance (+ balance amount))
    balance)
  (define (dispatch m)
    (cond ((eq? m 'withdraw) withdraw)
          ((eq? m 'deposit) deposit)
          (else (error "Unknown request -- MAKE-ACCOUNT"
                       m))))
  dispatch)
```

Show the environment structure generated by the sequence of interactions

```
(define acc (make-account 50))
```

```
((acc 'deposit) 40)
90
```

```
((acc 'withdraw) 60)
30
```

Where is the local state for `acc` kept? Suppose we define another account

```
(define acc2 (make-account 100))
```

How are the local states for the two accounts kept distinct? Which parts of the environment structure are shared between `acc` and `acc2`?

3.3   Modeling with Mutable Data

Chapter 2 dealt with compound data as a means for constructing computational objects that have several parts, in order to model real-world objects that have several aspects. In that chapter we introduced the discipline of data abstraction, according to which data structures are specified in terms of constructors, which create data objects, and selectors, which access the parts of compound data objects. But we now know that there is another aspect of data that chapter 2 did not address. The desire to model systems composed of objects that have changing state leads us to the need to modify compound data objects, as well as to construct and select from them. In order to model compound objects with changing state, we will design data abstractions to include, in addition to selectors and constructors, operations called *mutators*, which modify data objects. For instance, modeling a banking system requires us to change account balances. Thus, a data structure for representing bank accounts might admit an operation

(set-balance! ⟨*account*⟩ ⟨*new-value*⟩)

that changes the balance of the designated account to the designated new value. Data objects for which mutators are defined are known as *mutable data objects*.

Chapter 2 introduced pairs as a general-purpose "glue" for synthesizing compound data. We begin this section by defining basic mutators for pairs, so that pairs can serve as building blocks for constructing mutable data objects. These mutators greatly enhance the representational power of pairs, enabling us to build data structures other than the sequences and trees that we worked with in section 2.2. We also present some examples of simulations in which complex systems are modeled as collections of objects with local state.

3.3.1 Mutable List Structure

The basic operations on pairs—cons, car, and cdr—can be used to construct list structure and to select parts from list structure, but they are incapable of modifying list structure. The same is true of the list operations we have used so far, such as append and list, since these can be defined in terms of cons, car, and cdr. To modify list structures we need new operations.

The primitive mutators for pairs are set-car! and set-cdr!. Set-car! takes two arguments, the first of which must be a pair. It modifies this pair, replacing the car pointer by a pointer to the second argument of set-car!.[16]

As an example, suppose that x is bound to the list ((a b) c d) and y to the list (e f) as illustrated in figure 3.12. Evaluating the expression (set-car! x y) modifies the pair to which x is bound, replacing

---

[16]Set-car! and set-cdr! return implementation-dependent values. Like set!, they should be used only for their effect.

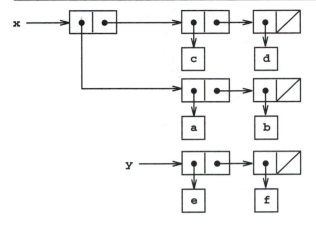

Figure 3.12   Lists x: ((a b) c d) and y: (e f).

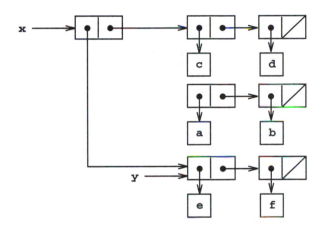

Figure 3.13   Effect of (set-car! x y) on the lists in figure 3.12.

its car by the value of y. The result of the operation is shown in figure 3.13. The structure x has been modified and would now be printed as ((e f) c d). The pairs representing the list (a b), identified by the pointer that was replaced, are now detached from the original structure.[17]

---

[17]We see from this that mutation operations on lists can create "garbage" that is not part of any accessible structure. We will see in section 5.3.2 that Lisp memory-management systems include a *garbage collector*, which identifies and recycles the memory space used by unneeded pairs.

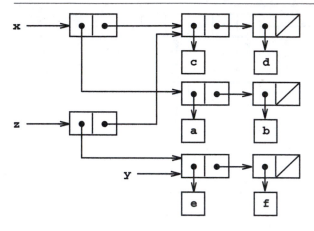

Figure 3.14   Effect of (define z (cons y (cdr x))) on the lists in figure 3.12.

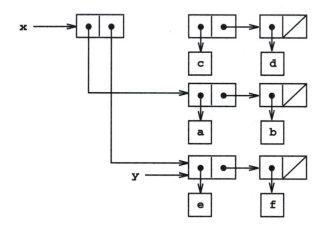

Figure 3.15   Effect of (set-cdr! x y) on the lists in figure 3.12.

Compare figure 3.13 with figure 3.14, which illustrates the result of executing (define z (cons y (cdr x))) with x and y bound to the original lists of figure 3.12. The variable z is now bound to a new pair created by the cons operation; the list to which x is bound is unchanged.

The set-cdr! operation is similar to set-car!. The only difference is that the cdr pointer of the pair, rather than the car pointer, is replaced. The effect of executing (set-cdr! x y) on the lists of figure 3.12 is shown in figure 3.15. Here the cdr pointer of x has been replaced by the pointer to (e f). Also, the list (c d), which used to be the cdr of x, is now detached from the structure.

Cons builds new list structure by creating new pairs, while `set-car!` and `set-cdr!` modify existing pairs. Indeed, we could implement cons in terms of the two mutators, together with a procedure `get-new-pair`, which returns a new pair that is not part of any existing list structure. We obtain the new pair, set its `car` and `cdr` pointers to the designated objects, and return the new pair as the result of the cons.[18]

```
(define (cons x y)
  (let ((new (get-new-pair)))
    (set-car! new x)
    (set-cdr! new y)
    new))
```

Exercise 3.12

The following procedure for appending lists was introduced in section 2.2.1:

```
(define (append x y)
  (if (null? x)
      y
      (cons (car x) (append (cdr x) y))))
```

Append forms a new list by successively consing the elements of x onto y. The procedure append! is similar to append, but it is a mutator rather than a constructor. It appends the lists by splicing them together, modifying the final pair of x so that its cdr is now y. (It is an error to call append! with an empty x.)

```
(define (append! x y)
  (set-cdr! (last-pair x) y)
  x)
```

Here `last-pair` is a procedure that returns the last pair in its argument:

```
(define (last-pair x)
  (if (null? (cdr x))
      x
      (last-pair (cdr x))))
```

Consider the interaction

```
(define x (list 'a 'b))

(define y (list 'c 'd))

(define z (append x y))
```

---

[18] Get-new-pair is one of the operations that must be implemented as part of the memory management required by a Lisp implementation. We will discuss this in section 5.3.1.

z
(a b c d)

```
(cdr x)
```
⟨ *response* ⟩

```
(define w (append! x y))
```

w
(a b c d)

```
(cdr x)
```
⟨ *response* ⟩

What are the missing ⟨ *response* ⟩s? Draw box-and-pointer diagrams to explain your answer.

Exercise 3.13

Consider the following make-cycle procedure, which uses the last-pair procedure defined in exercise 3.12:

```
(define (make-cycle x)
  (set-cdr! (last-pair x) x)
  x)
```

Draw a box-and-pointer diagram that shows the structure z created by

```
(define z (make-cycle (list 'a 'b 'c)))
```

What happens if we try to compute (last-pair z)?

Exercise 3.14

The following procedure is quite useful, although obscure:

```
(define (mystery x)
  (define (loop x y)
    (if (null? x)
        y
        (let ((temp (cdr x)))
          (set-cdr! x y)
          (loop temp x))))
  (loop x '()))
```

Loop uses the "temporary" variable temp to hold the old value of the cdr of x, since the set-cdr! on the next line destroys the cdr. Explain what mystery does in general. Suppose v is defined by (define v (list 'a 'b 'c 'd)). Draw the box-and-pointer diagram that represents the list to which v is bound. Suppose that we now evaluate (define w (mystery v)). Draw box-and-pointer diagrams that show the structures v and w after evaluating this expression. What would be printed as the values of v and w?

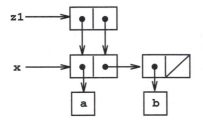

Figure 3.16   The list z1 formed by (cons x x).

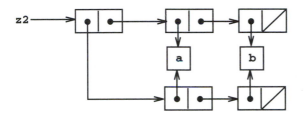

Figure 3.17   The list z2 formed by (cons (list 'a 'b) (list 'a 'b)).

Sharing and identity

We mentioned in section 3.1.3 the theoretical issues of "sameness" and "change" raised by the introduction of assignment. These issues arise in practice when individual pairs are *shared* among different data objects. For example, consider the structure formed by

```
(define x (list 'a 'b))
(define z1 (cons x x))
```

As shown in figure 3.16, z1 is a pair whose car and cdr both point to the same pair x. This sharing of x by the car and cdr of z1 is a consequence of the straightforward way in which cons is implemented. In general, using cons to construct lists will result in an interlinked structure of pairs in which many individual pairs are shared by many different structures.

In contrast to figure 3.16, figure 3.17 shows the structure created by

```
(define z2 (cons (list 'a 'b) (list 'a 'b)))
```

In this structure, the pairs in the two (a b) lists are distinct, although the actual symbols are shared.[19]

---

[19]The two pairs are distinct because each call to cons returns a new pair. The symbols are shared; in Scheme there is a unique symbol with any given name. Since Scheme provides no way to mutate a symbol, this sharing is undetectable. Note also that the sharing is what enables us to compare symbols using eq?, which simply checks equality of pointers.

When thought of as a list, z1 and z2 both represent "the same" list,
((a b) a b). In general, sharing is completely undetectable if we operate on lists using only cons, car, and cdr. However, if we allow mutators on list structure, sharing becomes significant. As an example of
the difference that sharing can make, consider the following procedure,
which modifies the car of the structure to which it is applied:

```
(define (set-to-wow! x)
  (set-car! (car x) 'wow)
  x)
```

Even though z1 and z2 are "the same" structure, applying set-to-wow!
to them yields different results. With z1, altering the car also changes
the cdr, because in z1 the car and the cdr are the same pair. With z2,
the car and cdr are distinct, so set-to-wow! modifies only the car:

```
z1
((a b) a b)

(set-to-wow! z1)
((wow b) wow b)

z2
((a b) a b)

(set-to-wow! z2)
((wow b) a b)
```

One way to detect sharing in list structures is to use the predicate eq?,
which we introduced in section 2.3.1 as a way to test whether two symbols are equal. More generally, (eq? x y) tests whether x and y are the
same object (that is, whether x and y are equal as pointers). Thus, with z1
and z2 as defined in figures 3.16 and 3.17, (eq? (car z1) (cdr z1))
is true and (eq? (car z2) (cdr z2)) is false.

As will be seen in the following sections, we can exploit sharing to
greatly extend the repertoire of data structures that can be represented
by pairs. On the other hand, sharing can also be dangerous, since modifications made to structures will also affect other structures that happen to share the modified parts. The mutation operations set-car! and

`set-cdr!` should be used with care; unless we have a good understanding of how our data objects are shared, mutation can have unanticipated results.[20]

Exercise 3.15

Draw box-and-pointer diagrams to explain the effect of `set-to-wow!` on the structures `z1` and `z2` above.

Exercise 3.16

Ben Bitdiddle decides to write a procedure to count the number of pairs in any list structure. "It's easy," he reasons. "The number of pairs in any structure is the number in the `car` plus the number in the `cdr` plus one more to count the current pair." So Ben writes the following procedure:

```
(define (count-pairs x)
  (if (not (pair? x))
      0
      (+ (count-pairs (car x))
         (count-pairs (cdr x))
         1)))
```

Show that this procedure is not correct. In particular, draw box-and-pointer diagrams representing list structures made up of exactly three pairs for which Ben's procedure would return 3; return 4; return 7; never return at all.

Exercise 3.17

Devise a correct version of the `count-pairs` procedure of exercise 3.16 that returns the number of distinct pairs in any structure. (Hint: Traverse the structure, maintaining an auxiliary data structure that is used to keep track of which pairs have already been counted.)

---

[20]The subtleties of dealing with sharing of mutable data objects reflect the underlying issues of "sameness" and "change" that were raised in section 3.1.3. We mentioned there that admitting change to our language requires that a compound object must have an "identity" that is something different from the pieces from which it is composed. In Lisp, we consider this "identity" to be the quality that is tested by eq?, i.e., by equality of pointers. Since in most Lisp implementations a pointer is essentially a memory address, we are "solving the problem" of defining the identity of objects by stipulating that a data object "itself" is the information stored in some particular set of memory locations in the computer. This suffices for simple Lisp programs, but is hardly a general way to resolve the issue of "sameness" in computational models.

Exercise 3.18

Write a procedure that examines a list and determines whether it contains a cycle, that is, whether a program that tried to find the end of the list by taking successive cdrs would go into an infinite loop. Exercise 3.13 constructed such lists.

Exercise 3.19

Redo exercise 3.18 using an algorithm that takes only a constant amount of space. (This requires a very clever idea.)

Mutation is just assignment

When we introduced compound data, we observed in section 2.1.3 that pairs can be represented purely in terms of procedures:

```
(define (cons x y)
  (define (dispatch m)
    (cond ((eq? m 'car) x)
          ((eq? m 'cdr) y)
          (else (error "Undefined operation -- CONS" m))))
  dispatch)

(define (car z) (z 'car))

(define (cdr z) (z 'cdr))
```

The same observation is true for mutable data. We can implement mutable data objects as procedures using assignment and local state. For instance, we can extend the above pair implementation to handle set-car! and set-cdr! in a manner analogous to the way we implemented bank accounts using make-account in section 3.1.1:

```
(define (cons x y)
  (define (set-x! v) (set! x v))
  (define (set-y! v) (set! y v))
  (define (dispatch m)
    (cond ((eq? m 'car) x)
          ((eq? m 'cdr) y)
          ((eq? m 'set-car!) set-x!)
          ((eq? m 'set-cdr!) set-y!)
          (else (error "Undefined operation -- CONS" m))))
  dispatch)

(define (car z) (z 'car))

(define (cdr z) (z 'cdr))
```

```
(define (set-car! z new-value)
  ((z 'set-car!) new-value)
  z)

(define (set-cdr! z new-value)
  ((z 'set-cdr!) new-value)
  z)
```

Assignment is all that is needed, theoretically, to account for the behavior of mutable data. As soon as we admit `set!` to our language, we raise all the issues, not only of assignment, but of mutable data in general.[21]

Exercise 3.20

Draw environment diagrams to illustrate the evaluation of the sequence of expressions

```
(define x (cons 1 2))
(define z (cons x x))
(set-car! (cdr z) 17)

(car x)
17
```

using the procedural implementation of pairs given above. (Compare exercise 3.11.)

3.3.2   Representing Queues

The mutators `set-car!` and `set-cdr!` enable us to use pairs to construct data structures that cannot be built with `cons`, `car`, and `cdr` alone. This section shows how to use pairs to represent a data structure called a queue. Section 3.3.3 will show how to represent data structures called tables.

A *queue* is a sequence in which items are inserted at one end (called the *rear* of the queue) and deleted from the other end (the *front*). Figure 3.18 shows an initially empty queue in which the items a and b are inserted. Then a is removed, c and d are inserted, and b is removed. Because items are always removed in the order in which they are inserted, a queue is sometimes called a *FIFO* (first in, first out) buffer.

---

[21]On the other hand, from the viewpoint of implementation, assignment requires us to modify the environment, which is itself a mutable data structure. Thus, assignment and mutation are equipotent: Each can be implemented in terms of the other.

Operation   Resulting Queue

```
(define q (make-queue))
(insert-queue! q 'a)      a
(insert-queue! q 'b)      a b
(delete-queue! q)         b
(insert-queue! q 'c)      b c
(insert-queue! q 'd)      b c d
(delete-queue! q)         c d
```

Figure 3.18   Queue operations.

In terms of data abstraction, we can regard a queue as defined by the following set of operations:

● a constructor:
(make-queue)
returns an empty queue (a queue containing no items).

● two selectors:
(empty-queue? ⟨*queue*⟩)
tests if the queue is empty.

(front-queue ⟨*queue*⟩)
returns the object at the front of the queue, signaling an error if the queue is empty; it does not modify the queue.

● two mutators:
(insert-queue! ⟨*queue*⟩ ⟨*item*⟩)
inserts the item at the rear of the queue and returns the modified queue as its value.

(delete-queue! ⟨*queue*⟩)
removes the item at the front of the queue and returns the modified queue as its value, signaling an error if the queue is empty before the deletion.

Because a queue is a sequence of items, we could certainly represent it as an ordinary list; the front of the queue would be the car of the list, inserting an item in the queue would amount to appending a new element at the end of the list, and deleting an item from the queue would just be taking the cdr of the list. However, this representation is ineffi-

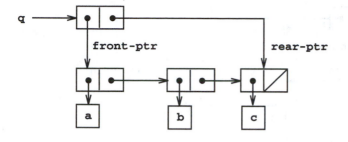

Figure 3.19   Implementation of a queue as a list with front and rear pointers.

cient, because in order to insert an item we must scan the list until we reach the end. Since the only method we have for scanning a list is by successive cdr operations, this scanning requires $\Theta(n)$ steps for a list of n items. A simple modification to the list representation overcomes this disadvantage by allowing the queue operations to be implemented so that they require $\Theta(1)$ steps; that is, so that the number of steps needed is independent of the length of the queue.

The difficulty with the list representation arises from the need to scan to find the end of the list. The reason we need to scan is that, although the standard way of representing a list as a chain of pairs readily provides us with a pointer to the beginning of the list, it gives us no easily accessible pointer to the end. The modification that avoids the drawback is to represent the queue as a list, together with an additional pointer that indicates the final pair in the list. That way, when we go to insert an item, we can consult the rear pointer and so avoid scanning the list.

A queue is represented, then, as a pair of pointers, front-ptr and rear-ptr, which indicate, respectively, the first and last pairs in an ordinary list. Since we would like the queue to be an identifiable object, we can use cons to combine the two pointers. Thus, the queue itself will be the cons of the two pointers. Figure 3.19 illustrates this representation.

To define the queue operations we use the following procedures, which enable us to select and to modify the front and rear pointers of a queue:

```
(define (front-ptr queue) (car queue))

(define (rear-ptr queue) (cdr queue))

(define (set-front-ptr! queue item) (set-car! queue item))

(define (set-rear-ptr! queue item) (set-cdr! queue item))
```

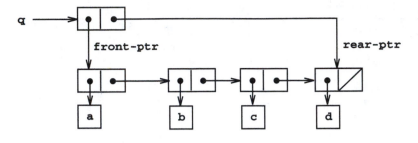

Figure 3.20 Result of using (insert-queue! q 'd) on the queue of figure 3.19.

Now we can implement the actual queue operations. We will consider a queue to be empty if its front pointer is the empty list:

```
(define (empty-queue? queue) (null? (front-ptr queue)))
```

The make-queue constructor returns, as an initially empty queue, a pair whose car and cdr are both the empty list:

```
(define (make-queue) (cons '() '()))
```

To select the item at the front of the queue, we return the car of the pair indicated by the front pointer:

```
(define (front-queue queue)
  (if (empty-queue? queue)
      (error "FRONT called with an empty queue" queue)
      (car (front-ptr queue))))
```

To insert an item in a queue, we follow the method whose result is indicated in figure 3.20. We first create a new pair whose car is the item to be inserted and whose cdr is the empty list. If the queue was initially empty, we set the front and rear pointers of the queue to this new pair. Otherwise, we modify the final pair in the queue to point to the new pair, and also set the rear pointer to the new pair.

```
(define (insert-queue! queue item)
  (let ((new-pair (cons item '())))
    (cond ((empty-queue? queue)
           (set-front-ptr! queue new-pair)
           (set-rear-ptr! queue new-pair)
           queue)
          (else
           (set-cdr! (rear-ptr queue) new-pair)
           (set-rear-ptr! queue new-pair)
           queue))))
```

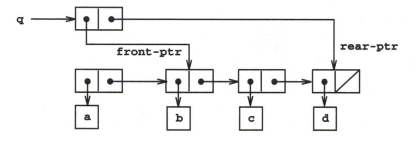

Figure 3.21 Result of using (`delete-queue!` q) on the queue of figure 3.20.

To delete the item at the front of the queue, we merely modify the front pointer so that it now points at the second item in the queue, which can be found by following the `cdr` pointer of the first item (see figure 3.21):[22]

```
(define (delete-queue! queue)
  (cond ((empty-queue? queue)
         (error "DELETE! called with an empty queue" queue))
        (else
         (set-front-ptr! queue (cdr (front-ptr queue)))
         queue)))
```

Exercise 3.21

Ben Bitdiddle decides to test the queue implementation described above. He types in the procedures to the Lisp interpreter and proceeds to try them out:

```
(define q1 (make-queue))

(insert-queue! q1 'a)
((a) a)

(insert-queue! q1 'b)
((a b) b)

(delete-queue! q1)
((b) b)

(delete-queue! q1)
(() b)
```

"It's all wrong!" he complains. "The interpreter's response shows that the last item is inserted into the queue twice. And when I delete both items, the second b

---

[22]If the first item is the final item in the queue, the front pointer will be the empty list after the deletion, which will mark the queue as empty; we needn't worry about updating the rear pointer, which will still point to the deleted item, because `empty-queue?` looks only at the front pointer.

is still there, so the queue isn't empty, even though it's supposed to be." Eva Lu Ator suggests that Ben has misunderstood what is happening. "It's not that the items are going into the queue twice," she explains. "It's just that the standard Lisp printer doesn't know how to make sense of the queue representation. If you want to see the queue printed correctly, you'll have to define your own print procedure for queues." Explain what Eva Lu is talking about. In particular, show why Ben's examples produce the printed results that they do. Define a procedure `print-queue` that takes a queue as input and prints the sequence of items in the queue.

Exercise 3.22

Instead of representing a queue as a pair of pointers, we can build a queue as a procedure with local state. The local state will consist of pointers to the beginning and the end of an ordinary list. Thus, the `make-queue` procedure will have the form

```
(define (make-queue)
  (let ((front-ptr ... )
        (rear-ptr ... ))
    ⟨ definitions of internal procedures ⟩
    (define (dispatch m) ...)
    dispatch))
```

Complete the definition of `make-queue` and provide implementations of the queue operations using this representation.

Exercise 3.23

A *deque* ("double-ended queue") is a sequence in which items can be inserted and deleted at either the front or the rear. Operations on deques are the constructor `make-deque`, the predicate `empty-deque?`, selectors `front-deque` and `rear-deque`, and mutators `front-insert-deque!`, `rear-insert-deque!`, `front-delete-deque!`, and `rear-delete-deque!`. Show how to represent deques using pairs, and give implementations of the operations.[23] All operations should be accomplished in $\Theta(1)$ steps.

3.3.3   Representing Tables

When we studied various ways of representing sets in chapter 2, we mentioned in section 2.3.3 the task of maintaining a table of records indexed by identifying keys. In the implementation of data-directed programming in section 2.4.3, we made extensive use of two-dimensional tables, in which information is stored and retrieved using two keys. Here we see how to build tables as mutable list structures.

---

[23]Be careful not to make the interpreter try to print a structure that contains cycles. (See exercise 3.13.)

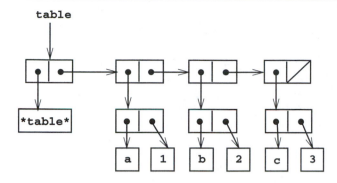

Figure 3.22   A table represented as a headed list.

We first consider a one-dimensional table, in which each value is stored under a single key. We implement the table as a list of records, each of which is implemented as a pair consisting of a key and the associated value. The records are glued together to form a list by pairs whose `cars` point to successive records. These gluing pairs are called the *backbone* of the table. In order to have a place that we can change when we add a new record to the table, we build the table as a *headed list*. A headed list has a special backbone pair at the beginning, which holds a dummy "record"—in this case the arbitrarily chosen symbol `*table*`. Figure 3.22 shows the box-and-pointer diagram for the table

```
a:    1
b:    2
c:    3
```

To extract information from a table we use the `lookup` procedure, which takes a key as argument and returns the associated value (or false if there is no value stored under that key). Lookup is defined in terms of the `assoc` operation, which expects a key and a list of records as arguments. Note that `assoc` never sees the dummy record. Assoc returns the record that has the given key as its `car`.[24] Lookup then checks to see that the resulting record returned by `assoc` is not false, and returns the value (the `cdr`) of the record.

---

[24]Because `assoc` uses `equal?`, it can recognize keys that are symbols, numbers, or list structure.

```
(define (lookup key table)
  (let ((record (assoc key (cdr table))))
    (if record
        (cdr record)
        false)))

(define (assoc key records)
  (cond ((null? records) false)
        ((equal? key (caar records)) (car records))
        (else (assoc key (cdr records)))))
```

To insert a value in a table under a specified key, we first use `assoc` to see if there is already a record in the table with this key. If not, we form a new record by `cons`ing the key with the value, and insert this at the head of the table's list of records, after the dummy record. If there already is a record with this key, we set the `cdr` of this record to the designated new value. The header of the table provides us with a fixed location to modify in order to insert the new record.[25]

```
(define (insert! key value table)
  (let ((record (assoc key (cdr table))))
    (if record
        (set-cdr! record value)
        (set-cdr! table
                  (cons (cons key value) (cdr table)))))
  'ok)
```

To construct a new table, we simply create a list containing the symbol `*table*`:

```
(define (make-table)
  (list '*table*))
```

Two-dimensional tables

In a two-dimensional table, each value is indexed by two keys. We can construct such a table as a one-dimensional table in which each key iden-

---

[25]Thus, the first backbone pair is the object that represents the table "itself"; that is, a pointer to the table is a pointer to this pair. This same backbone pair always starts the table. If we did not arrange things in this way, `insert!` would have to return a new value for the start of the table when it added a new record.

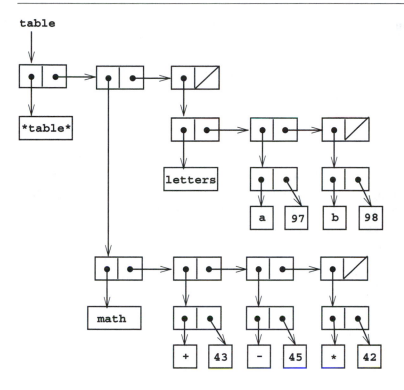

Figure 3.23   A two-dimensional table.

tifies a subtable. Figure 3.23 shows the box-and-pointer diagram for the table

```
math:
     +:   43
     -:   45
     *:   42
letters:
     a:   97
     b:   98
```

which has two subtables. (The subtables don't need a special header symbol, since the key that identifies the subtable serves this purpose.)

When we look up an item, we use the first key to identify the correct subtable. Then we use the second key to identify the record within the subtable.

```
(define (lookup key-1 key-2 table)
  (let ((subtable (assoc key-1 (cdr table))))
    (if subtable
        (let ((record (assoc key-2 (cdr subtable))))
          (if record
              (cdr record)
              false))
        false)))
```

To insert a new item under a pair of keys, we use `assoc` to see if there is a subtable stored under the first key. If not, we build a new subtable containing the single record (`key-2`, `value`) and insert it into the table under the first key. If a subtable already exists for the first key, we insert the new record into this subtable, using the insertion method for one-dimensional tables described above:

```
(define (insert! key-1 key-2 value table)
  (let ((subtable (assoc key-1 (cdr table))))
    (if subtable
        (let ((record (assoc key-2 (cdr subtable))))
          (if record
              (set-cdr! record value)
              (set-cdr! subtable
                        (cons (cons key-2 value)
                              (cdr subtable)))))
        (set-cdr! table
                  (cons (list key-1
                              (cons key-2 value))
                        (cdr table)))))
  'ok)
```

Creating local tables

The `lookup` and `insert!` operations defined above take the table as an argument. This enables us to use programs that access more than one table. Another way to deal with multiple tables is to have separate `lookup` and `insert!` procedures for each table. We can do this by representing a table procedurally, as an object that maintains an internal table as part of its local state. When sent an appropriate message, this "table object" supplies the procedure with which to operate on the internal table. Here is a generator for two-dimensional tables represented in this fashion:

```
(define (make-table)
  (let ((local-table (list '*table*)))
    (define (lookup key-1 key-2)
      (let ((subtable (assoc key-1 (cdr local-table))))
        (if subtable
            (let ((record (assoc key-2 (cdr subtable))))
              (if record
                  (cdr record)
                  false))
            false)))
    (define (insert! key-1 key-2 value)
      (let ((subtable (assoc key-1 (cdr local-table))))
        (if subtable
            (let ((record (assoc key-2 (cdr subtable))))
              (if record
                  (set-cdr! record value)
                  (set-cdr! subtable
                            (cons (cons key-2 value)
                                  (cdr subtable)))))
            (set-cdr! local-table
                      (cons (list key-1
                                  (cons key-2 value))
                            (cdr local-table)))))
      'ok)
    (define (dispatch m)
      (cond ((eq? m 'lookup-proc) lookup)
            ((eq? m 'insert-proc!) insert!)
            (else (error "Unknown operation -- TABLE" m))))
    dispatch))
```

Using `make-table`, we could implement the `get` and `put` operations used in section 2.4.3 for data-directed programming, as follows:

```
(define operation-table (make-table))
(define get (operation-table 'lookup-proc))
(define put (operation-table 'insert-proc!))
```

Get takes as arguments two keys, and put takes as arguments two keys and a value. Both operations access the same local table, which is encapsulated within the object created by the call to `make-table`.

Exercise 3.24

In the table implementations above, the keys are tested for equality using `equal?` (called by `assoc`). This is not always the appropriate test. For instance, we might have a table with numeric keys in which we don't need an exact match to the number we're looking up, but only a number within some tolerance of it. Design a table constructor `make-table` that takes as an argument a `same-key?` procedure that will be used to test "equality" of keys. `Make-table` should return a `dispatch` procedure that can be used to access appropriate `lookup` and `insert!` procedures for a local table.

Exercise 3.25

Generalizing one- and two-dimensional tables, show how to implement a table in which values are stored under an arbitrary number of keys and different values may be stored under different numbers of keys. The `lookup` and `insert!` procedures should take as input a list of keys used to access the table.

Exercise 3.26

To search a table as implemented above, one needs to scan through the list of records. This is basically the unordered list representation of section 2.3.3. For large tables, it may be more efficient to structure the table in a different manner. Describe a table implementation where the (key, value) records are organized using a binary tree, assuming that keys can be ordered in some way (e.g., numerically or alphabetically). (Compare exercise 2.66 of chapter 2.)

Exercise 3.27

Memoization (also called *tabulation*) is a technique that enables a procedure to record, in a local table, values that have previously been computed. This technique can make a vast difference in the performance of a program. A memoized procedure maintains a table in which values of previous calls are stored using as keys the arguments that produced the values. When the memoized procedure is asked to compute a value, it first checks the table to see if the value is already there and, if so, just returns that value. Otherwise, it computes the new value in the ordinary way and stores this in the table. As an example of memoization, recall from section 1.2.2 the exponential process for computing Fibonacci numbers:

```
(define (fib n)
  (cond ((= n 0) 0)
        ((= n 1) 1)
        (else (+ (fib (- n 1))
                 (fib (- n 2))))))
```

The memoized version of the same procedure is

```
(define memo-fib
  (memoize (lambda (n)
             (cond ((= n 0) 0)
                   ((= n 1) 1)
                   (else (+ (memo-fib (- n 1))
                            (memo-fib (- n 2))))))))
```

where the memoizer is defined as

```
(define (memoize f)
  (let ((table (make-table)))
    (lambda (x)
      (let ((previously-computed-result (lookup x table)))
        (or previously-computed-result
            (let ((result (f x)))
              (insert! x result table)
              result))))))
```

Draw an environment diagram to analyze the computation of (memo-fib 3). Explain why memo-fib computes the *n*th Fibonacci number in a number of steps proportional to *n*. Would the scheme still work if we had simply defined memo-fib to be (memoize fib)?

3.3.4   A Simulator for Digital Circuits

Designing complex digital systems, such as computers, is an important engineering activity. Digital systems are constructed by interconnecting simple elements. Although the behavior of these individual elements is simple, networks of them can have very complex behavior. Computer simulation of proposed circuit designs is an important tool used by digital systems engineers. In this section we design a system for performing digital logic simulations. This system typifies a kind of program called an *event-driven simulation*, in which actions ("events") trigger further events that happen at a later time, which in turn trigger more events, and so so.

Our computational model of a circuit will be composed of objects that correspond to the elementary components from which the circuit is constructed. There are *wires*, which carry *digital signals*. A digital signal may at any moment have only one of two possible values, 0 and 1. There are also various types of digital *function boxes*, which connect wires carrying input signals to other output wires. Such boxes produce output signals computed from their input signals. The output signal is delayed by a time that depends on the type of the function box. For example, an *inverter* is a primitive function box that inverts its input. If the input signal to an inverter changes to 0, then one inverter-delay later the inverter will change its output signal to 1. If the input signal to an inverter changes to 1, then one inverter-delay later the inverter will change its output signal to 0. We draw an inverter symbolically as in figure 3.24. An *and-gate*, also shown in figure 3.24, is a primitive function box with two inputs and one output. It drives its output signal to a value that is the *logical and* of the inputs. That is, if both of its input signals become 1, then one and-gate-delay time later the and-gate will force its output signal to

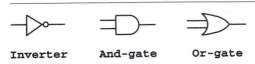

Inverter   **And-gate**   **Or-gate**

Figure 3.24   Primitive functions in the digital logic simulator.

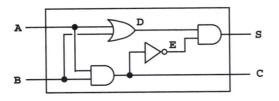

Figure 3.25   A half-adder circuit.

be 1; otherwise the output will be 0. An *or-gate* is a similar two-input primitive function box that drives its output signal to a value that is the *logical or* of the inputs. That is, the output will become 1 if at least one of the input signals is 1; otherwise the output will become 0.

We can connect primitive functions together to construct more complex functions. To accomplish this we wire the outputs of some function boxes to the inputs of other function boxes. For example, the *half-adder* circuit shown in figure 3.25 consists of an or-gate, two and-gates, and an inverter. It takes two input signals, A and B, and has two output signals, S and C. S will become 1 whenever precisely one of A and B is 1, and C will become 1 whenever A and B are both 1. We can see from the figure that, because of the delays involved, the outputs may be generated at different times. Many of the difficulties in the design of digital circuits arise from this fact.

We will now build a program for modeling the digital logic circuits we wish to study. The program will construct computational objects modeling the wires, which will "hold" the signals. Function boxes will be modeled by procedures that enforce the correct relationships among the signals.

One basic element of our simulation will be a procedure make-wire, which constructs wires. For example, we can construct six wires as follows:

```
(define a (make-wire))
(define b (make-wire))
(define c (make-wire))
```

```
(define d (make-wire))
(define e (make-wire))
(define s (make-wire))
```

We attach a function box to a set of wires by calling a procedure that constructs that kind of box. The arguments to the constructor procedure are the wires to be attached to the box. For example, given that we can construct and-gates, or-gates, and inverters, we can wire together the half-adder shown in figure 3.25:

```
(or-gate a b d)
```
ok

```
(and-gate a b c)
```
ok

```
(inverter c e)
```
ok

```
(and-gate d e s)
```
ok

Better yet, we can explicitly name this operation by defining a procedure `half-adder` that constructs this circuit, given the four external wires to be attached to the half-adder:

```
(define (half-adder a b s c)
  (let ((d (make-wire)) (e (make-wire)))
    (or-gate a b d)
    (and-gate a b c)
    (inverter c e)
    (and-gate d e s)
    'ok))
```

The advantage of making this definition is that we can use `half-adder` itself as a building block in creating more complex circuits. Figure 3.26, for example, shows a *full-adder* composed of two half-adders and an or-gate.[26] We can construct a full-adder as follows:

---

[26] A full-adder is a basic circuit element used in adding two binary numbers. Here A and B are the bits at corresponding positions in the two numbers to be added, and C_{in} is the carry bit from the addition one place to the right. The circuit generates SUM, which is the sum bit in the corresponding position, and C_{out}, which is the carry bit to be propagated to the left.

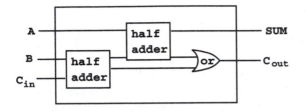

Figure 3.26   A full-adder circuit.

```
(define (full-adder a b c-in sum c-out)
  (let ((s (make-wire))
        (c1 (make-wire))
        (c2 (make-wire)))
    (half-adder b c-in s c1)
    (half-adder a s sum c2)
    (or-gate c1 c2 c-out)
    'ok))
```

Having defined full-adder as a procedure, we can now use it as a building block for creating still more complex circuits. (For example, see exercise 3.30.)

In essence, our simulator provides us with the tools to construct a language of circuits. If we adopt the general perspective on languages with which we approached the study of Lisp in section 1.1, we can say that the primitive function boxes form the primitive elements of the language, that wiring boxes together provides a means of combination, and that specifying wiring patterns as procedures serves as a means of abstraction.

Primitive function boxes

The primitive function boxes implement the "forces" by which a change in the signal on one wire influences the signals on other wires. To build function boxes, we use the following operations on wires:

- (get-signal ⟨*wire*⟩)
returns the current value of the signal on the wire.

- (set-signal! ⟨*wire*⟩ ⟨*new value*⟩)
changes the value of the signal on the wire to the new value.

- (add-action! ⟨*wire*⟩ ⟨*procedure of no arguments*⟩)
asserts that the designated procedure should be run whenever the signal on the wire changes value. Such procedures are the vehicles by which changes in the signal value on the wire are communicated to other wires.

In addition, we will make use of a procedure `after-delay` that takes a time delay and a procedure to be run and executes the given procedure after the given delay.

Using these procedures, we can define the primitive digital logic functions. To connect an input to an output through an inverter, we use `add-action!` to associate with the input wire a procedure that will be run whenever the signal on the input wire changes value. The procedure computes the `logical-not` of the input signal, and then, after one `inverter-delay`, sets the output signal to be this new value:

```
(define (inverter input output)
  (define (invert-input)
    (let ((new-value (logical-not (get-signal input))))
      (after-delay inverter-delay
                   (lambda ()
                     (set-signal! output new-value)))))
  (add-action! input invert-input)
  'ok)

(define (logical-not s)
  (cond ((= s 0) 1)
        ((= s 1) 0)
        (else (error "Invalid signal" s))))
```

An and-gate is a little more complex. The action procedure must be run if either of the inputs to the gate changes. It computes the `logical-and` (using a procedure analogous to `logical-not`) of the values of the signals on the input wires and sets up a change to the new value to occur on the output wire after one `and-gate-delay`.

```
(define (and-gate a1 a2 output)
  (define (and-action-procedure)
    (let ((new-value
           (logical-and (get-signal a1) (get-signal a2))))
      (after-delay and-gate-delay
                   (lambda ()
                     (set-signal! output new-value)))))
  (add-action! a1 and-action-procedure)
  (add-action! a2 and-action-procedure)
  'ok)
```

Exercise 3.28

Define an or-gate as a primitive function box. Your `or-gate` constructor should be similar to `and-gate`.

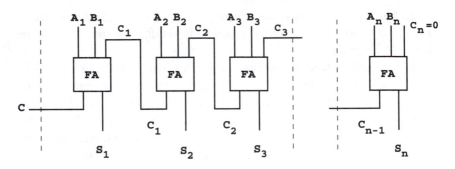

Figure 3.27   A ripple-carry adder for n-bit numbers.

Exercise 3.29

Another way to construct an or-gate is as a compound digital logic device, built from and-gates and inverters. Define a procedure `or-gate` that accomplishes this. What is the delay time of the or-gate in terms of `and-gate-delay` and `inverter-delay`?

Exercise 3.30

Figure 3.27 shows a *ripple-carry adder* formed by stringing together n full-adders. This is the simplest form of parallel adder for adding two n-bit binary numbers. The inputs $A_1, A_2, A_3, \ldots, A_n$ and $B_1, B_2, B_3, \ldots, B_n$ are the two binary numbers to be added (each A_k and B_k is a 0 or a 1). The circuit generates $S_1, S_2, S_3, \ldots, S_n$, the n bits of the sum, and C, the carry from the addition. Write a procedure `ripple-carry-adder` that generates this circuit. The procedure should take as arguments three lists of n wires each—the A_k, the B_k, and the S_k—and also another wire C. The major drawback of the ripple-carry adder is the need to wait for the carry signals to propagate. What is the delay needed to obtain the complete output from an n-bit ripple-carry adder, expressed in terms of the delays for and-gates, or-gates, and inverters?

Representing wires

A wire in our simulation will be a computational object with two local state variables: a `signal-value` (initially taken to be 0) and a collection of `action-procedures` to be run when the signal changes value. We implement the wire, using message-passing style, as a collection of local procedures together with a `dispatch` procedure that selects the appropriate local operation, just as we did with the simple bank-account object in section 3.1.1:

```
(define (make-wire)
  (let ((signal-value 0) (action-procedures '()))
    (define (set-my-signal! new-value)
      (if (not (= signal-value new-value))
          (begin (set! signal-value new-value)
                 (call-each action-procedures))
          'done))

    (define (accept-action-procedure! proc)
      (set! action-procedures (cons proc action-procedures))
      (proc))

    (define (dispatch m)
      (cond ((eq? m 'get-signal) signal-value)
            ((eq? m 'set-signal!) set-my-signal!)
            ((eq? m 'add-action!) accept-action-procedure!)
            (else (error "Unknown operation -- WIRE" m))))
    dispatch))
```

The local procedure set-my-signal! tests whether the new signal value
changes the signal on the wire. If so, it runs each of the action procedures, using the following procedure call-each, which calls each of the
items in a list of no-argument procedures:

```
(define (call-each procedures)
  (if (null? procedures)
      'done
      (begin
        ((car procedures))
        (call-each (cdr procedures)))))
```

The local procedure accept-action-procedure! adds the given procedure to the list of procedures to be run, and then runs the new procedure
once. (See exercise 3.31.)

With the local dispatch procedure set up as specified, we can provide
the following procedures to access the local operations on wires:[27]

---

[27]These procedures are simply syntactic sugar that allow us to use ordinary procedural
syntax to access the local procedures of objects. It is striking that we can interchange
the role of "procedures" and "data" in such a simple way. For example, if we write
(wire 'get-signal) we think of wire as a procedure that is called with the message get-signal as input. Alternatively, writing (get-signal wire) encourages us
to think of wire as a data object that is the input to a procedure get-signal. The truth
of the matter is that, in a language in which we can deal with procedures as objects, there
is no fundamental difference between "procedures" and "data," and we can choose our
syntactic sugar to allow us to program in whatever style we choose.

```
(define (get-signal wire)
  (wire 'get-signal))

(define (set-signal! wire new-value)
  ((wire 'set-signal!) new-value))

(define (add-action! wire action-procedure)
  ((wire 'add-action!) action-procedure))
```

Wires, which have time-varying signals and may be incrementally attached to devices, are typical of mutable objects. We have modeled them as procedures with local state variables that are modified by assignment. When a new wire is created, a new set of state variables is allocated (by the `let` expression in `make-wire`) and a new `dispatch` procedure is constructed and returned, capturing the environment with the new state variables.

The wires are shared among the various devices that have been connected to them. Thus, a change made by an interaction with one device will affect all the other devices attached to the wire. The wire communicates the change to its neighbors by calling the action procedures provided to it when the connections were established.

The agenda

The only thing needed to complete the simulator is `after-delay`. The idea here is that we maintain a data structure, called an *agenda*, that contains a schedule of things to do. The following operations are defined for agendas:

- (make-agenda)
returns a new empty agenda.

- (empty-agenda? ⟨*agenda*⟩)
is true if the specified agenda is empty.

- (first-agenda-item ⟨*agenda*⟩)
returns the first item on the agenda.

- (remove-first-agenda-item! ⟨*agenda*⟩)
modifies the agenda by removing the first item.

- (add-to-agenda! ⟨*time*⟩ ⟨*action*⟩ ⟨*agenda*⟩)
modifies the agenda by adding the given action procedure to be run at the specified time.

- (current-time ⟨*agenda*⟩)
returns the current simulation time.

The particular agenda that we use is denoted by `the-agenda`. The procedure `after-delay` adds new elements to `the-agenda`:

```
(define (after-delay delay action)
  (add-to-agenda! (+ delay (current-time the-agenda))
                  action
                  the-agenda))
```

The simulation is driven by the procedure `propagate`, which operates on `the-agenda`, executing each procedure on the agenda in sequence. In general, as the simulation runs, new items will be added to the agenda, and `propagate` will continue the simulation as long as there are items on the agenda:

```
(define (propagate)
  (if (empty-agenda? the-agenda)
      'done
      (let ((first-item (first-agenda-item the-agenda)))
        (first-item)
        (remove-first-agenda-item! the-agenda)
        (propagate))))
```

A sample simulation

The following procedure, which places a "probe" on a wire, shows the simulator in action. The probe tells the wire that, whenever its signal changes value, it should print the new signal value, together with the current time and a name that identifies the wire:

```
(define (probe name wire)
  (add-action! wire
               (lambda ()
                 (newline)
                 (display name)
                 (display " ")
                 (display (current-time the-agenda))
                 (display "  New-value = ")
                 (display (get-signal wire)))))
```

We begin by initializing the agenda and specifying delays for the primitive function boxes:

```
(define the-agenda (make-agenda))
(define inverter-delay 2)
(define and-gate-delay 3)
(define or-gate-delay 5)
```

Now we define four wires, placing probes on two of them:

```
(define input-1 (make-wire))
(define input-2 (make-wire))
(define sum (make-wire))
(define carry (make-wire))

(probe 'sum sum)
sum 0  New-value = 0

(probe 'carry carry)
carry 0  New-value = 0
```

Next we connect the wires in a half-adder circuit (as in figure 3.25), set the signal on input-1 to 1, and run the simulation:

```
(half-adder input-1 input-2 sum carry)
ok

(set-signal! input-1 1)
done

(propagate)
sum 8  New-value = 1
done
```

The sum signal changes to 1 at time 8. We are now eight time units from the beginning of the simulation. At this point, we can set the signal on input-2 to 1 and allow the values to propagate:

```
(set-signal! input-2 1)
done

(propagate)
carry 11  New-value = 1
sum 16  New-value = 0
done
```

The carry changes to 1 at time 11 and the sum changes to 0 at time 16.

Exercise 3.31

The internal procedure accept-action-procedure! defined in make-wire specifies that when a new action procedure is added to a wire, the procedure is immediately run. Explain why this initialization is necessary. In particular, trace through the half-adder example in the paragraphs above and say how the system's response would differ if we had defined accept-action-procedure! as

```
(define (accept-action-procedure! proc)
  (set! action-procedures (cons proc action-procedures)))
```

Implementing the agenda

Finally, we give details of the agenda data structure, which holds the procedures that are scheduled for future execution.

The agenda is made up of *time segments*. Each time segment is a pair consisting of a number (the time) and a queue (see exercise 3.32) that holds the procedures that are scheduled to be run during that time segment.

```
(define (make-time-segment time queue)
  (cons time queue))

(define (segment-time s) (car s))

(define (segment-queue s) (cdr s))
```

We will operate on the time-segment queues using the queue operations described in section 3.3.2.

The agenda itself is a one-dimensional table of time segments. It differs from the tables described in section 3.3.3 in that the segments will be sorted in order of increasing time. In addition, we store the *current time* (i.e., the time of the last action that was processed) at the head of the agenda. A newly constructed agenda has no time segments and has a current time of 0:[28]

```
(define (make-agenda) (list 0))

(define (current-time agenda) (car agenda))

(define (set-current-time! agenda time)
  (set-car! agenda time))

(define (segments agenda) (cdr agenda))

(define (set-segments! agenda segments)
  (set-cdr! agenda segments))

(define (first-segment agenda) (car (segments agenda)))

(define (rest-segments agenda) (cdr (segments agenda)))
```

---

[28]The agenda is a headed list, like the tables in section 3.3.3, but since the list is headed by the time, we do not need an additional dummy header (such as the *table* symbol used with tables).

An agenda is empty if it has no time segments:

```
(define (empty-agenda? agenda)
  (null? (segments agenda)))
```

To add an action to an agenda, we first check if the agenda is empty. If so, we create a time segment for the action and install this in the agenda. Otherwise, we scan the agenda, examining the time of each segment. If we find a segment for our appointed time, we add the action to the associated queue. If we reach a time later than the one to which we are appointed, we insert a new time segment into the agenda just before it. If we reach the end of the agenda, we must create a new time segment at the end.

```
(define (add-to-agenda! time action agenda)
  (define (belongs-before? segments)
    (or (null? segments)
        (< time (segment-time (car segments)))))
  (define (make-new-time-segment time action)
    (let ((q (make-queue)))
      (insert-queue! q action)
      (make-time-segment time q)))
  (define (add-to-segments! segments)
    (if (= (segment-time (car segments)) time)
        (insert-queue! (segment-queue (car segments))
                       action)
        (let ((rest (cdr segments)))
          (if (belongs-before? rest)
              (set-cdr!
               segments
               (cons (make-new-time-segment time action)
                     (cdr segments)))
              (add-to-segments! rest)))))
  (let ((segments (segments agenda)))
    (if (belongs-before? segments)
        (set-segments!
         agenda
         (cons (make-new-time-segment time action)
               segments))
        (add-to-segments! segments))))
```

The procedure that removes the first item from the agenda deletes the item at the front of the queue in the first time segment. If this deletion makes the time segment empty, we remove it from the list of segments:[29]

---

[29]Observe that the `if` expression in this procedure has no ⟨ *alternative* ⟩ expression. Such a "one-armed `if` statement" is used to decide whether to do something, rather than to select between two expressions. An `if` expression returns an unspecified value if the predicate is false and there is no ⟨ *alternative* ⟩.

```
(define (remove-first-agenda-item! agenda)
  (let ((q (segment-queue (first-segment agenda))))
    (delete-queue! q)
    (if (empty-queue? q)
        (set-segments! agenda (rest-segments agenda)))))
```

The first agenda item is found at the head of the queue in the first time segment. Whenever we extract an item, we also update the current time:[30]

```
(define (first-agenda-item agenda)
  (if (empty-agenda? agenda)
      (error "Agenda is empty -- FIRST-AGENDA-ITEM")
      (let ((first-seg (first-segment agenda)))
        (set-current-time! agenda (segment-time first-seg))
        (front-queue (segment-queue first-seg)))))
```

Exercise 3.32

The procedures to be run during each time segment of the agenda are kept in a queue. Thus, the procedures for each segment are called in the order in which they were added to the agenda (first in, first out). Explain why this order must be used. In particular, trace the behavior of an and-gate whose inputs change from 0,1 to 1,0 in the same segment and say how the behavior would differ if we stored a segment's procedures in an ordinary list, adding and removing procedures only at the front (last in, first out).

3.3.5   Propagation of Constraints

Computer programs are traditionally organized as one-directional computations, which perform operations on prespecified arguments to produce desired outputs. On the other hand, we often model systems in terms of relations among quantities. For example, a mathematical model of a mechanical structure might include the information that the deflection d of a metal rod is related to the force F on the rod, the length L of the rod, the cross-sectional area A, and the elastic modulus E via the equation

$$dAE = FL$$

Such an equation is not one-directional. Given any four of the quantities, we can use it to compute the fifth. Yet translating the equation into a

---

[30]In this way, the current time will always be the time of the action most recently processed. Storing this time at the head of the agenda ensures that it will still be available even if the associated time segment has been deleted.

traditional computer language would force us to choose one of the quantities to be computed in terms of the other four. Thus, a procedure for computing the area A could not be used to compute the deflection d, even though the computations of A and d arise from the same equation.[31]

In this section, we sketch the design of a language that enables us to work in terms of relations themselves. The primitive elements of the language are *primitive constraints*, which state that certain relations hold between quantities. For example, (adder a b c) specifies that the quantities a, b, and c must be related by the equation $a + b = c$, (multiplier x y z) expresses the constraint $xy = z$, and (constant 3.14 x) says that the value of x must be 3.14.

Our language provides a means of combining primitive constraints in order to express more complex relations. We combine constraints by constructing *constraint networks*, in which constraints are joined by *connectors*. A connector is an object that "holds" a value that may participate in one or more constraints. For example, we know that the relationship between Fahrenheit and Celsius temperatures is

$$9C = 5(F - 32)$$

Such a constraint can be thought of as a network consisting of primitive adder, multiplier, and constant constraints (figure 3.28). In the figure, we see on the left a multiplier box with three terminals, labeled $m1$, $m2$, and p. These connect the multiplier to the rest of the network as follows: The $m1$ terminal is linked to a connector C, which will hold the Celsius temperature. The $m2$ terminal is linked to a connector w, which is also linked to a constant box that holds 9. The p terminal, which the multiplier box constrains to be the product of $m1$ and $m2$, is linked to the p terminal of another multiplier box, whose $m2$ is connected to a constant 5 and whose $m1$ is connected to one of the terms in a sum.

Computation by such a network proceeds as follows: When a connector is given a value (by the user or by a constraint box to which it is linked), it awakens all of its associated constraints (except for the constraint that just awakened it) to inform them that it has a value. Each awakened constraint box then polls its connectors to see if there is enough information to determine a value for a connector. If so, the

---

[31]Constraint propagation first appeared in the incredibly forward-looking SKETCHPAD system of Ivan Sutherland (1963). A beautiful constraint-propagation system based on the Smalltalk language was developed by Alan Borning (1977) at Xerox Palo Alto Research Center. Sussman, Stallman, and Steele applied constraint propagation to electrical circuit analysis (Sussman and Stallman 1975; Sussman and Steele 1980). TK!Solver (Konopasek and Jayaraman 1984) is an extensive modeling environment based on constraints.

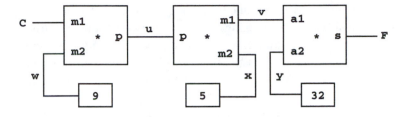

Figure 3.28   The relation $9C = 5(F - 32)$ expressed as a constraint network.

box sets that connector, which then awakens all of its associated constraints, and so on. For instance, in conversion between Celsius and Fahrenheit, w, x, and y are immediately set by the constant boxes to 9, 5, and 32, respectively. The connectors awaken the multipliers and the adder, which determine that there is not enough information to proceed. If the user (or some other part of the network) sets C to a value (say 25), the leftmost multiplier will be awakened, and it will set u to $25 \cdot 9 = 225$. Then u awakens the second multiplier, which sets v to 45, and v awakens the adder, which sets F to 77.

Using the constraint system
To use the constraint system to carry out the temperature computation outlined above, we first create two connectors, C and F, by calling the constructor make-connector, and link C and F in an appropriate network:

```
(define C (make-connector))
(define F (make-connector))
(celsius-fahrenheit-converter C F)
ok
```

The procedure that creates the network is defined as follows:

```
(define (celsius-fahrenheit-converter c f)
  (let ((u (make-connector))
        (v (make-connector))
        (w (make-connector))
        (x (make-connector))
        (y (make-connector)))
    (multiplier c w u)
    (multiplier v x u)
    (adder v y f)
    (constant 9 w)
    (constant 5 x)
    (constant 32 y)
    'ok))
```

This procedure creates the internal connectors u, v, w, x, and y, and links them as shown in figure 3.28 using the primitive constraint constructors adder, multiplier, and constant. Just as with the digital-circuit simulator of section 3.3.4, expressing these combinations of primitive elements in terms of procedures automatically provides our language with a means of abstraction for compound objects.

To watch the network in action, we can place probes on the connectors C and F, using a probe procedure similar to the one we used to monitor wires in section 3.3.4. Placing a probe on a connector will cause a message to be printed whenever the connector is given a value:

```
(probe "Celsius temp" C)
(probe "Fahrenheit temp" F)
```

Next we set the value of C to 25. (The third argument to set-value! tells C that this directive comes from the user.)

```
(set-value! C 25 'user)
Probe: Celsius temp = 25
Probe: Fahrenheit temp = 77
done
```

The probe on C awakens and reports the value. C also propagates its value through the network as described above. This sets F to 77, which is reported by the probe on F.

Now we can try to set F to a new value, say 212:

```
(set-value! F 212 'user)
Error! Contradiction (77 212)
```

The connector complains that it has sensed a contradiction: Its value is 77, and someone is trying to set it to 212. If we really want to reuse the network with new values, we can tell C to forget its old value:

```
(forget-value! C 'user)
Probe: Celsius temp = ?
Probe: Fahrenheit temp = ?
done
```

C finds that the user, who set its value originally, is now retracting that value, so C agrees to lose its value, as shown by the probe, and informs the rest of the network of this fact. This information eventually propagates to F, which now finds that it has no reason for continuing to believe that its own value is 77. Thus, F also gives up its value, as shown by the probe.

Now that F has no value, we are free to set it to 212:

```
(set-value! F 212 'user)
Probe: Fahrenheit temp = 212
Probe: Celsius temp = 100
done
```

This new value, when propagated through the network, forces C to have a value of 100, and this is registered by the probe on C. Notice that the very same network is being used to compute C given F and to compute F given C. This nondirectionality of computation is the distinguishing feature of constraint-based systems.

Implementing the constraint system

The constraint system is implemented via procedural objects with local state, in a manner very similar to the digital-circuit simulator of section 3.3.4. Although the primitive objects of the constraint system are somewhat more complex, the overall system is simpler, since there is no concern about agendas and logic delays.

The basic operations on connectors are the following:

- (has-value? ⟨*connector*⟩)
tells whether the connector has a value.

- (get-value ⟨*connector*⟩)
returns the connector's current value.

- (set-value! ⟨*connector*⟩ ⟨*new-value*⟩ ⟨*informant*⟩)
indicates that the informant is requesting the connector to set its value to the new value.

- (forget-value! ⟨*connector*⟩ ⟨*retractor*⟩)
tells the connector that the retractor is requesting it to forget its value.

- (connect ⟨*connector*⟩ ⟨*new-constraint*⟩)
tells the connector to participate in the new constraint.

The connectors communicate with the constraints by means of the procedures inform-about-value, which tells the given constraint that the connector has a value, and inform-about-no-value, which tells the constraint that the connector has lost its value.

Adder constructs an adder constraint among summand connectors a1 and a2 and a sum connector. An adder is implemented as a procedure with local state (the procedure me below):

```
(define (adder a1 a2 sum)
  (define (process-new-value)
    (cond ((and (has-value? a1) (has-value? a2))
           (set-value! sum
                       (+ (get-value a1) (get-value a2))
                       me))
          ((and (has-value? a1) (has-value? sum))
           (set-value! a2
                       (- (get-value sum) (get-value a1))
                       me))
          ((and (has-value? a2) (has-value? sum))
           (set-value! a1
                       (- (get-value sum) (get-value a2))
                       me))))
  (define (process-forget-value)
    (forget-value! sum me)
    (forget-value! a1 me)
    (forget-value! a2 me)
    (process-new-value))
  (define (me request)
    (cond ((eq? request 'I-have-a-value)
           (process-new-value))
          ((eq? request 'I-lost-my-value)
           (process-forget-value))
          (else
           (error "Unknown request -- ADDER" request))))
  (connect a1 me)
  (connect a2 me)
  (connect sum me)
  me)
```

Adder connects the new adder to the designated connectors and returns it as its value. The procedure me, which represents the adder, acts as a dispatch to the local procedures. The following "syntax interfaces" (see footnote 27 in section 3.3.4) are used in conjunction with the dispatch:

```
(define (inform-about-value constraint)
  (constraint 'I-have-a-value))
```

```
(define (inform-about-no-value constraint)
  (constraint 'I-lost-my-value))
```

The adder's local procedure process-new-value is called when the adder is informed that one of its connectors has a value. The adder first checks to see if both a1 and a2 have values. If so, it tells sum to set its value to the sum of the two addends. The informant argument to set-value! is me, which is the adder object itself. If a1 and a2 do not both have values, then the adder checks to see if perhaps a1 and sum have values. If so, it sets a2 to the difference of these two. Finally, if a2 and sum have values, this gives the adder enough information to set a1. If the adder is told that one of its connectors has lost a value, it requests that all of its connectors now lose their values. (Only those values that were set by this adder are actually lost.) Then it runs process-new-value. The reason for this last step is that one or more connectors may still have a value (that is, a connector may have had a value that was not originally set by the adder), and these values may need to be propagated back through the adder.

A multiplier is very similar to an adder. It will set its product to 0 if either of the factors is 0, even if the other factor is not known.

```
(define (multiplier m1 m2 product)
  (define (process-new-value)
    (cond ((or (and (has-value? m1) (= (get-value m1) 0))
               (and (has-value? m2) (= (get-value m2) 0)))
           (set-value! product 0 me))
          ((and (has-value? m1) (has-value? m2))
           (set-value! product
                       (* (get-value m1) (get-value m2))
                       me))
          ((and (has-value? product) (has-value? m1))
           (set-value! m2
                       (/ (get-value product) (get-value m1))
                       me))
          ((and (has-value? product) (has-value? m2))
           (set-value! m1
                       (/ (get-value product) (get-value m2))
                       me))))
  (define (process-forget-value)
    (forget-value! product me)
    (forget-value! m1 me)
    (forget-value! m2 me)
    (process-new-value))
  (define (me request)
    (cond ((eq? request 'I-have-a-value)
           (process-new-value))
          ((eq? request 'I-lost-my-value)
           (process-forget-value))
          (else
           (error "Unknown request -- MULTIPLIER" request))))
  (connect m1 me)
  (connect m2 me)
  (connect product me)
  me)
```

A `constant` constructor simply sets the value of the designated connector. Any `I-have-a-value` or `I-lost-my-value` message sent to the constant box will produce an error.

```
(define (constant value connector)
  (define (me request)
    (error "Unknown request -- CONSTANT" request))
  (connect connector me)
  (set-value! connector value me)
  me)
```

Finally, a probe prints a message about the setting or unsetting of the designated connector:

```
(define (probe name connector)
  (define (print-probe value)
    (newline)
    (display "Probe: ")
    (display name)
    (display " = ")
    (display value))
  (define (process-new-value)
    (print-probe (get-value connector)))
  (define (process-forget-value)
    (print-probe "?"))
  (define (me request)
    (cond ((eq? request 'I-have-a-value)
           (process-new-value))
          ((eq? request 'I-lost-my-value)
           (process-forget-value))
          (else
           (error "Unknown request -- PROBE" request))))
  (connect connector me)
  me)
```

Representing connectors

A connector is represented as a procedural object with local state variables `value`, the current value of the connector; `informant`, the object that set the connector's value; and `constraints`, a list of the constraints in which the connector participates.

```scheme
(define (make-connector)
  (let ((value false) (informant false) (constraints '()))
    (define (set-my-value newval setter)
      (cond ((not (has-value? me))
             (set! value newval)
             (set! informant setter)
             (for-each-except setter
                              inform-about-value
                              constraints))
            ((not (= value newval))
             (error "Contradiction" (list value newval)))
            (else 'ignored)))
    (define (forget-my-value retractor)
      (if (eq? retractor informant)
          (begin (set! informant false)
                 (for-each-except retractor
                                  inform-about-no-value
                                  constraints))
          'ignored))
    (define (connect new-constraint)
      (if (not (memq new-constraint constraints))
          (set! constraints
                (cons new-constraint constraints)))
      (if (has-value? me)
          (inform-about-value new-constraint))
      'done)
    (define (me request)
      (cond ((eq? request 'has-value?)
             (if informant true false))
            ((eq? request 'value) value)
            ((eq? request 'set-value!) set-my-value)
            ((eq? request 'forget) forget-my-value)
            ((eq? request 'connect) connect)
            (else (error "Unknown operation -- CONNECTOR"
                         request))))
    me))
```

The connector's local procedure set-my-value is called when there is a request to set the connector's value. If the connector does not currently have a value, it will set its value and remember as informant

the constraint that requested the value to be set.[32] Then the connector
will notify all of its participating constraints except the constraint that
requested the value to be set. This is accomplished using the following
iterator, which applies a designated procedure to all items in a list except
a given one:

```
(define (for-each-except exception procedure list)
  (define (loop items)
    (cond ((null? items) 'done)
          ((eq? (car items) exception) (loop (cdr items)))
          (else (procedure (car items))
                (loop (cdr items)))))
  (loop list))
```

If a connector is asked to forget its value, it runs the local procedure
forget-my-value, which first checks to make sure that the request is
coming from the same object that set the value originally. If so, the
connector informs its associated constraints about the loss of the value.

The local procedure connect adds the designated new constraint to
the list of constraints if it is not already in that list. Then, if the connector
has a value, it informs the new constraint of this fact.

The connector's procedure me serves as a dispatch to the other internal
procedures and also represents the connector as an object. The following
procedures provide a syntax interface for the dispatch:

```
(define (has-value? connector)
  (connector 'has-value?))

(define (get-value connector)
  (connector 'value))

(define (set-value! connector new-value informant)
  ((connector 'set-value!) new-value informant))

(define (forget-value! connector retractor)
  ((connector 'forget) retractor))

(define (connect connector new-constraint)
  ((connector 'connect) new-constraint))
```

---

[32]The setter might not be a constraint. In our temperature example, we used user as the
setter.

Exercise 3.33

Using primitive multiplier, adder, and constant constraints, define a procedure
averager that takes three connectors a, b, and c as inputs and establishes the
constraint that the value of c is the average of the values of a and b.

Exercise 3.34

Louis Reasoner wants to build a squarer, a constraint device with two terminals
such that the value of connector b on the second terminal will always be the
square of the value a on the first terminal. He proposes the following simple
device made from a multiplier:

```
(define (squarer a b)
  (multiplier a a b))
```

There is a serious flaw in this idea. Explain.

Exercise 3.35

Ben Bitdiddle tells Louis that one way to avoid the trouble in exercise 3.34 is
to define a squarer as a new primitive constraint. Fill in the missing portions in
Ben's outline for a procedure to implement such a constraint:

```
(define (squarer a b)
  (define (process-new-value)
    (if (has-value? b)
        (if (< (get-value b) 0)
            (error "square less than 0 -- SQUARER" (get-value b))
            ⟨alternative1⟩)
        ⟨alternative2⟩))
  (define (process-forget-value) ⟨body1⟩)
  (define (me request) ⟨body2⟩)
  ⟨rest of definition⟩
  me)
```

Exercise 3.36

Suppose we evaluate the following sequence of expressions in the global environment:

```
(define a (make-connector))
(define b (make-connector))
(set-value! a 10 'user)
```

At some time during evaluation of the set-value!, the following expression
from the connector's local procedure is evaluated:

```
(for-each-except setter inform-about-value constraints)
```

Draw an environment diagram showing the environment in which the above
expression is evaluated.

Exercise 3.37

The `celsius-fahrenheit-converter` procedure is cumbersome when compared with a more expression-oriented style of definition, such as

```
(define (celsius-fahrenheit-converter x)
  (c+ (c* (c/ (cv 9) (cv 5))
          x)
      (cv 32)))
```

```
(define C (make-connector))
(define F (celsius-fahrenheit-converter C))
```

Here c+, c*, etc. are the "constraint" versions of the arithmetic operations. For example, c+ takes two connectors as arguments and returns a connector that is related to these by an adder constraint:

```
(define (c+ x y)
  (let ((z (make-connector)))
    (adder x y z)
    z))
```

Define analogous procedures c-, c*, c/, and cv (constant value) that enable us to define compound constraints as in the converter example above.[33]

---

[33] The expression-oriented format is convenient because it avoids the need to name the intermediate expressions in a computation. Our original formulation of the constraint language is cumbersome in the same way that many languages are cumbersome when dealing with operations on compound data. For example, if we wanted to compute the product $(a + b) \cdot (c + d)$, where the variables represent vectors, we could work in "imperative style," using procedures that set the values of designated vector arguments but do not themselves return vectors as values:

```
(v-sum a b temp1)
(v-sum c d temp2)
(v-prod temp1 temp2 answer)
```

Alternatively, we could deal with expressions, using procedures that return vectors as values, and thus avoid explicitly mentioning temp1 and temp2:

```
(define answer (v-prod (v-sum a b) (v-sum c d)))
```

Since Lisp allows us to return compound objects as values of procedures, we can transform our imperative-style constraint language into an expression-oriented style as shown in this exercise. In languages that are impoverished in handling compound objects, such as Algol, Basic, and Pascal (unless one explicitly uses Pascal pointer variables), one is usually stuck with the imperative style when manipulating compound objects. Given the advantage of the expression-oriented format, one might ask if there is any reason to have implemented the system in imperative style, as we did in this section. One reason is that the non-expression-oriented constraint language provides a handle on constraint objects (e.g., the value of the adder procedure) as well as on connector objects. This is useful if we wish to extend the system with new operations that communicate with constraints directly rather than only indirectly via operations on connectors. Although it is easy to implement the expression-oriented style in terms of the imperative implementation, it is very difficult to do the converse.

3.4   Concurrency: Time Is of the Essence

We've seen the power of computational objects with local state as tools for modeling. Yet, as section 3.1.3 warned, this power extracts a price: the loss of referential transparency, giving rise to a thicket of questions about sameness and change, and the need to abandon the substitution model of evaluation in favor of the more intricate environment model.

The central issue lurking beneath the complexity of state, sameness, and change is that by introducing assignment we are forced to admit *time* into our computational models. Before we introduced assignment, all our programs were timeless, in the sense that any expression that has a value always has the same value. In contrast, recall the example of modeling withdrawals from a bank account and returning the resulting balance, introduced at the beginning of section 3.1.1:

```
(withdraw 25)
75

(withdraw 25)
50
```

Here successive evaluations of the same expression yield different values. This behavior arises from the fact that the execution of assignment statements (in this case, assignments to the variable `balance`) delineates *moments in time* when values change. The result of evaluating an expression depends not only on the expression itself, but also on whether the evaluation occurs before or after these moments. Building models in terms of computational objects with local state forces us to confront time as an essential concept in programming.

We can go further in structuring computational models to match our perception of the physical world. Objects in the world do not change one at a time in sequence. Rather we perceive them as acting *concurrently*— all at once. So it is often natural to model systems as collections of computational processes that execute concurrently. Just as we can make our programs modular by organizing models in terms of objects with separate local state, it is often appropriate to divide computational models into parts that evolve separately and concurrently. Even if the programs are to be executed on a sequential computer, the practice of writing programs as if they were to be executed concurrently forces the programmer to avoid inessential timing constraints and thus makes programs more modular.

In addition to making programs more modular, concurrent computation can provide a speed advantage over sequential computation. Sequential computers execute only one operation at a time, so the amount of time it takes to perform a task is proportional to the total number of operations performed.[34] However, if it is possible to decompose a problem into pieces that are relatively independent and need to communicate only rarely, it may be possible to allocate pieces to separate computing processors, producing a speed advantage proportional to the number of processors available.

Unfortunately, the complexities introduced by assignment become even more problematic in the presence of concurrency. The fact of concurrent execution, either because the world operates in parallel or because our computers do, entails additional complexity in our understanding of time.

3.4.1   The Nature of Time in Concurrent Systems

On the surface, time seems straightforward. It is an ordering imposed on events.[35] For any events A and B, either A occurs before B, A and B are simultaneous, or A occurs after B. For instance, returning to the bank account example, suppose that Peter withdraws \$10 and Paul withdraws \$25 from a joint account that initially contains \$100, leaving \$65 in the account. Depending on the order of the two withdrawals, the sequence of balances in the account is either \$100 $\rightarrow$ \$90 $\rightarrow$ \$65 or \$100 $\rightarrow$ \$75 $\rightarrow$ \$65. In a computer implementation of the banking system, this changing sequence of balances could be modeled by successive assignments to a variable `balance`.

In complex situations, however, such a view can be problematic. Suppose that Peter and Paul, and other people besides, are accessing the same bank account through a network of banking machines distributed all over the world. The actual sequence of balances in the account will depend critically on the detailed timing of the accesses and the details of the communication among the machines.

This indeterminacy in the order of events can pose serious problems in the design of concurrent systems. For instance, suppose that the with-

---

[34]Most real processors actually execute a few operations at a time, following a strategy called *pipelining*. Although this technique greatly improves the effective utilization of the hardware, it is used only to speed up the execution of a sequential instruction stream, while retaining the behavior of the sequential program.

[35]To quote some graffiti seen on a Cambridge building wall: "Time is a device that was invented to keep everything from happening at once."

drawals made by Peter and Paul are implemented as two separate processes sharing a common variable `balance`, each process specified by the procedure given in section 3.1.1:

```
(define (withdraw amount)
  (if (>= balance amount)
      (begin (set! balance (- balance amount))
             balance)
      "Insufficient funds"))
```

If the two processes operate independently, then Peter might test the balance and attempt to withdraw a legitimate amount. However, Paul might withdraw some funds in between the time that Peter checks the balance and the time Peter completes the withdrawal, thus invalidating Peter's test.

Things can be worse still. Consider the expression

```
(set! balance (- balance amount))
```

executed as part of each withdrawal process. This consists of three steps: (1) accessing the value of the `balance` variable; (2) computing the new balance; (3) setting `balance` to this new value. If Peter and Paul's withdrawals execute this statement concurrently, then the two withdrawals might interleave the order in which they access `balance` and set it to the new value.

The timing diagram in figure 3.29 depicts an order of events where `balance` starts at 100, Peter withdraws 10, Paul withdraws 25, and yet the final value of `balance` is 75. As shown in the diagram, the reason for this anomaly is that Paul's assignment of 75 to `balance` is made under the assumption that the value of `balance` to be decremented is 100. That assumption, however, became invalid when Peter changed `balance` to 90. This is a catastrophic failure for the banking system, because the total amount of money in the system is not conserved. Before the transactions, the total amount of money was $100. Afterwards, Peter has $10, Paul has $25, and the bank has $75.[36]

---

[36] An even worse failure for this system could occur if the two `set!` operations attempt to change the balance simultaneously, in which case the actual data appearing in memory might end up being a random combination of the information being written by the two processes. Most computers have interlocks on the primitive memory-write operations, which protect against such simultaneous access. Even this seemingly simple kind of protection, however, raises implementation challenges in the design of multiprocessing computers, where elaborate *cache-coherence* protocols are required to ensure that the various processors will maintain a consistent view of memory contents, despite the fact that data may be replicated ("cached") among the different processors to increase the speed of memory access.

The general phenomenon illustrated here is that several processes may share a common state variable. What makes this complicated is that more than one process may be trying to manipulate the shared state at the same time. For the bank account example, during each transaction, each customer should be able to act as if the other customers did not exist. When a customer changes the balance in a way that depends on the balance, he must be able to assume that, just before the moment of change, the balance is still what he thought it was.

Correct behavior of concurrent programs

The above example typifies the subtle bugs that can creep into concurrent programs. The root of this complexity lies in the assignments to variables that are shared among the different processes. We already know that we must be careful in writing programs that use set!, because the results of a computation depend on the order in which the assignments occur.[37] With concurrent processes we must be especially careful about assignments, because we may not be able to control the order of the assignments made by the different processes. If several such changes might be made concurrently (as with two depositors accessing a joint account) we need some way to ensure that our system behaves correctly. For example, in the case of withdrawals from a joint bank account, we must ensure that money is conserved. To make concurrent programs behave correctly, we may have to place some restrictions on concurrent execution.

One possible restriction on concurrency would stipulate that no two operations that change any shared state variables can occur at the same time. This is an extremely stringent requirement. For distributed banking, it would require the system designer to ensure that only one transaction could proceed at a time. This would be both inefficient and overly conservative. Figure 3.30 shows Peter and Paul sharing a bank account, where Paul has a private account as well. The diagram illustrates two withdrawals from the shared account (one by Peter and one by Paul) and a deposit to Paul's private account.[38] The two withdrawals from the shared account must not be concurrent (since both access and update the same account), and Paul's deposit and withdrawal must not be concur-

---

[37]The factorial program in section 3.1.3 illustrates this for a single sequential process.

[38]The columns show the contents of Peter's wallet, the joint account (in Bank1), Paul's wallet, and Paul's private account (in Bank2), before and after each withdrawal (W) and deposit (D). Peter withdraws $10 from Bank1; Paul deposits $5 in Bank2, then withdraws $25 from Bank1.

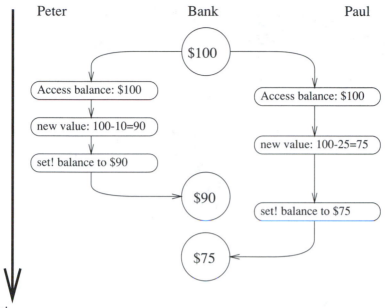

Peter   Bank   Paul

time

Figure 3.29   Timing diagram showing how interleaving the order of events in two banking withdrawals can lead to an incorrect final balance.

rent (since both access and update the amount in Paul's wallet). But there should be no problem permitting Paul's deposit to his private account to proceed concurrently with Peter's withdrawal from the shared account.

A less stringent restriction on concurrency would ensure that a concurrent system produces the same result as if the processes had run sequentially in some order. There are two important aspects to this requirement. First, it does not require the processes to actually run sequentially, but only to produce results that are the same *as if* they had run sequentially. For the example in figure 3.30, the designer of the bank account system can safely allow Paul's deposit and Peter's withdrawal to happen concurrently, because the net result will be the same as if the two operations had happened sequentially. Second, there may be more than one possible "correct" result produced by a concurrent program, because we require only that the result be the same as for *some* sequential order. For example, suppose that Peter and Paul's joint account starts out with $100, and Peter deposits $40 while Paul concurrently withdraws half the money in

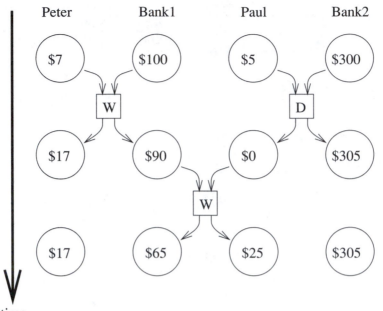

Figure 3.30 Concurrent deposits and withdrawals from a joint account in Bank1 and a private account in Bank2.

the account. Then sequential execution could result in the account balance being either $70 or $90 (see exercise 3.38).[39]

There are still weaker requirements for correct execution of concurrent programs. A program for simulating diffusion (say, the flow of heat in an object) might consist of a large number of processes, each one representing a small volume of space, that update their values concurrently. Each process repeatedly changes its value to the average of its own value and its neighbors' values. This algorithm converges to the right answer independent of the order in which the operations are done; there is no need for any restrictions on concurrent use of the shared values.

[39] A more formal way to express this idea is to say that concurrent programs are inherently *nondeterministic*. That is, they are described not by single-valued functions, but by functions whose results are sets of possible values. In section 4.3 we will study a language for expressing nondeterministic computations.

Exercise 3.38

Suppose that Peter, Paul, and Mary share a joint bank account that initially contains $100. Concurrently, Peter deposits $10, Paul withdraws $20, and Mary withdraws half the money in the account, by executing the following commands:

```
Peter:   (set! balance (+ balance 10))
Paul:    (set! balance (- balance 20))
Mary:    (set! balance (- balance (/ balance 2)))
```

a. List all the different possible values for balance after these three transactions have been completed, assuming that the banking system forces the three processes to run sequentially in some order.

b. What are some other values that could be produced if the system allows the processes to be interleaved? Draw timing diagrams like the one in figure 3.29 to explain how these values can occur.

3.4.2 Mechanisms for Controlling Concurrency

We've seen that the difficulty in dealing with concurrent processes is rooted in the need to consider the interleaving of the order of events in the different processes. For example, suppose we have two processes, one with three ordered events (a, b, c) and one with three ordered events (x, y, z). If the two processes run concurrently, with no constraints on how their execution is interleaved, then there are 20 different possible orderings for the events that are consistent with the individual orderings for the two processes:

$$
\begin{array}{llll}
(a, b, c, x, y, z) & (a, x, b, y, c, z) & (x, a, b, c, y, z) & (x, a, y, z, b, c) \\
(a, b, x, c, y, z) & (a, x, b, y, z, c) & (x, a, b, y, c, z) & (x, y, a, b, c, z) \\
(a, b, x, y, c, z) & (a, x, y, b, c, z) & (x, a, b, y, z, c) & (x, y, a, b, z, c) \\
(a, b, x, y, z, c) & (a, x, y, b, z, c) & (x, a, y, b, c, z) & (x, y, a, z, b, c) \\
(a, x, b, c, y, z) & (a, x, y, z, b, c) & (x, a, y, b, z, c) & (x, y, z, a, b, c)
\end{array}
$$

As programmers designing this system, we would have to consider the effects of each of these 20 orderings and check that each behavior is acceptable. Such an approach rapidly becomes unwieldy as the numbers of processes and events increase.

A more practical approach to the design of concurrent systems is to devise general mechanisms that allow us to constrain the interleaving of concurrent processes so that we can be sure that the program behavior is correct. Many mechanisms have been developed for this purpose. In this section, we describe one of them, the *serializer*.

Serializing access to shared state

Serialization implements the following idea: Processes will execute concurrently, but there will be certain collections of procedures that cannot be executed concurrently. More precisely, serialization creates distinguished sets of procedures such that only one execution of a procedure in each serialized set is permitted to happen at a time. If some procedure in the set is being executed, then a process that attempts to execute any procedure in the set will be forced to wait until the first execution has finished.

We can use serialization to control access to shared variables. For example, if we want to update a shared variable based on the previous value of that variable, we put the access to the previous value of the variable and the assignment of the new value to the variable in the same procedure. We then ensure that no other procedure that assigns to the variable can run concurrently with this procedure by serializing all of these procedures with the same serializer. This guarantees that the value of the variable cannot be changed between an access and the corresponding assignment.

Serializers in Scheme

To make the above mechanism more concrete, suppose that we have extended Scheme to include a procedure called `parallel-execute`:

```
(parallel-execute ⟨p₁⟩ ⟨p₂⟩ ... ⟨pₖ⟩)
```

Each ⟨p⟩ must be a procedure of no arguments. Parallel-execute creates a separate process for each ⟨p⟩, which applies ⟨p⟩ (to no arguments). These processes all run concurrently.[40]

As an example of how this is used, consider

```
(define x 10)

(parallel-execute (lambda () (set! x (* x x)))
                  (lambda () (set! x (+ x 1))))
```

This creates two concurrent processes—P_1, which sets x to x times x, and P_2, which increments x. After execution is complete, x will be left

---

[40]`Parallel-execute` is not part of standard Scheme, but it can be implemented in MIT Scheme. In our implementation, the new concurrent processes also run concurrently with the original Scheme process. Also, in our implementation, the value returned by `parallel-execute` is a special control object that can be used to halt the newly created processes.

with one of five possible values, depending on the interleaving of the events of P_1 and P_2:

101:   P_1 sets x to 100 and then P_2 increments x to 101.

121:   P_2 increments x to 11 and then P_1 sets x to x times x.

110:   P_2 changes x from 10 to 11 between the two times that P_1 accesses the value of x during the evaluation of (* x x).

11:   P_2 accesses x, then P_1 sets x to 100, then P_2 sets x.

100:   P_1 accesses x (twice), then P_2 sets x to 11, then P_1 sets x.

We can constrain the concurrency by using serialized procedures, which are created by *serializers*. Serializers are constructed by make-serializer, whose implementation is given below. A serializer takes a procedure as argument and returns a serialized procedure that behaves like the original procedure. All calls to a given serializer return serialized procedures in the same set.

Thus, in contrast to the example above, executing

```
(define x 10)

(define s (make-serializer))

(parallel-execute (s (lambda () (set! x (* x x))))
                  (s (lambda () (set! x (+ x 1)))))
```

can produce only two possible values for x, 101 or 121. The other possibilities are eliminated, because the execution of P_1 and P_2 cannot be interleaved.

Here is a version of the make-account procedure from section 3.1.1, where the deposits and withdrawals have been serialized:

```
(define (make-account balance)
  (define (withdraw amount)
    (if (>= balance amount)
        (begin (set! balance (- balance amount))
               balance)
        "Insufficient funds"))
  (define (deposit amount)
    (set! balance (+ balance amount))
    balance)
  (let ((protected (make-serializer)))
    (define (dispatch m)
      (cond ((eq? m 'withdraw) (protected withdraw))
            ((eq? m 'deposit) (protected deposit))
            ((eq? m 'balance) balance)
            (else (error "Unknown request -- MAKE-ACCOUNT"
                         m))))
    dispatch))
```

With this implementation, two processes cannot be withdrawing from or depositing into a single account concurrently. This eliminates the source of the error illustrated in figure 3.29, where Peter changes the account balance between the times when Paul accesses the balance to compute the new value and when Paul actually performs the assignment. On the other hand, each account has its own serializer, so that deposits and withdrawals for different accounts can proceed concurrently.

Exercise 3.39

Which of the five possibilities in the parallel execution shown above remain if we instead serialize execution as follows:

```
(define x 10)

(define s (make-serializer))

(parallel-execute (lambda () (set! x ((s (lambda () (* x x))))))
                  (s (lambda () (set! x (+ x 1)))))
```

Exercise 3.40

Give all possible values of x that can result from executing

```
(define x 10)

(parallel-execute (lambda () (set! x (* x x)))
                  (lambda () (set! x (* x x x))))
```

Which of these possibilities remain if we instead use serialized procedures:

```
(define x 10)

(define s (make-serializer))

(parallel-execute (s (lambda () (set! x (* x x))))
                  (s (lambda () (set! x (* x x x)))))
```

Exercise 3.41

Ben Bitdiddle worries that it would be better to implement the bank account as follows (where the commented line has been changed):

```
(define (make-account balance)
  (define (withdraw amount)
    (if (>= balance amount)
        (begin (set! balance (- balance amount))
               balance)
        "Insufficient funds"))
  (define (deposit amount)
    (set! balance (+ balance amount))
    balance)
  ;; continued on next page
```

```
(let ((protected (make-serializer)))
  (define (dispatch m)
    (cond ((eq? m 'withdraw) (protected withdraw))
          ((eq? m 'deposit) (protected deposit))
          ((eq? m 'balance)
           ((protected (lambda () balance))))  ; serialized
          (else (error "Unknown request -- MAKE-ACCOUNT"
                       m))))
  dispatch))
```

because allowing unserialized access to the bank balance can result in anomalous behavior. Do you agree? Is there any scenario that demonstrates Ben's concern?

Exercise 3.42

Ben Bitdiddle suggests that it's a waste of time to create a new serialized procedure in response to every `withdraw` and `deposit` message. He says that `make-account` could be changed so that the calls to `protected` are done outside the `dispatch` procedure. That is, an account would return the same serialized procedure (which was created at the same time as the account) each time it is asked for a withdrawal procedure.

```
(define (make-account balance)
  (define (withdraw amount)
    (if (>= balance amount)
        (begin (set! balance (- balance amount))
               balance)
        "Insufficient funds"))
  (define (deposit amount)
    (set! balance (+ balance amount))
    balance)
  (let ((protected (make-serializer)))
    (let ((protected-withdraw (protected withdraw))
          (protected-deposit (protected deposit)))
      (define (dispatch m)
        (cond ((eq? m 'withdraw) protected-withdraw)
              ((eq? m 'deposit) protected-deposit)
              ((eq? m 'balance) balance)
              (else (error "Unknown request -- MAKE-ACCOUNT"
                           m))))
      dispatch)))
```

Is this a safe change to make? In particular, is there any difference in what concurrency is allowed by these two versions of `make-account`?

Complexity of using multiple shared resources

Serializers provide a powerful abstraction that helps isolate the complexities of concurrent programs so that they can be dealt with carefully and (hopefully) correctly. However, while using serializers is relatively straightforward when there is only a single shared resource (such as a single bank account), concurrent programming can be treacherously difficult when there are multiple shared resources.

To illustrate one of the difficulties that can arise, suppose we wish to swap the balances in two bank accounts. We access each account to find the balance, compute the difference between the balances, withdraw this difference from one account, and deposit it in the other account. We could implement this as follows:[41]

```
(define (exchange account1 account2)
  (let ((difference (- (account1 'balance)
                       (account2 'balance))))
    ((account1 'withdraw) difference)
    ((account2 'deposit) difference)))
```

This procedure works well when only a single process is trying to do the exchange. Suppose, however, that Peter and Paul both have access to accounts *a*1, *a*2, and *a*3, and that Peter exchanges *a*1 and *a*2 while Paul concurrently exchanges *a*1 and *a*3. Even with account deposits and withdrawals serialized for individual accounts (as in the make-account procedure shown above in this section), exchange can still produce incorrect results. For example, Peter might compute the difference in the balances for *a*1 and *a*2, but then Paul might change the balance in *a*1 before Peter is able to complete the exchange.[42] For correct behavior, we must arrange for the exchange procedure to lock out any other concurrent accesses to the accounts during the entire time of the exchange.

One way we can accomplish this is by using both accounts' serializers to serialize the entire exchange procedure. To do this, we will arrange for access to an account's serializer. Note that we are deliberately breaking the modularity of the bank-account object by exposing the serializer. The following version of make-account is identical to the original version given in section 3.1.1, except that a serializer is provided to protect the balance variable, and the serializer is exported via message passing:

---

[41]We have simplified exchange by exploiting the fact that our deposit message accepts negative amounts. (This is a serious bug in our banking system!)

[42]If the account balances start out as $10, $20, and $30, then after any number of concurrent exchanges, the balances should still be $10, $20, and $30 in some order. Serializing the deposits to individual accounts is not sufficient to guarantee this. See exercise 3.43.

```
(define (make-account-and-serializer balance)
  (define (withdraw amount)
    (if (>= balance amount)
        (begin (set! balance (- balance amount))
               balance)
        "Insufficient funds"))
  (define (deposit amount)
    (set! balance (+ balance amount))
    balance)
  (let ((balance-serializer (make-serializer)))
    (define (dispatch m)
      (cond ((eq? m 'withdraw) withdraw)
            ((eq? m 'deposit) deposit)
            ((eq? m 'balance) balance)
            ((eq? m 'serializer) balance-serializer)
            (else (error "Unknown request -- MAKE-ACCOUNT"
                         m))))
    dispatch))
```

We can use this to do serialized deposits and withdrawals. However, unlike our earlier serialized account, it is now the responsibility of each user of bank-account objects to explicitly manage the serialization, for example as follows:[43]

```
(define (deposit account amount)
  (let ((s (account 'serializer))
        (d (account 'deposit)))
    ((s d) amount)))
```

Exporting the serializer in this way gives us enough flexibility to implement a serialized exchange program. We simply serialize the original exchange procedure with the serializers for both accounts:

```
(define (serialized-exchange account1 account2)
  (let ((serializer1 (account1 'serializer))
        (serializer2 (account2 'serializer)))
    ((serializer1 (serializer2 exchange))
     account1
     account2)))
```

Exercise 3.43

Suppose that the balances in three accounts start out as $10, $20, and $30, and that multiple processes run, exchanging the balances in the accounts. Argue that if the processes are run sequentially, after any number of concurrent exchanges,

---

[43]Exercise 3.45 investigates why deposits and withdrawals are no longer automatically serialized by the account.

the account balances should be $10, $20, and $30 in some order. Draw a timing diagram like the one in figure 3.29 to show how this condition can be violated if the exchanges are implemented using the first version of the account-exchange program in this section. On the other hand, argue that even with this exchange program, the sum of the balances in the accounts will be preserved. Draw a timing diagram to show how even this condition would be violated if we did not serialize the transactions on individual accounts.

Exercise 3.44

Consider the problem of transferring an amount from one account to another. Ben Bitdiddle claims that this can be accomplished with the following procedure, even if there are multiple people concurrently transferring money among multiple accounts, using any account mechanism that serializes deposit and withdrawal transactions, for example, the version of make-account in the text above.

```
(define (transfer from-account to-account amount)
  ((from-account 'withdraw) amount)
  ((to-account 'deposit) amount))
```

Louis Reasoner claims that there is a problem here, and that we need to use a more sophisticated method, such as the one required for dealing with the exchange problem. Is Louis right? If not, what is the essential difference between the transfer problem and the exchange problem? (You should assume that the balance in from-account is at least amount.)

Exercise 3.45

Louis Reasoner thinks our bank-account system is unnecessarily complex and error-prone now that deposits and withdrawals aren't automatically serialized. He suggests that make-account-and-serializer should have exported the serializer (for use by such procedures as serialized-exchange) in addition to (rather than instead of) using it to serialize accounts and deposits as make-account did. He proposes to redefine accounts as follows:

```
(define (make-account-and-serializer balance)
  (define (withdraw amount)
    (if (>= balance amount)
        (begin (set! balance (- balance amount))
               balance)
        "Insufficient funds"))
  (define (deposit amount)
    (set! balance (+ balance amount))
    balance)
  (let ((balance-serializer (make-serializer)))
    (define (dispatch m)
      (cond ((eq? m 'withdraw) (balance-serializer withdraw))
            ((eq? m 'deposit) (balance-serializer deposit))
            ((eq? m 'balance) balance)
            ((eq? m 'serializer) balance-serializer)
            (else (error "Unknown request -- MAKE-ACCOUNT"
                         m))))
    dispatch))
```

Then deposits are handled as with the original `make-account`:

```
(define (deposit account amount)
  ((account 'deposit) amount))
```

Explain what is wrong with Louis's reasoning. In particular, consider what happens when `serialized-exchange` is called.

Implementing serializers

We implement serializers in terms of a more primitive synchronization mechanism called a *mutex*. A mutex is an object that supports two operations—the mutex can be *acquired*, and the mutex can be *released*. Once a mutex has been acquired, no other acquire operations on that mutex may proceed until the mutex is released.[44] In our implementation, each serializer has an associated mutex. Given a procedure p, the serializer returns a procedure that acquires the mutex, runs p, and then releases the mutex. This ensures that only one of the procedures produced by the serializer can be running at once, which is precisely the serialization property that we need to guarantee.

```
(define (make-serializer)
  (let ((mutex (make-mutex)))
    (lambda (p)
      (define (serialized-p . args)
        (mutex 'acquire)
        (let ((val (apply p args)))
          (mutex 'release)
          val))
      serialized-p)))
```

The mutex is a mutable object (here we'll use a one-element list, which we'll refer to as a *cell*) that can hold the value true or false. When the value is false, the mutex is available to be acquired. When the value is true, the mutex is unavailable, and any process that attempts to acquire the mutex must wait.

---

[44]The term "mutex" is an abbreviation for *mutual exclusion*. The general problem of arranging a mechanism that permits concurrent processes to safely share resources is called the mutual exclusion problem. Our mutex is a simple variant of the *semaphore* mechanism (see exercise 3.47), which was introduced in the "THE" Multiprogramming System developed at the Technological University of Eindhoven and named for the university's initials in Dutch (Dijkstra 1968a). The acquire and release operations were originally called P and V, from the Dutch words *passeren* (to pass) and *vrijgeven* (to release), in reference to the semaphores used on railroad systems. Dijkstra's classic exposition (1968b) was one of the first to clearly present the issues of concurrency control, and showed how to use semaphores to handle a variety of concurrency problems.

Our mutex constructor `make-mutex` begins by initializing the cell contents to false. To acquire the mutex, we test the cell. If the mutex is available, we set the cell contents to true and proceed. Otherwise, we wait in a loop, attempting to acquire over and over again, until we find that the mutex is available.[45] To release the mutex, we set the cell contents to false.

```
(define (make-mutex)
  (let ((cell (list false)))
    (define (the-mutex m)
      (cond ((eq? m 'acquire)
             (if (test-and-set! cell)
                 (the-mutex 'acquire)))  ; retry
            ((eq? m 'release) (clear! cell))))
    the-mutex))

(define (clear! cell)
  (set-car! cell false))
```

`Test-and-set!` tests the cell and returns the result of the test. In addition, if the test was false, `test-and-set!` sets the cell contents to true before returning false. We can express this behavior as the following procedure:

```
(define (test-and-set! cell)
  (if (car cell)
      true
      (begin (set-car! cell true)
             false)))
```

However, this implementation of `test-and-set!` does not suffice as it stands. There is a crucial subtlety here, which is the essential place where concurrency control enters the system: The `test-and-set!` operation must be performed *atomically*. That is, we must guarantee that, once a process has tested the cell and found it to be false, the cell contents will actually be set to true before any other process can test the cell. If we do not make this guarantee, then the mutex can fail in a way similar to the bank-account failure in figure 3.29. (See exercise 3.46.)

---

[45]In most time-shared operating systems, processes that are blocked by a mutex do not waste time "busy-waiting" as above. Instead, the system schedules another process to run while the first is waiting, and the blocked process is awakened when the mutex becomes available.

The actual implementation of `test-and-set!` depends on the details of how our system runs concurrent processes. For example, we might be executing concurrent processes on a sequential processor using a time-slicing mechanism that cycles through the processes, permitting each process to run for a short time before interrupting it and moving on to the next process. In that case, `test-and-set!` can work by disabling time slicing during the testing and setting.[46] Alternatively, multiprocessing computers provide instructions that support atomic operations directly in hardware.[47]

Exercise 3.46

Suppose that we implement `test-and-set!` using an ordinary procedure as shown in the text, without attempting to make the operation atomic. Draw a timing diagram like the one in figure 3.29 to demonstrate how the mutex implementation can fail by allowing two processes to acquire the mutex at the same time.

Exercise 3.47

A semaphore (of size *n*) is a generalization of a mutex. Like a mutex, a semaphore supports acquire and release operations, but it is more general in that up to *n* processes can acquire it concurrently. Additional processes that attempt to

---

[46]In MIT Scheme for a single processor, which uses a time-slicing model, `test-and-set!` can be implemented as follows:

```
(define (test-and-set! cell)
  (without-interrupts
   (lambda ()
     (if (car cell)
         true
         (begin (set-car! cell true)
                false)))))
```

`Without-interrupts` disables time-slicing interrupts while its procedure argument is being executed.

[47]There are many variants of such instructions—including test-and-set, test-and-clear, swap, compare-and-exchange, load-reserve, and store-conditional—whose design must be carefully matched to the machine's processor–memory interface. One issue that arises here is to determine what happens if two processes attempt to acquire the same resource at exactly the same time by using such an instruction. This requires some mechanism for making a decision about which process gets control. Such a mechanism is called an *arbiter*. Arbiters usually boil down to some sort of hardware device. Unfortunately, it is possible to prove that one cannot physically construct a fair arbiter that works 100% of the time unless one allows the arbiter an arbitrarily long time to make its decision. The fundamental phenomenon here was originally observed by the fourteenth-century French philosopher Jean Buridan in his commentary on Aristotle's *De caelo*. Buridan argued that a perfectly rational dog placed between two equally attractive sources of food will starve to death, because it is incapable of deciding which to go to first.

acquire the semaphore must wait for release operations. Give implementations of semaphores

a. in terms of mutexes

b. in terms of atomic `test-and-set!` operations.

Deadlock

Now that we have seen how to implement serializers, we can see that account exchanging still has a problem, even with the `serialized-exchange` procedure above. Imagine that Peter attempts to exchange $a1$ with $a2$ while Paul concurrently attempts to exchange $a2$ with $a1$. Suppose that Peter's process reaches the point where it has entered a serialized procedure protecting $a1$ and, just after that, Paul's process enters a serialized procedure protecting $a2$. Now Peter cannot proceed (to enter a serialized procedure protecting $a2$) until Paul exits the serialized procedure protecting $a2$. Similarly, Paul cannot proceed until Peter exits the serialized procedure protecting $a1$. Each process is stalled forever, waiting for the other. This situation is called a *deadlock*. Deadlock is always a danger in systems that provide concurrent access to multiple shared resources.

One way to avoid the deadlock in this situation is to give each account a unique identification number and rewrite `serialized-exchange` so that a process will always attempt to enter a procedure protecting the lowest-numbered account first. Although this method works well for the exchange problem, there are other situations that require more sophisticated deadlock-avoidance techniques, or where deadlock cannot be avoided at all. (See exercises 3.48 and 3.49.)[48]

Exercise 3.48

Explain in detail why the deadlock-avoidance method described above, (i.e., the accounts are numbered, and each process attempts to acquire the smaller-numbered account first) avoids deadlock in the exchange problem. Rewrite `serialized-exchange` to incorporate this idea. (You will also need to modify `make-account` so that each account is created with a number, which can be accessed by sending an appropriate message.)

---

[48]The general technique for avoiding deadlock by numbering the shared resources and acquiring them in order is due to Havender (1968). Situations where deadlock cannot be avoided require *deadlock-recovery* methods, which entail having processes "back out" of the deadlocked state and try again. Deadlock-recovery mechanisms are widely used in database management systems, a topic that is treated in detail in Gray and Reuter 1993.

Exercise 3.49

Give a scenario where the deadlock-avoidance mechanism described above does not work. (Hint: In the exchange problem, each process knows in advance which accounts it will need to get access to. Consider a situation where a process must get access to some shared resources before it can know which additional shared resources it will require.)

Concurrency, time, and communication

We've seen how programming concurrent systems requires controlling the ordering of events when different processes access shared state, and we've seen how to achieve this control through judicious use of serializers. But the problems of concurrency lie deeper than this, because, from a fundamental point of view, it's not always clear what is meant by "shared state."

Mechanisms such as `test-and-set!` require processes to examine a global shared flag at arbitrary times. This is problematic and inefficient to implement in modern high-speed processors, where due to optimization techniques such as pipelining and cached memory, the contents of memory may not be in a consistent state at every instant. In contemporary multiprocessing systems, therefore, the serializer paradigm is being supplanted by new approaches to concurrency control.[49]

The problematic aspects of shared state also arise in large, distributed systems. For instance, imagine a distributed banking system where individual branch banks maintain local values for bank balances and periodically compare these with values maintained by other branches. In such a system the value of "the account balance" would be undetermined, except right after synchronization. If Peter deposits money in an account he holds jointly with Paul, when should we say that the account balance has changed—when the balance in the local branch changes, or not until after the synchronization? And if Paul accesses the account from a different branch, what are the reasonable constraints to place on the banking system such that the behavior is "correct"? The only thing that might matter for correctness is the behavior observed by Peter and Paul individually

---

[49]One such alternative to serialization is called *barrier synchronization*. The programmer permits concurrent processes to execute as they please, but establishes certain synchronization points ("barriers") through which no process can proceed until all the processes have reached the barrier. Modern processors provide machine instructions that permit programmers to establish synchronization points at places where consistency is required. The PowerPC^{TM}, for example, includes for this purpose two instructions called SYNC and EIEIO (Enforced In-order Execution of Input/Output).

and the "state" of the account immediately after synchronization. Questions about the "real" account balance or the order of events between synchronizations may be irrelevant or meaningless.[50]

The basic phenomenon here is that synchronizing different processes, establishing shared state, or imposing an order on events requires communication among the processes. In essence, any notion of time in concurrency control must be intimately tied to communication.[51] It is intriguing that a similar connection between time and communication also arises in the Theory of Relativity, where the speed of light (the fastest signal that can be used to synchronize events) is a fundamental constant relating time and space. The complexities we encounter in dealing with time and state in our computational models may in fact mirror a fundamental complexity of the physical universe.

3.5   Streams

We've gained a good understanding of assignment as a tool in modeling, as well as an appreciation of the complex problems that assignment raises. It is time to ask whether we could have gone about things in a different way, so as to avoid some of these problems. In this section, we explore an alternative approach to modeling state, based on data structures called *streams*. As we shall see, streams can mitigate some of the complexity of modeling state.

Let's step back and review where this complexity comes from. In an attempt to model real-world phenomena, we made some apparently reasonable decisions: We modeled real-world objects with local state by computational objects with local variables. We identified time variation in the real world with time variation in the computer. We implemented the time variation of the states of the model objects in the computer with assignments to the local variables of the model objects.

Is there another approach? Can we avoid identifying time in the computer with time in the modeled world? Must we make the model change

---

[50]This may seem like a strange point of view, but there are systems that work this way. International charges to credit-card accounts, for example, are normally cleared on a per-country basis, and the charges made in different countries are periodically reconciled. Thus the account balance may be different in different countries.

[51]For distributed systems, this perspective was pursued by Lamport (1978), who showed how to use communication to establish "global clocks" that can be used to establish orderings on events in distributed systems.

with time in order to model phenomena in a changing world? Think about the issue in terms of mathematical functions. We can describe the time-varying behavior of a quantity x as a function of time $x(t)$. If we concentrate on x instant by instant, we think of it as a changing quantity. Yet if we concentrate on the entire time history of values, we do not emphasize change—the function itself does not change.[52]

If time is measured in discrete steps, then we can model a time function as a (possibly infinite) sequence. In this section, we will see how to model change in terms of sequences that represent the time histories of the systems being modeled. To accomplish this, we introduce new data structures called *streams*. From an abstract point of view, a stream is simply a sequence. However, we will find that the straightforward implementation of streams as lists (as in section 2.2.1) doesn't fully reveal the power of stream processing. As an alternative, we introduce the technique of *delayed evaluation*, which enables us to represent very large (even infinite) sequences as streams.

Stream processing lets us model systems that have state without ever using assignment or mutable data. This has important implications, both theoretical and practical, because we can build models that avoid the drawbacks inherent in introducing assignment. On the other hand, the stream framework raises difficulties of its own, and the question of which modeling technique leads to more modular and more easily maintained systems remains open.

3.5.1 Streams Are Delayed Lists

As we saw in section 2.2.3, sequences can serve as standard interfaces for combining program modules. We formulated powerful abstractions for manipulating sequences, such as map, filter, and accumulate, that capture a wide variety of operations in a manner that is both succinct and elegant.

Unfortunately, if we represent sequences as lists, this elegance is bought at the price of severe inefficiency with respect to both the time and space required by our computations. When we represent manipulations on sequences as transformations of lists, our programs must construct and copy data structures (which may be huge) at every step of a process.

---

[52]Physicists sometimes adopt this view by introducing the "world lines" of particles as a device for reasoning about motion. We've also already mentioned (section 2.2.3) that this is the natural way to think about signal-processing systems. We will explore applications of streams to signal processing in section 3.5.3.

To see why this is true, let us compare two programs for computing the sum of all the prime numbers in an interval. The first program is written in standard iterative style:[53]

```
(define (sum-primes a b)
  (define (iter count accum)
    (cond ((> count b) accum)
          ((prime? count) (iter (+ count 1) (+ count accum)))
          (else (iter (+ count 1) accum))))
  (iter a 0))
```

The second program performs the same computation using the sequence operations of section 2.2.3:

```
(define (sum-primes a b)
  (accumulate +
              0
              (filter prime? (enumerate-interval a b))))
```

In carrying out the computation, the first program needs to store only the sum being accumulated. In contrast, the filter in the second program cannot do any testing until enumerate-interval has constructed a complete list of the numbers in the interval. The filter generates another list, which in turn is passed to accumulate before being collapsed to form a sum. Such large intermediate storage is not needed by the first program, which we can think of as enumerating the interval incrementally, adding each prime to the sum as it is generated.

The inefficiency in using lists becomes painfully apparent if we use the sequence paradigm to compute the second prime in the interval from 10,000 to 1,000,000 by evaluating the expression

```
(car (cdr (filter prime?
                  (enumerate-interval 10000 1000000))))
```

This expression does find the second prime, but the computational overhead is outrageous. We construct a list of almost a million integers, filter this list by testing each element for primality, and then ignore almost all of the result. In a more traditional programming style, we would interleave the enumeration and the filtering, and stop when we reached the second prime.

---

[53] Assume that we have a predicate prime? (e.g., as in section 1.2.6) that tests for primality.

Streams are a clever idea that allows one to use sequence manipulations without incurring the costs of manipulating sequences as lists. With streams we can achieve the best of both worlds: We can formulate programs elegantly as sequence manipulations, while attaining the efficiency of incremental computation. The basic idea is to arrange to construct a stream only partially, and to pass the partial construction to the program that consumes the stream. If the consumer attempts to access a part of the stream that has not yet been constructed, the stream will automatically construct just enough more of itself to produce the required part, thus preserving the illusion that the entire stream exists. In other words, although we will write programs as if we were processing complete sequences, we design our stream implementation to automatically and transparently interleave the construction of the stream with its use.

On the surface, streams are just lists with different names for the procedures that manipulate them. There is a constructor, `cons-stream`, and two selectors, `stream-car` and `stream-cdr`, which satisfy the constraints

```
(stream-car (cons-stream x y)) = x

(stream-cdr (cons-stream x y)) = y
```

There is a distinguishable object, `the-empty-stream`, which cannot be the result of any `cons-stream` operation, and which can be identified with the predicate `stream-null?`.[54] Thus we can make and use streams, in just the same way as we can make and use lists, to represent aggregate data arranged in a sequence. In particular, we can build stream analogs of the list operations from chapter 2, such as `list-ref`, `map`, and `for-each`:[55]

```
(define (stream-ref s n)
  (if (= n 0)
      (stream-car s)
      (stream-ref (stream-cdr s) (- n 1))))
```

---

[54]In the MIT implementation, `the-empty-stream` is the same as the empty list ' (), and `stream-null?` is the same as `null?`.

[55]This should bother you. The fact that we are defining such similar procedures for streams and lists indicates that we are missing some underlying abstraction. Unfortunately, in order to exploit this abstraction, we will need to exert finer control over the process of evaluation than we can at present. We will discuss this point further at the end of section 3.5.4. In section 4.2, we'll develop a framework that unifies lists and streams.

```
(define (stream-map proc s)
  (if (stream-null? s)
      the-empty-stream
      (cons-stream (proc (stream-car s))
                   (stream-map proc (stream-cdr s)))))

(define (stream-for-each proc s)
  (if (stream-null? s)
      'done
      (begin (proc (stream-car s))
             (stream-for-each proc (stream-cdr s)))))
```

Stream-for-each is useful for viewing streams:

```
(define (display-stream s)
  (stream-for-each display-line s))

(define (display-line x)
  (newline)
  (display x))
```

To make the stream implementation automatically and transparently interleave the construction of a stream with its use, we will arrange for the cdr of a stream to be evaluated when it is accessed by the stream-cdr procedure rather than when the stream is constructed by cons-stream. This implementation choice is reminiscent of our discussion of rational numbers in section 2.1.2, where we saw that we can choose to implement rational numbers so that the reduction of numerator and denominator to lowest terms is performed either at construction time or at selection time. The two rational-number implementations produce the same data abstraction, but the choice has an effect on efficiency. There is a similar relationship between streams and ordinary lists. As a data abstraction, streams are the same as lists. The difference is the time at which the elements are evaluated. With ordinary lists, both the car and the cdr are evaluated at construction time. With streams, the cdr is evaluated at selection time.

Our implementation of streams will be based on a special form called delay. Evaluating (delay ⟨*exp*⟩) does not evaluate the expression ⟨*exp*⟩, but rather returns a so-called *delayed object*, which we can think of as a "promise" to evaluate ⟨*exp*⟩ at some future time. As a companion to delay, there is a procedure called force that takes a delayed object as argument and performs the evaluation—in effect, forcing the delay to fulfill its promise. We will see below how delay and force can be implemented, but first let us use these to construct streams.

Cons-stream is a special form defined so that

```
(cons-stream ⟨a⟩ ⟨b⟩)
```

is equivalent to

```
(cons ⟨a⟩ (delay ⟨b⟩))
```

What this means is that we will construct streams using pairs. However, rather than placing the value of the rest of the stream into the cdr of the pair we will put there a promise to compute the rest if it is ever requested. Stream-car and stream-cdr can now be defined as procedures:

```
(define (stream-car stream) (car stream))

(define (stream-cdr stream) (force (cdr stream)))
```

Stream-car selects the car of the pair; stream-cdr selects the cdr of the pair and evaluates the delayed expression found there to obtain the rest of the stream.[56]

The stream implementation in action

To see how this implementation behaves, let us analyze the "outrageous" prime computation we saw above, reformulated in terms of streams:

```
(stream-car
 (stream-cdr
  (stream-filter prime?
                 (stream-enumerate-interval 10000 1000000))))
```

We will see that it does indeed work efficiently.

We begin by calling stream-enumerate-interval with the arguments 10,000 and 1,000,000. Stream-enumerate-interval is the stream analog of enumerate-interval (section 2.2.3):

```
(define (stream-enumerate-interval low high)
  (if (> low high)
      the-empty-stream
      (cons-stream
       low
       (stream-enumerate-interval (+ low 1) high))))
```

---

[56]Although stream-car and stream-cdr can be defined as procedures, cons-stream must be a special form. If cons-stream were a procedure, then, according to our model of evaluation, evaluating (cons-stream ⟨a⟩ ⟨b⟩) would automatically cause ⟨b⟩ to be evaluated, which is precisely what we do not want to happen. For the same reason, delay must be a special form, though force can be an ordinary procedure.

and thus the result returned by `stream-enumerate-interval`, formed by the `cons-stream`, is[57]

```
(cons 10000
      (delay (stream-enumerate-interval 10001 1000000)))
```

That is, `stream-enumerate-interval` returns a stream represented as a pair whose `car` is 10,000 and whose `cdr` is a promise to enumerate more of the interval if so requested. This stream is now filtered for primes, using the stream analog of the `filter` procedure (section 2.2.3):

```
(define (stream-filter pred stream)
  (cond ((stream-null? stream) the-empty-stream)
        ((pred (stream-car stream))
         (cons-stream (stream-car stream)
                      (stream-filter pred
                                     (stream-cdr stream))))
        (else (stream-filter pred (stream-cdr stream)))))
```

`Stream-filter` tests the `stream-car` of the stream (the `car` of the pair, which is 10,000). Since this is not prime, `stream-filter` examines the `stream-cdr` of its input stream. The call to `stream-cdr` forces evaluation of the delayed `stream-enumerate-interval`, which now returns

```
(cons 10001
      (delay (stream-enumerate-interval 10002 1000000)))
```

`Stream-filter` now looks at the `stream-car` of this stream, 10,001, sees that this is not prime either, forces another `stream-cdr`, and so on, until `stream-enumerate-interval` yields the prime 10,007, whereupon `stream-filter`, according to its definition, returns

```
(cons-stream (stream-car stream)
             (stream-filter pred (stream-cdr stream)))
```

which in this case is

```
(cons 10007
      (delay
        (stream-filter
          prime?
          (cons 10008
                (delay
                  (stream-enumerate-interval 10009
                                             1000000))))))
```

---

[57]The numbers shown here do not really appear in the delayed expression. What actually appears is the original expression, in an environment in which the variables are bound to the appropriate numbers. For example, `(+ low 1)` with `low` bound to 10,000 actually appears where 10001 is shown.

This result is now passed to `stream-cdr` in our original expression. This forces the delayed `stream-filter`, which in turn keeps forcing the delayed `stream-enumerate-interval` until it finds the next prime, which is 10,009. Finally, the result passed to `stream-car` in our original expression is

```
(cons 10009
      (delay
        (stream-filter
         prime?
         (cons 10010
               (delay
                 (stream-enumerate-interval 10011
                                            1000000))))))
```

`Stream-car` returns 10,009, and the computation is complete. Only as many integers were tested for primality as were necessary to find the second prime, and the interval was enumerated only as far as was necessary to feed the prime filter.

In general, we can think of delayed evaluation as "demand-driven" programming, whereby each stage in the stream process is activated only enough to satisfy the next stage. What we have done is to decouple the actual order of events in the computation from the apparent structure of our procedures. We write procedures as if the streams existed "all at once" when, in reality, the computation is performed incrementally, as in traditional programming styles.

Implementing `delay` and `force`

Although `delay` and `force` may seem like mysterious operations, their implementation is really quite straightforward. `Delay` must package an expression so that it can be evaluated later on demand, and we can accomplish this simply by treating the expression as the body of a procedure. `Delay` can be a special form such that

```
(delay ⟨exp⟩)
```

is syntactic sugar for

```
(lambda () ⟨exp⟩)
```

`Force` simply calls the procedure (of no arguments) produced by `delay`, so we can implement `force` as a procedure:

```
(define (force delayed-object)
  (delayed-object))
```

This implementation suffices for `delay` and `force` to work as advertised, but there is an important optimization that we can include. In many applications, we end up forcing the same delayed object many times. This can lead to serious inefficiency in recursive programs involving streams. (See exercise 3.57.) The solution is to build delayed objects so that the first time they are forced, they store the value that is computed. Subsequent forcings will simply return the stored value without repeating the computation. In other words, we implement `delay` as a special-purpose memoized procedure similar to the one described in exercise 3.27. One way to accomplish this is to use the following procedure, which takes as argument a procedure (of no arguments) and returns a memoized version of the procedure. The first time the memoized procedure is run, it saves the computed result. On subsequent evaluations, it simply returns the result.

```
(define (memo-proc proc)
  (let ((already-run? false) (result false))
    (lambda ()
      (if (not already-run?)
          (begin (set! result (proc))
                 (set! already-run? true)
                 result)
          result))))
```

`Delay` is then defined so that (`delay` ⟨*exp*⟩) is equivalent to

(`memo-proc` (`lambda` () ⟨*exp*⟩))

and `force` is as defined previously.[58]

Exercise 3.50

Complete the following definition, which generalizes `stream-map` to allow procedures that take multiple arguments, analogous to `map` in section 2.2.3, footnote 12.

---

[58]There are many possible implementations of streams other than the one described in this section. Delayed evaluation, which is the key to making streams practical, was inherent in Algol 60's *call-by-name* parameter-passing method. The use of this mechanism to implement streams was first described by Landin (1965). Delayed evaluation for streams was introduced into Lisp by Friedman and Wise (1976). In their implementation, `cons` always delays evaluating its arguments, so that lists automatically behave as streams. The memoizing optimization is also known as *call-by-need*. The Algol community would refer to our original delayed objects as *call-by-name thunks* and to the optimized versions as *call-by-need thunks*.

```
(define (stream-map proc . argstreams)
  (if ((⟨??⟩) (car argstreams))
      the-empty-stream
      ((⟨??⟩)
       (apply proc (map ⟨??⟩ argstreams))
       (apply stream-map
              (cons proc (map ⟨??⟩ argstreams))))))
```

Exercise 3.51

In order to take a closer look at delayed evaluation, we will use the following procedure, which simply returns its argument after printing it:

```
(define (show x)
  (display-line x)
  x)
```

What does the interpreter print in response to evaluating each expression in the following sequence?[59]

```
(define x (stream-map show (stream-enumerate-interval 0 10)))
```

```
(stream-ref x 5)
```

```
(stream-ref x 7)
```

Exercise 3.52

Consider the sequence of expressions

```
(define sum 0)
```

```
(define (accum x)
  (set! sum (+ x sum))
  sum)
```

```
(define seq (stream-map accum (stream-enumerate-interval 1 20)))
(define y (stream-filter even? seq))
(define z (stream-filter (lambda (x) (= (remainder x 5) 0))
                         seq))
```

```
(stream-ref y 7)
```

```
(display-stream z)
```

---

[59]Exercises such as 3.51 and 3.52 are valuable for testing our understanding of how `delay` works. On the other hand, intermixing delayed evaluation with printing—and, even worse, with assignment—is extremely confusing, and instructors of courses on computer languages have traditionally tormented their students with examination questions such as the ones in this section. Needless to say, writing programs that depend on such subtleties is odious programming style. Part of the power of stream processing is that it lets us ignore the order in which events actually happen in our programs. Unfortunately, this is precisely what we cannot afford to do in the presence of assignment, which forces us to be concerned with time and change.

What is the value of sum after each of the above expressions is evaluated? What is the printed response to evaluating the stream-ref and display-stream expressions? Would these responses differ if we had implemented (delay ⟨*exp*⟩) simply as (lambda () ⟨*exp*⟩) without using the optimization provided by memo-proc? Explain.

3.5.2   Infinite Streams

We have seen how to support the illusion of manipulating streams as complete entities even though, in actuality, we compute only as much of the stream as we need to access. We can exploit this technique to represent sequences efficiently as streams, even if the sequences are very long. What is more striking, we can use streams to represent sequences that are infinitely long. For instance, consider the following definition of the stream of positive integers:

```
(define (integers-starting-from n)
  (cons-stream n (integers-starting-from (+ n 1))))

(define integers (integers-starting-from 1))
```

This makes sense because integers will be a pair whose car is 1 and whose cdr is a promise to produce the integers beginning with 2. This is an infinitely long stream, but in any given time we can examine only a finite portion of it. Thus, our programs will never know that the entire infinite stream is not there.

Using integers we can define other infinite streams, such as the stream of integers that are not divisible by 7:

```
(define (divisible? x y) (= (remainder x y) 0))

(define no-sevens
  (stream-filter (lambda (x) (not (divisible? x 7)))
                 integers))
```

Then we can find integers not divisible by 7 simply by accessing elements of this stream:

```
(stream-ref no-sevens 100)
117
```

In analogy with integers, we can define the infinite stream of Fibonacci numbers:

```
(define (fibgen a b)
  (cons-stream a (fibgen b (+ a b))))
```

```
(define fibs (fibgen 0 1))
```

Fibs is a pair whose car is 0 and whose cdr is a promise to evaluate
(fibgen 1 1). When we evaluate this delayed (fibgen 1 1), it will
produce a pair whose car is 1 and whose cdr is a promise to evaluate
(fibgen 1 2), and so on.

For a look at a more exciting infinite stream, we can generalize the
no-sevens example to construct the infinite stream of prime numbers,
using a method known as the *sieve of Eratosthenes*.[60] We start with
the integers beginning with 2, which is the first prime. To get the rest
of the primes, we start by filtering the multiples of 2 from the rest of
the integers. This leaves a stream beginning with 3, which is the next
prime. Now we filter the multiples of 3 from the rest of this stream. This
leaves a stream beginning with 5, which is the next prime, and so on. In
other words, we construct the primes by a sieving process, described as
follows: To sieve a stream S, form a stream whose first element is the first
element of S and the rest of which is obtained by filtering all multiples
of the first element of S out of the rest of S and sieving the result. This
process is readily described in terms of stream operations:

```
(define (sieve stream)
  (cons-stream
   (stream-car stream)
   (sieve (stream-filter
           (lambda (x)
             (not (divisible? x (stream-car stream))))
           (stream-cdr stream)))))

(define primes (sieve (integers-starting-from 2)))
```

Now to find a particular prime we need only ask for it:

```
(stream-ref primes 50)
233
```

---

[60]Eratosthenes, a third-century B.C. Alexandrian Greek philosopher, is famous for giving the first accurate estimate of the circumference of the Earth, which he computed by
observing shadows cast at noon on the day of the summer solstice. Eratosthenes's sieve
method, although ancient, has formed the basis for special-purpose hardware "sieves" that,
until recently, were the most powerful tools in existence for locating large primes. Since
the 70s, however, these methods have been superseded by outgrowths of the probabilistic
techniques discussed in section 1.2.6.

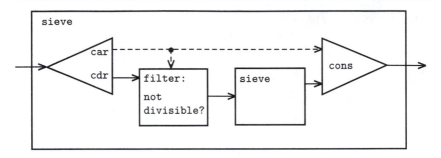

Figure 3.31   The prime sieve viewed as a signal-processing system.

It is interesting to contemplate the signal-processing system set up by
sieve, shown in the "Henderson diagram" in figure 3.31.[61] The input
stream feeds into an "unconser" that separates the first element of the
stream from the rest of the stream. The first element is used to construct
a divisibility filter, through which the rest is passed, and the output of the
filter is fed to another sieve box. Then the original first element is consed
onto the output of the internal sieve to form the output stream. Thus,
not only is the stream infinite, but the signal processor is also infinite,
because the sieve contains a sieve within it.

Defining streams implicitly

The integers and fibs streams above were defined by specifying "generating" procedures that explicitly compute the stream elements one by
one. An alternative way to specify streams is to take advantage of delayed evaluation to define streams implicitly. For example, the following
expression defines the stream ones to be an infinite stream of ones:

```
(define ones (cons-stream 1 ones))
```

This works much like the definition of a recursive procedure: ones is
a pair whose car is 1 and whose cdr is a promise to evaluate ones.
Evaluating the cdr gives us again a 1 and a promise to evaluate ones,
and so on.

---

[61] We have named these figures after Peter Henderson, who was the first person to show
us diagrams of this sort as a way of thinking about stream processing. Each solid line
represents a stream of values being transmitted. The dashed line from the car to the cons
and the filter indicates that this is a single value rather than a stream.

We can do more interesting things by manipulating streams with operations such as `add-streams`, which produces the elementwise sum of two given streams:[62]

```
(define (add-streams s1 s2)
  (stream-map + s1 s2))
```

Now we can define the integers as follows:

```
(define integers (cons-stream 1 (add-streams ones integers)))
```

This defines `integers` to be a stream whose first element is 1 and the rest of which is the sum of `ones` and `integers`. Thus, the second element of `integers` is 1 plus the first element of `integers`, or 2; the third element of `integers` is 1 plus the second element of `integers`, or 3; and so on. This definition works because, at any point, enough of the `integers` stream has been generated so that we can feed it back into the definition to produce the next integer.

We can define the Fibonacci numbers in the same style:

```
(define fibs
  (cons-stream 0
               (cons-stream 1
                            (add-streams (stream-cdr fibs)
                                         fibs)))))
```

This definition says that `fibs` is a stream beginning with 0 and 1, such that the rest of the stream can be generated by adding `fibs` to itself shifted by one place:

```
    1   1   2   3   5   8  13  21  ... = (stream-cdr fibs)
    0   1   1   2   3   5   8  13  ... = fibs
───────────────────────────────────
0   1   1   2   3   5   8  13  21  34  ... = fibs
```

`Scale-stream` is another useful procedure in formulating such stream definitions. This multiplies each item in a stream by a given constant:

```
(define (scale-stream stream factor)
  (stream-map (lambda (x) (* x factor)) stream))
```

---

[62]This uses the generalized version of `stream-map` from exercise 3.50.

For example,

```
(define double (cons-stream 1 (scale-stream double 2)))
```

produces the stream of powers of 2: $1, 2, 4, 8, 16, 32, \ldots$.

An alternate definition of the stream of primes can be given by starting with the integers and filtering them by testing for primality. We will need the first prime, 2, to get started:

```
(define primes
  (cons-stream
   2
   (stream-filter prime? (integers-starting-from 3))))
```

This definition is not so straightforward as it appears, because we will test whether a number n is prime by checking whether n is divisible by a prime (not by just any integer) less than or equal to $\sqrt{n}$:

```
(define (prime? n)
  (define (iter ps)
    (cond ((> (square (stream-car ps)) n) true)
          ((divisible? n (stream-car ps)) false)
          (else (iter (stream-cdr ps)))))
  (iter primes))
```

This is a recursive definition, since primes is defined in terms of the prime? predicate, which itself uses the primes stream. The reason this procedure works is that, at any point, enough of the primes stream has been generated to test the primality of the numbers we need to check next. That is, for every n we test for primality, either n is not prime (in which case there is a prime already generated that divides it) or n is prime (in which case there is a prime already generated—i.e., a prime less than n—that is greater than $\sqrt{n}$).[63]

Exercise 3.53

Without running the program, describe the elements of the stream defined by

```
(define s (cons-stream 1 (add-streams s s)))
```

---

[63]This last point is very subtle and relies on the fact that $p_{n+1} \leq p_n^2$. (Here, p_k denotes the kth prime.) Estimates such as these are very difficult to establish. The ancient proof by Euclid that there are an infinite number of primes shows that $p_{n+1} \leq p_1 p_2 \cdots p_n + 1$, and no substantially better result was proved until 1851, when the Russian mathematician P. L. Chebyshev established that $p_{n+1} \leq 2p_n$ for all n. This result, originally conjectured in 1845, is known as *Bertrand's hypothesis*. A proof can be found in section 22.3 of Hardy and Wright 1960.

Exercise 3.54

Define a procedure `mul-streams`, analogous to `add-streams`, that produces the elementwise product of its two input streams. Use this together with the stream of `integers` to complete the following definition of the stream whose nth element (counting from 0) is $n + 1$ factorial:

```
(define factorials (cons-stream 1 (mul-streams ⟨??⟩ ⟨??⟩)))
```

Exercise 3.55

Define a procedure `partial-sums` that takes as argument a stream S and returns the stream whose elements are S_0, $S_0 + S_1$, $S_0 + S_1 + S_2$, ... For example, `(partial-sums integers)` should be the stream $1, 3, 6, 10, 15, \ldots$.

Exercise 3.56

A famous problem, first raised by R. Hamming, is to enumerate, in ascending order with no repetitions, all positive integers with no prime factors other than 2, 3, or 5. One obvious way to do this is to simply test each integer in turn to see whether it has any factors other than 2, 3, and 5. But this is very inefficient, since, as the integers get larger, fewer and fewer of them fit the requirement. As an alternative, let us call the required stream of numbers S and notice the following facts about it.

- S begins with 1.
- The elements of (`scale-stream` S 2) are also elements of S.
- The same is true for (`scale-stream` S 3) and (`scale-stream` 5 S).
- These are all the elements of S.

Now all we have to do is combine elements from these sources. For this we define a procedure `merge` that combines two ordered streams into one ordered result stream, eliminating repetitions:

```
(define (merge s1 s2)
  (cond ((stream-null? s1) s2)
        ((stream-null? s2) s1)
        (else
         (let ((s1car (stream-car s1))
               (s2car (stream-car s2)))
           (cond ((< s1car s2car)
                  (cons-stream s1car (merge (stream-cdr s1) s2)))
                 ((> s1car s2car)
                  (cons-stream s2car (merge s1 (stream-cdr s2))))
                 (else
                  (cons-stream s1car
                               (merge (stream-cdr s1)
                                      (stream-cdr s2)))))))))
```

Then the required stream may be constructed with `merge`, as follows:

```
(define S (cons-stream 1 (merge ⟨??⟩ ⟨??⟩)))
```

Fill in the missing expressions in the places marked ⟨ *??* ⟩ above.

Exercise 3.57

How many additions are performed when we compute the nth Fibonacci number using the definition of fibs based on the add-streams procedure? Show that the number of additions would be exponentially greater if we had implemented (delay $\langle exp \rangle$) simply as (lambda () $\langle exp \rangle$), without using the optimization provided by the memo-proc procedure described in section 3.5.1.[64]

Exercise 3.58

Give an interpretation of the stream computed by the following procedure:

```
(define (expand num den radix)
  (cons-stream
    (quotient (* num radix) den)
    (expand (remainder (* num radix) den) den radix)))
```

(Quotient is a primitive that returns the integer quotient of two integers.) What are the successive elements produced by (expand 1 7 10)? What is produced by (expand 3 8 10)?

Exercise 3.59

In section 2.5.3 we saw how to implement a polynomial arithmetic system representing polynomials as lists of terms. In a similar way, we can work with *power series*, such as

$$e^x = 1 + x + \frac{x^2}{2} + \frac{x^3}{3 \cdot 2} + \frac{x^4}{4 \cdot 3 \cdot 2} + \cdots,$$

$$\cos x = 1 - \frac{x^2}{2} + \frac{x^4}{4 \cdot 3 \cdot 2} - \cdots,$$

$$\sin x = x - \frac{x^3}{3 \cdot 2} + \frac{x^5}{5 \cdot 4 \cdot 3 \cdot 2} - \cdots,$$

represented as infinite streams. We will represent the series $a_0 + a_1x + a_2x^2 + a_3x^3 + \cdots$ as the stream whose elements are the coefficients $a_0, a_1, a_2, a_3, \ldots$.

a. The integral of the series $a_0 + a_1x + a_2x^2 + a_3x^3 + \cdots$ is the series

$$c + a_0x + \frac{1}{2}a_1x^2 + \frac{1}{3}a_2x^3 + \frac{1}{4}a_3x^4 + \cdots$$

where c is any constant. Define a procedure integrate-series that takes as input a stream $a_0, a_1, a_2, \ldots$ representing a power series and returns the stream

---

[64]This exercise shows how call-by-need is closely related to ordinary memoization as described in exercise 3.27. In that exercise, we used assignment to explicitly construct a local table. Our call-by-need stream optimization effectively constructs such a table automatically, storing values in the previously forced parts of the stream.

$a_0, \frac{1}{2}a_1, \frac{1}{3}a_2, \ldots$ of coefficients of the non-constant terms of the integral of the series. (Since the result has no constant term, it doesn't represent a power series; when we use `integrate-series`, we will cons on the appropriate constant.)

b. The function $x \mapsto e^x$ is its own derivative. This implies that e^x and the integral of e^x are the same series, except for the constant term, which is $e^0 = 1$. Accordingly, we can generate the series for e^x as

```
(define exp-series
  (cons-stream 1 (integrate-series exp-series)))
```

Show how to generate the series for sine and cosine, starting from the facts that the derivative of sine is cosine and the derivative of cosine is the negative of sine:

```
(define cosine-series
  (cons-stream 1 ⟨??⟩))

(define sine-series
  (cons-stream 0 ⟨??⟩))
```

Exercise 3.60

With power series represented as streams of coefficients as in exercise 3.59, adding series is implemented by `add-streams`. Complete the definition of the following procedure for multiplying series:

```
(define (mul-series s1 s2)
  (cons-stream ⟨??⟩ (add-streams ⟨??⟩ ⟨??⟩)))
```

You can test your procedure by verifying that $sin^2x + cos^2x = 1$, using the series from exercise 3.59.

Exercise 3.61

Let S be a power series (exercise 3.59) whose constant term is 1. Suppose we want to find the power series $1/S$, that is, the series X such that $S \cdot X = 1$. Write $S = 1 + S_R$ where S_R is the part of S after the constant term. Then we can solve for X as follows:

$$
\begin{aligned}
S \cdot X &= 1 \\
(1 + S_R) \cdot X &= 1 \\
X + S_R \cdot X &= 1 \\
X &= 1 - S_R \cdot X
\end{aligned}
$$

In other words, X is the power series whose constant term is 1 and whose higher-order terms are given by the negative of S_R times X. Use this idea to write a procedure `invert-unit-series` that computes $1/S$ for a power series S with constant term 1. You will need to use `mul-series` from exercise 3.60.

Exercise 3.62

Use the results of exercises 3.60 and 3.61 to define a procedure `div-series` that divides two power series. `Div-series` should work for any two series, provided that the denominator series begins with a nonzero constant term. (If the denominator has a zero constant term, then `div-series` should signal an error.) Show how to use `div-series` together with the result of exercise 3.59 to generate the power series for tangent.

3.5.3   Exploiting the Stream Paradigm

Streams with delayed evaluation can be a powerful modeling tool, providing many of the benefits of local state and assignment. Moreover, they avoid some of the theoretical tangles that accompany the introduction of assignment into a programming language.

The stream approach can be illuminating because it allows us to build systems with different module boundaries than systems organized around assignment to state variables. For example, we can think of an entire time series (or signal) as a focus of interest, rather than the values of the state variables at individual moments. This makes it convenient to combine and compare components of state from different moments.

Formulating iterations as stream processes

In section 1.2.1, we introduced iterative processes, which proceed by updating state variables. We know now that we can represent state as a "timeless" stream of values rather than as a set of variables to be updated. Let's adopt this perspective in revisiting the square-root procedure from section 1.1.7. Recall that the idea is to generate a sequence of better and better guesses for the square root of x by applying over and over again the procedure that improves guesses:

```
(define (sqrt-improve guess x)
  (average guess (/ x guess)))
```

In our original `sqrt` procedure, we made these guesses be the successive values of a state variable. Instead we can generate the infinite stream of guesses, starting with an initial guess of 1:[65]

---

[65]We can't use `let` to bind the local variable `guesses`, because the value of `guesses` depends on `guesses` itself. Exercise 3.63 addresses why we want a local variable here.

```
(define (sqrt-stream x)
  (define guesses
    (cons-stream 1.0
                 (stream-map (lambda (guess)
                               (sqrt-improve guess x))
                             guesses)))
  guesses)

(display-stream (sqrt-stream 2))
1.
1.5
1.4166666666666665
1.4142156862745097
1.4142135623746899
...
```

We can generate more and more terms of the stream to get better and better guesses. If we like, we can write a procedure that keeps generating terms until the answer is good enough. (See exercise 3.64.)

Another iteration that we can treat in the same way is to generate an approximation to π, based upon the alternating series that we saw in section 1.3.1:

$$\frac{\pi}{4} = 1 - \frac{1}{3} + \frac{1}{5} - \frac{1}{7} + \cdots$$

We first generate the stream of summands of the series (the reciprocals of the odd integers, with alternating signs). Then we take the stream of sums of more and more terms (using the partial-sums procedure of exercise 3.55) and scale the result by 4:

```
(define (pi-summands n)
  (cons-stream (/ 1.0 n)
               (stream-map - (pi-summands (+ n 2)))))

(define pi-stream
  (scale-stream (partial-sums (pi-summands 1)) 4))

(display-stream pi-stream)
4.
2.666666666666667
3.466666666666667
2.8952380952380956
3.3396825396825403
2.9760461760461765
3.2837384837384844
3.017071817071818
...
```

This gives us a stream of better and better approximations to π, although the approximations converge rather slowly. Eight terms of the sequence bound the value of π between 3.284 and 3.017.

So far, our use of the stream of states approach is not much different from updating state variables. But streams give us an opportunity to do some interesting tricks. For example, we can transform a stream with a *sequence accelerator* that converts a sequence of approximations to a new sequence that converges to the same value as the original, only faster.

One such accelerator, due to the eighteenth-century Swiss mathematician Leonhard Euler, works well with sequences that are partial sums of alternating series (series of terms with alternating signs). In Euler's technique, if S_n is the nth term of the original sum sequence, then the accelerated sequence has terms

$$S_{n+1} - \frac{(S_{n+1} - S_n)^2}{S_{n-1} - 2S_n + S_{n+1}}$$

Thus, if the original sequence is represented as a stream of values, the transformed sequence is given by

```
(define (euler-transform s)
  (let ((s0 (stream-ref s 0))          ; S_{n-1}
        (s1 (stream-ref s 1))          ; S_n
        (s2 (stream-ref s 2)))         ; S_{n+1}
    (cons-stream (- s2 (/ (square (- s2 s1))
                          (+ s0 (* -2 s1) s2)))
                 (euler-transform (stream-cdr s)))))
```

We can demonstrate Euler acceleration with our sequence of approximations to π:

```
(display-stream (euler-transform pi-stream))
3.166666666666667
3.1333333333333337
3.1452380952380956
3.13968253968254
3.1427128427128435
3.1408813408813416
3.142071817071818
3.1412548236077655
...
```

Even better, we can accelerate the accelerated sequence, and recursively accelerate that, and so on. Namely, we create a stream of streams (a structure we'll call a *tableau*) in which each stream is the transform of the preceding one:

```
(define (make-tableau transform s)
  (cons-stream s
               (make-tableau transform
                             (transform s))))
```

The tableau has the form

$$
\begin{array}{cccccc}
s_{00} & s_{01} & s_{02} & s_{03} & s_{04} & \cdots \\
       & s_{10} & s_{11} & s_{12} & s_{13} & \cdots \\
       &   & s_{20} & s_{21} & s_{22} & \cdots \\
       &   &   & \cdots &   &
\end{array}
$$

Finally, we form a sequence by taking the first term in each row of the tableau:

```
(define (accelerated-sequence transform s)
  (stream-map stream-car
              (make-tableau transform s)))
```

We can demonstrate this kind of "super-acceleration" of the π sequence:

```
(display-stream (accelerated-sequence euler-transform
                                      pi-stream))
4.
3.166666666666667
3.142105263157895
3.141599357319005
3.1415927140337785
3.1415926539752927
3.1415926535911765
3.141592653589778
...
```

The result is impressive. Taking eight terms of the sequence yields the correct value of π to 14 decimal places. If we had used only the original π sequence, we would need to compute on the order of 10^{13} terms (i.e., expanding the series far enough so that the individual terms are less then 10^{-13}) to get that much accuracy!

We could have implemented these acceleration techniques without using streams. But the stream formulation is particularly elegant and convenient because the entire sequence of states is available to us as a data structure that can be manipulated with a uniform set of operations.

Exercise 3.63

Louis Reasoner asks why the `sqrt-stream` procedure was not written in the following more straightforward way, without the local variable `guesses`:

```
(define (sqrt-stream x)
  (cons-stream 1.0
               (stream-map (lambda (guess)
                             (sqrt-improve guess x))
                           (sqrt-stream x)))))
```

Alyssa P. Hacker replies that this version of the procedure is considerably less efficient because it performs redundant computation. Explain Alyssa's answer. Would the two versions still differ in efficiency if our implementation of `delay` used only `(lambda () ⟨exp⟩)` without using the optimization provided by `memo-proc` (section 3.5.1)?

Exercise 3.64

Write a procedure `stream-limit` that takes as arguments a stream and a number (the tolerance). It should examine the stream until it finds two successive elements that differ in absolute value by less than the tolerance, and return the second of the two elements. Using this, we could compute square roots up to a given tolerance by

```
(define (sqrt x tolerance)
  (stream-limit (sqrt-stream x) tolerance))
```

Exercise 3.65

Use the series

$$\ln 2 = 1 - \frac{1}{2} + \frac{1}{3} - \frac{1}{4} + \cdots$$

to compute three sequences of approximations to the natural logarithm of 2, in the same way we did above for π. How rapidly do these sequences converge?

Infinite streams of pairs

In section 2.2.3, we saw how the sequence paradigm handles traditional nested loops as processes defined on sequences of pairs. If we generalize this technique to infinite streams, then we can write programs that are not easily represented as loops, because the "looping" must range over an infinite set.

For example, suppose we want to generalize the `prime-sum-pairs` procedure of section 2.2.3 to produce the stream of pairs of *all* integers (i, j) with $i \leq j$ such that $i + j$ is prime. If `int-pairs` is the sequence of all pairs of integers (i, j) with $i \leq j$, then our required stream is simply[66]

```
(stream-filter (lambda (pair)
                 (prime? (+ (car pair) (cadr pair))))
               int-pairs)
```

Our problem, then, is to produce the stream `int-pairs`. More generally, suppose we have two streams $S = (S_i)$ and $T = (T_j)$, and imagine the infinite rectangular array

$$
\begin{array}{cccc}
(S_0, T_0) & (S_0, T_1) & (S_0, T_2) & \cdots \\
(S_1, T_0) & (S_1, T_1) & (S_1, T_2) & \cdots \\
(S_2, T_0) & (S_2, T_1) & (S_2, T_2) & \cdots \\
\cdots
\end{array}
$$

We wish to generate a stream that contains all the pairs in the array that lie on or above the diagonal, i.e., the pairs

$$
\begin{array}{cccc}
(S_0, T_0) & (S_0, T_1) & (S_0, T_2) & \cdots \\
           & (S_1, T_1) & (S_1, T_2) & \cdots \\
           &   & (S_2, T_2) & \cdots \\
           &   & \cdots
\end{array}
$$

(If we take both S and T to be the stream of integers, then this will be our desired stream `int-pairs`.)

Call the general stream of pairs (`pairs S T`), and consider it to be composed of three parts: the pair (S_0, T_0), the rest of the pairs in the first row, and the remaining pairs:[67]

$$
\begin{array}{c|ccc}
(S_0, T_0) & (S_0, T_1) & (S_0, T_2) & \cdots \\
\hline
           & (S_1, T_1) & (S_1, T_2) & \cdots \\
           &   & (S_2, T_2) & \cdots \\
           &   & \cdots
\end{array}
$$

Observe that the third piece in this decomposition (pairs that are not in the first row) is (recursively) the pairs formed from (`stream-cdr S`)

---

[66] As in section 2.2.3, we represent a pair of integers as a list rather than a Lisp pair.

[67] See exercise 3.68 for some insight into why we chose this decomposition.

and (stream-cdr T). Also note that the second piece (the rest of the first row) is

```
(stream-map (lambda (x) (list (stream-car s) x))
            (stream-cdr t))
```

Thus we can form our stream of pairs as follows:

```
(define (pairs s t)
  (cons-stream
   (list (stream-car s) (stream-car t))
   (⟨ combine-in-some-way ⟩
        (stream-map (lambda (x) (list (stream-car s) x))
                    (stream-cdr t))
        (pairs (stream-cdr s) (stream-cdr t)))))
```

In order to complete the procedure, we must choose some way to combine the two inner streams. One idea is to use the stream analog of the append procedure from section 2.2.1:

```
(define (stream-append s1 s2)
  (if (stream-null? s1)
      s2
      (cons-stream (stream-car s1)
                   (stream-append (stream-cdr s1) s2))))
```

This is unsuitable for infinite streams, however, because it takes all the elements from the first stream before incorporating the second stream. In particular, if we try to generate all pairs of positive integers using

```
(pairs integers integers)
```

our stream of results will first try to run through all pairs with the first integer equal to 1, and hence will never produce pairs with any other value of the first integer.

To handle infinite streams, we need to devise an order of combination that ensures that every element will eventually be reached if we let our program run long enough. An elegant way to accomplish this is with the following interleave procedure:[68]

---

[68]The precise statement of the required property on the order of combination is as follows: There should be a function f of two arguments such that the pair corresponding to element i of the first stream and element j of the second stream will appear as element number $f(i, j)$ of the output stream. The trick of using interleave to accomplish this was shown to us by David Turner, who employed it in the language KRC (Turner 1981).

```
(define (interleave s1 s2)
  (if (stream-null? s1)
      s2
      (cons-stream (stream-car s1)
                   (interleave s2 (stream-cdr s1)))))
```

Since `interleave` takes elements alternately from the two streams, every element of the second stream will eventually find its way into the interleaved stream, even if the first stream is infinite.

We can thus generate the required stream of pairs as

```
(define (pairs s t)
  (cons-stream
    (list (stream-car s) (stream-car t))
    (interleave
      (stream-map (lambda (x) (list (stream-car s) x))
                  (stream-cdr t))
      (pairs (stream-cdr s) (stream-cdr t)))))
```

Exercise 3.66

Examine the stream `(pairs integers integers)`. Can you make any general comments about the order in which the pairs are placed into the stream? For example, about how many pairs precede the pair (1,100)? the pair (99,100)? the pair (100,100)? (If you can make precise mathematical statements here, all the better. But feel free to give more qualitative answers if you find yourself getting bogged down.)

Exercise 3.67

Modify the `pairs` procedure so that `(pairs integers integers)` will produce the stream of *all* pairs of integers (i, j) (without the condition $i \le j$). Hint: You will need to mix in an additional stream.

Exercise 3.68

Louis Reasoner thinks that building a stream of pairs from three parts is unnecessarily complicated. Instead of separating the pair (S_0, T_0) from the rest of the pairs in the first row, he proposes to work with the whole first row, as follows:

```
(define (pairs s t)
  (interleave
    (stream-map (lambda (x) (list (stream-car s) x))
                t)
    (pairs (stream-cdr s) (stream-cdr t))))
```

Does this work? Consider what happens if we evaluate `(pairs integers integers)` using Louis's definition of `pairs`.

Exercise 3.69

Write a procedure `triples` that takes three infinite streams, S, T, and U, and produces the stream of triples (S_i, T_j, U_k) such that $i \le j \le k$. Use `triples` to generate the stream of all Pythagorean triples of positive integers, i.e., the triples (i, j, k) such that $i \le j$ and $i^2 + j^2 = k^2$.

Exercise 3.70

It would be nice to be able to generate streams in which the pairs appear in some useful order, rather than in the order that results from an *ad hoc* interleaving process. We can use a technique similar to the `merge` procedure of exercise 3.56, if we define a way to say that one pair of integers is "less than" another. One way to do this is to define a "weighting function" $W(i, j)$ and stipulate that (i_1, j_1) is less than (i_2, j_2) if $W(i_1, j_1) < W(i_2, j_2)$. Write a procedure `merge-weighted` that is like `merge`, except that `merge-weighted` takes an additional argument `weight`, which is a procedure that computes the weight of a pair, and is used to determine the order in which elements should appear in the resulting merged stream.[69] Using this, generalize `pairs` to a procedure `weighted-pairs` that takes two streams, together with a procedure that computes a weighting function, and generates the stream of pairs, ordered according to weight. Use your procedure to generate

a. the stream of all pairs of positive integers (i, j) with $i \le j$ ordered according to the sum $i + j$

b. the stream of all pairs of positive integers (i, j) with $i \le j$, where neither i nor j is divisible by 2, 3, or 5, and the pairs are ordered according to the sum $2i + 3j + 5ij$.

Exercise 3.71

Numbers that can be expressed as the sum of two cubes in more than one way are sometimes called *Ramanujan numbers*, in honor of the mathematician Srinivasa Ramanujan.[70] Ordered streams of pairs provide an elegant solution to the problem of computing these numbers. To find a number that can be written as the sum of two cubes in two different ways, we need only generate the stream of pairs of integers (i, j) weighted according to the sum $i^3 + j^3$ (see exercise 3.70), then search the stream for two consecutive pairs with the same weight. Write a procedure to generate the Ramanujan numbers. The first such number is 1,729. What are the next five?

---

[69] We will require that the weighting function be such that the weight of a pair increases as we move out along a row or down along a column of the array of pairs.

[70] To quote from G. H. Hardy's obituary of Ramanujan (Hardy 1921): "It was Mr. Littlewood (I believe) who remarked that 'every positive integer was one of his friends.' I remember once going to see him when he was lying ill at Putney. I had ridden in taxi-cab No. 1729, and remarked that the number seemed to me a rather dull one, and that I hoped it was not an unfavorable omen. 'No,' he replied, 'it is a very interesting number; it is the smallest number expressible as the sum of two cubes in two different ways.'" The trick of using weighted pairs to generate the Ramanujan numbers was shown to us by Charles Leiserson.

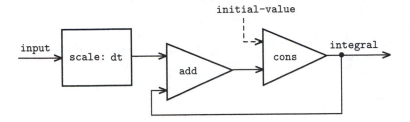

Figure 3.32   The `integral` procedure viewed as a signal-processing system.

Exercise 3.72
In a similar way to exercise 3.71 generate a stream of all numbers that can be written as the sum of two squares in three different ways (showing how they can be so written).

Streams as signals
We began our discussion of streams by describing them as computational analogs of the "signals" in signal-processing systems. In fact, we can use streams to model signal-processing systems in a very direct way, representing the values of a signal at successive time intervals as consecutive elements of a stream. For instance, we can implement an *integrator* or *summer* that, for an input stream $x = (x_i)$, an initial value C, and a small increment dt, accumulates the sum

$$S_i = C + \sum_{j=1}^{i} x_j \, dt$$

and returns the stream of values $S = (S_i)$. The following `integral` procedure is reminiscent of the "implicit style" definition of the stream of integers (section 3.5.2):

```
(define (integral integrand initial-value dt)
  (define int
    (cons-stream initial-value
                 (add-streams (scale-stream integrand dt)
                              int)))
  int)
```

Figure 3.32 is a picture of a signal-processing system that corresponds to the `integral` procedure. The input stream is scaled by dt and passed through an adder, whose output is passed back through the same adder. The self-reference in the definition of `int` is reflected in the figure by the feedback loop that connects the output of the adder to one of the inputs.

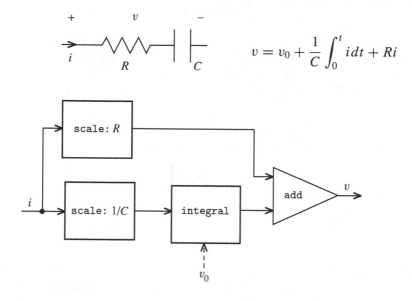

$$v = v_0 + \frac{1}{C} \int_0^t i\,dt + Ri$$

Figure 3.33   An RC circuit and the associated signal-flow diagram.

Exercise 3.73

We can model electrical circuits using streams to represent the values of currents
or voltages at a sequence of times. For instance, suppose we have an *RC circuit*
consisting of a resistor of resistance R and a capacitor of capacitance C in series.
The voltage response v of the circuit to an injected current i is determined by the
formula in figure 3.33, whose structure is shown by the accompanying signal-
flow diagram.

   Write a procedure RC that models this circuit. RC should take as inputs the
values of R, C, and dt and should return a procedure that takes as inputs a stream
representing the current i and an initial value for the capacitor voltage v_0 and
produces as output the stream of voltages v. For example, you should be able to
use RC to model an RC circuit with $R = 5$ ohms, $C = 1$ farad, and a 0.5-second
time step by evaluating (define RC1 (RC 5 1 0.5)). This defines RC1 as a
procedure that takes a stream representing the time sequence of currents and an
initial capacitor voltage and produces the output stream of voltages.

Exercise 3.74

Alyssa P. Hacker is designing a system to process signals coming from physical
sensors. One important feature she wishes to produce is a signal that describes
the *zero crossings* of the input signal. That is, the resulting signal should be $+1$
whenever the input signal changes from negative to positive, -1 whenever the
input signal changes from positive to negative, and 0 otherwise. (Assume that

the sign of a 0 input is positive.) For example, a typical input signal with its associated zero-crossing signal would be

```
... 1  2  1.5  1  0.5  -0.1  -2  -3  -2  -0.5  0.2  3  4 ...
... 0  0   0   0   0    -1   0   0   0    0    1   0  0 ...
```

In Alyssa's system, the signal from the sensor is represented as a stream `sense-data` and the stream `zero-crossings` is the corresponding stream of zero crossings. Alyssa first writes a procedure `sign-change-detector` that takes two values as arguments and compares the signs of the values to produce an appropriate 0, 1, or −1. She then constructs her zero-crossing stream as follows:

```
(define (make-zero-crossings input-stream last-value)
  (cons-stream
   (sign-change-detector (stream-car input-stream) last-value)
   (make-zero-crossings (stream-cdr input-stream)
                        (stream-car input-stream))))

(define zero-crossings (make-zero-crossings sense-data 0))
```

Alyssa's boss, Eva Lu Ator, walks by and suggests that this program is approximately equivalent to the following one, which uses the generalized version of `stream-map` from exercise 3.50:

```
(define zero-crossings
  (stream-map sign-change-detector sense-data ⟨expression⟩))
```

Complete the program by supplying the indicated ⟨ *expression* ⟩.

Exercise 3.75

Unfortunately, Alyssa's zero-crossing detector in exercise 3.74 proves to be insufficient, because the noisy signal from the sensor leads to spurious zero crossings. Lem E. Tweakit, a hardware specialist, suggests that Alyssa smooth the signal to filter out the noise before extracting the zero crossings. Alyssa takes his advice and decides to extract the zero crossings from the signal constructed by averaging each value of the sense data with the previous value. She explains the problem to her assistant, Louis Reasoner, who attempts to implement the idea, altering Alyssa's program as follows:

```
(define (make-zero-crossings input-stream last-value)
  (let ((avpt (/ (+ (stream-car input-stream) last-value) 2)))
    (cons-stream (sign-change-detector avpt last-value)
                 (make-zero-crossings (stream-cdr input-stream)
                                      avpt))))
```

This does not correctly implement Alyssa's plan. Find the bug that Louis has installed and fix it without changing the structure of the program. (Hint: You will need to increase the number of arguments to `make-zero-crossings`.)

Exercise 3.76

Eva Lu Ator has a criticism of Louis's approach in exercise 3.75. The program he wrote is not modular, because it intermixes the operation of smoothing with the zero-crossing extraction. For example, the extractor should not have to be changed if Alyssa finds a better way to condition her input signal. Help Louis by writing a procedure `smooth` that takes a stream as input and produces a stream in which each element is the average of two successive input stream elements. Then use `smooth` as a component to implement the zero-crossing detector in a more modular style.

3.5.4   Streams and Delayed Evaluation

The `integral` procedure at the end of the preceding section shows how we can use streams to model signal-processing systems that contain feedback loops. The feedback loop for the adder shown in figure 3.32 is modeled by the fact that `integral`'s internal stream `int` is defined in terms of itself:

```
(define int
  (cons-stream initial-value
               (add-streams (scale-stream integrand dt)
                            int)))
```

The interpreter's ability to deal with such an implicit definition depends on the `delay` that is incorporated into `cons-stream`. Without this delay, the interpreter could not construct `int` before evaluating both arguments to `cons-stream`, which would require that `int` already be defined. In general, `delay` is crucial for using streams to model signal-processing systems that contain loops. Without `delay`, our models would have to be formulated so that the inputs to any signal-processing component would be fully evaluated before the output could be produced. This would outlaw loops.

Unfortunately, stream models of systems with loops may require uses of `delay` beyond the "hidden" `delay` supplied by `cons-stream`. For instance, figure 3.34 shows a signal-processing system for solving the differential equation $dy/dt = f(y)$ where f is a given function. The figure shows a mapping component, which applies f to its input signal, linked in a feedback loop to an integrator in a manner very similar to that of the analog computer circuits that are actually used to solve such equations.

Assuming we are given an initial value y_0 for y, we could try to model this system using the procedure

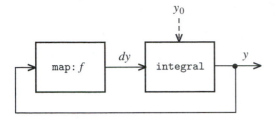

Figure 3.34   An "analog computer circuit" that solves the equation $dy/dt = f(y)$.

```
(define (solve f y0 dt)
  (define y (integral dy y0 dt))
  (define dy (stream-map f y))
  y)
```

This procedure does not work, because in the first line of `solve` the call to `integral` requires that the input `dy` be defined, which does not happen until the second line of `solve`.

On the other hand, the intent of our definition does make sense, because we can, in principle, begin to generate the `y` stream without knowing `dy`. Indeed, `integral` and many other stream operations have properties similar to those of `cons-stream`, in that we can generate part of the answer given only partial information about the arguments. For `integral`, the first element of the output stream is the specified `initial-value`. Thus, we can generate the first element of the output stream without evaluating the integrand `dy`. Once we know the first element of `y`, the `stream-map` in the second line of `solve` can begin working to generate the first element of `dy`, which will produce the next element of `y`, and so on.

To take advantage of this idea, we will redefine `integral` to expect the integrand stream to be a *delayed argument*. `Integral` will force the integrand to be evaluated only when it is required to generate more than the first element of the output stream:

```
(define (integral delayed-integrand initial-value dt)
  (define int
    (cons-stream initial-value
                 (let ((integrand (force delayed-integrand)))
                   (add-streams (scale-stream integrand dt)
                                int)))))
  int)
```

Now we can implement our `solve` procedure by delaying the evaluation of dy in the definition of y:[71]

```
(define (solve f y0 dt)
  (define y (integral (delay dy) y0 dt))
  (define dy (stream-map f y))
  y)
```

In general, every caller of `integral` must now `delay` the integrand argument. We can demonstrate that the `solve` procedure works by approximating $e \approx 2.718$ by computing the value at $y = 1$ of the solution to the differential equation $dy/dt = y$ with initial condition $y(0) = 1$:

```
(stream-ref (solve (lambda (y) y) 1 0.001) 1000)
2.716924
```

Exercise 3.77

The `integral` procedure used above was analogous to the "implicit" definition of the infinite stream of integers in section 3.5.2. Alternatively, we can give a definition of `integral` that is more like `integers-starting-from` (also in section 3.5.2):

```
(define (integral integrand initial-value dt)
  (cons-stream initial-value
               (if (stream-null? integrand)
                   the-empty-stream
                   (integral (stream-cdr integrand)
                             (+ (* dt (stream-car integrand))
                                initial-value)
                             dt))))
```

When used in systems with loops, this procedure has the same problem as does our original version of `integral`. Modify the procedure so that it expects the `integrand` as a delayed argument and hence can be used in the `solve` procedure shown above.

Exercise 3.78

Consider the problem of designing a signal-processing system to study the homogeneous second-order linear differential equation

$$\frac{d^2y}{dt^2} - a\frac{dy}{dt} - by = 0$$

---

[71] This procedure is not guaranteed to work in all Scheme implementations, although for any implementation there is a simple variation that will work. The problem has to do with subtle differences in the ways that Scheme implementations handle internal definitions. (See section 4.1.6.)

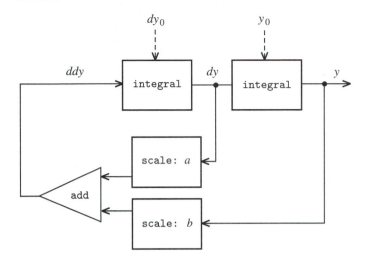

Figure 3.35 Signal-flow diagram for the solution to a second-order linear differential equation.

The output stream, modeling y, is generated by a network that contains a loop. This is because the value of d^2y/dt^2 depends upon the values of y and dy/dt and both of these are determined by integrating d^2y/dt^2. The diagram we would like to encode is shown in figure 3.35. Write a procedure `solve-2nd` that takes as arguments the constants a, b, and dt and the initial values y_0 and dy_0 for y and dy/dt and generates the stream of successive values of y.

Exercise 3.79

Generalize the `solve-2nd` procedure of exercise 3.78 so that it can be used to solve general second-order differential equations $d^2y/dt^2 = f(dy/dt, y)$.

Exercise 3.80

A *series RLC circuit* consists of a resistor, a capacitor, and an inductor connected in series, as shown in figure 3.36. If R, L, and C are the resistance, inductance, and capacitance, then the relations between voltage (v) and current (i) for the three components are described by the equations

$$v_R = i_R R$$
$$v_L = L\frac{di_L}{dt}$$
$$i_C = C\frac{dv_C}{dt}$$

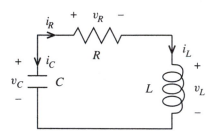

Figure 3.36   A series RLC circuit.

and the circuit connections dictate the relations

$$i_R = i_L = -i_C$$
$$v_C = v_L + v_R$$

Combining these equations shows that the state of the circuit (summarized by v_C, the voltage across the capacitor, and i_L, the current in the inductor) is described by the pair of differential equations

$$\frac{dv_C}{dt} = -\frac{i_L}{C}$$
$$\frac{di_L}{dt} = \frac{1}{L}v_C - \frac{R}{L}i_L$$

The signal-flow diagram representing this system of differential equations is shown in figure 3.37.

Write a procedure RLC that takes as arguments the parameters R, L, and C of the circuit and the time increment dt. In a manner similar to that of the RC procedure of exercise 3.73, RLC should produce a procedure that takes the initial values of the state variables, v_{C_0} and i_{L_0}, and produces a pair (using cons) of the streams of states v_C and i_L. Using RLC, generate the pair of streams that models the behavior of a series RLC circuit with $R = 1$ ohm, $C = 0.2$ farad, $L = 1$ henry, $dt = 0.1$ second, and initial values $i_{L_0} = 0$ amps and $v_{C_0} = 10$ volts.

Normal-order evaluation

The examples in this section illustrate how the explicit use of delay and force provides great programming flexibility, but the same examples also show how this can make our programs more complex. Our new integral procedure, for instance, gives us the power to model systems with loops, but we must now remember that integral should be called with a delayed integrand, and every procedure that uses integral must be aware of this. In effect, we have created two classes of procedures: ordinary procedures and procedures that take delayed arguments. In gen-

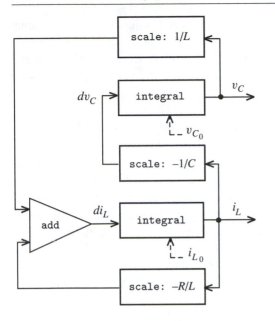

Figure 3.37   A signal-flow diagram for the solution to a series RLC circuit.

eral, creating separate classes of procedures forces us to create separate classes of higher-order procedures as well.[72]

One way to avoid the need for two different classes of procedures is to make all procedures take delayed arguments. We could adopt a model of evaluation in which all arguments to procedures are automatically delayed and arguments are forced only when they are actually needed (for example, when they are required by a primitive operation). This would transform our language to use normal-order evaluation, which we

---

[72]This is a small reflection, in Lisp, of the difficulties that conventional strongly typed languages such as Pascal have in coping with higher-order procedures. In such languages, the programmer must specify the data types of the arguments and the result of each procedure: number, logical value, sequence, and so on. Consequently, we could not express an abstraction such as "map a given procedure `proc` over all the elements in a sequence" by a single higher-order procedure such as `stream-map`. Rather, we would need a different mapping procedure for each different combination of argument and result data types that might be specified for a `proc`. Maintaining a practical notion of "data type" in the presence of higher-order procedures raises many difficult issues. One way of dealing with this problem is illustrated by the language ML (Gordon, Milner, and Wadsworth 1979), whose "polymorphic data types" include templates for higher-order transformations between data types. Moreover, data types for most procedures in ML are never explicitly declared by the programmer. Instead, ML includes a *type-inferencing* mechanism that uses information in the environment to deduce the data types for newly defined procedures.

first described when we introduced the substitution model for evaluation in section 1.1.5. Converting to normal-order evaluation provides a uniform and elegant way to simplify the use of delayed evaluation, and this would be a natural strategy to adopt if we were concerned only with stream processing. In section 4.2, after we have studied the evaluator, we will see how to transform our language in just this way. Unfortunately, including delays in procedure calls wreaks havoc with our ability to design programs that depend on the order of events, such as programs that use assignment, mutate data, or perform input or output. Even the single `delay` in `cons-stream` can cause great confusion, as illustrated by exercises 3.51 and 3.52. As far as anyone knows, mutability and delayed evaluation do not mix well in programming languages, and devising ways to deal with both of these at once is an active area of research.

3.5.5   Modularity of Functional Programs and Modularity of Objects

As we saw in section 3.1.2, one of the major benefits of introducing assignment is that we can increase the modularity of our systems by encapsulating, or "hiding," parts of the state of a large system within local variables. Stream models can provide an equivalent modularity without the use of assignment. As an illustration, we can reimplement the Monte Carlo estimation of π, which we examined in section 3.1.2, from a stream-processing point of view.

The key modularity issue was that we wished to hide the internal state of a random-number generator from programs that used random numbers. We began with a procedure `rand-update`, whose successive values furnished our supply of random numbers, and used this to produce a random-number generator:

```
(define rand
  (let ((x random-init))
    (lambda ()
      (set! x (rand-update x))
      x)))
```

In the stream formulation there is no random-number generator *per se*, just a stream of random numbers produced by successive calls to `rand-update`:

```
(define random-numbers
  (cons-stream random-init
               (stream-map rand-update random-numbers)))
```

We use this to construct the stream of outcomes of the Cesàro experiment performed on consecutive pairs in the `random-numbers` stream:

```
(define cesaro-stream
  (map-successive-pairs (lambda (r1 r2) (= (gcd r1 r2) 1))
                        random-numbers))

(define (map-successive-pairs f s)
  (cons-stream
   (f (stream-car s) (stream-car (stream-cdr s)))
   (map-successive-pairs f (stream-cdr (stream-cdr s)))))
```

The `cesaro-stream` is now fed to a `monte-carlo` procedure, which produces a stream of estimates of probabilities. The results are then converted into a stream of estimates of π. This version of the program doesn't need a parameter telling how many trials to perform. Better estimates of π (from performing more experiments) are obtained by looking farther into the `pi` stream:

```
(define (monte-carlo experiment-stream passed failed)
  (define (next passed failed)
    (cons-stream
     (/ passed (+ passed failed))
     (monte-carlo
      (stream-cdr experiment-stream) passed failed)))
  (if (stream-car experiment-stream)
      (next (+ passed 1) failed)
      (next passed (+ failed 1))))

(define pi
  (stream-map (lambda (p) (sqrt (/ 6 p)))
              (monte-carlo cesaro-stream 0 0)))
```

There is considerable modularity in this approach, because we still can formulate a general `monte-carlo` procedure that can deal with arbitrary experiments. Yet there is no assignment or local state.

Exercise 3.81

Exercise 3.6 discussed generalizing the random-number generator to allow one to reset the random-number sequence so as to produce repeatable sequences of "random" numbers. Produce a stream formulation of this same generator that operates on an input stream of requests to `generate` a new random number or to `reset` the sequence to a specified value and that produces the desired stream of random numbers. Don't use assignment in your solution.

Exercise 3.82

Redo exercise 3.5 on Monte Carlo integration in terms of streams. The stream version of `estimate-integral` will not have an argument telling how many trials to perform. Instead, it will produce a stream of estimates based on successively more trials.

A functional-programming view of time

Let us now return to the issues of objects and state that were raised at the beginning of this chapter and examine them in a new light. We introduced assignment and mutable objects to provide a mechanism for modular construction of programs that model systems with state. We constructed computational objects with local state variables and used assignment to modify these variables. We modeled the temporal behavior of the objects in the world by the temporal behavior of the corresponding computational objects.

Now we have seen that streams provide an alternative way to model objects with local state. We can model a changing quantity, such as the local state of some object, using a stream that represents the time history of successive states. In essence, we represent time explicitly, using streams, so that we decouple time in our simulated world from the sequence of events that take place during evaluation. Indeed, because of the presence of `delay` there may be little relation between simulated time in the model and the order of events during the evaluation.

In order to contrast these two approaches to modeling, let us reconsider the implementation of a "withdrawal processor" that monitors the balance in a bank account. In section 3.1.3 we implemented a simplified version of such a processor:

```
(define (make-simplified-withdraw balance)
  (lambda (amount)
    (set! balance (- balance amount))
    balance))
```

Calls to `make-simplified-withdraw` produce computational objects, each with a local state variable `balance` that is decremented by successive calls to the object. The object takes an `amount` as an argument and returns the new balance. We can imagine the user of a bank account typing a sequence of inputs to such an object and observing the sequence of returned values shown on a display screen.

Alternatively, we can model a withdrawal processor as a procedure that takes as input a balance and a stream of amounts to withdraw and produces the stream of successive balances in the account:

```
(define (stream-withdraw balance amount-stream)
  (cons-stream
   balance
   (stream-withdraw (- balance (stream-car amount-stream))
                    (stream-cdr amount-stream))))
```

Stream-withdraw implements a well-defined mathematical function whose output is fully determined by its input. Suppose, however, that the input amount-stream is the stream of successive values typed by the user and that the resulting stream of balances is displayed. Then, from the perspective of the user who is typing values and watching results, the stream process has the same behavior as the object created by make-simplified-withdraw. However, with the stream version, there is no assignment, no local state variable, and consequently none of the theoretical difficulties that we encountered in section 3.1.3. Yet the system has state!

This is really remarkable. Even though stream-withdraw implements a well-defined mathematical function whose behavior does not change, the user's perception here is one of interacting with a system that has a changing state. One way to resolve this paradox is to realize that it is the user's temporal existence that imposes state on the system. If the user could step back from the interaction and think in terms of streams of balances rather than individual transactions, the system would appear stateless.[73]

From the point of view of one part of a complex process, the other parts appear to change with time. They have hidden time-varying local state. If we wish to write programs that model this kind of natural decomposition in our world (as we see it from our viewpoint as a part of that world) with structures in our computer, we make computational objects that are not functional—they must change with time. We model state with local state variables, and we model the changes of state with assignments to those variables. By doing this we make the time of execution of a computation model time in the world that we are part of, and thus we get "objects" in our computer.

Modeling with objects is powerful and intuitive, largely because this matches the perception of interacting with a world of which we are part. However, as we've seen repeatedly throughout this chapter, these models raise thorny problems of constraining the order of events and of synchro-

---

[73] Similarly in physics, when we observe a moving particle, we say that the position (state) of the particle is changing. However, from the perspective of the particle's world line in space-time there is no change involved.

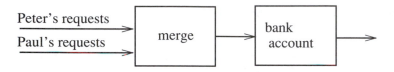

Figure 3.38   A joint bank account, modeled by merging two streams of transaction requests.

nizing multiple processes. The possibility of avoiding these problems has stimulated the development of *functional programming languages*, which do not include any provision for assignment or mutable data. In such a language, all procedures implement well-defined mathematical functions of their arguments, whose behavior does not change. The functional approach is extremely attractive for dealing with concurrent systems.[74]

On the other hand, if we look closely, we can see time-related problems creeping into functional models as well. One particularly troublesome area arises when we wish to design interactive systems, especially ones that model interactions between independent entities. For instance, consider once more the implementation a banking system that permits joint bank accounts. In a conventional system using assignment and objects, we would model the fact that Peter and Paul share an account by having both Peter and Paul send their transaction requests to the same bank-account object, as we saw in section 3.1.3. From the stream point of view, where there are no "objects" *per se*, we have already indicated that a bank account can be modeled as a process that operates on a stream of transaction requests to produce a stream of responses. Accordingly, we could model the fact that Peter and Paul have a joint bank account by merging Peter's stream of transaction requests with Paul's stream of requests and feeding the result to the bank-account stream process, as shown in figure 3.38.

The trouble with this formulation is in the notion of *merge*. It will not do to merge the two streams by simply taking alternately one request from Peter and one request from Paul. Suppose Paul accesses the account only very rarely. We could hardly force Peter to wait for Paul to access the account before he could issue a second transaction. However such a

---

[74]John Backus, the inventor of Fortran, gave high visibility to functional programming when he was awarded the ACM Turing award in 1978. His acceptance speech (Backus 1978) strongly advocated the functional approach. A good overview of functional programming is given in Henderson 1980 and in Darlington, Henderson, and Turner 1982.

merge is implemented, it must interleave the two transaction streams in some way that is constrained by "real time" as perceived by Peter and Paul, in the sense that, if Peter and Paul meet, they can agree that certain transactions were processed before the meeting, and other transactions were processed after the meeting.[75] This is precisely the same constraint that we had to deal with in section 3.4.1, where we found the need to introduce explicit synchronization to ensure a "correct" order of events in concurrent processing of objects with state. Thus, in an attempt to support the functional style, the need to merge inputs from different agents reintroduces the same problems that the functional style was meant to eliminate.

We began this chapter with the goal of building computational models whose structure matches our perception of the real world we are trying to model. We can model the world as a collection of separate, time-bound, interacting objects with state, or we can model the world as a single, timeless, stateless unity. Each view has powerful advantages, but neither view alone is completely satisfactory. A grand unification has yet to emerge.[76]

---

[75]Observe that, for any two streams, there is in general more than one acceptable order of interleaving. Thus, technically, "merge" is a relation rather than a function—the answer is not a deterministic function of the inputs. We already mentioned (footnote 39) that nondeterminism is essential when dealing with concurrency. The merge relation illustrates the same essential nondeterminism, from the functional perspective. In section 4.3, we will look at nondeterminism from yet another point of view.

[76]The object model approximates the world by dividing it into separate pieces. The functional model does not modularize along object boundaries. The object model is useful when the unshared state of the "objects" is much larger than the state that they share. An example of a place where the object viewpoint fails is quantum mechanics, where thinking of things as individual particles leads to paradoxes and confusions. Unifying the object view with the functional view may have little to do with programming, but rather with fundamental epistemological issues.

4

Metalinguistic Abstraction

> ... It's in words that the magic is—Abracadabra, Open
> Sesame, and the rest—but the magic words in one story
> aren't magical in the next. The real magic is to
> understand which words work, and when, and for what;
> the trick is to learn the trick.
> ... And those words are made from the letters of our
> alphabet: a couple-dozen squiggles we can draw with the
> pen. This is the key! And the treasure, too, if we can
> only get our hands on it! It's as if—as if the key to the
> treasure *is* the treasure!
>
> John Barth, *Chimera*

In our study of program design, we have seen that expert programmers
control the complexity of their designs with the same general techniques
used by designers of all complex systems. They combine primitive
elements to form compound objects, they abstract compound objects
to form higher-level building blocks, and they preserve modularity by
adopting appropriate large-scale views of system structure. In illustrating these techniques, we have used Lisp as a language for describing
processes and for constructing computational data objects and processes
to model complex phenomena in the real world. However, as we confront increasingly complex problems, we will find that Lisp, or indeed
any fixed programming language, is not sufficient for our needs. We must
constantly turn to new languages in order to express our ideas more effectively. Establishing new languages is a powerful strategy for controlling
complexity in engineering design; we can often enhance our ability to
deal with a complex problem by adopting a new language that enables
us to describe (and hence to think about) the problem in a different way,
using primitives, means of combination, and means of abstraction that
are particularly well suited to the problem at hand.[1]

---

[1] The same idea is pervasive throughout all of engineering. For example, electrical engineers use many different languages for describing circuits. Two of these are the language
of electrical *networks* and the language of electrical *systems*. The network language emphasizes the physical modeling of devices in terms of discrete electrical elements. The

Programming is endowed with a multitude of languages. There are physical languages, such as the machine languages for particular computers. These languages are concerned with the representation of data and control in terms of individual bits of storage and primitive machine instructions. The machine-language programmer is concerned with using the given hardware to erect systems and utilities for the efficient implementation of resource-limited computations. High-level languages, erected on a machine-language substrate, hide concerns about the representation of data as collections of bits and the representation of programs as sequences of primitive instructions. These languages have means of combination and abstraction, such as procedure definition, that are appropriate to the larger-scale organization of systems.

Metalinguistic abstraction—establishing new languages—plays an important role in all branches of engineering design. It is particularly important to computer programming, because in programming not only can we formulate new languages but we can also implement these languages by constructing evaluators. An *evaluator* (or *interpreter*) for a programming language is a procedure that, when applied to an expression of the language, performs the actions required to evaluate that expression.

It is no exaggeration to regard this as the most fundamental idea in programming:

> The evaluator, which determines the meaning of expressions in a programming language, is just another program.

To appreciate this point is to change our images of ourselves as programmers. We come to see ourselves as designers of languages, rather than only users of languages designed by others.

In fact, we can regard almost any program as the evaluator for some language. For instance, the polynomial manipulation system of section 2.5.3 embodies the rules of polynomial arithmetic and implements

---

primitive objects of the network language are primitive electrical components such as resistors, capacitors, inductors, and transistors, which are characterized in terms of physical variables called voltage and current. When describing circuits in the network language, the engineer is concerned with the physical characteristics of a design. In contrast, the primitive objects of the system language are signal-processing modules such as filters and amplifiers. Only the functional behavior of the modules is relevant, and signals are manipulated without concern for their physical realization as voltages and currents. The system language is erected on the network language, in the sense that the elements of signal-processing systems are constructed from electrical networks. Here, however, the concerns are with the large-scale organization of electrical devices to solve a given application problem; the physical feasibility of the parts is assumed. This layered collection of languages is another example of the stratified design technique illustrated by the picture language of section 2.2.4.

them in terms of operations on list-structured data. If we augment this system with procedures to read and print polynomial expressions, we have the core of a special-purpose language for dealing with problems in symbolic mathematics. The digital-logic simulator of section 3.3.4 and the constraint propagator of section 3.3.5 are legitimate languages in their own right, each with its own primitives, means of combination, and means of abstraction. Seen from this perspective, the technology for coping with large-scale computer systems merges with the technology for building new computer languages, and computer science itself becomes no more (and no less) than the discipline of constructing appropriate descriptive languages.

We now embark on a tour of the technology by which languages are established in terms of other languages. In this chapter we shall use Lisp as a base, implementing evaluators as Lisp procedures. Lisp is particularly well suited to this task, because of its ability to represent and manipulate symbolic expressions. We will take the first step in understanding how languages are implemented by building an evaluator for Lisp itself. The language implemented by our evaluator will be a subset of the Scheme dialect of Lisp that we use in this book. Although the evaluator described in this chapter is written for a particular dialect of Lisp, it contains the essential structure of an evaluator for any expression-oriented language designed for writing programs for a sequential machine. (In fact, most language processors contain, deep within them, a little "Lisp" evaluator.) The evaluator has been simplified for the purposes of illustration and discussion, and some features have been left out that would be important to include in a production-quality Lisp system. Nevertheless, this simple evaluator is adequate to execute most of the programs in this book.[2]

An important advantage of making the evaluator accessible as a Lisp program is that we can implement alternative evaluation rules by describing these as modifications to the evaluator program. One place where we can use this power to good effect is to gain extra control over the ways in which computational models embody the notion of time, which was so central to the discussion in chapter 3. There, we mitigated some of the complexities of state and assignment by using streams to decouple the representation of time in the world from time in the computer. Our stream programs, however, were sometimes cumbersome, because they

---

[2]The most important features that our evaluator leaves out are mechanisms for handling errors and supporting debugging. For a more extensive discussion of evaluators, see Friedman, Wand, and Haynes 1992, which gives an exposition of programming languages that proceeds via a sequence of evaluators written in Scheme.

were constrained by the applicative-order evaluation of Scheme. In section 4.2, we'll change the underlying language to provide for a more elegant approach, by modifying the evaluator to provide for *normal-order evaluation*.

Section 4.3 implements a more ambitious linguistic change, whereby expressions have many values, rather than just a single value. In this language of *nondeterministic computing*, it is natural to express processes that generate all possible values for expressions and then search for those values that satisfy certain constraints. In terms of models of computation and time, this is like having time branch into a set of "possible futures" and then searching for appropriate time lines. With our nondeterministic evaluator, keeping track of multiple values and performing searches are handled automatically by the underlying mechanism of the language.

In section 4.4 we implement a *logic-programming* language in which knowledge is expressed in terms of relations, rather than in terms of computations with inputs and outputs. Even though this makes the language drastically different from Lisp, or indeed from any conventional language, we will see that the logic-programming evaluator shares the essential structure of the Lisp evaluator.

4.1   The Metacircular Evaluator

Our evaluator for Lisp will be implemented as a Lisp program. It may seem circular to think about evaluating Lisp programs using an evaluator that is itself implemented in Lisp. However, evaluation is a process, so it is appropriate to describe the evaluation process using Lisp, which, after all, is our tool for describing processes.[3] An evaluator that is written in the same language that it evaluates is said to be *metacircular*.

The metacircular evaluator is essentially a Scheme formulation of the environment model of evaluation described in section 3.2. Recall that the model has two basic parts:

1. To evaluate a combination (a compound expression other than a special form), evaluate the subexpressions and then apply the value of the operator subexpression to the values of the operand subexpressions.

---

[3]Even so, there will remain important aspects of the evaluation process that are not elucidated by our evaluator. The most important of these are the detailed mechanisms by which procedures call other procedures and return values to their callers. We will address these issues in chapter 5, where we take a closer look at the evaluation process by implementing the evaluator as a simple register machine.

2. To apply a compound procedure to a set of arguments, evaluate the body of the procedure in a new environment. To construct this environment, extend the environment part of the procedure object by a frame in which the formal parameters of the procedure are bound to the arguments to which the procedure is applied.

These two rules describe the essence of the evaluation process, a basic cycle in which expressions to be evaluated in environments are reduced to procedures to be applied to arguments, which in turn are reduced to new expressions to be evaluated in new environments, and so on, until we get down to symbols, whose values are looked up in the environment, and to primitive procedures, which are applied directly (see figure 4.1).[4] This evaluation cycle will be embodied by the interplay between the two critical procedures in the evaluator, `eval` and `apply`, which are described in section 4.1.1 (see figure 4.1).

The implementation of the evaluator will depend upon procedures that define the *syntax* of the expressions to be evaluated. We will use data abstraction to make the evaluator independent of the representation of the language. For example, rather than committing to a choice that an assignment is to be represented by a list beginning with the symbol `set!` we use an abstract predicate `assignment?` to test for an assignment, and we use abstract selectors `assignment-variable` and `assignment-value` to access the parts of an assignment. Implementation of expressions

---

[4]If we grant ourselves the ability to apply primitives, then what remains for us to implement in the evaluator? The job of the evaluator is not to specify the primitives of the language, but rather to provide the connective tissue—the means of combination and the means of abstraction—that binds a collection of primitives to form a language. Specifically:

• The evaluator enables us to deal with nested expressions. For example, although simply applying primitives would suffice for evaluating the expression (+ 1 6), it is not adequate for handling (+ 1 (* 2 3)). As far as the primitive procedure + is concerned, its arguments must be numbers, and it would choke if we passed it the expression (* 2 3) as an argument. One important role of the evaluator is to choreograph procedure composition so that (* 2 3) is reduced to 6 before being passed as an argument to +.

• The evaluator allows us to use variables. For example, the primitive procedure for addition has no way to deal with expressions such as (+ x 1). We need an evaluator to keep track of variables and obtain their values before invoking the primitive procedures.

• The evaluator allows us to define compound procedures. This involves keeping track of procedure definitions, knowing how to use these definitions in evaluating expressions, and providing a mechanism that enables procedures to accept arguments.

• The evaluator provides the special forms, which must be evaluated differently from procedure calls.

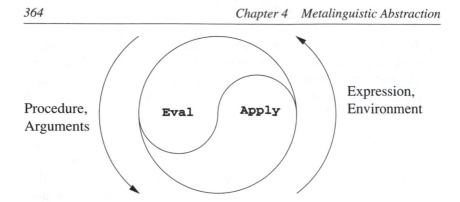

Figure 4.1   The eval–apply cycle exposes the essence of a computer language.

will be described in detail in section 4.1.2. There are also operations, described in section 4.1.3, that specify the representation of procedures and environments. For example, `make-procedure` constructs compound procedures, `lookup-variable-value` accesses the values of variables, and `apply-primitive-procedure` applies a primitive procedure to a given list of arguments.

4.1.1   The Core of the Evaluator

The evaluation process can be described as the interplay between two procedures: `eval` and `apply`.

Eval

`Eval` takes as arguments an expression and an environment. It classifies the expression and directs its evaluation. `Eval` is structured as a case analysis of the syntactic type of the expression to be evaluated. In order to keep the procedure general, we express the determination of the type of an expression abstractly, making no commitment to any particular representation for the various types of expressions. Each type of expression has a predicate that tests for it and an abstract means for selecting its parts. This *abstract syntax* makes it easy to see how we can change the syntax of the language by using the same evaluator, but with a different collection of syntax procedures.

Primitive expressions

• For self-evaluating expressions, such as numbers, `eval` returns the expression itself.

• `Eval` must look up variables in the environment to find their values.

Special forms

• For quoted expressions, eval returns the expression that was quoted.

• An assignment to (or a definition of) a variable must recursively call eval to compute the new value to be associated with the variable. The environment must be modified to change (or create) the binding of the variable.

• An if expression requires special processing of its parts, so as to evaluate the consequent if the predicate is true, and otherwise to evaluate the alternative.

• A lambda expression must be transformed into an applicable procedure by packaging together the parameters and body specified by the lambda expression with the environment of the evaluation.

• A begin expression requires evaluating its sequence of expressions in the order in which they appear.

• A case analysis (cond) is transformed into a nest of if expressions and then evaluated.

Combinations

• For a procedure application, eval must recursively evaluate the operator part and the operands of the combination. The resulting procedure and arguments are passed to apply, which handles the actual procedure application.

Here is the definition of eval:

```
(define (eval exp env)
  (cond ((self-evaluating? exp) exp)
        ((variable? exp) (lookup-variable-value exp env))
        ((quoted? exp) (text-of-quotation exp))
        ((assignment? exp) (eval-assignment exp env))
        ((definition? exp) (eval-definition exp env))
        ((if? exp) (eval-if exp env))
        ((lambda? exp)
         (make-procedure (lambda-parameters exp)
                         (lambda-body exp)
                         env))
        ((begin? exp)
         (eval-sequence (begin-actions exp) env))
        ((cond? exp) (eval (cond->if exp) env))
        ((application? exp)
         (apply (eval (operator exp) env)
                (list-of-values (operands exp) env)))
        (else
         (error "Unknown expression type -- EVAL" exp))))
```

For clarity, `eval` has been implemented as a case analysis using `cond`. The disadvantage of this is that our procedure handles only a few distinguishable types of expressions, and no new ones can be defined without editing the definition of `eval`. In most Lisp implementations, dispatching on the type of an expression is done in a data-directed style. This allows a user to add new types of expressions that `eval` can distinguish, without modifying the definition of `eval` itself. (See exercise 4.3.)

Apply

`Apply` takes two arguments, a procedure and a list of arguments to which the procedure should be applied. `Apply` classifies procedures into two kinds: It calls `apply-primitive-procedure` to apply primitives; it applies compound procedures by sequentially evaluating the expressions that make up the body of the procedure. The environment for the evaluation of the body of a compound procedure is constructed by extending the base environment carried by the procedure to include a frame that binds the parameters of the procedure to the arguments to which the procedure is to be applied. Here is the definition of `apply`:

```
(define (apply procedure arguments)
  (cond ((primitive-procedure? procedure)
         (apply-primitive-procedure procedure arguments))
        ((compound-procedure? procedure)
         (eval-sequence
           (procedure-body procedure)
           (extend-environment
             (procedure-parameters procedure)
             arguments
             (procedure-environment procedure))))
        (else
         (error
           "Unknown procedure type -- APPLY" procedure))))
```

Procedure arguments

When `eval` processes a procedure application, it uses `list-of-values` to produce the list of arguments to which the procedure is to be applied. `List-of-values` takes as an argument the operands of the combination. It evaluates each operand and returns a list of the corresponding values:[5]

---

[5]We could have simplified the `application?` clause in `eval` by using `map` (and stipulating that `operands` returns a list) rather than writing an explicit `list-of-values` procedure. We chose not to use `map` here to emphasize the fact that the evaluator can be implemented without any use of higher-order procedures (and thus could be written in a language that doesn't have higher-order procedures), even though the language that it supports will include higher-order procedures.

```
(define (list-of-values exps env)
  (if (no-operands? exps)
      '()
      (cons (eval (first-operand exps) env)
            (list-of-values (rest-operands exps) env))))
```

Conditionals

Eval-if evaluates the predicate part of an if expression in the given environment. If the result is true, eval-if evaluates the consequent, otherwise it evaluates the alternative:

```
(define (eval-if exp env)
  (if (true? (eval (if-predicate exp) env))
      (eval (if-consequent exp) env)
      (eval (if-alternative exp) env)))
```

The use of true? in eval-if highlights the issue of the connection between an implemented language and an implementation language. The if-predicate is evaluated in the language being implemented and thus yields a value in that language. The interpreter predicate true? translates that value into a value that can be tested by the if in the implementation language: The metacircular representation of truth might not be the same as that of the underlying Scheme.[6]

Sequences

Eval-sequence is used by apply to evaluate the sequence of expressions in a procedure body and by eval to evaluate the sequence of expressions in a begin expression. It takes as arguments a sequence of expressions and an environment, and evaluates the expressions in the order in which they occur. The value returned is the value of the final expression.

```
(define (eval-sequence exps env)
  (cond ((last-exp? exps) (eval (first-exp exps) env))
        (else (eval (first-exp exps) env)
              (eval-sequence (rest-exps exps) env))))
```

Assignments and definitions

The following procedure handles assignments to variables. It calls eval to find the value to be assigned and transmits the variable and the re-

---

[6]In this case, the language being implemented and the implementation language are the same. Contemplation of the meaning of true? here yields expansion of consciousness without the abuse of substance.

sulting value to `set-variable-value!` to be installed in the designated environment.

```
(define (eval-assignment exp env)
  (set-variable-value! (assignment-variable exp)
                       (eval (assignment-value exp) env)
                       env)
  'ok)
```

Definitions of variables are handled in a similar manner.[7]

```
(define (eval-definition exp env)
  (define-variable! (definition-variable exp)
                    (eval (definition-value exp) env)
                    env)
  'ok)
```

We have chosen here to return the symbol ok as the value of an assignment or a definition.[8]

Exercise 4.1

Notice that we cannot tell whether the metacircular evaluator evaluates operands from left to right or from right to left. Its evaluation order is inherited from the underlying Lisp: If the arguments to `cons` in `list-of-values` are evaluated from left to right, then `list-of-values` will evaluate operands from left to right; and if the arguments to `cons` are evaluated from right to left, then `list-of-values` will evaluate operands from right to left.

Write a version of `list-of-values` that evaluates operands from left to right regardless of the order of evaluation in the underlying Lisp. Also write a version of `list-of-values` that evaluates operands from right to left.

4.1.2   Representing Expressions

The evaluator is reminiscent of the symbolic differentiation program discussed in section 2.3.2. Both programs operate on symbolic expressions. In both programs, the result of operating on a compound expression is determined by operating recursively on the pieces of the expression and combining the results in a way that depends on the type of the expression. In both programs we used data abstraction to decouple the general

---

[7]This implementation of `define` ignores a subtle issue in the handling of internal definitions, although it works correctly in most cases. We will see what the problem is and how to solve it in section 4.1.6.

[8]As we said when we introduced `define` and `set!`, these values are implementation-dependent in Scheme—that is, the implementor can choose what value to return.

rules of operation from the details of how expressions are represented. In the differentiation program this meant that the same differentiation procedure could deal with algebraic expressions in prefix form, in infix form, or in some other form. For the evaluator, this means that the syntax of the language being evaluated is determined solely by the procedures that classify and extract pieces of expressions.

Here is the specification of the syntax of our language:

• The only self-evaluating items are numbers and strings:

```
(define (self-evaluating? exp)
  (cond ((number? exp) true)
        ((string? exp) true)
        (else false)))
```

• Variables are represented by symbols:

```
(define (variable? exp) (symbol? exp))
```

• Quotations have the form (quote ⟨*text-of-quotation*⟩):[9]

```
(define (quoted? exp)
  (tagged-list? exp 'quote))
```

```
(define (text-of-quotation exp) (cadr exp))
```

Quoted? is defined in terms of the procedure tagged-list?, which identifies lists beginning with a designated symbol:

```
(define (tagged-list? exp tag)
  (if (pair? exp)
      (eq? (car exp) tag)
      false))
```

• Assignments have the form (set! ⟨*var*⟩ ⟨*value*⟩):

```
(define (assignment? exp)
  (tagged-list? exp 'set!))
```

```
(define (assignment-variable exp) (cadr exp))
```

```
(define (assignment-value exp) (caddr exp))
```

---

[9]As mentioned in section 2.3.1, the evaluator sees a quoted expression as a list beginning with quote, even if the expression is typed with the quotation mark. For example, the expression 'a would be seen by the evaluator as (quote a). See exercise 2.55.

• Definitions have the form

```
(define ⟨var⟩ ⟨value⟩)
```

or the form

```
(define ((⟨var⟩ ⟨parameter₁⟩ ... ⟨parameterₙ⟩))
  ⟨body⟩))
```

The latter form (standard procedure definition) is syntactic sugar for

```
(define ⟨var⟩
  (lambda (⟨parameter₁⟩ ... ⟨parameterₙ⟩)
    ⟨body⟩)))
```

The corresponding syntax procedures are the following:

```
(define (definition? exp)
  (tagged-list? exp 'define))

(define (definition-variable exp)
  (if (symbol? (cadr exp))
      (cadr exp)
      (caadr exp)))

(define (definition-value exp)
  (if (symbol? (cadr exp))
      (caddr exp)
      (make-lambda (cdadr exp)     ; formal parameters
                   (cddr exp))))   ; body
```

• Lambda expressions are lists that begin with the symbol `lambda`:

```
(define (lambda? exp) (tagged-list? exp 'lambda))

(define (lambda-parameters exp) (cadr exp))

(define (lambda-body exp) (cddr exp))
```

We also provide a constructor for `lambda` expressions, which is used by `definition-value`, above:

```
(define (make-lambda parameters body)
  (cons 'lambda (cons parameters body)))
```

• Conditionals begin with `if` and have a predicate, a consequent, and an (optional) alternative. If the expression has no alternative part, we provide `false` as the alternative.[10]

```
(define (if? exp) (tagged-list? exp 'if))

(define (if-predicate exp) (cadr exp))

(define (if-consequent exp) (caddr exp))

(define (if-alternative exp)
  (if (not (null? (cdddr exp)))
      (cadddr exp)
      'false))
```

We also provide a constructor for `if` expressions, to be used by `cond->if` to transform `cond` expressions into `if` expressions:

```
(define (make-if predicate consequent alternative)
  (list 'if predicate consequent alternative))
```

• Begin packages a sequence of expressions into a single expression. We include syntax operations on `begin` expressions to extract the actual sequence from the `begin` expression, as well as selectors that return the first expression and the rest of the expressions in the sequence.[11]

```
(define (begin? exp) (tagged-list? exp 'begin))

(define (begin-actions exp) (cdr exp))

(define (last-exp? seq) (null? (cdr seq)))

(define (first-exp seq) (car seq))

(define (rest-exps seq) (cdr seq))
```

---

[10]The value of an `if` expression when the predicate is false and there is no alternative is unspecified in Scheme; we have chosen here to make it false. We will support the use of the variables `true` and `false` in expressions to be evaluated by binding them in the global environment. See section 4.1.4.

[11]These selectors for a list of expressions—and the corresponding ones for a list of operands—are not intended as a data abstraction. They are introduced as mnemonic names for the basic list operations in order to make it easier to understand the explicit-control evaluator in section 5.4.

We also include a constructor `sequence->exp` (for use by `cond->if`) that transforms a sequence into a single expression, using `begin` if necessary:

```
(define (sequence->exp seq)
  (cond ((null? seq) seq)
        ((last-exp? seq) (first-exp seq))
        (else (make-begin seq))))

(define (make-begin seq) (cons 'begin seq))
```

• A procedure application is any compound expression that is not one of the above expression types. The `car` of the expression is the operator, and the `cdr` is the list of operands:

```
(define (application? exp) (pair? exp))

(define (operator exp) (car exp))

(define (operands exp) (cdr exp))

(define (no-operands? ops) (null? ops))

(define (first-operand ops) (car ops))

(define (rest-operands ops) (cdr ops))
```

Derived expressions

Some special forms in our language can be defined in terms of expressions involving other special forms, rather than being implemented directly. One example is `cond`, which can be implemented as a nest of `if` expressions. For example, we can reduce the problem of evaluating the expression

```
(cond ((> x 0) x)
      ((= x 0) (display 'zero) 0)
      (else (- x)))
```

to the problem of evaluating the following expression involving `if` and `begin` expressions:

```
(if (> x 0)
    x
    (if (= x 0)
        (begin (display 'zero)
               0)
        (- x)))
```

Implementing the evaluation of cond in this way simplifies the evaluator because it reduces the number of special forms for which the evaluation process must be explicitly specified.

We include syntax procedures that extract the parts of a cond expression, and a procedure cond->if that transforms cond expressions into if expressions. A case analysis begins with cond and has a list of predicate-action clauses. A clause is an else clause if its predicate is the symbol else.[12]

```
(define (cond? exp) (tagged-list? exp 'cond))

(define (cond-clauses exp) (cdr exp))

(define (cond-else-clause? clause)
  (eq? (cond-predicate clause) 'else))

(define (cond-predicate clause) (car clause))

(define (cond-actions clause) (cdr clause))

(define (cond->if exp)
  (expand-clauses (cond-clauses exp)))

(define (expand-clauses clauses)
  (if (null? clauses)
      'false                               ; no else clause
      (let ((first (car clauses))
            (rest (cdr clauses)))
        (if (cond-else-clause? first)
            (if (null? rest)
                (sequence->exp (cond-actions first))
                (error "ELSE clause isn't last -- COND->IF"
                       clauses))
            (make-if (cond-predicate first)
                     (sequence->exp (cond-actions first))
                     (expand-clauses rest))))))
```

Expressions (such as cond) that we choose to implement as syntactic transformations are called *derived expressions*. Let expressions are also derived expressions (see exercise 4.6).[13]

---

[12]The value of a cond expression when all the predicates are false and there is no else clause is unspecified in Scheme; we have chosen here to make it false.

[13]Practical Lisp systems provide a mechanism that allows a user to add new derived expressions and specify their implementation as syntactic transformations without modifying the evaluator. Such a user-defined transformation is called a *macro*. Although it is easy

Exercise 4.2

Louis Reasoner plans to reorder the cond clauses in eval so that the clause
for procedure applications appears before the clause for assignments. He argues
that this will make the interpreter more efficient: Since programs usually contain
more applications than assignments, definitions, and so on, his modified eval
will usually check fewer clauses than the original eval before identifying the
type of an expression.

a. What is wrong with Louis's plan? (Hint: What will Louis's evaluator do with
the expression (define x 3)?)

b. Louis is upset that his plan didn't work. He is willing to go to any lengths to
make his evaluator recognize procedure applications before it checks for most
other kinds of expressions. Help him by changing the syntax of the evaluated
language so that procedure applications start with call. For example, instead of
(factorial 3) we will now have to write (call factorial 3) and instead
of (+ 1 2) we will have to write (call + 1 2).

Exercise 4.3

Rewrite eval so that the dispatch is done in data-directed style. Compare this
with the data-directed differentiation procedure of exercise 2.73. (You may use
the car of a compound expression as the type of the expression, as is appropriate
for the syntax implemented in this section.) .

Exercise 4.4

Recall the definitions of the special forms and and or from chapter 1:

• and: The expressions are evaluated from left to right. If any expression evaluates to false, false is returned; any remaining expressions are not evaluated.
If all the expressions evaluate to true values, the value of the last expression is
returned. If there are no expressions then true is returned.

• or: The expressions are evaluated from left to right. If any expression evaluates to a true value, that value is returned; any remaining expressions are not
evaluated. If all expressions evaluate to false, or if there are no expressions, then
false is returned.

Install and and or as new special forms for the evaluator by defining appropriate
syntax procedures and evaluation procedures eval-and and eval-or. Alternatively, show how to implement and and or as derived expressions.

---

to add an elementary mechanism for defining macros, the resulting language has subtle
name-conflict problems. There has been much research on mechanisms for macro definition that do not cause these difficulties. See, for example, Kohlbecker 1986, Clinger and
Rees 1991, and Hanson 1991.

Exercise 4.5

Scheme allows an additional syntax for cond clauses, (⟨ *test* ⟩ => ⟨ *recipient* ⟩).
If ⟨ *test* ⟩ evaluates to a true value, then ⟨ *recipient* ⟩ is evaluated. Its value must
be a procedure of one argument; this procedure is then invoked on the value of
the ⟨ *test* ⟩, and the result is returned as the value of the cond expression. For
example

```
(cond ((assoc 'b '((a 1) (b 2))) => cadr)
      (else false))
```

returns 2. Modify the handling of cond so that it supports this extended syntax.

Exercise 4.6

Let expressions are derived expressions, because

```
(let (((⟨var₁⟩ ⟨exp₁⟩) ... ((⟨varₙ⟩ ⟨expₙ⟩)))
  ⟨body⟩))
```

is equivalent to

```
((lambda (⟨var₁⟩ ... ⟨varₙ⟩)
    ⟨body⟩)
  ⟨exp₁⟩
  .
  .
  .
  ⟨expₙ⟩))
```

Implement a syntactic transformation let->combination that reduces evaluating let expressions to evaluating combinations of the type shown above, and
add the appropriate clause to eval to handle let expressions.

Exercise 4.7

Let* is similar to let, except that the bindings of the let variables are performed sequentially from left to right, and each binding is made in an environment in which all of the preceding bindings are visible. For example

```
(let* ((x 3)
       (y (+ x 2))
       (z (+ x y 5)))
  (* x z))
```

returns 39. Explain how a let* expression can be rewritten as a set of nested
let expressions, and write a procedure let*->nested-lets that performs this
transformation. If we have already implemented let (exercise 4.6) and we want
to extend the evaluator to handle let*, is it sufficient to add a clause to eval
whose action is

```
(eval (let*->nested-lets exp) env)
```

or must we explicitly expand let* in terms of non-derived expressions?

Exercise 4.8

"Named `let`" is a variant of `let` that has the form

```
(let ⟨var⟩ ⟨bindings⟩ ⟨body⟩)
```

The ⟨*bindings*⟩ and ⟨*body*⟩ are just as in ordinary `let`, except that ⟨*var*⟩ is bound within ⟨*body*⟩ to a procedure whose body is ⟨*body*⟩ and whose parameters are the variables in the ⟨*bindings*⟩. Thus, one can repeatedly execute the ⟨*body*⟩ by invoking the procedure named ⟨*var*⟩. For example, the iterative Fibonacci procedure (section 1.2.2) can be rewritten using named `let` as follows:

```
(define (fib n)
  (let fib-iter ((a 1)
                 (b 0)
                 (count n))
    (if (= count 0)
        b
        (fib-iter (+ a b) a (- count 1)))))
```

Modify `let->combination` of exercise 4.6 to also support named `let`.

Exercise 4.9

Many languages support a variety of iteration constructs, such as `do`, `for`, `while`, and `until`. In Scheme, iterative processes can be expressed in terms of ordinary procedure calls, so special iteration constructs provide no essential gain in computational power. On the other hand, such constructs are often convenient. Design some iteration constructs, give examples of their use, and show how to implement them as derived expressions.

Exercise 4.10

By using data abstraction, we were able to write an `eval` procedure that is independent of the particular syntax of the language to be evaluated. To illustrate this, design and implement a new syntax for Scheme by modifying the procedures in this section, without changing `eval` or `apply`.

4.1.3   Evaluator Data Structures

In addition to defining the external syntax of expressions, the evaluator implementation must also define the data structures that the evaluator manipulates internally, as part of the execution of a program, such as the representation of procedures and environments and the representation of true and false.

Testing of predicates

For conditionals, we accept anything to be true that is not the explicit `false` object.

```
(define (true? x)
  (not (eq? x false)))

(define (false? x)
  (eq? x false))
```

Representing procedures

To handle primitives, we assume that we have available the following procedures:

- (apply-primitive-procedure ⟨*proc*⟩ ⟨*args*⟩)

applies the given primitive procedure to the argument values in the list ⟨*args*⟩ and returns the result of the application.

- (primitive-procedure? ⟨*proc*⟩)

tests whether ⟨*proc*⟩ is a primitive procedure.

These mechanisms for handling primitives are further described in section 4.1.4.

Compound procedures are constructed from parameters, procedure bodies, and environments using the constructor make-procedure:

```
(define (make-procedure parameters body env)
  (list 'procedure parameters body env))

(define (compound-procedure? p)
  (tagged-list? p 'procedure))

(define (procedure-parameters p) (cadr p))

(define (procedure-body p) (caddr p))

(define (procedure-environment p) (cadddr p))
```

Operations on Environments

The evaluator needs operations for manipulating environments. As explained in section 3.2, an environment is a sequence of frames, where each frame is a table of bindings that associate variables with their corresponding values. We use the following operations for manipulating environments:

- (lookup-variable-value ⟨*var*⟩ ⟨*env*⟩)

returns the value that is bound to the symbol ⟨*var*⟩ in the environment ⟨*env*⟩, or signals an error if the variable is unbound.

• (extend-environment ⟨*variables*⟩ ⟨*values*⟩ ⟨*base-env*⟩)
returns a new environment, consisting of a new frame in which the symbols in the list ⟨*variables*⟩ are bound to the corresponding elements in the list ⟨*values*⟩, where the enclosing environment is the environment ⟨*base-env*⟩.

• (define-variable! ⟨*var*⟩ ⟨*value*⟩ ⟨*env*⟩)
adds to the first frame in the environment ⟨*env*⟩ a new binding that associates the variable ⟨*var*⟩ with the value ⟨*value*⟩.

• (set-variable-value! ⟨*var*⟩ ⟨*value*⟩ ⟨*env*⟩)
changes the binding of the variable ⟨*var*⟩ in the environment ⟨*env*⟩ so that the variable is now bound to the value ⟨*value*⟩, or signals an error if the variable is unbound.

To implement these operations we represent an environment as a list of frames. The enclosing environment of an environment is the cdr of the list. The empty environment is simply the empty list.

```
(define (enclosing-environment env) (cdr env))

(define (first-frame env) (car env))

(define the-empty-environment '())
```

Each frame of an environment is represented as a pair of lists: a list of the variables bound in that frame and a list of the associated values.[14]

```
(define (make-frame variables values)
  (cons variables values))

(define (frame-variables frame) (car frame))

(define (frame-values frame) (cdr frame))

(define (add-binding-to-frame! var val frame)
  (set-car! frame (cons var (car frame)))
  (set-cdr! frame (cons val (cdr frame))))
```

To extend an environment by a new frame that associates variables with values, we make a frame consisting of the list of variables and the

---

[14]Frames are not really a data abstraction in the following code: Set-variable-value! and define-variable! use set-car! to directly modify the values in a frame. The purpose of the frame procedures is to make the environment-manipulation procedures easy to read.

list of values, and we adjoin this to the environment. We signal an error
if the number of variables does not match the number of values.

```
(define (extend-environment vars vals base-env)
  (if (= (length vars) (length vals))
      (cons (make-frame vars vals) base-env)
      (if (< (length vars) (length vals))
          (error "Too many arguments supplied" vars vals)
          (error "Too few arguments supplied" vars vals))))
```

To look up a variable in an environment, we scan the list of variables
in the first frame. If we find the desired variable, we return the corresponding element in the list of values. If we do not find the variable in
the current frame, we search the enclosing environment, and so on. If we
reach the empty environment, we signal an "unbound variable" error.

```
(define (lookup-variable-value var env)
  (define (env-loop env)
    (define (scan vars vals)
      (cond ((null? vars)
             (env-loop (enclosing-environment env)))
            ((eq? var (car vars))
             (car vals))
            (else (scan (cdr vars) (cdr vals)))))
    (if (eq? env the-empty-environment)
        (error "Unbound variable" var)
        (let ((frame (first-frame env)))
          (scan (frame-variables frame)
                (frame-values frame)))))
  (env-loop env))
```

To set a variable to a new value in a specified environment, we scan
for the variable, just as in lookup-variable-value, and change the
corresponding value when we find it.

```
(define (set-variable-value! var val env)
  (define (env-loop env)
    (define (scan vars vals)
      (cond ((null? vars)
             (env-loop (enclosing-environment env)))
            ((eq? var (car vars))
             (set-car! vals val))
            (else (scan (cdr vars) (cdr vals)))))
    (if (eq? env the-empty-environment)
        (error "Unbound variable -- SET!" var)
        (let ((frame (first-frame env)))
          (scan (frame-variables frame)
                (frame-values frame)))))
  (env-loop env))
```

To define a variable, we search the first frame for a binding for the variable, and change the binding if it exists (just as in `set-variable-value!`). If no such binding exists, we adjoin one to the first frame.

```
(define (define-variable! var val env)
  (let ((frame (first-frame env)))
    (define (scan vars vals)
      (cond ((null? vars)
             (add-binding-to-frame! var val frame))
            ((eq? var (car vars))
             (set-car! vals val))
            (else (scan (cdr vars) (cdr vals)))))
    (scan (frame-variables frame)
          (frame-values frame))))
```

The method described here is only one of many plausible ways to represent environments. Since we used data abstraction to isolate the rest of the evaluator from the detailed choice of representation, we could change the environment representation if we wanted to. (See exercise 4.11.) In a production-quality Lisp system, the speed of the evaluator's environment operations—especially that of variable lookup—has a major impact on the performance of the system. The representation described here, although conceptually simple, is not efficient and would not ordinarily be used in a production system.[15]

Exercise 4.11

Instead of representing a frame as a pair of lists, we can represent a frame as a list of bindings, where each binding is a name-value pair. Rewrite the environment operations to use this alternative representation.

Exercise 4.12

The procedures `set-variable-value!`, `define-variable!`, and `lookup-variable-value` can be expressed in terms of more abstract procedures for traversing the environment structure. Define abstractions that capture the common patterns and redefine the three procedures in terms of these abstractions.

Exercise 4.13

Scheme allows us to create new bindings for variables by means of `define`, but provides no way to get rid of bindings. Implement for the evaluator a special

---

[15]The drawback of this representation (as well as the variant in exercise 4.11) is that the evaluator may have to search through many frames in order to find the binding for a given variable. (Such an approach is referred to as *deep binding*.) One way to avoid this inefficiency is to make use of a strategy called *lexical addressing*, which will be discussed in section 5.5.6.

form `make-unbound!` that removes the binding of a given symbol from the environment in which the `make-unbound!` expression is evaluated. This problem is not completely specified. For example, should we remove only the binding in the first frame of the environment? Complete the specification and justify any choices you make.

4.1.4   Running the Evaluator as a Program

Given the evaluator, we have in our hands a description (expressed in Lisp) of the process by which Lisp expressions are evaluated. One advantage of expressing the evaluator as a program is that we can run the program. This gives us, running within Lisp, a working model of how Lisp itself evaluates expressions. This can serve as a framework for experimenting with evaluation rules, as we shall do later in this chapter.

Our evaluator program reduces expressions ultimately to the application of primitive procedures. Therefore, all that we need to run the evaluator is to create a mechanism that calls on the underlying Lisp system to model the application of primitive procedures.

There must be a binding for each primitive procedure name, so that when `eval` evaluates the operator of an application of a primitive, it will find an object to pass to `apply`. We thus set up a global environment that associates unique objects with the names of the primitive procedures that can appear in the expressions we will be evaluating. The global environment also includes bindings for the symbols `true` and `false`, so that they can be used as variables in expressions to be evaluated.

```
(define (setup-environment)
  (let ((initial-env
          (extend-environment (primitive-procedure-names)
                              (primitive-procedure-objects)
                              the-empty-environment)))
    (define-variable! 'true true initial-env)
    (define-variable! 'false false initial-env)
    initial-env))

(define the-global-environment (setup-environment))
```

It does not matter how we represent the primitive procedure objects, so long as `apply` can identify and apply them by using the procedures `primitive-procedure?` and `apply-primitive-procedure`. We have chosen to represent a primitive procedure as a list beginning with the symbol `primitive` and containing a procedure in the underlying Lisp that implements that primitive.

```
(define (primitive-procedure? proc)
  (tagged-list? proc 'primitive))
```

```
(define (primitive-implementation proc) (cadr proc))
```

Setup-environment will get the primitive names and implementation procedures from a list:[16]

```
(define primitive-procedures
  (list (list 'car car)
        (list 'cdr cdr)
        (list 'cons cons)
        (list 'null? null?)
        ⟨more primitives⟩
        ))
```

```
(define (primitive-procedure-names)
  (map car
       primitive-procedures))
```

```
(define (primitive-procedure-objects)
  (map (lambda (proc) (list 'primitive (cadr proc)))
       primitive-procedures))
```

To apply a primitive procedure, we simply apply the implementation procedure to the arguments, using the underlying Lisp system:[17]

```
(define (apply-primitive-procedure proc args)
  (apply-in-underlying-scheme
   (primitive-implementation proc) args))
```

---

[16]Any procedure defined in the underlying Lisp can be used as a primitive for the metacircular evaluator. The name of a primitive installed in the evaluator need not be the same as the name of its implementation in the underlying Lisp; the names are the same here because the metacircular evaluator implements Scheme itself. Thus, for example, we could put (list 'first car) or (list 'square (lambda (x) (* x x))) in the list of primitive-procedures.

[17]Apply-in-underlying-scheme is the apply procedure we have used in earlier chapters. The metacircular evaluator's apply procedure (section 4.1.1) models the working of this primitive. Having two different things called apply leads to a technical problem in running the metacircular evaluator, because defining the metacircular evaluator's apply will mask the definition of the primitive. One way around this is to rename the metacircular apply to avoid conflict with the name of the primitive procedure. We have assumed instead that we have saved a reference to the underlying apply by doing

(define apply-in-underlying-scheme apply)

before defining the metacircular apply. This allows us to access the original version of apply under a different name.

For convenience in running the metacircular evaluator, we provide a *driver loop* that models the read-eval-print loop of the underlying Lisp system. It prints a *prompt*, reads an input expression, evaluates this expression in the global environment, and prints the result. We precede each printed result by an *output prompt* so as to distinguish the value of the expression from other output that may be printed.[18]

```
(define input-prompt ";;; M-Eval input:")
(define output-prompt ";;; M-Eval value:")

(define (driver-loop)
  (prompt-for-input input-prompt)
  (let ((input (read)))
    (let ((output (eval input the-global-environment)))
      (announce-output output-prompt)
      (user-print output)))
  (driver-loop))

(define (prompt-for-input string)
  (newline) (newline) (display string) (newline))

(define (announce-output string)
  (newline) (display string) (newline))
```

We use a special printing procedure, user-print, to avoid printing the environment part of a compound procedure, which may be a very long list (or may even contain cycles).

```
(define (user-print object)
  (if (compound-procedure? object)
      (display (list 'compound-procedure
                     (procedure-parameters object)
                     (procedure-body object)
                     '<procedure-env>))
      (display object)))
```

Now all we need to do to run the evaluator is to initialize the global environment and start the driver loop. Here is a sample interaction:

```
(define the-global-environment (setup-environment))
```

---

[18]The primitive procedure read waits for input from the user, and returns the next complete expression that is typed. For example, if the user types (+ 23 x), read returns a three-element list containing the symbol +, the number 23, and the symbol x. If the user types 'x, read returns a two-element list containing the symbol quote and the symbol x.

```
(driver-loop)
```

```
;;; M-Eval input:
(define (append x y)
  (if (null? x)
      y
      (cons (car x)
            (append (cdr x) y))))
;;; M-Eval value:
ok
```

```
;;; M-Eval input:
(append '(a b c) '(d e f))
;;; M-Eval value:
(a b c d e f)
```

Exercise 4.14

Eva Lu Ator and Louis Reasoner are each experimenting with the metacircular evaluator. Eva types in the definition of map, and runs some test programs that use it. They work fine. Louis, in contrast, has installed the system version of map as a primitive for the metacircular evaluator. When he tries it, things go terribly wrong. Explain why Louis's map fails even though Eva's works.

4.1.5   Data as Programs

In thinking about a Lisp program that evaluates Lisp expressions, an analogy might be helpful. One operational view of the meaning of a program is that a program is a description of an abstract (perhaps infinitely large) machine. For example, consider the familiar program to compute factorials:

```
(define (factorial n)
  (if (= n 1)
      1
      (* (factorial (- n 1)) n)))
```

We may regard this program as the description of a machine containing parts that decrement, multiply, and test for equality, together with a two-position switch and another factorial machine. (The factorial machine is infinite because it contains another factorial machine within it.) Figure 4.2 is a flow diagram for the factorial machine, showing how the parts are wired together.

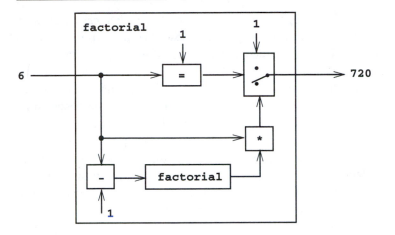

Figure 4.2   The factorial program, viewed as an abstract machine.

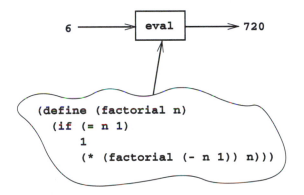

Figure 4.3   The evaluator emulating a factorial machine.

In a similar way, we can regard the evaluator as a very special machine that takes as input a description of a machine. Given this input, the evaluator configures itself to emulate the machine described. For example, if we feed our evaluator the definition of `factorial`, as shown in figure 4.3, the evaluator will be able to compute factorials.

From this perspective, our evaluator is seen to be a *universal machine*. It mimics other machines when these are described as Lisp programs.[19] This is striking. Try to imagine an analogous evaluator for electrical circuits. This would be a circuit that takes as input a signal encoding the plans for some other circuit, such as a filter. Given this input, the circuit evaluator would then behave like a filter with the same description. Such a universal electrical circuit is almost unimaginably complex. It is remarkable that the program evaluator is a rather simple program.[20]

Another striking aspect of the evaluator is that it acts as a bridge between the data objects that are manipulated by our programming language and the programming language itself. Imagine that the evaluator program (implemented in Lisp) is running, and that a user is typing expressions to the evaluator and observing the results. From the perspective of the user, an input expression such as (* x x) is an expression in the programming language, which the evaluator should execute. From the perspective of the evaluator, however, the expression is simply a list (in this case, a list of three symbols: *, x, and x) that is to be manipulated according to a well-defined set of rules.

That the user's programs are the evaluator's data need not be a source of confusion. In fact, it is sometimes convenient to ignore this distinction,

---

[19]The fact that the machines are described in Lisp is inessential. If we give our evaluator a Lisp program that behaves as an evaluator for some other language, say C, the Lisp evaluator will emulate the C evaluator, which in turn can emulate any machine described as a C program. Similarly, writing a Lisp evaluator in C produces a C program that can execute any Lisp program. The deep idea here is that any evaluator can emulate any other. Thus, the notion of "what can in principle be computed" (ignoring practicalities of time and memory required) is independent of the language or the computer, and instead reflects an underlying notion of *computability*. This was first demonstrated in a clear way by Alan M. Turing (1912–1954), whose 1936 paper laid the foundations for theoretical computer science. In the paper, Turing presented a simple computational model—now known as a *Turing machine*—and argued that any "effective process" can be formulated as a program for such a machine. (This argument is known as the *Church-Turing thesis*.) Turing then implemented a universal machine, i.e., a Turing machine that behaves as an evaluator for Turing-machine programs. He used this framework to demonstrate that there are well-posed problems that cannot be computed by Turing machines (see exercise 4.15), and so by implication cannot be formulated as "effective processes." Turing went on to make fundamental contributions to practical computer science as well. For example, he invented the idea of structuring programs using general-purpose subroutines. See Hodges 1983 for a biography of Turing.

[20]Some people find it counterintuitive that an evaluator, which is implemented by a relatively simple procedure, can emulate programs that are more complex than the evaluator itself. The existence of a universal evaluator machine is a deep and wonderful property of computation. *Recursion theory*, a branch of mathematical logic, is concerned with logical limits of computation. Douglas Hofstadter's beautiful book *Gödel, Escher, Bach* (1979) explores some of these ideas.

and to give the user the ability to explicitly evaluate a data object as a Lisp expression, by making eval available for use in programs. Many Lisp dialects provide a primitive eval procedure that takes as arguments an expression and an environment and evaluates the expression relative to the environment.[21] Thus,

```
(eval '(* 5 5) user-initial-environment)
```

and

```
(eval (cons '* (list 5 5)) user-initial-environment)
```

will both return 25.[22]

Exercise 4.15

Given a one-argument procedure p and an object a, p is said to "halt" on a if evaluating the expression (p a) returns a value (as opposed to terminating with an error message or running forever). Show that it is impossible to write a procedure halts? that correctly determines whether p halts on a for any procedure p and object a. Use the following reasoning: If you had such a procedure halts?, you could implement the following program:

```
(define (run-forever) (run-forever))

(define (try p)
  (if (halts? p p)
      (run-forever)
      'halted))
```

Now consider evaluating the expression (try try) and show that any possible outcome (either halting or running forever) violates the intended behavior of halts?.[23]

---

[21] Warning: This eval primitive is not identical to the eval procedure we implemented in section 4.1.1, because it uses *actual* Scheme environments rather than the sample environment structures we built in section 4.1.3. These actual environments cannot be manipulated by the user as ordinary lists; they must be accessed via eval or other special operations. Similarly, the apply primitive we saw earlier is not identical to the metacircular apply, because it uses actual Scheme procedures rather than the procedure objects we constructed in sections 4.1.3 and 4.1.4.

[22] The MIT implementation of Scheme includes eval, as well as a symbol user-initial-environment that is bound to the initial environment in which the user's input expressions are evaluated.

[23] Although we stipulated that halts? is given a procedure object, notice that this reasoning still applies even if halts? can gain access to the procedure's text and its environment. This is Turing's celebrated *Halting Theorem*, which gave the first clear example of a *non-computable* problem, i.e., a well-posed task that cannot be carried out as a computational procedure.

4.1.6   Internal Definitions

Our environment model of evaluation and our metacircular evaluator execute definitions in sequence, extending the environment frame one definition at a time. This is particularly convenient for interactive program
development, in which the programmer needs to freely mix the application of procedures with the definition of new procedures. However, if
we think carefully about the internal definitions used to implement block
structure (introduced in section 1.1.8), we will find that name-by-name
extension of the environment may not be the best way to define local
variables.

Consider a procedure with internal definitions, such as

```
(define (f x)
  (define (even? n)
    (if (= n 0)
        true
        (odd? (- n 1))))
  (define (odd? n)
    (if (= n 0)
        false
        (even? (- n 1))))
  ⟨ rest of body of f ⟩)
```

Our intention here is that the name odd? in the body of the procedure
even? should refer to the procedure odd? that is defined after even?.
The scope of the name odd? is the entire body of f, not just the portion
of the body of f starting at the point where the define for odd? occurs.
Indeed, when we consider that odd? is itself defined in terms of even?—
so that even? and odd? are mutually recursive procedures—we see that
the only satisfactory interpretation of the two defines is to regard them
as if the names even? and odd? were being added to the environment
simultaneously. More generally, in block structure, the scope of a local
name is the entire procedure body in which the define is evaluated.

As it happens, our interpreter will evaluate calls to f correctly, but
for an "accidental" reason: Since the definitions of the internal procedures come first, no calls to these procedures will be evaluated until all
of them have been defined. Hence, odd? will have been defined by the
time even? is executed. In fact, our sequential evaluation mechanism
will give the same result as a mechanism that directly implements simultaneous definition for any procedure in which the internal definitions

come first in a body and evaluation of the value expressions for the defined variables doesn't actually use any of the defined variables. (For
an example of a procedure that doesn't obey these restrictions, so that
sequential definition isn't equivalent to simultaneous definition, see exercise 4.19.)[24]

There is, however, a simple way to treat definitions so that internally
defined names have truly simultaneous scope—just create all local variables that will be in the current environment before evaluating any of the
value expressions. One way to do this is by a syntax transformation on
lambda expressions. Before evaluating the body of a lambda expression,
we "scan out" and eliminate all the internal definitions in the body. The
internally defined variables will be created with a let and then set to
their values by assignment. For example, the procedure

```
(lambda ⟨vars⟩
  (define u ⟨e1⟩)
  (define v ⟨e2⟩)
  ⟨e3⟩)
```

would be transformed into

```
(lambda ⟨vars⟩
  (let ((u '*unassigned*)
        (v '*unassigned*))
    (set! u ⟨e1⟩)
    (set! v ⟨e2⟩)
    ⟨e3⟩))
```

where *unassigned* is a special symbol that causes looking up a variable to signal an error if an attempt is made to use the value of the not-
yet-assigned variable.

An alternative strategy for scanning out internal definitions is shown
in exercise 4.18. Unlike the transformation shown above, this enforces

---

[24]Wanting programs to not depend on this evaluation mechanism is the reason for the
"management is not responsible" remark in footnote 28 of chapter 1. By insisting that
internal definitions come first and do not use each other while the definitions are being
evaluated, the IEEE standard for Scheme leaves implementors some choice in the mechanism used to evaluate these definitions. The choice of one evaluation rule rather than another here may seem like a small issue, affecting only the interpretation of "badly formed"
programs. However, we will see in section 5.5.6 that moving to a model of simultaneous
scoping for internal definitions avoids some nasty difficulties that would otherwise arise in
implementing a compiler.

the restriction that the defined variables' values can be evaluated without using any of the variables' values.[25]

Exercise 4.16

In this exercise we implement the method just described for interpreting internal definitions. We assume that the evaluator supports `let` (see exercise 4.6).

a. Change `lookup-variable-value` (section 4.1.3) to signal an error if the value it finds is the symbol `*unassigned*`.

b. Write a procedure `scan-out-defines` that takes a procedure body and returns an equivalent one that has no internal definitions, by making the transformation described above.

c. Install `scan-out-defines` in the interpreter, either in `make-procedure` or in `procedure-body` (see section 4.1.3). Which place is better? Why?

Exercise 4.17

Draw diagrams of the environment in effect when evaluating the expression ⟨*e3*⟩ in the procedure in the text, comparing how this will be structured when definitions are interpreted sequentially with how it will be structured if definitions are scanned out as described. Why is there an extra frame in the transformed program? Explain why this difference in environment structure can never make a difference in the behavior of a correct program. Design a way to make the interpreter implement the "simultaneous" scope rule for internal definitions without constructing the extra frame.

Exercise 4.18

Consider an alternative strategy for scanning out definitions that translates the example in the text to

```
(lambda ⟨vars⟩
  (let ((u '*unassigned*)
        (v '*unassigned*))
    (let ((a ⟨e1⟩)
          (b ⟨e2⟩))
      (set! u a)
      (set! v b))
    ⟨e3⟩))
```

Here a and b are meant to represent new variable names, created by the interpreter, that do not appear in the user's program. Consider the `solve` procedure from section 3.5.4:

---

[25]The IEEE standard for Scheme allows for different implementation strategies by specifying that it is up to the programmer to obey this restriction, not up to the implementation to enforce it. Some Scheme implementations, including MIT Scheme, use the transformation shown above. Thus, some programs that don't obey this restriction will in fact run in such implementations.

```
(define (solve f y0 dt)
  (define y (integral (delay dy) y0 dt))
  (define dy (stream-map f y))
  y)
```

Will this procedure work if internal definitions are scanned out as shown in this exercise? What if they are scanned out as shown in the text? Explain.

Exercise 4.19

Ben Bitdiddle, Alyssa P. Hacker, and Eva Lu Ator are arguing about the desired result of evaluating the expression

```
(let ((a 1))
  (define (f x)
    (define b (+ a x))
    (define a 5)
    (+ a b))
  (f 10))
```

Ben asserts that the result should be obtained using the sequential rule for define: b is defined to be 11, then a is defined to be 5, so the result is 16. Alyssa objects that mutual recursion requires the simultaneous scope rule for internal procedure definitions, and that it is unreasonable to treat procedure names differently from other names. Thus, she argues for the mechanism implemented in exercise 4.16. This would lead to a being unassigned at the time that the value for b is to be computed. Hence, in Alyssa's view the procedure should produce an error. Eva has a third opinion. She says that if the definitions of a and b are truly meant to be simultaneous, then the value 5 for a should be used in evaluating b. Hence, in Eva's view a should be 5, b should be 15, and the result should be 20. Which (if any) of these viewpoints do you support? Can you devise a way to implement internal definitions so that they behave as Eva prefers?[26]

Exercise 4.20

Because internal definitions look sequential but are actually simultaneous, some people prefer to avoid them entirely, and use the special form letrec instead. Letrec looks like let, so it is not surprising that the variables it binds are bound simultaneously and have the same scope as each other. The sample procedure f above can be written without internal definitions, but with exactly the same meaning, as

---

[26]The MIT implementors of Scheme support Alyssa on the following grounds: Eva is in principle correct—the definitions should be regarded as simultaneous. But it seems difficult to implement a general, efficient mechanism that does what Eva requires. In the absence of such a mechanism, it is better to generate an error in the difficult cases of simultaneous definitions (Alyssa's notion) than to produce an incorrect answer (as Ben would have it).

```
(define (f x)
  (letrec ((even?
             (lambda (n)
               (if (= n 0)
                   true
                   (odd? (- n 1)))))
           (odd?
             (lambda (n)
               (if (= n 0)
                   false
                   (even? (- n 1))))))
    ⟨ rest of body of f ⟩))
```

Letrec expressions, which have the form

```
(letrec (((⟨var₁⟩ ⟨exp₁⟩)) ... ((⟨varₙ⟩ ⟨expₙ⟩)))
  ⟨body⟩)
```

are a variation on let in which the expressions ⟨ exp_k ⟩ that provide the initial values for the variables ⟨ var_k ⟩ are evaluated in an environment that includes all the letrec bindings. This permits recursion in the bindings, such as the mutual recursion of even? and odd? in the example above, or the evaluation of 10 factorial with

```
(letrec ((fact
           (lambda (n)
             (if (= n 1)
                 1
                 (* n (fact (- n 1)))))))
  (fact 10))
```

a. Implement letrec as a derived expression, by transforming a letrec expression into a let expression as shown in the text above or in exercise 4.18. That is, the letrec variables should be created with a let and then be assigned their values with set!.

b. Louis Reasoner is confused by all this fuss about internal definitions. The way he sees it, if you don't like to use define inside a procedure, you can just use let. Illustrate what is loose about his reasoning by drawing an environment diagram that shows the environment in which the ⟨ rest of body of f ⟩ is evaluated during evaluation of the expression (f 5), with f defined as in this exercise. Draw an environment diagram for the same evaluation, but with let in place of letrec in the definition of f.

Exercise 4.21

Amazingly, Louis's intuition in exercise 4.20 is correct. It is indeed possible to specify recursive procedures without using letrec (or even define), although the method for accomplishing this is much more subtle than Louis imagined.

The following expression computes 10 factorial by applying a recursive factorial procedure:[27]

```
((lambda (n)
   ((lambda (fact)
      (fact fact n))
    (lambda (ft k)
      (if (= k 1)
          1
          (* k (ft ft (- k 1)))))))
 10)
```

a. Check (by evaluating the expression) that this really does compute factorials. Devise an analogous expression for computing Fibonacci numbers.

b. Consider the following procedure, which includes mutually recursive internal definitions:

```
(define (f x)
  (define (even? n)
    (if (= n 0)
        true
        (odd? (- n 1))))
  (define (odd? n)
    (if (= n 0)
        false
        (even? (- n 1))))
  (even? x))
```

Fill in the missing expressions to complete an alternative definition of f, which uses neither internal definitions nor letrec:

```
(define (f x)
  ((lambda (even? odd?)
     (even? even? odd? x))
   (lambda (ev? od? n)
     (if (= n 0) true (od? <??> <??> <??>)))
   (lambda (ev? od? n)
     (if (= n 0) false (ev? <??> <??> <??>)))))
```

4.1.7   Separating Syntactic Analysis from Execution

The evaluator implemented above is simple, but it is very inefficient, because the syntactic analysis of expressions is interleaved with their execution. Thus if a program is executed many times, its syntax is analyzed

---

[27]This example illustrates a programming trick for formulating recursive procedures without using define. The most general trick of this sort is the *Y operator*, which can be used to give a "pure λ-calculus" implementation of recursion. (See Stoy 1977 for details on the lambda calculus, and Gabriel 1988 for an exposition of the *Y* operator in Scheme.)

many times. Consider, for example, evaluating (factorial 4) using
the following definition of factorial:

```
(define (factorial n)
  (if (= n 1)
      1
      (* (factorial (- n 1)) n)))
```

Each time factorial is called, the evaluator must determine that
the body is an if expression and extract the predicate. Only then can
it evaluate the predicate and dispatch on its value. Each time it evaluates the expression (* (factorial (- n 1)) n), or the subexpressions (factorial (- n 1)) and (- n 1), the evaluator must perform
the case analysis in eval to determine that the expression is an application, and must extract its operator and operands. This analysis is expensive. Performing it repeatedly is wasteful.

We can transform the evaluator to be significantly more efficient by
arranging things so that syntactic analysis is performed only once.[28] We
split eval, which takes an expression and an environment, into two parts.
The procedure analyze takes only the expression. It performs the syntactic analysis and returns a new procedure, the *execution procedure*, that
encapsulates the work to be done in executing the analyzed expression.
The execution procedure takes an environment as its argument and completes the evaluation. This saves work because analyze will be called
only once on an expression, while the execution procedure may be called
many times.

With the separation into analysis and execution, eval now becomes

```
(define (eval exp env)
  ((analyze exp) env))
```

The result of calling analyze is the execution procedure to be applied
to the environment. The analyze procedure is the same case analysis as
performed by the original eval of section 4.1.1, except that the procedures to which we dispatch perform only analysis, not full evaluation:

---

[28]This technique is an integral part of the compilation process, which we shall discuss in
chapter 5. Jonathan Rees wrote a Scheme interpreter like this in about 1982 for the T
project (Rees and Adams 1982). Marc Feeley (1986) (see also Feeley and Lapalme 1987)
independently invented this technique in his master's thesis.

```
(define (analyze exp)
  (cond ((self-evaluating? exp)
         (analyze-self-evaluating exp))
        ((quoted? exp) (analyze-quoted exp))
        ((variable? exp) (analyze-variable exp))
        ((assignment? exp) (analyze-assignment exp))
        ((definition? exp) (analyze-definition exp))
        ((if? exp) (analyze-if exp))
        ((lambda? exp) (analyze-lambda exp))
        ((begin? exp) (analyze-sequence (begin-actions exp)))
        ((cond? exp) (analyze (cond->if exp)))
        ((application? exp) (analyze-application exp))
        (else
         (error "Unknown expression type -- ANALYZE" exp))))
```

Here is the simplest syntactic analysis procedure, which handles self-evaluating expressions. It returns an execution procedure that ignores its environment argument and just returns the expression:

```
(define (analyze-self-evaluating exp)
  (lambda (env) exp))
```

For a quoted expression, we can gain a little efficiency by extracting the text of the quotation only once, in the analysis phase, rather than in the execution phase.

```
(define (analyze-quoted exp)
  (let ((qval (text-of-quotation exp)))
    (lambda (env) qval)))
```

Looking up a variable value must still be done in the execution phase, since this depends upon knowing the environment.[29]

```
(define (analyze-variable exp)
  (lambda (env) (lookup-variable-value exp env)))
```

Analyze-assignment also must defer actually setting the variable until the execution, when the environment has been supplied. However, the fact that the assignment-value expression can be analyzed (recursively) during analysis is a major gain in efficiency, because the

---

[29]There is, however, an important part of the variable search that *can* be done as part of the syntactic analysis. As we will show in section 5.5.6, one can determine the position in the environment structure where the value of the variable will be found, thus obviating the need to scan the environment for the entry that matches the variable.

assignment-value expression will now be analyzed only once. The
same holds true for definitions.

```
(define (analyze-assignment exp)
  (let ((var (assignment-variable exp))
        (vproc (analyze (assignment-value exp))))
    (lambda (env)
      (set-variable-value! var (vproc env) env)
      'ok)))

(define (analyze-definition exp)
  (let ((var (definition-variable exp))
        (vproc (analyze (definition-value exp))))
    (lambda (env)
      (define-variable! var (vproc env) env)
      'ok)))
```

For if expressions, we extract and analyze the predicate, consequent,
and alternative at analysis time.

```
(define (analyze-if exp)
  (let ((pproc (analyze (if-predicate exp)))
        (cproc (analyze (if-consequent exp)))
        (aproc (analyze (if-alternative exp))))
    (lambda (env)
      (if (true? (pproc env))
          (cproc env)
          (aproc env)))))
```

Analyzing a lambda expression also achieves a major gain in efficiency: We analyze the lambda body only once, even though procedures
resulting from evaluation of the lambda may be applied many times.

```
(define (analyze-lambda exp)
  (let ((vars (lambda-parameters exp))
        (bproc (analyze-sequence (lambda-body exp))))
    (lambda (env) (make-procedure vars bproc env))))
```

Analysis of a sequence of expressions (as in a begin or the body of a
lambda expression) is more involved.[30] Each expression in the sequence
is analyzed, yielding an execution procedure. These execution procedures are combined to produce an execution procedure that takes an environment as argument and sequentially calls each individual execution
procedure with the environment as argument.

---

[30]See exercise 4.23 for some insight into the processing of sequences.

```
(define (analyze-sequence exps)
  (define (sequentially proc1 proc2)
    (lambda (env) (proc1 env) (proc2 env)))
  (define (loop first-proc rest-procs)
    (if (null? rest-procs)
        first-proc
        (loop (sequentially first-proc (car rest-procs))
              (cdr rest-procs))))
  (let ((procs (map analyze exps)))
    (if (null? procs)
        (error "Empty sequence -- ANALYZE"))
    (loop (car procs) (cdr procs))))
```

To analyze an application, we analyze the operator and operands and
construct an execution procedure that calls the operator execution procedure (to obtain the actual procedure to be applied) and the operand execution procedures (to obtain the actual arguments). We then pass these to
`execute-application`, which is the analog of `apply` in section 4.1.1.
Execute-application differs from `apply` in that the procedure body
for a compound procedure has already been analyzed, so there is no need
to do further analysis. Instead, we just call the execution procedure for
the body on the extended environment.

```
(define (analyze-application exp)
  (let ((fproc (analyze (operator exp)))
        (aprocs (map analyze (operands exp))))
    (lambda (env)
      (execute-application (fproc env)
                           (map (lambda (aproc) (aproc env))
                                aprocs)))))
```

```
(define (execute-application proc args)
  (cond ((primitive-procedure? proc)
         (apply-primitive-procedure proc args))
        ((compound-procedure? proc)
         ((procedure-body proc)
          (extend-environment (procedure-parameters proc)
                              args
                              (procedure-environment proc))))
        (else
         (error
          "Unknown procedure type -- EXECUTE-APPLICATION"
          proc))))
```

Our new evaluator uses the same data structures, syntax procedures,
and run-time support procedures as in sections 4.1.2, 4.1.3, and 4.1.4.

Exercise 4.22

Extend the evaluator in this section to support the special form `let`. (See exercise 4.6.)

Exercise 4.23

Alyssa P. Hacker doesn't understand why `analyze-sequence` needs to be so complicated. All the other analysis procedures are straightforward transformations of the corresponding evaluation procedures (or `eval` clauses) in section 4.1.1. She expected `analyze-sequence` to look like this:

```
(define (analyze-sequence exps)
  (define (execute-sequence procs env)
    (cond ((null? (cdr procs)) ((car procs) env))
          (else ((car procs) env)
                (execute-sequence (cdr procs) env))))
  (let ((procs (map analyze exps)))
    (if (null? procs)
        (error "Empty sequence -- ANALYZE"))
    (lambda (env) (execute-sequence procs env))))
```

Eva Lu Ator explains to Alyssa that the version in the text does more of the work of evaluating a sequence at analysis time. Alyssa's sequence-execution procedure, rather than having the calls to the individual execution procedures built in, loops through the procedures in order to call them: In effect, although the individual expressions in the sequence have been analyzed, the sequence itself has not been.

Compare the two versions of `analyze-sequence`. For example, consider the common case (typical of procedure bodies) where the sequence has just one expression. What work will the execution procedure produced by Alyssa's program do? What about the execution procedure produced by the program in the text above? How do the two versions compare for a sequence with two expressions?

Exercise 4.24

Design and carry out some experiments to compare the speed of the original metacircular evaluator with the version in this section. Use your results to estimate the fraction of time that is spent in analysis versus execution for various procedures.

4.2   Variations on a Scheme—Lazy Evaluation

Now that we have an evaluator expressed as a Lisp program, we can experiment with alternative choices in language design simply by modifying the evaluator. Indeed, new languages are often invented by first writing an evaluator that embeds the new language within an existing high-level language. For example, if we wish to discuss some aspect of a proposed modification to Lisp with another member of the Lisp community, we can supply an evaluator that embodies the change. The recipient can then experiment with the new evaluator and send back comments as further modifications. Not only does the high-level implementation base make it easier to test and debug the evaluator; in addition, the embedding enables the designer to snarf[31] features from the underlying language, just as our embedded Lisp evaluator uses primitives and control structure from the underlying Lisp. Only later (if ever) need the designer go to the trouble of building a complete implementation in a low-level language or in hardware. In this section and the next we explore some variations on Scheme that provide significant additional expressive power.

4.2.1   Normal Order and Applicative Order

In section 1.1, where we began our discussion of models of evaluation, we noted that Scheme is an *applicative-order* language, namely, that all the arguments to Scheme procedures are evaluated when the procedure is applied. In contrast, *normal-order* languages delay evaluation of procedure arguments until the actual argument values are needed. Delaying evaluation of procedure arguments until the last possible moment (e.g., until they are required by a primitive operation) is called *lazy evaluation*.[32] Consider the procedure

```
(define (try a b)
  (if (= a 0) 1 b))
```

Evaluating (try 0 (/ 1 0)) generates an error in Scheme. With lazy evaluation, there would be no error. Evaluating the expression would return 1, because the argument (/ 1 0) would never be evaluated.

An example that exploits lazy evaluation is the definition of a procedure unless

```
(define (unless condition usual-value exceptional-value)
  (if condition exceptional-value usual-value))
```

---

[31] Snarf: "To grab, especially a large document or file for the purpose of using it either with or without the owner's permission." Snarf down: "To snarf, sometimes with the connotation of absorbing, processing, or understanding." (These definitions were snarfed from Steele et al. 1983. See also Raymond 1993.)

[32] The difference between the "lazy" terminology and the "normal-order" terminology is somewhat fuzzy. Generally, "lazy" refers to the mechanisms of particular evaluators, while "normal-order" refers to the semantics of languages, independent of any particular evaluation strategy. But this is not a hard-and-fast distinction, and the two terminologies are often used interchangeably.

that can be used in expressions such as

```
(unless (= b 0)
        (/ a b)
        (begin (display "exception: returning 0")
               0))
```

This won't work in an applicative-order language because both the usual value and the exceptional value will be evaluated before unless is called (compare exercise 1.6). An advantage of lazy evaluation is that some procedures, such as unless, can do useful computation even if evaluation of some of their arguments would produce errors or would not terminate.

If the body of a procedure is entered before an argument has been evaluated we say that the procedure is *non-strict* in that argument. If the argument is evaluated before the body of the procedure is entered we say that the procedure is *strict* in that argument.[33] In a purely applicative-order language, all procedures are strict in each argument. In a purely normal-order language, all compound procedures are non-strict in each argument, and primitive procedures may be either strict or non-strict. There are also languages (see exercise 4.31) that give programmers detailed control over the strictness of the procedures they define.

A striking example of a procedure that can usefully be made non-strict is cons (or, in general, almost any constructor for data structures). One can do useful computation, combining elements to form data structures and operating on the resulting data structures, even if the values of the elements are not known. It makes perfect sense, for instance, to compute the length of a list without knowing the values of the individual elements in the list. We will exploit this idea in section 4.2.3 to implement the streams of chapter 3 as lists formed of non-strict cons pairs.

Exercise 4.25

Suppose that (in ordinary applicative-order Scheme) we define unless as shown above and then define factorial in terms of unless as

```
(define (factorial n)
  (unless (= n 1)
          (* n (factorial (- n 1)))
          1))
```

---

[33]The "strict" versus "non-strict" terminology means essentially the same thing as "applicative-order" versus "normal-order," except that it refers to individual procedures and arguments rather than to the language as a whole. At a conference on programming languages you might hear someone say, "The normal-order language Hassle has certain strict primitives. Other procedures take their arguments by lazy evaluation."

What happens if we attempt to evaluate (`factorial 5`)? Will our definitions work in a normal-order language?

Exercise 4.26

Ben Bitdiddle and Alyssa P. Hacker disagree over the importance of lazy evaluation for implementing things such as `unless`. Ben points out that it's possible to implement `unless` in applicative order as a special form. Alyssa counters that, if one did that, `unless` would be merely syntax, not a procedure that could be used in conjunction with higher-order procedures. Fill in the details on both sides of the argument. Show how to implement `unless` as a derived expression (like `cond` or `let`), and give an example of a situation where it might be useful to have `unless` available as a procedure, rather than as a special form.

4.2.2   An Interpreter with Lazy Evaluation

In this section we will implement a normal-order language that is the same as Scheme except that compound procedures are non-strict in each argument. Primitive procedures will still be strict. It is not difficult to modify the evaluator of section 4.1.1 so that the language it interprets behaves this way. Almost all the required changes center around procedure application.

The basic idea is that, when applying a procedure, the interpreter must determine which arguments are to be evaluated and which are to be delayed. The delayed arguments are not evaluated; instead, they are transformed into objects called *thunks*.[34] The thunk must contain the information required to produce the value of the argument when it is needed, as if it had been evaluated at the time of the application. Thus, the thunk must contain the argument expression and the environment in which the procedure application is being evaluated.

The process of evaluating the expression in a thunk is called *forcing*.[35] In general, a thunk will be forced only when its value is needed: when it is passed to a primitive procedure that will use the value of the thunk; when it is the value of a predicate of a conditional; and when it is the value of an operator that is about to be applied as a procedure. One design choice we have available is whether or not to *memoize* thunks, as we did

---

[34]The word *thunk* was invented by an informal working group that was discussing the implementation of call-by-name in Algol 60. They observed that most of the analysis of ("thinking about") the expression could be done at compile time; thus, at run time, the expression would already have been "thunk" about (Ingerman et al. 1960).

[35]This is analogous to the use of `force` on the delayed objects that were introduced in chapter 3 to represent streams. The critical difference between what we are doing here and what we did in chapter 3 is that we are building delaying and forcing into the evaluator, and thus making this uniform and automatic throughout the language.

with delayed objects in section 3.5.1. With memoization, the first time a
thunk is forced, it stores the value that is computed. Subsequent forcings
simply return the stored value without repeating the computation. We'll
make our interpreter memoize, because this is more efficient for many
applications. There are tricky considerations here, however.[36]

Modifying the evaluator

The main difference between the lazy evaluator and the one in section 4.1
is in the handling of procedure applications in eval and apply.

The application? clause of eval becomes

```
((application? exp)
 (apply (actual-value (operator exp) env)
        (operands exp)
        env))
```

This is almost the same as the application? clause of eval in section 4.1.1. For lazy evaluation, however, we call apply with the operand
expressions, rather than the arguments produced by evaluating them.
Since we will need the environment to construct thunks if the arguments
are to be delayed, we must pass this as well. We still evaluate the operator, because apply needs the actual procedure to be applied in order to
dispatch on its type (primitive versus compound) and apply it.

Whenever we need the actual value of an expression, we use

```
(define (actual-value exp env)
  (force-it (eval exp env)))
```

instead of just eval, so that if the expression's value is a thunk, it will be
forced.

Our new version of apply is also almost the same as the version in section 4.1.1. The difference is that eval has passed in unevaluated operand
expressions: For primitive procedures (which are strict), we evaluate all
the arguments before applying the primitive; for compound procedures

---

[36]Lazy evaluation combined with memoization is sometimes referred to as *call-by-need*
argument passing, in contrast to *call-by-name* argument passing. (Call-by-name, introduced in Algol 60, is similar to non-memoized lazy evaluation.) As language designers,
we can build our evaluator to memoize, not to memoize, or leave this an option for programmers (exercise 4.31). As you might expect from chapter 3, these choices raise issues
that become both subtle and confusing in the presence of assignments. (See exercises 4.27
and 4.29.) An excellent article by Clinger (1982) attempts to clarify the multiple dimen-
sions of confusion that arise here.

(which are non-strict) we delay all the arguments before applying the procedure.

```
(define (apply procedure arguments env)
  (cond ((primitive-procedure? procedure)
         (apply-primitive-procedure
          procedure
          (list-of-arg-values arguments env)))    ; changed
        ((compound-procedure? procedure)
         (eval-sequence
          (procedure-body procedure)
          (extend-environment
           (procedure-parameters procedure)
           (list-of-delayed-args arguments env)  ; changed
           (procedure-environment procedure))))
        (else
         (error
          "Unknown procedure type -- APPLY" procedure))))
```

The procedures that process the arguments are just like `list-of-values` from section 4.1.1, except that `list-of-delayed-args` delays the arguments instead of evaluating them, and `list-of-arg-values` uses actual-value instead of eval:

```
(define (list-of-arg-values exps env)
  (if (no-operands? exps)
      '()
      (cons (actual-value (first-operand exps) env)
            (list-of-arg-values (rest-operands exps)
                                env))))

(define (list-of-delayed-args exps env)
  (if (no-operands? exps)
      '()
      (cons (delay-it (first-operand exps) env)
            (list-of-delayed-args (rest-operands exps)
                                  env))))
```

The other place we must change the evaluator is in the handling of `if`, where we must use `actual-value` instead of `eval` to get the value of the predicate expression before testing whether it is true or false:

```
(define (eval-if exp env)
  (if (true? (actual-value (if-predicate exp) env))
      (eval (if-consequent exp) env)
      (eval (if-alternative exp) env)))
```

Finally, we must change the `driver-loop` procedure (section 4.1.4) to use `actual-value` instead of `eval`, so that if a delayed value is propagated back to the read-eval-print loop, it will be forced before being printed. We also change the prompts to indicate that this is the lazy evaluator:

```
(define input-prompt ";;; L-Eval input:")
(define output-prompt ";;; L-Eval value:")

(define (driver-loop)
  (prompt-for-input input-prompt)
  (let ((input (read)))
    (let ((output
            (actual-value input the-global-environment)))
      (announce-output output-prompt)
      (user-print output)))
  (driver-loop))
```

With these changes made, we can start the evaluator and test it. The successful evaluation of the `try` expression discussed in section 4.2.1 indicates that the interpreter is performing lazy evaluation:

```
(define the-global-environment (setup-environment))

(driver-loop)

;;; L-Eval input:
(define (try a b)
  (if (= a 0) 1 b))
;;; L-Eval value:
ok

;;; L-Eval input:
(try 0 (/ 1 0))
;;; L-Eval value:
1
```

Representing thunks

Our evaluator must arrange to create thunks when procedures are applied to arguments and to force these thunks later. A thunk must package an expression together with the environment, so that the argument can be produced later. To force the thunk, we simply extract the expression and environment from the thunk and evaluate the expression in the environment. We use `actual-value` rather than `eval` so that in case the value of the expression is itself a thunk, we will force that, and so on, until we reach something that is not a thunk:

```
(define (force-it obj)
  (if (thunk? obj)
      (actual-value (thunk-exp obj) (thunk-env obj))
      obj))
```

One easy way to package an expression with an environment is to make a list containing the expression and the environment. Thus, we create a thunk as follows:

```
(define (delay-it exp env)
  (list 'thunk exp env))

(define (thunk? obj)
  (tagged-list? obj 'thunk))

(define (thunk-exp thunk) (cadr thunk))

(define (thunk-env thunk) (caddr thunk))
```

Actually, what we want for our interpreter is not quite this, but rather thunks that have been memoized. When a thunk is forced, we will turn it into an evaluated thunk by replacing the stored expression with its value and changing the `thunk` tag so that it can be recognized as already evaluated.[37]

```
(define (evaluated-thunk? obj)
  (tagged-list? obj 'evaluated-thunk))

(define (thunk-value evaluated-thunk) (cadr evaluated-thunk))
```

---

[37]Notice that we also erase the `env` from the thunk once the expression's value has been computed. This makes no difference in the values returned by the interpreter. It does help save space, however, because removing the reference from the thunk to the `env` once it is no longer needed allows this structure to be *garbage-collected* and its space recycled, as we will discuss in section 5.3.

Similarly, we could have allowed unneeded environments in the memoized delayed objects of section 3.5.1 to be garbage-collected, by having `memo-proc` do something like `(set! proc '())` to discard the procedure `proc` (which includes the environment in which the `delay` was evaluated) after storing its value.

```
(define (force-it obj)
  (cond ((thunk? obj)
         (let ((result (actual-value
                        (thunk-exp obj)
                        (thunk-env obj)))))
           (set-car! obj 'evaluated-thunk)
           (set-car! (cdr obj) result)      ; replace exp with its value
           (set-cdr! (cdr obj) '())         ; forget unneeded env
           result))
        ((evaluated-thunk? obj)
         (thunk-value obj))
        (else obj)))
```

Notice that the same `delay-it` procedure works both with and without memoization.

Exercise 4.27

Suppose we type in the following definitions to the lazy evaluator:

```
(define count 0)

(define (id x)
  (set! count (+ count 1))
  x)
```

Give the missing values in the following sequence of interactions, and explain your answers.[38]

```
(define w (id (id 10)))

;;; L-Eval input:
count
;;; L-Eval value:
⟨response⟩

;;; L-Eval input:
w
;;; L-Eval value:
⟨response⟩

;;; L-Eval input:
count
;;; L-Eval value:
⟨response⟩
```

---

[38]This exercise demonstrates that the interaction between lazy evaluation and side effects can be very confusing. This is just what you might expect from the discussion in chapter 3.

Exercise 4.28

Eval uses `actual-value` rather than `eval` to evaluate the operator before passing it to `apply`, in order to force the value of the operator. Give an example that demonstrates the need for this forcing.

Exercise 4.29

Exhibit a program that you would expect to run much more slowly without memoization than with memoization. Also, consider the following interaction, where the `id` procedure is defined as in exercise 4.27 and `count` starts at 0:

```
(define (square x)
  (* x x))

;;; L-Eval input:
(square (id 10))
;;; L-Eval value:
⟨response⟩

;;; L-Eval input:
count
;;; L-Eval value:
⟨response⟩
```

Give the responses both when the evaluator memoizes and when it does not.

Exercise 4.30

Cy D. Fect, a reformed C programmer, is worried that some side effects may never take place, because the lazy evaluator doesn't force the expressions in a sequence. Since the value of an expression in a sequence other than the last one is not used (the expression is there only for its effect, such as assigning to a variable or printing), there can be no subsequent use of this value (e.g., as an argument to a primitive procedure) that will cause it to be forced. Cy thus thinks that when evaluating sequences, we must force all expressions in the sequence except the final one. He proposes to modify `eval-sequence` from section 4.1.1 to use `actual-value` rather than `eval`:

```
(define (eval-sequence exps env)
  (cond ((last-exp? exps) (eval (first-exp exps) env))
        (else (actual-value (first-exp exps) env)
              (eval-sequence (rest-exps exps) env))))
```

a. Ben Bitdiddle thinks Cy is wrong. He shows Cy the `for-each` procedure described in exercise 2.23, which gives an important example of a sequence with side effects:

```
(define (for-each proc items)
  (if (null? items)
      'done
      (begin (proc (car items))
             (for-each proc (cdr items)))))
```

He claims that the evaluator in the text (with the original `eval-sequence`) handles this correctly:

```
;;; L-Eval input:
(for-each (lambda (x) (newline) (display x))
          (list 57 321 88))
57
321
88
;;; L-Eval value:
done
```

Explain why Ben is right about the behavior of `for-each`.

b. Cy agrees that Ben is right about the `for-each` example, but says that that's not the kind of program he was thinking about when he proposed his change to `eval-sequence`. He defines the following two procedures in the lazy evaluator:

```
(define (p1 x)
  (set! x (cons x '(2)))
  x)

(define (p2 x)
  (define (p e)
    e
    x)
  (p (set! x (cons x '(2)))))
```

What are the values of `(p1 1)` and `(p2 1)` with the original `eval-sequence`? What would the values be with Cy's proposed change to `eval-sequence`?

c. Cy also points out that changing `eval-sequence` as he proposes does not affect the behavior of the example in part a. Explain why this is true.

d. How do you think sequences ought to be treated in the lazy evaluator? Do you like Cy's approach, the approach in the text, or some other approach?

Exercise 4.31

The approach taken in this section is somewhat unpleasant, because it makes an incompatible change to Scheme. It might be nicer to implement lazy evaluation as an *upward-compatible extension*, that is, so that ordinary Scheme programs will work as before. We can do this by extending the syntax of procedure declarations to let the user control whether or not arguments are to be delayed. While we're at it, we may as well also give the user the choice between delaying with and without memoization. For example, the definition

```
(define (f a (b lazy) c (d lazy-memo))
  ...)
```

would define f to be a procedure of four arguments, where the first and third arguments are evaluated when the procedure is called, the second argument is delayed, and the fourth argument is both delayed and memoized. Thus, ordinary procedure definitions will produce the same behavior as ordinary Scheme, while adding the `lazy-memo` declaration to each parameter of every compound procedure will produce the behavior of the lazy evaluator defined in this section. Design and implement the changes required to produce such an extension to Scheme. You will have to implement new syntax procedures to handle the new syntax for `define`. You must also arrange for `eval` or `apply` to determine when arguments are to be delayed, and to force or delay arguments accordingly, and you must arrange for forcing to memoize or not, as appropriate.

4.2.3   Streams as Lazy Lists

In section 3.5.1, we showed how to implement streams as delayed lists. We introduced special forms `delay` and `cons-stream`, which allowed us to construct a "promise" to compute the `cdr` of a stream, without actually fulfilling that promise until later. We could use this general technique of introducing special forms whenever we need more control over the evaluation process, but this is awkward. For one thing, a special form is not a first-class object like a procedure, so we cannot use it together with higher-order procedures.[39] Additionally, we were forced to create streams as a new kind of data object similar but not identical to lists, and this required us to reimplement many ordinary list operations (`map`, `append`, and so on) for use with streams.

With lazy evaluation, streams and lists can be identical, so there is no need for special forms or for separate list and stream operations. All we need to do is to arrange matters so that `cons` is non-strict. One way to accomplish this is to extend the lazy evaluator to allow for non-strict primitives, and to implement `cons` as one of these. An easier way is to recall (section 2.1.3) that there is no fundamental need to implement `cons` as a primitive at all. Instead, we can represent pairs as procedures:[40]

```
(define (cons x y)
  (lambda (m) (m x y)))

(define (car z)
  (z (lambda (p q) p)))

(define (cdr z)
  (z (lambda (p q) q)))
```

---

[39]This is precisely the issue with the `unless` procedure, as in exercise 4.26.

[40]This is the procedural representation described in exercise 2.4. Essentially any procedural representation (e.g., a message-passing implementation) would do as well. Notice that we can install these definitions in the lazy evaluator simply by typing them at the driver loop. If we had originally included `cons`, `car`, and `cdr` as primitives in the global environment, they will be redefined. (Also see exercises 4.33 and 4.34.)

In terms of these basic operations, the standard definitions of the list operations will work with infinite lists (streams) as well as finite ones, and the stream operations can be implemented as list operations. Here are some examples:

```
(define (list-ref items n)
  (if (= n 0)
      (car items)
      (list-ref (cdr items) (- n 1)))))

(define (map proc items)
  (if (null? items)
      '()
      (cons (proc (car items))
            (map proc (cdr items))))))

(define (scale-list items factor)
  (map (lambda (x) (* x factor))
       items))

(define (add-lists list1 list2)
  (cond ((null? list1) list2)
        ((null? list2) list1)
        (else (cons (+ (car list1) (car list2))
                    (add-lists (cdr list1) (cdr list2))))))

(define ones (cons 1 ones))

(define integers (cons 1 (add-lists ones integers)))

;;; L-Eval input:
(list-ref integers 17)
;;; L-Eval value:
18
```

Note that these lazy lists are even lazier than the streams of chapter 3: The car of the list, as well as the cdr, is delayed.[41] In fact, even accessing the car or cdr of a lazy pair need not force the value of a list element. The value will be forced only when it is really needed—e.g., for use as the argument of a primitive, or to be printed as an answer.

Lazy pairs also help with the problem that arose with streams in section 3.5.4, where we found that formulating stream models of systems

---

[41]This permits us to create delayed versions of more general kinds of list structures, not just sequences. Hughes 1990 discusses some applications of "lazy trees."

with loops may require us to sprinkle our programs with explicit `delay` operations, beyond the ones supplied by `cons-stream`. With lazy evaluation, all arguments to procedures are delayed uniformly. For instance, we can implement procedures to integrate lists and solve differential equations as we originally intended in section 3.5.4:

```
(define (integral integrand initial-value dt)
  (define int
    (cons initial-value
          (add-lists (scale-list integrand dt)
                     int)))
  int)

(define (solve f y0 dt)
  (define y (integral dy y0 dt))
  (define dy (map f y))
  y)

;;; L-Eval input:
(list-ref (solve (lambda (x) x) 1 0.001) 1000)
;;; L-Eval value:
2.716924
```

Exercise 4.32

Give some examples that illustrate the difference between the streams of chapter 3 and the "lazier" lazy lists described in this section. How can you take advantage of this extra laziness?

Exercise 4.33

Ben Bitdiddle tests the lazy list implementation given above by evaluating the expression

```
(car '(a b c))
```

To his surprise, this produces an error. After some thought, he realizes that the "lists" obtained by reading in quoted expressions are different from the lists manipulated by the new definitions of `cons`, `car`, and `cdr`. Modify the evaluator's treatment of quoted expressions so that quoted lists typed at the driver loop will produce true lazy lists.

Exercise 4.34

Modify the driver loop for the evaluator so that lazy pairs and lists will print in some reasonable way. (What are you going to do about infinite lists?) You may also need to modify the representation of lazy pairs so that the evaluator can identify them in order to print them.

4.3   Variations on a Scheme—Nondeterministic Computing

In this section, we extend the Scheme evaluator to support a programming paradigm called *nondeterministic computing* by building into the evaluator a facility to support automatic search. This is a much more profound change to the language than the introduction of lazy evaluation in section 4.2.

Nondeterministic computing, like stream processing, is useful for "generate and test" applications. Consider the task of starting with two lists of positive integers and finding a pair of integers—one from the first list and one from the second list—whose sum is prime. We saw how to handle this with finite sequence operations in section 2.2.3 and with infinite streams in section 3.5.3. Our approach was to generate the sequence of all possible pairs and filter these to select the pairs whose sum is prime. Whether we actually generate the entire sequence of pairs first as in chapter 2, or interleave the generating and filtering as in chapter 3, is immaterial to the essential image of how the computation is organized.

The nondeterministic approach evokes a different image. Imagine simply that we choose (in some way) a number from the first list and a number from the second list and require (using some mechanism) that their sum be prime. This is expressed by following procedure:

```
(define (prime-sum-pair list1 list2)
  (let ((a (an-element-of list1))
        (b (an-element-of list2)))
    (require (prime? (+ a b)))
    (list a b)))
```

It might seem as if this procedure merely restates the problem, rather than specifying a way to solve it. Nevertheless, this is a legitimate nondeterministic program.[42]

The key idea here is that expressions in a nondeterministic language can have more than one possible value. For instance, `an-element-of`

---

[42]We assume that we have previously defined a procedure `prime?` that tests whether numbers are prime. Even with `prime?` defined, the `prime-sum-pair` procedure may look suspiciously like the unhelpful "pseudo-Lisp" attempt to define the square-root function, which we described at the beginning of section 1.1.7. In fact, a square-root procedure along those lines can actually be formulated as a nondeterministic program. By incorporating a search mechanism into the evaluator, we are eroding the distinction between purely declarative descriptions and imperative specifications of how to compute answers. We'll go even farther in this direction in section 4.4.

might return any element of the given list. Our nondeterministic program evaluator will work by automatically choosing a possible value and keeping track of the choice. If a subsequent requirement is not met, the evaluator will try a different choice, and it will keep trying new choices until the evaluation succeeds, or until we run out of choices. Just as the lazy evaluator freed the programmer from the details of how values are delayed and forced, the nondeterministic program evaluator will free the programmer from the details of how choices are made.

It is instructive to contrast the different images of time evoked by nondeterministic evaluation and stream processing. Stream processing uses lazy evaluation to decouple the time when the stream of possible answers is assembled from the time when the actual stream elements are produced. The evaluator supports the illusion that all the possible answers are laid out before us in a timeless sequence. With nondeterministic evaluation, an expression represents the exploration of a set of possible worlds, each determined by a set of choices. Some of the possible worlds lead to dead ends, while others have useful values. The nondeterministic program evaluator supports the illusion that time branches, and that our programs have different possible execution histories. When we reach a dead end, we can revisit a previous choice point and proceed along a different branch.

The nondeterministic program evaluator implemented below is called the `amb` evaluator because it is based on a new special form called `amb`. We can type the above definition of `prime-sum-pair` at the `amb` evaluator driver loop (along with definitions of `prime?`, `an-element-of`, and `require`) and run the procedure as follows:

```
;;; Amb-Eval input:
(prime-sum-pair '(1 3 5 8) '(20 35 110))
;;; Starting a new problem
;;; Amb-Eval value:
(3 20)
```

The value returned was obtained after the evaluator repeatedly chose elements from each of the lists, until a successful choice was made.

Section 4.3.1 introduces `amb` and explains how it supports nondeterminism through the evaluator's automatic search mechanism. Section 4.3.2 presents examples of nondeterministic programs, and section 4.3.3 gives the details of how to implement the `amb` evaluator by modifying the ordinary Scheme evaluator.

4.3.1   Amb and Search

To extend Scheme to support nondeterminism, we introduce a new special form called amb.[43] The expression (amb $\langle e_1 \rangle$ $\langle e_2 \rangle$ ... $\langle e_n \rangle$) returns the value of one of the n expressions $\langle e_i \rangle$ "ambiguously." For example, the expression

```
(list (amb 1 2 3) (amb 'a 'b))
```

can have six possible values:

```
(1 a)    (1 b)    (2 a)    (2 b)    (3 a)    (3 b)
```

Amb with a single choice produces an ordinary (single) value.

Amb with no choices—the expression (amb)—is an expression with no acceptable values. Operationally, we can think of (amb) as an expression that when evaluated causes the computation to "fail": The computation aborts and no value is produced. Using this idea, we can express the requirement that a particular predicate expression p must be true as follows:

```
(define (require p)
  (if (not p) (amb)))
```

With amb and `require`, we can implement the an-element-of procedure used above:

```
(define (an-element-of items)
  (require (not (null? items)))
  (amb (car items) (an-element-of (cdr items))))
```

An-element-of fails if the list is empty. Otherwise it ambiguously returns either the first element of the list or an element chosen from the rest of the list.

We can also express infinite ranges of choices. The following procedure potentially returns any integer greater than or equal to some given n:

```
(define (an-integer-starting-from n)
  (amb n (an-integer-starting-from (+ n 1))))
```

This is like the stream procedure `integers-starting-from` described in section 3.5.2, but with an important difference: The stream procedure

---

[43]The idea of amb for nondeterministic programming was first described in 1961 by John McCarthy (see McCarthy 1967).

returns an object that represents the sequence of all integers beginning with n, whereas the amb procedure returns a single integer.[44]

Abstractly, we can imagine that evaluating an amb expression causes time to split into branches, where the computation continues on each branch with one of the possible values of the expression. We say that amb represents a *nondeterministic choice point*. If we had a machine with a sufficient number of processors that could be dynamically allocated, we could implement the search in a straightforward way. Execution would proceed as in a sequential machine, until an amb expression is encountered. At this point, more processors would be allocated and initialized to continue all of the parallel executions implied by the choice. Each processor would proceed sequentially as if it were the only choice, until it either terminates by encountering a failure, or it further subdivides, or it finishes.[45]

On the other hand, if we have a machine that can execute only one process (or a few concurrent processes), we must consider the alternatives sequentially. One could imagine modifying an evaluator to pick at random a branch to follow whenever it encounters a choice point. Random choice, however, can easily lead to failing values. We might try running the evaluator over and over, making random choices and hoping to find a non-failing value, but it is better to *systematically search* all possible execution paths. The amb evaluator that we will develop and work with in this section implements a systematic search as follows: When the evaluator encounters an application of amb, it initially selects the first alternative. This selection may itself lead to a further choice. The evaluator will always initially choose the first alternative at each choice point. If a

---

[44]In actuality, the distinction between nondeterministically returning a single choice and returning all choices depends somewhat on our point of view. From the perspective of the code that uses the value, the nondeterministic choice returns a single value. From the perspective of the programmer designing the code, the nondeterministic choice potentially returns all possible values, and the computation branches so that each value is investigated separately.

[45]One might object that this is a hopelessly inefficient mechanism. It might require millions of processors to solve some easily stated problem this way, and most of the time most of those processors would be idle. This objection should be taken in the context of history. Memory used to be considered just such an expensive commodity. In 1964 a megabyte of RAM cost about $400,000. Now every personal computer has many megabytes of RAM, and most of the time most of that RAM is unused. It is hard to underestimate the cost of mass-produced electronics.

choice results in a failure, then the evaluator automagically[46] *backtracks* to the most recent choice point and tries the next alternative. If it runs out of alternatives at any choice point, the evaluator will back up to the previous choice point and resume from there. This process leads to a search strategy known as *depth-first search* or *chronological backtracking*.[47]

Driver loop

The driver loop for the `amb` evaluator has some unusual properties. It reads an expression and prints the value of the first non-failing execution, as in the `prime-sum-pair` example shown above. If we want to see the value of the next successful execution, we can ask the interpreter to backtrack and attempt to generate a second non-failing execution. This is signaled by typing the symbol `try-again`. If any expression except `try-again` is given, the interpreter will start a new problem, discarding the unexplored alternatives in the previous problem. Here is a sample interaction:

---

[46]Automagically: "Automatically, but in a way which, for some reason (typically because it is too complicated, or too ugly, or perhaps even too trivial), the speaker doesn't feel like explaining." (Steele 1983, Raymond 1993)

[47]The integration of automatic search strategies into programming languages has had a long and checkered history. The first suggestions that nondeterministic algorithms might be elegantly encoded in a programming language with search and automatic backtracking came from Robert Floyd (1967). Carl Hewitt (1969) invented a programming language called Planner that explicitly supported automatic chronological backtracking, providing for a built-in depth-first search strategy. Sussman, Winograd, and Charniak (1971) implemented a subset of this language, called MicroPlanner, which was used to support work in problem solving and robot planning. Similar ideas, arising from logic and theorem proving, led to the genesis in Edinburgh and Marseille of the elegant language Prolog (which we will discuss in section 4.4). After sufficient frustration with automatic search, McDermott and Sussman (1972) developed a language called Conniver, which included mechanisms for placing the search strategy under programmer control. This proved unwieldy, however, and Sussman and Stallman (1975) found a more tractable approach while investigating methods of symbolic analysis for electrical circuits. They developed a non-chronological backtracking scheme that was based on tracing out the logical dependencies connecting facts, a technique that has come to be known as *dependency-directed backtracking*. Although their method was complex, it produced reasonably efficient programs because it did little redundant search. Doyle (1979) and McAllester (1978, 1980) generalized and clarified the methods of Stallman and Sussman, developing a new paradigm for formulating search that is now called *truth maintenance*. Modern problem-solving systems all use some form of truth-maintenance system as a substrate. See Forbus and deKleer 1993 for a discussion of elegant ways to build truth-maintenance systems and applications using truth maintenance. Zabih, McAllester, and Chapman 1987 describes a nondeterministic extension to Scheme that is based on amb; it is similar to the interpreter described in this section, but more sophisticated, because it uses dependency-directed backtracking rather than chronological backtracking. Winston 1992 gives an introduction to both kinds of backtracking.

```
;;; Amb-Eval input:
(prime-sum-pair '(1 3 5 8) '(20 35 110))
;;; Starting a new problem
;;; Amb-Eval value:
(3 20)

;;; Amb-Eval input:
try-again
;;; Amb-Eval value:
(3 110)

;;; Amb-Eval input:
try-again
;;; Amb-Eval value:
(8 35)

;;; Amb-Eval input:
try-again
;;; There are no more values of
(prime-sum-pair (quote (1 3 5 8)) (quote (20 35 110)))

;;; Amb-Eval input:
(prime-sum-pair '(19 27 30) '(11 36 58))
;;; Starting a new problem
;;; Amb-Eval value:
(30 11)
```

Exercise 4.35

Write a procedure `an-integer-between` that returns an integer between two given bounds. This can be used to implement a procedure that finds Pythagorean triples, i.e., triples of integers (i, j, k) between the given bounds such that $i \leq j$ and $i^2 + j^2 = k^2$, as follows:

```
(define (a-pythagorean-triple-between low high)
  (let ((i (an-integer-between low high)))
    (let ((j (an-integer-between i high)))
      (let ((k (an-integer-between j high)))
        (require (= (+ (* i i) (* j j)) (* k k)))
        (list i j k)))))
```

Exercise 4.36

Exercise 3.69 discussed how to generate the stream of *all* Pythagorean triples, with no upper bound on the size of the integers to be searched. Explain why simply replacing `an-integer-between` by `an-integer-starting-from` in the procedure in exercise 4.35 is not an adequate way to generate arbitrary Pythagorean triples. Write a procedure that actually will accomplish this. (That is, write a procedure for which repeatedly typing `try-again` would in principle eventually generate all Pythagorean triples.)

Exercise 4.37

Ben Bitdiddle claims that the following method for generating Pythagorean triples is more efficient than the one in exercise 4.35. Is he correct? (Hint: Consider the number of possibilities that must be explored.)

```
(define (a-pythagorean-triple-between low high)
  (let ((i (an-integer-between low high))
        (hsq (* high high)))
    (let ((j (an-integer-between i high)))
      (let ((ksq (+ (* i i) (* j j))))
        (require (>= hsq ksq))
        (let ((k (sqrt ksq)))
          (require (integer? k))
          (list i j k)))))))
```

4.3.2   Examples of Nondeterministic Programs

Section 4.3.3 describes the implementation of the amb evaluator. First, however, we give some examples of how it can be used. The advantage of nondeterministic programming is that we can suppress the details of how search is carried out, thereby expressing our programs at a higher level of abstraction.

Logic Puzzles

The following puzzle (taken from Dinesman 1968) is typical of a large class of simple logic puzzles:

> Baker, Cooper, Fletcher, Miller, and Smith live on different floors of an apartment house that contains only five floors. Baker does not live on the top floor. Cooper does not live on the bottom floor. Fletcher does not live on either the top or the bottom floor. Miller lives on a higher floor than does Cooper. Smith does not live on a floor adjacent to Fletcher's. Fletcher does not live on a floor adjacent to Cooper's. Where does everyone live?

We can determine who lives on each floor in a straightforward way by enumerating all the possibilities and imposing the given restrictions:[48]

---

[48] Our program uses the following procedure to determine if the elements of a list are distinct:

```
(define (distinct? items)
  (cond ((null? items) true)
        ((null? (cdr items)) true)
        ((member (car items) (cdr items)) false)
        (else (distinct? (cdr items)))))
```

Member is like memq except that it uses equal? instead of eq? to test for equality.

```
(define (multiple-dwelling)
  (let ((baker (amb 1 2 3 4 5))
        (cooper (amb 1 2 3 4 5))
        (fletcher (amb 1 2 3 4 5))
        (miller (amb 1 2 3 4 5))
        (smith (amb 1 2 3 4 5)))
    (require
     (distinct? (list baker cooper fletcher miller smith)))
    (require (not (= baker 5)))
    (require (not (= cooper 1)))
    (require (not (= fletcher 5)))
    (require (not (= fletcher 1)))
    (require (> miller cooper))
    (require (not (= (abs (- smith fletcher)) 1)))
    (require (not (= (abs (- fletcher cooper)) 1)))
    (list (list 'baker baker)
          (list 'cooper cooper)
          (list 'fletcher fletcher)
          (list 'miller miller)
          (list 'smith smith))))
```

Evaluating the expression (multiple-dwelling) produces the result

```
((baker 3) (cooper 2) (fletcher 4) (miller 5) (smith 1))
```

Although this simple procedure works, it is very slow. Exercises 4.39 and 4.40 discuss some possible improvements.

Exercise 4.38

Modify the multiple-dwelling procedure to omit the requirement that Smith and Fletcher do not live on adjacent floors. How many solutions are there to this modified puzzle?

Exercise 4.39

Does the order of the restrictions in the multiple-dwelling procedure affect the answer? Does it affect the time to find an answer? If you think it matters, demonstrate a faster program obtained from the given one by reordering the restrictions. If you think it does not matter, argue your case.

Exercise 4.40

In the multiple dwelling problem, how many sets of assignments are there of people to floors, both before and after the requirement that floor assignments be distinct? It is very inefficient to generate all possible assignments of people to floors and then leave it to backtracking to eliminate them. For example, most of the restrictions depend on only one or two of the person-floor variables, and can thus be imposed before floors have been selected for all the people. Write and demonstrate a much more efficient nondeterministic procedure that solves this problem based upon generating only those possibilities that are not already ruled out by previous restrictions. (Hint: This will require a nest of let expressions.)

Exercise 4.41

Write an ordinary Scheme program to solve the multiple dwelling puzzle.

Exercise 4.42

Solve the following "Liars" puzzle (from Phillips 1934):

Five schoolgirls sat for an examination. Their parents—so they thought—
showed an undue degree of interest in the result. They therefore agreed
that, in writing home about the examination, each girl should make one
true statement and one untrue one. The following are the relevant passages
from their letters:

- Betty: "Kitty was second in the examination. I was only third."
- Ethel: "You'll be glad to hear that I was on top. Joan was second."
- Joan: "I was third, and poor old Ethel was bottom."
- Kitty: "I came out second. Mary was only fourth."
- Mary: "I was fourth. Top place was taken by Betty."

What in fact was the order in which the five girls were placed?

Exercise 4.43

Use the amb evaluator to solve the following puzzle:[49]

Mary Ann Moore's father has a yacht and so has each of his four friends:
Colonel Downing, Mr. Hall, Sir Barnacle Hood, and Dr. Parker. Each of
the five also has one daughter and each has named his yacht after a daughter of one of the others. Sir Barnacle's yacht is the Gabrielle, Mr. Moore
owns the Lorna; Mr. Hall the Rosalind. The Melissa, owned by Colonel
Downing, is named after Sir Barnacle's daughter. Gabrielle's father owns
the yacht that is named after Dr. Parker's daughter. Who is Lorna's father?

Try to write the program so that it runs efficiently (see exercise 4.40). Also
determine how many solutions there are if we are not told that Mary Ann's last
name is Moore.

Exercise 4.44

Exercise 2.42 described the "eight-queens puzzle" of placing queens on a chessboard so that no two attack each other. Write a nondeterministic program to
solve this puzzle.

Parsing natural language

Programs designed to accept natural language as input usually start by
attempting to *parse* the input, that is, to match the input against some
grammatical structure. For example, we might try to recognize simple

---

[49]This is taken from a booklet called "Problematical Recreations," published in the 1960s
by Litton Industries, where it is attributed to the *Kansas State Engineer*.

sentences consisting of an article followed by a noun followed by a verb, such as "The cat eats." To accomplish such an analysis, we must be able to identify the parts of speech of individual words. We could start with some lists that classify various words:[50]

```
(define nouns '(noun student professor cat class))

(define verbs '(verb studies lectures eats sleeps))

(define articles '(article the a))
```

We also need a *grammar*, that is, a set of rules describing how grammatical elements are composed from simpler elements. A very simple grammar might stipulate that a sentence always consists of two pieces— a noun phrase followed by a verb—and that a noun phrase consists of an article followed by a noun. With this grammar, the sentence "The cat eats" is parsed as follows:

```
(sentence (noun-phrase (article the) (noun cat))
          (verb eats))
```

We can generate such a parse with a simple program that has separate procedures for each of the grammatical rules. To parse a sentence, we identify its two constituent pieces and return a list of these two elements, tagged with the symbol `sentence`:

```
(define (parse-sentence)
  (list 'sentence
        (parse-noun-phrase)
        (parse-word verbs)))
```

A noun phrase, similarly, is parsed by finding an article followed by a noun:

```
(define (parse-noun-phrase)
  (list 'noun-phrase
        (parse-word articles)
        (parse-word nouns)))
```

At the lowest level, parsing boils down to repeatedly checking that the next unparsed word is a member of the list of words for the required part of speech. To implement this, we maintain a global variable

---

[50]Here we use the convention that the first element of each list designates the part of speech for the rest of the words in the list.

unparsed, which is the input that has not yet been parsed. Each time
we check a word, we require that *unparsed* must be non-empty and
that it should begin with a word from the designated list. If so, we remove that word from *unparsed* and return the word together with its
part of speech (which is found at the head of the list):[51]

```
(define (parse-word word-list)
  (require (not (null? *unparsed*)))
  (require (memq (car *unparsed*) (cdr word-list)))
  (let ((found-word (car *unparsed*)))
    (set! *unparsed* (cdr *unparsed*))
    (list (car word-list) found-word)))
```

To start the parsing, all we need to do is set *unparsed* to be the
entire input, try to parse a sentence, and check that nothing is left over:

```
(define *unparsed* '())

(define (parse input)
  (set! *unparsed* input)
  (let ((sent (parse-sentence)))
    (require (null? *unparsed*))
    sent))
```

We can now try the parser and verify that it works for our simple test
sentence:

```
;;; Amb-Eval input:
(parse '(the cat eats))
;;; Starting a new problem
;;; Amb-Eval value:
(sentence (noun-phrase (article the) (noun cat)) (verb eats))
```

The amb evaluator is useful here because it is convenient to express
the parsing constraints with the aid of require. Automatic search and
backtracking really pay off, however, when we consider more complex
grammars where there are choices for how the units can be decomposed.

Let's add to our grammar a list of prepositions:

```
(define prepositions '(prep for to in by with))
```

---

[51]Notice that parse-word uses set! to modify the unparsed input list. For this to work,
our amb evaluator must undo the effects of set! operations when it backtracks.

and define a prepositional phrase (e.g., "for the cat") to be a preposition followed by a noun phrase:

```
(define (parse-prepositional-phrase)
  (list 'prep-phrase
        (parse-word prepositions)
        (parse-noun-phrase)))
```

Now we can define a sentence to be a noun phrase followed by a verb phrase, where a verb phrase can be either a verb or a verb phrase extended by a prepositional phrase:[52]

```
(define (parse-sentence)
  (list 'sentence
        (parse-noun-phrase)
        (parse-verb-phrase)))

(define (parse-verb-phrase)
  (define (maybe-extend verb-phrase)
    (amb verb-phrase
         (maybe-extend (list 'verb-phrase
                             verb-phrase
                             (parse-prepositional-phrase)))))
  (maybe-extend (parse-word verbs)))
```

While we're at it, we can also elaborate the definition of noun phrases to permit such things as "a cat in the class." What we used to call a noun phrase, we'll now call a simple noun phrase, and a noun phrase will now be either a simple noun phrase or a noun phrase extended by a prepositional phrase:

```
(define (parse-simple-noun-phrase)
  (list 'simple-noun-phrase
        (parse-word articles)
        (parse-word nouns)))

(define (parse-noun-phrase)
  (define (maybe-extend noun-phrase)
    (amb noun-phrase
         (maybe-extend (list 'noun-phrase
                             noun-phrase
                             (parse-prepositional-phrase)))))
  (maybe-extend (parse-simple-noun-phrase)))
```

---

[52]Observe that this definition is recursive—a verb may be followed by any number of prepositional phrases.

Our new grammar lets us parse more complex sentences. For example

```
(parse '(the student with the cat sleeps in the class))
```

produces

```
(sentence
 (noun-phrase
  (simple-noun-phrase (article the) (noun student))
  (prep-phrase (prep with)
               (simple-noun-phrase
                (article the) (noun cat))))
 (verb-phrase
  (verb sleeps)
  (prep-phrase (prep in)
               (simple-noun-phrase
                (article the) (noun class)))))
```

Observe that a given input may have more than one legal parse. In the sentence "The professor lectures to the student with the cat," it may be that the professor is lecturing with the cat, or that the student has the cat. Our nondeterministic program finds both possibilities:

```
(parse '(the professor lectures to the student with the cat))
```

produces

```
(sentence
 (simple-noun-phrase (article the) (noun professor))
 (verb-phrase
  (verb-phrase
   (verb lectures)
   (prep-phrase (prep to)
                (simple-noun-phrase
                 (article the) (noun student))))
  (prep-phrase (prep with)
               (simple-noun-phrase
                (article the) (noun cat)))))
```

Asking the evaluator to try again yields

```
(sentence
 (simple-noun-phrase (article the) (noun professor))
 (verb-phrase
  (verb lectures)
  (prep-phrase (prep to)
               (noun-phrase
                (simple-noun-phrase
                 (article the) (noun student))
                (prep-phrase (prep with)
                             (simple-noun-phrase
                              (article the) (noun cat)))))))
```

Exercise 4.45

With the grammar given above, the following sentence can be parsed in five different ways: "The professor lectures to the student in the class with the cat." Give the five parses and explain the differences in shades of meaning among them.

Exercise 4.46

The evaluators in sections 4.1 and 4.2 do not determine what order operands are evaluated in. We will see that the amb evaluator evaluates them from left to right. Explain why our parsing program wouldn't work if the operands were evaluated in some other order.

Exercise 4.47

Louis Reasoner suggests that, since a verb phrase is either a verb or a verb phrase followed by a prepositional phrase, it would be much more straightforward to define the procedure parse-verb-phrase as follows (and similarly for noun phrases):

```
(define (parse-verb-phrase)
  (amb (parse-word verbs)
       (list 'verb-phrase
             (parse-verb-phrase)
             (parse-prepositional-phrase))))
```

Does this work? Does the program's behavior change if we interchange the order of expressions in the amb?

Exercise 4.48

Extend the grammar given above to handle more complex sentences. For example, you could extend noun phrases and verb phrases to include adjectives and adverbs, or you could handle compound sentences.[53]

Exercise 4.49

Alyssa P. Hacker is more interested in generating interesting sentences than in parsing them. She reasons that by simply changing the procedure `parse-word` so that it ignores the "input sentence" and instead always succeeds and generates an appropriate word, we can use the programs we had built for parsing to do generation instead. Implement Alyssa's idea, and show the first half-dozen or so sentences generated.[54]

4.3.3   Implementing the Amb Evaluator

The evaluation of an ordinary Scheme expression may return a value, may never terminate, or may signal an error. In nondeterministic Scheme the evaluation of an expression may in addition result in the discovery of a dead end, in which case evaluation must backtrack to a previous choice point. The interpretation of nondeterministic Scheme is complicated by this extra case.

We will construct the amb evaluator for nondeterministic Scheme by modifying the analyzing evaluator of section 4.1.7.[55] As in the analyzing evaluator, evaluation of an expression is accomplished by calling an execution procedure produced by analysis of that expression. The difference between the interpretation of ordinary Scheme and the interpretation of nondeterministic Scheme will be entirely in the execution procedures.

---

[53]This kind of grammar can become arbitrarily complex, but it is only a toy as far as real language understanding is concerned. Real natural-language understanding by computer requires an elaborate mixture of syntactic analysis and interpretation of meaning. On the other hand, even toy parsers can be useful in supporting flexible command languages for programs such as information-retrieval systems. Winston 1992 discusses computational approaches to real language understanding and also the applications of simple grammars to command languages.

[54]Although Alyssa's idea works just fine (and is surprisingly simple), the sentences that it generates are a bit boring—they don't sample the possible sentences of this language in a very interesting way. In fact, the grammar is highly recursive in many places, and Alyssa's technique "falls into" one of these recursions and gets stuck. See exercise 4.50 for a way to deal with this.

[55]We chose to implement the lazy evaluator in section 4.2 as a modification of the ordinary metacircular evaluator of section 4.1.1. In contrast, we will base the amb evaluator on the analyzing evaluator of section 4.1.7, because the execution procedures in that evaluator provide a convenient framework for implementing backtracking.

Execution procedures and continuations

Recall that the execution procedures for the ordinary evaluator take one argument: the environment of execution. In contrast, the execution procedures in the amb evaluator take three arguments: the environment, and two procedures called *continuation procedures*. The evaluation of an expression will finish by calling one of these two continuations: If the evaluation results in a value, the *success continuation* is called with that value; if the evaluation results in the discovery of a dead end, the *failure continuation* is called. Constructing and calling appropriate continuations is the mechanism by which the nondeterministic evaluator implements backtracking.

It is the job of the success continuation to receive a value and proceed with the computation. Along with that value, the success continuation is passed another failure continuation, which is to be called subsequently if the use of that value leads to a dead end.

It is the job of the failure continuation to try another branch of the nondeterministic process. The essence of the nondeterministic language is in the fact that expressions may represent choices among alternatives. The evaluation of such an expression must proceed with one of the indicated alternative choices, even though it is not known in advance which choices will lead to acceptable results. To deal with this, the evaluator picks one of the alternatives and passes this value to the success continuation. Together with this value, the evaluator constructs and passes along a failure continuation that can be called later to choose a different alternative.

A failure is triggered during evaluation (that is, a failure continuation is called) when a user program explicitly rejects the current line of attack (for example, a call to `require` may result in execution of (amb), an expression that always fails—see section 4.3.1). The failure continuation in hand at that point will cause the most recent choice point to choose another alternative. If there are no more alternatives to be considered at that choice point, a failure at an earlier choice point is triggered, and so on. Failure continuations are also invoked by the driver loop in response to a `try-again` request, to find another value of the expression.

In addition, if a side-effect operation (such as assignment to a variable) occurs on a branch of the process resulting from a choice, it may be necessary, when the process finds a dead end, to undo the side effect before making a new choice. This is accomplished by having the side-effect operation produce a failure continuation that undoes the side effect and propagates the failure.

In summary, failure continuations are constructed by

• amb expressions—to provide a mechanism to make alternative choices if the current choice made by the amb expression leads to a dead end;

• the top-level driver—to provide a mechanism to report failure when the choices are exhausted;

• assignments—to intercept failures and undo assignments during back-tracking.

Failures are initiated only when a dead end is encountered. This occurs

• if the user program executes (amb);

• if the user types try-again at the top-level driver.

Failure continuations are also called during processing of a failure:

• When the failure continuation created by an assignment finishes undoing a side effect, it calls the failure continuation it intercepted, in order to propagate the failure back to the choice point that led to this assignment or to the top level.

• When the failure continuation for an amb runs out of choices, it calls the failure continuation that was originally given to the amb, in order to propagate the failure back to the previous choice point or to the top level.

Structure of the evaluator

The syntax- and data-representation procedures for the amb evaluator, and also the basic analyze procedure, are identical to those in the evaluator of section 4.1.7, except for the fact that we need additional syntax procedures to recognize the amb special form:[56]

```
(define (amb? exp) (tagged-list? exp 'amb))
```

```
(define (amb-choices exp) (cdr exp))
```

We must also add to the dispatch in analyze a clause that will recognize this special form and generate an appropriate execution procedure:

```
((amb? exp) (analyze-amb exp))
```

---

[56]We assume that the evaluator supports let (see exercise 4.22), which we have used in our nondeterministic programs.

The top-level procedure ambeval (similar to the version of eval given in section 4.1.7) analyzes the given expression and applies the resulting execution procedure to the given environment, together with two given continuations:

```
(define (ambeval exp env succeed fail)
  ((analyze exp) env succeed fail))
```

A success continuation is a procedure of two arguments: the value just obtained and another failure continuation to be used if that value leads to a subsequent failure. A failure continuation is a procedure of no arguments. So the general form of an execution procedure is

```
(lambda (env succeed fail)
  ;; succeed is (lambda (value fail) ...)
  ;; fail is (lambda () ...)
  ...)
```

For example, executing

```
(ambeval ⟨exp⟩
         the-global-environment
         (lambda (value fail) value)
         (lambda () 'failed))
```

will attempt to evaluate the given expression and will return either the expression's value (if the evaluation succeeds) or the symbol failed (if the evaluation fails). The call to ambeval in the driver loop shown below uses much more complicated continuation procedures, which continue the loop and support the try-again request.

Most of the complexity of the amb evaluator results from the mechanics of passing the continuations around as the execution procedures call each other. In going through the following code, you should compare each of the execution procedures with the corresponding procedure for the ordinary evaluator given in section 4.1.7.

Simple expressions

The execution procedures for the simplest kinds of expressions are essentially the same as those for the ordinary evaluator, except for the need to manage the continuations. The execution procedures simply succeed with the value of the expression, passing along the failure continuation that was passed to them.

```
(define (analyze-self-evaluating exp)
  (lambda (env succeed fail)
    (succeed exp fail)))

(define (analyze-quoted exp)
  (let ((qval (text-of-quotation exp)))
    (lambda (env succeed fail)
      (succeed qval fail))))

(define (analyze-variable exp)
  (lambda (env succeed fail)
    (succeed (lookup-variable-value exp env)
             fail)))

(define (analyze-lambda exp)
  (let ((vars (lambda-parameters exp))
        (bproc (analyze-sequence (lambda-body exp))))
    (lambda (env succeed fail)
      (succeed (make-procedure vars bproc env)
               fail))))
```

Notice that looking up a variable always "succeeds." If lookup-variable-value fails to find the variable, it signals an error, as usual. Such a "failure" indicates a program bug—a reference to an unbound variable; it is not an indication that we should try another nondeterministic choice instead of the one that is currently being tried.

Conditionals and sequences

Conditionals are also handled in a similar way as in the ordinary evaluator. The execution procedure generated by analyze-if invokes the predicate execution procedure pproc with a success continuation that checks whether the predicate value is true and goes on to execute either the consequent or the alternative. If the execution of pproc fails, the original failure continuation for the if expression is called.

```
(define (analyze-if exp)
  (let ((pproc (analyze (if-predicate exp)))
        (cproc (analyze (if-consequent exp)))
        (aproc (analyze (if-alternative exp))))
    (lambda (env succeed fail)
      (pproc env
             ;; success continuation for evaluating the predicate
             ;; to obtain pred-value
             (lambda (pred-value fail2)
               (if (true? pred-value)
                   (cproc env succeed fail2)
                   (aproc env succeed fail2)))
             ;; failure continuation for evaluating the predicate
             fail))))
```

Sequences are also handled in the same way as in the previous evaluator, except for the machinations in the subprocedure `sequentially` that are required for passing the continuations. Namely, to sequentially execute a and then b, we call a with a success continuation that calls b.

```
(define (analyze-sequence exps)
  (define (sequentially a b)
    (lambda (env succeed fail)
      (a env
          ;; success continuation for calling a
          (lambda (a-value fail2)
            (b env succeed fail2))
          ;; failure continuation for calling a
          fail)))
  (define (loop first-proc rest-procs)
    (if (null? rest-procs)
        first-proc
        (loop (sequentially first-proc (car rest-procs))
              (cdr rest-procs))))
  (let ((procs (map analyze exps)))
    (if (null? procs)
        (error "Empty sequence -- ANALYZE"))
    (loop (car procs) (cdr procs))))
```

Definitions and assignments

Definitions are another case where we must go to some trouble to manage the continuations, because it is necessary to evaluate the definition-value expression before actually defining the new variable. To accomplish this, the definition-value execution procedure `vproc` is called with the environment, a success continuation, and the failure continuation. If the execution of `vproc` succeeds, obtaining a value `val` for the defined variable, the variable is defined and the success is propagated:

```
(define (analyze-definition exp)
  (let ((var (definition-variable exp))
        (vproc (analyze (definition-value exp))))
    (lambda (env succeed fail)
      (vproc env
             (lambda (val fail2)
               (define-variable! var val env)
               (succeed 'ok fail2))
             fail))))
```

Assignments are more interesting. This is the first place where we really use the continuations, rather than just passing them around. The execution procedure for assignments starts out like the one for definitions. It first attempts to obtain the new value to be assigned to the variable. If this evaluation of vproc fails, the assignment fails.

If vproc succeeds, however, and we go on to make the assignment, we must consider the possibility that this branch of the computation might later fail, which will require us to backtrack out of the assignment. Thus, we must arrange to undo the assignment as part of the backtracking process.[57]

This is accomplished by giving vproc a success continuation (marked with the comment "*1*" below) that saves the old value of the variable before assigning the new value to the variable and proceeding from the assignment. The failure continuation that is passed along with the value of the assignment (marked with the comment "*2*" below) restores the old value of the variable before continuing the failure. That is, a successful assignment provides a failure continuation that will intercept a subsequent failure; whatever failure would otherwise have called fail2 calls this procedure instead, to undo the assignment before actually calling fail2.

```
(define (analyze-assignment exp)
  (let ((var (assignment-variable exp))
        (vproc (analyze (assignment-value exp))))
    (lambda (env succeed fail)
      (vproc env
             (lambda (val fail2)         ; *1*
               (let ((old-value
                      (lookup-variable-value var env)))
                 (set-variable-value! var val env)
                 (succeed 'ok
                          (lambda ()      ; *2*
                            (set-variable-value! var
                                                 old-value
                                                 env)
                            (fail2)))))
             fail))))
```

---

[57] We didn't worry about undoing definitions, since we can assume that internal definitions are scanned out (section 4.1.6).

Procedure applications

The execution procedure for applications contains no new ideas except for the technical complexity of managing the continuations. This complexity arises in analyze-application, due to the need to keep track of the success and failure continuations as we evaluate the operands. We use a procedure get-args to evaluate the list of operands, rather than a simple map as in the ordinary evaluator.

```
(define (analyze-application exp)
  (let ((fproc (analyze (operator exp)))
        (aprocs (map analyze (operands exp))))
    (lambda (env succeed fail)
      (fproc env
             (lambda (proc fail2)
               (get-args aprocs
                         env
                         (lambda (args fail3)
                           (execute-application
                            proc args succeed fail3))
                         fail2))
             fail))))
```

In get-args, notice how cdring down the list of aproc execution procedures and consing up the resulting list of args is accomplished by calling each aproc in the list with a success continuation that recursively calls get-args. Each of these recursive calls to get-args has a success continuation whose value is the cons of the newly obtained argument onto the list of accumulated arguments:

```
(define (get-args aprocs env succeed fail)
  (if (null? aprocs)
      (succeed '() fail)
      ((car aprocs) env
                    ;; success continuation for this aproc
                    (lambda (arg fail2)
                      (get-args (cdr aprocs)
                                env
                                ;; success continuation for recursive
                                ;; call to get-args
                                (lambda (args fail3)
                                  (succeed (cons arg args)
                                           fail3))
                                fail2))
                    fail)))
```

The actual procedure application, which is performed by execute-application, is accomplished in the same way as for the ordinary evaluator, except for the need to manage the continuations.

```
(define (execute-application proc args succeed fail)
  (cond ((primitive-procedure? proc)
         (succeed (apply-primitive-procedure proc args)
                  fail))
        ((compound-procedure? proc)
         ((procedure-body proc)
          (extend-environment (procedure-parameters proc)
                              args
                              (procedure-environment proc))
          succeed
          fail))
        (else
         (error
          "Unknown procedure type -- EXECUTE-APPLICATION"
          proc))))
```

Evaluating amb expressions

The amb special form is the key element in the nondeterministic language. Here we see the essence of the interpretation process and the reason for keeping track of the continuations. The execution procedure for amb defines a loop try-next that cycles through the execution procedures for all the possible values of the amb expression. Each execution procedure is called with a failure continuation that will try the next one. When there are no more alternatives to try, the entire amb expression fails.

```
(define (analyze-amb exp)
  (let ((cprocs (map analyze (amb-choices exp))))
    (lambda (env succeed fail)
      (define (try-next choices)
        (if (null? choices)
            (fail)
            ((car choices) env
                           succeed
                           (lambda ()
                             (try-next (cdr choices))))))
      (try-next cprocs))))
```

Driver loop

The driver loop for the amb evaluator is complex, due to the mechanism that permits the user to try again in evaluating an expression. The driver uses a procedure called internal-loop, which takes as argument a procedure try-again. The intent is that calling try-again should go on to the next untried alternative in the nondeterministic evaluation. Internal-loop either calls try-again in response to the user typing try-again at the driver loop, or else starts a new evaluation by calling ambeval.

The failure continuation for this call to ambeval informs the user that there are no more values and re-invokes the driver loop.

The success continuation for the call to ambeval is more subtle. We print the obtained value and then invoke the internal loop again with a try-again procedure that will be able to try the next alternative. This next-alternative procedure is the second argument that was passed to the success continuation. Ordinarily, we think of this second argument as a failure continuation to be used if the current evaluation branch later fails. In this case, however, we have completed a successful evaluation, so we can invoke the "failure" alternative branch in order to search for additional successful evaluations.

```
(define input-prompt ";;; Amb-Eval input:")
(define output-prompt ";;; Amb-Eval value:")

(define (driver-loop)
  (define (internal-loop try-again)
    (prompt-for-input input-prompt)
    (let ((input (read)))
      (if (eq? input 'try-again)
          (try-again)
          (begin
            (newline)
            (display ";;; Starting a new problem ")
            (ambeval input
                     the-global-environment
                     ;; ambeval success
                     (lambda (val next-alternative)
                       (announce-output output-prompt)
                       (user-print val)
                       (internal-loop next-alternative))
                     ;; ambeval failure
                     (lambda ()
                       (announce-output
                        ";;; There are no more values of")
                       (user-print input)
                       (driver-loop)))))))
  (internal-loop
   (lambda ()
     (newline)
     (display ";;; There is no current problem")
     (driver-loop))))
```

The initial call to `internal-loop` uses a `try-again` procedure that complains that there is no current problem and restarts the driver loop. This is the behavior that will happen if the user types `try-again` when there is no evaluation in progress.

Exercise 4.50

Implement a new special form `ramb` that is like `amb` except that it searches alternatives in a random order, rather than from left to right. Show how this can help with Alyssa's problem in exercise 4.49.

Exercise 4.51

Implement a new kind of assignment called `permanent-set!` that is not undone upon failure. For example, we can choose two distinct elements from a list and count the number of trials required to make a successful choice as follows:

```
(define count 0)

(let ((x (an-element-of '(a b c)))
      (y (an-element-of '(a b c))))
  (permanent-set! count (+ count 1))
  (require (not (eq? x y)))
  (list x y count))
;;; Starting a new problem
;;; Amb-Eval value:
(a b 2)

;;; Amb-Eval input:
try-again
;;; Amb-Eval value:
(a c 3)
```

What values would have been displayed if we had used `set!` here rather than `permanent-set!`?

Exercise 4.52

Implement a new construct called `if-fail` that permits the user to catch the failure of an expression. `If-fail` takes two expressions. It evaluates the first expression as usual and returns as usual if the evaluation succeeds. If the evaluation fails, however, the value of the second expression is returned, as in the following example:

```
;;; Amb-Eval input:
(if-fail (let ((x (an-element-of '(1 3 5))))
           (require (even? x))
           x)
         'all-odd)
;;; Starting a new problem
;;; Amb-Eval value:
all-odd
```

```
;;; Amb-Eval input:
(if-fail (let ((x (an-element-of '(1 3 5 8))))
           (require (even? x))
           x)
         'all-odd)
;;; Starting a new problem
;;; Amb-Eval value:
8
```

Exercise 4.53

With `permanent-set!` as described in exercise 4.51 and `if-fail` as in exercise 4.52, what will be the result of evaluating

```
(let ((pairs '()))
  (if-fail (let ((p (prime-sum-pair '(1 3 5 8) '(20 35 110))))
             (permanent-set! pairs (cons p pairs))
             (amb))
           pairs))
```

Exercise 4.54

If we had not realized that `require` could be implemented as an ordinary procedure that uses amb, to be defined by the user as part of a nondeterministic program, we would have had to implement it as a special form. This would require syntax procedures

```
(define (require? exp) (tagged-list? exp 'require))
```

```
(define (require-predicate exp) (cadr exp))
```

and a new clause in the dispatch in `analyze`

```
((require? exp) (analyze-require exp))
```

as well the procedure `analyze-require` that handles `require` expressions. Complete the following definition of `analyze-require`.

```
(define (analyze-require exp)
  (let ((pproc (analyze (require-predicate exp))))
    (lambda (env succeed fail)
      (pproc env
             (lambda (pred-value fail2)
               (if ⟨??⟩
                   ⟨??⟩
                   (succeed 'ok fail2)))
             fail))))
```

4.4   Logic Programming

In chapter 1 we stressed that computer science deals with imperative (how to) knowledge, whereas mathematics deals with declarative (what is) knowledge. Indeed, programming languages require that the programmer express knowledge in a form that indicates the step-by-step methods for solving particular problems. On the other hand, high-level languages provide, as part of the language implementation, a substantial amount of methodological knowledge that frees the user from concern with numerous details of how a specified computation will progress.

Most programming languages, including Lisp, are organized around computing the values of mathematical functions. Expression-oriented languages (such as Lisp, Fortran, and Algol) capitalize on the "pun" that an expression that describes the value of a function may also be interpreted as a means of computing that value. Because of this, most programming languages are strongly biased toward unidirectional computations (computations with well-defined inputs and outputs). There are, however, radically different programming languages that relax this bias. We saw one such example in section 3.3.5, where the objects of computation were arithmetic constraints. In a constraint system the direction and the order of computation are not so well specified; in carrying out a computation the system must therefore provide more detailed "how to" knowledge than would be the case with an ordinary arithmetic computation. This does not mean, however, that the user is released altogether from the responsibility of providing imperative knowledge. There are many constraint networks that implement the same set of constraints, and the user must choose from the set of mathematically equivalent networks a suitable network to specify a particular computation.

The nondeterministic program evaluator of section 4.3 also moves away from the view that programming is about constructing algorithms for computing unidirectional functions. In a nondeterministic language, expressions can have more than one value, and, as a result, the computation is dealing with relations rather than with single-valued functions. Logic programming extends this idea by combining a relational vision of programming with a powerful kind of symbolic pattern matching called *unification.*[58]

---

[58]Logic programming has grown out of a long history of research in automatic theorem proving. Early theorem-proving programs could accomplish very little, because they exhaustively searched the space of possible proofs. The major breakthrough that made such

This approach, when it works, can be a very powerful way to write programs. Part of the power comes from the fact that a single "what is" fact can be used to solve a number of different problems that would have different "how to" components. As an example, consider the append operation, which takes two lists as arguments and combines their elements to form a single list. In a procedural language such as Lisp, we could define append in terms of the basic list constructor cons, as we did in section 2.2.1:

```
(define (append x y)
  (if (null? x)
      y
      (cons (car x) (append (cdr x) y))))
```

This procedure can be regarded as a translation into Lisp of the following two rules, the first of which covers the case where the first list is empty and the second of which handles the case of a nonempty list, which is a cons of two parts:

- For any list y, the empty list and y append to form y.

- For any u, v, y, and z, (cons u v) and y append to form (cons u z) if v and y append to form z.[59]

---

a search plausible was the discovery in the early 1960s of the *unification algorithm* and the *resolution principle* (Robinson 1965). Resolution was used, for example, by Green and Raphael (1968) (see also Green 1969) as the basis for a deductive question-answering system. During most of this period, researchers concentrated on algorithms that are guaranteed to find a proof if one exists. Such algorithms were difficult to control and to direct toward a proof. Hewitt (1969) recognized the possibility of merging the control structure of a programming language with the operations of a logic-manipulation system, leading to the work in automatic search mentioned in section 4.3.1 (footnote 47). At the same time that this was being done, Colmerauer, in Marseille, was developing rule-based systems for manipulating natural language (see Colmerauer et al. 1973). He invented a programming language called Prolog for representing those rules. Kowalski (1973; 1979), in Edinburgh, recognized that execution of a Prolog program could be interpreted as proving theorems (using a proof technique called linear Horn-clause resolution). The merging of the last two strands led to the logic-programming movement. Thus, in assigning credit for the development of logic programming, the French can point to Prolog's genesis at the University of Marseille, while the British can highlight the work at the University of Edinburgh. According to people at MIT, logic programming was developed by these groups in an attempt to figure out what Hewitt was talking about in his brilliant but impenetrable Ph.D. thesis. For a history of logic programming, see Robinson 1983.

[59]To see the correspondence between the rules and the procedure, let x in the procedure (where x is nonempty) correspond to (cons u v) in the rule. Then z in the rule corresponds to the append of (cdr x) and y.

Using the append procedure, we can answer questions such as

Find the append of (a b) and (c d).

But the same two rules are also sufficient for answering the following sorts of questions, which the procedure can't answer:

Find a list y that appends with (a b) to produce (a b c d).

Find all x and y that append to form (a b c d).

In a logic programming language, the programmer writes an append "procedure" by stating the two rules about append given above. "How to" knowledge is provided automatically by the interpreter to allow this single pair of rules to be used to answer all three types of questions about append.[60]

Contemporary logic programming languages (including the one we implement here) have substantial deficiencies, in that their general "how to" methods can lead them into spurious infinite loops or other undesirable behavior. Logic programming is an active field of research in computer science.[61]

Earlier in this chapter we explored the technology of implementing interpreters and described the elements that are essential to an interpreter for a Lisp-like language (indeed, to an interpreter for any conventional language). Now we will apply these ideas to discuss an interpreter for a logic programming language. We call this language the *query language*, because it is very useful for retrieving information from data bases by for-

---

[60]This certainly does not relieve the user of the entire problem of how to compute the answer. There are many different mathematically equivalent sets of rules for formulating the append relation, only some of which can be turned into effective devices for computing in any direction. In addition, sometimes "what is" information gives no clue "how to" compute an answer. For example, consider the problem of computing the y such that $y^2 = x$.

[61]Interest in logic programming peaked during the early 80s when the Japanese government began an ambitious project aimed at building superfast computers optimized to run logic programming languages. The speed of such computers was to be measured in LIPS (Logical Inferences Per Second) rather than the usual FLOPS (FLoating-point Operations Per Second). Although the project succeeded in developing hardware and software as originally planned, the international computer industry moved in a different direction. See Feigenbaum and Shrobe 1993 for an overview evaluation of the Japanese project. The logic programming community has also moved on to consider relational programming based on techniques other than simple pattern matching, such as the ability to deal with numerical constraints such as the ones illustrated in the constraint-propagation system of section 3.3.5.

mulating *queries*, or questions, expressed in the language. Even though the query language is very different from Lisp, we will find it convenient to describe the language in terms of the same general framework we have been using all along: as a collection of primitive elements, together with means of combination that enable us to combine simple elements to create more complex elements and means of abstraction that enable us to regard complex elements as single conceptual units. An interpreter for a logic programming language is considerably more complex than an interpreter for a language like Lisp. Nevertheless, we will see that our query-language interpreter contains many of the same elements found in the interpreter of section 4.1. In particular, there will be an "eval" part that classifies expressions according to type and an "apply" part that implements the language's abstraction mechanism (procedures in the case of Lisp, and *rules* in the case of logic programming). Also, a central role is played in the implementation by a frame data structure, which determines the correspondence between symbols and their associated values. One additional interesting aspect of our query-language implementation is that we make substantial use of streams, which were introduced in chapter 3.

4.4.1   Deductive Information Retrieval

Logic programming excels in providing interfaces to data bases for information retrieval. The query language we shall implement in this chapter is designed to be used in this way.

In order to illustrate what the query system does, we will show how it can be used to manage the data base of personnel records for Microshaft, a thriving high-technology company in the Boston area. The language provides pattern-directed access to personnel information and can also take advantage of general rules in order to make logical deductions.

A sample data base

The personnel data base for Microshaft contains *assertions* about company personnel. Here is the information about Ben Bitdiddle, the resident computer wizard:

```
(address (Bitdiddle Ben) (Slumerville (Ridge Road) 10))
(job (Bitdiddle Ben) (computer wizard))
(salary (Bitdiddle Ben) 60000)
```

Each assertion is a list (in this case a triple) whose elements can themselves be lists.

As resident wizard, Ben is in charge of the company's computer division, and he supervises two programmers and one technician. Here is the information about them:

```
(address (Hacker Alyssa P) (Cambridge (Mass Ave) 78))
(job (Hacker Alyssa P) (computer programmer))
(salary (Hacker Alyssa P) 40000)
(supervisor (Hacker Alyssa P) (Bitdiddle Ben))

(address (Fect Cy D) (Cambridge (Ames Street) 3))
(job (Fect Cy D) (computer programmer))
(salary (Fect Cy D) 35000)
(supervisor (Fect Cy D) (Bitdiddle Ben))

(address (Tweakit Lem E) (Boston (Bay State Road) 22))
(job (Tweakit Lem E) (computer technician))
(salary (Tweakit Lem E) 25000)
(supervisor (Tweakit Lem E) (Bitdiddle Ben))
```

There is also a programmer trainee, who is supervised by Alyssa:

```
(address (Reasoner Louis) (Slumerville (Pine Tree Road) 80))
(job (Reasoner Louis) (computer programmer trainee))
(salary (Reasoner Louis) 30000)
(supervisor (Reasoner Louis) (Hacker Alyssa P))
```

All of these people are in the computer division, as indicated by the word `computer` as the first item in their job descriptions.

Ben is a high-level employee. His supervisor is the company's big wheel himself:

```
(supervisor (Bitdiddle Ben) (Warbucks Oliver))

(address (Warbucks Oliver) (Swellesley (Top Heap Road)))
(job (Warbucks Oliver) (administration big wheel))
(salary (Warbucks Oliver) 150000)
```

Besides the computer division supervised by Ben, the company has an accounting division, consisting of a chief accountant and his assistant:

```
(address (Scrooge Eben) (Weston (Shady Lane) 10))
(job (Scrooge Eben) (accounting chief accountant))
(salary (Scrooge Eben) 75000)
(supervisor (Scrooge Eben) (Warbucks Oliver))
```

```
(address (Cratchet Robert) (Allston (N Harvard Street) 16))
(job (Cratchet Robert) (accounting scrivener))
(salary (Cratchet Robert) 18000)
(supervisor (Cratchet Robert) (Scrooge Eben))
```

There is also a secretary for the big wheel:

```
(address (Aull DeWitt) (Slumerville (Onion Square) 5))
(job (Aull DeWitt) (administration secretary))
(salary (Aull DeWitt) 25000)
(supervisor (Aull DeWitt) (Warbucks Oliver))
```

The data base also contains assertions about which kinds of jobs can be done by people holding other kinds of jobs. For instance, a computer wizard can do the jobs of both a computer programmer and a computer technician:

```
(can-do-job (computer wizard) (computer programmer))
(can-do-job (computer wizard) (computer technician))
```

A computer programmer could fill in for a trainee:

```
(can-do-job (computer programmer)
            (computer programmer trainee))
```

Also, as is well known,

```
(can-do-job (administration secretary)
            (administration big wheel))
```

Simple queries

The query language allows users to retrieve information from the data base by posing queries in response to the system's prompt. For example, to find all computer programmers one can say

```
;;; Query input:
(job ?x (computer programmer))
```

The system will respond with the following items:

```
;;; Query results:
(job (Hacker Alyssa P) (computer programmer))
(job (Fect Cy D) (computer programmer))
```

The input query specifies that we are looking for entries in the data base that match a certain *pattern*. In this example, the pattern specifies entries consisting of three items, of which the first is the literal symbol job, the second can be anything, and the third is the literal list (computer programmer). The "anything" that can be the second item in the matching list is specified by a *pattern variable*, ?x. The general form of a pattern variable is a symbol, taken to be the name of the variable, preceded by a question mark. We will see below why it is useful to specify names for pattern variables rather than just putting ? into patterns to represent "anything." The system responds to a simple query by showing all entries in the data base that match the specified pattern.

A pattern can have more than one variable. For example, the query

```
(address ?x ?y)
```

will list all the employees' addresses.

A pattern can have no variables, in which case the query simply determines whether that pattern is an entry in the data base. If so, there will be one match; if not, there will be no matches.

The same pattern variable can appear more than once in a query, specifying that the same "anything" must appear in each position. This is why variables have names. For example,

```
(supervisor ?x ?x)
```

finds all people who supervise themselves (though there are no such assertions in our sample data base).

The query

```
(job ?x (computer ?type))
```

matches all job entries whose third item is a two-element list whose first item is computer:

```
(job (Bitdiddle Ben) (computer wizard))
(job (Hacker Alyssa P) (computer programmer))
(job (Fect Cy D) (computer programmer))
(job (Tweakit Lem E) (computer technician))
```

This same pattern does *not* match

```
(job (Reasoner Louis) (computer programmer trainee))
```

because the third item in the entry is a list of three elements, and the pattern's third item specifies that there should be two elements. If we wanted to change the pattern so that the third item could be any list beginning with computer, we could specify[62]

```
(job ?x (computer . ?type))
```

For example,

```
(computer . ?type)
```

matches the data

```
(computer programmer trainee)
```

with ?type as the list (programmer trainee). It also matches the data

```
(computer programmer)
```

with ?type as the list (programmer), and matches the data

```
(computer)
```

with ?type as the empty list ().

We can describe the query language's processing of simple queries as follows:

• The system finds all assignments to variables in the query pattern that *satisfy* the pattern—that is, all sets of values for the variables such that if the pattern variables are *instantiated with* (replaced by) the values, the result is in the data base.

• The system responds to the query by listing all instantiations of the query pattern with the variable assignments that satisfy it.

Note that if the pattern has no variables, the query reduces to a determination of whether that pattern is in the data base. If so, the empty assignment, which assigns no values to variables, satisfies that pattern for that data base.

---

[62]This uses the dotted-tail notation introduced in exercise 2.20.

Exercise 4.55

Give simple queries that retrieve the following information from the data base:

a. all people supervised by Ben Bitdiddle;

b. the names and jobs of all people in the accounting division;

c. the names and addresses of all people who live in Slumerville.

Compound queries

Simple queries form the primitive operations of the query language. In order to form compound operations, the query language provides means of combination. One thing that makes the query language a logic programming language is that the means of combination mirror the means of combination used in forming logical expressions: and, or, and not. (Here and, or, and not are not the Lisp primitives, but rather operations built into the query language.)

We can use and as follows to find the addresses of all the computer programmers:

```
(and (job ?person (computer programmer))
     (address ?person ?where))
```

The resulting output is

```
(and (job (Hacker Alyssa P) (computer programmer))
     (address (Hacker Alyssa P) (Cambridge (Mass Ave) 78)))
```

```
(and (job (Fect Cy D) (computer programmer))
     (address (Fect Cy D) (Cambridge (Ames Street) 3)))
```

In general,

```
(and ⟨query₁⟩ ⟨query₂⟩ ... ⟨queryₙ⟩)
```

is satisfied by all sets of values for the pattern variables that simultaneously satisfy $\langle query_1 \rangle \dots \langle query_n \rangle$.

As for simple queries, the system processes a compound query by finding all assignments to the pattern variables that satisfy the query, then displaying instantiations of the query with those values.

Another means of constructing compound queries is through or. For example,

```
(or (supervisor ?x (Bitdiddle Ben))
    (supervisor ?x (Hacker Alyssa P)))
```

will find all employees supervised by Ben Bitdiddle or Alyssa P. Hacker:

```
(or (supervisor (Hacker Alyssa P) (Bitdiddle Ben))
    (supervisor (Hacker Alyssa P) (Hacker Alyssa P)))

(or (supervisor (Fect Cy D) (Bitdiddle Ben))
    (supervisor (Fect Cy D) (Hacker Alyssa P)))

(or (supervisor (Tweakit Lem E) (Bitdiddle Ben))
    (supervisor (Tweakit Lem E) (Hacker Alyssa P)))

(or (supervisor (Reasoner Louis) (Bitdiddle Ben))
    (supervisor (Reasoner Louis) (Hacker Alyssa P)))
```

In general,

```
(or ⟨query₁⟩ ⟨query₂⟩ ... ⟨queryₙ⟩)
```

is satisfied by all sets of values for the pattern variables that satisfy at
least one of ⟨$query_1$⟩ ... ⟨$query_n$⟩.

Compound queries can also be formed with not. For example,

```
(and (supervisor ?x (Bitdiddle Ben))
     (not (job ?x (computer programmer))))
```

finds all people supervised by Ben Bitdiddle who are not computer programmers. In general,

```
(not ⟨query₁⟩)
```

is satisfied by all assignments to the pattern variables that do not satisfy
⟨$query_1$⟩.[63]

The final combining form is called lisp-value. When lisp-value
is the first element of a pattern, it specifies that the next element is a
Lisp predicate to be applied to the rest of the (instantiated) elements as
arguments. In general,

```
(lisp-value ⟨predicate⟩ ⟨arg₁⟩ ... ⟨argₙ⟩)
```

will be satisfied by assignments to the pattern variables for which the
⟨predicate⟩ applied to the instantiated ⟨arg_1⟩ ... ⟨arg_n⟩ is true. For

---

[63] Actually, this description of not is valid only for simple cases. The real behavior of not
is more complex. We will examine not's peculiarities in sections 4.4.2 and 4.4.3.

example, to find all people whose salary is greater than $30,000 we could write[64]

```
(and (salary ?person ?amount)
     (lisp-value > ?amount 30000))
```

Exercise 4.56

Formulate compound queries that retrieve the following information:

a. the names of all people who are supervised by Ben Bitdiddle, together with their addresses;

b. all people whose salary is less than Ben Bitdiddle's, together with their salary and Ben Bitdiddle's salary;

c. all people who are supervised by someone who is not in the computer division, together with the supervisor's name and job.

Rules

In addition to primitive queries and compound queries, the query language provides means for abstracting queries. These are given by *rules*. The rule

```
(rule (lives-near ?person-1 ?person-2)
      (and (address ?person-1 (?town . ?rest-1))
           (address ?person-2 (?town . ?rest-2))
           (not (same ?person-1 ?person-2))))
```

specifies that two people live near each other if they live in the same town. The final not clause prevents the rule from saying that all people live near themselves. The same relation is defined by a very simple rule:[65]

```
(rule (same ?x ?x))
```

---

[64]Lisp-value should be used only to perform an operation not provided in the query language. In particular, it should not be used to test equality (since that is what the matching in the query language is designed to do) or inequality (since that can be done with the same rule shown below).

[65]Notice that we do not need same in order to make two things be the same: We just use the same pattern variable for each—in effect, we have one thing instead of two things in the first place. For example, see ?town in the lives-near rule and ?middle-manager in the wheel rule below. Same is useful when we want to force two things to be different, such as ?person-1 and ?person-2 in the lives-near rule. Although using the same pattern variable in two parts of a query forces the same value to appear in both places, using different pattern variables does not force different values to appear. (The values assigned to different pattern variables may be the same or different.)

The following rule declares that a person is a "wheel" in an organization if he supervises someone who is in turn a supervisor:

```
(rule (wheel ?person)
      (and (supervisor ?middle-manager ?person)
           (supervisor ?x ?middle-manager)))
```

The general form of a rule is

```
(rule ⟨conclusion⟩ ⟨body⟩)
```

where ⟨*conclusion*⟩ is a pattern and ⟨*body*⟩ is any query.[66] We can think of a rule as representing a large (even infinite) set of assertions, namely all instantiations of the rule conclusion with variable assignments that satisfy the rule body. When we described simple queries (patterns), we said that an assignment to variables satisfies a pattern if the instantiated pattern is in the data base. But the pattern needn't be explicitly in the data base as an assertion. It can be an implicit assertion implied by a rule. For example, the query

```
(lives-near ?x (Bitdiddle Ben))
```

results in

```
(lives-near (Reasoner Louis) (Bitdiddle Ben))
(lives-near (Aull DeWitt) (Bitdiddle Ben))
```

To find all computer programmers who live near Ben Bitdiddle, we can ask

```
(and (job ?x (computer programmer))
     (lives-near ?x (Bitdiddle Ben)))
```

As in the case of compound procedures, rules can be used as parts of other rules (as we saw with the `lives-near` rule above) or even be defined recursively. For instance, the rule

```
(rule (outranked-by ?staff-person ?boss)
      (or (supervisor ?staff-person ?boss)
          (and (supervisor ?staff-person ?middle-manager)
               (outranked-by ?middle-manager ?boss))))
```

says that a staff person is outranked by a boss in the organization if the boss is the person's supervisor or (recursively) if the person's supervisor is outranked by the boss.

---

[66]We will also allow rules without bodies, as in `same`, and we will interpret such a rule to mean that the rule conclusion is satisfied by any values of the variables.

Exercise 4.57

Define a rule that says that person 1 can replace person 2 if either person 1 does the same job as person 2 or someone who does person 1's job can also do person 2's job, and if person 1 and person 2 are not the same person. Using your rule, give queries that find the following:

a. all people who can replace Cy D. Fect;

b. all people who can replace someone who is being paid more than they are, together with the two salaries.

Exercise 4.58

Define a rule that says that a person is a "big shot" in a division if the person works in the division but does not have a supervisor who works in the division.

Exercise 4.59

Ben Bitdiddle has missed one meeting too many. Fearing that his habit of forgetting meetings could cost him his job, Ben decides to do something about it. He adds all the weekly meetings of the firm to the Microshaft data base by asserting the following:

```
(meeting accounting (Monday 9am))
(meeting administration (Monday 10am))
(meeting computer (Wednesday 3pm))
(meeting administration (Friday 1pm))
```

Each of the above assertions is for a meeting of an entire division. Ben also adds an entry for the company-wide meeting that spans all the divisions. All of the company's employees attend this meeting.

```
(meeting whole-company (Wednesday 4pm))
```

a. On Friday morning, Ben wants to query the data base for all the meetings that occur that day. What query should he use?

b. Alyssa P. Hacker is unimpressed. She thinks it would be much more useful to be able to ask for her meetings by specifying her name. So she designs a rule that says that a person's meetings include all whole-company meetings plus all meetings of that person's division. Fill in the body of Alyssa's rule.

```
(rule (meeting-time ?person ?day-and-time)
      ⟨ rule-body ⟩)
```

c. Alyssa arrives at work on Wednesday morning and wonders what meetings she has to attend that day. Having defined the above rule, what query should she make to find this out?

Exercise 4.60

By giving the query

```
(lives-near ?person (Hacker Alyssa P))
```

Alyssa P. Hacker is able to find people who live near her, with whom she can ride to work. On the other hand, when she tries to find all pairs of people who live near each other by querying

```
(lives-near ?person-1 ?person-2)
```

she notices that each pair of people who live near each other is listed twice; for example,

```
(lives-near (Hacker Alyssa P) (Fect Cy D))
(lives-near (Fect Cy D) (Hacker Alyssa P))
```

Why does this happen? Is there a way to find a list of people who live near each other, in which each pair appears only once? Explain.

Logic as programs

We can regard a rule as a kind of logical implication: *If* an assignment of values to pattern variables satisfies the body, *then* it satisfies the conclusion. Consequently, we can regard the query language as having the ability to perform *logical deductions* based upon the rules. As an example, consider the append operation described at the beginning of section 4.4. As we said, append can be characterized by the following two rules:

- For any list y, the empty list and y append to form y.

- For any u, v, y, and z, (cons u v) and y append to form (cons u z) if v and y append to form z.

To express this in our query language, we define two rules for a relation

```
(append-to-form x y z)
```

which we can interpret to mean "x and y append to form z":

```
(rule (append-to-form () ?y ?y))

(rule (append-to-form (?u . ?v) ?y (?u . ?z))
      (append-to-form ?v ?y ?z))
```

The first rule has no body, which means that the conclusion holds for any value of ?y. Note how the second rule makes use of dotted-tail notation to name the car and cdr of a list.

Given these two rules, we can formulate queries that compute the append of two lists:

```
;;; Query input:
(append-to-form (a b) (c d) ?z)
;;; Query results:
(append-to-form (a b) (c d) (a b c d))
```

What is more striking, we can use the same rules to ask the question "Which list, when appended to (a b), yields (a b c d)?" This is done as follows:

```
;;; Query input:
(append-to-form (a b) ?y (a b c d))
;;; Query results:
(append-to-form (a b) (c d) (a b c d))
```

We can also ask for all pairs of lists that append to form (a b c d):

```
;;; Query input:
(append-to-form ?x ?y (a b c d))
;;; Query results:
(append-to-form () (a b c d) (a b c d))
(append-to-form (a) (b c d) (a b c d))
(append-to-form (a b) (c d) (a b c d))
(append-to-form (a b c) (d) (a b c d))
(append-to-form (a b c d) () (a b c d))
```

The query system may seem to exhibit quite a bit of intelligence in using the rules to deduce the answers to the queries above. Actually, as we will see in the next section, the system is following a well-determined algorithm in unraveling the rules. Unfortunately, although the system works impressively in the append case, the general methods may break down in more complex cases, as we will see in section 4.4.3.

Exercise 4.61

The following rules implement a next-to relation that finds adjacent elements of a list:

```
(rule (?x next-to ?y in (?x ?y . ?u)))

(rule (?x next-to ?y in (?v . ?z))
      (?x next-to ?y in ?z))
```

What will the response be to the following queries?

```
(?x next-to ?y in (1 (2 3) 4))
```

```
(?x next-to 1 in (2 1 3 1))
```

Exercise 4.62

Define rules to implement the `last-pair` operation of exercise 2.17, which returns a list containing the last element of a nonempty list. Check your rules on queries such as (last-pair (3) ?x), (last-pair (1 2 3) ?x), and (last-pair (2 ?x) (3)). Do your rules work correctly on queries such as (last-pair ?x (3))?

Exercise 4.63

The following data base (see Genesis 4) traces the genealogy of the descendants of Ada back to Adam, by way of Cain:

```
(son Adam Cain)
(son Cain Enoch)
(son Enoch Irad)
(son Irad Mehujael)
(son Mehujael Methushael)
(son Methushael Lamech)
(wife Lamech Ada)
(son Ada Jabal)
(son Ada Jubal)
```

Formulate rules such as "If *S* is the son of *F*, and *F* is the son of *G*, then *S* is the grandson of *G*" and "If *W* is the wife of *M*, and *S* is the son of *W*, then *S* is the son of *M*" (which was supposedly more true in biblical times than today) that will enable the query system to find the grandson of Cain; the sons of Lamech; the grandsons of Methushael. (See exercise 4.69 for some rules to deduce more complicated relationships.)

4.4.2   How the Query System Works

In section 4.4.4 we will present an implementation of the query interpreter as a collection of procedures. In this section we give an overview that explains the general structure of the system independent of low-level implementation details. After describing the implementation of the interpreter, we will be in a position to understand some of its limitations and some of the subtle ways in which the query language's logical operations differ from the operations of mathematical logic.

It should be apparent that the query evaluator must perform some kind of search in order to match queries against facts and rules in the data base. One way to do this would be to implement the query system as a nondeterministic program, using the `amb` evaluator of section 4.3 (see exercise 4.78). Another possibility is to manage the search with the aid of streams. Our implementation follows this second approach.

The query system is organized around two central operations called *pattern matching* and *unification*. We first describe pattern matching and explain how this operation, together with the organization of information in terms of streams of frames, enables us to implement both simple and compound queries. We next discuss unification, a generalization of pattern matching needed to implement rules. Finally, we show how the entire query interpreter fits together through a procedure that classifies expressions in a manner analogous to the way eval classifies expressions for the interpreter described in section 4.1.

Pattern matching

A *pattern matcher* is a program that tests whether some datum fits a specified pattern. For example, the data list ((a b) c (a b)) matches the pattern (?x c ?x) with the pattern variable ?x bound to (a b). The same data list matches the pattern (?x ?y ?z) with ?x and ?z both bound to (a b) and ?y bound to c. It also matches the pattern ((?x ?y) c (?x ?y)) with ?x bound to a and ?y bound to b. However, it does not match the pattern (?x a ?y), since that pattern specifies a list whose second element is the symbol a.

The pattern matcher used by the query system takes as inputs a pattern, a datum, and a *frame* that specifies bindings for various pattern variables. It checks whether the datum matches the pattern in a way that is consistent with the bindings already in the frame. If so, it returns the given frame augmented by any bindings that may have been determined by the match. Otherwise, it indicates that the match has failed.

For example, using the pattern (?x ?y ?x) to match (a b a) given an empty frame will return a frame specifying that ?x is bound to a and ?y is bound to b. Trying the match with the same pattern, the same datum, and a frame specifying that ?y is bound to a will fail. Trying the match with the same pattern, the same datum, and a frame in which ?y is bound to b and ?x is unbound will return the given frame augmented by a binding of ?x to a.

The pattern matcher is all the mechanism that is needed to process simple queries that don't involve rules. For instance, to process the query

```
(job ?x (computer programmer))
```

we scan through all assertions in the data base and select those that match the pattern with respect to an initially empty frame. For each match we find, we use the frame returned by the match to instantiate the pattern with a value for ?x.

Streams of frames

The testing of patterns against frames is organized through the use of streams. Given a single frame, the matching process runs through the

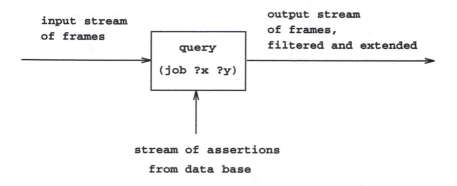

Figure 4.4   A query processes a stream of frames.

data-base entries one by one. For each data-base entry, the matcher generates either a special symbol indicating that the match has failed or an extension to the frame. The results for all the data-base entries are collected into a stream, which is passed through a filter to weed out the failures. The result is a stream of all the frames that extend the given frame via a match to some assertion in the data base.[67]

In our system, a query takes an input stream of frames and performs the above matching operation for every frame in the stream, as indicated in figure 4.4. That is, for each frame in the input stream, the query generates a new stream consisting of all extensions to that frame by matches to assertions in the data base. All these streams are then combined to form one huge stream, which contains all possible extensions of every frame in the input stream. This stream is the output of the query.

To answer a simple query, we use the query with an input stream consisting of a single empty frame. The resulting output stream contains all extensions to the empty frame (that is, all answers to our query). This stream of frames is then used to generate a stream of copies of the original query pattern with the variables instantiated by the values in each frame, and this is the stream that is finally printed.

---

[67]Because matching is generally very expensive, we would like to avoid applying the full matcher to every element of the data base. This is usually arranged by breaking up the process into a fast, coarse match and the final match. The coarse match filters the data base to produce a small set of candidates for the final match. With care, we can arrange our data base so that some of the work of coarse matching can be done when the data base is constructed rather then when we want to select the candidates. This is called *indexing* the data base. There is a vast technology built around data-base-indexing schemes. Our implementation, described in section 4.4.4, contains a simple-minded form of such an optimization.

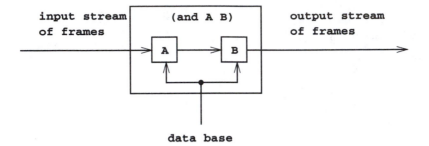

Figure 4.5   The and combination of two queries is produced by operating on the stream of frames in series.

Compound queries

The real elegance of the stream-of-frames implementation is evident when we deal with compound queries. The processing of compound queries makes use of the ability of our matcher to demand that a match be consistent with a specified frame. For example, to handle the and of two queries, such as

```
(and (can-do-job ?x (computer programmer trainee))
     (job ?person ?x))
```

(informally, "Find all people who can do the job of a computer programmer trainee"), we first find all entries that match the pattern

```
(can-do-job ?x (computer programmer trainee))
```

This produces a stream of frames, each of which contains a binding for ?x. Then for each frame in the stream we find all entries that match

```
(job ?person ?x)
```

in a way that is consistent with the given binding for ?x. Each such match will produce a frame containing bindings for ?x and ?person. The and of two queries can be viewed as a series combination of the two component queries, as shown in figure 4.5. The frames that pass through the first query filter are filtered and further extended by the second query.

Figure 4.6 shows the analogous method for computing the or of two queries as a parallel combination of the two component queries. The input stream of frames is extended separately by each query. The two resulting streams are then merged to produce the final output stream.

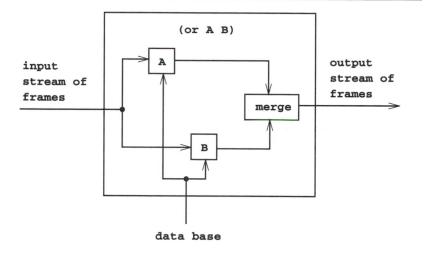

Figure 4.6   The `or` combination of two queries is produced by operating on the stream of frames in parallel and merging the results.

Even from this high-level description, it is apparent that the processing of compound queries can be slow. For example, since a query may produce more than one output frame for each input frame, and each query in an `and` gets its input frames from the previous query, an `and` query could, in the worst case, have to perform a number of matches that is exponential in the number of queries (see exercise 4.76).[68] Though systems for handling only simple queries are quite practical, dealing with complex queries is extremely difficult.[69]

From the stream-of-frames viewpoint, the `not` of some query acts as a filter that removes all frames for which the query can be satisfied. For instance, given the pattern

```
(not (job ?x (computer programmer)))
```

we attempt, for each frame in the input stream, to produce extension frames that satisfy `(job ?x (computer programmer))`. We remove from the input stream all frames for which such extensions exist. The result is a stream consisting of only those frames in which the binding for

---

[68] But this kind of exponential explosion is not common in `and` queries because the added conditions tend to reduce rather than expand the number of frames produced.

[69] There is a large literature on data-base-management systems that is concerned with how to handle complex queries efficiently.

?x does not satisfy (job ?x (computer programmer)). For example, in processing the query

```
(and (supervisor ?x ?y)
     (not (job ?x (computer programmer)))))
```

the first clause will generate frames with bindings for ?x and ?y. The not clause will then filter these by removing all frames in which the binding for ?x satisfies the restriction that ?x is a computer programmer.[70]

The lisp-value special form is implemented as a similar filter on frame streams. We use each frame in the stream to instantiate any variables in the pattern, then apply the Lisp predicate. We remove from the input stream all frames for which the predicate fails.

Unification

In order to handle rules in the query language, we must be able to find the rules whose conclusions match a given query pattern. Rule conclusions are like assertions except that they can contain variables, so we will need a generalization of pattern matching—called *unification*—in which both the "pattern" and the "datum" may contain variables.

A unifier takes two patterns, each containing constants and variables, and determines whether it is possible to assign values to the variables that will make the two patterns equal. If so, it returns a frame containing these bindings. For example, unifying (?x a ?y) and (?y ?z a) will specify a frame in which ?x, ?y, and ?z must all be bound to a. On the other hand, unifying (?x ?y a) and (?x b ?y) will fail, because there is no value for ?y that can make the two patterns equal. (For the second elements of the patterns to be equal, ?y would have to be b; however, for the third elements to be equal, ?y would have to be a.) The unifier used in the query system, like the pattern matcher, takes a frame as input and performs unifications that are consistent with this frame.

The unification algorithm is the most technically difficult part of the query system. With complex patterns, performing unification may seem to require deduction. To unify (?x ?x) and ((a ?y c) (a b ?z)), for example, the algorithm must infer that ?x should be (a b c), ?y should be b, and ?z should be c. We may think of this process as solving a set of equations among the pattern components. In general, these are simultaneous equations, which may require substantial manipulation to

---

[70]There is a subtle difference between this filter implementation of not and the usual meaning of not in mathematical logic. See section 4.4.3.

solve.[71]   For example, unifying (?x ?x) and ((a ?y c) (a b ?z)) may be thought of as specifying the simultaneous equations

```
?x = (a ?y c)
?x = (a b ?z)
```

These equations imply that

```
(a ?y c) = (a b ?z)
```

which in turn implies that

```
a = a, ?y = b, c = ?z,
```

and hence that

```
?x = (a b c)
```

In a successful pattern match, all pattern variables become bound, and the values to which they are bound contain only constants. This is also true of all the examples of unification we have seen so far. In general, however, a successful unification may not completely determine the variable values; some variables may remain unbound and others may be bound to values that contain variables.

Consider the unification of (?x a) and ((b ?y) ?z). We can deduce that ?x = (b ?y) and a = ?z, but we cannot further solve for ?x or ?y. The unification doesn't fail, since it is certainly possible to make the two patterns equal by assigning values to ?x and ?y. Since this match in no way restricts the values ?y can take on, no binding for ?y is put into the result frame. The match does, however, restrict the value of ?x. Whatever value ?y has, ?x must be (b ?y). A binding of ?x to the pattern (b ?y) is thus put into the frame. If a value for ?y is later determined and added to the frame (by a pattern match or unification that is required to be consistent with this frame), the previously bound ?x will refer to this value.[72]

---

[71] In one-sided pattern matching, all the equations that contain pattern variables are explicit and already solved for the unknown (the pattern variable).

[72] Another way to think of unification is that it generates the most general pattern that is a specialization of the two input patterns. That is, the unification of (?x a) and ((b ?y) ?z) is ((b ?y) a), and the unification of (?x a ?y) and (?y ?z a), discussed above, is (a a a). For our implementation, it is more convenient to think of the result of unification as a frame rather than a pattern.

Applying rules

Unification is the key to the component of the query system that makes inferences from rules. To see how this is accomplished, consider processing a query that involves applying a rule, such as

```
(lives-near ?x (Hacker Alyssa P))
```

To process this query, we first use the ordinary pattern-match procedure described above to see if there are any assertions in the data base that match this pattern. (There will not be any in this case, since our data base includes no direct assertions about who lives near whom.) The next step is to attempt to unify the query pattern with the conclusion of each rule. We find that the pattern unifies with the conclusion of the rule

```
(rule (lives-near ?person-1 ?person-2)
      (and (address ?person-1 (?town . ?rest-1))
           (address ?person-2 (?town . ?rest-2))
           (not (same ?person-1 ?person-2))))
```

resulting in a frame specifying that ?person-2 is bound to (Hacker Alyssa P) and that ?x should be bound to (have the same value as) ?person-1. Now, relative to this frame, we evaluate the compound query given by the body of the rule. Successful matches will extend this frame by providing a binding for ?person-1, and consequently a value for ?x, which we can use to instantiate the original query pattern.

In general, the query evaluator uses the following method to apply a rule when trying to establish a query pattern in a frame that specifies bindings for some of the pattern variables:

• Unify the query with the conclusion of the rule to form, if successful, an extension of the original frame.

• Relative to the extended frame, evaluate the query formed by the body of the rule.

Notice how similar this is to the method for applying a procedure in the eval/apply evaluator for Lisp:

• Bind the procedure's parameters to its arguments to form a frame that extends the original procedure environment.

• Relative to the extended environment, evaluate the expression formed by the body of the procedure.

The similarity between the two evaluators should come as no surprise. Just as procedure definitions are the means of abstraction in Lisp, rule definitions are the means of abstraction in the query language. In each case, we unwind the abstraction by creating appropriate bindings and evaluating the rule or procedure body relative to these.

Simple queries

We saw earlier in this section how to evaluate simple queries in the absence of rules. Now that we have seen how to apply rules, we can describe how to evaluate simple queries by using both rules and assertions.

Given the query pattern and a stream of frames, we produce, for each frame in the input stream, two streams:

- a stream of extended frames obtained by matching the pattern against all assertions in the data base (using the pattern matcher), and

- a stream of extended frames obtained by applying all possible rules (using the unifier).[73]

Appending these two streams produces a stream that consists of all the ways that the given pattern can be satisfied consistent with the original frame. These streams (one for each frame in the input stream) are now all combined to form one large stream, which therefore consists of all the ways that any of the frames in the original input stream can be extended to produce a match with the given pattern.

The query evaluator and the driver loop

Despite the complexity of the underlying matching operations, the system is organized much like an evaluator for any language. The procedure that coordinates the matching operations is called `qeval`, and it plays a role analogous to that of the `eval` procedure for Lisp. Qeval takes as inputs a query and a stream of frames. Its output is a stream of frames, corresponding to successful matches to the query pattern, that extend some frame in the input stream, as indicated in figure 4.4. Like `eval`, `qeval` classifies the different types of expressions (queries) and dispatches to an appropriate procedure for each. There is a procedure for each special form (`and`, `or`, `not`, and `lisp-value`) and one for simple queries.

---

[73] Since unification is a generalization of matching, we could simplify the system by using the unifier to produce both streams. Treating the easy case with the simple matcher, however, illustrates how matching (as opposed to full-blown unification) can be useful in its own right.

The driver loop, which is analogous to the `driver-loop` procedure for the other evaluators in this chapter, reads queries from the terminal. For each query, it calls `qeval` with the query and a stream that consists of a single empty frame. This will produce the stream of all possible matches (all possible extensions to the empty frame). For each frame in the resulting stream, it instantiates the original query using the values of the variables found in the frame. This stream of instantiated queries is then printed.[74]

The driver also checks for the special command `assert!`, which signals that the input is not a query but rather an assertion or rule to be added to the data base. For instance,

```
(assert! (job (Bitdiddle Ben) (computer wizard)))

(assert! (rule (wheel ?person)
               (and (supervisor ?middle-manager ?person)
                    (supervisor ?x ?middle-manager))))
```

4.4.3   Is Logic Programming Mathematical Logic?

The means of combination used in the query language may at first seem identical to the operations `and`, `or`, and `not` of mathematical logic, and the application of query-language rules is in fact accomplished through a legitimate method of inference.[75] This identification of the query language with mathematical logic is not really valid, though, because the query language provides a *control structure* that interprets the logical statements procedurally. We can often take advantage of this control structure. For example, to find all of the supervisors of programmers we could formulate a query in either of two logically equivalent forms:

---

[74]The reason we use streams (rather than lists) of frames is that the recursive application of rules can generate infinite numbers of values that satisfy a query. The delayed evaluation embodied in streams is crucial here: The system will print responses one by one as they are generated, regardless of whether there are a finite or infinite number of responses.

[75]That a particular method of inference is legitimate is not a trivial assertion. One must prove that if one starts with true premises, only true conclusions can be derived. The method of inference represented by rule applications is *modus ponens*, the familiar method of inference that says that if A is true and A *implies* B is true, then we may conclude that B is true.

```
(and (job ?x (computer programmer))
     (supervisor ?x ?y))
```

or

```
(and (supervisor ?x ?y)
     (job ?x (computer programmer)))
```

If a company has many more supervisors than programmers (the usual case), it is better to use the first form rather than the second because the data base must be scanned for each intermediate result (frame) produced by the first clause of the and.

The aim of logic programming is to provide the programmer with techniques for decomposing a computational problem into two separate problems: "what" is to be computed, and "how" this should be computed. This is accomplished by selecting a subset of the statements of mathematical logic that is powerful enough to be able to describe anything one might want to compute, yet weak enough to have a controllable procedural interpretation. The intention here is that, on the one hand, a program specified in a logic programming language should be an effective program that can be carried out by a computer. Control ("how" to compute) is effected by using the order of evaluation of the language. We should be able to arrange the order of clauses and the order of subgoals within each clause so that the computation is done in an order deemed to be effective and efficient. At the same time, we should be able to view the result of the computation ("what" to compute) as a simple consequence of the laws of logic.

Our query language can be regarded as just such a procedurally interpretable subset of mathematical logic. An assertion represents a simple fact (an atomic proposition). A rule represents the implication that the rule conclusion holds for those cases where the rule body holds. A rule has a natural procedural interpretation: To establish the conclusion of the rule, establish the body of the rule. Rules, therefore, specify computations. However, because rules can also be regarded as statements of mathematical logic, we can justify any "inference" accomplished by a logic program by asserting that the same result could be obtained by working entirely within mathematical logic.[76]

Infinite loops

A consequence of the procedural interpretation of logic programs is that it is possible to construct hopelessly inefficient programs for solving certain problems. An extreme case of inefficiency occurs when the system falls into infinite loops in making deductions. As a simple example, suppose we are setting up a data base of famous marriages, including

```
(assert! (married Minnie Mickey))
```

If we now ask

```
(married Mickey ?who)
```

we will get no response, because the system doesn't know that if *A* is married to *B*, then *B* is married to *A*. So we assert the rule

```
(assert! (rule (married ?x ?y)
               (married ?y ?x)))
```

and again query

```
(married Mickey ?who)
```

Unfortunately, this will drive the system into an infinite loop, as follows:

● The system finds that the `married` rule is applicable; that is, the rule conclusion (married ?x ?y) successfully unifies with the query pattern (married Mickey ?who) to produce a frame in which ?x is bound to Mickey and ?y is bound to ?who. So the interpreter proceeds to evaluate the rule body (married ?y ?x) in this frame—in effect, to process the query (married ?who Mickey).

---

[76]We must qualify this statement by agreeing that, in speaking of the "inference" accomplished by a logic program, we assume that the computation terminates. Unfortunately, even this qualified statement is false for our implementation of the query language (and also false for programs in Prolog and most other current logic programming languages) because of our use of not and lisp-value. As we will describe below, the not implemented in the query language is not always consistent with the not of mathematical logic, and lisp-value introduces additional complications. We could implement a language consistent with mathematical logic by simply removing not and lisp-value from the language and agreeing to write programs using only simple queries, and, and or. However, this would greatly restrict the expressive power of the language. One of the major concerns of research in logic programming is to find ways to achieve more consistency with mathematical logic without unduly sacrificing expressive power.

- One answer appears directly as an assertion in the data base: (married Minnie Mickey).

- The married rule is also applicable, so the interpreter again evaluates the rule body, which this time is equivalent to (married Mickey ?who).

The system is now in an infinite loop. Indeed, whether the system will find the simple answer (married Minnie Mickey) before it goes into the loop depends on implementation details concerning the order in which the system checks the items in the data base. This is a very simple example of the kinds of loops that can occur. Collections of interrelated rules can lead to loops that are much harder to anticipate, and the appearance of a loop can depend on the order of clauses in an and (see exercise 4.64) or on low-level details concerning the order in which the system processes queries.[77]

Problems with not

Another quirk in the query system concerns not. Given the data base of section 4.4.1, consider the following two queries:

```
(and (supervisor ?x ?y)
     (not (job ?x (computer programmer))))

(and (not (job ?x (computer programmer)))
     (supervisor ?x ?y))
```

These two queries do not produce the same result. The first query begins by finding all entries in the data base that match (supervisor ?x ?y), and then filters the resulting frames by removing the ones in which the value of ?x satisfies (job ?x (computer programmer)). The second query begins by filtering the incoming frames to remove those that can satisfy (job ?x (computer programmer)). Since the only incoming frame is empty, it checks the data base to see if there are any patterns

---

[77]This is not a problem of the logic but one of the procedural interpretation of the logic provided by our interpreter. We could write an interpreter that would not fall into a loop here. For example, we could enumerate all the proofs derivable from our assertions and our rules in a breadth-first rather than a depth-first order. However, such a system makes it more difficult to take advantage of the order of deductions in our programs. One attempt to build sophisticated control into such a program is described in deKleer et al. 1977. Another technique, which does not lead to such serious control problems, is to put in special knowledge, such as detectors for particular kinds of loops (exercise 4.67). However, there can be no general scheme for reliably preventing a system from going down infinite paths in performing deductions. Imagine a diabolical rule of the form "To show $P(x)$ is true, show that $P(f(x))$ is true," for some suitably chosen function f.

that satisfy (job ?x (computer programmer)). Since there generally
are entries of this form, the not clause filters out the empty frame and
returns an empty stream of frames. Consequently, the entire compound
query returns an empty stream.

The trouble is that our implementation of not really is meant to serve
as a filter on values for the variables. If a not clause is processed with
a frame in which some of the variables remain unbound (as does ?x in
the example above), the system will produce unexpected results. Similar
problems occur with the use of lisp-value—the Lisp predicate can't
work if some of its arguments are unbound. See exercise 4.77.

There is also a much more serious way in which the not of the query
language differs from the not of mathematical logic. In logic, we interpret the statement "not *P*" to mean that *P* is not true. In the query
system, however, "not *P*" means that *P* is not deducible from the knowledge in the data base. For example, given the personnel data base of
section 4.4.1, the system would happily deduce all sorts of not statements, such as that Ben Bitdiddle is not a baseball fan, that it is not
raining outside, and that 2 +2 is not 4.[78] In other words, the not of logic
programming languages reflects the so-called *closed world assumption*
that all relevant information has been included in the data base.[79]

Exercise 4.64

Louis Reasoner mistakenly deletes the outranked-by rule (section 4.4.1) from
the data base. When he realizes this, he quickly reinstalls it. Unfortunately, he
makes a slight change in the rule, and types it in as

```
(rule (outranked-by ?staff-person ?boss)
      (or (supervisor ?staff-person ?boss)
          (and (outranked-by ?middle-manager ?boss)
               (supervisor ?staff-person ?middle-manager)))))
```

Just after Louis types this information into the system, DeWitt Aull comes by to
find out who outranks Ben Bitdiddle. He issues the query

```
(outranked-by (Bitdiddle Ben) ?who)
```

After answering, the system goes into an infinite loop. Explain why.

---

[78]Consider the query (not (baseball-fan (Bitdiddle Ben))). The system finds
that (baseball-fan (Bitdiddle Ben)) is not in the data base, so the empty frame
does not satisfy the pattern and is not filtered out of the initial stream of frames. The result
of the query is thus the empty frame, which is used to instantiate the input query to produce
(not (baseball-fan (Bitdiddle Ben))).

[79]A discussion and justification of this treatment of not can be found in the article by
Clark (1978).

Exercise 4.65

Cy D. Fect, looking forward to the day when he will rise in the organization, gives a query to find all the wheels (using the `wheel` rule of section 4.4.1):

```
(wheel ?who)
```

To his surprise, the system responds

```
;;; Query results:
(wheel (Warbucks Oliver))
(wheel (Bitdiddle Ben))
(wheel (Warbucks Oliver))
(wheel (Warbucks Oliver))
(wheel (Warbucks Oliver))
```

Why is Oliver Warbucks listed four times?

Exercise 4.66

Ben has been generalizing the query system to provide statistics about the company. For example, to find the total salaries of all the computer programmers one will be able to say

```
(sum ?amount
      (and (job ?x (computer programmer))
           (salary ?x ?amount)))
```

In general, Ben's new system allows expressions of the form

```
(accumulation-function ⟨variable⟩
                       ⟨query pattern⟩)
```

where `accumulation-function` can be things like `sum`, `average`, or `maximum`. Ben reasons that it should be a cinch to implement this. He will simply feed the query pattern to `qeval`. This will produce a stream of frames. He will then pass this stream through a mapping function that extracts the value of the designated variable from each frame in the stream and feed the resulting stream of values to the accumulation function. Just as Ben completes the implementation and is about to try it out, Cy walks by, still puzzling over the `wheel` query result in exercise 4.65. When Cy shows Ben the system's response, Ben groans, "Oh, no, my simple accumulation scheme won't work!"

What has Ben just realized? Outline a method he can use to salvage the situation.

Exercise 4.67

Devise a way to install a loop detector in the query system so as to avoid the kinds of simple loops illustrated in the text and in exercise 4.64. The general idea is that the system should maintain some sort of history of its current chain of deductions and should not begin processing a query that it is already working on. Describe what kind of information (patterns and frames) is included in this history, and how the check should be made. (After you study the details of the query-system implementation in section 4.4.4, you may want to modify the system to include your loop detector.)

Exercise 4.68

Define rules to implement the `reverse` operation of exercise 2.18, which returns a list containing the same elements as a given list in reverse order. (Hint: Use `append-to-form`.) Can your rules answer both (reverse (1 2 3) ?x) and (reverse ?x (1 2 3))?

Exercise 4.69

Beginning with the data base and the rules you formulated in exercise 4.63, devise a rule for adding "greats" to a grandson relationship. This should enable the system to deduce that Irad is the great-grandson of Adam, or that Jabal and Jubal are the great-great-great-great-great-grandsons of Adam. (Hint: Represent the fact about Irad, for example, as ((great grandson) Adam Irad). Write rules that determine if a list ends in the word `grandson`. Use this to express a rule that allows one to derive the relationship ((great . ?rel) ?x ?y), where ?rel is a list ending in `grandson`.) Check your rules on queries such as ((great grandson) ?g ?ggs) and (?relationship Adam Irad).

4.4.4   Implementing the Query System

Section 4.4.2 described how the query system works. Now we fill in the details by presenting a complete implementation of the system.

4.4.4.1   The Driver Loop and Instantiation

The driver loop for the query system repeatedly reads input expressions. If the expression is a rule or assertion to be added to the data base, then the information is added. Otherwise the expression is assumed to be a query. The driver passes this query to the evaluator `qeval` together with an initial frame stream consisting of a single empty frame. The result of the evaluation is a stream of frames generated by satisfying the query with variable values found in the data base. These frames are used to form a new stream consisting of copies of the original query in which the variables are instantiated with values supplied by the stream of frames, and this final stream is printed at the terminal:

```
(define input-prompt ";;; Query input:")
(define output-prompt ";;; Query results:")
```

```
(define (query-driver-loop)
  (prompt-for-input input-prompt)
  (let ((q (query-syntax-process (read))))
    (cond ((assertion-to-be-added? q)
           (add-rule-or-assertion! (add-assertion-body q))
           (newline)
           (display "Assertion added to data base.")
           (query-driver-loop))
          (else
           (newline)
           (display output-prompt)
           (display-stream
            (stream-map
             (lambda (frame)
               (instantiate q
                            frame
                            (lambda (v f)
                              (contract-question-mark v))))
             (qeval q (singleton-stream '()))))
           (query-driver-loop)))))
```

Here, as in the other evaluators in this chapter, we use an abstract syntax
for the expressions of the query language. The implementation of the
expression syntax, including the predicate `assertion-to-be-added?`
and the selector `add-assertion-body`, is given in section 4.4.4.7. Add-
rule-or-assertion! is defined in section 4.4.4.5.

Before doing any processing on an input expression, the driver loop
transforms it syntactically into a form that makes the processing more
efficient. This involves changing the representation of pattern variables.
When the query is instantiated, any variables that remain unbound are
transformed back to the input representation before being printed. These
transformations are performed by the two procedures `query-syntax-
process` and `contract-question-mark` (section 4.4.4.7).

To instantiate an expression, we copy it, replacing any variables in the
expression by their values in a given frame. The values are themselves
instantiated, since they could contain variables (for example, if ?x in
exp is bound to ?y as the result of unification and ?y is in turn bound
to 5). The action to take if a variable cannot be instantiated is given by a
procedural argument to `instantiate`.

```
(define (instantiate exp frame unbound-var-handler)
  (define (copy exp)
    (cond ((var? exp)
           (let ((binding (binding-in-frame exp frame)))
             (if binding
                 (copy (binding-value binding))
                 (unbound-var-handler exp frame))))
          ((pair? exp)
           (cons (copy (car exp)) (copy (cdr exp))))
          (else exp)))
  (copy exp))
```

The procedures that manipulate bindings are defined in section 4.4.4.8.

4.4.4.2 The Evaluator

The qeval procedure, called by the query-driver-loop, is the basic
evaluator of the query system. It takes as inputs a query and a stream of
frames, and it returns a stream of extended frames. It identifies special
forms by a data-directed dispatch using get and put, just as we did in
implementing generic operations in chapter 2. Any query that is not identified as a special form is assumed to be a simple query, to be processed
by simple-query.

```
(define (qeval query frame-stream)
  (let ((qproc (get (type query) 'qeval)))
    (if qproc
        (qproc (contents query) frame-stream)
        (simple-query query frame-stream))))
```

Type and contents, defined in section 4.4.4.7, implement the abstract
syntax of the special forms.

Simple queries

The simple-query procedure handles simple queries. It takes as arguments a simple query (a pattern) together with a stream of frames, and
it returns the stream formed by extending each frame by all data-base
matches of the query.

```
(define (simple-query query-pattern frame-stream)
  (stream-flatmap
   (lambda (frame)
     (stream-append-delayed
      (find-assertions query-pattern frame)
      (delay (apply-rules query-pattern frame))))
   frame-stream))
```

For each frame in the input stream, we use `find-assertions` (section 4.4.4.3) to match the pattern against all assertions in the data base, producing a stream of extended frames, and we use `apply-rules` (section 4.4.4.4) to apply all possible rules, producing another stream of extended frames. These two streams are combined (using `stream-append-delayed`, section 4.4.4.6) to make a stream of all the ways that the given pattern can be satisfied consistent with the original frame (see exercise 4.71). The streams for the individual input frames are combined using `stream-flatmap` (section 4.4.4.6) to form one large stream of all the ways that any of the frames in the original input stream can be extended to produce a match with the given pattern.

Compound queries

And queries are handled as illustrated in figure 4.5 by the `conjoin` procedure. `Conjoin` takes as inputs the conjuncts and the frame stream and returns the stream of extended frames. First, `conjoin` processes the stream of frames to find the stream of all possible frame extensions that satisfy the first query in the conjunction. Then, using this as the new frame stream, it recursively applies `conjoin` to the rest of the queries.

```
(define (conjoin conjuncts frame-stream)
  (if (empty-conjunction? conjuncts)
      frame-stream
      (conjoin (rest-conjuncts conjuncts)
               (qeval (first-conjunct conjuncts)
                      frame-stream))))
```

The expression

```
(put 'and 'qeval conjoin)
```

sets up `qeval` to dispatch to `conjoin` when an `and` form is encountered.

Or queries are handled similarly, as shown in figure 4.6. The output streams for the various disjuncts of the `or` are computed separately and merged using the `interleave-delayed` procedure from section 4.4.4.6. (See exercises 4.71 and 4.72.)

```
(define (disjoin disjuncts frame-stream)
  (if (empty-disjunction? disjuncts)
      the-empty-stream
      (interleave-delayed
       (qeval (first-disjunct disjuncts) frame-stream)
       (delay (disjoin (rest-disjuncts disjuncts)
                       frame-stream)))))
```

```
(put 'or 'qeval disjoin)
```

The predicates and selectors for the syntax of conjuncts and disjuncts are given in section 4.4.4.7.

Filters

Not is handled by the method outlined in section 4.4.2. We attempt to extend each frame in the input stream to satisfy the query being negated, and we include a given frame in the output stream only if it cannot be extended.

```
(define (negate operands frame-stream)
  (stream-flatmap
    (lambda (frame)
      (if (stream-null? (qeval (negated-query operands)
                               (singleton-stream frame)))
          (singleton-stream frame)
          the-empty-stream))
    frame-stream))

(put 'not 'qeval negate)
```

Lisp-value is a filter similar to not. Each frame in the stream is used to instantiate the variables in the pattern, the indicated predicate is applied, and the frames for which the predicate returns false are filtered out of the input stream. An error results if there are unbound pattern variables.

```
(define (lisp-value call frame-stream)
  (stream-flatmap
    (lambda (frame)
      (if (execute
            (instantiate
              call
              frame
              (lambda (v f)
                (error "Unknown pat var -- LISP-VALUE" v))))
          (singleton-stream frame)
          the-empty-stream))
    frame-stream))

(put 'lisp-value 'qeval lisp-value)
```

Execute, which applies the predicate to the arguments, must eval the predicate expression to get the procedure to apply. However, it must not evaluate the arguments, since they are already the actual arguments, not expressions whose evaluation (in Lisp) will produce the arguments. Note that `execute` is implemented using `eval` and `apply` from the underlying Lisp system.

```
(define (execute exp)
  (apply (eval (predicate exp) user-initial-environment)
         (args exp)))
```

The `always-true` special form provides for a query that is always satisfied. It ignores its contents (normally empty) and simply passes through all the frames in the input stream. Always-true is used by the `rule-body` selector (section 4.4.4.7) to provide bodies for rules that were defined without bodies (that is, rules whose conclusions are always satisfied).

```
(define (always-true ignore frame-stream) frame-stream)

(put 'always-true 'qeval always-true)
```

The selectors that define the syntax of `not` and `lisp-value` are given in section 4.4.4.7.

4.4.4.3   Finding Assertions by Pattern Matching

`Find-assertions`, called by `simple-query` (section 4.4.4.2), takes as input a pattern and a frame. It returns a stream of frames, each extending the given one by a data-base match of the given pattern. It uses `fetch-assertions` (section 4.4.4.5) to get a stream of all the assertions in the data base that should be checked for a match against the pattern and the frame. The reason for `fetch-assertions` here is that we can often apply simple tests that will eliminate many of the entries in the data base from the pool of candidates for a successful match. The system would still work if we eliminated `fetch-assertions` and simply checked a stream of all assertions in the data base, but the computation would be less efficient because we would need to make many more calls to the matcher.

```
(define (find-assertions pattern frame)
  (stream-flatmap (lambda (datum)
                    (check-an-assertion datum pattern frame))
                  (fetch-assertions pattern frame)))
```

`Check-an-assertion` takes as arguments a pattern, a data object (assertion), and a frame and returns either a one-element stream containing the extended frame or `the-empty-stream` if the match fails.

```
(define (check-an-assertion assertion query-pat query-frame)
  (let ((match-result
          (pattern-match query-pat assertion query-frame)))
    (if (eq? match-result 'failed)
        the-empty-stream
        (singleton-stream match-result))))
```

The basic pattern matcher returns either the symbol `failed` or an extension of the given frame. The basic idea of the matcher is to check the pattern against the data, element by element, accumulating bindings for the pattern variables. If the pattern and the data object are the same, the match succeeds and we return the frame of bindings accumulated so far. Otherwise, if the pattern is a variable we extend the current frame by binding the variable to the data, so long as this is consistent with the bindings already in the frame. If the pattern and the data are both pairs, we (recursively) match the `car` of the pattern against the `car` of the data to produce a frame; in this frame we then match the `cdr` of the pattern against the `cdr` of the data. If none of these cases are applicable, the match fails and we return the symbol `failed`.

```
(define (pattern-match pat dat frame)
  (cond ((eq? frame 'failed) 'failed)
        ((equal? pat dat) frame)
        ((var? pat) (extend-if-consistent pat dat frame))
        ((and (pair? pat) (pair? dat))
         (pattern-match (cdr pat)
                        (cdr dat)
                        (pattern-match (car pat)
                                       (car dat)
                                       frame)))
        (else 'failed)))
```

Here is the procedure that extends a frame by adding a new binding, if this is consistent with the bindings already in the frame:

```
(define (extend-if-consistent var dat frame)
  (let ((binding (binding-in-frame var frame)))
    (if binding
        (pattern-match (binding-value binding) dat frame)
        (extend var dat frame))))
```

If there is no binding for the variable in the frame, we simply add the binding of the variable to the data. Otherwise we match, in the frame, the data against the value of the variable in the frame. If the stored value contains only constants, as it must if it was stored during pattern match-

ing by `extend-if-consistent`, then the match simply tests whether
the stored and new values are the same. If so, it returns the unmodi-
fied frame; if not, it returns a failure indication. The stored value may,
however, contain pattern variables if it was stored during unification (see
section 4.4.4.4). The recursive match of the stored pattern against the
new data will add or check bindings for the variables in this pattern. For
example, suppose we have a frame in which `?x` is bound to `(f ?y)` and
`?y` is unbound, and we wish to augment this frame by a binding of `?x` to
`(f b)`. We look up `?x` and find that it is bound to `(f ?y)`. This leads
us to match `(f ?y)` against the proposed new value `(f b)` in the same
frame. Eventually this match extends the frame by adding a binding of
`?y` to b. `?X` remains bound to `(f ?y)`. We never modify a stored binding
and we never store more than one binding for a given variable.

   The procedures used by `extend-if-consistent` to manipulate bindings are defined in section 4.4.4.8.

Patterns with dotted tails

If a pattern contains a dot followed by a pattern variable, the pattern variable matches the rest of the data list (rather than the next element of the
data list), just as one would expect with the dotted-tail notation described
in exercise 2.20. Although the pattern matcher we have just implemented
doesn't look for dots, it does behave as we want. This is because the Lisp
`read` primitive, which is used by `query-driver-loop` to read the query
and represent it as a list structure, treats dots in a special way.

   When `read` sees a dot, instead of making the next item be the next
element of a list (the `car` of a `cons` whose `cdr` will be the rest of the
list) it makes the next item be the `cdr` of the list structure. For example,
the list structure produced by `read` for the pattern `(computer ?type)`
could be constructed by evaluating the expression `(cons 'computer
(cons '?type '()))`, and that for `(computer . ?type)` could be
constructed by evaluating the expression `(cons 'computer '?type)`.

   Thus, as `pattern-match` recursively compares `car`s and `cdr`s of a
data list and a pattern that had a dot, it eventually matches the variable
after the dot (which is a `cdr` of the pattern) against a sublist of the data
list, binding the variable to that list. For example, matching the pattern
`(computer . ?type)` against `(computer programmer trainee)` will
match `?type` against the list `(programmer trainee)`.

4.4.4.4   Rules and Unification

`Apply-rules` is the rule analog of `find-assertions` (section 4.4.4.3).
It takes as input a pattern and a frame, and it forms a stream of extension

frames by applying rules from the data base. Stream-flatmap maps apply-a-rule down the stream of possibly applicable rules (selected by fetch-rules, section 4.4.4.5) and combines the resulting streams of frames.

```
(define (apply-rules pattern frame)
  (stream-flatmap (lambda (rule)
                    (apply-a-rule rule pattern frame))
                  (fetch-rules pattern frame)))
```

Apply-a-rule applies rules using the method outlined in section 4.4.2. It first augments its argument frame by unifying the rule conclusion with the pattern in the given frame. If this succeeds, it evaluates the rule body in this new frame.

Before any of this happens, however, the program renames all the variables in the rule with unique new names. The reason for this is to prevent the variables for different rule applications from becoming confused with each other. For instance, if two rules both use a variable named ?x, then each one may add a binding for ?x to the frame when it is applied. These two ?x's have nothing to do with each other, and we should not be fooled into thinking that the two bindings must be consistent. Rather than rename variables, we could devise a more clever environment structure; however, the renaming approach we have chosen here is the most straightforward, even if not the most efficient. (See exercise 4.79.) Here is the apply-a-rule procedure:

```
(define (apply-a-rule rule query-pattern query-frame)
  (let ((clean-rule (rename-variables-in rule)))
    (let ((unify-result
            (unify-match query-pattern
                         (conclusion clean-rule)
                         query-frame)))
      (if (eq? unify-result 'failed)
          the-empty-stream
          (qeval (rule-body clean-rule)
                 (singleton-stream unify-result))))))
```

The selectors rule-body and conclusion that extract parts of a rule are defined in section 4.4.4.7.

We generate unique variable names by associating a unique identifier (such as a number) with each rule application and combining this identifier with the original variable names. For example, if the rule-application identifier is 7, we might change each ?x in the rule to ?x-7 and each ?y in the rule to ?y-7. (Make-new-variable and new-rule-application-id are included with the syntax procedures in section 4.4.4.7.)

```
(define (rename-variables-in rule)
  (let ((rule-application-id (new-rule-application-id)))
    (define (tree-walk exp)
      (cond ((var? exp)
             (make-new-variable exp rule-application-id))
            ((pair? exp)
             (cons (tree-walk (car exp))
                   (tree-walk (cdr exp))))
            (else exp)))
    (tree-walk rule)))
```

The unification algorithm is implemented as a procedure that takes as inputs two patterns and a frame and returns either the extended frame or the symbol failed. The unifier is like the pattern matcher except that it is symmetrical—variables are allowed on both sides of the match. Unify-match is basically the same as pattern-match, except that there is extra code (marked "***" below) to handle the case where the object on the right side of the match is a variable.

```
(define (unify-match p1 p2 frame)
  (cond ((eq? frame 'failed) 'failed)
        ((equal? p1 p2) frame)
        ((var? p1) (extend-if-possible p1 p2 frame))
        ((var? p2) (extend-if-possible p2 p1 frame))   ; ***
        ((and (pair? p1) (pair? p2))
         (unify-match (cdr p1)
                      (cdr p2)
                      (unify-match (car p1)
                                   (car p2)
                                   frame)))
        (else 'failed)))
```

In unification, as in one-sided pattern matching, we want to accept a proposed extension of the frame only if it is consistent with existing bindings. The procedure extend-if-possible used in unification is the same as the extend-if-consistent used in pattern matching except for two special checks, marked "***" in the program below. In the first case, if the variable we are trying to match is not bound, but the value we are trying to match it with is itself a (different) variable, it is necessary to check to see if the value is bound, and if so, to match its value. If both parties to the match are unbound, we may bind either to the other.

The second check deals with attempts to bind a variable to a pattern that includes that variable. Such a situation can occur whenever a variable is repeated in both patterns. Consider, for example, unifying the two patterns (?x ?x) and (?y ⟨ *expression involving* ?y ⟩) in a frame where both ?x and ?y are unbound. First ?x is matched against ?y, making a binding of ?x to ?y. Next, the same ?x is matched against the given expression involving ?y. Since ?x is already bound to ?y, this results in matching ?y against the expression. If we think of the unifier as finding a set of values for the pattern variables that make the patterns the same, then these patterns imply instructions to find a ?y such that ?y is equal to the expression involving ?y. There is no general method for solving such equations, so we reject such bindings; these cases are recognized by the predicate depends-on?.[80] On the other hand, we do not want to reject attempts to bind a variable to itself. For example, consider unifying (?x ?x) and (?y ?y). The second attempt to bind ?x to ?y matches ?y (the stored value of ?x) against ?y (the new value of ?x). This is taken care of by the equal? clause of unify-match.

---

[80] In general, unifying ?y with an expression involving ?y would require our being able to find a fixed point of the equation ?y = ⟨ *expression involving* ?y ⟩. It is sometimes possible to syntactically form an expression that appears to be the solution. For example, ?y = (f ?y) seems to have the fixed point (f (f (f ...))), which we can produce by beginning with the expression (f ?y) and repeatedly substituting (f ?y) for ?y. Unfortunately, not every such equation has a meaningful fixed point. The issues that arise here are similar to the issues of manipulating infinite series in mathematics. For example, we know that 2 is the solution to the equation $y = 1 + y/2$. Beginning with the expression $1 + y/2$ and repeatedly substituting $1 + y/2$ for y gives

$$2 = y = 1 + y/2 = 1 + (1 + y/2)/2 = 1 + 1/2 + y/4 = \cdots,$$

which leads to

$$2 = 1 + 1/2 + 1/4 + 1/8 + \cdots.$$

However, if we try the same manipulation beginning with the observation that -1 is the solution to the equation $y = 1 + 2y$, we obtain

$$-1 = y = 1 + 2y = 1 + 2(1 + 2y) = 1 + 2 + 4y = \cdots,$$

which leads to

$$-1 = 1 + 2 + 4 + 8 + \cdots.$$

Although the formal manipulations used in deriving these two equations are identical, the first result is a valid assertion about infinite series but the second is not. Similarly, for our unification results, reasoning with an arbitrary syntactically constructed expression may lead to errors.

```
(define (extend-if-possible var val frame)
  (let ((binding (binding-in-frame var frame)))
    (cond (binding
           (unify-match
            (binding-value binding) val frame))
          ((var? val)                        ; ***
           (let ((binding (binding-in-frame val frame)))
             (if binding
                 (unify-match
                  var (binding-value binding) frame)
                 (extend var val frame))))
          ((depends-on? val var frame)       ; ***
           'failed)
          (else (extend var val frame)))))
```

Depends-on? is a predicate that tests whether an expression proposed to be the value of a pattern variable depends on the variable. This must be done relative to the current frame because the expression may contain occurrences of a variable that already has a value that depends on our test variable. The structure of depends-on? is a simple recursive tree walk in which we substitute for the values of variables whenever necessary.

```
(define (depends-on? exp var frame)
  (define (tree-walk e)
    (cond ((var? e)
           (if (equal? var e)
               true
               (let ((b (binding-in-frame e frame)))
                 (if b
                     (tree-walk (binding-value b))
                     false))))
          ((pair? e)
           (or (tree-walk (car e))
               (tree-walk (cdr e))))
          (else false)))
  (tree-walk exp))
```

4.4.4.5   Maintaining the Data Base

One important problem in designing logic programming languages is that of arranging things so that as few irrelevant data-base entries as possible will be examined in checking a given pattern. In our system, in addition to storing all assertions in one big stream, we store all assertions whose cars are constant symbols in separate streams, in a table indexed by the symbol. To fetch an assertion that may match a pattern, we first check to see if the car of the pattern is a constant symbol. If so, we return (to be tested using the matcher) all the stored assertions that have the same car. If the pattern's car is not a constant symbol, we return all the stored assertions. Cleverer methods could also take advantage of information in the frame, or try also to optimize the case where the car of the pattern is not a constant symbol. We avoid building our criteria for indexing (using the car, handling only the case of constant symbols) into the program; instead we call on predicates and selectors that embody our criteria.

```
(define THE-ASSERTIONS the-empty-stream)

(define (fetch-assertions pattern frame)
  (if (use-index? pattern)
      (get-indexed-assertions pattern)
      (get-all-assertions)))

(define (get-all-assertions) THE-ASSERTIONS)

(define (get-indexed-assertions pattern)
  (get-stream (index-key-of pattern) 'assertion-stream))
```

Get-stream looks up a stream in the table and returns an empty stream if nothing is stored there.

```
(define (get-stream key1 key2)
  (let ((s (get key1 key2)))
    (if s s the-empty-stream)))
```

Rules are stored similarly, using the car of the rule conclusion. Rule conclusions are arbitrary patterns, however, so they differ from assertions in that they can contain variables. A pattern whose car is a constant symbol can match rules whose conclusions start with a variable as well as rules whose conclusions have the same car. Thus, when fetching rules that might match a pattern whose car is a constant symbol we fetch all rules whose conclusions start with a variable as well as those whose conclusions have the same car as the pattern. For this purpose we store all rules whose conclusions start with a variable in a separate stream in our table, indexed by the symbol ?.

```
(define THE-RULES the-empty-stream)

(define (fetch-rules pattern frame)
  (if (use-index? pattern)
      (get-indexed-rules pattern)
      (get-all-rules)))

(define (get-all-rules) THE-RULES)
```

```
(define (get-indexed-rules pattern)
  (stream-append
   (get-stream (index-key-of pattern) 'rule-stream)
   (get-stream '? 'rule-stream)))
```

Add-rule-or-assertion! is used by query-driver-loop to add assertions and rules to the data base. Each item is stored in the index, if appropriate, and in a stream of all assertions or rules in the data base.

```
(define (add-rule-or-assertion! assertion)
  (if (rule? assertion)
      (add-rule! assertion)
      (add-assertion! assertion)))

(define (add-assertion! assertion)
  (store-assertion-in-index assertion)
  (let ((old-assertions THE-ASSERTIONS))
    (set! THE-ASSERTIONS
          (cons-stream assertion old-assertions))
    'ok))

(define (add-rule! rule)
  (store-rule-in-index rule)
  (let ((old-rules THE-RULES))
    (set! THE-RULES (cons-stream rule old-rules))
    'ok))
```

To actually store an assertion or a rule, we check to see if it can be indexed. If so, we store it in the appropriate stream.

```
(define (store-assertion-in-index assertion)
  (if (indexable? assertion)
      (let ((key (index-key-of assertion)))
        (let ((current-assertion-stream
               (get-stream key 'assertion-stream)))
          (put key
               'assertion-stream
               (cons-stream assertion
                            current-assertion-stream))))))

(define (store-rule-in-index rule)
  (let ((pattern (conclusion rule)))
    (if (indexable? pattern)
        (let ((key (index-key-of pattern)))
          (let ((current-rule-stream
                 (get-stream key 'rule-stream)))
            (put key
                 'rule-stream
                 (cons-stream rule
                              current-rule-stream)))))))
```

The following procedures define how the data-base index is used. A pattern (an assertion or a rule conclusion) will be stored in the table if it starts with a variable or a constant symbol.

```
(define (indexable? pat)
  (or (constant-symbol? (car pat))
      (var? (car pat))))
```

The key under which a pattern is stored in the table is either ? (if it starts with a variable) or the constant symbol with which it starts.

```
(define (index-key-of pat)
  (let ((key (car pat)))
    (if (var? key) '? key)))
```

The index will be used to retrieve items that might match a pattern if the pattern starts with a constant symbol.

```
(define (use-index? pat)
  (constant-symbol? (car pat)))
```

Exercise 4.70

What is the purpose of the `let` bindings in the procedures `add-assertion!` and `add-rule!`? What would be wrong with the following implementation of `add-assertion!`? Hint: Recall the definition of the infinite stream of ones in section 3.5.2: `(define ones (cons-stream 1 ones))`.

```
(define (add-assertion! assertion)
  (store-assertion-in-index assertion)
  (set! THE-ASSERTIONS
        (cons-stream assertion THE-ASSERTIONS))
  'ok)
```

4.4.4.6   Stream Operations

The query system uses a few stream operations that were not presented in chapter 3.

`Stream-append-delayed` and `interleave-delayed` are just like `stream-append` and `interleave` (section 3.5.3), except that they take a delayed argument (like the `integral` procedure in section 3.5.4). This postpones looping in some cases (see exercise 4.71).

```
(define (stream-append-delayed s1 delayed-s2)
  (if (stream-null? s1)
      (force delayed-s2)
      (cons-stream
       (stream-car s1)
       (stream-append-delayed (stream-cdr s1) delayed-s2))))
```

```
(define (interleave-delayed s1 delayed-s2)
  (if (stream-null? s1)
      (force delayed-s2)
      (cons-stream
       (stream-car s1)
       (interleave-delayed (force delayed-s2)
                           (delay (stream-cdr s1))))))
```

Stream-flatmap, which is used throughout the query evaluator to map a procedure over a stream of frames and combine the resulting streams of frames, is the stream analog of the flatmap procedure introduced for ordinary lists in section 2.2.3. Unlike ordinary flatmap, however, we accumulate the streams with an interleaving process, rather than simply appending them (see exercises 4.72 and 4.73).

```
(define (stream-flatmap proc s)
  (flatten-stream (stream-map proc s)))
```

```
(define (flatten-stream stream)
  (if (stream-null? stream)
      the-empty-stream
      (interleave-delayed
       (stream-car stream)
       (delay (flatten-stream (stream-cdr stream))))))
```

The evaluator also uses the following simple procedure to generate a stream consisting of a single element:

```
(define (singleton-stream x)
  (cons-stream x the-empty-stream))
```

4.4.4.7   Query Syntax Procedures

Type and contents, used by qeval (section 4.4.4.2), specify that a special form is identified by the symbol in its car. They are the same as the type-tag and contents procedures in section 2.4.2, except for the error message.

```
(define (type exp)
  (if (pair? exp)
      (car exp)
      (error "Unknown expression TYPE" exp)))
```

```
(define (contents exp)
  (if (pair? exp)
      (cdr exp)
      (error "Unknown expression CONTENTS" exp)))
```

The following procedures, used by query-driver-loop (in section 4.4.4.1), specify that rules and assertions are added to the data base by expressions of the form (assert! ⟨*rule-or-assertion*⟩):

```
(define (assertion-to-be-added? exp)
  (eq? (type exp) 'assert!))

(define (add-assertion-body exp)
  (car (contents exp)))
```

Here are the syntax definitions for the and, or, not, and lisp-value special forms (section 4.4.4.2):

```
(define (empty-conjunction? exps) (null? exps))
(define (first-conjunct exps) (car exps))
(define (rest-conjuncts exps) (cdr exps))

(define (empty-disjunction? exps) (null? exps))
(define (first-disjunct exps) (car exps))
(define (rest-disjuncts exps) (cdr exps))

(define (negated-query exps) (car exps))

(define (predicate exps) (car exps))
(define (args exps) (cdr exps))
```

The following three procedures define the syntax of rules:

```
(define (rule? statement)
  (tagged-list? statement 'rule))

(define (conclusion rule) (cadr rule))

(define (rule-body rule)
  (if (null? (cddr rule))
      '(always-true)
      (caddr rule)))
```

Query-driver-loop (section 4.4.4.1) calls query-syntax-process to transform pattern variables in the expression, which have the form ?symbol, into the internal format (? symbol). That is to say, a pattern such as (job ?x ?y) is actually represented internally by the system as (job (? x) (? y)). This increases the efficiency of query processing, since it means that the system can check to see if an expression is a

pattern variable by checking whether the car of the expression is the
symbol ?, rather than having to extract characters from the symbol. The
syntax transformation is accomplished by the following procedure:[81]

```
(define (query-syntax-process exp)
  (map-over-symbols expand-question-mark exp))

(define (map-over-symbols proc exp)
  (cond ((pair? exp)
         (cons (map-over-symbols proc (car exp))
               (map-over-symbols proc (cdr exp))))
        ((symbol? exp) (proc exp))
        (else exp)))

(define (expand-question-mark symbol)
  (let ((chars (symbol->string symbol)))
    (if (string=? (substring chars 0 1) "?")
        (list '?
              (string->symbol
               (substring chars 1 (string-length chars))))
        symbol)))
```

Once the variables are transformed in this way, the variables in a pattern are lists starting with ?, and the constant symbols (which need to be
recognized for data-base indexing, section 4.4.4.5) are just the symbols.

```
(define (var? exp)
  (tagged-list? exp '?))

(define (constant-symbol? exp) (symbol? exp))
```

Unique variables are constructed during rule application (in section
4.4.4.4) by means of the following procedures. The unique identifier for
a rule application is a number, which is incremented each time a rule is
applied.

---

[81]Most Lisp systems give the user the ability to modify the ordinary read procedure to
perform such transformations by defining *reader macro characters*. Quoted expressions
are already handled in this way: The reader automatically translates 'expression into
(quote expression) before the evaluator sees it. We could arrange for ?expression
to be transformed into (? expression) in the same way; however, for the sake of clarity
we have included the transformation procedure here explicitly.

Expand-question-mark and contract-question-mark use several procedures
with string in their names. These are Scheme primitives.

```
(define rule-counter 0)

(define (new-rule-application-id)
  (set! rule-counter (+ 1 rule-counter))
  rule-counter)

(define (make-new-variable var rule-application-id)
  (cons '? (cons rule-application-id (cdr var))))
```

When `query-driver-loop` instantiates the query to print the answer, it converts any unbound pattern variables back to the right form for printing, using

```
(define (contract-question-mark variable)
  (string->symbol
   (string-append "?"
     (if (number? (cadr variable))
         (string-append (symbol->string (caddr variable))
                        "-"
                        (number->string (cadr variable)))
         (symbol->string (cadr variable))))))
```

4.4.4.8　Frames and Bindings

Frames are represented as lists of bindings, which are variable-value pairs:

```
(define (make-binding variable value)
  (cons variable value))

(define (binding-variable binding)
  (car binding))

(define (binding-value binding)
  (cdr binding))

(define (binding-in-frame variable frame)
  (assoc variable frame))

(define (extend variable value frame)
  (cons (make-binding variable value) frame))
```

Exercise 4.71

Louis Reasoner wonders why the `simple-query` and `disjoin` procedures (section 4.4.4.2) are implemented using explicit `delay` operations, rather than being defined as follows:

```
(define (simple-query query-pattern frame-stream)
  (stream-flatmap
    (lambda (frame)
      (stream-append (find-assertions query-pattern frame)
                     (apply-rules query-pattern frame)))
   frame-stream))

(define (disjoin disjuncts frame-stream)
  (if (empty-disjunction? disjuncts)
      the-empty-stream
      (interleave
        (qeval (first-disjunct disjuncts) frame-stream)
        (disjoin (rest-disjuncts disjuncts) frame-stream))))
```

Can you give examples of queries where these simpler definitions would lead to
undesirable behavior?

Exercise 4.72

Why do `disjoin` and `stream-flatmap` interleave the streams rather than simply append them? Give examples that illustrate why interleaving works better.
(Hint: Why did we use `interleave` in section 3.5.3?)

Exercise 4.73

Why does `flatten-stream` use `delay` explicitly? What would be wrong with
defining it as follows:

```
(define (flatten-stream stream)
  (if (stream-null? stream)
      the-empty-stream
      (interleave
        (stream-car stream)
        (flatten-stream (stream-cdr stream)))))
```

Exercise 4.74

Alyssa P. Hacker proposes to use a simpler version of `stream-flatmap` in
`negate`, `lisp-value`, and `find-assertions`. She observes that the procedure that is mapped over the frame stream in these cases always produces either
the empty stream or a singleton stream, so no interleaving is needed when combining these streams.

a. Fill in the missing expressions in Alyssa's program.

```
(define (simple-stream-flatmap proc s)
  (simple-flatten (stream-map proc s)))

(define (simple-flatten stream)
  (stream-map ⟨??⟩
              (stream-filter ⟨??⟩ stream)))
```

b. Does the query system's behavior change if we change it in this way?

Exercise 4.75

Implement for the query language a new special form called unique. Unique should succeed if there is precisely one item in the data base satisfying a specified query. For example,

```
(unique (job ?x (computer wizard)))
```

should print the one-item stream

```
(unique (job (Bitdiddle Ben) (computer wizard)))
```

since Ben is the only computer wizard, and

```
(unique (job ?x (computer programmer)))
```

should print the empty stream, since there is more than one computer programmer. Moreover,

```
(and (job ?x ?j) (unique (job ?anyone ?j)))
```

should list all the jobs that are filled by only one person, and the people who fill them.

There are two parts to implementing unique. The first is to write a procedure that handles this special form, and the second is to make qeval dispatch to that procedure. The second part is trivial, since qeval does its dispatching in a data-directed way. If your procedure is called uniquely-asserted, all you need to do is

```
(put 'unique 'qeval uniquely-asserted)
```

and qeval will dispatch to this procedure for every query whose type (car) is the symbol unique.

The real problem is to write the procedure uniquely-asserted. This should take as input the contents (cdr) of the unique query, together with a stream of frames. For each frame in the stream, it should use qeval to find the stream of all extensions to the frame that satisfy the given query. Any stream that does not have exactly one item in it should be eliminated. The remaining streams should be passed back to be accumulated into one big stream that is the result of the unique query. This is similar to the implementation of the not special form.

Test your implementation by forming a query that lists all people who supervise precisely one person.

Exercise 4.76

Our implementation of and as a series combination of queries (figure 4.5) is elegant, but it is inefficient because in processing the second query of the and we must scan the data base for each frame produced by the first query. If the data base has N elements, and a typical query produces a number of output frames proportional to N (say N/k), then scanning the data base for each frame produced by the first query will require N^2/k calls to the pattern matcher. Another approach would be to process the two clauses of the and separately, then look for all pairs of output frames that are compatible. If each query produces N/k output frames, then this means that we must perform N^2/k^2 compatibility checks—a factor of k fewer than the number of matches required in our current method.

Devise an implementation of and that uses this strategy. You must implement a procedure that takes two frames as inputs, checks whether the bindings in the frames are compatible, and, if so, produces a frame that merges the two sets of bindings. This operation is similar to unification.

Exercise 4.77

In section 4.4.3 we saw that not and lisp-value can cause the query language to give "wrong" answers if these filtering operations are applied to frames in which variables are unbound. Devise a way to fix this shortcoming. One idea is to perform the filtering in a "delayed" manner by appending to the frame a "promise" to filter that is fulfilled only when enough variables have been bound to make the operation possible. We could wait to perform filtering until all other operations have been performed. However, for efficiency's sake, we would like to perform filtering as soon as possible so as to cut down on the number of intermediate frames generated.

Exercise 4.78

Redesign the query language as a nondeterministic program to be implemented using the evaluator of section 4.3, rather than as a stream process. In this approach, each query will produce a single answer (rather than the stream of all answers) and the user can type try-again to see more answers. You should find that much of the mechanism we built in this section is subsumed by nondeterministic search and backtracking. You will probably also find, however, that your new query language has subtle differences in behavior from the one implemented here. Can you find examples that illustrate this difference?

Exercise 4.79

When we implemented the Lisp evaluator in section 4.1, we saw how to use local environments to avoid name conflicts between the parameters of procedures. For example, in evaluating

```
(define (square x)
  (* x x))

(define (sum-of-squares x y)
  (+ (square x) (square y)))

(sum-of-squares 3 4)
```

there is no confusion between the x in square and the x in sum-of-squares, because we evaluate the body of each procedure in an environment that is specially constructed to contain bindings for the local variables. In the query system, we used a different strategy to avoid name conflicts in applying rules. Each time we apply a rule we rename the variables with new names that are guaranteed to be unique. The analogous strategy for the Lisp evaluator would be to do away with local environments and simply rename the variables in the body of a procedure each time we apply the procedure.

Implement for the query language a rule-application method that uses environments rather than renaming. See if you can build on your environment structure to create constructs in the query language for dealing with large systems, such as the rule analog of block-structured procedures. Can you relate any of this to the problem of making deductions in a context (e.g., "If I supposed that P were true, then I would be able to deduce A and B.") as a method of problem solving? (This problem is open-ended. A good answer is probably worth a Ph.D.)

5

Computing with Register Machines

> My aim is to show that the heavenly machine is not a
> kind of divine, live being, but a kind of clockwork (and
> he who believes that a clock has soul attributes the
> maker's glory to the work), insofar as nearly all the
> manifold motions are caused by a most simple and
> material force, just as all motions of the clock are caused
> by a single weight.
>
> Johannes Kepler (letter to Herwart von Hohenburg, 1605)

We began this book by studying processes and by describing processes in terms of procedures written in Lisp. To explain the meanings of these procedures, we used a succession of models of evaluation: the substitution model of chapter 1, the environment model of chapter 3, and the metacircular evaluator of chapter 4. Our examination of the metacircular evaluator, in particular, dispelled much of the mystery of how Lisp-like languages are interpreted. But even the metacircular evaluator leaves important questions unanswered, because it fails to elucidate the mechanisms of control in a Lisp system. For instance, the evaluator does not explain how the evaluation of a subexpression manages to return a value to the expression that uses this value, nor does the evaluator explain how some recursive procedures generate iterative processes (that is, are evaluated using constant space) whereas other recursive procedures generate recursive processes. These questions remain unanswered because the metacircular evaluator is itself a Lisp program and hence inherits the control structure of the underlying Lisp system. In order to provide a more complete description of the control structure of the Lisp evaluator, we must work at a more primitive level than Lisp itself.

In this chapter we will describe processes in terms of the step-by-step operation of a traditional computer. Such a computer, or *register machine*, sequentially executes *instructions* that manipulate the contents of a fixed set of storage elements called *registers*. A typical register-machine instruction applies a primitive operation to the contents of some registers and assigns the result to another register. Our descriptions of processes executed by register machines will look very much like "machine-language" programs for traditional computers. However, instead of focusing on the machine language of any particular computer, we will examine several Lisp procedures and design a specific register machine to execute each procedure. Thus, we will approach our task from the perspective of a hardware architect rather than that of a machine-language computer programmer. In designing register machines, we will develop mechanisms for implementing important programming constructs such as recursion. We will also present a language for describing designs for register machines. In section 5.2 we will implement a Lisp program that uses these descriptions to simulate the machines we design.

Most of the primitive operations of our register machines are very simple. For example, an operation might add the numbers fetched from two registers, producing a result to be stored into a third register. Such an operation can be performed by easily described hardware. In order to deal with list structure, however, we will also use the memory operations car, cdr, and cons, which require an elaborate storage-allocation mechanism. In section 5.3 we study their implementation in terms of more elementary operations.

In section 5.4, after we have accumulated experience formulating simple procedures as register machines, we will design a machine that carries out the algorithm described by the metacircular evaluator of section 4.1. This will fill in the gap in our understanding of how Scheme expressions are interpreted, by providing an explicit model for the mechanisms of control in the evaluator. In section 5.5 we will study a simple compiler that translates Scheme programs into sequences of instructions that can be executed directly with the registers and operations of the evaluator register machine.

5.1   Designing Register Machines

To design a register machine, we must design its *data paths* (registers and operations) and the *controller* that sequences these operations. To illustrate the design of a simple register machine, let us examine Euclid's Algorithm, which is used to compute the greatest common divisor (GCD) of two integers. As we saw in section 1.2.5, Euclid's Algorithm can be carried out by an iterative process, as specified by the following procedure:

```
(define (gcd a b)
  (if (= b 0)
      a
      (gcd b (remainder a b))))
```

A machine to carry out this algorithm must keep track of two numbers, *a* and *b*, so let us assume that these numbers are stored in two registers with those names. The basic operations required are testing whether the contents of register b is zero and computing the remainder of the contents of register a divided by the contents of register b. The remainder operation is a complex process, but assume for the moment that we have a primitive device that computes remainders. On each cycle of the GCD algorithm, the contents of register a must be replaced by the contents of register b, and the contents of b must be replaced by the remainder of the old contents of a divided by the old contents of b. It would be convenient if these replacements could be done simultaneously, but in our model of register machines we will assume that only one register can be assigned a new value at each step. To accomplish the replacements, our machine will use a third "temporary" register, which we call t. (First the remainder will be placed in t, then the contents of b will be placed in a, and finally the remainder stored in t will be placed in b.)

We can illustrate the registers and operations required for this machine by using the data-path diagram shown in figure 5.1. In this diagram, the registers (a, b, and t) are represented by rectangles. Each way to assign a value to a register is indicated by an arrow with an X behind the head, pointing from the source of data to the register. We can think of the X as a button that, when pushed, allows the value at the source to "flow" into the designated register. The label next to each button is the name we will use to refer to the button. The names are arbitrary, and can be chosen to have mnemonic value (for example, a<-b denotes pushing the button that assigns the contents of register b to register a). The source of data for a register can be another register (as in the a<-b assignment), an operation result (as in the t<-r assignment), or a constant (a built-in value that cannot be changed, represented in a data-path diagram by a triangle containing the constant).

An operation that computes a value from constants and the contents of registers is represented in a data-path diagram by a trapezoid containing a name for the operation. For example, the box marked rem in figure 5.1 represents an operation that computes the remainder of the contents of the registers a and b to which it is attached. Arrows (without buttons) point from the input registers and constants to the box, and arrows connect the operation's output value to registers. A test is represented by a circle containing a name for the test. For example, our GCD machine has an operation that tests whether the contents of register b is zero. A test also has arrows from its input registers and constants, but it has no output arrows; its value is used by the controller rather than by the data paths.

Overall, the data-path diagram shows the registers and operations that are required for the machine and how they must be connected. If we view the arrows as wires and the X buttons as switches, the data-path diagram is very like the wiring diagram for a machine that could be constructed from electrical components.

In order for the data paths to actually compute GCDs, the buttons must be pushed in the correct sequence. We will describe this sequence in terms of a controller diagram, as illustrated in figure 5.2. The elements of the controller diagram indicate how the data-path components should be operated. The rectangular boxes in the controller diagram identify data-path buttons to be pushed, and the arrows describe the sequencing from one step to the next. The diamond in the diagram represents a decision. One of the two sequencing arrows will be followed, depending on the value of the data-path test identified in the diamond. We can interpret the controller in terms of a physical analogy: Think of the diagram as a maze in which a marble is rolling. When the marble rolls into a box, it pushes the data-path button that is named by the box. When the marble rolls into a decision node (such as the test for $b = 0$), it leaves the node on the path determined by the result of the indicated test. Taken together, the data paths and the controller completely describe a machine for computing GCDs. We start the controller (the rolling marble) at the place marked start, after placing numbers in registers a and b. When the controller reaches done, we will find the value of the GCD in register a.

Exercise 5.1

Design a register machine to compute factorials using the iterative algorithm specified by the following procedure. Draw data-path and controller diagrams for this machine.

```
(define (factorial n)
  (define (iter product counter)
    (if (> counter n)
        product
        (iter (* counter product)
              (+ counter 1))))
  (iter 1 1))
```

5.1.1 A Language for Describing Register Machines

Data-path and controller diagrams are adequate for representing simple machines such as GCD, but they are unwieldy for describing large machines such as a Lisp interpreter. To make it possible to deal with com-

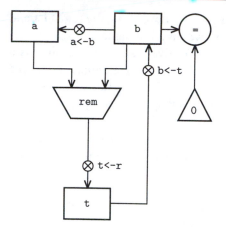

Figure 5.1   Data paths for a GCD machine.

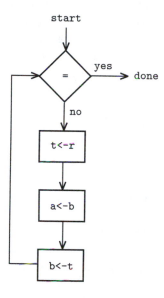

Figure 5.2   Controller for a GCD machine.

plex machines, we will create a language that presents, in textual form, all the information given by the data-path and controller diagrams. We will start with a notation that directly mirrors the diagrams.

We define the data paths of a machine by describing the registers and the operations. To describe a register, we give it a name and specify the buttons that control assignment to it. We give each of these buttons a name and specify the source of the data that enters the register under the button's control. (The source is a register, a constant, or an operation.) To describe an operation, we give it a name and specify its inputs (registers or constants).

We define the controller of a machine as a sequence of *instructions* together with *labels* that identify *entry points* in the sequence. An instruction is one of the following:

• The name of a data-path button to push to assign a value to a register. (This corresponds to a box in the controller diagram.)

• A `test` instruction, that performs a specified test.

• A conditional branch (`branch` instruction) to a location indicated by a controller label, based on the result of the previous test. (The test and branch together correspond to a diamond in the controller diagram.) If the test is false, the controller should continue with the next instruction in the sequence. Otherwise, the controller should continue with the instruction after the label.

• An unconditional branch (`goto` instruction) naming a controller label at which to continue execution.

The machine starts at the beginning of the controller instruction sequence and stops when execution reaches the end of the sequence. Except when a branch changes the flow of control, instructions are executed in the order in which they are listed.

Figure 5.3 shows the GCD machine described in this way. This example only hints at the generality of these descriptions, since the GCD machine is a very simple case: Each register has only one button, and each button and test is used only once in the controller.

Unfortunately, it is difficult to read such a description. In order to understand the controller instructions we must constantly refer back to the definitions of the button names and the operation names, and to understand what the buttons do we may have to refer to the definitions of the operation names. We will thus transform our notation to combine the information from the data-path and controller descriptions so that we see it all together.

To obtain this form of description, we will replace the arbitrary button and operation names by the definitions of their behavior. That is, instead

```
(data-paths
 (registers
  ((name a)
   (buttons ((name a<-b) (source (register b)))))
  ((name b)
   (buttons ((name b<-t) (source (register t)))))
  ((name t)
   (buttons ((name t<-r) (source (operation rem)))))))

 (operations
  ((name rem)
   (inputs (register a) (register b)))
  ((name =)
   (inputs (register b) (constant 0)))))
```

```
(controller
 test-b                          ; label
   (test =)                      ; test
   (branch (label gcd-done))     ; conditional branch
   (t<-r)                        ; button push
   (a<-b)                        ; button push
   (b<-t)                        ; button push
   (goto (label test-b))         ; unconditional branch
 gcd-done)                       ; label
```

Figure 5.3   A specification of the GCD machine.

of saying (in the controller) "Push button `t<-r`" and separately saying
(in the data paths) "Button `t<-r` assigns the value of the `rem` operation
to register `t`" and "The `rem` operation's inputs are the contents of registers
`a` and `b`," we will say (in the controller) "Push the button that assigns to
register `t` the value of the `rem` operation on the contents of registers `a`
and `b`." Similarly, instead of saying (in the controller) "Perform the `=`
test" and separately saying (in the data paths) "The `=` test operates on the
contents of register `b` and the constant 0," we will say "Perform the `=` test
on the contents of register `b` and the constant 0." We will omit the data-
path description, leaving only the controller sequence. Thus, the GCD
machine is described as follows:

```
(controller
 test-b
   (test (op =) (reg b) (const 0))
   (branch (label gcd-done))
   (assign t (op rem) (reg a) (reg b))
   (assign a (reg b))
   (assign b (reg t))
   (goto (label test-b))
 gcd-done)
```

This form of description is easier to read than the kind illustrated in figure 5.3, but it also has disadvantages:

• It is more verbose for large machines, because complete descriptions of the data-path elements are repeated whenever the elements are mentioned in the controller instruction sequence. (This is not a problem in the GCD example, because each operation and button is used only once.) Moreover, repeating the data-path descriptions obscures the actual data-path structure of the machine; it is not obvious for a large machine how many registers, operations, and buttons there are and how they are interconnected.

• Because the controller instructions in a machine definition look like Lisp expressions, it is easy to forget that they are not arbitrary Lisp expressions. They can notate only legal machine operations. For example, operations can operate directly only on constants and the contents of registers, not on the results of other operations.

In spite of these disadvantages, we will use this register-machine language throughout this chapter, because we will be more concerned with understanding controllers than with understanding the elements and connections in data paths. We should keep in mind, however, that data-path design is crucial in designing real machines.

Exercise 5.2

Use the register-machine language to describe the iterative factorial machine of exercise 5.1.

Actions

Let us modify the GCD machine so that we can type in the numbers whose GCD we want and get the answer printed at our terminal. We will not discuss how to make a machine that can read and print, but will assume (as we do when we use `read` and `display` in Scheme) that they are available as primitive operations.[1]

`Read` is like the operations we have been using in that it produces a value that can be stored in a register. But `read` does not take inputs from any registers; its value depends on something that happens outside the parts of the machine we are designing. We will allow our machine's operations to have such behavior, and thus will draw and notate the use of `read` just as we do any other operation that computes a value.

---

[1] This assumption glosses over a great deal of complexity. Usually a large portion of the implementation of a Lisp system is dedicated to making reading and printing work.

Print, on the other hand, differs from the operations we have been using in a fundamental way: It does not produce an output value to be stored in a register. Though it has an effect, this effect is not on a part of the machine we are designing. We will refer to this kind of operation as an *action*. We will represent an action in a data-path diagram just as we represent an operation that computes a value—as a trapezoid that contains the name of the action. Arrows point to the action box from any inputs (registers or constants). We also associate a button with the action. Pushing the button makes the action happen. To make a controller push an action button we use a new kind of instruction called perform. Thus, the action of printing the contents of register a is represented in a controller sequence by the instruction

```
(perform (op print) (reg a))
```

Figure 5.4 shows the data paths and controller for the new GCD machine. Instead of having the machine stop after printing the answer, we have made it start over, so that it repeatedly reads a pair of numbers, computes their GCD, and prints the result. This structure is like the driver loops we used in the interpreters of chapter 4.

5.1.2   Abstraction in Machine Design

We will often define a machine to include "primitive" operations that are actually very complex. For example, in sections 5.4 and 5.5 we will treat Scheme's environment manipulations as primitive. Such abstraction is valuable because it allows us to ignore the details of parts of a machine so that we can concentrate on other aspects of the design. The fact that we have swept a lot of complexity under the rug, however, does not mean that a machine design is unrealistic. We can always replace the complex "primitives" by simpler primitive operations.

Consider the GCD machine. The machine has an instruction that computes the remainder of the contents of registers a and b and assigns the result to register t. If we want to construct the GCD machine without using a primitive remainder operation, we must specify how to compute remainders in terms of simpler operations, such as subtraction. Indeed, we can write a Scheme procedure that finds remainders in this way:

```
(define (remainder n d)
  (if (< n d)
      n
      (remainder (- n d) d)))
```

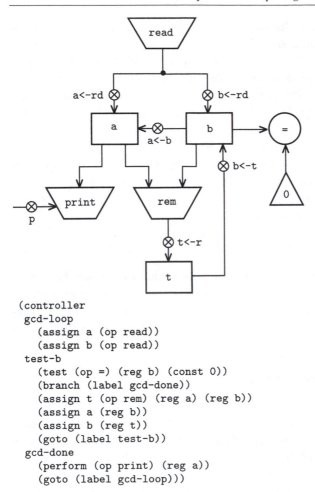

```
(controller
 gcd-loop
   (assign a (op read))
   (assign b (op read))
 test-b
   (test (op =) (reg b) (const 0))
   (branch (label gcd-done))
   (assign t (op rem) (reg a) (reg b))
   (assign a (reg b))
   (assign b (reg t))
   (goto (label test-b))
 gcd-done
   (perform (op print) (reg a))
   (goto (label gcd-loop)))
```

Figure 5.4   A GCD machine that reads inputs and prints results.

We can thus replace the remainder operation in the GCD machine's data paths with a subtraction operation and a comparison test. Figure 5.5 shows the data paths and controller for the elaborated machine. The instruction

```
(assign t (op rem) (reg a) (reg b))
```

in the GCD controller definition is replaced by a sequence of instructions that contains a loop, as shown in figure 5.6.

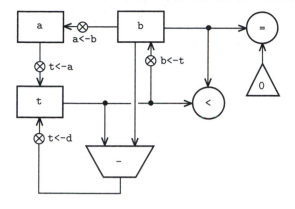

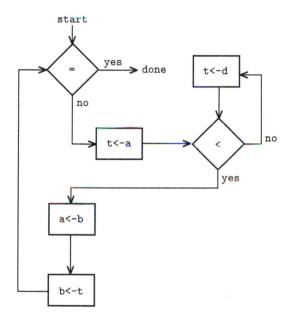

Figure 5.5   Data paths and controller for the elaborated GCD machine.

```
(controller
 test-b
   (test (op =) (reg b) (const 0))
   (branch (label gcd-done))
   (assign t (reg a))
 rem-loop
   (test (op <) (reg t) (reg b))
   (branch (label rem-done))
   (assign t (op -) (reg t) (reg b))
   (goto (label rem-loop))
 rem-done
   (assign a (reg b))
   (assign b (reg t))
   (goto (label test-b))
 gcd-done)
```

Figure 5.6   Controller instruction sequence for the GCD machine in figure 5.5.

Exercise 5.3

Design a machine to compute square roots using Newton's method, as described in section 1.1.7:

```
(define (sqrt x)
  (define (good-enough? guess)
    (< (abs (- (square guess) x)) 0.001))
  (define (improve guess)
    (average guess (/ x guess)))
  (define (sqrt-iter guess)
    (if (good-enough? guess)
        guess
        (sqrt-iter (improve guess))))
  (sqrt-iter 1.0))
```

Begin by assuming that good-enough? and improve operations are available as primitives. Then show how to expand these in terms of arithmetic operations. Describe each version of the sqrt machine design by drawing a data-path diagram and writing a controller definition in the register-machine language.

5.1.3   Subroutines

When designing a machine to perform a computation, we would often prefer to arrange for components to be shared by different parts of the computation rather than duplicate the components. Consider a machine that includes two GCD computations—one that finds the GCD of the contents of registers a and b and one that finds the GCD of the contents of registers c and d. We might start by assuming we have a primitive gcd operation, then expand the two instances of gcd in terms of more primitive operations. Figure 5.7 shows just the GCD portions of the resulting

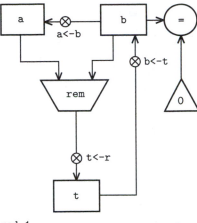 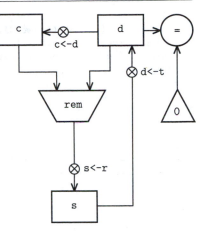

```
gcd-1
 (test (op =) (reg b) (const 0))
 (branch (label after-gcd-1))
 (assign t (op rem) (reg a) (reg b))
 (assign a (reg b))
 (assign b (reg t))
 (goto (label gcd-1))
after-gcd-1
   ⋮

gcd-2
 (test (op =) (reg d) (const 0))
 (branch (label after-gcd-2))
 (assign s (op rem) (reg c) (reg d))
 (assign c (reg d))
 (assign d (reg s))
 (goto (label gcd-2))
after-gcd-2
```

Figure 5.7 Portions of the data paths and controller sequence for a machine with two GCD computations.

machine's data paths, without showing how they connect to the rest of the machine. The figure also shows the corresponding portions of the machine's controller sequence.

This machine has two remainder operation boxes and two boxes for testing equality. If the duplicated components are complicated, as is the remainder box, this will not be an economical way to build the machine. We can avoid duplicating the data-path components by using the same components for both GCD computations, provided that doing so will not affect the rest of the larger machine's computation. If the values in registers a and b are not needed by the time the controller gets to gcd-2 (or if these values can be moved to other registers for safekeeping), we can

```
gcd-1
 (test (op =) (reg b) (const 0))
 (branch (label after-gcd-1))
 (assign t (op rem) (reg a) (reg b))
 (assign a (reg b))
 (assign b (reg t))
 (goto (label gcd-1))
after-gcd-1
   .
   .
   .

gcd-2
 (test (op =) (reg b) (const 0))
 (branch (label after-gcd-2))
 (assign t (op rem) (reg a) (reg b))
 (assign a (reg b))
 (assign b (reg t))
 (goto (label gcd-2))
after-gcd-2
```

Figure 5.8   Portions of the controller sequence for a machine that uses the same data-path components for two different GCD computations.

change the machine so that it uses registers a and b, rather than registers c and d, in computing the second GCD as well as the first. If we do this, we obtain the controller sequence shown in figure 5.8.

We have removed the duplicate data-path components (so that the data paths are again as in figure 5.1), but the controller now has two GCD sequences that differ only in their entry-point labels. It would be better to replace these two sequences by branches to a single sequence—a gcd *subroutine*—at the end of which we branch back to the correct place in the main instruction sequence. We can accomplish this as follows: Before branching to gcd, we place a distinguishing value (such as 0 or 1) into a special register, continue. At the end of the gcd subroutine we return either to after-gcd-1 or to after-gcd-2, depending on the value of the continue register. Figure 5.9 shows the relevant portion of the resulting controller sequence, which includes only a single copy of the gcd instructions.

This is a reasonable approach for handling small problems, but it would be awkward if there were many instances of GCD computations in the controller sequence. To decide where to continue executing after the gcd subroutine, we would need tests in the data paths and branch instructions in the controller for all the places that use gcd. A more powerful method for implementing subroutines is to have the continue register hold the label of the entry point in the controller sequence at which execution should continue when the subroutine is finished. Implementing

```
gcd
  (test (op =) (reg b) (const 0))
  (branch (label gcd-done))
  (assign t (op rem) (reg a) (reg b))
  (assign a (reg b))
  (assign b (reg t))
  (goto (label gcd))
gcd-done
  (test (op =) (reg continue) (const 0))
  (branch (label after-gcd-1))
  (goto (label after-gcd-2))
    ⋮
```

;; Before branching to gcd from the first place where
;; it is needed, we place 0 in the continue *register*
```
  (assign continue (const 0))
  (goto (label gcd))
after-gcd-1
    ⋮
```

;; Before the second use of gcd, we place 1 in the continue *register*
```
  (assign continue (const 1))
  (goto (label gcd))
after-gcd-2
```

Figure 5.9 Using a `continue` register to avoid the duplicate controller sequence in figure 5.8.

```
gcd
  (test (op =) (reg b) (const 0))
  (branch (label gcd-done))
  (assign t (op rem) (reg a) (reg b))
  (assign a (reg b))
  (assign b (reg t))
  (goto (label gcd))
gcd-done
  (goto (reg continue))
    ⋮
```

;; Before calling gcd, we assign to continue
;; the label to which gcd should return.
```
  (assign continue (label after-gcd-1))
  (goto (label gcd))
after-gcd-1
    ⋮
```

;; Here is the second call to gcd, with a different continuation.
```
  (assign continue (label after-gcd-2))
  (goto (label gcd))
after-gcd-2
```

Figure 5.10 Assigning labels to the `continue` register simplifies and generalizes the strategy shown in figure 5.9.

this strategy requires a new kind of connection between the data paths and the controller of a register machine: There must be a way to assign to a register a label in the controller sequence in such a way that this value can be fetched from the register and used to continue execution at the designated entry point.

To reflect this ability, we will extend the `assign` instruction of the register-machine language to allow a register to be assigned as value a label from the controller sequence (as a special kind of constant). We will also extend the `goto` instruction to allow execution to continue at the entry point described by the contents of a register rather than only at an entry point described by a constant label. Using these new constructs we can terminate the gcd subroutine with a branch to the location stored in the `continue` register. This leads to the controller sequence shown in figure 5.10.

A machine with more than one subroutine could use multiple continuation registers (e.g., `gcd-continue`, `factorial-continue`) or we could have all subroutines share a single `continue` register. Sharing is more economical, but we must be careful if we have a subroutine (`sub1`) that calls another subroutine (`sub2`). Unless `sub1` saves the contents of `continue` in some other register before setting up `continue` for the call to `sub2`, `sub1` will not know where to go when it is finished. The mechanism developed in the next section to handle recursion also provides a better solution to this problem of nested subroutine calls.

5.1.4   Using a Stack to Implement Recursion

With the ideas illustrated so far, we can implement any iterative process by specifying a register machine that has a register corresponding to each state variable of the process. The machine repeatedly executes a controller loop, changing the contents of the registers, until some termination condition is satisfied. At each point in the controller sequence, the state of the machine (representing the state of the iterative process) is completely determined by the contents of the registers (the values of the state variables).

Implementing recursive processes, however, requires an additional mechanism. Consider the following recursive method for computing factorials, which we first examined in section 1.2.1:

```
(define (factorial n)
  (if (= n 1)
      1
      (* (factorial (- n 1)) n)))
```

As we see from the procedure, computing $n!$ requires computing $(n-1)!$. Our GCD machine, modeled on the procedure

```
(define (gcd a b)
  (if (= b 0)
      a
      (gcd b (remainder a b)))))
```

similarly had to compute another GCD. But there is an important difference between the gcd procedure, which reduces the original computation to a new GCD computation, and factorial, which requires computing another factorial as a subproblem. In GCD, the answer to the new GCD computation is the answer to the original problem. To compute the next GCD, we simply place the new arguments in the input registers of the GCD machine and reuse the machine's data paths by executing the same controller sequence. When the machine is finished solving the final GCD problem, it has completed the entire computation.

In the case of factorial (or any recursive process) the answer to the new factorial subproblem is not the answer to the original problem. The value obtained for $(n-1)!$ must be multiplied by n to get the final answer. If we try to imitate the GCD design, and solve the factorial subproblem by decrementing the n register and rerunning the factorial machine, we will no longer have available the old value of n by which to multiply the result. We thus need a second factorial machine to work on the subproblem. This second factorial computation itself has a factorial subproblem, which requires a third factorial machine, and so on. Since each factorial machine contains another factorial machine within it, the total machine contains an infinite nest of similar machines and hence cannot be constructed from a fixed, finite number of parts.

Nevertheless, we can implement the factorial process as a register machine if we can arrange to use the same components for each nested instance of the machine. Specifically, the machine that computes $n!$ should use the same components to work on the subproblem of computing $(n-1)!$, on the subproblem for $(n-2)!$, and so on. This is plausible because, although the factorial process dictates that an unbounded number of copies of the same machine are needed to perform a computation, only one of these copies needs to be active at any given time. When the machine encounters a recursive subproblem, it can suspend work on the main problem, reuse the same physical parts to work on the subproblem, then continue the suspended computation.

In the subproblem, the contents of the registers will be different than they were in the main problem. (In this case the n register is decremented.) In order to be able to continue the suspended computation, the machine must save the contents of any registers that will be needed after the subproblem is solved so that these can be restored to continue the suspended computation. In the case of factorial, we will save the old value of n, to be restored when we are finished computing the factorial of the decremented n register.[2]

Since there is no *a priori* limit on the depth of nested recursive calls, we may need to save an arbitrary number of register values. These values must be restored in the reverse of the order in which they were saved, since in a nest of recursions the last subproblem to be entered is the first to be finished. This dictates the use of a *stack*, or "last in, first out" data structure, to save register values. We can extend the register-machine language to include a stack by adding two kinds of instructions: Values are placed on the stack using a `save` instruction and restored from the stack using a `restore` instruction. After a sequence of values has been saved on the stack, a sequence of `restores` will retrieve these values in reverse order.[3]

With the aid of the stack, we can reuse a single copy of the factorial machine's data paths for each factorial subproblem. There is a similar design issue in reusing the controller sequence that operates the data paths. To reexecute the factorial computation, the controller cannot simply loop back to the beginning, as with an iterative process, because after solving the $(n - 1)!$ subproblem the machine must still multiply the result by n. The controller must suspend its computation of $n!$, solve the $(n-1)!$ subproblem, then continue its computation of $n!$. This view of the factorial computation suggests the use of the subroutine mechanism described in section 5.1.3, which has the controller use a `continue` register to transfer to the part of the sequence that solves a subproblem and then continue where it left off on the main problem. We can thus make a factorial subroutine that returns to the entry point stored in the `continue` register. Around each subroutine call, we save and restore `continue` just as we

---

[2]One might argue that we don't need to save the old n; after we decrement it and solve the subproblem, we could simply increment it to recover the old value. Although this strategy works for factorial, it cannot work in general, since the old value of a register cannot always be computed from the new one.

[3]In section 5.3 we will see how to implement a stack in terms of more primitive operations.

do the n register, since each "level" of the factorial computation will use the same `continue` register. That is, the factorial subroutine must put a new value in `continue` when it calls itself for a subproblem, but it will need the old value in order to return to the place that called it to solve a subproblem.

Figure 5.11 shows the data paths and controller for a machine that implements the recursive `factorial` procedure. The machine has a stack and three registers, called n, `val`, and `continue`. To simplify the data-path diagram, we have not named the register-assignment buttons, only the stack-operation buttons (`sc` and `sn` to save registers, `rc` and `rn` to restore registers). To operate the machine, we put in register n the number whose factorial we wish to compute and start the machine. When the machine reaches `fact-done`, the computation is finished and the answer will be found in the `val` register. In the controller sequence, n and `continue` are saved before each recursive call and restored upon return from the call. Returning from a call is accomplished by branching to the location stored in `continue`. `Continue` is initialized when the machine starts so that the last return will go to `fact-done`. The `val` register, which holds the result of the factorial computation, is not saved before the recursive call, because the old contents of `val` is not useful after the subroutine returns. Only the new value, which is the value produced by the subcomputation, is needed.

Although in principle the factorial computation requires an infinite machine, the machine in figure 5.11 is actually finite except for the stack, which is potentially unbounded. Any particular physical implementation of a stack, however, will be of finite size, and this will limit the depth of recursive calls that can be handled by the machine. This implementation of factorial illustrates the general strategy for realizing recursive algorithms as ordinary register machines augmented by stacks. When a recursive subproblem is encountered, we save on the stack the registers whose current values will be required after the subproblem is solved, solve the recursive subproblem, then restore the saved registers and continue execution on the main problem. The `continue` register must always be saved. Whether there are other registers that need to be saved depends on the particular machine, since not all recursive computations need the original values of registers that are modified during solution of the subproblem (see exercise 5.4).

A double recursion

Let us examine a more complex recursive process, the tree-recursive computation of the Fibonacci numbers, which we introduced in section 1.2.2:

```
(define (fib n)
  (if (< n 2)
      n
      (+ (fib (- n 1)) (fib (- n 2))))))
```

Just as with factorial, we can implement the recursive Fibonacci computation as a register machine with registers n, val, and continue. The machine is more complex than the one for factorial, because there are two places in the controller sequence where we need to perform recursive calls—once to compute Fib($n - 1$) and once to compute Fib($n - 2$). To set up for each of these calls, we save the registers whose values will be needed later, set the n register to the number whose Fib we need to compute recursively ($n - 1$ or $n - 2$), and assign to continue the entry point in the main sequence to which to return (afterfib-n-1 or afterfib-n-2, respectively). We then go to fib-loop. When we return from the recursive call, the answer is in val. Figure 5.12 shows the controller sequence for this machine.

Exercise 5.4

Specify register machines that implement each of the following procedures. For each machine, write a controller instruction sequence and draw a diagram showing the data paths.

a. Recursive exponentiation:

```
(define (expt b n)
  (if (= n 0)
      1
      (* b (expt b (- n 1))))))
```

b. Iterative exponentiation:

```
(define (expt b n)
  (define (expt-iter counter product)
    (if (= counter 0)
        product
        (expt-iter (- counter 1) (* b product))))
  (expt-iter n 1))
```

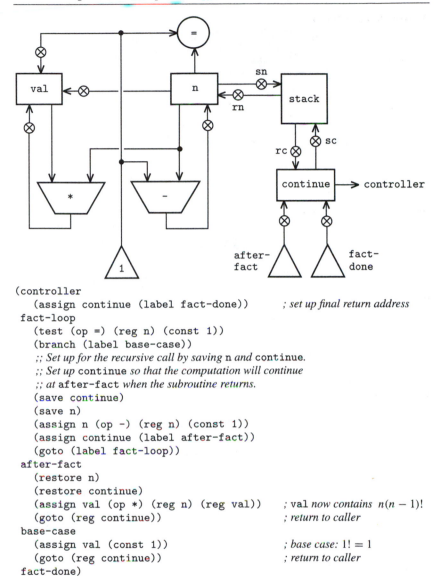

```
(controller
    (assign continue (label fact-done))          ; set up final return address
 fact-loop
    (test (op =) (reg n) (const 1))
    (branch (label base-case))
    ;; Set up for the recursive call by saving n and continue.
    ;; Set up continue so that the computation will continue
    ;; at after-fact when the subroutine returns.
    (save continue)
    (save n)
    (assign n (op -) (reg n) (const 1))
    (assign continue (label after-fact))
    (goto (label fact-loop))
 after-fact
    (restore n)
    (restore continue)
    (assign val (op *) (reg n) (reg val))        ; val now contains n(n - 1)!
    (goto (reg continue))                        ; return to caller
 base-case
    (assign val (const 1))                       ; base case: 1! = 1
    (goto (reg continue))                        ; return to caller
 fact-done)
```

Figure 5.11   A recursive factorial machine.

```
(controller
  (assign continue (label fib-done))
 fib-loop
  (test (op <) (reg n) (const 2))
  (branch (label immediate-answer))
  ;; set up to compute Fib(n − 1)
  (save continue)
  (assign continue (label afterfib-n-1))
  (save n)                               ; save old value of n
  (assign n (op -) (reg n) (const 1)) ; clobber n to n − 1
  (goto (label fib-loop))                ; perform recursive call
 afterfib-n-1                            ; upon return, val contains Fib(n − 1)
  (restore n)
  (restore continue)
  ;; set up to compute Fib(n − 2)
  (assign n (op -) (reg n) (const 2))
  (save continue)
  (assign continue (label afterfib-n-2))
  (save val)                             ; save Fib(n − 1)
  (goto (label fib-loop))
 afterfib-n-2                            ; upon return, val contains Fib(n − 2)
  (assign n (reg val))                   ; n now contains Fib(n − 2)
  (restore val)                          ; val now contains Fib(n − 1)
  (restore continue)
  (assign val                            ;  Fib(n − 1) + Fib(n − 2)
          (op +) (reg val) (reg n))
  (goto (reg continue))                  ; return to caller, answer is in val
 immediate-answer
  (assign val (reg n))                   ; base case:  Fib(n) = n
  (goto (reg continue))
 fib-done)
```

Figure 5.12   Controller for a machine to compute Fibonacci numbers.

Exercise 5.5

Hand-simulate the factorial and Fibonacci machines, using some nontrivial input (requiring execution of at least one recursive call). Show the contents of the stack at each significant point in the execution.

Exercise 5.6

Ben Bitdiddle observes that the Fibonacci machine's controller sequence has an extra save and an extra restore, which can be removed to make a faster machine. Where are these instructions?

5.1.5   Instruction Summary

A controller instruction in our register-machine language has one of the following forms, where each ⟨ *input$_i$* ⟩ is either (reg ⟨ *register-name* ⟩) or (const ⟨ *constant-value* ⟩).

These instructions were introduced in section 5.1.1:

`(assign ⟨`*register-name*`⟩ (reg ⟨`*register-name*`⟩))`

`(assign ⟨`*register-name*`⟩ (const ⟨`*constant-value*`⟩))`

`(assign ⟨`*register-name*`⟩ (op ⟨`*operation-name*`⟩) ⟨`*input₁*`⟩ ... ⟨`*inputₙ*`⟩)`

`(perform (op ⟨`*operation-name*`⟩) ⟨`*input₁*`⟩ ... ⟨`*inputₙ*`⟩)`

`(test (op ⟨`*operation-name*`⟩) ⟨`*input₁*`⟩ ... ⟨`*inputₙ*`⟩)`

`(branch (label ⟨`*label-name*`⟩))`

`(goto (label ⟨`*label-name*`⟩))`

The use of registers to hold labels was introduced in section 5.1.3:

`(assign ⟨`*register-name*`⟩ (label ⟨`*label-name*`⟩))`

`(goto (reg ⟨`*register-name*`⟩))`

Instructions to use the stack were introduced in section 5.1.4:

`(save ⟨`*register-name*`⟩)`

`(restore ⟨`*register-name*`⟩)`

The only kind of ⟨*constant-value*⟩ we have seen so far is a number, but later we will use strings, symbols, and lists. For example, `(const "abc")` is the string `"abc"`, `(const abc)` is the symbol abc, `(const (a b c))` is the list `(a b c)`, and `(const ())` is the empty list.

5.2   A Register-Machine Simulator

In order to gain a good understanding of the design of register machines, we must test the machines we design to see if they perform as expected. One way to test a design is to hand-simulate the operation of the controller, as in exercise 5.5. But this is extremely tedious for all but the simplest machines. In this section we construct a simulator for machines described in the register-machine language. The simulator is a Scheme program with four interface procedures. The first uses a description of a register machine to construct a model of the machine (a data structure whose parts correspond to the parts of the machine to be simulated), and the other three allow us to simulate the machine by manipulating the model:

(make-machine ⟨*register-names*⟩ ⟨*operations*⟩ ⟨*controller*⟩)
constructs and returns a model of the machine with the given registers, operations, and controller.

(set-register-contents! ⟨*machine-model*⟩ ⟨*register-name*⟩ ⟨*value*⟩)
stores a value in a simulated register in the given machine.

(get-register-contents ⟨*machine-model*⟩ ⟨*register-name*⟩)
returns the contents of a simulated register in the given machine.

(start ⟨*machine-model*⟩)
simulates the execution of the given machine, starting from the beginning of the controller sequence and stopping when it reaches the end of the sequence.

As an example of how these procedures are used, we can define gcd-machine to be a model of the GCD machine of section 5.1.1 as follows:

```
(define gcd-machine
  (make-machine
   '(a b t)
   (list (list 'rem remainder) (list '= =))
   '(test-b
       (test (op =) (reg b) (const 0))
       (branch (label gcd-done))
       (assign t (op rem) (reg a) (reg b))
       (assign a (reg b))
       (assign b (reg t))
       (goto (label test-b))
     gcd-done)))
```

The first argument to make-machine is a list of register names. The next argument is a table (a list of two-element lists) that pairs each operation name with a Scheme procedure that implements the operation (that is, produces the same output value given the same input values). The last argument specifies the controller as a list of labels and machine instructions, as in section 5.1.

To compute GCDs with this machine, we set the input registers, start the machine, and examine the result when the simulation terminates:

```
(set-register-contents! gcd-machine 'a 206)
done

(set-register-contents! gcd-machine 'b 40)
done

(start gcd-machine)
done

(get-register-contents gcd-machine 'a)
2
```

This computation will run much more slowly than a gcd procedure written in Scheme, because we will simulate low-level machine instructions, such as assign, by much more complex operations.

Exercise 5.7

Use the simulator to test the machines you designed in exercise 5.4.

5.2.1   The Machine Model

The machine model generated by make-machine is represented as a procedure with local state using the message-passing techniques developed in chapter 3. To build this model, make-machine begins by calling the procedure make-new-machine to construct the parts of the machine model that are common to all register machines. This basic machine model constructed by make-new-machine is essentially a container for some registers and a stack, together with an execution mechanism that processes the controller instructions one by one.

Make-machine then extends this basic model (by sending it messages) to include the registers, operations, and controller of the particular machine being defined. First it allocates a register in the new machine for each of the supplied register names and installs the designated operations in the machine. Then it uses an *assembler* (described below in section 5.2.2) to transform the controller list into instructions for the new machine and installs these as the machine's instruction sequence. Make-machine returns as its value the modified machine model.

```
(define (make-machine register-names ops controller-text)
  (let ((machine (make-new-machine)))
    (for-each (lambda (register-name)
                ((machine 'allocate-register) register-name))
              register-names)
    ((machine 'install-operations) ops)
    ((machine 'install-instruction-sequence)
     (assemble controller-text machine))
    machine))
```

Registers

We will represent a register as a procedure with local state, as in chapter 3. The procedure `make-register` creates a register that holds a value that can be accessed or changed:

```
(define (make-register name)
  (let ((contents '*unassigned*))
    (define (dispatch message)
      (cond ((eq? message 'get) contents)
            ((eq? message 'set)
             (lambda (value) (set! contents value)))
            (else
             (error "Unknown request -- REGISTER" message))))
    dispatch))
```

The following procedures are used to access registers:

```
(define (get-contents register)
  (register 'get))

(define (set-contents! register value)
  ((register 'set) value))
```

The stack

We can also represent a stack as a procedure with local state. The procedure `make-stack` creates a stack whose local state consists of a list of the items on the stack. A stack accepts requests to push an item onto the stack, to pop the top item off the stack and return it, and to `initialize` the stack to empty.

```
(define (make-stack)
  (let ((s '()))
    (define (push x)
      (set! s (cons x s)))
    (define (pop)
      (if (null? s)
          (error "Empty stack -- POP")
          (let ((top (car s)))
            (set! s (cdr s))
            top)))
    (define (initialize)
      (set! s '())
      'done)
    (define (dispatch message)
      (cond ((eq? message 'push) push)
            ((eq? message 'pop) (pop))
            ((eq? message 'initialize) (initialize))
            (else (error "Unknown request -- STACK"
                         message))))
    dispatch))
```

The following procedures are used to access stacks:

```
(define (pop stack)
  (stack 'pop))
```

```
(define (push stack value)
  ((stack 'push) value))
```

The basic machine

The make-new-machine procedure, shown in figure 5.13, constructs an object whose local state consists of a stack, an initially empty instruction sequence, a list of operations that initially contains an operation to initialize the stack, and a *register table* that initially contains two registers, named flag and pc (for "program counter"). The internal procedure allocate-register adds new entries to the register table, and the internal procedure lookup-register looks up registers in the table.

The flag register is used to control branching in the simulated machine. Test instructions set the contents of flag to the result of the test (true or false). Branch instructions decide whether or not to branch by examining the contents of flag.

The pc register determines the sequencing of instructions as the machine runs. This sequencing is implemented by the internal procedure execute. In the simulation model, each machine instruction is a data structure that includes a procedure of no arguments, called the *instruc-*

tion execution procedure, such that calling this procedure simulates executing the instruction. As the simulation runs, pc points to the place in the instruction sequence beginning with the next instruction to be executed. Execute gets that instruction, executes it by calling the instruction execution procedure, and repeats this cycle until there are no more instructions to execute (i.e., until pc points to the end of the instruction sequence).

As part of its operation, each instruction execution procedure modifies pc to indicate the next instruction to be executed. Branch and goto instructions change pc to point to the new destination. All other instructions simply advance pc, making it point to the next instruction in the sequence. Observe that each call to execute calls execute again, but this does not produce an infinite loop because running the instruction execution procedure changes the contents of pc.

Make-new-machine returns a dispatch procedure that implements message-passing access to the internal state. Notice that starting the machine is accomplished by setting pc to the beginning of the instruction sequence and calling execute.

For convenience, we provide an alternate procedural interface to a machine's start operation, as well as procedures to set and examine register contents, as specified at the beginning of section 5.2:

```
(define (start machine)
  (machine 'start))

(define (get-register-contents machine register-name)
  (get-contents (get-register machine register-name)))

(define (set-register-contents! machine register-name value)
  (set-contents! (get-register machine register-name) value)
  'done)
```

These procedures (and many procedures in sections 5.2.2 and 5.2.3) use the following to look up the register with a given name in a given machine:

```
(define (get-register machine reg-name)
  ((machine 'get-register) reg-name))
```

```
(define (make-new-machine)
  (let ((pc (make-register 'pc))
        (flag (make-register 'flag))
        (stack (make-stack))
        (the-instruction-sequence '()))
    (let ((the-ops
           (list (list 'initialize-stack
                       (lambda () (stack 'initialize)))))
          (register-table
           (list (list 'pc pc) (list 'flag flag))))
      (define (allocate-register name)
        (if (assoc name register-table)
            (error "Multiply defined register: " name)
            (set! register-table
                  (cons (list name (make-register name))
                        register-table)))
        'register-allocated)
      (define (lookup-register name)
        (let ((val (assoc name register-table)))
          (if val
              (cadr val)
              (error "Unknown register:" name))))
      (define (execute)
        (let ((insts (get-contents pc)))
          (if (null? insts)
              'done
              (begin
                ((instruction-execution-proc (car insts)))
                (execute)))))
      (define (dispatch message)
        (cond ((eq? message 'start)
               (set-contents! pc the-instruction-sequence)
               (execute))
              ((eq? message 'install-instruction-sequence)
               (lambda (seq) (set! the-instruction-sequence seq)))
              ((eq? message 'allocate-register) allocate-register)
              ((eq? message 'get-register) lookup-register)
              ((eq? message 'install-operations)
               (lambda (ops) (set! the-ops (append the-ops ops))))
              ((eq? message 'stack) stack)
              ((eq? message 'operations) the-ops)
              (else (error "Unknown request -- MACHINE" message))))
      dispatch)))
```

Figure 5.13   The make-new-machine procedure, which implements the basic machine model.

5.2.2 The Assembler

The assembler transforms the sequence of controller expressions for a machine into a corresponding list of machine instructions, each with its execution procedure. Overall, the assembler is much like the evaluators we studied in chapter 4—there is an input language (in this case, the register-machine language) and we must perform an appropriate action for each type of expression in the language.

The technique of producing an execution procedure for each instruction is just what we used in section 4.1.7 to speed up the evaluator by separating analysis from runtime execution. As we saw in chapter 4, much useful analysis of Scheme expressions could be performed without knowing the actual values of variables. Here, analogously, much useful analysis of register-machine-language expressions can be performed without knowing the actual contents of machine registers. For example, we can replace references to registers by pointers to the register objects, and we can replace references to labels by pointers to the place in the instruction sequence that the label designates.

Before it can generate the instruction execution procedures, the assembler must know what all the labels refer to, so it begins by scanning the controller text to separate the labels from the instructions. As it scans the text, it constructs both a list of instructions and a table that associates each label with a pointer into that list. Then the assembler augments the instruction list by inserting the execution procedure for each instruction.

The `assemble` procedure is the main entry to the assembler. It takes the controller text and the machine model as arguments and returns the instruction sequence to be stored in the model. Assemble calls `extract-labels` to build the initial instruction list and label table from the supplied controller text. The second argument to `extract-labels` is a procedure to be called to process these results: This procedure uses `update-insts!` to generate the instruction execution procedures and insert them into the instruction list, and returns the modified list.

```
(define (assemble controller-text machine)
  (extract-labels controller-text
    (lambda (insts labels)
      (update-insts! insts labels machine)
      insts)))
```

Extract-labels takes as arguments a list `text` (the sequence of controller instruction expressions) and a `receive` procedure. Receive will be called with two values: (1) a list `insts` of instruction data structures, each containing an instruction from `text`; and (2) a table called `labels`, which associates each label from `text` with the position in the list `insts` that the label designates.

```
(define (extract-labels text receive)
  (if (null? text)
      (receive '() '())
      (extract-labels (cdr text)
        (lambda (insts labels)
          (let ((next-inst (car text)))
            (if (symbol? next-inst)
                (receive insts
                         (cons (make-label-entry next-inst
                                                 insts)
                               labels))
                (receive (cons (make-instruction next-inst
                                                 insts)
                               labels)))))))))
```

Extract-labels works by sequentially scanning the elements of the text and accumulating the `insts` and the `labels`. If an element is a symbol (and thus a label) an appropriate entry is added to the `labels` table. Otherwise the element is accumulated onto the `insts` list.[4]

---

[4]Using the `receive` procedure here is a way to get `extract-labels` to effectively return two values—`labels` and `insts`—without explicitly making a compound data structure to hold them. An alternative implementation, which returns an explicit pair of values, is

```
(define (extract-labels text)
  (if (null? text)
      (cons '() '())
      (let ((result (extract-labels (cdr text))))
        (let ((insts (car result)) (labels (cdr result)))
          (let ((next-inst (car text)))
            (if (symbol? next-inst)
                (cons insts
                      (cons (make-label-entry next-inst insts) labels))
                (cons (cons (make-instruction next-inst) insts)
                      labels)))))))
```

which would be called by `assemble` as follows:

```
(define (assemble controller-text machine)
  (let ((result (extract-labels controller-text)))
    (let ((insts (car result)) (labels (cdr result)))
      (update-insts! insts labels machine)
      insts)))
```

You can consider our use of `receive` as demonstrating an elegant way to return multiple values, or simply an excuse to show off a programming trick. An argument like `receive` that is the next procedure to be invoked is called a "continuation." Recall that we also used continuations to implement the backtracking control structure in the amb evaluator in section 4.3.3.

Update-insts! modifies the instruction list, which initially contains only the text of the instructions, to include the corresponding execution procedures:

```
(define (update-insts! insts labels machine)
  (let ((pc (get-register machine 'pc))
        (flag (get-register machine 'flag))
        (stack (machine 'stack))
        (ops (machine 'operations)))
    (for-each
     (lambda (inst)
       (set-instruction-execution-proc!
        inst
        (make-execution-procedure
         (instruction-text inst) labels machine
          pc flag stack ops)))
     insts)))
```

The machine instruction data structure simply pairs the instruction text with the corresponding execution procedure. The execution procedure is not yet available when extract-labels constructs the instruction, and is inserted later by update-insts!.

```
(define (make-instruction text)
  (cons text '()))

(define (instruction-text inst)
  (car inst))

(define (instruction-execution-proc inst)
  (cdr inst))

(define (set-instruction-execution-proc! inst proc)
  (set-cdr! inst proc))
```

The instruction text is not used by our simulator, but it is handy to keep around for debugging (see exercise 5.16).

Elements of the label table are pairs:

```
(define (make-label-entry label-name insts)
  (cons label-name insts))
```

Entries will be looked up in the table with

```
(define (lookup-label labels label-name)
  (let ((val (assoc label-name labels)))
    (if val
        (cdr val)
        (error "Undefined label -- ASSEMBLE" label-name))))
```

Exercise 5.8

The following register-machine code is ambiguous, because the label `here` is defined more than once:

```
start
  (goto (label here))
here
  (assign a (const 3))
  (goto (label there))
here
  (assign a (const 4))
  (goto (label there))
there
```

With the simulator as written, what will the contents of register a be when control reaches `there`? Modify the `extract-labels` procedure so that the assembler will signal an error if the same label name is used to indicate two different locations.

5.2.3   Generating Execution Procedures for Instructions

The assembler calls `make-execution-procedure` to generate the execution procedure for an instruction. Like the `analyze` procedure in the evaluator of section 4.1.7, this dispatches on the type of instruction to generate the appropriate execution procedure.

```
(define (make-execution-procedure inst labels machine
                                  pc flag stack ops)
  (cond ((eq? (car inst) 'assign)
         (make-assign inst machine labels ops pc))
        ((eq? (car inst) 'test)
         (make-test inst machine labels ops flag pc))
        ((eq? (car inst) 'branch)
         (make-branch inst machine labels flag pc))
        ((eq? (car inst) 'goto)
         (make-goto inst machine labels pc))
        ((eq? (car inst) 'save)
         (make-save inst machine stack pc))
        ((eq? (car inst) 'restore)
         (make-restore inst machine stack pc))
        ((eq? (car inst) 'perform)
         (make-perform inst machine labels ops pc))
        (else (error "Unknown instruction type -- ASSEMBLE"
                     inst))))
```

For each type of instruction in the register-machine language, there is a generator that builds an appropriate execution procedure. The details of these procedures determine both the syntax and meaning of the individual instructions in the register-machine language. We use data abstraction to isolate the detailed syntax of register-machine expressions from the general execution mechanism, as we did for evaluators in section 4.1.2, by using syntax procedures to extract and classify the parts of an instruction.

Assign instructions

The make-assign procedure handles assign instructions:

```
(define (make-assign inst machine labels operations pc)
  (let ((target
          (get-register machine (assign-reg-name inst)))
        (value-exp (assign-value-exp inst)))
    (let ((value-proc
            (if (operation-exp? value-exp)
                (make-operation-exp
                 value-exp machine labels operations)
                (make-primitive-exp
                 (car value-exp) machine labels))))
      (lambda ()                          ; execution procedure for assign
        (set-contents! target (value-proc))
        (advance-pc pc)))))
```

Make-assign extracts the target register name (the second element of the instruction) and the value expression (the rest of the list that forms the instruction) from the assign instruction using the selectors

```
(define (assign-reg-name assign-instruction)
  (cadr assign-instruction))

(define (assign-value-exp assign-instruction)
  (cddr assign-instruction))
```

The register name is looked up with get-register to produce the target register object. The value expression is passed to make-operation-exp if the value is the result of an operation, and to make-primitive-exp otherwise. These procedures (shown below) parse the value expression and produce an execution procedure for the value. This is a procedure of no arguments, called value-proc, which will be evaluated during the simulation to produce the actual value to be assigned to the register. Notice that the work of looking up the register name and parsing the value expression is performed just once, at assembly time, not every time the instruction is simulated. This saving of work is the reason we use execution procedures, and corresponds directly to the saving in work we obtained by separating program analysis from execution in the evaluator of section 4.1.7.

The result returned by `make-assign` is the execution procedure for the `assign` instruction. When this procedure is called (by the machine model's `execute` procedure), it sets the contents of the target register to the result obtained by executing `value-proc`. Then it advances the `pc` to the next instruction by running the procedure

```
(define (advance-pc pc)
  (set-contents! pc (cdr (get-contents pc))))
```

Advance-pc is the normal termination for all instructions except `branch` and `goto`.

Test, `branch`, and `goto` instructions

Make-test handles `test` instructions in a similar way. It extracts the expression that specifies the condition to be tested and generates an execution procedure for it. At simulation time, the procedure for the condition is called, the result is assigned to the `flag` register, and the `pc` is advanced:

```
(define (make-test inst machine labels operations flag pc)
  (let ((condition (test-condition inst)))
    (if (operation-exp? condition)
        (let ((condition-proc
               (make-operation-exp
                condition machine labels operations)))
          (lambda ()
            (set-contents! flag (condition-proc))
            (advance-pc pc)))
        (error "Bad TEST instruction -- ASSEMBLE" inst))))

(define (test-condition test-instruction)
  (cdr test-instruction))
```

The execution procedure for a `branch` instruction checks the contents of the `flag` register and either sets the contents of the `pc` to the branch destination (if the branch is taken) or else just advances the `pc` (if the branch is not taken). Notice that the indicated destination in a `branch` instruction must be a label, and the `make-branch` procedure enforces this. Notice also that the label is looked up at assembly time, not each time the `branch` instruction is simulated.

```
(define (make-branch inst machine labels flag pc)
  (let ((dest (branch-dest inst)))
    (if (label-exp? dest)
        (let ((insts
                (lookup-label labels (label-exp-label dest))))
          (lambda ()
            (if (get-contents flag)
                (set-contents! pc insts)
                (advance-pc pc))))
        (error "Bad BRANCH instruction -- ASSEMBLE" inst))))

(define (branch-dest branch-instruction)
  (cadr branch-instruction))
```

A goto instruction is similar to a branch, except that the destination may be specified either as a label or as a register, and there is no condition to check—the pc is always set to the new destination.

```
(define (make-goto inst machine labels pc)
  (let ((dest (goto-dest inst)))
    (cond ((label-exp? dest)
           (let ((insts
                   (lookup-label labels
                                 (label-exp-label dest))))
             (lambda () (set-contents! pc insts))))
          ((register-exp? dest)
           (let ((reg
                   (get-register machine
                                 (register-exp-reg dest))))
             (lambda ()
               (set-contents! pc (get-contents reg)))))
          (else (error "Bad GOTO instruction -- ASSEMBLE"
                       inst)))))

(define (goto-dest goto-instruction)
  (cadr goto-instruction))
```

Other instructions

The stack instructions save and restore simply use the stack with the designated register and advance the pc:

```
(define (make-save inst machine stack pc)
  (let ((reg (get-register machine
                           (stack-inst-reg-name inst))))
    (lambda ()
      (push stack (get-contents reg))
      (advance-pc pc))))
```

```
(define (make-restore inst machine stack pc)
  (let ((reg (get-register machine
                           (stack-inst-reg-name inst))))
    (lambda ()
      (set-contents! reg (pop stack))
      (advance-pc pc))))

(define (stack-inst-reg-name stack-instruction)
  (cadr stack-instruction))
```

The final instruction type, handled by `make-perform`, generates an execution procedure for the action to be performed. At simulation time, the action procedure is executed and the pc advanced.

```
(define (make-perform inst machine labels operations pc)
  (let ((action (perform-action inst)))
    (if (operation-exp? action)
        (let ((action-proc
               (make-operation-exp
                action machine labels operations)))
          (lambda ()
            (action-proc)
            (advance-pc pc)))
        (error "Bad PERFORM instruction -- ASSEMBLE" inst))))

(define (perform-action inst) (cdr inst))
```

Execution procedures for subexpressions

The value of a reg, label, or const expression may be needed for assignment to a register (`make-assign`) or for input to an operation (`make-operation-exp`, below). The following procedure generates execution procedures to produce values for these expressions during the simulation:

```
(define (make-primitive-exp exp machine labels)
  (cond ((constant-exp? exp)
         (let ((c (constant-exp-value exp)))
           (lambda () c)))
        ((label-exp? exp)
         (let ((insts
                (lookup-label labels
                              (label-exp-label exp))))
           (lambda () insts)))
        ((register-exp? exp)
         (let ((r (get-register machine
                                (register-exp-reg exp))))
           (lambda () (get-contents r))))
        (else
         (error "Unknown expression type -- ASSEMBLE" exp))))
```

The syntax of `reg`, `label`, and `const` expressions is determined by

```
(define (register-exp? exp) (tagged-list? exp 'reg))

(define (register-exp-reg exp) (cadr exp))

(define (constant-exp? exp) (tagged-list? exp 'const))

(define (constant-exp-value exp) (cadr exp))

(define (label-exp? exp) (tagged-list? exp 'label))

(define (label-exp-label exp) (cadr exp))
```

Assign, `perform`, and `test` instructions may include the application of a machine operation (specified by an op expression) to some operands (specified by `reg` and `const` expressions). The following procedure produces an execution procedure for an "operation expression"—a list containing the operation and operand expressions from the instruction:

```
(define (make-operation-exp exp machine labels operations)
  (let ((op (lookup-prim (operation-exp-op exp) operations)))
       (aprocs
         (map (lambda (e)
                  (make-primitive-exp e machine labels))
              (operation-exp-operands exp))))
    (lambda ()
      (apply op (map (lambda (p) (p)) aprocs)))))
```

The syntax of operation expressions is determined by

```
(define (operation-exp? exp)
  (and (pair? exp) (tagged-list? (car exp) 'op)))

(define (operation-exp-op operation-exp)
  (cadr (car operation-exp)))

(define (operation-exp-operands operation-exp)
  (cdr operation-exp))
```

Observe that the treatment of operation expressions is very much like the treatment of procedure applications by the `analyze-application` procedure in the evaluator of section 4.1.7 in that we generate an execution procedure for each operand. At simulation time, we call the operand procedures and apply the Scheme procedure that simulates the operation to the resulting values. The simulation procedure is found by looking up the operation name in the operation table for the machine:

```
(define (lookup-prim symbol operations)
  (let ((val (assoc symbol operations)))
    (if val
        (cadr val)
        (error "Unknown operation -- ASSEMBLE" symbol))))
```

Exercise 5.9

The treatment of machine operations above permits them to operate on labels as well as on constants and the contents of registers. Modify the expression-processing procedures to enforce the condition that operations can be used only with registers and constants.

Exercise 5.10

Design a new syntax for register-machine instructions and modify the simulator to use your new syntax. Can you implement your new syntax without changing any part of the simulator except the syntax procedures in this section?

Exercise 5.11

When we introduced save and restore in section 5.1.4, we didn't specify what would happen if you tried to restore a register that was not the last one saved, as in the sequence

```
(save y)
(save x)
(restore y)
```

There are several reasonable possibilities for the meaning of restore:

a. (restore y) puts into y the last value saved on the stack, regardless of what register that value came from. This is the way our simulator behaves. Show how to take advantage of this behavior to eliminate one instruction from the Fibonacci machine of section 5.1.4 (figure 5.12).

b. (restore y) puts into y the last value saved on the stack, but only if that value was saved from y; otherwise, it signals an error. Modify the simulator to behave this way. You will have to change save to put the register name on the stack along with the value.

c. (restore y) puts into y the last value saved from y regardless of what other registers were saved after y and not restored. Modify the simulator to behave this way. You will have to associate a separate stack with each register. You should make the initialize-stack operation initialize all the register stacks.

Exercise 5.12

The simulator can be used to help determine the data paths required for implementing a machine with a given controller. Extend the assembler to store the following information in the machine model:

• a list of all instructions, with duplicates removed, sorted by instruction type (assign, goto, and so on);

• a list (without duplicates) of the registers used to hold entry points (these are the registers referenced by goto instructions);

• a list (without duplicates) of the registers that are saved or restored;

• for each register, a list (without duplicates) of the sources from which it is assigned (for example, the sources for register val in the factorial machine of figure 5.11 are (const 1) and ((op *) (reg n) (reg val))).

Extend the message-passing interface to the machine to provide access to this new information. To test your analyzer, define the Fibonacci machine from figure 5.12 and examine the lists you constructed.

Exercise 5.13

Modify the simulator so that it uses the controller sequence to determine what registers the machine has rather than requiring a list of registers as an argument to make-machine. Instead of pre-allocating the registers in make-machine, you can allocate them one at a time when they are first seen during assembly of the instructions.

5.2.4   Monitoring Machine Performance

Simulation is useful not only for verifying the correctness of a proposed machine design but also for measuring the machine's performance. For example, we can install in our simulation program a "meter" that measures the number of stack operations used in a computation. To do this, we modify our simulated stack to keep track of the number of times registers are saved on the stack and the maximum depth reached by the stack, and add a message to the stack's interface that prints the statistics, as shown below. We also add an operation to the basic machine model to print the stack statistics, by initializing the-ops in make-new-machine to

```
(list (list 'initialize-stack
            (lambda () (stack 'initialize)))
      (list 'print-stack-statistics
            (lambda () (stack 'print-statistics)))))
```

Here is the new version of `make-stack`:

```
(define (make-stack)
  (let ((s '())
        (number-pushes 0)
        (max-depth 0)
        (current-depth 0))
    (define (push x)
      (set! s (cons x s))
      (set! number-pushes (+ 1 number-pushes))
      (set! current-depth (+ 1 current-depth))
      (set! max-depth (max current-depth max-depth)))
    (define (pop)
      (if (null? s)
          (error "Empty stack -- POP")
          (let ((top (car s)))
            (set! s (cdr s))
            (set! current-depth (- current-depth 1))
            top)))
    (define (initialize)
      (set! s '())
      (set! number-pushes 0)
      (set! max-depth 0)
      (set! current-depth 0)
      'done)
    (define (print-statistics)
      (newline)
      (display (list 'total-pushes  '= number-pushes
                     'maximum-depth '= max-depth)))
    (define (dispatch message)
      (cond ((eq? message 'push) push)
            ((eq? message 'pop) (pop))
            ((eq? message 'initialize) (initialize))
            ((eq? message 'print-statistics)
             (print-statistics))
            (else
             (error "Unknown request -- STACK" message))))
    dispatch))
```

Exercises 5.15 through 5.19 describe other useful monitoring and debugging features that can be added to the register-machine simulator.

Exercise 5.14

Measure the number of pushes and the maximum stack depth required to compute $n!$ for various small values of n using the factorial machine shown in figure 5.11. From your data determine formulas in terms of n for the total number of push operations and the maximum stack depth used in computing $n!$ for any $n > 1$. Note that each of these is a linear function of n and is thus determined by two constants. In order to get the statistics printed, you will have to augment the factorial machine with instructions to initialize the stack and print the statistics. You may want to also modify the machine so that it repeatedly reads a value for n, computes the factorial, and prints the result (as we did for the GCD machine in figure 5.4), so that you will not have to repeatedly invoke get-register-contents, set-register-contents!, and start.

Exercise 5.15

Add *instruction counting* to the register machine simulation. That is, have the machine model keep track of the number of instructions executed. Extend the machine model's interface to accept a new message that prints the value of the instruction count and resets the count to zero.

Exercise 5.16

Augment the simulator to provide for *instruction tracing*. That is, before each instruction is executed, the simulator should print the text of the instruction. Make the machine model accept trace-on and trace-off messages to turn tracing on and off.

Exercise 5.17

Extend the instruction tracing of exercise 5.16 so that before printing an instruction, the simulator prints any labels that immediately precede that instruction in the controller sequence. Be careful to do this in a way that does not interfere with instruction counting (exercise 5.15). You will have to make the simulator retain the necessary label information.

Exercise 5.18

Modify the make-register procedure of section 5.2.1 so that registers can be traced. Registers should accept messages that turn tracing on and off. When a register is traced, assigning a value to the register should print the name of the register, the old contents of the register, and the new contents being assigned. Extend the interface to the machine model to permit you to turn tracing on and off for designated machine registers.

Exercise 5.19

Alyssa P. Hacker wants a *breakpoint* feature in the simulator to help her debug her machine designs. You have been hired to install this feature for her. She wants to be able to specify a place in the controller sequence where the simulator will stop and allow her to examine the state of the machine. You are to implement a procedure

```
(set-breakpoint ⟨machine⟩ ⟨label⟩ ⟨n⟩)
```

that sets a breakpoint just before the nth instruction after the given label. For example,

```
(set-breakpoint gcd-machine 'test-b 4)
```

installs a breakpoint in `gcd-machine` just before the assignment to register a. When the simulator reaches the breakpoint it should print the label and the offset of the breakpoint and stop executing instructions. Alyssa can then use `get-register-contents` and `set-register-contents!` to manipulate the state of the simulated machine. She should then be able to continue execution by saying

```
(proceed-machine ⟨machine⟩)
```

She should also be able to remove a specific breakpoint by means of

```
(cancel-breakpoint ⟨machine⟩ ⟨label⟩ ⟨n⟩)
```

or to remove all breakpoints by means of

```
(cancel-all-breakpoints ⟨machine⟩)
```

5.3   Storage Allocation and Garbage Collection

In section 5.4, we will show how to implement a Scheme evaluator as a register machine. In order to simplify the discussion, we will assume that our register machines can be equipped with a *list-structured memory*, in which the basic operations for manipulating list-structured data are primitive. Postulating the existence of such a memory is a useful abstraction when one is focusing on the mechanisms of control in a Scheme interpreter, but this does not reflect a realistic view of the actual primitive data operations of contemporary computers. To obtain a more complete picture of how a Lisp system operates, we must investigate how list structure can be represented in a way that is compatible with conventional computer memories.

There are two considerations in implementing list structure. The first is purely an issue of representation: how to represent the "box-and-pointer" structure of Lisp pairs, using only the storage and addressing capabilities of typical computer memories. The second issue concerns the management of memory as a computation proceeds. The operation of a Lisp system depends crucially on the ability to continually create new data objects. These include objects that are explicitly created by the Lisp procedures being interpreted as well as structures created by the interpreter itself, such as environments and argument lists. Although the constant creation of new data objects would pose no problem on a computer with an infinite amount of rapidly addressable memory, computer memories are available only in finite sizes (more's the pity). Lisp systems thus provide an *automatic storage allocation* facility to support the illusion of an infinite memory. When a data object is no longer needed, the memory allocated to it is automatically recycled and used to construct new data objects. There are various techniques for providing such automatic storage allocation. The method we shall discuss in this section is called *garbage collection*.

5.3.1 Memory as Vectors

A conventional computer memory can be thought of as an array of cubbyholes, each of which can contain a piece of information. Each cubbyhole has a unique name, called its *address* or *location*. Typical memory systems provide two primitive operations: one that fetches the data stored in a specified location and one that assigns new data to a specified location. Memory addresses can be incremented to support sequential access to some set of the cubbyholes. More generally, many important data operations require that memory addresses be treated as data, which can be stored in memory locations and manipulated in machine registers. The representation of list structure is one application of such *address arithmetic*.

To model computer memory, we use a new kind of data structure called a *vector*. Abstractly, a vector is a compound data object whose individual elements can be accessed by means of an integer index in an amount of time that is independent of the index.[5] In order to describe memory operations, we use two primitive Scheme procedures for manipulating vectors:

- (vector-ref ⟨*vector*⟩ ⟨*n*⟩) returns the *n*th element of the vector.

- (vector-set! ⟨*vector*⟩ ⟨*n*⟩ ⟨*value*⟩) sets the *n*th element of the vector to the designated value.

For example, if v is a vector, then (vector-ref v 5) gets the fifth entry in the vector v and (vector-set! v 5 7) changes the value of the fifth

---

[5]We could represent memory as lists of items. However, the access time would then not be independent of the index, since accessing the *n*th element of a list requires $n - 1$ cdr operations.

entry of the vector v to 7.[6] For computer memory, this access can be implemented through the use of address arithmetic to combine a *base address* that specifies the beginning location of a vector in memory with an *index* that specifies the offset of a particular element of the vector.

Representing Lisp data

We can use vectors to implement the basic pair structures required for a list-structured memory. Let us imagine that computer memory is divided into two vectors: the-cars and the-cdrs. We will represent list structure as follows: A pointer to a pair is an index into the two vectors. The car of the pair is the entry in the-cars with the designated index, and the cdr of the pair is the entry in the-cdrs with the designated index. We also need a representation for objects other than pairs (such as numbers and symbols) and a way to distinguish one kind of data from another. There are many methods of accomplishing this, but they all reduce to using *typed pointers*, that is, to extending the notion of "pointer" to include information on data type.[7] The data type enables the system to distinguish a pointer to a pair (which consists of the "pair" data type and an index into the memory vectors) from pointers to other kinds of data (which consist of some other data type and whatever is being used to represent data of that type). Two data objects are considered to be the same (eq?) if their pointers are identical.[8] Figure 5.14 illustrates the use of this method to represent the list ((1 2) 3 4), whose box-and-pointer diagram is also shown. We use letter prefixes to denote the data-type information. Thus, a pointer to the pair with index 5 is denoted p5, the empty list is denoted by the pointer e0, and a pointer to the number 4

---

[6]For completeness, we should specify a make-vector operation that constructs vectors. However, in the present application we will use vectors only to model fixed divisions of the computer memory.

[7]This is precisely the same "tagged data" idea we introduced in chapter 2 for dealing with generic operations. Here, however, the data types are included at the primitive machine level rather than constructed through the use of lists.

[8]Type information may be encoded in a variety of ways, depending on the details of the machine on which the Lisp system is to be implemented. The execution efficiency of Lisp programs will be strongly dependent on how cleverly this choice is made, but it is difficult to formulate general design rules for good choices. The most straightforward way to implement typed pointers is to allocate a fixed set of bits in each pointer to be a *type field* that encodes the data type. Important questions to be addressed in designing such a representation include the following: How many type bits are required? How large must the vector indices be? How efficiently can the primitive machine instructions be used to manipulate the type fields of pointers? Machines that include special hardware for the efficient handling of type fields are said to have *tagged architectures*.

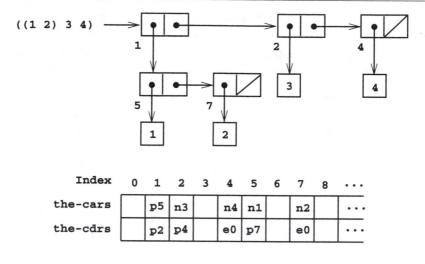

Figure 5.14 Box-and-pointer and memory-vector representations of the list
((1 2) 3 4).

is denoted n4. In the box-and-pointer diagram, we have indicated at
the lower left of each pair the vector index that specifies where the car
and cdr of the pair are stored. The blank locations in the-cars and
the-cdrs may contain parts of other list structures (not of interest here).

A pointer to a number, such as n4, might consist of a type indicating
numeric data together with the actual representation of the number 4.[9]
To deal with numbers that are too large to be represented in the fixed
amount of space allocated for a single pointer, we could use a distinct
bignum data type, for which the pointer designates a list in which the
parts of the number are stored.[10]

A symbol might be represented as a typed pointer that designates a
sequence of the characters that form the symbol's printed representation.
This sequence is constructed by the Lisp reader when the character string
is initially encountered in input. Since we want two instances of a symbol to be recognized as the "same" symbol by eq? and we want eq? to
be a simple test for equality of pointers, we must ensure that if the reader

---

[9]This decision on the representation of numbers determines whether eq?, which tests
equality of pointers, can be used to test for equality of numbers. If the pointer contains the
number itself, then equal numbers will have the same pointer. But if the pointer contains
the index of a location where the number is stored, equal numbers will be guaranteed to
have equal pointers only if we are careful never to store the same number in more than one
location.

[10]This is just like writing a number as a sequence of digits, except that each "digit" is a
number between 0 and the largest number that can be stored in a single pointer.

sees the same character string twice, it will use the same pointer (to the same sequence of characters) to represent both occurrences. To accomplish this, the reader maintains a table, traditionally called the *obarray*, of all the symbols it has ever encountered. When the reader encounters a character string and is about to construct a symbol, it checks the obarray to see if it has ever before seen the same character string. If it has not, it uses the characters to construct a new symbol (a typed pointer to a new character sequence) and enters this pointer in the obarray. If the reader has seen the string before, it returns the symbol pointer stored in the obarray. This process of replacing character strings by unique pointers is called *interning* symbols.

Implementing the primitive list operations

Given the above representation scheme, we can replace each "primitive" list operation of a register machine with one or more primitive vector operations. We will use two registers, the-cars and the-cdrs, to identify the memory vectors, and will assume that vector-ref and vector-set! are available as primitive operations. We also assume that numeric operations on pointers (such as incrementing a pointer, using a pair pointer to index a vector, or adding two numbers) use only the index portion of the typed pointer.

For example, we can make a register machine support the instructions

```
(assign ⟨reg₁⟩ (op car) (reg ⟨reg₂⟩))
```

```
(assign ⟨reg₁⟩ (op cdr) (reg ⟨reg₂⟩))
```

if we implement these, respectively, as

```
(assign ⟨reg₁⟩ (op vector-ref) (reg the-cars) (reg ⟨reg₂⟩))
```

```
(assign ⟨reg₁⟩ (op vector-ref) (reg the-cdrs) (reg ⟨reg₂⟩))
```

The instructions

```
(perform (op set-car!) (reg ⟨reg₁⟩) (reg ⟨reg₂⟩))
```

```
(perform (op set-cdr!) (reg ⟨reg₁⟩) (reg ⟨reg₂⟩))
```

are implemented as

```
(perform
 (op vector-set!) (reg the-cars) (reg ⟨reg₁⟩) (reg ⟨reg₂⟩))
```

```
(perform
 (op vector-set!) (reg the-cdrs) (reg ⟨reg₁⟩) (reg ⟨reg₂⟩))
```

Cons is performed by allocating an unused index and storing the arguments to cons in the-cars and the-cdrs at that indexed vector position. We presume that there is a special register, free, that always holds a pair pointer containing the next available index, and that we can increment the index part of that pointer to find the next free location.[11] For example, the instruction

```
(assign ⟨reg₁⟩ (op cons) (reg ⟨reg₂⟩) (reg ⟨reg₃⟩))
```

is implemented as the following sequence of vector operations:[12]

```
(perform
 (op vector-set!) (reg the-cars) (reg free) (reg ⟨reg₂⟩))
(perform
 (op vector-set!) (reg the-cdrs) (reg free) (reg ⟨reg₃⟩))
(assign ⟨reg₁⟩ (reg free))
(assign free (op +) (reg free) (const 1))
```

The eq? operation

```
(op eq?) (reg ⟨reg₁⟩) (reg ⟨reg₂⟩)
```

simply tests the equality of all fields in the registers, and predicates such as pair?, null?, symbol?, and number? need only check the type field.

Implementing stacks

Although our register machines use stacks, we need do nothing special here, since stacks can be modeled in terms of lists. The stack can be a list of the saved values, pointed to by a special register the-stack. Thus, (save ⟨reg⟩) can be implemented as

```
(assign the-stack (op cons) (reg ⟨reg⟩) (reg the-stack))
```

Similarly, (restore ⟨reg⟩) can be implemented as

```
(assign ⟨reg⟩ (op car) (reg the-stack))
(assign the-stack (op cdr) (reg the-stack))
```

---

[11]There are other ways of finding free storage. For example, we could link together all the unused pairs into a *free list*. Our free locations are consecutive (and hence can be accessed by incrementing a pointer) because we are using a compacting garbage collector, as we will see in section 5.3.2.

[12]This is essentially the implementation of cons in terms of set-car! and set-cdr!, as described in section 3.3.1. The operation get-new-pair used in that implementation is realized here by the free pointer.

and (perform (op initialize-stack)) can be implemented as

(assign the-stack (const ()))

These operations can be further expanded in terms of the vector operations given above. In conventional computer architectures, however, it
is usually advantageous to allocate the stack as a separate vector. Then
pushing and popping the stack can be accomplished by incrementing or
decrementing an index into that vector.

Exercise 5.20

Draw the box-and-pointer representation and the memory-vector representation
(as in figure 5.14) of the list structure produced by

```
(define x (cons 1 2))
(define y (list x x))
```

with the free pointer initially p1. What is the final value of free? What
pointers represent the values of x and y ?

Exercise 5.21

Implement register machines for the following procedures. Assume that the list-
structure memory operations are available as machine primitives.

a. Recursive count-leaves:

```
(define (count-leaves tree)
  (cond ((null? tree) 0)
        ((not (pair? tree)) 1)
        (else (+ (count-leaves (car tree))
                 (count-leaves (cdr tree))))))
```

b. Recursive count-leaves with explicit counter:

```
(define (count-leaves tree)
  (define (count-iter tree n)
    (cond ((null? tree) n)
          ((not (pair? tree)) (+ n 1))
          (else (count-iter (cdr tree)
                            (count-iter (car tree) n)))))
  (count-iter tree 0))
```

Exercise 5.22

Exercise 3.12 of section 3.3.1 presented an append procedure that appends two
lists to form a new list and an append! procedure that splices two lists together.
Design a register machine to implement each of these procedures. Assume that
the list-structure memory operations are available as primitive operations.

5.3.2   Maintaining the Illusion of Infinite Memory

The representation method outlined in section 5.3.1 solves the problem of implementing list structure, provided that we have an infinite amount of memory. With a real computer we will eventually run out of free space in which to construct new pairs.[13] However, most of the pairs generated in a typical computation are used only to hold intermediate results. After these results are accessed, the pairs are no longer needed— they are *garbage*. For instance, the computation

```
(accumulate + 0 (filter odd? (enumerate-interval 0 n)))
```

constructs two lists: the enumeration and the result of filtering the enumeration. When the accumulation is complete, these lists are no longer needed, and the allocated memory can be reclaimed. If we can arrange to collect all the garbage periodically, and if this turns out to recycle memory at about the same rate at which we construct new pairs, we will have preserved the illusion that there is an infinite amount of memory.

In order to recycle pairs, we must have a way to determine which allocated pairs are not needed (in the sense that their contents can no longer influence the future of the computation). The method we shall examine for accomplishing this is known as *garbage collection*. Garbage collection is based on the observation that, at any moment in a Lisp interpretation, the only objects that can affect the future of the computation are those that can be reached by some succession of car and cdr operations starting from the pointers that are currently in the machine registers.[14] Any memory cell that is not so accessible may be recycled.

There are many ways to perform garbage collection. The method we shall examine here is called *stop-and-copy*. The basic idea is to divide memory into two halves: "working memory" and "free memory." When cons constructs pairs, it allocates these in working memory. When work-

---

[13]This may not be true eventually, because memories may get large enough so that it would be impossible to run out of free memory in the lifetime of the computer. For example, there are about 3×10^{13}, microseconds in a year, so if we were to cons once per microsecond we would need about 10^{15} cells of memory to build a machine that could operate for 30 years without running out of memory. That much memory seems absurdly large by today's standards, but it is not physically impossible. On the other hand, processors are getting faster and a future computer may have large numbers of processors operating in parallel on a single memory, so it may be possible to use up memory much faster than we have postulated.

[14]We assume here that the stack is represented as a list as described in section 5.3.1, so that items on the stack are accessible via the pointer in the stack register.

ing memory is full, we perform garbage collection by locating all the useful pairs in working memory and copying these into consecutive locations in free memory. (The useful pairs are located by tracing all the car and cdr pointers, starting with the machine registers.) Since we do not copy the garbage, there will presumably be additional free memory that we can use to allocate new pairs. In addition, nothing in the working memory is needed, since all the useful pairs in it have been copied. Thus, if we interchange the roles of working memory and free memory, we can continue processing; new pairs will be allocated in the new working memory (which was the old free memory). When this is full, we can copy the useful pairs into the new free memory (which was the old working memory).[15]

Implementation of a stop-and-copy garbage collector

We now use our register-machine language to describe the stop-and-copy algorithm in more detail. We will assume that there is a register called root that contains a pointer to a structure that eventually points at all accessible data. This can be arranged by storing the contents of all the machine registers in a pre-allocated list pointed at by root just before starting garbage collection.[16] We also assume that, in addition to the current working memory, there is free memory available into which we can

---

[15]This idea was invented and first implemented by Minsky, as part of the implementation of Lisp for the PDP-1 at the MIT Research Laboratory of Electronics. It was further developed by Fenichel and Yochelson (1969) for use in the Lisp implementation for the Multics time-sharing system. Later, Baker (1978) developed a "real-time" version of the method, which does not require the computation to stop during garbage collection. Baker's idea was extended by Hewitt, Lieberman, and Moon (see Lieberman and Hewitt 1983) to take advantage of the fact that some structure is more volatile and other structure is more permanent.

An alternative commonly used garbage-collection technique is the *mark-sweep* method. This consists of tracing all the structure accessible from the machine registers and marking each pair we reach. We then scan all of memory, and any location that is unmarked is "swept up" as garbage and made available for reuse. A full discussion of the mark-sweep method can be found in Allen 1978.

The Minsky-Fenichel-Yochelson algorithm is the dominant algorithm in use for large-memory systems because it examines only the useful part of memory. This is in contrast to mark-sweep, in which the sweep phase must check all of memory. A second advantage of stop-and-copy is that it is a *compacting* garbage collector. That is, at the end of the garbage-collection phase the useful data will have been moved to consecutive memory locations, with all garbage pairs compressed out. This can be an extremely important performance consideration in machines with virtual memory, in which accesses to widely separated memory addresses may require extra paging operations.

[16]This list of registers does not include the registers used by the storage-allocation system—root, the-cars, the-cdrs, and the other registers that will be introduced in this section.

copy the useful data. The current working memory consists of vectors whose base addresses are in registers called `the-cars` and `the-cdrs`, and the free memory is in registers called `new-cars` and `new-cdrs`.

Garbage collection is triggered when we exhaust the free cells in the current working memory, that is, when a `cons` operation attempts to increment the `free` pointer beyond the end of the memory vector. When the garbage-collection process is complete, the `root` pointer will point into the new memory, all objects accessible from the `root` will have been moved to the new memory, and the `free` pointer will indicate the next place in the new memory where a new pair can be allocated. In addition, the roles of working memory and new memory will have been interchanged—new pairs will be constructed in the new memory, beginning at the place indicated by `free`, and the (previous) working memory will be available as the new memory for the next garbage collection. Figure 5.15 shows the arrangement of memory just before and just after garbage collection.

The state of the garbage-collection process is controlled by maintaining two pointers: `free` and `scan`. These are initialized to point to the beginning of the new memory. The algorithm begins by relocating the pair pointed at by `root` to the beginning of the new memory. The pair is copied, the `root` pointer is adjusted to point to the new location, and the `free` pointer is incremented. In addition, the old location of the pair is marked to show that its contents have been moved. This marking is done as follows: In the `car` position, we place a special tag that signals that this is an already-moved object. (Such an object is traditionally called a *broken heart*.)[17] In the `cdr` position we place a *forwarding address* that points at the location to which the object has been moved.

After relocating the root, the garbage collector enters its basic cycle. At each step in the algorithm, the `scan` pointer (initially pointing at the relocated root) points at a pair that has been moved to the new memory but whose `car` and `cdr` pointers still refer to objects in the old memory. These objects are each relocated, and the `scan` pointer is incremented. To relocate an object (for example, the object indicated by the `car` pointer of the pair we are scanning) we check to see if the object has already been moved (as indicated by the presence of a broken-heart tag in the `car` position of the object). If the object has not already been moved, we copy it to the place indicated by `free`, update `free`, set up a broken

---

[17]The term *broken heart* was coined by David Cressey, who wrote a garbage collector for MDL, a dialect of Lisp developed at MIT during the early 1970s.

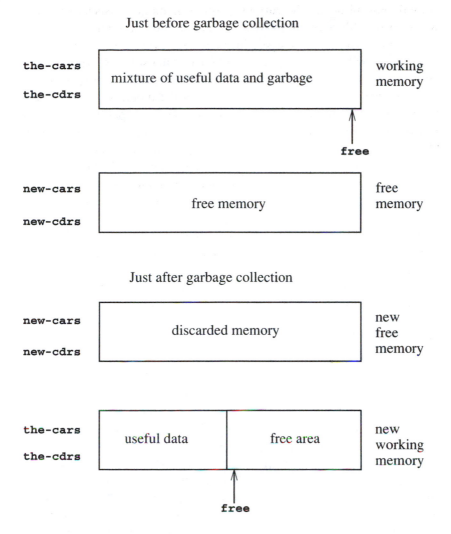

Figure 5.15   Reconfiguration of memory by the garbage-collection process.

heart at the object's old location, and update the pointer to the object (in this example, the `car` pointer of the pair we are scanning) to point to the new location. If the object has already been moved, its forwarding address (found in the `cdr` position of the broken heart) is substituted for the pointer in the pair being scanned. Eventually, all accessible objects will have been moved and scanned, at which point the `scan` pointer will overtake the `free` pointer and the process will terminate.

We can specify the stop-and-copy algorithm as a sequence of instructions for a register machine. The basic step of relocating an object is accomplished by a subroutine called `relocate-old-result-in-new`. This subroutine gets its argument, a pointer to the object to be relocated, from a register named `old`. It relocates the designated object (incrementing `free` in the process), puts a pointer to the relocated object into a register called `new`, and returns by branching to the entry point stored in the register `relocate-continue`. To begin garbage collection, we invoke this subroutine to relocate the `root` pointer, after initializing `free` and `scan`. When the relocation of `root` has been accomplished, we install the new pointer as the new `root` and enter the main loop of the garbage collector.

```
begin-garbage-collection
  (assign free (const 0))
  (assign scan (const 0))
  (assign old (reg root))
  (assign relocate-continue (label reassign-root))
  (goto (label relocate-old-result-in-new))
reassign-root
  (assign root (reg new))
  (goto (label gc-loop))
```

In the main loop of the garbage collector we must determine whether there are any more objects to be scanned. We do this by testing whether the `scan` pointer is coincident with the `free` pointer. If the pointers are equal, then all accessible objects have been relocated, and we branch to `gc-flip`, which cleans things up so that we can continue the interrupted computation. If there are still pairs to be scanned, we call the relocate subroutine to relocate the `car` of the next pair (by placing the `car` pointer in `old`). The `relocate-continue` register is set up so that the subroutine will return to update the `car` pointer.

```
gc-loop
  (test (op =) (reg scan) (reg free))
  (branch (label gc-flip))
  (assign old (op vector-ref) (reg new-cars) (reg scan))
  (assign relocate-continue (label update-car))
  (goto (label relocate-old-result-in-new))
```

At `update-car`, we modify the `car` pointer of the pair being scanned, then proceed to relocate the `cdr` of the pair. We return to `update-cdr` when that relocation has been accomplished. After relocating and updating the `cdr`, we are finished scanning that pair, so we continue with the main loop.

```
update-car
  (perform
    (op vector-set!) (reg new-cars) (reg scan) (reg new))
  (assign old (op vector-ref) (reg new-cdrs) (reg scan))
  (assign relocate-continue (label update-cdr))
  (goto (label relocate-old-result-in-new))

update-cdr
  (perform
    (op vector-set!) (reg new-cdrs) (reg scan) (reg new))
  (assign scan (op +) (reg scan) (const 1))
  (goto (label gc-loop))
```

The subroutine `relocate-old-result-in-new` relocates objects as follows: If the object to be relocated (pointed at by `old`) is not a pair, then we return the same pointer to the object unchanged (in `new`). (For example, we may be scanning a pair whose `car` is the number 4. If we represent the `car` by n4, as described in section 5.3.1, then we want the "relocated" `car` pointer to still be n4.) Otherwise, we must perform the relocation. If the `car` position of the pair to be relocated contains a broken-heart tag, then the pair has in fact already been moved, so we retrieve the forwarding address (from the `cdr` position of the broken heart) and return this in `new`. If the pointer in `old` points at a yet-unmoved pair, then we move the pair to the first free cell in new memory (pointed at by `free`) and set up the broken heart by storing a broken-heart tag and forwarding address at the old location. `Relocate-old-result-in-new` uses a register `oldcr` to hold the `car` or the `cdr` of the object pointed at by `old`.[18]

---

[18]The garbage collector uses the low-level predicate `pointer-to-pair?` instead of the list-structure `pair?` operation because in a real system there might be various things that are treated as pairs for garbage-collection purposes. For example, in a Scheme system that conforms to the IEEE standard a procedure object may be implemented as a special kind of "pair" that doesn't satisfy the `pair?` predicate. For simulation purposes, `pointer-to-pair?` can be implemented as `pair?`.

```
relocate-old-result-in-new
  (test (op pointer-to-pair?) (reg old))
  (branch (label pair))
  (assign new (reg old))
  (goto (reg relocate-continue))
pair
  (assign oldcr (op vector-ref) (reg the-cars) (reg old))
  (test (op broken-heart?) (reg oldcr))
  (branch (label already-moved))
  (assign new (reg free))   ; new location for pair
  ;; Update free pointer.
  (assign free (op +) (reg free) (const 1))
  ;; Copy the car and cdr to new memory.
  (perform (op vector-set!)
          (reg new-cars) (reg new) (reg oldcr))
  (assign oldcr (op vector-ref) (reg the-cdrs) (reg old))
  (perform (op vector-set!)
          (reg new-cdrs) (reg new) (reg oldcr))
  ;; Construct the broken heart.
  (perform (op vector-set!)
          (reg the-cars) (reg old) (const broken-heart))
  (perform
   (op vector-set!) (reg the-cdrs) (reg old) (reg new))
  (goto (reg relocate-continue))
already-moved
  (assign new (op vector-ref) (reg the-cdrs) (reg old))
  (goto (reg relocate-continue))
```

At the very end of the garbage-collection process, we interchange the role of old and new memories by interchanging pointers: interchanging the-cars with new-cars, and the-cdrs with new-cdrs. We will then be ready to perform another garbage collection the next time memory runs out.

```
gc-flip
  (assign temp (reg the-cdrs))
  (assign the-cdrs (reg new-cdrs))
  (assign new-cdrs (reg temp))
  (assign temp (reg the-cars))
  (assign the-cars (reg new-cars))
  (assign new-cars (reg temp))
```

5.4   The Explicit-Control Evaluator

In section 5.1 we saw how to transform simple Scheme programs into descriptions of register machines. We will now perform this transformation on a more complex program, the metacircular evaluator of sections 4.1.1–4.1.4, which shows how the behavior of a Scheme interpreter can be described in terms of the procedures `eval` and `apply`. The *explicit-control evaluator* that we develop in this section shows how the underlying procedure-calling and argument-passing mechanisms used in the evaluation process can be described in terms of operations on registers and stacks. In addition, the explicit-control evaluator can serve as an implementation of a Scheme interpreter, written in a language that is very similar to the native machine language of conventional computers. The evaluator can be executed by the register-machine simulator of section 5.2. Alternatively, it can be used as a starting point for building a machine-language implementation of a Scheme evaluator, or even a special-purpose machine for evaluating Scheme expressions. Figure 5.16 shows such a hardware implementation: a silicon chip that acts as an evaluator for Scheme. The chip designers started with the data-path and controller specifications for a register machine similar to the evaluator described in this section and used design automation programs to construct the integrated-circuit layout.[19]

Registers and operations

In designing the explicit-control evaluator, we must specify the operations to be used in our register machine. We described the metacircular evaluator in terms of abstract syntax, using procedures such as `quoted?` and `make-procedure`. In implementing the register machine, we could expand these procedures into sequences of elementary list-structure memory operations, and implement these operations on our register machine. However, this would make our evaluator very long, obscuring the basic structure with details. To clarify the presentation, we will include as primitive operations of the register machine the syntax procedures given in section 4.1.2 and the procedures for representing environments and other run-time data given in sections 4.1.3 and 4.1.4.

---

[19]See Batali et al. 1982 for more information on the chip and the method by which it was designed.

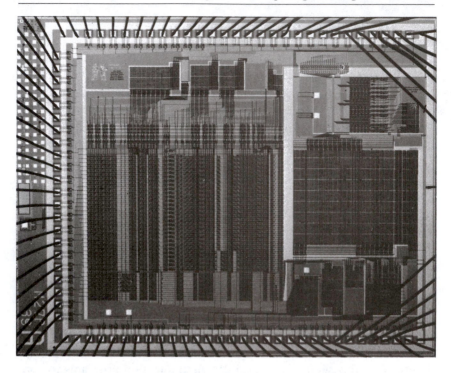

Figure 5.16   A silicon-chip implementation of an evaluator for Scheme.

In order to completely specify an evaluator that could be programmed in a low-level machine language or implemented in hardware, we would replace these operations by more elementary operations, using the list-structure implementation we described in section 5.3.

Our Scheme evaluator register machine includes a stack and seven registers: `exp`, `env`, `val`, `continue`, `proc`, `argl`, and `unev`. Exp is used to hold the expression to be evaluated, and `env` contains the environment in which the evaluation is to be performed. At the end of an evaluation, `val` contains the value obtained by evaluating the expression in the designated environment. The `continue` register is used to implement recursion, as explained in section 5.1.4. (The evaluator needs to call itself recursively, since evaluating an expression requires evaluating its subexpressions.) The registers `proc`, `argl`, and `unev` are used in evaluating combinations.

We will not provide a data-path diagram to show how the registers and operations of the evaluator are connected, nor will we give the complete list of machine operations. These are implicit in the evaluator's controller, which will be presented in detail.

5.4.1   The Core of the Explicit-Control Evaluator

The central element in the evaluator is the sequence of instructions beginning at `eval-dispatch`. This corresponds to the `eval` procedure of the metacircular evaluator described in section 4.1.1. When the controller starts at `eval-dispatch`, it evaluates the expression specified by exp in the environment specified by env. When evaluation is complete, the controller will go to the entry point stored in `continue`, and the val register will hold the value of the expression. As with the metacircular `eval`, the structure of `eval-dispatch` is a case analysis on the syntactic type of the expression to be evaluated.[20]

```
eval-dispatch
  (test (op self-evaluating?) (reg exp))
  (branch (label ev-self-eval))
  (test (op variable?) (reg exp))
  (branch (label ev-variable))
  (test (op quoted?) (reg exp))
  (branch (label ev-quoted))
  (test (op assignment?) (reg exp))
  (branch (label ev-assignment))
  (test (op definition?) (reg exp))
  (branch (label ev-definition))
  (test (op if?) (reg exp))
  (branch (label ev-if))
  (test (op lambda?) (reg exp))
  (branch (label ev-lambda))
  (test (op begin?) (reg exp))
  (branch (label ev-begin))
  (test (op application?) (reg exp))
  (branch (label ev-application))
  (goto (label unknown-expression-type))
```

Evaluating simple expressions

Numbers and strings (which are self-evaluating), variables, quotations, and `lambda` expressions have no subexpressions to be evaluated. For these, the evaluator simply places the correct value in the val register and continues execution at the entry point specified by `continue`. Evaluation of simple expressions is performed by the following controller code:

---

[20]In our controller, the dispatch is written as a sequence of `test` and `branch` instructions. Alternatively, it could have been written in a data-directed style (and in a real system it probably would have been) to avoid the need to perform sequential tests and to facilitate the definition of new expression types. A machine designed to run Lisp would probably include a `dispatch-on-type` instruction that would efficiently execute such data-directed dispatches.

```
ev-self-eval
  (assign val (reg exp))
  (goto (reg continue))
ev-variable
  (assign val (op lookup-variable-value) (reg exp) (reg env))
  (goto (reg continue))
ev-quoted
  (assign val (op text-of-quotation) (reg exp))
  (goto (reg continue))
ev-lambda
  (assign unev (op lambda-parameters) (reg exp))
  (assign exp (op lambda-body) (reg exp))
  (assign val (op make-procedure)
              (reg unev) (reg exp) (reg env))
  (goto (reg continue))
```

Observe how `ev-lambda` uses the `unev` and `exp` registers to hold the parameters and body of the lambda expression so that they can be passed to the `make-procedure` operation, along with the environment in `env`.

Evaluating procedure applications

A procedure application is specified by a combination containing an operator and operands. The operator is a subexpression whose value is a procedure, and the operands are subexpressions whose values are the arguments to which the procedure should be applied. The metacircular `eval` handles applications by calling itself recursively to evaluate each element of the combination, and then passing the results to `apply`, which performs the actual procedure application. The explicit-control evaluator does the same thing; these recursive calls are implemented by `goto` instructions, together with use of the stack to save registers that will be restored after the recursive call returns. Before each call we will be careful to identify which registers must be saved (because their values will be needed later).[21]

We begin the evaluation of an application by evaluating the operator to produce a procedure, which will later be applied to the evaluated operands. To evaluate the operator, we move it to the `exp` register and go to `eval-dispatch`. The environment in the `env` register is already

---

[21]This is an important but subtle point in translating algorithms from a procedural language, such as Lisp, to a register-machine language. As an alternative to saving only what is needed, we could save all the registers (except `val`) before each recursive call. This is called a *framed-stack* discipline. This would work but might save more registers than necessary; this could be an important consideration in a system where stack operations are expensive. Saving registers whose contents will not be needed later may also hold onto useless data that could otherwise be garbage-collected, freeing space to be reused.

the correct one in which to evaluate the operator. However, we save `env` because we will need it later to evaluate the operands. We also extract the operands into `unev` and save this on the stack. We set up `continue` so that `eval-dispatch` will resume at `ev-appl-did-operator` after the operator has been evaluated. First, however, we save the old value of `continue`, which tells the controller where to continue after the application.

```
ev-application
  (save continue)
  (save env)
  (assign unev (op operands) (reg exp))
  (save unev)
  (assign exp (op operator) (reg exp))
  (assign continue (label ev-appl-did-operator))
  (goto (label eval-dispatch))
```

Upon returning from evaluating the operator subexpression, we proceed to evaluate the operands of the combination and to accumulate the resulting arguments in a list, held in `argl`. First we restore the unevaluated operands and the environment. We initialize `argl` to an empty list. Then we assign to the `proc` register the procedure that was produced by evaluating the operator. If there are no operands, we go directly to `apply-dispatch`. Otherwise we save `proc` on the stack and start the argument-evaluation loop:[22]

```
ev-appl-did-operator
  (restore unev)                      ; the operands
  (restore env)
  (assign argl (op empty-arglist))
  (assign proc (reg val))             ; the operator
  (test (op no-operands?) (reg unev))
  (branch (label apply-dispatch))
  (save proc)
```

---

[22]We add to the evaluator data-structure procedures in section 4.1.3 the following two procedures for manipulating argument lists:

```
(define (empty-arglist) '())
```

```
(define (adjoin-arg arg arglist)
  (append arglist (list arg)))
```

We also use an additional syntax procedure to test for the last operand in a combination:

```
(define (last-operand? ops)
  (null? (cdr ops)))
```

Each cycle of the argument-evaluation loop evaluates an operand from the list in `unev` and accumulates the result into `argl`. To evaluate an operand, we place it in the `exp` register and go to `eval-dispatch`, after setting `continue` so that execution will resume with the argument-accumulation phase. But first we save the arguments accumulated so far (held in `argl`), the environment (held in `env`), and the remaining operands to be evaluated (held in `unev`). A special case is made for the evaluation of the last operand, which is handled at `ev-appl-last-arg`.

```
ev-appl-operand-loop
  (save argl)
  (assign exp (op first-operand) (reg unev))
  (test (op last-operand?) (reg unev))
  (branch (label ev-appl-last-arg))
  (save env)
  (save unev)
  (assign continue (label ev-appl-accumulate-arg))
  (goto (label eval-dispatch))
```

When an operand has been evaluated, the value is accumulated into the list held in `argl`. The operand is then removed from the list of unevaluated operands in `unev`, and the argument-evaluation continues.

```
ev-appl-accumulate-arg
  (restore unev)
  (restore env)
  (restore argl)
  (assign argl (op adjoin-arg) (reg val) (reg argl))
  (assign unev (op rest-operands) (reg unev))
  (goto (label ev-appl-operand-loop))
```

Evaluation of the last argument is handled differently. There is no need to save the environment or the list of unevaluated operands before going to `eval-dispatch`, since they will not be required after the last operand is evaluated. Thus, we return from the evaluation to a special entry point `ev-appl-accum-last-arg`, which restores the argument list, accumulates the new argument, restores the saved procedure, and goes off to perform the application.[23]

---

[23]The optimization of treating the last operand specially is known as *evlis tail recursion* (see Wand 1980). We could be somewhat more efficient in the argument evaluation loop if we made evaluation of the first operand a special case too. This would permit us to postpone initializing `argl` until after evaluating the first operand, so as to avoid saving `argl` in this case. The compiler in section 5.5 performs this optimization. (Compare the `construct-arglist` procedure of section 5.5.3.)

```
ev-appl-last-arg
  (assign continue (label ev-appl-accum-last-arg))
  (goto (label eval-dispatch))
ev-appl-accum-last-arg
  (restore argl)
  (assign argl (op adjoin-arg) (reg val) (reg argl))
  (restore proc)
  (goto (label apply-dispatch))
```

The details of the argument-evaluation loop determine the order in which the interpreter evaluates the operands of a combination (e.g., left to right or right to left—see exercise 3.8). This order is not determined by the metacircular evaluator, which inherits its control structure from the underlying Scheme in which it is implemented.[24] Because the first-operand selector (used in ev-appl-operand-loop to extract successive operands from unev) is implemented as car and the rest-operands selector is implemented as cdr, the explicit-control evaluator will evaluate the operands of a combination in left-to-right order.

Procedure application

The entry point apply-dispatch corresponds to the apply procedure of the metacircular evaluator. By the time we get to apply-dispatch, the proc register contains the procedure to apply and argl contains the list of evaluated arguments to which it must be applied. The saved value of continue (originally passed to eval-dispatch and saved at ev-application), which tells where to return with the result of the procedure application, is on the stack. When the application is complete, the controller transfers to the entry point specified by the saved continue, with the result of the application in val. As with the metacircular apply, there are two cases to consider. Either the procedure to be applied is a primitive or it is a compound procedure.

```
apply-dispatch
  (test (op primitive-procedure?) (reg proc))
  (branch (label primitive-apply))
  (test (op compound-procedure?) (reg proc))
  (branch (label compound-apply))
  (goto (label unknown-procedure-type))
```

---

[24]The order of operand evaluation in the metacircular evaluator is determined by the order of evaluation of the arguments to cons in the procedure list-of-values of section 4.1.1 (see exercise 4.1).

We assume that each primitive is implemented so as to obtain its arguments from argl and place its result in val. To specify how the machine handles primitives, we would have to provide a sequence of controller instructions to implement each primitive and arrange for primitive-apply to dispatch to the instructions for the primitive identified by the contents of proc. Since we are interested in the structure of the evaluation process rather than the details of the primitives, we will instead just use an apply-primitive-procedure operation that applies the procedure in proc to the arguments in argl. For the purpose of simulating the evaluator with the simulator of section 5.2 we use the procedure apply-primitive-procedure, which calls on the underlying Scheme system to perform the application, just as we did for the metacircular evaluator in section 4.1.4. After computing the value of the primitive application, we restore continue and go to the designated entry point.

```
primitive-apply
  (assign val (op apply-primitive-procedure)
              (reg proc)
              (reg argl))
  (restore continue)
  (goto (reg continue))
```

To apply a compound procedure, we proceed just as with the metacircular evaluator. We construct a frame that binds the procedure's parameters to the arguments, use this frame to extend the environment carried by the procedure, and evaluate in this extended environment the sequence of expressions that forms the body of the procedure. Ev-sequence, described below in section 5.4.2, handles the evaluation of the sequence.

```
compound-apply
  (assign unev (op procedure-parameters) (reg proc))
  (assign env (op procedure-environment) (reg proc))
  (assign env (op extend-environment)
              (reg unev) (reg argl) (reg env))
  (assign unev (op procedure-body) (reg proc))
  (goto (label ev-sequence))
```

Compound-apply is the only place in the interpreter where the env register is ever assigned a new value. Just as in the metacircular evaluator, the new environment is constructed from the environment carried by the procedure, together with the argument list and the corresponding list of variables to be bound.

5.4.2 Sequence Evaluation and Tail Recursion

The portion of the explicit-control evaluator at ev-sequence is analogous to the metacircular evaluator's eval-sequence procedure. It handles sequences of expressions in procedure bodies or in explicit begin expressions.

Explicit begin expressions are evaluated by placing the sequence of expressions to be evaluated in unev, saving continue on the stack, and jumping to ev-sequence.

```
ev-begin
  (assign unev (op begin-actions) (reg exp))
  (save continue)
  (goto (label ev-sequence))
```

The implicit sequences in procedure bodies are handled by jumping to ev-sequence from compound-apply, at which point continue is already on the stack, having been saved at ev-application.

The entries at ev-sequence and ev-sequence-continue form a loop that successively evaluates each expression in a sequence. The list of unevaluated expressions is kept in unev. Before evaluating each expression, we check to see if there are additional expressions to be evaluated in the sequence. If so, we save the rest of the unevaluated expressions (held in unev) and the environment in which these must be evaluated (held in env) and call eval-dispatch to evaluate the expression. The two saved registers are restored upon the return from this evaluation, at ev-sequence-continue.

The final expression in the sequence is handled differently, at the entry point ev-sequence-last-exp. Since there are no more expressions to be evaluated after this one, we need not save unev or env before going to eval-dispatch. The value of the whole sequence is the value of the last expression, so after the evaluation of the last expression there is nothing left to do except continue at the entry point currently held on the stack (which was saved by ev-application or ev-begin.) Rather than setting up continue to arrange for eval-dispatch to return here and then restoring continue from the stack and continuing at that entry point, we restore continue from the stack before going to eval-dispatch, so that eval-dispatch will continue at that entry point after evaluating the expression.

```
ev-sequence
  (assign exp (op first-exp) (reg unev))
  (test (op last-exp?) (reg unev))
  (branch (label ev-sequence-last-exp))
  (save unev)
  (save env)
  (assign continue (label ev-sequence-continue))
  (goto (label eval-dispatch))
ev-sequence-continue
  (restore env)
  (restore unev)
  (assign unev (op rest-exps) (reg unev))
  (goto (label ev-sequence))
ev-sequence-last-exp
  (restore continue)
  (goto (label eval-dispatch))
```

Tail recursion

In chapter 1 we said that the process described by a procedure such as

```
(define (sqrt-iter guess x)
  (if (good-enough? guess x)
      guess
      (sqrt-iter (improve guess x)
                 x)))
```

is an iterative process. Even though the procedure is syntactically recursive (defined in terms of itself), it is not logically necessary for an evaluator to save information in passing from one call to sqrt-iter to the next.[25] An evaluator that can execute a procedure such as sqrt-iter without requiring increasing storage as the procedure continues to call itself is called a *tail-recursive* evaluator. The metacircular implementation of the evaluator in chapter 4 does not specify whether the evaluator is tail-recursive, because that evaluator inherits its mechanism for saving state from the underlying Scheme. With the explicit-control evaluator, however, we can trace through the evaluation process to see when procedure calls cause a net accumulation of information on the stack.

Our evaluator is tail-recursive, because in order to evaluate the final expression of a sequence we transfer directly to eval-dispatch without saving any information on the stack. Hence, evaluating the final expression in a sequence—even if it is a procedure call (as in sqrt-iter, where the if expression, which is the last expression in the procedure

---

[25]We saw in section 5.1 how to implement such a process with a register machine that had no stack; the state of the process was stored in a fixed set of registers.

body, reduces to a call to `sqrt-iter`)—will not cause any information to be accumulated on the stack.[26]

If we did not think to take advantage of the fact that it was unnecessary to save information in this case, we might have implemented `eval-sequence` by treating all the expressions in a sequence in the same way—saving the registers, evaluating the expression, returning to restore the registers, and repeating this until all the expressions have been evaluated:[27]

```
ev-sequence
  (test (op no-more-exps?) (reg unev))
  (branch (label ev-sequence-end))
  (assign exp (op first-exp) (reg unev))
  (save unev)
  (save env)
  (assign continue (label ev-sequence-continue))
  (goto (label eval-dispatch))
ev-sequence-continue
  (restore env)
  (restore unev)
  (assign unev (op rest-exps) (reg unev))
  (goto (label ev-sequence))
ev-sequence-end
  (restore continue)
  (goto (reg continue))
```

This may seem like a minor change to our previous code for evaluation of a sequence: The only difference is that we go through the save-restore cycle for the last expression in a sequence as well as for the others. The interpreter will still give the same value for any expression. But this change is fatal to the tail-recursive implementation, because we must now return after evaluating the final expression in a sequence in order to undo the (useless) register saves. These extra saves will accumulate during a nest of procedure calls. Consequently, processes such as `sqrt-iter` will require space proportional to the number of iterations rather than requiring constant space. This difference can be significant.

---

[26]This implementation of tail recursion in `ev-sequence` is one variety of a well-known optimization technique used by many compilers. In compiling a procedure that ends with a procedure call, one can replace the call by a jump to the called procedure's entry point. Building this strategy into the interpreter, as we have done in this section, provides the optimization uniformly throughout the language.

[27]We can define `no-more-exps?` as follows:

```
(define (no-more-exps? seq) (null? seq))
```

For example, with tail recursion, an infinite loop can be expressed using only the procedure-call mechanism:

```
(define (count n)
  (newline)
  (display n)
  (count (+ n 1)))
```

Without tail recursion, such a procedure would eventually run out of stack space, and expressing a true iteration would require some control mechanism other than procedure call.

5.4.3   Conditionals, Assignments, and Definitions

As with the metacircular evaluator, special forms are handled by selectively evaluating fragments of the expression. For an `if` expression, we must evaluate the predicate and decide, based on the value of predicate, whether to evaluate the consequent or the alternative.

Before evaluating the predicate, we save the `if` expression itself so that we can later extract the consequent or alternative. We also save the environment, which we will need later in order to evaluate the consequent or the alternative, and we save `continue`, which we will need later in order to return to the evaluation of the expression that is waiting for the value of the `if`.

```
ev-if
  (save exp)                       ; save expression for later
  (save env)
  (save continue)
  (assign continue (label ev-if-decide))
  (assign exp (op if-predicate) (reg exp))
  (goto (label eval-dispatch))    ; evaluate the predicate
```

When we return from evaluating the predicate, we test whether it was true or false and, depending on the result, place either the consequent or the alternative in `exp` before going to `eval-dispatch`. Notice that restoring `env` and `continue` here sets up `eval-dispatch` to have the correct environment and to continue at the right place to receive the value of the `if` expression.

```
ev-if-decide
  (restore continue)
  (restore env)
  (restore exp)
  (test (op true?) (reg val))
  (branch (label ev-if-consequent))
```

```
ev-if-alternative
  (assign exp (op if-alternative) (reg exp))
  (goto (label eval-dispatch))
ev-if-consequent
  (assign exp (op if-consequent) (reg exp))
  (goto (label eval-dispatch))
```

Assignments and definitions

Assignments are handled by `ev-assignment`, which is reached from `eval-dispatch` with the assignment expression in exp. The code at `ev-assignment` first evaluates the value part of the expression and then installs the new value in the environment. `Set-variable-value!` is assumed to be available as a machine operation.

```
ev-assignment
  (assign unev (op assignment-variable) (reg exp))
  (save unev)                          ; save variable for later
  (assign exp (op assignment-value) (reg exp))
  (save env)
  (save continue)
  (assign continue (label ev-assignment-1))
  (goto (label eval-dispatch))    ; evaluate the assignment value
ev-assignment-1
  (restore continue)
  (restore env)
  (restore unev)
  (perform
   (op set-variable-value!) (reg unev) (reg val) (reg env))
  (assign val (const ok))
  (goto (reg continue))
```

Definitions are handled in a similar way:

```
ev-definition
  (assign unev (op definition-variable) (reg exp))
  (save unev)                          ; save variable for later
  (assign exp (op definition-value) (reg exp))
  (save env)
  (save continue)
  (assign continue (label ev-definition-1))
  (goto (label eval-dispatch))    ; evaluate the definition value
ev-definition-1
  (restore continue)
  (restore env)
  (restore unev)
  (perform
   (op define-variable!) (reg unev) (reg val) (reg env))
  (assign val (const ok))
  (goto (reg continue))
```

Exercise 5.23

Extend the evaluator to handle derived expressions such as cond, let, and so on (section 4.1.2). You may "cheat" and assume that the syntax transformers such as cond->if are available as machine operations.[28]

Exercise 5.24

Implement cond as a new basic special form without reducing it to if. You will have to construct a loop that tests the predicates of successive cond clauses until you find one that is true, and then use ev-sequence to evaluate the actions of the clause.

Exercise 5.25

Modify the evaluator so that it uses normal-order evaluation, based on the lazy evaluator of section 4.2.

5.4.4   Running the Evaluator

With the implementation of the explicit-control evaluator we come to the end of a development, begun in chapter 1, in which we have explored successively more precise models of the evaluation process. We started with the relatively informal substitution model, then extended this in chapter 3 to the environment model, which enabled us to deal with state and change. In the metacircular evaluator of chapter 4, we used Scheme itself as a language for making more explicit the environment structure constructed during evaluation of an expression. Now, with register machines, we have taken a close look at the evaluator's mechanisms for storage management, argument passing, and control. At each new level of description, we have had to raise issues and resolve ambiguities that were not apparent at the previous, less precise treatment of evaluation. To understand the behavior of the explicit-control evaluator, we can simulate it and monitor its performance.

We will install a driver loop in our evaluator machine. This plays the role of the driver-loop procedure of section 4.1.4. The evaluator will repeatedly print a prompt, read an expression, evaluate the expression by going to eval-dispatch, and print the result. The following

---

[28]This isn't really cheating. In an actual implementation built from scratch, we would use our explicit-control evaluator to interpret a Scheme program that performs source-level transformations like cond->if in a syntax phase that runs before execution.

instructions form the beginning of the explicit-control evaluator's controller sequence:[29]

```
read-eval-print-loop
  (perform (op initialize-stack))
  (perform
   (op prompt-for-input) (const ";;; EC-Eval input:"))
  (assign exp (op read))
  (assign env (op get-global-environment))
  (assign continue (label print-result))
  (goto (label eval-dispatch))
print-result
  (perform
   (op announce-output) (const ";;; EC-Eval value:"))
  (perform (op user-print) (reg val))
  (goto (label read-eval-print-loop))
```

When we encounter an error in a procedure (such as the "unknown procedure type error" indicated at `apply-dispatch`), we print an error message and return to the driver loop.[30]

```
unknown-expression-type
  (assign val (const unknown-expression-type-error))
  (goto (label signal-error))

unknown-procedure-type
  (restore continue)      ; clean up stack (from apply-dispatch)
  (assign val (const unknown-procedure-type-error))
  (goto (label signal-error))

signal-error
  (perform (op user-print) (reg val))
  (goto (label read-eval-print-loop))
```

---

[29] We assume here that `read` and the various printing operations are available as primitive machine operations, which is useful for our simulation, but completely unrealistic in practice. These are actually extremely complex operations. In practice, they would be implemented using low-level input-output operations such as transferring single characters to and from a device.

To support the `get-global-environment` operation we define

```
(define the-global-environment (setup-environment))

(define (get-global-environment)
  the-global-environment)
```

[30] There are other errors that we would like the interpreter to handle, but these are not so simple. See exercise 5.30.

For the purposes of the simulation, we initialize the stack each time through the driver loop, since it might not be empty after an error (such as an undefined variable) interrupts an evaluation.[31]

If we combine all the code fragments presented in sections 5.4.1–5.4.4, we can create an evaluator machine model that we can run using the register-machine simulator of section 5.2.

```
(define eceval
  (make-machine
    '(exp env val proc argl continue unev)
    eceval-operations
    '(
      read-eval-print-loop
        ⟨ entire machine controller as given above ⟩
    )))
```

We must define Scheme procedures to simulate the operations used as primitives by the evaluator. These are the same procedures we used for the metacircular evaluator in section 4.1, together with the few additional ones defined in footnotes throughout section 5.4.

```
(define eceval-operations
  (list (list 'self-evaluating? self-evaluating)
        ⟨complete list of operations for eceval machine⟩))
```

Finally, we can initialize the global environment and run the evaluator:

```
(define the-global-environment (setup-environment))

(start eceval)

;;; EC-Eval input:
(define (append x y)
  (if (null? x)
      y
      (cons (car x)
            (append (cdr x) y))))
;;; EC-Eval value:
ok

;;; EC-Eval input:
(append '(a b c) '(d e f))
;;; EC-Eval value:
(a b c d e f)
```

---

[31] We could perform the stack initialization only after errors, but doing it in the driver loop will be convenient for monitoring the evaluator's performance, as described below.

Of course, evaluating expressions in this way will take much longer than if we had directly typed them into Scheme, because of the multiple levels of simulation involved. Our expressions are evaluated by the explicit-control-evaluator machine, which is being simulated by a Scheme program, which is itself being evaluated by the Scheme interpreter.

Monitoring the performance of the evaluator

Simulation can be a powerful tool to guide the implementation of evaluators. Simulations make it easy not only to explore variations of the register-machine design but also to monitor the performance of the simulated evaluator. For example, one important factor in performance is how efficiently the evaluator uses the stack. We can observe the number of stack operations required to evaluate various expressions by defining the evaluator register machine with the version of the simulator that collects statistics on stack use (section 5.2.4), and adding an instruction at the evaluator's `print-result` entry point to print the statistics:

```
print-result
  (perform (op print-stack-statistics)) ; added instruction
  (perform
   (op announce-output) (const ";;; EC-Eval value:"))
  ... ; same as before
```

Interactions with the evaluator now look like this:

```
;;; EC-Eval input:
(define (factorial n)
  (if (= n 1)
      1
      (* (factorial (- n 1)) n)))
(total-pushes = 3 maximum-depth = 3)
;;; EC-Eval value:
ok

;;; EC-Eval input:
(factorial 5)
(total-pushes = 144 maximum-depth = 28)
;;; EC-Eval value:
120
```

Note that the driver loop of the evaluator reinitializes the stack at the start of each interaction, so that the statistics printed will refer only to stack operations used to evaluate the previous expression.

Exercise 5.26

Use the monitored stack to explore the tail-recursive property of the evaluator (section 5.4.2). Start the evaluator and define the iterative `factorial` procedure from section 1.2.1:

```
(define (factorial n)
  (define (iter product counter)
    (if (> counter n)
        product
        (iter (* counter product)
              (+ counter 1))))
  (iter 1 1))
```

Run the procedure with some small values of n. Record the maximum stack depth and the number of pushes required to compute $n!$ for each of these values.

a. You will find that the maximum depth required to evaluate $n!$ is independent of n. What is that depth?

b. Determine from your data a formula in terms of n for the total number of push operations used in evaluating $n!$ for any $n \geq 1$. Note that the number of operations used is a linear function of n and is thus determined by two constants.

Exercise 5.27

For comparison with exercise 5.26, explore the behavior of the following procedure for computing factorials recursively:

```
(define (factorial n)
  (if (= n 1)
      1
      (* (factorial (- n 1)) n)))
```

By running this procedure with the monitored stack, determine, as a function of n, the maximum depth of the stack and the total number of pushes used in evaluating $n!$ for $n \geq 1$. (Again, these functions will be linear.) Summarize your experiments by filling in the following table with the appropriate expressions in terms of n:

	Maximum depth	Number of pushes
Recursive factorial		
Iterative factorial		

The maximum depth is a measure of the amount of space used by the evaluator in carrying out the computation, and the number of pushes correlates well with the time required.

Exercise 5.28

Modify the definition of the evaluator by changing `eval-sequence` as described in section 5.4.2 so that the evaluator is no longer tail-recursive. Rerun your experiments from exercises 5.26 and 5.27 to demonstrate that both versions of the `factorial` procedure now require space that grows linearly with their input.

Exercise 5.29

Monitor the stack operations in the tree-recursive Fibonacci computation:

```
(define (fib n)
  (if (< n 2)
      n
      (+ (fib (- n 1)) (fib (- n 2))))))
```

a. Give a formula in terms of n for the maximum depth of the stack required to compute Fib(n) for $n \geq 2$. Hint: In section 1.2.2 we argued that the space used by this process grows linearly with n.

b. Give a formula for the total number of pushes used to compute Fib(n) for $n \geq 2$. You should find that the number of pushes (which correlates well with the time used) grows exponentially with n. Hint: Let $S(n)$ be the number of pushes used in computing Fib(n). You should be able to argue that there is a formula that expresses $S(n)$ in terms of $S(n-1)$, $S(n-2)$, and some fixed "overhead" constant k that is independent of n. Give the formula, and say what k is. Then show that $S(n)$ can be expressed as aFib($n + 1$) $+ b$ and give the values of a and b.

Exercise 5.30

Our evaluator currently catches and signals only two kinds of errors—unknown expression types and unknown procedure types. Other errors will take us out of the evaluator read-eval-print loop. When we run the evaluator using the register-machine simulator, these errors are caught by the underlying Scheme system. This is analogous to the computer crashing when a user program makes an error.[32] It is a large project to make a real error system work, but it is well worth the effort to understand what is involved here.

a. Errors that occur in the evaluation process, such as an attempt to access an unbound variable, could be caught by changing the lookup operation to make it return a distinguished condition code, which cannot be a possible value of any user variable. The evaluator can test for this condition code and then do what is necessary to go to `signal-error`. Find all of the places in the evaluator where such a change is necessary and fix them. This is lots of work.

---

[32]Regrettably, this is the normal state of affairs in conventional compiler-based language systems such as C. In UNIX™ the system "dumps core," and in DOS/Windows™ it becomes catatonic. The Macintosh™ displays a picture of an exploding bomb and offers you the opportunity to reboot the computer—if you're lucky.

b. Much worse is the problem of handling errors that are signaled by applying primitive procedures, such as an attempt to divide by zero or an attempt to extract the `car` of a symbol. In a professionally written high-quality system, each primitive application is checked for safety as part of the primitive. For example, every call to `car` could first check that the argument is a pair. If the argument is not a pair, the application would return a distinguished condition code to the evaluator, which would then report the failure. We could arrange for this in our register-machine simulator by making each primitive procedure check for applicability and returning an appropriate distinguished condition code on failure. Then the `primitive-apply` code in the evaluator can check for the condition code and go to `signal-error` if necessary. Build this structure and make it work. This is a major project.

5.5   Compilation

The explicit-control evaluator of section 5.4 is a register machine whose controller interprets Scheme programs. In this section we will see how to run Scheme programs on a register machine whose controller is not a Scheme interpreter.

The explicit-control evaluator machine is universal—it can carry out any computational process that can be described in Scheme. The evaluator's controller orchestrates the use of its data paths to perform the desired computation. Thus, the evaluator's data paths are universal: They are sufficient to perform any computation we desire, given an appropriate controller.[33]

Commercial general-purpose computers are register machines organized around a collection of registers and operations that constitute an efficient and convenient universal set of data paths. The controller for a general-purpose machine is an interpreter for a register-machine language like the one we have been using. This language is called the *native language* of the machine, or simply *machine language*. Programs written in machine language are sequences of instructions that use the machine's data paths. For example, the explicit-control evaluator's instruction sequence can be thought of as a machine-language program for a general-purpose computer rather than as the controller for a specialized interpreter machine.

---

[33]This is a theoretical statement. We are not claiming that the evaluator's data paths are a particularly convenient or efficient set of data paths for a general-purpose computer. For example, they are not very good for implementing high-performance floating-point calculations or calculations that intensively manipulate bit vectors.

There are two common strategies for bridging the gap between higher-level languages and register-machine languages. The explicit-control evaluator illustrates the strategy of interpretation. An interpreter written in the native language of a machine configures the machine to execute programs written in a language (called the *source language*) that may differ from the native language of the machine performing the evaluation. The primitive procedures of the source language are implemented as a library of subroutines written in the native language of the given machine. A program to be interpreted (called the *source program*) is represented as a data structure. The interpreter traverses this data structure, analyzing the source program. As it does so, it simulates the intended behavior of the source program by calling appropriate primitive subroutines from the library.

In this section, we explore the alternative strategy of *compilation*. A compiler for a given source language and machine translates a source program into an equivalent program (called the *object program*) written in the machine's native language. The compiler that we implement in this section translates programs written in Scheme into sequences of instructions to be executed using the explicit-control evaluator machine's data paths.[34]

Compared with interpretation, compilation can provide a great increase in the efficiency of program execution, as we will explain below in the overview of the compiler. On the other hand, an interpreter provides a more powerful environment for interactive program development and debugging, because the source program being executed is available at run time to be examined and modified. In addition, because the entire library of primitives is present, new programs can be constructed and added to the system during debugging.

In view of the complementary advantages of compilation and interpretation, modern program-development environments pursue a mixed strategy. Lisp interpreters are generally organized so that interpreted procedures and compiled procedures can call each other. This enables a programmer to compile those parts of a program that are assumed to be

---

[34]Actually, the machine that runs compiled code can be simpler than the interpreter machine, because we won't use the exp and unev registers. The interpreter used these to hold pieces of unevaluated expressions. With the compiler, however, these expressions get built into the compiled code that the register machine will run. For the same reason, we don't need the machine operations that deal with expression syntax. But compiled code will use a few additional machine operations (to represent compiled procedure objects) that didn't appear in the explicit-control evaluator machine.

debugged, thus gaining the efficiency advantage of compilation, while retaining the interpretive mode of execution for those parts of the program that are in the flux of interactive development and debugging. In section 5.5.7, after we have implemented the compiler, we will show how to interface it with our interpreter to produce an integrated interpreter-compiler development system.

An overview of the compiler

Our compiler is much like our interpreter, both in its structure and in the function it performs. Accordingly, the mechanisms used by the compiler for analyzing expressions will be similar to those used by the interpreter. Moreover, to make it easy to interface compiled and interpreted code, we will design the compiler to generate code that obeys the same conventions of register usage as the interpreter: The environment will be kept in the env register, argument lists will be accumulated in argl, a procedure to be applied will be in proc, procedures will return their answers in val, and the location to which a procedure should return will be kept in continue. In general, the compiler translates a source program into an object program that performs essentially the same register operations as would the interpreter in evaluating the same source program.

This description suggests a strategy for implementing a rudimentary compiler: We traverse the expression in the same way the interpreter does. When we encounter a register instruction that the interpreter would perform in evaluating the expression, we do not execute the instruction but instead accumulate it into a sequence. The resulting sequence of instructions will be the object code. Observe the efficiency advantage of compilation over interpretation. Each time the interpreter evaluates an expression—for example, (f 84 96)—it performs the work of classifying the expression (discovering that this is a procedure application) and testing for the end of the operand list (discovering that there are two operands). With a compiler, the expression is analyzed only once, when the instruction sequence is generated at compile time. The object code produced by the compiler contains only the instructions that evaluate the operator and the two operands, assemble the argument list, and apply the procedure (in proc) to the arguments (in argl).

This is the same kind of optimization we implemented in the analyzing evaluator of section 4.1.7. But there are further opportunities to gain efficiency in compiled code. As the interpreter runs, it follows a process that must be applicable to any expression in the language. In contrast, a given segment of compiled code is meant to execute some particular expression. This can make a big difference, for example in the use of the stack to save registers. When the interpreter evaluates an expression, it must be prepared for any contingency. Before evaluating a subexpression, the interpreter saves all registers that will be needed later, because the subexpression might require an arbitrary evaluation. A compiler, on the other hand, can exploit the structure of the particular expression it is processing to generate code that avoids unnecessary stack operations.

As a case in point, consider the combination (f 84 96). Before the interpreter evaluates the operator of the combination, it prepares for this evaluation by saving the registers containing the operands and the environment, whose values will be needed later. The interpreter then evaluates the operator to obtain the result in val, restores the saved registers, and finally moves the result from val to proc. However, in the particular expression we are dealing with, the operator is the symbol f, whose evaluation is accomplished by the machine operation lookup-variable-value, which does not alter any registers. The compiler that we implement in this section will take advantage of this fact and generate code that evaluates the operator using the instruction

```
(assign proc (op lookup-variable-value) (const f) (reg env))
```

This code not only avoids the unnecessary saves and restores but also assigns the value of the lookup directly to proc, whereas the interpreter would obtain the result in val and then move this to proc.

A compiler can also optimize access to the environment. Having analyzed the code, the compiler can in many cases know in which frame a particular variable will be located and access that frame directly, rather than performing the lookup-variable-value search. We will discuss how to implement such variable access in section 5.5.6. Until then, however, we will focus on the kind of register and stack optimizations described above. There are many other optimizations that can be performed by a compiler, such as coding primitive operations "in line" instead of using a general apply mechanism (see exercise 5.38); but we will not emphasize these here. Our main goal in this section is to illustrate the compilation process in a simplified (but still interesting) context.

5.5.1   Structure of the Compiler

In section 4.1.7 we modified our original metacircular interpreter to separate analysis from execution. We analyzed each expression to produce an execution procedure that took an environment as argument and performed the required operations. In our compiler, we will do essentially the same analysis. Instead of producing execution procedures, however, we will generate sequences of instructions to be run by our register machine.

The procedure `compile` is the top-level dispatch in the compiler. It corresponds to the `eval` procedure of section 4.1.1, the `analyze` procedure of section 4.1.7, and the `eval-dispatch` entry point of the explicit-control-evaluator in section 5.4.1. The compiler, like the interpreters, uses the expression-syntax procedures defined in section 4.1.2.[35] Compile performs a case analysis on the syntactic type of the expression to be compiled. For each type of expression, it dispatches to a specialized *code generator*:

```
(define (compile exp target linkage)
  (cond ((self-evaluating? exp)
         (compile-self-evaluating exp target linkage))
        ((quoted? exp) (compile-quoted exp target linkage))
        ((variable? exp)
         (compile-variable exp target linkage))
        ((assignment? exp)
         (compile-assignment exp target linkage))
        ((definition? exp)
         (compile-definition exp target linkage))
        ((if? exp) (compile-if exp target linkage))
        ((lambda? exp) (compile-lambda exp target linkage))
        ((begin? exp)
         (compile-sequence (begin-actions exp)
                           target
                           linkage))
        ((cond? exp) (compile (cond->if exp) target linkage))
        ((application? exp)
         (compile-application exp target linkage))
        (else
         (error "Unknown expression type -- COMPILE" exp))))
```

----

[35]Notice, however, that our compiler is a Scheme program, and the syntax procedures that it uses to manipulate expressions are the actual Scheme procedures used with the metacircular evaluator. For the explicit-control evaluator, in contrast, we assumed that equivalent syntax operations were available as operations for the register machine. (Of course, when we simulated the register machine in Scheme, we used the actual Scheme procedures in our register machine simulation.)

Targets and linkages

Compile and the code generators that it calls take two arguments in addition to the expression to compile. There is a *target*, which specifies the register in which the compiled code is to return the value of the expression. There is also a *linkage descriptor*, which describes how the code resulting from the compilation of the expression should proceed when it has finished its execution. The linkage descriptor can require that the code do one of the following three things:

- continue at the next instruction in sequence (this is specified by the linkage descriptor next),

- return from the procedure being compiled (this is specified by the linkage descriptor return), or

- jump to a named entry point (this is specified by using the designated label as the linkage descriptor).

For example, compiling the expression 5 (which is self-evaluating) with a target of the val register and a linkage of next should produce the instruction

```
(assign val (const 5))
```

Compiling the same expression with a linkage of return should produce the instructions

```
(assign val (const 5))
(goto (reg continue))
```

In the first case, execution will continue with the next instruction in the sequence. In the second case, we will return from a procedure call. In both cases, the value of the expression will be placed into the target val register.

Instruction sequences and stack usage

Each code generator returns an *instruction sequence* containing the object code it has generated for the expression. Code generation for a compound expression is accomplished by combining the output from simpler code generators for component expressions, just as evaluation of a compound expression is accomplished by evaluating the component expressions.

The simplest method for combining instruction sequences is a procedure called `append-instruction-sequences`. It takes as arguments any number of instruction sequences that are to be executed sequentially; it appends them and returns the combined sequence. That is, if $\langle seq_1 \rangle$ and $\langle seq_2 \rangle$ are sequences of instructions, then evaluating

```
(append-instruction-sequences ⟨seq₁⟩ ⟨seq₂⟩)
```

produces the sequence

$\langle seq_1 \rangle$
$\langle seq_2 \rangle$

Whenever registers might need to be saved, the compiler's code generators use `preserving`, which is a more subtle method for combining instruction sequences. Preserving takes three arguments: a set of registers and two instruction sequences that are to be executed sequentially. It appends the sequences in such a way that the contents of each register in the set is preserved over the execution of the first sequence, if this is needed for the execution of the second sequence. That is, if the first sequence modifies the register and the second sequence actually needs the register's original contents, then `preserving` wraps a `save` and a `restore` of the register around the first sequence before appending the sequences. Otherwise, `preserving` simply returns the appended instruction sequences. Thus, for example,

```
(preserving (list ⟨reg₁⟩ ⟨reg₂⟩) ⟨seq₁⟩ ⟨seq₂⟩)
```

produces one of the following four sequences of instructions, depending on how $\langle seq_1 \rangle$ and $\langle seq_2 \rangle$ use $\langle reg_1 \rangle$ and $\langle reg_2 \rangle$:

$\langle seq_1 \rangle$ $\langle seq_2 \rangle$	`(save` $\langle reg_1 \rangle$`)` $\langle seq_1 \rangle$ `(restore` $\langle reg_1 \rangle$`)` $\langle seq_2 \rangle$	`(save` $\langle reg_2 \rangle$`)` $\langle seq1 \rangle$ `(restore` $\langle reg_2 \rangle$`)` $\langle seq2 \rangle$	`(save` $\langle reg_2 \rangle$`)` `(save` $\langle reg_1 \rangle$`)` $\langle seq_1 \rangle$ `(restore` $\langle reg_1 \rangle$`)` `(restore` $\langle reg_2 \rangle$`)` $\langle seq_2 \rangle$

By using `preserving` to combine instruction sequences the compiler avoids unnecessary stack operations. This also isolates the details of whether or not to generate `save` and `restore` instructions within the `preserving` procedure, separating them from the concerns that arise in writing each of the individual code generators. In fact no `save` or `restore` instructions are explicitly produced by the code generators.

In principle, we could represent an instruction sequence simply as a list of instructions. Append-instruction-sequences could then combine instruction sequences by performing an ordinary list append. However, preserving would then be a complex operation, because it would have to analyze each instruction sequence to determine how the sequence uses its registers. Preserving would be inefficient as well as complex, because it would have to analyze each of its instruction sequence arguments, even though these sequences might themselves have been constructed by calls to preserving, in which case their parts would have already been analyzed. To avoid such repetitious analysis we will associate with each instruction sequence some information about its register use. When we construct a basic instruction sequence we will provide this information explicitly, and the procedures that combine instruction sequences will derive register-use information for the combined sequence from the information associated with the component sequences.

An instruction sequence will contain three pieces of information:

• the set of registers that must be initialized before the instructions in the sequence are executed (these registers are said to be *needed* by the sequence),

• the set of registers whose values are modified by the instructions in the sequence, and

• the actual instructions (also called *statements*) in the sequence.

We will represent an instruction sequence as a list of its three parts. The constructor for instruction sequences is thus

```
(define (make-instruction-sequence needs modifies statements)
  (list needs modifies statements))
```

For example, the two-instruction sequence that looks up the value of the variable x in the current environment, assigns the result to val, and then returns, requires registers env and continue to have been initialized, and modifies register val. This sequence would therefore be constructed as

```
(make-instruction-sequence '(env continue) '(val)
 '((assign val
           (op lookup-variable-value) (const x) (reg env))
   (goto (reg continue))))
```

We sometimes need to construct an instruction sequence with no statements:

```
(define (empty-instruction-sequence)
  (make-instruction-sequence '() '() '()))
```

The procedures for combining instruction sequences are shown in section 5.5.4.

Exercise 5.31

In evaluating a procedure application, the explicit-control evaluator always saves and restores the `env` register around the evaluation of the operator, saves and restores `env` around the evaluation of each operand (except the final one), saves and restores `argl` around the evaluation of each operand, and saves and restores `proc` around the evaluation of the operand sequence. For each of the following combinations, say which of these `save` and `restore` operations are superfluous and thus could be eliminated by the compiler's `preserving` mechanism:

```
(f 'x 'y)
```

```
((f) 'x 'y)
```

```
(f (g 'x) y)
```

```
(f (g 'x) 'y)
```

Exercise 5.32

Using the `preserving` mechanism, the compiler will avoid saving and restoring env around the evaluation of the operator of a combination in the case where the operator is a symbol. We could also build such optimizations into the evaluator. Indeed, the explicit-control evaluator of section 5.4 already performs a similar optimization, by treating combinations with no operands as a special case.

a. Extend the explicit-control evaluator to recognize as a separate class of expressions combinations whose operator is a symbol, and to take advantage of this fact in evaluating such expressions.

b. Alyssa P. Hacker suggests that by extending the evaluator to recognize more and more special cases we could incorporate all the compiler's optimizations, and that this would eliminate the advantage of compilation altogether. What do you think of this idea?

5.5.2   Compiling Expressions

In this section and the next we implement the code generators to which the `compile` procedure dispatches.

Compiling linkage code

In general, the output of each code generator will end with instructions—generated by the procedure `compile-linkage`—that implement the required linkage. If the linkage is `return` then we must generate the instruction (goto (reg continue)). This needs the `continue` register and does not modify any registers. If the linkage is `next`, then we needn't include any additional instructions. Otherwise, the linkage is a label, and we generate a `goto` to that label, an instruction that does not need or modify any registers.[36]

```
(define (compile-linkage linkage)
  (cond ((eq? linkage 'return)
         (make-instruction-sequence '(continue) '()
          '((goto (reg continue)))))
        ((eq? linkage 'next)
         (empty-instruction-sequence))
        (else
         (make-instruction-sequence '() '()
          `((goto (label ,linkage)))))))
```

The linkage code is appended to an instruction sequence by `preserving` the `continue` register, since a `return` linkage will require the `continue` register: If the given instruction sequence modifies `continue` and the linkage code needs it, `continue` will be saved and restored.

```
(define (end-with-linkage linkage instruction-sequence)
  (preserving '(continue)
   instruction-sequence
   (compile-linkage linkage)))
```

Compiling simple expressions

The code generators for self-evaluating expressions, quotations, and variables construct instruction sequences that assign the required value to the target register and then proceed as specified by the linkage descriptor.

```
(define (compile-self-evaluating exp target linkage)
  (end-with-linkage linkage
   (make-instruction-sequence '() (list target)
    `((assign ,target (const ,exp))))))
```

---

[36]This procedure uses a feature of Lisp called *backquote* (or *quasiquote*) that is handy for constructing lists. Preceding a list with a backquote symbol is much like quoting it, except that anything in the list that is flagged with a comma is evaluated.

For example, if the value of `linkage` is the symbol `branch25`, then the expression `((goto (label ,linkage)))` evaluates to the list ((goto (label branch25))). Similarly, if the value of x is the list (a b c), then `(1 2 ,(car x))` evaluates to the list (1 2 a).

```
(define (compile-quoted exp target linkage)
  (end-with-linkage linkage
    (make-instruction-sequence '() (list target)
     `((assign ,target (const ,(text-of-quotation exp)))))))

(define (compile-variable exp target linkage)
  (end-with-linkage linkage
    (make-instruction-sequence '(env) (list target)
     `((assign ,target
                (op lookup-variable-value)
                (const ,exp)
                (reg env))))))
```

All these assignment instructions modify the target register, and the one
that looks up a variable needs the env register.

Assignments and definitions are handled much as they are in the interpreter. We recursively generate code that computes the value to be
assigned to the variable, and append to it a two-instruction sequence that
actually sets or defines the variable and assigns the value of the whole expression (the symbol ok) to the target register. The recursive compilation
has target val and linkage next so that the code will put its result into
val and continue with the code that is appended after it. The appending is done preserving env, since the environment is needed for setting
or defining the variable and the code for the variable value could be the
compilation of a complex expression that might modify the registers in
arbitrary ways.

```
(define (compile-assignment exp target linkage)
  (let ((var (assignment-variable exp))
        (get-value-code
          (compile (assignment-value exp) 'val 'next)))
    (end-with-linkage linkage
      (preserving '(env)
        get-value-code
        (make-instruction-sequence '(env val) (list target)
         `((perform (op set-variable-value!)
                     (const ,var)
                     (reg val)
                     (reg env))
           (assign ,target (const ok))))))))
```

```
(define (compile-definition exp target linkage)
  (let ((var (definition-variable exp)))
        (get-value-code
          (compile (definition-value exp) 'val 'next)))
    (end-with-linkage linkage
     (preserving '(env)
       get-value-code
       (make-instruction-sequence '(env val) (list target)
        `((perform (op define-variable!)
                   (const ,var)
                   (reg val)
                   (reg env))
          (assign ,target (const ok)))))))))
```

The appended two-instruction sequence requires env and val and modifies the target. Note that although we preserve env for this sequence, we do not preserve val, because the get-value-code is designed to explicitly place its result in val for use by this sequence. (In fact, if we did preserve val, we would have a bug, because this would cause the previous contents of val to be restored right after the get-value-code is run.)

Compiling conditional expressions

The code for an if expression compiled with a given target and linkage has the form

```
⟨compilation of predicate, target val, linkage next⟩
(test (op false?) (reg val))
(branch (label false-branch))
true-branch
⟨compilation of consequent with given target and given linkage or after-if⟩
false-branch
⟨compilation of alternative with given target and linkage⟩
after-if
```

To generate this code, we compile the predicate, consequent, and alternative, and combine the resulting code with instructions to test the predicate result and with newly generated labels to mark the true and false branches and the end of the conditional.[37] In this arrangement of code, we must branch around the true branch if the test is false. The only slight complication is in how the linkage for the true branch should be handled. If the linkage for the conditional is `return` or a label, then the true and false branches will both use this same linkage. If the linkage is `next`, the true branch ends with a jump around the code for the false branch to the label at the end of the conditional.

```
(define (compile-if exp target linkage)
  (let ((t-branch (make-label 'true-branch))
        (f-branch (make-label 'false-branch))
        (after-if (make-label 'after-if)))
    (let ((consequent-linkage
            (if (eq? linkage 'next) after-if linkage)))
      (let ((p-code (compile (if-predicate exp) 'val 'next))
            (c-code
              (compile
                (if-consequent exp) target consequent-linkage))
            (a-code
              (compile (if-alternative exp) target linkage)))
        (preserving '(env continue)
          p-code
          (append-instruction-sequences
            (make-instruction-sequence '(val) '()
              `((test (op false?) (reg val))
                (branch (label ,f-branch))))
            (parallel-instruction-sequences
              (append-instruction-sequences t-branch c-code)
              (append-instruction-sequences f-branch a-code))
            after-if))))))
```

Env is preserved around the predicate code because it could be needed by the true and false branches, and `continue` is preserved because it could

---

[37]We can't just use the labels `true-branch`, `false-branch`, and `after-if` as shown above, because there might be more than one `if` in the program. The compiler uses the procedure `make-label` to generate labels. `Make-label` takes a symbol as argument and returns a new symbol that begins with the given symbol. For example, successive calls to `(make-label 'a)` would return a1, a2, and so on. `Make-label` can be implemented similarly to the generation of unique variable names in the query language, as follows:

```
(define label-counter 0)

(define (new-label-number)
  (set! label-counter (+ 1 label-counter))
  label-counter)

(define (make-label name)
  (string->symbol
    (string-append (symbol->string name)
                   (number->string (new-label-number)))))
```

be needed by the linkage code in those branches. The code for the true
and false branches (which are not executed sequentially) is appended using a special combiner `parallel-instruction-sequences` described
in section 5.5.4.

   Note that `cond` is a derived expression, so all that the compiler needs
to do handle it is to apply the `cond->if` transformer (from section 4.1.2)
and compile the resulting `if` expression.

Compiling sequences

The compilation of sequences (from procedure bodies or explicit `begin`
expressions) parallels their evaluation. Each expression of the sequence
is compiled—the last expression with the linkage specified for the sequence, and the other expressions with linkage `next` (to execute the rest
of the sequence). The instruction sequences for the individual expressions are appended to form a single instruction sequence, such that `env`
(needed for the rest of the sequence) and `continue` (possibly needed for
the linkage at the end of the sequence) are preserved.

```
(define (compile-sequence seq target linkage)
  (if (last-exp? seq)
      (compile (first-exp seq) target linkage)
      (preserving '(env continue)
       (compile (first-exp seq) target 'next)
       (compile-sequence (rest-exps seq) target linkage))))
```

Compiling `lambda` expressions

Lambda expressions construct procedures. The object code for a `lambda`
expression must have the form

⟨ *construct procedure object and assign it to target register* ⟩
⟨ *linkage* ⟩

When we compile the `lambda` expression, we also generate the code
for the procedure body. Although the body won't be executed at the
time of procedure construction, it is convenient to insert it into the object
code right after the code for the `lambda`. If the linkage for the `lambda`
expression is a label or `return`, this is fine. But if the linkage is `next`,
we will need to skip around the code for the procedure body by using a
linkage that jumps to a label that is inserted after the body. The object
code thus has the form

⟨ *construct procedure object and assign it to target register* ⟩
⟨ *code for given linkage* ⟩ *or* `(goto (label after-lambda))`
⟨ *compilation of procedure body* ⟩
`after-lambda`

Compile-lambda generates the code for constructing the procedure object followed by the code for the procedure body. The procedure object will be constructed at run time by combining the current environment (the environment at the point of definition) with the entry point to the compiled procedure body (a newly generated label).[38]

```
(define (compile-lambda exp target linkage)
  (let ((proc-entry (make-label 'entry))
        (after-lambda (make-label 'after-lambda)))
    (let ((lambda-linkage
           (if (eq? linkage 'next) after-lambda linkage)))
      (append-instruction-sequences
       (tack-on-instruction-sequence
        (end-with-linkage lambda-linkage
         (make-instruction-sequence '(env) (list target)
          `((assign ,target
                    (op make-compiled-procedure)
                    (label ,proc-entry)
                    (reg env)))))
        (compile-lambda-body exp proc-entry))
       after-lambda))))
```

Compile-lambda uses the special combiner tack-on-instruction-sequence (section 5.5.4) rather than append-instruction-sequences to append the procedure body to the lambda expression code, because the body is not part of the sequence of instructions that will be executed when the combined sequence is entered; rather, it is in the sequence only because that was a convenient place to put it.

Compile-lambda-body constructs the code for the body of the procedure. This code begins with a label for the entry point. Next come instructions that will cause the run-time evaluation environment to switch to the correct environment for evaluating the procedure body—namely, the definition environment of the procedure, extended to include the bindings of the formal parameters to the arguments with which the pro-

---

[38] We need machine operations to implement a data structure for representing compiled procedures, analogous to the structure for compound procedures described in section 4.1.3:

```
(define (make-compiled-procedure entry env)
  (list 'compiled-procedure entry env))

(define (compiled-procedure? proc)
  (tagged-list? proc 'compiled-procedure))

(define (compiled-procedure-entry c-proc) (cadr c-proc))

(define (compiled-procedure-env c-proc) (caddr c-proc))
```

cedure is called. After this comes the code for the sequence of expressions that makes up the procedure body. The sequence is compiled with linkage `return` and target `val` so that it will end by returning from the procedure with the procedure result in `val`.

```
(define (compile-lambda-body exp proc-entry)
  (let ((formals (lambda-parameters exp)))
    (append-instruction-sequences
     (make-instruction-sequence '(env proc argl) '(env)
      `(,proc-entry
        (assign env (op compiled-procedure-env) (reg proc))
        (assign env
                (op extend-environment)
                (const ,formals)
                (reg argl)
                (reg env))))
     (compile-sequence (lambda-body exp) 'val 'return))))
```

5.5.3   Compiling Combinations

The essence of the compilation process is the compilation of procedure applications. The code for a combination compiled with a given target and linkage has the form

⟨*compilation of operator, target* `proc`*, linkage* next ⟩
⟨*evaluate operands and construct argument list in* `argl` ⟩
⟨*compilation of procedure call with given target and linkage* ⟩

The registers env, `proc`, and `argl` may have to be saved and restored during evaluation of the operator and operands. Note that this is the only place in the compiler where a target other than `val` is specified.

The required code is generated by `compile-application`. This recursively compiles the operator, to produce code that puts the procedure to be applied into `proc`, and compiles the operands, to produce code that evaluates the individual operands of the application. The instruction sequences for the operands are combined (by `construct-arglist`) with code that constructs the list of arguments in `argl`, and the resulting argument-list code is combined with the procedure code and the code that performs the procedure call (produced by `compile-procedure-call`). In appending the code sequences, the env register must be preserved around the evaluation of the operator (since evaluating the operator might modify env, which will be needed to evaluate the operands), and the proc register must be preserved around the construction of the argument list (since evaluating the operands might modify proc, which will be needed for the actual procedure application). Continue must also be preserved throughout, since it is needed for the linkage in the procedure call.

```
(define (compile-application exp target linkage)
  (let ((proc-code (compile (operator exp) 'proc 'next))
        (operand-codes
          (map (lambda (operand) (compile operand 'val 'next))
               (operands exp))))
    (preserving '(env continue)
     proc-code
     (preserving '(proc continue)
      (construct-arglist operand-codes)
      (compile-procedure-call target linkage)))))
```

The code to construct the argument list will evaluate each operand into val and then cons that value onto the argument list being accumulated in argl. Since we cons the arguments onto argl in sequence, we must start with the last argument and end with the first, so that the arguments will appear in order from first to last in the resulting list. Rather than waste an instruction by initializing argl to the empty list to set up for this sequence of evaluations, we make the first code sequence construct the initial argl. The general form of the argument-list construction is thus as follows:

⟨*compilation of last operand, targeted to* val⟩
(assign argl (op list) (reg val))
⟨*compilation of next operand, targeted to* val⟩
(assign argl (op cons) (reg val) (reg argl))
. . .
⟨*compilation of first operand, targeted to* val⟩
(assign argl (op cons) (reg val) (reg argl))

Argl must be preserved around each operand evaluation except the first (so that arguments accumulated so far won't be lost), and env must be preserved around each operand evaluation except the last (for use by subsequent operand evaluations).

Compiling this argument code is a bit tricky, because of the special treatment of the first operand to be evaluated and the need to preserve argl and env in different places. The construct-arglist procedure takes as arguments the code that evaluates the individual operands. If there are no operands at all, it simply emits the instruction

```
(assign argl (const ()))
```

Otherwise, `construct-arglist` creates code that initializes `argl` with the last argument, and appends code that evaluates the rest of the arguments and adjoins them to `argl` in succession. In order to process the arguments from last to first, we must reverse the list of operand code sequences from the order supplied by `compile-application`.

```
(define (construct-arglist operand-codes)
  (let ((operand-codes (reverse operand-codes)))
    (if (null? operand-codes)
        (make-instruction-sequence '() '(argl)
         '((assign argl (const ()))))
        (let ((code-to-get-last-arg
                (append-instruction-sequences
                 (car operand-codes)
                 (make-instruction-sequence '(val) '(argl)
                  '((assign argl (op list) (reg val)))))))
          (if (null? (cdr operand-codes))
              code-to-get-last-arg
              (preserving '(env)
               code-to-get-last-arg
               (code-to-get-rest-args
                (cdr operand-codes))))))))

(define (code-to-get-rest-args operand-codes)
  (let ((code-for-next-arg
          (preserving '(argl)
           (car operand-codes)
           (make-instruction-sequence '(val argl) '(argl)
            '((assign argl
               (op cons) (reg val) (reg argl)))))))
    (if (null? (cdr operand-codes))
        code-for-next-arg
        (preserving '(env)
         code-for-next-arg
         (code-to-get-rest-args (cdr operand-codes))))))
```

Applying procedures

After evaluating the elements of a combination, the compiled code must apply the procedure in `proc` to the arguments in `argl`. The code performs essentially the same dispatch as the `apply` procedure in the metacircular evaluator of section 4.1.1 or the `apply-dispatch` entry point in the explicit-control evaluator of section 5.4.1. It checks whether the procedure to be applied is a primitive procedure or a compiled procedure. For a primitive procedure, it uses `apply-primitive-procedure`; we will see shortly how it handles compiled procedures. The procedure-application code has the following form:

```
(test (op primitive-procedure?) (reg proc))
(branch (label primitive-branch))
compiled-branch
⟨ code to apply compiled procedure with given target and appropriate linkage ⟩
primitive-branch
 (assign ⟨ target ⟩
         (op apply-primitive-procedure)
         (reg proc)
         (reg argl))
⟨ linkage ⟩
after-call
```

Observe that the compiled branch must skip around the primitive branch.
Therefore, if the linkage for the original procedure call was next, the
compound branch must use a linkage that jumps to a label that is inserted
after the primitive branch. (This is similar to the linkage used for the true
branch in compile-if.)

```
(define (compile-procedure-call target linkage)
  (let ((primitive-branch (make-label 'primitive-branch))
        (compiled-branch (make-label 'compiled-branch))
        (after-call (make-label 'after-call)))
    (let ((compiled-linkage
           (if (eq? linkage 'next) after-call linkage)))
      (append-instruction-sequences
       (make-instruction-sequence '(proc) '()
        `((test (op primitive-procedure?) (reg proc))
          (branch (label ,primitive-branch))))
       (parallel-instruction-sequences
        (append-instruction-sequences
         compiled-branch
         (compile-proc-appl target compiled-linkage))
        (append-instruction-sequences
         primitive-branch
         (end-with-linkage linkage
          (make-instruction-sequence '(proc argl)
                                     (list target)
           `((assign ,target
                     (op apply-primitive-procedure)
                     (reg proc)
                     (reg argl)))))))
       after-call))))
```

The primitive and compound branches, like the true and false branches in
compile-if, are appended using parallel-instruction-sequences
rather than the ordinary append-instruction-sequences, because
they will not be executed sequentially.

Applying compiled procedures

The code that handles procedure application is the most subtle part of the compiler, even though the instruction sequences it generates are very short. A compiled procedure (as constructed by `compile-lambda`) has an entry point, which is a label that designates where the code for the procedure starts. The code at this entry point computes a result in `val` and returns by executing the instruction (`goto (reg continue)`). Thus, we might expect the code for a compiled-procedure application (to be generated by `compile-proc-appl`) with a given target and linkage to look like this if the linkage is a label

```
(assign continue (label proc-return))
(assign val (op compiled-procedure-entry) (reg proc))
(goto (reg val))
proc-return
(assign ⟨target⟩ (reg val))    ; included if target is not val
(goto (label ⟨linkage⟩))       ; linkage code
```

or like this if the linkage is `return`.

```
(save continue)
(assign continue (label proc-return))
(assign val (op compiled-procedure-entry) (reg proc))
(goto (reg val))
proc-return
(assign ⟨target⟩ (reg val))    ; included if target is not val
(restore continue)
(goto (reg continue))          ; linkage code
```

This code sets up `continue` so that the procedure will return to a label `proc-return` and jumps to the procedure's entry point. The code at `proc-return` transfers the procedure's result from `val` to the target register (if necessary) and then jumps to the location specified by the linkage. (The linkage is always `return` or a label, because `compile-procedure-call` replaces a next linkage for the compound-procedure branch by an `after-call` label.)

In fact, if the target is not `val`, that is exactly the code our compiler will generate.[39] Usually, however, the target is `val` (the only time the compiler specifies a different register is when targeting the evaluation of an operator to `proc`), so the procedure result is put directly into the target register and there is no need to return to a special location that copies it. Instead, we simplify the code by setting up `continue` so that

---

[39] Actually, we signal an error when the target is not `val` and the linkage is `return`, since the only place we request `return` linkages is in compiling procedures, and our convention is that procedures return their values in `val`.

the procedure will "return" directly to the place specified by the caller's linkage:

```
⟨ set up continue for linkage ⟩
(assign val (op compiled-procedure-entry) (reg proc))
(goto (reg val))
```

If the linkage is a label, we set up `continue` so that the procedure will return to that label. (That is, the `(goto (reg continue))` the procedure ends with becomes equivalent to the `(goto (label ⟨ linkage ⟩))` at `proc-return` above.)

```
(assign continue (label ⟨ linkage ⟩))
(assign val (op compiled-procedure-entry) (reg proc))
(goto (reg val))
```

If the linkage is `return`, we don't need to set up `continue` at all: It already holds the desired location. (That is, the `(goto (reg continue))` the procedure ends with goes directly to the place where the `(goto (reg continue))` at `proc-return` would have gone.)

```
(assign val (op compiled-procedure-entry) (reg proc))
(goto (reg val))
```

With this implementation of the `return` linkage, the compiler generates tail-recursive code. Calling a procedure as the final step in a procedure body does a direct transfer, without saving any information on the stack.

Suppose instead that we had handled the case of a procedure call with a linkage of `return` and a target of `val` as shown above for a non-`val` target. This would destroy tail recursion. Our system would still give the same value for any expression. But each time we called a procedure, we would save `continue` and return after the call to undo the (useless) save. These extra saves would accumulate during a nest of procedure calls.[40]

---

[40]Making a compiler generate tail-recursive code might seem like a straightforward idea. But most compilers for common languages, including C and Pascal, do not do this, and therefore these languages cannot represent iterative processes in terms of procedure call alone. The difficulty with tail recursion in these languages is that their implementations use the stack to store procedure arguments and local variables as well as return addresses. The Scheme implementations described in this book store arguments and variables in memory to be garbage-collected. The reason for using the stack for variables and arguments is that it avoids the need for garbage collection in languages that would not otherwise require it, and is generally believed to be more efficient. Sophisticated Lisp compilers can, in fact, use the stack for arguments without destroying tail recursion. (See Hanson 1990 for a description.) There is also some debate about whether stack allocation is actually more efficient than garbage collection in the first place, but the details seem to hinge on fine points of computer architecture. (See Appel 1987 and Miller and Rozas 1994 for opposing views on this issue.)

Compile-proc-appl generates the above procedure-application code by considering four cases, depending on whether the target for the call is val and whether the linkage is return. Observe that the instruction sequences are declared to modify all the registers, since executing the procedure body can change the registers in arbitrary ways.[41] Also note that the code sequence for the case with target val and linkage return is declared to need continue: Even though continue is not explicitly used in the two-instruction sequence, we must be sure that continue will have the correct value when we enter the compiled procedure.

```
(define (compile-proc-appl target linkage)
  (cond ((and (eq? target 'val) (not (eq? linkage 'return)))
         (make-instruction-sequence '(proc) all-regs
          '((assign continue (label ,linkage))
            (assign val (op compiled-procedure-entry)
                        (reg proc))
            (goto (reg val)))))
        ((and (not (eq? target 'val))
              (not (eq? linkage 'return)))
         (let ((proc-return (make-label 'proc-return)))
           (make-instruction-sequence '(proc) all-regs
            '((assign continue (label ,proc-return))
              (assign val (op compiled-procedure-entry)
                          (reg proc))
              (goto (reg val))
              ,proc-return
              (assign ,target (reg val))
              (goto (label ,linkage))))))
        ((and (eq? target 'val) (eq? linkage 'return))
         (make-instruction-sequence '(proc continue) all-regs
          '((assign val (op compiled-procedure-entry)
                        (reg proc))
            (goto (reg val)))))
        ((and (not (eq? target 'val)) (eq? linkage 'return))
         (error "return linkage, target not val -- COMPILE"
                target))))
```

5.5.4   Combining Instruction Sequences

This section describes the details on how instruction sequences are represented and combined. Recall from section 5.5.1 that an instruction sequence is represented as a list of the registers needed, the registers

---

[41]The variable all-regs is bound to the list of names of all the registers:

```
(define all-regs '(env proc val argl continue))
```

modified, and the actual instructions. We will also consider a label (symbol) to be a degenerate case of an instruction sequence, which doesn't
need or modify any registers. So to determine the registers needed and
modified by instruction sequences we use the selectors

```
(define (registers-needed s)
  (if (symbol? s) '() (car s)))

(define (registers-modified s)
  (if (symbol? s) '() (cadr s)))

(define (statements s)
  (if (symbol? s) (list s) (caddr s)))
```

and to determine whether a given sequence needs or modifies a given
register we use the predicates

```
(define (needs-register? seq reg)
  (memq reg (registers-needed seq)))

(define (modifies-register? seq reg)
  (memq reg (registers-modified seq)))
```

In terms of these predicates and selectors, we can implement the various
instruction sequence combiners used throughout the compiler.

The basic combiner is `append-instruction-sequences`. This takes
as arguments an arbitrary number of instruction sequences that are to be
executed sequentially and returns an instruction sequence whose statements are the statements of all the sequences appended together. The
subtle point is to determine the registers that are needed and modified
by the resulting sequence. It modifies those registers that are modified
by any of the sequences; it needs those registers that must be initialized before the first sequence can be run (the registers needed by the
first sequence), together with those registers needed by any of the other
sequences that are not initialized (modified) by sequences preceding it.

The sequences are appended two at a time by `append-2-sequences`.
This takes two instruction sequences seq1 and seq2 and returns the instruction sequence whose statements are the statements of seq1 followed
by the statements of seq2, whose modified registers are those registers
that are modified by either seq1 or seq2, and whose needed registers
are the registers needed by seq1 together with those registers needed by
seq2 that are not modified by seq1. (In terms of set operations, the new
set of needed registers is the union of the set of registers needed by seq1
with the set difference of the registers needed by seq2 and the registers

modified by seq1.) Thus, append-instruction-sequences is implemented as follows:

```
(define (append-instruction-sequences . seqs)
  (define (append-2-sequences seq1 seq2)
    (make-instruction-sequence
      (list-union (registers-needed seq1)
                  (list-difference (registers-needed seq2)
                                   (registers-modified seq1)))
      (list-union (registers-modified seq1)
                  (registers-modified seq2))
      (append (statements seq1) (statements seq2))))
  (define (append-seq-list seqs)
    (if (null? seqs)
        (empty-instruction-sequence)
        (append-2-sequences (car seqs)
                            (append-seq-list (cdr seqs)))))
  (append-seq-list seqs))
```

This procedure uses some simple operations for manipulating sets represented as lists, similar to the (unordered) set representation described
in section 2.3.3:

```
(define (list-union s1 s2)
  (cond ((null? s1) s2)
        ((memq (car s1) s2) (list-union (cdr s1) s2))
        (else (cons (car s1) (list-union (cdr s1) s2)))))

(define (list-difference s1 s2)
  (cond ((null? s1) '())
        ((memq (car s1) s2) (list-difference (cdr s1) s2))
        (else (cons (car s1)
                    (list-difference (cdr s1) s2)))))
```

Preserving, the second major instruction sequence combiner, takes
a list of registers regs and two instruction sequences seq1 and seq2
that are to be executed sequentially. It returns an instruction sequence
whose statements are the statements of seq1 followed by the statements
of seq2, with appropriate save and restore instructions around seq1
to protect the registers in regs that are modified by seq1 but needed by
seq2. To accomplish this, preserving first creates a sequence that has
the required saves followed by the statements of seq1 followed by the
required restores. This sequence needs the registers being saved and
restored in addition to the registers needed by seq1, and modifies the
registers modified by seq1 except for the ones being saved and restored.

This augmented sequence and seq2 are then appended in the usual way. The following procedure implements this strategy recursively, walking down the list of registers to be preserved:[42]

```
(define (preserving regs seq1 seq2)
  (if (null? regs)
      (append-instruction-sequences seq1 seq2)
      (let ((first-reg (car regs)))
        (if (and (needs-register? seq2 first-reg)
                 (modifies-register? seq1 first-reg))
            (preserving (cdr regs)
             (make-instruction-sequence
              (list-union (list first-reg)
                          (registers-needed seq1))
              (list-difference (registers-modified seq1)
                               (list first-reg))
              (append `((save ,first-reg))
                      (statements seq1)
                      `((restore ,first-reg))))
             seq2)
            (preserving (cdr regs) seq1 seq2)))))
```

Another sequence combiner, tack-on-instruction-sequence, is used by compile-lambda to append a procedure body to another sequence. Because the procedure body is not "in line" to be executed as part of the combined sequence, its register use has no impact on the register use of the sequence in which it is embedded. We thus ignore the procedure body's sets of needed and modified registers when we tack it onto the other sequence.

```
(define (tack-on-instruction-sequence seq body-seq)
  (make-instruction-sequence
   (registers-needed seq)
   (registers-modified seq)
   (append (statements seq) (statements body-seq))))
```

Compile-if and compile-procedure-call use a special combiner called parallel-instruction-sequences to append the two alternative branches that follow a test. The two branches will never be executed sequentially; for any particular evaluation of the test, one branch or the other will be entered. Because of this, the registers needed by the sec-

---

[42]Note that preserving calls append with three arguments. Though the definition of append shown in this book accepts only two arguments, Scheme standardly provides an append procedure that takes an arbitrary number of arguments.

ond branch are still needed by the combined sequence, even if these are
modified by the first branch.

```
(define (parallel-instruction-sequences seq1 seq2)
  (make-instruction-sequence
    (list-union (registers-needed seq1)
                (registers-needed seq2))
    (list-union (registers-modified seq1)
                (registers-modified seq2))
    (append (statements seq1) (statements seq2))))
```

5.5.5   An Example of Compiled Code

Now that we have seen all the elements of the compiler, let us examine an
example of compiled code to see how things fit together. We will compile
the definition of a recursive `factorial` procedure by calling `compile`:

```
(compile
 '(define (factorial n)
    (if (= n 1)
        1
        (* (factorial (- n 1)) n)))
 'val
 'next)
```

We have specified that the value of the `define` expression should be
placed in the `val` register. We don't care what the compiled code does
after executing the `define`, so our choice of next as the linkage descriptor is arbitrary.

Compile determines that the expression is a definition, so it calls
`compile-definition` to compile code to compute the value to be assigned (targeted to `val`), followed by code to install the definition, followed by code to put the value of the `define` (which is the symbol `ok`)
into the target register, followed finally by the linkage code. Env is preserved around the computation of the value, because it is needed in order
to install the definition. Because the linkage is `next`, there is no linkage
code in this case. The skeleton of the compiled code is thus

```
⟨ save env if modified by code to compute value ⟩
⟨ compilation of definition value, target val, linkage next ⟩
⟨ restore env if saved above ⟩
(perform (op define-variable!)
         (const factorial)
         (reg val)
         (reg env))
(assign val (const ok))
```

The expression that is to be compiled to produce the value for the variable factorial is a lambda expression whose value is the procedure that computes factorials. Compile handles this by calling compile-lambda, which compiles the procedure body, labels it as a new entry point, and generates the instruction that will combine the procedure body at the new entry point with the run-time environment and assign the result to val. The sequence then skips around the compiled procedure code, which is inserted at this point. The procedure code itself begins by extending the procedure's definition environment by a frame that binds the formal parameter n to the procedure argument. Then comes the actual procedure body. Since this code for the value of the variable doesn't modify the env register, the optional save and restore shown above aren't generated. (The procedure code at entry2 isn't executed at this point, so its use of env is irrelevant.) Therefore, the skeleton for the compiled code becomes

```
(assign val (op make-compiled-procedure)
            (label entry2)
            (reg env))
(goto (label after-lambda1))
entry2
  (assign env (op compiled-procedure-env) (reg proc))
  (assign env (op extend-environment)
            (const (n))
            (reg argl)
            (reg env))
  ⟨compilation of procedure body⟩
after-lambda1
  (perform (op define-variable!)
            (const factorial)
            (reg val)
            (reg env))
  (assign val (const ok))
```

A procedure body is always compiled (by compile-lambda-body) as a sequence with target val and linkage return. The sequence in this case consists of a single if expression:

```
(if (= n 1)
    1
    (* (factorial (- n 1)) n))
```

Compile-if generates code that first computes the predicate (targeted to val), then checks the result and branches around the true branch if the predicate is false. Env and continue are preserved around the predicate code, since they may be needed for the rest of the `if` expression. Since the `if` expression is the final expression (and only expression) in the sequence making up the procedure body, its target is `val` and its linkage is `return`, so the true and false branches are both compiled with target `val` and linkage `return`. (That is, the value of the conditional, which is the value computed by either of its branches, is the value of the procedure.)

```
⟨ save continue, env if modified by predicate and needed by branches ⟩
⟨ compilation of predicate, target val, linkage next ⟩
⟨ restore continue, env if saved above ⟩
(test (op false?) (reg val))
(branch (label false-branch4))
true-branch5
  ⟨ compilation of true branch, target val, linkage return ⟩
false-branch4
  ⟨ compilation of false branch, target val, linkage return ⟩
after-if3
```

The predicate (= n 1) is a procedure call. This looks up the operator (the symbol =) and places this value in `proc`. It then assembles the arguments 1 and the value of n into `argl`. Then it tests whether `proc` contains a primitive or a compound procedure, and dispatches to a primitive branch or a compound branch accordingly. Both branches resume at the `after-call` label. The requirements to preserve registers around the evaluation of the operator and operands don't result in any saving of registers, because in this case those evaluations don't modify the registers in question.

```
(assign proc
          (op lookup-variable-value) (const =) (reg env))
(assign val (const 1))
(assign argl (op list) (reg val))
(assign val (op lookup-variable-value) (const n) (reg env))
(assign argl (op cons) (reg val) (reg argl))
(test (op primitive-procedure?) (reg proc))
(branch (label primitive-branch17))
compiled-branch16
  (assign continue (label after-call15))
  (assign val (op compiled-procedure-entry) (reg proc))
  (goto (reg val))
primitive-branch17
  (assign val (op apply-primitive-procedure)
              (reg proc)
              (reg argl))
after-call15
```

The true branch, which is the constant 1, compiles (with target `val` and linkage `return`) to

```
(assign val (const 1))
(goto (reg continue))
```

The code for the false branch is another a procedure call, where the procedure is the value of the symbol `*`, and the arguments are `n` and the result of another procedure call (a call to `factorial`). Each of these calls sets up `proc` and `argl` and its own primitive and compound branches. Figure 5.17 shows the complete compilation of the definition of the `factorial` procedure. Notice that the possible `save` and `restore` of `continue` and `env` around the predicate, shown above, are in fact generated, because these registers are modified by the procedure call in the predicate and needed for the procedure call and the `return` linkage in the branches.

Exercise 5.33

Consider the following definition of a factorial procedure, which is slightly different from the one given above:

```
(define (factorial-alt n)
  (if (= n 1)
      1
      (* n (factorial-alt (- n 1)))))
```

Compile this procedure and compare the resulting code with that produced for `factorial`. Explain any differences you find. Does either program execute more efficiently than the other?

Exercise 5.34

Compile the iterative factorial procedure

```
(define (factorial n)
  (define (iter product counter)
    (if (> counter n)
        product
        (iter (* counter product)
              (+ counter 1))))
  (iter 1 1))
```

Annotate the resulting code, showing the essential difference between the code for iterative and recursive versions of `factorial` that makes one process build up stack space and the other run in constant stack space.

Exercise 5.35

What expression was compiled to produce the code shown in figure 5.18?

Exercise 5.36

What order of evaluation does our compiler produce for operands of a combination? Is it left-to-right, right-to-left, or some other order? Where in the compiler is this order determined? Modify the compiler so that it produces some other order of evaluation. (See the discussion of order of evaluation for the explicit-control evaluator in section 5.4.1.) How does changing the order of operand evaluation affect the efficiency of the code that constructs the argument list?

Exercise 5.37

One way to understand the compiler's `preserving` mechanism for optimizing stack usage is to see what extra operations would be generated if we did not use this idea. Modify `preserving` so that it always generates the `save` and `restore` operations. Compile some simple expressions and identify the unnecessary stack operations that are generated. Compare the code to that generated with the `preserving` mechanism intact.

Exercise 5.38

Our compiler is clever about avoiding unnecessary stack operations, but it is not clever at all when it comes to compiling calls to the primitive procedures of the language in terms of the primitive operations supplied by the machine. For example, consider how much code is compiled to compute (+ a 1): The code sets up an argument list in `argl`, puts the primitive addition procedure (which it finds by looking up the symbol + in the environment) into `proc`, and tests whether the procedure is primitive or compound. The compiler always generates code to perform the test, as well as code for primitive and compound branches (only one of which will be executed). We have not shown the part of the controller that implements primitives, but we presume that these instructions make use of primitive arithmetic operations in the machine's data paths. Consider how much less code would be generated if the compiler could *open-code* primitives—that is, if it could generate code to directly use these primitive machine operations. The expression (+ a 1) might be compiled into something as simple as [43]

```
(assign val (op lookup-variable-value) (const a) (reg env))
(assign val (op +) (reg val) (const 1))
```

In this exercise we will extend our compiler to support open coding of selected primitives. Special-purpose code will be generated for calls to these primitive

---

[43] We have used the same symbol + here to denote both the source-language procedure and the machine operation. In general there will not be a one-to-one correspondence between primitives of the source language and primitives of the machine.

```
;; construct the procedure and skip over code for the procedure body
  (assign val
          (op make-compiled-procedure) (label entry2) (reg env))
  (goto (label after-lambda1))

entry2        ; calls to factorial will enter here
  (assign env (op compiled-procedure-env) (reg proc))
  (assign env
          (op extend-environment) (const (n)) (reg argl) (reg env))
;; begin actual procedure body
  (save continue)
  (save env)

;; compute (= n 1)
  (assign proc (op lookup-variable-value) (const =) (reg env))
  (assign val (const 1))
  (assign argl (op list) (reg val))
  (assign val (op lookup-variable-value) (const n) (reg env))
  (assign argl (op cons) (reg val) (reg argl))
  (test (op primitive-procedure?) (reg proc))
  (branch (label primitive-branch17))
compiled-branch16
  (assign continue (label after-call15))
  (assign val (op compiled-procedure-entry) (reg proc))
  (goto (reg val))
primitive-branch17
  (assign val (op apply-primitive-procedure) (reg proc) (reg argl))

after-call15     ; val now contains result of (= n 1)
  (restore env)
  (restore continue)
  (test (op false?) (reg val))
  (branch (label false-branch4))
true-branch5    ; return 1
  (assign val (const 1))
  (goto (reg continue))


false-branch4
;; compute and return (* (factorial (- n 1)) n)
  (assign proc (op lookup-variable-value) (const *) (reg env))
  (save continue)
  (save proc)     ; save * procedure
  (assign val (op lookup-variable-value) (const n) (reg env))
  (assign argl (op list) (reg val))
  (save argl)     ; save partial argument list for *

;; compute (factorial (- n 1)), which is the other argument for *
  (assign proc
          (op lookup-variable-value) (const factorial) (reg env))
  (save proc)     ; save factorial procedure
```

Figure 5.17 Compilation of the definition of the factorial procedure (continued on next page).

```
;; compute (- n 1), which is the argument for factorial
  (assign proc (op lookup-variable-value) (const -) (reg env))
  (assign val (const 1))
  (assign argl (op list) (reg val))
  (assign val (op lookup-variable-value) (const n) (reg env))
  (assign argl (op cons) (reg val) (reg argl))
  (test (op primitive-procedure?) (reg proc))
  (branch (label primitive-branch8))
compiled-branch7
  (assign continue (label after-call6))
  (assign val (op compiled-procedure-entry) (reg proc))
  (goto (reg val))
primitive-branch8
  (assign val (op apply-primitive-procedure) (reg proc) (reg argl))

after-call6      ; val now contains result of (- n 1)
  (assign argl (op list) (reg val))
  (restore proc)  ; restore factorial
;; apply factorial
  (test (op primitive-procedure?) (reg proc))
  (branch (label primitive-branch11))
compiled-branch10
  (assign continue (label after-call9))
  (assign val (op compiled-procedure-entry) (reg proc))
  (goto (reg val))
primitive-branch11
  (assign val (op apply-primitive-procedure) (reg proc) (reg argl))

after-call9        ; val now contains result of (factorial (- n 1))
  (restore argl)  ; restore partial argument list for *
  (assign argl (op cons) (reg val) (reg argl))
  (restore proc)  ; restore *
  (restore continue)
;; apply * and return its value
  (test (op primitive-procedure?) (reg proc))
  (branch (label primitive-branch14))
compiled-branch13
;; note that a compound procedure here is called tail-recursively
  (assign val (op compiled-procedure-entry) (reg proc))
  (goto (reg val))
primitive-branch14
  (assign val (op apply-primitive-procedure) (reg proc) (reg argl))
  (goto (reg continue))
after-call12
after-if3
after-lambda1
;; assign the procedure to the variable factorial
  (perform
   (op define-variable!) (const factorial) (reg val) (reg env))
  (assign val (const ok))
```

Figure 5.17   (continued)

```
(assign val (op make-compiled-procedure) (label entry16)
                                         (reg env))
(goto (label after-lambda15))
entry16
(assign env (op compiled-procedure-env) (reg proc))
(assign env
        (op extend-environment) (const (x)) (reg argl) (reg env))
(assign proc (op lookup-variable-value) (const +) (reg env))
(save continue)
(save proc)
(save env)
(assign proc (op lookup-variable-value) (const g) (reg env))
(save proc)
(assign proc (op lookup-variable-value) (const +) (reg env))
(assign val (const 2))
(assign argl (op list) (reg val))
(assign val (op lookup-variable-value) (const x) (reg env))
(assign argl (op cons) (reg val) (reg argl))
(test (op primitive-procedure?) (reg proc))
(branch (label primitive-branch19))
compiled-branch18
(assign continue (label after-call17))
(assign val (op compiled-procedure-entry) (reg proc))
(goto (reg val))
primitive-branch19
(assign val (op apply-primitive-procedure) (reg proc) (reg argl))
after-call17
(assign argl (op list) (reg val))
(restore proc)
(test (op primitive-procedure?) (reg proc))
(branch (label primitive-branch22))
compiled-branch21
(assign continue (label after-call20))
(assign val (op compiled-procedure-entry) (reg proc))
(goto (reg val))
primitive-branch22
(assign val (op apply-primitive-procedure) (reg proc) (reg argl))
```

Figure 5.18   An example of compiler output (continued on next page). See exercise 5.35.

procedures instead of the general procedure-application code. In order to support this, we will augment our machine with special argument registers arg1 and arg2. The primitive arithmetic operations of the machine will take their inputs from arg1 and arg2. The results may be put into val, arg1, or arg2.

The compiler must be able to recognize the application of an open-coded primitive in the source program. We will augment the dispatch in the compile procedure to recognize the names of these primitives in addition to the reserved

```
after-call20
  (assign argl (op list) (reg val))
  (restore env)
  (assign val (op lookup-variable-value) (const x) (reg env))
  (assign argl (op cons) (reg val) (reg argl))
  (restore proc)
  (restore continue)
  (test (op primitive-procedure?) (reg proc))
  (branch (label primitive-branch25))
compiled-branch24
  (assign val (op compiled-procedure-entry) (reg proc))
  (goto (reg val))
primitive-branch25
  (assign val (op apply-primitive-procedure) (reg proc) (reg argl))
  (goto (reg continue))
after-call23
after-lambda15
  (perform (op define-variable!) (const f) (reg val) (reg env))
  (assign val (const ok))
```

Figure 5.18   (continued)

words (the special forms) it currently recognizes.[44] For each special form our compiler has a code generator. In this exercise we will construct a family of code generators for the open-coded primitives.

a. The open-coded primitives, unlike the special forms, all need their operands evaluated. Write a code generator `spread-arguments` for use by all the open-coding code generators. `Spread-arguments` should take an operand list and compile the given operands targeted to successive argument registers. Note that an operand may contain a call to an open-coded primitive, so argument registers will have to be preserved during operand evaluation.

b. For each of the primitive procedures =, *, -, and +, write a code generator that takes a combination with that operator, together with a target and a linkage descriptor, and produces code to spread the arguments into the registers and then perform the operation targeted to the given target with the given linkage. You need only handle expressions with two operands. Make `compile` dispatch to these code generators.

c. Try your new compiler on the `factorial` example. Compare the resulting code with the result produced without open coding.

d. Extend your code generators for + and * so that they can handle expressions with arbitrary numbers of operands. An expression with more than two operands will have to be compiled into a sequence of operations, each with only two inputs.

---

[44]Making the primitives into reserved words is in general a bad idea, since a user cannot then rebind these names to different procedures. Moreover, if we add reserved words to a compiler that is in use, existing programs that define procedures with these names will stop working. See exercise 5.44 for ideas on how to avoid this problem.

5.5.6   Lexical Addressing

One of the most common optimizations performed by compilers is the optimization of variable lookup. Our compiler, as we have implemented it so far, generates code that uses the `lookup-variable-value` operation of the evaluator machine. This searches for a variable by comparing it with each variable that is currently bound, working frame by frame outward through the run-time environment. This search can be expensive if the frames are deeply nested or if there are many variables. For example, consider the problem of looking up the value of x while evaluating the expression (* x y z) in an application of the procedure that is returned by

```
(let ((x 3) (y 4))
  (lambda (a b c d e)
    (let ((y (* a b x))
          (z (+ c d x)))
      (* x y z))))
```

Since a `let` expression is just syntactic sugar for a `lambda` combination, this expression is equivalent to

```
((lambda (x y)
   (lambda (a b c d e)
     ((lambda (y z) (* x y z))
      (* a b x)
      (+ c d x))))
 3
 4)
```

Each time `lookup-variable-value` searches for x, it must determine that the symbol x is not eq? to y or z (in the first frame), nor to a, b, c, d, or e (in the second frame). We will assume, for the moment, that our programs do not use `define`—that variables are bound only with `lambda`. Because our language is lexically scoped, the run-time environment for any expression will have a structure that parallels the lexical structure of the program in which the expression appears.[45] Thus, the compiler can know, when it analyzes the above expression, that each time the procedure is applied the variable x in (* x y z) will be found two frames out from the current frame and will be the first variable in that frame.

We can exploit this fact by inventing a new kind of variable-lookup operation, `lexical-address-lookup`, that takes as arguments an en-

---

[45]This is not true if we allow internal definitions, unless we scan them out. See exercise 5.43.

vironment and a *lexical address* that consists of two numbers: a *frame number*, which specifies how many frames to pass over, and a *displacement number*, which specifies how many variables to pass over in that frame. `Lexical-address-lookup` will produce the value of the variable stored at that lexical address relative to the current environment. If we add the `lexical-address-lookup` operation to our machine, we can make the compiler generate code that references variables using this operation, rather than `lookup-variable-value`. Similarly, our compiled code can use a new `lexical-address-set!` operation instead of `set-variable-value!`.

In order to generate such code, the compiler must be able to determine the lexical address of a variable it is about to compile a reference to. The lexical address of a variable in a program depends on where one is in the code. For example, in the following program, the address of x in expression ⟨*e1*⟩ is (2,0)—two frames back and the first variable in the frame. At that point y is at address (0,0) and c is at address (1,2). In expression ⟨*e2*⟩, x is at (1,0), y is at (1,1), and c is at (0,2).

```
((lambda (x y)
   (lambda (a b c d e)
     ((lambda (y z) ⟨e1⟩)
      ⟨e2⟩
      (+ c d x))))
 3
 4)
```

One way for the compiler to produce code that uses lexical addressing is to maintain a data structure called a *compile-time environment*. This keeps track of which variables will be at which positions in which frames in the run-time environment when a particular variable-access operation is executed. The compile-time environment is a list of frames, each containing a list of variables. (There will of course be no values bound to the variables, since values are not computed at compile time.) The compile-time environment becomes an additional argument to `compile` and is passed along to each code generator. The top-level call to `compile` uses an empty compile-time environment. When a `lambda` body is compiled, `compile-lambda-body` extends the compile-time environment by a frame containing the procedure's parameters, so that the sequence making up the body is compiled with that extended environment. At each point in the compilation, `compile-variable` and `compile-assignment` use the compile-time environment in order to generate the appropriate lexical addresses.

Exercises 5.39 through 5.43 describe how to complete this sketch of the lexical-addressing strategy in order to incorporate lexical lookup into the compiler. Exercise 5.44 describes another use for the compile-time environment.

Exercise 5.39

Write a procedure `lexical-address-lookup` that implements the new lookup operation. It should take two arguments—a lexical address and a run-time environment—and return the value of the variable stored at the specified lexical address. `Lexical-address-lookup` should signal an error if the value of the variable is the symbol `*unassigned*`.[46] Also write a procedure `lexical-address-set!` that implements the operation that changes the value of the variable at a specified lexical address.

Exercise 5.40

Modify the compiler to maintain the compile-time environment as described above. That is, add a compile-time-environment argument to `compile` and the various code generators, and extend it in `compile-lambda-body`.

Exercise 5.41

Write a procedure `find-variable` that takes as arguments a variable and a compile-time environment and returns the lexical address of the variable with respect to that environment. For example, in the program fragment that is shown above, the compile-time environment during the compilation of expression $\langle e1 \rangle$ is `((y z) (a b c d e) (x y))`. Find-variable should produce

```
(find-variable 'c '((y z) (a b c d e) (x y)))
(1 2)

(find-variable 'x '((y z) (a b c d e) (x y)))
(2 0)

(find-variable 'w '((y z) (a b c d e) (x y)))
not-found
```

Exercise 5.42

Using `find-variable` from exercise 5.41, rewrite `compile-variable` and `compile-assignment` to output lexical-address instructions. In cases where `find-variable` returns `not-found` (that is, where the variable is not in the compile-time environment), you should have the code generators use the evaluator operations, as before, to search for the binding. (The only place a variable that is not found at compile time can be is in the global environment, which

---

[46]This is the modification to variable lookup required if we implement the scanning method to eliminate internal definitions (exercise 5.43). We will need to eliminate these definitions in order for lexical addressing to work.

is part of the run-time environment but is not part of the compile-time environment.[47] Thus, if you wish, you may have the evaluator operations look directly in the global environment, which can be obtained with the operation (op get-global-environment), instead of having them search the whole run-time environment found in env.) Test the modified compiler on a few simple cases, such as the nested lambda combination at the beginning of this section.

Exercise 5.43

We argued in section 4.1.6 that internal definitions for block structure should not be considered "real" defines. Rather, a procedure body should be interpreted as if the internal variables being defined were installed as ordinary lambda variables initialized to their correct values using set!. Section 4.1.6 and exercise 4.16 showed how to modify the metacircular interpreter to accomplish this by scanning out internal definitions. Modify the compiler to perform the same transformation before it compiles a procedure body.

Exercise 5.44

In this section we have focused on the use of the compile-time environment to produce lexical addresses. But there are other uses for compile-time environments. For instance, in exercise 5.38 we increased the efficiency of compiled code by open-coding primitive procedures. Our implementation treated the names of open-coded procedures as reserved words. If a program were to rebind such a name, the mechanism described in exercise 5.38 would still open-code it as a primitive, ignoring the new binding. For example, consider the procedure

```
(lambda (+ * a b x y)
  (+ (* a x) (* b y)))
```

which computes a linear combination of x and y. We might call it with arguments +matrix, *matrix, and four matrices, but the open-coding compiler would still open-code the + and the * in (+ (* a x) (* b y)) as primitive + and *. Modify the open-coding compiler to consult the compile-time environment in order to compile the correct code for expressions involving the names of primitive procedures. (The code will work correctly as long as the program does not define or set! these names.)

5.5.7 Interfacing Compiled Code to the Evaluator

We have not yet explained how to load compiled code into the evaluator machine or how to run it. We will assume that the explicit-control-

---

[47]Lexical addresses cannot be used to access variables in the global environment, because these names can be defined and redefined interactively at any time. With internal definitions scanned out, as in exercise 5.43, the only definitions the compiler sees are those at top level, which act on the global environment. Compilation of a definition does not cause the defined name to be entered in the compile-time environment.

evaluator machine has been defined as in section 5.4.4, with the additional operations specified in footnote 38. We will implement a procedure `compile-and-go` that compiles a Scheme expression, loads the resulting object code into the evaluator machine, and causes the machine to run the code in the evaluator global environment, print the result, and enter the evaluator's driver loop. We will also modify the evaluator so that interpreted expressions can call compiled procedures as well as interpreted ones. We can then put a compiled procedure into the machine and use the evaluator to call it:

```
(compile-and-go
 '(define (factorial n)
    (if (= n 1)
        1
        (* (factorial (- n 1)) n))))
 ;;; EC-Eval value:
ok

 ;;; EC-Eval input:
(factorial 5)
;;; EC-Eval value:
120
```

To allow the evaluator to handle compiled procedures (for example, to evaluate the call to `factorial` above), we need to change the code at `apply-dispatch` (section 5.4.1) so that it recognizes compiled procedures (as distinct from compound or primitive procedures) and transfers control directly to the entry point of the compiled code:[48]

```
apply-dispatch
  (test (op primitive-procedure?) (reg proc))
  (branch (label primitive-apply))
  (test (op compound-procedure?) (reg proc))
  (branch (label compound-apply))
  (test (op compiled-procedure?) (reg proc))
  (branch (label compiled-apply))
  (goto (label unknown-procedure-type))

compiled-apply
  (restore continue)
  (assign val (op compiled-procedure-entry) (reg proc))
  (goto (reg val))
```

---

[48]Of course, compiled procedures as well as interpreted procedures are compound (nonprimitive). For compatibility with the terminology used in the explicit-control evaluator, in this section we will use "compound" to mean interpreted (as opposed to compiled).

Note the restore of `continue` at `compiled-apply`. Recall that the evaluator was arranged so that at `apply-dispatch`, the continuation would be at the top of the stack. The compiled code entry point, on the other hand, expects the continuation to be in `continue`, so `continue` must be restored before the compiled code is executed.

To enable us to run some compiled code when we start the evaluator machine, we add a `branch` instruction at the beginning of the evaluator machine, which causes the machine to go to a new entry point if the `flag` register is set.[49]

```
(branch (label external-entry))        ; branches if flag is set
read-eval-print-loop
  (perform (op initialize-stack))
  ...
```

`External-entry` assumes that the machine is started with `val` containing the location of an instruction sequence that puts a result into `val` and ends with `(goto (reg continue))`. Starting at this entry point jumps to the location designated by `val`, but first assigns `continue` so that execution will return to `print-result`, which prints the value in `val` and then goes to the beginning of the evaluator's read-eval-print loop.[50]

```
external-entry
  (perform (op initialize-stack))
  (assign env (op get-global-environment))
  (assign continue (label print-result))
  (goto (reg val))
```

---

[49]Now that the evaluator machine starts with a `branch`, we must always initialize the `flag` register before starting the evaluator machine. To start the machine at its ordinary read-eval-print loop, we could use

```
(define (start-eceval)
  (set! the-global-environment (setup-environment))
  (set-register-contents! eceval 'flag false)
  (start eceval))
```

[50]Since a compiled procedure is an object that the system may try to print, we also modify the system print operation `user-print` (from section 4.1.4) so that it will not attempt to print the components of a compiled procedure:

```
(define (user-print object)
  (cond ((compound-procedure? object)
         (display (list 'compound-procedure
                        (procedure-parameters object)
                        (procedure-body object)
                        '<procedure-env>)))
        ((compiled-procedure? object)
         (display '<compiled-procedure>))
        (else (display object))))
```

Now we can use the following procedure to compile a procedure definition, execute the compiled code, and run the read-eval-print loop so we can try the procedure. Because we want the compiled code to return to the location in continue with its result in val, we compile the expression with a target of val and a linkage of return. In order to transform the object code produced by the compiler into executable instructions for the evaluator register machine, we use the procedure assemble from the register-machine simulator (section 5.2.2). We then initialize the val register to point to the list of instructions, set the flag so that the evaluator will go to external-entry, and start the evaluator.

```
(define (compile-and-go expression)
  (let ((instructions
         (assemble (statements
                    (compile expression 'val 'return))
                   eceval)))
    (set! the-global-environment (setup-environment))
    (set-register-contents! eceval 'val instructions)
    (set-register-contents! eceval 'flag true)
    (start eceval)))
```

If we have set up stack monitoring, as at the end of section 5.4.4, we can examine the stack usage of compiled code:

```
(compile-and-go
 '(define (factorial n)
    (if (= n 1)
        1
        (* (factorial (- n 1)) n))))

(total-pushes = 0 maximum-depth = 0)
;;; EC-Eval value:
ok


;;; EC-Eval input:
(factorial 5)
(total-pushes = 31 maximum-depth = 14)
;;; EC-Eval value:
120
```

Compare this example with the evaluation of (factorial 5) using the interpreted version of the same procedure, shown at the end of section 5.4.4. The interpreted version required 144 pushes and a maximum stack depth of 28. This illustrates the optimization that results from our compilation strategy.

Interpretation and compilation

With the programs in this section, we can now experiment with the alternative execution strategies of interpretation and compilation.[51] An interpreter raises the machine to the level of the user program; a compiler lowers the user program to the level of the machine language. We can regard the Scheme language (or any programming language) as a coherent family of abstractions erected on the machine language. Interpreters are good for interactive program development and debugging because the steps of program execution are organized in terms of these abstractions, and are therefore more intelligible to the programmer. Compiled code can execute faster, because the steps of program execution are organized in terms of the machine language, and the compiler is free to make optimizations that cut across the higher-level abstractions.[52]

The alternatives of interpretation and compilation also lead to different strategies for porting languages to new computers. Suppose that we wish to implement Lisp for a new machine. One strategy is to begin with the explicit-control evaluator of section 5.4 and translate its instructions to instructions for the new machine. A different strategy is to begin with the compiler and change the code generators so that they generate code for the new machine. The second strategy allows us to run any Lisp program on the new machine by first compiling it with the compiler running on our original Lisp system, and linking it with a compiled version of the

---

[51]We can do even better by extending the compiler to allow compiled code to call interpreted procedures. See exercise 5.47.

[52]Independent of the strategy of execution, we incur significant overhead if we insist that errors encountered in execution of a user program be detected and signaled, rather than being allowed to kill the system or produce wrong answers. For example, an out-of-bounds array reference can be detected by checking the validity of the reference before performing it. The overhead of checking, however, can be many times the cost of the array reference itself, and a programmer should weigh speed against safety in determining whether such a check is desirable. A good compiler should be able to produce code with such checks, should avoid redundant checks, and should allow programmers to control the extent and type of error checking in the compiled code.

Compilers for popular languages, such as C and C++, put hardly any error-checking operations into running code, so as to make things run as fast as possible. As a result, it falls to programmers to explicitly provide error checking. Unfortunately, people often neglect to do this, even in critical applications where speed is not a constraint. Their programs lead fast and dangerous lives. For example, the notorious "Worm" that paralyzed the Internet in 1988 exploited the UNIX[TM] operating system's failure to check whether the input buffer has overflowed in the finger daemon. (See Spafford 1989.)

run-time library.[53] Better yet, we can compile the compiler itself, and run this on the new machine to compile other Lisp programs.[54] Or we can compile one of the interpreters of section 4.1 to produce an interpreter that runs on the new machine.

Exercise 5.45

By comparing the stack operations used by compiled code to the stack operations used by the evaluator for the same computation, we can determine the extent to which the compiler optimizes use of the stack, both in speed (reducing the total number of stack operations) and in space (reducing the maximum stack depth). Comparing this optimized stack use to the performance of a special-purpose machine for the same computation gives some indication of the quality of the compiler.

a. Exercise 5.27 asked you to determine, as a function of n, the number of pushes and the maximum stack depth needed by the evaluator to compute $n!$ using the recursive factorial procedure given above. Exercise 5.14 asked you to do the same measurements for the special-purpose factorial machine shown in figure 5.11. Now perform the same analysis using the compiled `factorial` procedure.

Take the ratio of the number of pushes in the compiled version to the number of pushes in the interpreted version, and do the same for the maximum stack depth. Since the number of operations and the stack depth used to compute $n!$ are linear in n, these ratios should approach constants as n becomes large. What are these constants? Similarly, find the ratios of the stack usage in the special-purpose machine to the usage in the interpreted version.

Compare the ratios for special-purpose versus interpreted code to the ratios for compiled versus interpreted code. You should find that the special-purpose machine does much better than the compiled code, since the hand-tailored controller code should be much better than what is produced by our rudimentary general-purpose compiler.

b. Can you suggest improvements to the compiler that would help it generate code that would come closer in performance to the hand-tailored version?

---

[53]Of course, with either the interpretation or the compilation strategy we must also implement for the new machine storage allocation, input and output, and all the various operations that we took as "primitive" in our discussion of the evaluator and compiler. One strategy for minimizing work here is to write as many of these operations as possible in Lisp and then compile them for the new machine. Ultimately, everything reduces to a small kernel (such as garbage collection and the mechanism for applying actual machine primitives) that is hand-coded for the new machine.

[54] This strategy leads to amusing tests of correctness of the compiler, such as checking whether the compilation of a program on the new machine, using the compiled compiler, is identical with the compilation of the program on the original Lisp system. Tracking down the source of differences is fun but often frustrating, because the results are extremely sensitive to minuscule details.

Exercise 5.46

Carry out an analysis like the one in exercise 5.45 to determine the effectiveness of compiling the tree-recursive Fibonacci procedure

```
(define (fib n)
  (if (< n 2)
      n
      (+ (fib (- n 1)) (fib (- n 2)))))
```

compared to the effectiveness of using the special-purpose Fibonacci machine of figure 5.12. (For measurement of the interpreted performance, see exercise 5.29.) For Fibonacci, the time resource used is not linear in *n*; hence the ratios of stack operations will not approach a limiting value that is independent of *n*.

Exercise 5.47

This section described how to modify the explicit-control evaluator so that interpreted code can call compiled procedures. Show how to modify the compiler so that compiled procedures can call not only primitive procedures and compiled procedures, but interpreted procedures as well. This requires modifying compile-procedure-call to handle the case of compound (interpreted) procedures. Be sure to handle all the same target and linkage combinations as in compile-proc-appl. To do the actual procedure application, the code needs to jump to the evaluator's compound-apply entry point. This label cannot be directly referenced in object code (since the assembler requires that all labels referenced by the code it is assembling be defined there), so we will add a register called compapp to the evaluator machine to hold this entry point, and add an instruction to initialize it:

```
(assign compapp (label compound-apply))
(branch (label external-entry))        ; branches if flag is set
read-eval-print-loop
  ...
```

To test your code, start by defining a procedure f that calls a procedure g. Use compile-and-go to compile the definition of f and start the evaluator. Now, typing at the evaluator, define g and try to call f.

Exercise 5.48

The compile-and-go interface implemented in this section is awkward, since the compiler can be called only once (when the evaluator machine is started). Augment the compiler-interpreter interface by providing a compile-and-run primitive that can be called from within the explicit-control evaluator as follows:

```
;;; EC-Eval input:
(compile-and-run
 '(define (factorial n)
    (if (= n 1)
        1
        (* (factorial (- n 1)) n))))
;;; EC-Eval value:
ok

;;; EC-Eval input:
(factorial 5)
;;; EC-Eval value:
120
```

Exercise 5.49

As an alternative to using the explicit-control evaluator's read-eval-print loop, design a register machine that performs a read-compile-execute-print loop. That is, the machine should run a loop that reads an expression, compiles it, assembles and executes the resulting code, and prints the result. This is easy to run in our simulated setup, since we can arrange to call the procedures `compile` and `assemble` as "register-machine operations."

Exercise 5.50

Use the compiler to compile the metacircular evaluator of section 4.1 and run this program using the register-machine simulator. (To compile more than one definition at a time, you can package the definitions in a `begin`.) The resulting interpreter will run very slowly because of the multiple levels of interpretation, but getting all the details to work is an instructive exercise.

Exercise 5.51

Develop a rudimentary implementation of Scheme in C (or some other low-level language of your choice) by translating the explicit-control evaluator of section 5.4 into C. In order to run this code you will need to also provide appropriate storage-allocation routines and other run-time support.

Exercise 5.52

As a counterpoint to exercise 5.51, modify the compiler so that it compiles Scheme procedures into sequences of C instructions. Compile the metacircular evaluator of section 4.1 to produce a Scheme interpreter written in C.

References

Abelson, Harold, Andrew Berlin, Jacob Katzenelson, William McAllister, Guillermo Rozas, Gerald Jay Sussman, and Jack Wisdom. 1992. The Supercomputer Toolkit: A general framework for special-purpose computing. *International Journal of High-Speed Electronics* 3(3):337–361.

Allen, John. 1978. *Anatomy of Lisp.* New York: McGraw-Hill.

ANSI X3.226-1994. *American National Standard for Information Systems— Programming Language—Common Lisp.*

Appel, Andrew W. 1987. Garbage collection can be faster than stack allocation. *Information Processing Letters* 25(4):275–279.

Backus, John. 1978. Can programming be liberated from the von Neumann style? *Communications of the ACM* 21(8):613–641.

Baker, Henry G., Jr. 1978. List processing in real time on a serial computer. *Communications of the ACM* 21(4):280–293.

Batali, John, Neil Mayle, Howard Shrobe, Gerald Jay Sussman, and Daniel Weise. 1982. The Scheme-81 architecture—System and chip. In *Proceedings of the MIT Conference on Advanced Research in VLSI,* edited by Paul Penfield, Jr. Dedham, MA: Artech House.

Borning, Alan. 1977. ThingLab—An object-oriented system for building simulations using constraints. In *Proceedings of the 5th International Joint Conference on Artificial Intelligence.*

Borodin, Alan, and Ian Munro. 1975. *The Computational Complexity of Algebraic and Numeric Problems.* New York: American Elsevier.

Chaitin, Gregory J. 1975. Randomness and mathematical proof. *Scientific American* 232(5):47–52.

Church, Alonzo. 1941. *The Calculi of Lambda-Conversion.* Princeton, N.J.: Princeton University Press.

Clark, Keith L. 1978. Negation as failure. In *Logic and Data Bases.* New York: Plenum Press, pp. 293–322.

Clinger, William. 1982. Nondeterministic call by need is neither lazy nor by name. In *Proceedings of the ACM Symposium on Lisp and Functional Programming,* pp. 226–234.

Clinger, William, and Jonathan Rees. 1991. Macros that work. In *Proceedings of the 1991 ACM Conference on Principles of Programming Languages,* pp. 155–162.

Colmerauer A., H. Kanoui, R. Pasero, and P. Roussel. 1973. Un système de communication homme-machine en français. Technical report, Groupe Intelligence Artificielle, Université d'Aix Marseille, Luminy.

Cormen, Thomas, Charles Leiserson, and Ronald Rivest. 1990. *Introduction to Algorithms.* Cambridge, MA: MIT Press.

Darlington, John, Peter Henderson, and David Turner. 1982. *Functional Programming and Its Applications.* New York: Cambridge University Press.

Dijkstra, Edsger W. 1968a. The structure of the "THE" multiprogramming system. *Communications of the ACM* 11(5):341–346.

Dijkstra, Edsger W. 1968b. Cooperating sequential processes. In *Programming Languages,* edited by F. Genuys. New York: Academic Press, pp. 43–112.

Dinesman, Howard P. 1968. *Superior Mathematical Puzzles.* New York: Simon and Schuster.

deKleer, Johan, Jon Doyle, Guy Steele, and Gerald J. Sussman. 1977. AMORD: Explicit control of reasoning. In *Proceedings of the ACM Symposium on Artificial Intelligence and Programming Languages,* pp. 116–125.

Doyle, Jon. 1979. A truth maintenance system. *Artificial Intelligence* 12:231–272.

Feigenbaum, Edward, and Howard Shrobe. 1993. The Japanese National Fifth Generation Project: Introduction, survey, and evaluation. In *Future Generation Computer Systems,* vol. 9, pp. 105–117.

Feeley, Marc. 1986. Deux approches à l'implantation du language Scheme. Masters thesis, Université de Montréal.

Feeley, Marc and Guy Lapalme. 1987. Using closures for code generation. *Journal of Computer Languages* 12(1):47–66.

Feller, William. 1957. *An Introduction to Probability Theory and Its Applications,* volume 1. New York: John Wiley & Sons.

Fenichel, R., and J. Yochelson. 1969. A Lisp garbage collector for virtual memory computer systems. *Communications of the ACM* 12(11):611–612.

Floyd, Robert. 1967. Nondeterministic algorithms. *JACM,* 14(4):636–644.

Forbus, Kenneth D., and Johan deKleer. 1993. *Building Problem Solvers.* Cambridge, MA: MIT Press.

Friedman, Daniel P., and David S. Wise. 1976. CONS should not evaluate its arguments. In *Automata, Languages, and Programming: Third International Colloquium,* edited by S. Michaelson and R. Milner, pp. 257–284.

Friedman, Daniel P., Mitchell Wand, and Christopher T. Haynes. 1992. *Essentials of Programming Languages.* Cambridge, MA: MIT Press/McGraw-Hill.

Gabriel, Richard P. 1988. The Why of *Y. Lisp Pointers* 2(2):15–25.

Goldberg, Adele, and David Robson. 1983. *Smalltalk-80: The Language and Its Implementation.* Reading, MA: Addison-Wesley.

Gordon, Michael, Robin Milner, and Christopher Wadsworth. 1979. *Edinburgh LCF.* Lecture Notes in Computer Science, volume 78. New York: Springer-Verlag.

Gray, Jim, and Andreas Reuter. 1993. *Transaction Processing: Concepts and Models.* San Mateo, CA: Morgan-Kaufman.

Green, Cordell. 1969. Application of theorem proving to problem solving. In *Proceedings of the International Joint Conference on Artificial Intelligence,* pp. 219–240.

Green, Cordell, and Bertram Raphael. 1968. The use of theorem-proving techniques in question-answering systems. In *Proceedings of the ACM National Conference,* pp. 169–181.

Griss, Martin L. 1981. Portable Standard Lisp, a brief overview. Utah Symbolic Computation Group Operating Note 58, University of Utah.

Guttag, John V. 1977. Abstract data types and the development of data structures. *Communications of the ACM* 20(6):397–404.

Hamming, Richard W. 1980. *Coding and Information Theory.* Englewood Cliffs, N.J.: Prentice-Hall.

Hanson, Christopher P. 1990. Efficient stack allocation for tail-recursive languages. In *Proceedings of ACM Conference on Lisp and Functional Programming,* pp. 106–118.

Hanson, Christopher P. 1991. A syntactic closures macro facility. *Lisp Pointers,* 4(3).

Hardy, Godfrey H. 1921. Srinivasa Ramanujan. *Proceedings of the London Mathematical Society* XIX(2).

Hardy, Godfrey H., and E. M. Wright. 1960. *An Introduction to the Theory of Numbers.* 4th edition. New York: Oxford University Press.

Havender, J. 1968. Avoiding deadlocks in multi-tasking systems. *IBM Systems Journal* 7(2):74–84.

Hearn, Anthony C. 1969. Standard Lisp. Technical report AIM-90, Artificial Intelligence Project, Stanford University.

Henderson, Peter. 1980. *Functional Programming: Application and Implementation.* Englewood Cliffs, N.J.: Prentice-Hall.

Henderson. Peter. 1982. Functional Geometry. In *Conference Record of the 1982 ACM Symposium on Lisp and Functional Programming,* pp. 179–187.

Hewitt, Carl E. 1969. PLANNER: A language for proving theorems in robots. In *Proceedings of the International Joint Conference on Artificial Intelligence,* pp. 295–301.

Hewitt, Carl E. 1977. Viewing control structures as patterns of passing messages. *Journal of Artificial Intelligence* 8(3):323–364.

Hoare, C. A. R. 1972. Proof of correctness of data representations. *Acta Informatica* 1(1).

Hodges, Andrew. 1983. *Alan Turing: The Enigma.* New York: Simon and Schuster.

Hofstadter, Douglas R. 1979. *Gödel, Escher, Bach: An Eternal Golden Braid.* New York: Basic Books.

Hughes, R. J. M. 1990. Why functional programming matters. In *Research Topics in Functional Programming,* edited by David Turner. Reading, MA: Addison-Wesley, pp. 17–42.

IEEE Std 1178–1990. 1990. *IEEE Standard for the Scheme Programming Language.*

Ingerman, Peter, Edgar Irons, Kirk Sattley, and Wallace Feurzeig; assisted by M. Lind, Herbert Kanner, and Robert Floyd. 1960. THUNKS: A way of compiling procedure statements, with some comments on procedure declarations. Unpublished manuscript. (Also, private communication from Wallace Feurzeig.)

Kaldewaij, Anne. 1990. *Programming: The Derivation of Algorithms.* New York: Prentice-Hall.

Kohlbecker, Eugene Edmund, Jr. 1986. Syntactic extensions in the programming language Lisp. Ph.D. thesis, Indiana University.

Konopasek, Milos, and Sundaresan Jayaraman. 1984. *The TK!Solver Book: A Guide to Problem-Solving in Science, Engineering, Business, and Education.* Berkeley, CA: Osborne/McGraw-Hill.

Knuth, Donald E. 1973. *Fundamental Algorithms.* Volume 1 of *The Art of Computer Programming.* 2nd edition. Reading, MA: Addison-Wesley.

Knuth, Donald E. 1981. *Seminumerical Algorithms.* Volume 2 of *The Art of Computer Programming.* 2nd edition. Reading, MA: Addison-Wesley.

Kowalski, Robert. 1973. Predicate logic as a programming language. Technical report 70, Department of Computational Logic, School of Artificial Intelligence, University of Edinburgh.

Kowalski, Robert. 1979. *Logic for Problem Solving.* New York: North-Holland.

Lamport, Leslie. 1978. Time, clocks, and the ordering of events in a distributed system. *Communications of the ACM* 21(7):558–565.

Lampson, Butler, J. J. Horning, R. London, J. G. Mitchell, and G. K. Popek. 1981. Report on the programming language Euclid. Technical report, Computer Systems Research Group, University of Toronto.

Landin, Peter. 1965. A correspondence between Algol 60 and Church's lambda notation: Part I. *Communications of the ACM* 8(2):89–101.

Lieberman, Henry, and Carl E. Hewitt. 1983. A real-time garbage collector based on the lifetimes of objects. *Communications of the ACM* 26(6):419–429.

Liskov, Barbara H., and Stephen N. Zilles. 1975. Specification techniques for data abstractions. *IEEE Transactions on Software Engineering* 1(1):7–19.

McAllester, David Allen. 1978. A three-valued truth-maintenance system. Memo 473, MIT Artificial Intelligence Laboratory.

McAllester, David Allen. 1980. An outlook on truth maintenance. Memo 551, MIT Artificial Intelligence Laboratory.

McCarthy, John. 1960. Recursive functions of symbolic expressions and their computation by machine. *Communications of the ACM* 3(4):184–195.

McCarthy, John. 1967. A basis for a mathematical theory of computation. In *Computer Programing and Formal Systems*, edited by P. Braffort and D. Hirschberg. North-Holland.

McCarthy, John. 1978. The history of Lisp. In *Proceedings of the ACM SIG-PLAN Conference on the History of Programming Languages*.

McCarthy, John, P. W. Abrahams, D. J. Edwards, T. P. Hart, and M. I. Levin. 1965. *Lisp 1.5 Programmer's Manual*. 2nd edition. Cambridge, MA: MIT Press.

McDermott, Drew, and Gerald Jay Sussman. 1972. Conniver reference manual. Memo 259, MIT Artificial Intelligence Laboratory.

Miller, Gary L. 1976. Riemann's Hypothesis and tests for primality. *Journal of Computer and System Sciences* 13(3):300–317.

Miller, James S., and Guillermo J. Rozas. 1994. Garbage collection is fast, but a stack is faster. Memo 1462, MIT Artificial Intelligence Laboratory.

Moon, David. 1978. MacLisp reference manual, Version 0. Technical report, MIT Laboratory for Computer Science.

Moon, David, and Daniel Weinreb. 1981. Lisp machine manual. Technical report, MIT Artificial Intelligence Laboratory.

Morris, J. H., Eric Schmidt, and Philip Wadler. 1980. Experience with an applicative string processing language. In *Proceedings of the 7th Annual ACM SIGACT/SIGPLAN Symposium on the Principles of Programming Languages*.

Phillips, Hubert. 1934. *The Sphinx Problem Book*. London: Faber and Faber.

Pitman, Kent. 1983. The revised MacLisp Manual (Saturday evening edition). Technical report 295, MIT Laboratory for Computer Science.

Rabin, Michael O. 1980. Probabilistic algorithm for testing primality. *Journal of Number Theory* 12:128–138.

Raymond, Eric. 1993. *The New Hacker's Dictionary.* 2nd edition. Cambridge, MA: MIT Press.

Raynal, Michel. 1986. *Algorithms for Mutual Exclusion.* Cambridge, MA: MIT Press.

Rees, Jonathan A., and Norman I. Adams IV. 1982. T: A dialect of Lisp or, lambda: The ultimate software tool. In *Conference Record of the 1982 ACM Symposium on Lisp and Functional Programming,* pp. 114–122.

Rees, Jonathan, and William Clinger (eds). 1991. The revised[4] report on the algorithmic language Scheme. *Lisp Pointers,* 4(3).

Rivest, Ronald, Adi Shamir, and Leonard Adleman. 1977. A method for obtaining digital signatures and public-key cryptosystems. Technical memo LCS/TM82, MIT Laboratory for Computer Science.

Robinson, J. A. 1965. A machine-oriented logic based on the resolution principle. *Journal of the ACM* 12(1):23.

Robinson, J. A. 1983. Logic programming—Past, present, and future. *New Generation Computing* 1:107–124.

Spafford, Eugene H. 1989. The Internet Worm: Crisis and aftermath. *Communications of the ACM* 32(6):678–688.

Steele, Guy Lewis, Jr. 1977. Debunking the "expensive procedure call" myth. In *Proceedings of the National Conference of the ACM,* pp. 153–62.

Steele, Guy Lewis, Jr. 1982. An overview of Common Lisp. In *Proceedings of the ACM Symposium on Lisp and Functional Programming,* pp. 98–107.

Steele, Guy Lewis, Jr. 1990. *Common Lisp: The Language.* 2nd edition. Digital Press.

Steele, Guy Lewis, Jr., and Gerald Jay Sussman. 1975. Scheme: An interpreter for the extended lambda calculus. Memo 349, MIT Artificial Intelligence Laboratory.

Steele, Guy Lewis, Jr., Donald R. Woods, Raphael A. Finkel, Mark R. Crispin, Richard M. Stallman, and Geoffrey S. Goodfellow. 1983. *The Hacker's Dictionary.* New York: Harper & Row.

Stoy, Joseph E. 1977. *Denotational Semantics.* Cambridge, MA: MIT Press.

Sussman, Gerald Jay, and Richard M. Stallman. 1975. Heuristic techniques in computer-aided circuit analysis. *IEEE Transactions on Circuits and Systems* CAS-22(11):857–865.

Sussman, Gerald Jay, and Guy Lewis Steele Jr. 1980. Constraints—A language for expressing almost-hierachical descriptions. *AI Journal* 14:1–39.

Sussman, Gerald Jay, and Jack Wisdom. 1992. Chaotic evolution of the solar system. *Science* 257:256–262.

Sussman, Gerald Jay, Terry Winograd, and Eugene Charniak. 1971. Microplanner reference manual. Memo 203A, MIT Artificial Intelligence Laboratory.

Sutherland, Ivan E. 1963. SKETCHPAD: A man-machine graphical communication system. Technical report 296, MIT Lincoln Laboratory.

Teitelman, Warren. 1974. Interlisp reference manual. Technical report, Xerox Palo Alto Research Center.

Thatcher, James W., Eric G. Wagner, and Jesse B. Wright. 1978. Data type specification: Parameterization and the power of specification techniques. In *Conference Record of the Tenth Annual ACM Symposium on Theory of Computing*, pp. 119-132.

Turner, David. 1981. The future of applicative languages. In *Proceedings of the 3rd European Conference on Informatics,* Lecture Notes in Computer Science, volume 123. New York: Springer-Verlag, pp. 334–348.

Wand, Mitchell. 1980. Continuation-based program transformation strategies. *Journal of the ACM* 27(1):164–180.

Waters, Richard C. 1979. A method for analyzing loop programs. *IEEE Transactions on Software Engineering* 5(3):237–247.

Winograd, Terry. 1971. Procedures as a representation for data in a computer program for understanding natural language. Technical report AI TR-17, MIT Artificial Intelligence Laboratory.

Winston, Patrick. 1992. *Artificial Intelligence.* 3rd edition. Reading, MA: Addison-Wesley.

Zabih, Ramin, David McAllester, and David Chapman. 1987. Non-deterministic Lisp with dependency-directed backtracking. *AAAI-87*, pp. 59–64.

Zippel, Richard. 1979. Probabilistic algorithms for sparse polynomials. Ph.D. dissertation, Department of Electrical Engineering and Computer Science, MIT.

Zippel, Richard. 1993. *Effective Polynomial Computation.* Boston, MA: Kluwer Academic Publishers.

List of Exercises

Index

Any inaccuracies in this index may be explained by the fact that it has been prepared with the help of a computer.

Donald E. Knuth, *Fundamental Algorithms* (Volume 1 of *The Art of Computer Programming*)

Page numbers for code definitions are in italics.
Page numbers followed by *n* indicate footnotes.